Programming with Visual Basic.NET for Business

PHILIP A. KONEMAN

PEARSON
Prentice
Hall

Prentice Hall
Upper Saddle River, New Jersey, 07458

Library of Congress Cataloging-in-Publication Data

Koneman, Philip A.
    Programming with Visual Basic.NET for business / Philip A. Koneman.
        p. cm.
    ISBN 0-13-047368-5
1. Microsoft Visual BASIC.   2. BASIC (Computer program language)
3. Microsoft .NET.   I. Title.
    QA76.9.D3 K6563 2003
    005.2'768—dc21

                                                        2002151876

Publisher and Vice President: Natalie E. Anderson
Executive Editor: Jodi McPherson
Senior Project Managers, Editorial: Eileen Clark and Thomas Park
Editorial Assistant: Jodi Bolognese
Development Editor: Christine Wright
Marketing Manager: Sharon Turkovich
Manager, Production: Gail Steier de Acevedo
Project Manager, Production: Audri Anna Bazlen
Associate Director, Manufacturing: Vincent Scelta
Manufacturing Buyer: Natacha St. Hill Moore
Design Manager: Maria Lange
Art Director: Pat Smythe
Interior Designer: John Romer
Cover Design: Pat Smythe
Cover Photo: Artville
Line Art Studio: Matrix Publishing Services
Full-Service Composition: Impressions Book and Journal Services, Inc.
Cover Printer: Phoenix
Printer/Binder: Quebecor World-Dubuque

Credits and acknowledgments borrowed from other sources and reproduced, with permission, in this textbook appear on the appropriate page within the text.

10 9 8 7 6 5 4 3 2 1

ISBN 0-13-047368-5

I dedicate this book to my wife, Tanya,
who is my constant companion and soulmate,
and our children—Megan, Jonathan, and Andrew—
who make our lives full and bring us joy.

BRIEF CONTENTS

CONTENTS

9

Object-Oriented Programming with Visual Basic.NET

10

Creating Distributed Web Applications by Using ASP.NET

Appendix B
Numeric Data Types and Type Conversions

Glossary

Index

ACHNOWLEDGMENTS

Writing a book of this magnitude is truly a team effort. I would like to acknowledge the contributions of those who made this book possible. First I would like to acknowledge the careful editorial work of Christine Wright, the Developmental Editor for this book. She carefully reviewed each chapter and provided insightful feedback for making the book applicable to students who are learning programming. She also did a great job of summarizing the feedback provided by the reviewers and at the same time kept the larger picture of presenting a unified and consistent style. I would also like to acknowledge the efforts of the CIS team at Prentice Hall. Special thanks to Jodi McPherson, Executive Editor, who crafted a vision for the *.NET for Business* series. Her insight into how this book addresses the needs of the higher education market is invaluable. Thanks also to Eileen Clark, Thomas Park, and Audri Anna Bazlen, who kept the production schedule moving forward. I also thank John Ferguson and Maria Murphy of Impressions Book and Journal Services, Inc. who worked long hours to prepare the book for composition. Thanks also to Melissa Edwards, who worked tirelessly to complete the Instructor Resources.

I'd also like to thank the technical editors, Ric Pavese of the Community College of Baltimore County and Fawzi Noman of Sam Houston State University, and the supplement authors, Kurt Kominek of Northeast State Technical Community College, who wrote the Instructor's Manual, Pati Milligan of Baylor University who created the PowerPoint presentations, and Marvin Harris of Lansing Community College who wrote the Test Bank.

Finally, thanks to the many reviewers who provided invaluable feedback:

- Gary R. Armstrong, Shippensburg University
- Douglas B. Bock, Southern Illinois University-Edwardsville
- Kuanchin Chen, Western Michigan University
- John S. DaPonte, Southern Connecticut State University
- Allen Dooley, Pasadena City College
- Mickie Goodro, Casper College
- David G. Grebner, Lansing Community College
- Brian Howard, Bridgewater College
- Dana Johnson, North Dakota State University
- Kurt W. Kominek, Northeast State Technical Community College
- Charles Lee, Riverside College
- Scott Lord, Bainbridge College
- Diane Murphey, Oklahoma Panhandle State University
- Christopher Panell, Heald College
- Diane Perreault, California State University-Sacramento
- Anita Philipp, Oklahoma City Community College
- Barry Schoenhaut, Rockland Community College
- Jack Van Deventer, Washington State University

ABOUT THE AUTHOR

Dr. Koneman manages the Certification Department at J.D. Edwards, a leading provider of integrated, Web-enabled applications designed to assist large- and medium-size companies improve business performance. In this role, Dr. Koneman manages the certification products and processes for validating the knowledge and skills of J.D. Edward's consultants and Business Partners. Prior to joining J.D. Edwards, he spent 10 years in Higher Education as an Associate Professor of Computer Information Systems at Colorado Christian University. He has taught courses in Computer Applications, Database Management, Multimedia Design, Visual Basic, and Business Ethics.

Dr. Koneman has a wide professional portfolio that includes writing, consulting, and software development. He has written for the Prentice Hall Select Series. He has worked with companies such as CertiPort, Inc. as a consultant in certification development. As the former President of Instructional Design Consultants, Inc., Dr. Koneman managed the design and development of CD-ROM instructional materials for medical technology education, and in 1995 his company was awarded the Denver Business Journal's Most Innovative New Products Award in Biotechnology for GermWare, an interactive CD-ROM for learning microbiology.

Dr. Koneman received his Ph.D. from the School of Education at the University of Colorado at Denver. His research interests include computer-based learning, educational testing and measurement, and ethical issues regarding computers and technology in a post-modern society.

PREFACE

Visual Studio.NET

The .NET platform is central to Microsoft's goal of making a digital world a reality. On February 13, 2002, Microsoft officially launched Visual Studio.NET, and Bill Gates reinforced the vision for the .NET strategy by emphasizing the goal of a digital world—being able to get information at any time, any place, on any device, using the common infrastructure of the Internet.

Visual Basic.NET continues the tradition of the visual development tool first released in 1991. With the release of Visual Studio.NET, Visual Basic is now a true object-oriented language. This book teaches programming concepts with Visual Basic.NET, emphasizing programs that support all aspects of creating Windows and ASP.NET Web applications for business that obtain input, perform data processing, generate output, and store program data for later use.

Introduction

This text introduces learners to creating desktop and Web-based applications by using Microsoft Visual Basic.NET. It covers introductory and intermediate topics and is targeted to students with no programming experience for whom Visual Basic is the first introduction to programming as well as students who understand either structured or object-oriented programming and are now learning the Visual Basic environment. A hallmark of this text is its comprehensive approach to programming, utilizing integrated cases that build from chapter to chapter and are based on common business problems and the processes integral to solving these problems. This text also emphasizes data storage and therefore uses cases in which programming results are stored and retrieved. Finally, this text covers important topics such as distributed Web applications, printing and reporting by using Crystal Reports, and packaging and deploying applications.

Features

This book has a number of features to support how students learn to program with Visual Basic.NET and how instructors can effectively cover the topics that are central to Visual Basic.NET and the .NET Framework.

1. **Performance Objectives**. The performance objectives at the beginning of each chapter describe what students will know and be able to do after completing the chapter. The concepts covered in each performance objective are summarized at the end of the chapter.

2. **Teaching Examples.** Multiple teaching examples appear in each chapter, using a business-oriented Visual Basic.NET project to illustrate and explain the topics in the chapter. The solution files for these examples are available to students and instructors. Students can open the solution files to see what is being taught, and instructors can use the solution files to walk through the chapter topics.

3. **Code Examples.** As a Visual Basic.NET feature is first presented, learners are presented with code examples that demonstrate how to write the code to implement the feature. In addition to the code statements in the chapter, all the code examples are included in the Teaching Example projects so students can open the projects and view the code statements in the Visual Studio Code Editor.

4. **Illustrations.** Multiple illustrations add visual appeal and reinforce learning. Illustrations include line art that visually represents key concepts and screen captures of the Visual Basic.NET solutions.

5. **Tips and Troubleshooting.** Feature boxes, popular with both students and instructors, are included throughout the text. They contain material that might be useful for performing a task or alert students to problems they might encounter while completing a task.

6. **Check Points.** These boxes provide brief review questions designed to assess the student's understanding of a given task or topic or remind them of a related topic. Answers are provided in the box or in the paragraph following the box.

7. **Hands-On Programming Examples.** Each chapter includes a comprehensive Hands-On Programming Example demonstrating a concept in an application that addresses a specific business problem or process. Additionally, learners are able to see different methods for solving a problem or implementing a process. Although no one example follows through every chapter in the book, the sets of examples are organized according to the specific topics where each is appropriate.

8. **A consistent programming methodology.** Each Hands-On Programming Example features a four-step methodology for creating Visual Basic applications:

    a. **Plan the application:** Determine inputs and outputs, draw the form layout, determine the required controls, and write pseudocode explaining the program's functionality.

    b. **Design the user interface:** Create the form, add controls to the form, and set control properties.

    c. **Write the code:** Write the Visual Basic statements that carry out the actions of the program.

    d. **Run the application:** Run the application to test its functionality and to debug the program

9. **Key Terms.** The key terms for each chapter are defined as each term is first introduced. The terms are also summarized at the end of the chapter, and the book includes a comprehensive glossary with definitions of over 400 terms.

10. **End-of-Chapter Materials.** The end-of-chapter materials reinforce the concepts presented in each chapter and its Hands-On Programming Examples. The end-of-chapter materials include a comprehensive

Summary for each concept or topic; multiple-choice, true/false, and short-answer questions that assess how well students comprehend the chapter objectives; and additional Exercises and Case Studies that instructors can use as assignments, including:

- **Guided Exercises** that reinforce the concepts presented in the chapter.

- **Case Studies** that allow students to apply what they have learned in a new way.

11. **New Features in .NET.** In addition to covering the core topics for learning programming, this text also includes chapters addressing new features in the .NET Framework, including Web Forms, ADO.NET, XML, and Crystal Reports.

12. **Packaging and Deploying Applications.** Appendix A covers a new feature in Visual Studio.NET, packaging and deployment projects. In Appendix A students learn to package Windows applications and ASP.NET projects for distribution.

STUDENT AND INSTRUCTOR RESOURCES

Instructor's Resources

INSTRUCTOR'S RESOURCE CD-ROM

The Instructor's Resource CD-ROM that is available with the book contains:

- Instructor's Manual in Word and PDF.
- Solutions to all questions and exercises from the book and web site
- PowerPoint lectures
- A Windows-based test manager and the associated test bank in Word format.
- Visual Basic. NET solution and data files.

The CD also includes the .NET Framework redistributable file for installing the .NET Framework on computers that do not have Visual Studio.NET installed. The .NET Framework is required to run the solutions that are packaged for deployment.

Tools for Online Learning

WWW.PRENHALL.COM/KONEMAN

This text is accompanied by a companion Web site at www.prenhall.com/koneman This website is designed to bring you and your students a richer, more interactive Web experience. The companion website contains all of the student data files as well as a password protected site for instructors.

DATA FILES

The programs from each chapter are copied to your computer when you install the data files. There are two archives for installing the files: the **Student archive** and the **Instructor archive**. Both archives are available for download from the Prentice Hall Website. The Student and Instructor archive is also included on the **Instructor Resource CD**. The archives include the following folders for each chapter:

EXAMPLES

These are the solution files for the sample programs shown in each chapter before the Hands-On Programming Example. The examples are included in both the Student and Instructor archives.

STUDENT FILES

These folders contain the files students need to complete the Hands-On Programming Example, Guided Exercises, and Case Study exercises. The Student Files are included in both the Student and Instructor archives.

INSTRUCTOR FILES

These folders contain the completed solutions for each Hands-On Programming Example, Guided Exercise, and Case Study exercise. The Instructor Folders are available in the Instructors archive only.

The data file archives include a *ReadMe* file with information about installing and running the solutions contained in each archive.

Required Software

WINDOWS APPLICATION PROJECTS

To complete the Windows Application projects in this book you need the following software installed on your computer:

- Microsoft Windows® XP Professional, Microsoft Windows 2000 Professional, or Windows NT® 4.0 Workstation
- Visual Studio.NET or Visual Basic.NET

ASP.NET WEB APPLICATION PROJECTS

To complete the ASP.NET Web Application projects, you need the following software:

- Internet Information Systems (IIS) or Internet Information Server 4.0 (available with the Windows NT 4 Option Pack)
- Internet Explorer 5.0 or later

Typing Code Statements in the Code Editor

To complete the Hands-on exercise and End of chapter exercises, you will enter code statements in the Visual Code Editor. When you create Visual Basic.NET applications, some code statements are generated automatically. For those you will enter, you must press ⏎Enter at the end of each line of code. If word wrap is enabled for the Code Editor, the code will wrap in the Code pane. In this book we will indicate a line of code using indentation. Consider the code statements shown on Page 174 of Chapter 4:

```
'Declare variables for calculating the loan payment
Dim sngPrincipal, sngRate As Single
Dim intTerm As Integer
Dim decPayment As Decimal
'Perform data validation
If IsNumeric(txtPrincipal.Text) = False Or
    Val(txtPrincipal.Text) < 50000 Or Val(txtPrincipal.Text) >
    200000 Then
MsgBox("The loan principal must be a number at least 50000 and
    not greater than 200000. Please try again.",
    MsgBoxStyle.Critical, "Invalid Data")
```

Type as one statement, and press ⏎Enter after typing *Then*

Type as one statement, and press ⏎Enter after typing "*Invalid Data*")

As you type the code statements, remember that each code statement appears as indented, so you will need to type the entire statement before pressing ⏎Enter.

Some of the code statements use the continuation character (_) to make the code statements easier to read in the Code Editor. When you enter code statements that include the continuation character, the continuation character signifies the end of a line. Type the underscore character and then press ⏎Enter. Consider the code shown on page 175 of Chapter 4:

```
'Populate the list box with the schedule
lstSchedule.Items.Add _
    ("Payment #" & intPayment & vbTab & vbTab & _
    Format(decPpmt, "c") & vbTab & vbTab & _
    Format(decIPmt, "c") & vbTab & vbTab & _
    Format(decBalance, "c"))
```

Although this is one code statement, since the statement includes four instances of the continuation character, type each line and press ⏎Enter after typing each continuation character.

Understanding Programming Concepts and Writing a Simple Visual Basic Application

Computers are truly remarkable machines. The tasks you can accomplish with a computer vary from writing a paper for school to balancing a checkbook or watching a DVD movie. Computers are flexible for a simple reason: computers run programs that perform specific tasks. In this book, you will learn how to use Visual Studio.NET, Microsoft's latest development suite, and the programming language Visual Basic.NET to create computer programs.

Performance Objectives

At the conclusion of this chapter, you will be able to:

- Understand and explain programs, programming, Visual Studio.NET, and Visual Basic.NET.
- Launch Visual Studio.NET and customize the Visual Studio.NET integrated development environment (IDE).
- Create and save a Visual Basic.NET project.
- Get online help in Visual Studio.NET.
- Define objects, properties, events, and methods.
- Display the Toolbox.
- Explain how design time and run time differ.
- Differentiate between procedural and event-driven programming.
- List the four-step process for developing Visual Basic applications.
- Open a project and add controls to the form.
- Set properties of objects at design time and run time.
- Write code to perform specific methods in response to specific events.
- Save and run a project.
- Close a Visual Basic.NET project and exit Visual Studio.NET.

What Programs Do

Computer programs process information from one form to another. The simplest computer programs receive input, process the information, and produce meaningful output for the user. This simple information-processing model is represented in Figure 1.1.

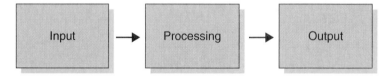

FIGURE 1.1. *Information processing model*

A ***computer program*** is a set of instructions that tells the computer hardware how to obtain input, what action to perform, and what output to produce. Computer programs are also called ***applications***. Computer programs range from very simple, such as the Windows Notepad used for creating text documents, to very complex, such as applications that allow companies to automate every aspect of their business.

The power of computers is that they can store information for later use. Many computer applications, including some you will create in the chapters ahead, allow users to store work and then retrieve this work later. An application that browses records in a database and allows you to input new records or edit existing records is an example of a program that supports the input, processing, output, and storage (IPOS) cycle shown in Figure 1.2.

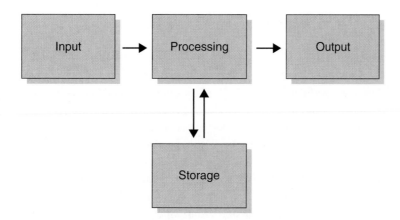

FIGURE 1.2. *The IPOS cycle*

Computer programs solve business problems. Calculating the withholding taxes and other payroll data for your employees, calculating the value of your inventory, or determining the best payment scenario for a personal loan are all examples of business problems computers solve. In this book, you will learn how to create programs that solve simple business problems or manipulate business data and run in the Windows environment.

Computer Programming

Why should you be interested in learning how to write computer programs? The field of computer programming includes a variety of job roles for creating and maintaining the programs that people run on computers as part of their daily work. Depending on your geographical location, entry-level programmers earn a median annual salary anywhere from $40,000 to $70,000. Whether you are writing the next release of a software application, customizing an existing application for a customer, or creating an application that links your cell phone to your e-mail account, there are many careers awaiting qualified computer programmers.

Computer programming involves creating the applications that enable end users to profit from the power and capabilities of computer hardware. Programming involves identifying the inputs and outputs that allow businesses to use computers to automate routine tasks. Programmers are professionals who create the applications to support the business needs of computer users. Programmers analyze the end user's identified requirements and then use commercial programming tools to create applications that provide those users with the data and information they need.

To create the computer applications that solve specific business problems, programmers use commercial programming tools that contain one or more programming languages. A *programming language* is an organized set of statements or commands that tell the computer what to do. The program statements or commands are written instructions called *code* that describe exactly what the program will do. The code is written according to specific rules called *syntax* that are specific to the programming language being used to create the application. The programming language you will learn in this text is Visual Basic.NET, which is one of the programming languages available in Visual Studio.NET. Now that you understand what programs, programmers, and programming languages do, we can begin to explore Visual Studio.NET.

Using Visual Studio.NET

Visual Studio.NET is Microsoft's development tool for creating Windows and Web applications. A *development tool* is a set of programs for developing applications. A *Windows application* has the Windows interface and is designed to run on a desktop computer in the Microsoft Windows environment. The *interface*, also called the *user interface*, is what users see on the screen and what they interact with when using a program. If a program runs in the Windows environment, the *Graphical User Interface (GUI)* typically includes forms, menus, buttons, text boxes, and other objects the user sees when the application runs. A *Web application* runs from a Web server, displays the user interface by using a Web browser, and includes *Web forms pages* that have a Web interface. Programmers can use Visual Studio.NET to develop computer programs that run on a single computer or share data over the Internet regardless of operating system and device.

Now that you have an idea of what Visual Studio.NET is, let's take a look at the tool.

LAUNCHING VISUAL STUDIO.NET

As with other Windows applications, you can launch Visual Studio.NET by using the Start button or by using the file management tools in Windows to locate an existing file and open it. In the steps that follow, you will use the Windows Start button to Launch Visual Studio.NET.

To Launch Visual Studio.NET:

1. Click Start and select All Programs, Microsoft Visual Studio.NET.
2. Select Microsoft Visual Studio.NET, as shown in Figure 1.3.

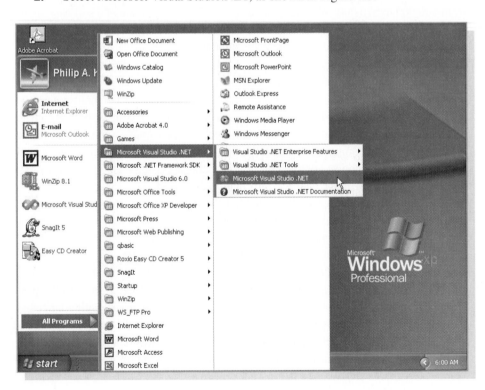

FIGURE 1.3. *Launching Microsoft Visual Studio.NET*

After a few seconds, the Visual Studio.NET Splash Screen appears. Depending on how Visual Studio.NET is configured or set up initially on your computer, the development environment Start Page will be similar to what is shown in Figure 1.4.

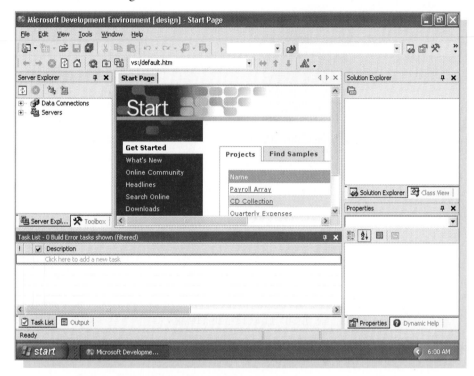

FIGURE 1.4. *Visual Studio.NET development environment Start Page*

A *development environment* is the comprehensive set of tools and features you use to develop (create), debug (find and fix errors), and deploy (distribute to users or customers) applications. In Visual Studio.NET, the features you use are made available in an integrated development environment. An *integrated development environment (IDE)* is a development environment in which all the features are made available within a common interface. You write your programs by using the IDE.

You can customize the development environment so its tools are available when and where you want them. You can even have Visual Studio.NET customize itself based on how you choose to work within the environment. If your screen does not match the interface shown in Figure 1.4, you can customize the IDE by choosing a *profile*, a collection of settings that defines the appearance of the IDE. Let's see how you can customize your environment by using a profile to set preferences for the IDE.

If you have already customized your environment and want to retain your settings, you do not need to complete the following task.

To customize the development environment:

1. Close any windows except the Start Page that appear on the screen.

2. Click **My Profile** on the Start Page. If **My Profile** isn't visible, use the scroll bar in the Start Page window to display it. The Start Page now displays the settings you can change to customize the development environment.

3. Select **Student Developer** in the *Profile:* drop-down list. The Start Page and the development environment will now appear in the view shown in Figure 1.5. A *view* defines how the interface elements appear on the screen. This view includes the Solution Explorer, Dynamic Help, the Start Page, and the Task List.

If the Start Page is not visible, click Help, Show Start Page.

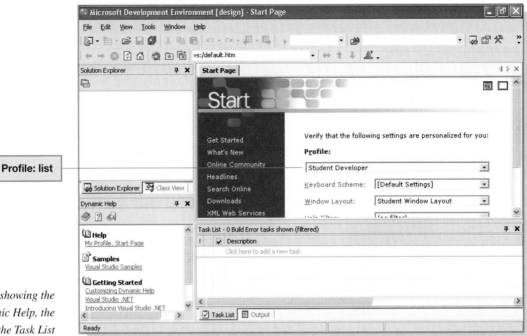

FIGURE 1.5. *View showing the Solution Explorer, Dynamic Help, the Start Page, and the Task List*

4.   Select **Visual Studio Developer** in the *Profile:* drop-down list. These are the settings you will use for all projects in this book.

5.   Click **Get Started** on the Start Page. Your screen should now look like Figure 1.6.

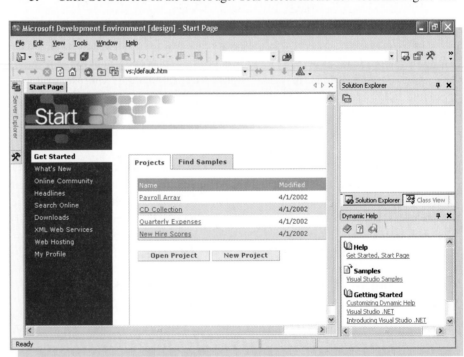

FIGURE 1.6. *The IDE after clicking Get Started*

ARRANGING WINDOWS IN THE IDE

In Figure 1.6, notice the windows in the IDE: the Start Page, Solution Explorer, and Dynamic Help. A *tool window* is listed on the View menu, and the current application and its add-ins will define the specific tool windows available. An example of a tool window is the Solution Explorer. You will learn about the Solution Explorer later in this chapter.

To view and modify the current options for the environment:

1. Click **Tools**, **Options**. The Options dialog box appears.

2. Check your settings to verify that your current settings match those shown in Figure 1.7.

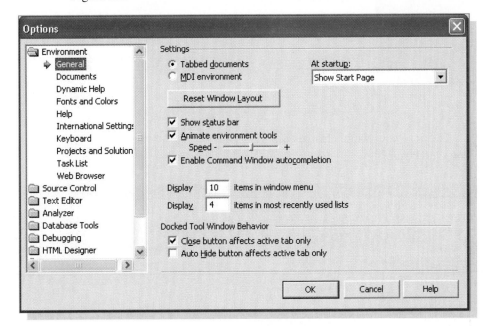

FIGURE 1.7. *The Options dialog box*

3. When you finish, click **OK**.

HIDING TOOL WINDOWS AUTOMATICALLY

You can set a tool window to hide automatically by using a *pushpin*, a small icon in the tool window that determines whether the window will display and hide automatically. This feature is called *Auto Hide*. The orientation of the pushpin displays the current setting. Figure 1.8 shows the pushpin for the Solution Explorer tool window. Notice the orientation of the pushpin. In this example, Auto Hide is turned off for this window.

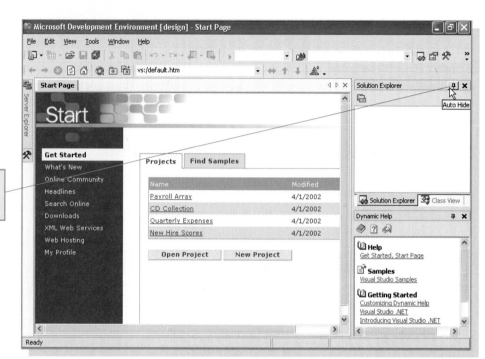

Pushpin indicating that Auto Hide is turned off

FIGURE 1.8. *The pushpin for the Solution Explorer tool window*

Clicking the pushpin changes the Auto Hide setting for the window. Figure 1.9 shows this change.

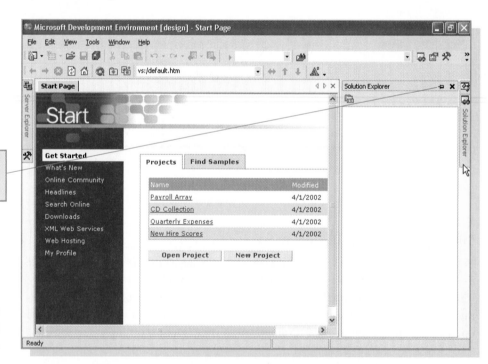

Pushpin indicating that Auto Hide is turned on

FIGURE 1.9. *Changing the Auto Hide setting of the Solution Explorer tool window*

Remember that the orientation of the pushpin indicates whether Auto Hide is activated.

Notice the orientation of the pin and the button that has appeared on the right border of the window. When you move the pointer out of the window, the tool window snaps to the side of the application window and appears as a tab. If you move the pointer over the tab on the side of the window, the window is again displayed (try it). Auto Hide is a great feature for keeping the IDE uncluttered while also providing immediate access to the development tools you need. To turn off Auto Hide, click the pushpin again.

DOCKING TOOL WINDOWS

Visual Studio.NET includes another feature for managing tool windows in the IDE. You can dock and undock a tool window by selecting or clearing **Dockable** on the Window menu. When a tool window is *dockable*, it floats on top of the other windows or snaps to a side of the application window. Figure 1.10 shows the Solution Explorer window as a dockable window.

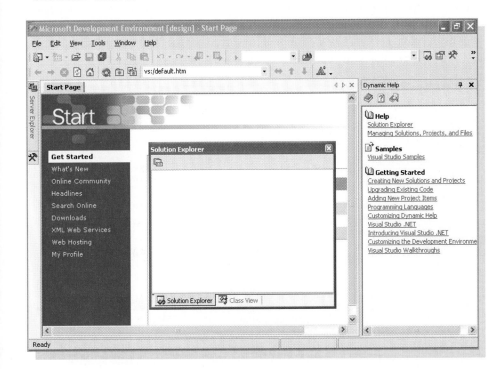

FIGURE 1.10. *The Solution Explorer as a dockable window*

You have just successfully started Visual Studio.NET and customized your development environment. Before we go any further, we need to examine Visual Basic.NET, the most important tool you'll be using within Visual Studio.NET.

Using Visual Basic.NET

You are now aware that Visual Studio.NET is a tool for creating computer programs. You can use any of the programming languages in Visual Studio.NET to create your applications. You even have the option of using more than one language for creating your solutions. Because this book is about programming with Visual Basic.NET, we will use only one of the languages available in Visual Studio.NET.

USING THE VISUAL BASIC.NET LANGUAGE

All Visual Basic code is contained within a procedure. In fact, every line of code in your application is contained inside some kind of procedure. A *procedure* is a block of Visual Basic statements. Before writing procedures, you need to know how Visual Studio.NET stores the Visual Basic.NET code you will create.

Tip At times we will refer to Visual Studio.NET, and at other times our references will be to Visual Basic.NET specifically. What's the difference? Visual Studio.NET is the integrated development environment that includes the languages and tools you use to create computer programs. Visual Basic.NET is one of the language options available in the development environment, and we will reference Visual Basic.NET when describing how to use this language within the IDE for solving a specific problem.

Solutions, Projects, and Files

To create an application by using Visual Studio.NET, you must first create a solution and then add one or more projects to the solution. A *solution* is the starting point for creating applications in Visual Studio.NET. Think of a solution as the container or receptacle (like a box or package) that manages all the individual pieces that make up your application. You create a solution in Visual Studio.NET. The solutions you create contain one or more *projects*. You create a project by using any Visual Studio.NET language, such as Visual Basic.NET. A project contains the *files* that provide the solution with its functionality or allow the solution to work. The IDE organizes solutions, projects, and files and holds all your work in the hierarchy shown in Figure 1.11.

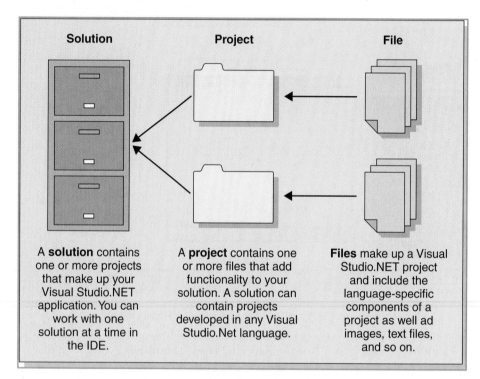

FIGURE 1.11. *Hierarchy showing a solution, its projects, and the project files*

Solution	Project	File
A **solution** contains one or more projects that make up your Visual Studio.NET application. You can work with one solution at a time in the IDE.	A **project** contains one or more files that add functionality to your solution. A solution can contain projects developed in any Visual Studio.Net language.	**Files** make up a Visual Studio.NET project and include the language-specific components of a project as well ad images, text files, and so on.

Creating a new Visual Basic.NET project

You have already started Visual Studio.NET and customized the development environment view. Follow these steps to create a new Visual Basic.NET project.

To Create a New Visual Basic.NET Project:

1. Click **File**, **New**, **Project**, as shown in Figure 1.12. The New Project dialog box opens.

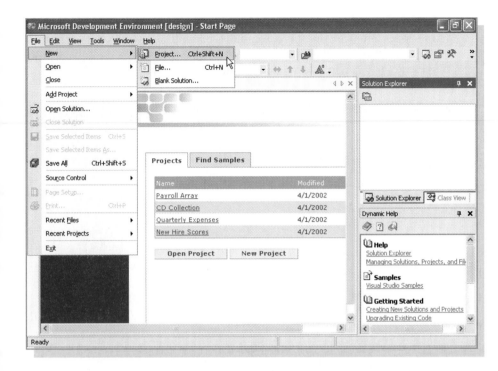

FIGURE 1.12. *Creating a new Visual Basic.NET project*

By default, the Visual Basic Projects folder should be open in the *Project Types:* list, the **Windows Application** template should be selected, and *WindowsApplication1* should appear in the **Name:** text box, as shown in Figure 1.13.

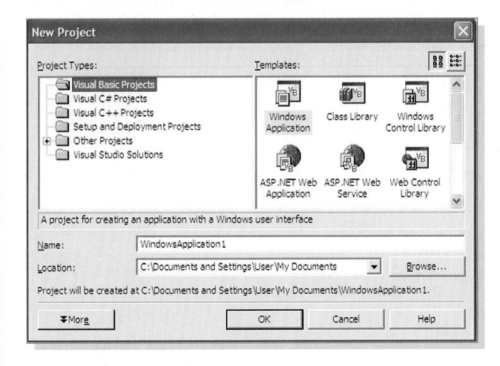

FIGURE 1.13. *The New Project dialog box*

When you create Windows applications by using Visual Studio.NET, the IDE uses the project name to create a new folder for each project you create. This makes it much easier to manage the files generated by the development environment as you work with the project.

2.   Select **Windows Application1** in the **Name:** box. Type About Form as the name for this project.

3.   Click the **Browse** button to navigate to the network or hard-disk location where you will save your projects. Although you can use a floppy disk for sav-

ing your work, you might want to use a network drive or hard disk when you run your projects. In this example, you will use *C:\Documents and Settings\VBNET* to store this project. When the name of your project matches the name shown in Figure 1.14, click **OK**.

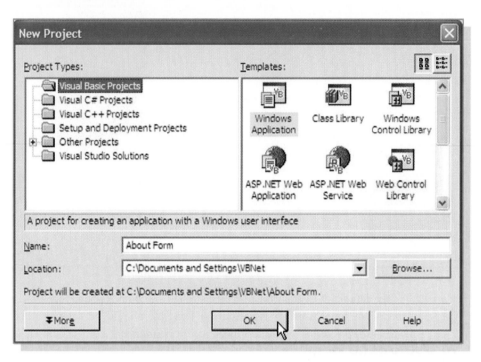

FIGURE 1.14. *Naming and storing your Windows Application project*

Visual Basic.NET now displays the project shown in Figure 1.15.

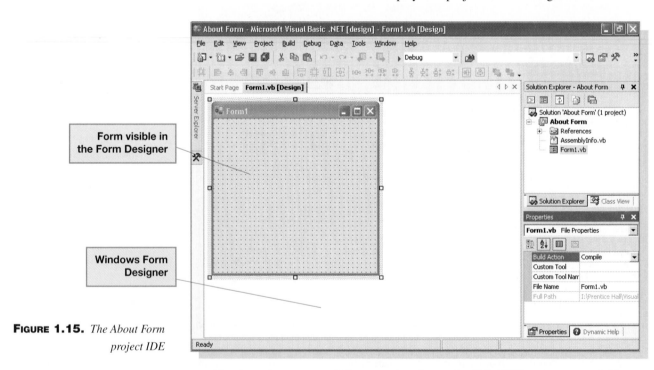

FIGURE 1.15. *The About Form project IDE*

You have just successfully created and saved a VB.NET project named About Form.

If you look closely at Figure 1.15, you will notice that the Solution Explorer window within the development environment has changed from the way it looked in Figure 1.12. When you create a project, Visual Studio.NET automatically generates a solution. Recall that a solution is a container for the projects and solution items you can build into an application. A solution usually has one or more related projects, and a single solution can consist of multiple projects.

The Solution Explorer provides you with an organized view of your solution, projects, and their files. The Solution Explorer uses a common tree-view interface so you can expand and collapse the listings contained in a project.

The form appears in the ***Windows Form Designer*** as shown in Figure 1.15. This is the visual workspace for creating the interface for your application.

As you continue to learn about the Visual Studio IDE, you might have specific questions about how to accomplish certain tasks. As with any application, knowing how to obtain help when you need it is important. With the complexity of Visual Studio, your success depends in part on your ability to obtain help when you need it.

Obtaining Help in Visual Studio

Fortunately, Visual Studio.NET has an extensive help system. As with Help in other Microsoft applications, you can obtain help dynamically, viewing a list of help contents, or search for help by using a word or phrase. You can also use Help to connect to the Web and thereby greatly increase the number of help topics that might be useful to you.

To Use Online Help:

1.   Click **Help**, **Search**, as shown in Figure 1.16.

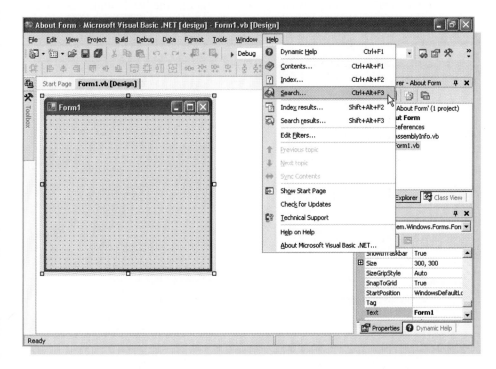

FIGURE 1.16. *Using Online Help in Visual Studio.NET*

The Search window appears as a new window in the Solution Explorer window, as shown in Figure 1.17.

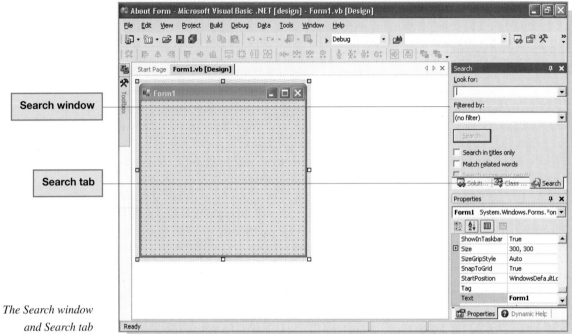

FIGURE 1.17. *The Search window and Search tab*

FIGURE 1.18. *Using the Search window*

2.   Type `designing windows applications` in the **Look for:** text box.

3.   Click the **Filtered by:** button and select Visual Basic and Related. When your settings match those shown in Figure 1.18, click **Search**.

4.   The Search Results window appears at the bottom of the IDE. The Enterprise Developer version of Visual Studio.NET returns the list of topics shown in Figure 1.19.

FIGURE 1.19. *The Search Results window*

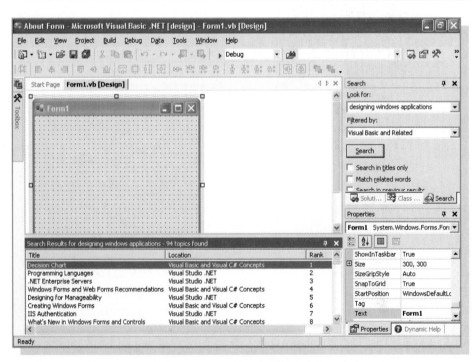

5. Double-click the **Creating Windows Forms** topic. A new tab with the help topic as the name of the tab now appears in the IDE, as shown in Figure 1.20. The **Creating Windows Forms** tab identifies the document window that contains the help topic you selected.

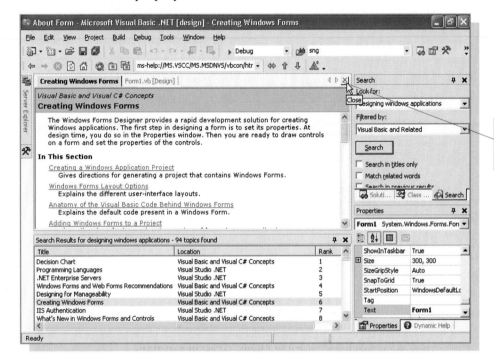

FIGURE 1.20. *The Creating Windows Forms document window*

A ***document window*** is created dynamically when you open or create files or other items. A list of open document windows appears in the Window menu.

You can scroll down the topic in the window to view its entire contents. You can select a related topic from the Search Results window or enter another search topic in the **Look for:** text box. You can also obtain help by any of the methods available on the Help menu.

6. With the help topic active in the Forms window, click the **Close** button shown in Figure 1.20. This closes the help topic and removes its tab from the IDE.

7. Click the **Close** button in the **Search Results** window.

8. Click the **Close** button in the **Search window** to close it, and click the **Solution Explorer** tab to display the Solution Explorer. The IDE once again appears as shown in Figure 1.15.

You have just learned how to get online help in Visual Studio.NET.

When you use Visual Basic.NET to create applications, you work with a variety of objects. In fact, nearly everything you do in Visual Basic.NET involves objects. Before we can go any further with our VB.NET project, you must become familiar with objects.

Objects, Properties, Events, and Methods

At the most fundamental level, an object is anything that is a part of your Visual Basic.NET application. An ***object*** is a combination of code and data you can treat as a single unit. An object can be part of your application, such as a menu, button, text box, or other control on a form. A form is also an object, and the entire application itself is an object.

How you manage your document windows depends greatly on the interface mode you select on the General page of the Environment folder in the Options dialog box. You can choose to work in either Multiple Document Interface (MDI) or Tabbed Documents mode. This book uses the Tabbed Documents mode.

As you work with Visual Studio.NET, you will develop your own preferences for obtaining online help. Using the Search window lets you quickly locate a list of topics and drill down to those that seem most applicable.

When you create a new project, Visual Studio adds a new form named *Form1* to the development environment.

Each project requires at least one form. Remember that a form is an object that acts as a container for the controls a user interacts with when using the application. ***Controls*** are objects such as buttons, text boxes, list boxes, labels, or other interface elements that make up the user interface. For example, if your application contains buttons, each button is a control. The buttons, along with other controls, are contained in the form. Thus controls are one kind of object you use when creating applications.

To learn more about forms and controls, look at an application that performs simple math calculations. Figure 1.21 shows the program interface.

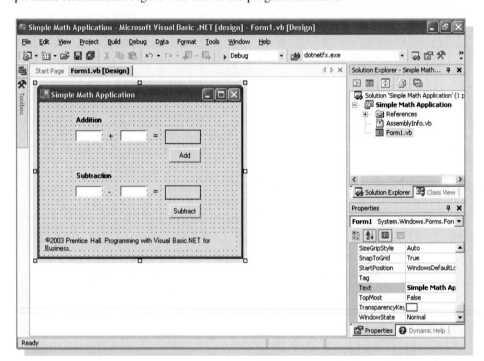

FIGURE 1.21. *Interface for the Simple Math Application*

The form for this application contains three controls commonly added to Visual Basic forms: text boxes, labels, and buttons. To add common controls to the forms contained in a project, you use the ***Toolbox***. The Toolbox holds a series of vertically oriented tabs containing the tools you need to create controls. You can access the Toolbox from the View menu or by clicking the Toolbox button in the IDE. The Toolbox window is currently set to Auto Hide because this is the default for the Visual Studio Developer profile. Let's look at the toolbox and explore its contents.

To display the Toolbox:

1. Move the pointer over the Toolbox tab that appears at the left of the IDE.

2. Because the Toolbox has its Auto Hide property set, it will look like Figure 1.22.

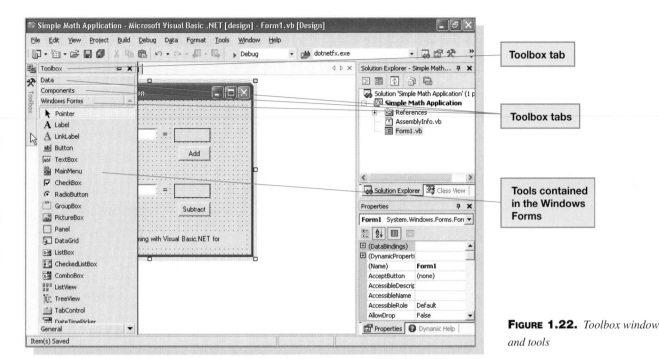

FIGURE 1.22. *Toolbox window and tools*

The tools in the Toolbox are organized according to the tabs you see in the Toolbox window. Figure 1.22 displays the tools that are on the Windows Forms tab.

3. Move the pointer out of the Toolbox tab. The Toolbox disappears.

OBJECT PROPERTIES

Whether they are forms or controls, all objects have characteristics known as properties, which appear in the Properties window when you select the object. The properties of form objects differ from the properties of control objects on a form. The form shown in Figure 1.21 has a **Name property**, *Form1*, and a **Text property**, *Simple Math Application*, that appear in the title bar of the form.

You can tell that the form is active (currently selected) because of the selection handles that appear on the corners and sides of the form. Now look at Figure 1.23. The selection handles around the *Subtract* button indicate that this control is selected. Notice as well that the Name property of the control is *btnSubtract*.

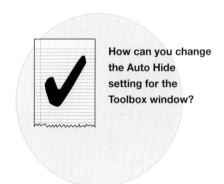

How can you change the Auto Hide setting for the Toolbox window?

You can use an object's selection handles to resize the object, which also changes the object's size property. You will learn more about the Name property for controls later in this chapter.

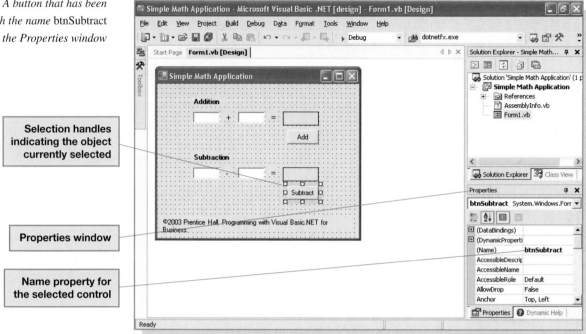

The properties of an object vary, depending on the type of object. Many objects share some of the same properties, such as the **Name** property. Buttons have different properties than text boxes, which have different properties than labels.

Now that you know what an object is, let's examine what an object does.

EVENTS

Some objects are containers for information, while other objects perform actions. In the following example, the application performs two simple math functions: addition and subtraction. The interface includes four text boxes for entering the values to add or subtract and a button for performing the math calculation.

The program inputs are the values entered by the user, the processing is the addition or subtraction of the values, and the output is the result of a calculation. The code for each button determines how to perform the calculations. An *event* is an action that triggers a program instruction. In this example, the buttons respond to a click event, which happens when a user clicks a button when the program is running. An object's code specifies what the object will do in response to an event. When you write code that responds to the click event, the application performs a task in response to a user clicking the button. The processing for this example is as follows:

Addition: First Value + Second Value = Result

Subtraction: First Value – Second Value = Result

The events of an object vary, depending on the object type. For example, buttons have events that differ from those of labels and text boxes.

OBJECT METHODS

The methods of an object determine which actions an event can trigger. A *method* is a specific action an object can perform when the application is running. For example, button controls have a **Hide** method and a **Show** method. If you do not want a button to be visible when the application is running, you can use the Hide method to make the button invisible. To make the button visible, use the Show method.

How do properties, events, and methods differ? In general, `properties` characterize an object's *appearance*. For example, the **Text** property of a button indicates the text contained by the button. `Events` are the actions to which a control *responds*. For example, code for a button's click event causes the program to perform an action when a user clicks a button. `Methods` characterize an object's *behavior*. For example, the state of being visible or invisible is a method supported by many objects in Visual Basic.NET.

Setting Properties at Design Time or Run Time

You can change the properties of an object in either design time or run time. It is common to set specific properties of an object, such as the object's name, at design time. *Design time* is the state of the application while you are working with a project in the development environment. Notice the word [Design] in the title bar of your project in Figure 1.23. This indicates that the application is currently in design time. You can change the properties of the object by using the Properties window, also shown in Figure 1.23.

To change the properties of an object at design time, select the object and then set or change the properties for the object in the Properties window.

Run time is the state of the application while it is running. You change an object's properties during run time by writing code that responds to specific events. The code appears in the form of an assignment statement, which is a statement in code that refers to the property and assigns a setting. The following examples show the general format for constructing an assignment statement and using an assignment statement to change the Text property of a control.

Assignment Statements: General Format

```
Object.Property = Value
```

Assignment Statement: Example

```
txtLastName.Text = "Smith"
```

The text in an assignment statement is a ***text string*** of one or more characters. To join multiple text strings so that the information displayed in the Text property of the text box appears on multiple lines, you use the ***ampersand symbol*** (&) between the strings to connect the individual text strings into a single string. The process of joining multiple elements such as text is ***concatenation***. The ampersand character *concatenates*, or joins, the text strings.

Naming Objects

The naming scheme you choose for objects is a big help toward understanding the logical flow of an application. Microsoft recommends that you make names long enough to be meaningful but short enough to be easily understood. Unique names differentiate the objects in your application. Expressive names function as an aid to a human reader. You might want to use names that a reader can easily comprehend. Although the rules for naming objects are simple—the first character of the name must be an alphabetic character or an underscore—most programmers follow a specific naming convention for the objects in a Visual Basic project so that the objects can easily be identified.

Modified-Hungarian Notation was originally developed for C++ by Microsoft's Chief Architect Dr. Charles Simonyi, who introduced a naming convention that adds a prefix to the identifier name to indicate the functional type of the identifier. Although Microsoft recommends you do not use Hungarian notation for some program elements, such as naming controls on your forms, it remains a common standard.

You will see that Microsoft uses Hungarian notation for many of the code samples in Visual Studio.NET. It is one technique that helps programmers produce consistent code. Two relevant articles are on Microsoft's MSDN knowledge base. Visit the MSDN knowledge base Website at: http://support.microsoft.com

Use the search tool to locate the following articles:

Article Q110264 (consulting standards)
Article Q173738 (C Hungarian naming conventions)

The specific naming conventions used in Visual Basic applications vary widely, and this range of practices is even reflected in the Visual Basic and Visual Studio.NET examples you will find on Microsoft's Website and in the Visual Studio.NET documentation. For consistency, we will use Modified-Hungarian Notation in this book.

When you work with other programmers, it is important to work by a standard so the other programmers will be familiar with the objects you create. The most common standard for naming controls in Visual Studio.NET is *Modified-Hungarian Notation*. This standard became widely used inside Microsoft and is accepted in the programming community.

Table 1.1 lists the Modified-Hungarian notation for naming some of the controls used in this chapter. The name for each object begins with a three-character, lowercase prefix, followed by a descriptive name of the object that begins with a capital letter.

Table 1.1: The Visual Basic.NET Modified-Hungarian Object Naming Convention

Type of Object or Control	Prefix	Example of an Object Name
Button	btn	btnExit
Form	frm	frmTempConv
Label	lbl	lblTitle
List box	lst	lstInterestRate
Picture box	pic	picLogo
Text box	txt	txtFirstName

Now that you have a better understanding of objects, properties, events, and methods, let's make sure you understand how programming in Visual Basic.NET differs from programming in other languages. These differences influence how you will develop your projects.

UNDERSTANDING PROCEDURAL AND EVENT-DRIVEN PROGRAMMING

The steps you take to design a program will differ depending on the programming language you use to create the program. Although all software development projects require you to define the problem to be solved, identify the inputs and outputs, and create and test the program, the type of programming language you'll use to create the program will vary. In Visual Basic.NET, the IDE provides the tools you need to create applications that run in the Windows environment and respond to user events.

Assume you need to create an application that displays a message on the computer screen when the program runs. This chapter shows you how to create two versions of the **Hello World** application that displays the message *Hello World!* on the screen. To understand the capabilities of Visual Basic.NET, take a look at a simple, text-based programming solution for creating the **Hello World** application.

Procedural Programming

Some programming languages, such as BASIC, COBOL, FORTRAN, and Pascal, are procedural languages. In a procedural language, the program specifies the sequence of all operations in a step-by-step manner, and the order of the program statements determines how the computer program will carry out a specific task.

Let's look first at how a procedural application displays *Hello World!* on the screen. Here is the program code for displaying a message on the screen by using a procedural programming language:

```
10 REM ============================================================
20 REM Copyright 2003 Prentice Hall
30 REM Programming with Visual Basic.NET for Business
40 REM Chapter 1: Simple procedural program example
50 REM "Hello World!"
60 REM ============================================================
70 PRINT "Programming with Visual Basic.NET for Business"
80 PRINT ""
90 PRINT "Hello World!"
100 END
```

This program was written in QBASIC, an early Microsoft text-based version of the BASIC programming language. QBASIC is a text-based interface that displays a *command prompt* when the program runs. In a command prompt environment such as MS-DOS, you indicate what actions the computer is to perform by typing a statement at the prompt and pressing the ⏎Enter key. In this example, the program results are displayed on the screen as text.

Each line of program code in our example is numbered. The first six lines (numbered 10 through 60) include a statement interpreted by the program, called a *keyword*. In this case, the keyword is **REM**, which stands for *remark*. A *remark* is a comment the programmer adds to the code, often to document what the program is doing. Lines 70 through 90 use the **PRINT** keyword to instruct the computer to display the text included in quotes on the screen. Line 100 includes the END keyword, which indicates the end of the code statements.

Figure 1.24 shows how the program code appears when written in the QBasic Editor, which is the QBasic text-based development environment.

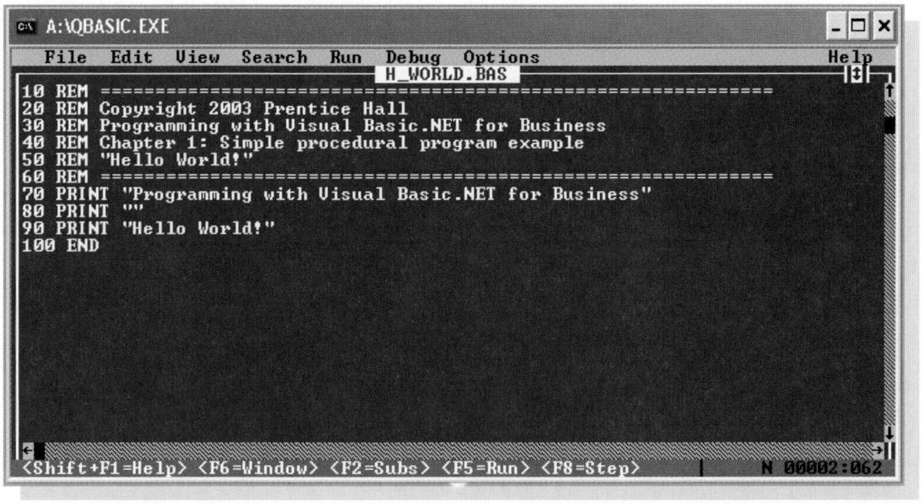

FIGURE 1.24. *Program code in QBasic Editor*

When the program runs, each line is loaded into the computer's memory before the subsequent lines run. There is no user interaction with this program; there are no user events. The computer simply displays text on the screen. Because the user is not given any opportunity to determine the program results, and the message that displays cannot be changed without changing the program code, the program is known as *hard-coded*. Figure 1.25 shows the result.

FIGURE 1.25. *Interface for the QBasic Hello World application*

The procedural program in the example displays text on the screen. The program flow in procedural programs is determined by the order of the instructions. Now compare what you've learned about procedural programming to event-driven programming.

Event Driven Programming

Visual Basic.NET is an *event-driven language*. In an event-driven language, you write program code that responds to specific events. The program logic in an event-driven language is not limited to any specific sequence of events you must anticipate while developing the program.

Visual Basic.NET is also an object-oriented language. You can use an object-oriented language to create objects that respond to events in different ways, and you build programs by combining objects. You use an object-oriented language to create reusable programming objects, which reduces development time.

Let's take a look at a Visual Basic.NET version of the **Hello World!** program. Figure 1.26 shows the program interface as it appears in the Visual Studio.NET IDE.

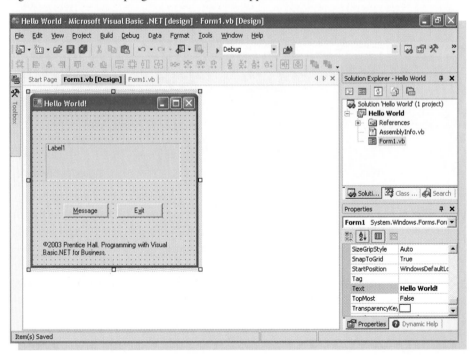

FIGURE 1.26. *Interface for the Visual Basic.NET Hello World application*

In Figure 1.26, the Solution Explorer displays a single form named *Form1.vb*. The form contains two buttons and two labels. So what makes this program event driven? When the program runs, it waits for a user event, such as clicking a button. Figure 1.27 shows the code that handles the events associated with clicking the buttons that appear on the form.

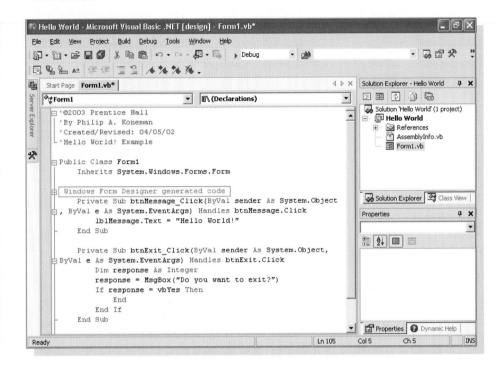

FIGURE 1.27. *Code for button click events in the Hello World application*

The code runs in no predetermined order. If the user clicks the **Message** button, the text shown in Figure 1.28 is displayed in a label on the form.

When the procedure associated with clicking the Message button runs, the program does not terminate. Rather, the program continues to run and can accept another event at any time. You can continue to click the **Message** button, and each time you do, the code associated with this event will run. Or, you can run the code for another event by clicking the **Exit** button, which runs the procedure associated with this event. Figure 1.29 shows the message box that appears when the **Exit** button is clicked.

FIGURE 1.28. *Viewing the results of a click event*

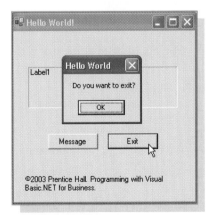

FIGURE 1.29. *Message box after clicking Exit button*

The message box contains a button control that has program code associated with it. If you click **OK**, the application will terminate. You can also click the **Close** button in the message box to run another procedure and remove the message box from the screen.

Now consider how the event-driven Visual Basic.NET application illustrated differs from the procedural QBasic program. Although both programs are written with the Basic language and will therefore have some similarities, there are also significant differences. The QBasic procedural example is run from a command prompt. The procedural program gathers input from the keyboard and prints the results to the screen, using a text-based interface. There are no message boxes, no buttons to click, and no graphical user interface for displaying the results.

The Visual Basic.NET example includes specific interface elements or controls such as buttons, message boxes, and labels on a form that will be displayed to the user *and* the code that gives the program its functionality. The program code is not run sequentially when the application starts but only when the user initiates an event. In the case of clicking a button, the user initiates an event through a specific action.

Before creating an application, you need to determine what information to gather from the user, how to store the information, how the program will act on this information, and how to return the results to the user. These considerations often dictate whether procedural or event-driven programming is preferable for your application.

Even though event-driven, object-oriented languages are more flexible than procedural languages, event-driven applications require more work than procedural applications. Let's look at a process that will help you handle the work required in event-driven, object-oriented applications in Visual Basic.NET.

Steps for Planning and Creating Visual Basic.NET Applications

Have you ever started a project and not been able to complete it as you originally intended? If you are like most of us, you know how even the best ideas sometimes go awry and good intentions are sidetracked by factors you did not anticipate at the outset. Perhaps things cost more than originally estimated, a necessary process is more complex than you anticipated, you changed your mind in the midst of the task to expand the original vision, or finishing the project simply is taking more time than predicted.

You might be thinking that planning is necessary only for complex projects. Do you need a plan for creating simple Visual Basic.NET projects that will run on a single computer? Yes, you do.

Before creating an application, you need to determine:

- What information to gather from the user
- How to store the information
- How the program will act on this information
- How to return the program results to the user
- These considerations often dictate how you design the application. After you have determined how you will distribute your application (as a Windows application or as a Web application), you are ready to create it.

Although the applications you will create in these chapters are relatively simple, mastering a four-step process for your applications will help when your projects become more complex. The four-step process is:

1. **Plan** the application.
2. **Design** the user interface and set the properties of objects.
3. **Write** code to handle events.
4. **Run** the application to verify that it successfully does what it is designed to do.

To learn about each step in the process, let's apply the process to designing a temperature conversion application.

Although some applications are designed to display information onscreen, other applications perform calculations and produce a result. Assume that the company you work for has its corporate offices in New York and subsidiary offices in Toronto and London. The company has a Web cam at each office that shows a live picture of the front entrance and, with the picture, displays the current temperature and humidity index. Employees in New York are used to seeing the temperature in Fahrenheit, while employees in London and Toronto are more familiar with Celsius. Therefore, your company includes a temperature conversion application on its corporate network.

1. PLAN THE APPLICATION

After you have decided that your temperature conversion project will be a Windows desktop application, you are ready to begin planning. The program will receive the following inputs and produce the following outputs:

Inputs	Outputs
Temperature to convert	Converted temperature

The user enters a temperature to convert into a text box. The converted temperature displays in a label. The user clicks a button to perform the desired conversion: Fahrenheit to Celsius, or Celsius to Fahrenheit. The formulas for calculating the conversion are as follows:

$$\text{Celsius to Fahrenheit:} \quad (9/5)\,C + 32$$

$$\text{Fahrenheit to Celsius:} \quad 5/9\,(F - 32)$$

The first step is to draw a diagram or mock-up of the user interface on a piece of paper. Figure 1.30 shows a drawing of the user interface.

The drawing, created on a legal pad, shows the approximate location and Name property of each control. This design document is essential for actually creating the form and controls that comprise the user interface.

Then name the controls and specify the properties you will set at design time. When you plan a Visual Basic application, you set some object properties at design time and others at run time. When you add controls to a form, many of the properties have a default setting, and some of these you change at design time. When you use your mock-up to create the form, you will also want to refer to Table 1.2, which lists the properties of each control you will set at design time. For the properties not listed, use the default setting.

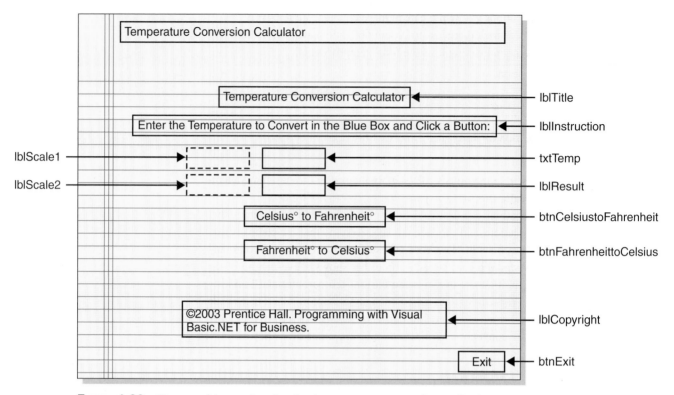

FIGURE 1.30. *Diagram of the user interface for the temperature conversion application*

Table 1.2: Object Properties for the Temperature Conversion Application

Object Name	Property	Setting
Form1	StartPosition	CenterScreen
	Size	576, 384
lblTitle	Text	Temperature Conversion Calculator
	Font	Arial, 18pt, style=Bold
	ForeColor	Navy
lblInstruction	Text	Enter the temperature to convert in the blue box and press a button.
	Font	Arial, 12pt, style=Bold
lblScale1	Text	None
	Font	Arial, 9pt
lblScale2	Text	None
	Font	Arial, 9pt
txtTemp	Text	None
	BackColor	192, 255, 255
	BorderStyle	Fixed3D
	Font	Arial, 12pt, style=Bold
lblResult	Text	None
	BackColor	255, 255, 192
	BorderStyle	Fixed3D
	Font	Arial, 12pt, style=Bold
btnCelsiusToFahrenheit	Text	Celsius° to Fahrenheit°
btnFahrenheitToCelsius	Text	Fahrenheit° to Celsius°

Table 1.2: *(continued)*

Object Name	Property	Setting
lblCopyright	Text	©2003 Prentice Hall. Programming with Visual Basic.NET for Business.
btnExit	Text	Exit

Finally, write the program events as pseudocode. ***Pseudocode*** is English-like statements that express in simple terms what the program will do. An example of the pseudocode for a program that performs a temperature conversion follows:

1. Get a value of the temperature to convert from the user.

2. Have the user tell the program which calculation to perform.

3. Perform the calculation.

4. Display the result.

Because the form contains three buttons, the pseudocode shown in Table 1.3 lists the procedure associated with the click event for each button. For this project, the event handled by all three buttons occurs when the button is clicked.

Table 1.3: Pseudocode for the Temperature Conversion Application

Event Procedure	Action
btnCelsiusToFahrenheit	Perform the Celsius to Fahrenheit conversion for the value entered in the txtTemp text box. Display the result of the calculation as the Text property of the lblResult label.
btnFahrenheitToCelsius	Perform the Fahrenheit to Celsius conversion for the value entered in the txtTemp text box. Display the result of the calculation as the Text property of the lblResult label.
btnExit_Click	Exit the project

You can then use your plan as a blueprint for designing the user interface.

2. DESIGN THE USER INTERFACE

In this step, you will design the user interface for the application. The user interface includes all the program components the end user will see and interact with, including objects such as forms and the controls for gathering input, making selections, performing actions, and displaying program results. Common control objects include labels, text boxes, and buttons. A *label* displays text as a caption that cannot be edited by the user. It is common to use labels for titles on forms. A *text box* contains text that the user can enter and change. A *button* runs an event procedure. You can add controls to the form by dragging a tool from the Toolbox to your Windows form.

After you create a form and add controls to it, you then set the properties for each object. One of the first properties you normally set for the objects in a project is the Name property, because you will always refer to an object by its name when you reference it in code.

Using the information in the preceding sections, you as the programmer would use the IDE to create the Windows form and associated controls shown in Figure 1.31.

Tip

Every object must have a unique Name property.

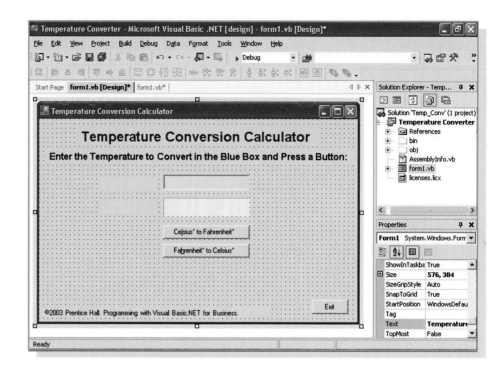

FIGURE 1.31. *Creating the Windows form and controls for the temperature conversion application*

3. WRITE THE CODE

After designing the user interface, you plan and write the program code that will give your application functionality or allow the application to work. The pseudocode you created in Step 1 describes the program's functionality in simple English-like terms, but when you write the code, you must include statements that follow the Visual Basic.NET syntax. In this step, you will plan the detailed program procedures that respond to specific events and then write the code statements that carry out these actions. For each pseudocode statement, write a Visual Basic.NET code statement.

In Visual Studio.NET, you write code by using the ***Code Editor***, which opens a document window in the IDE and displays all the code statements for an application. The Code Editor is the document window you use to enter the program statements that give your program its functionality.

The code for your application typically begins with remarks, also called ***comments***, which are internal documentation that explain what the code accomplishes. ***Documentation*** includes anything that helps someone understand the program. ***Internal documentation*** usually consists of comments added to the program statements to help programmers understand the purpose of the program code. ***External documentation*** refers to any documents that explain the application. For commercial programs, external documentation usually includes the user's manual and the online help system.

Internal documentation does nothing at run time but is invaluable at design time to help you understand why an application is designed as it is. A standard programming convention is to add documentation at the beginning of a program's code as well as before specific code sections. Comments provide information about the application, such as the programmer, the date the application was created, and a brief description of the specific task that each procedure accomplishes.

You add comments to the code by entering an apostrophe character (') before the text for the comment. In the Code Editor window, comments appear as green text. In this book, we will use the following format for entering comments at the beginning of each application:

Tip

When you use the Windows Form Designer to add controls to a form and set the properties, Visual Studio.NET automatically adds code to the Code Editor. This code will appear if you click the plus sign (+) that appears next to the Windows Form Designer-generated code region in the Code Editor. Make sure you do not modify this code in the Code Editor.

```
' 2003 Prentice Hall
'By [Enter your name here. . .]
'Date Created/Revised: [Enter the date here. . .]
'[Enter the application title here. . .]
```

The code for the temperature conversion application follows. You can enter the code directly into the Code Editor.

```
'©2003 Prentice Hall
'Philip A. Koneman
'Created/Revised: 04/05/02
'Temperature Conversion Example
Public Class Form1
  Inherits System.Windows.Forms.Form
Private Sub btnCelsiusToFahrenheit_Click(ByVal sender As
      System.Object, ByVal e As System.EventArgs) Handles
      btnCelsiusToFahrenheit.Click
    lblResult.Text = (9 / 5) * Val(txtTemp.Text) + 32
    lblScale1.Text = "Celsius°"
    lblScale2.Text = "Fahrenheit°"
  End Sub
  Private Sub btnFahrenheitToCelsius_Click(ByVal sender As
      System.Object, ByVal e As System.EventArgs) Handles
      btnFahrenheitToCelsius.Click
    lblResult.Text = (5 / 9) * (Val(txtTemp.Text) - 32)
    lblScale1.Text = "Fahrenheit°"
    lblScale2.Text = "Celsius°"
  End Sub
  Private Sub cmdExit_Click(ByVal sender As Object, ByVal e As
      System.EventArgs) Handles cmdExit.Click
    End
  End Sub
End Class
```

When you create code procedures in Visual Studio.NET, the IDE creates some of the code statements for you.

This code uses the **Val** function to convert the number appearing in the text box to a numeric value that Visual Basic.NET can use in a calculation. The **Val** function will not read any character it cannot recognize as part of a number, such as a dollar sign ($) or a comma (,). You can use this function to convert numbers entered as text to numbers you can use in calculations. You will learn more about the **Val** function in Chapter 2.

The code appears in the Code Editor as shown in Figure 1.32.

The Visual Studio.NET IDE contains two kinds of windows. In what kind of window does the Code Editor appear?

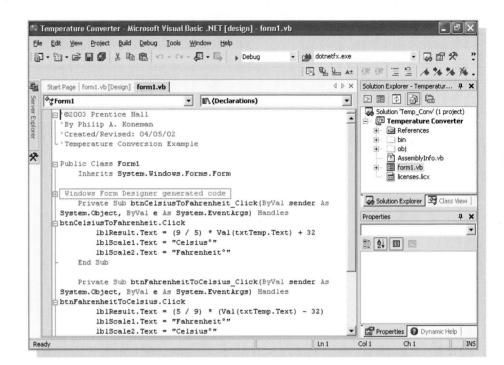

FIGURE 1.32. *Code Editor displaying the code for the temperature conversion application*

After you have completed the steps of designing the user interface, setting the object properties, and writing the code, you are ready to run your application.

4. RUN THE APPLICATION

You normally run an application while you are developing it to test the code's functionality. It is important to test and debug the applications you create. ***Testing*** is the process of running the application to locate any errors. A program error is a ***bug***, so ***debugging*** is the process of identifying, correcting, and eliminating errors in your application. When you run an application, Visual Studio switches to ***debug mode***. In debug mode, Visual Studio flags errors that occur when the application is running. Most applications check for common data-entry errors, such as entering a letter rather than a number. Other times, an error might trigger an event, such as when you try to print records from a database but the printer is not turned on.

During this step, you can use a number of tools for debugging your application. You can debug your application by simply testing its functionality or by using the many debugging tools available from the Debug menu. You will learn how to use the Visual Studio.NET debugger in the second Guided Exercise in Chapter 2.

When you run the application from within the Visual Basic.NET development environment, it will appear as shown in Figure 1.33. In this case, we entered 275 into the *txtTemp* text box, and then we clicked the *btnFahrenheitToCelsius* button. The result of 135 appears as the Text property of the *lblResult* label.

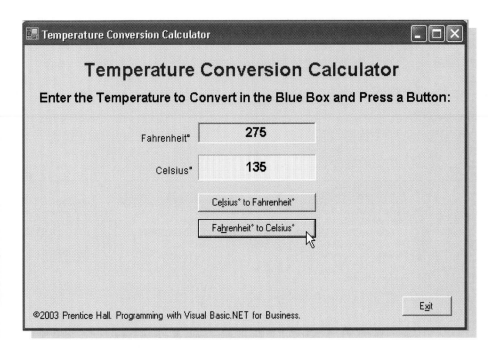

FIGURE 1.33. *Running the temperature conversion application*

As you can see, planning and designing even a simple application requires that you follow a process or methodology to determine the purpose of the application, the objects that will support an interface to allow users to use the program, and the program code that provides functionality to the application.

Now that you have seen the process demonstrated, you will have the opportunity to plan and design your first Visual Basic application.

☛ HANDS-ON PROGRAMMING EXAMPLE

CREATING AN *ABOUT* FORM

Many applications include a form that displays information about the program. In the Windows environment, information about an application often shows in a dialog box when the user selects an option from the Help menu. The dialog box or the form usually displays license and version information about the application. Figure 1.34 shows the dialog box that appears when you select **About Microsoft Visual Basic.NET** from the Help menu in the IDE.

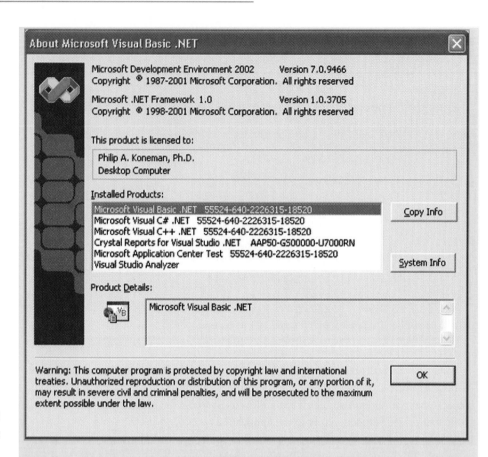

FIGURE 1.34. *About Microsoft Visual Basic.NET dialog box*

Your form should be generic enough to provide the kind of information that is normally included in an *About* dialog box, yet also specific to the applications you will create in this book. Many *About* forms display a company logo, the program title, and other information that is deemed important to communicate to the user. This form will display the name of the application and allow the user to select information about the application version and licensing information by clicking the appropriate button.

The form, when finished, will appear as shown in Figure 1.35.

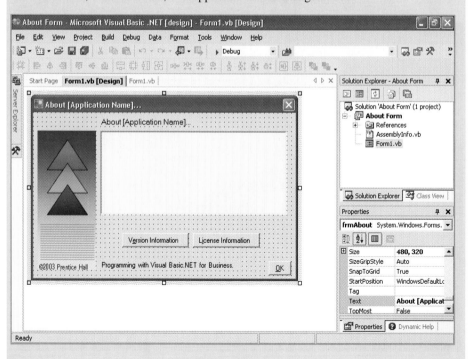

FIGURE 1.35. *Interface for About form*

When the form appears, there is no information in the text box located in the center of the form. Clicking the **Version Information** or **License Information** button displays the appropriate information. Clicking the OK button hides the form.

You are now ready to design your own *About Form* dialog box that you can add to any Windows application you create in Visual Basic.NET. Because Visual Basic.NET is object-oriented, you will be able to use this form in other applications you create. The solution you will create consists of a single form. You will create the form according to the specifications identified in the planning phase. When you design the interface, you will add the appropriate controls to the form and then write the program code. After running the application to ensure that it handles events as specified in the design, you will be able to add this form to any Visual Basic.NET solution.

Plan the Application

The first step in planning an application is determining the inputs and outputs. This application displays information onscreen, so the inputs and outputs are as follows:

Inputs	Outputs
User selection	Version information, license information

The inputs are the decisions the user makes about which program information to display or a decision to close the form by using the OK button.

Draw a visual representation of the application on a blank piece of paper. Figure 1.36 shows a drawing of the user interface and the name of each control on the form.

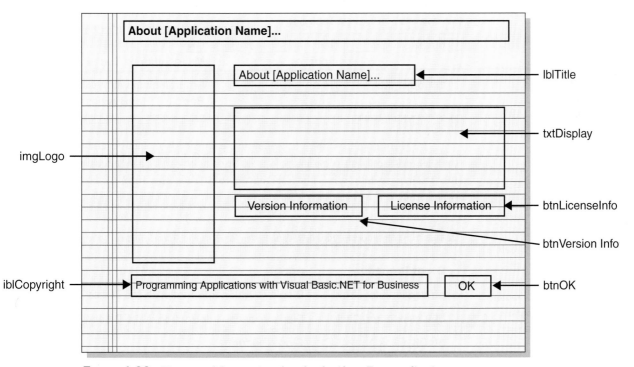

FIGURE 1.36. *Diagram of the user interface for the About Form application*

Table 1.4 lists the object control properties you will set at design time.

Table 1.4: *Object control properties for the About Form application*

Object Name	Control Property	Setting
frmAbout	StartPosition FormBorderStyle MaximizeBox MinimizeBox Size Text Image	CenterScreen Fixed3D False False 480, 320 About [Application Name].. AboutLogo.bmp
picLogo	Text	About [Application Name]..
lblTitle	Font Text	Microsoft Sans Serif, 9.75pt
txtDisplay	BackColor Multiline TabStop TabIndex	Info (Use the System tab to set the BackColor) True False 0
btnVersionInfo	Text TabIndex	V&ersion Information 1
btnLicenseInfo	Text TabIndex	L&icense Information 2
btnOK	Text Font	OK Microsoft Sans Serif, 8.25pt
lblCopyright	Text	Programming with Visual Basic.NET for Business.

The form contains three buttons, and each needs to handle a click event. The buttons for displaying version and license information will change the Text property of the *txtDisplay* text box. The OK button will hide the form. Table 1.5 lists the pseudocode for the event procedures.

Table 1.5: *Pseudocode for the Event Procedures in the About Form Application*

Event Procedure	Action
btnVersionInfo_Click	Display version information in the Display text box.
btnLicenseInfo_Click	Display license information in the Display text box.
btnOK_Click	Close the form.

Now that you have the planning documents for the application, you are ready to begin designing the user interface in the IDE.

Tip

Normally a form contains a button to exit or terminate the application. Because the goal of this project is to create a form you can add to any Visual Basic.NET solution, it is more appropriate to hide the form rather than to terminate the application. Therefore, this form does not contain an exit button.

Design the User Interface

Copy the *AboutLogo.bmp* image file from your student data disk to the *About Form* network or disk folder where you created the *About Form* solution earlier in the chapter. You will need this image when you set the image property of the *picLogo* control. After completing this task, launch Visual Studio.NET. You are now ready to open the application.

To Open an Existing Application:

1. Click **File**, **Open Solution**.
2. Open the *About Form* folder on your network location or data disk. Highlight the *About Form* solution file and click **Open**, as shown in Figure 1.37.

FIGURE 1.37. *Opening the existing About Form solution*

3. Depending on the state of Visual Studio when the project was last open, you might have multiple windows open on the screen. Click **My Profile** on the Start Page, choose **Visual Developer** in the **Profile:** list, and click **Get Started** on the Start Page.
4. Right-click the *Form1.vb* file in the Solution Explorer and choose **View Designer**, as shown in Figure 1.38, to display the form in the Windows Form Designer.

If the Start Page is not visible, click **Help, Show Start Page.**

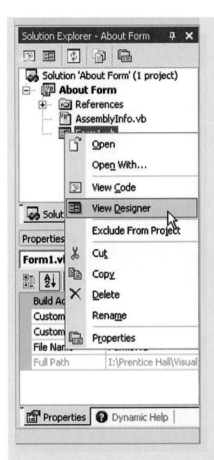

FIGURE 1.38. *Choosing View Designer in the Solution Explorer window*

When you set or modify properties in the Properties window, you are changing the properties at design time.

Whenever you make a change to the application, an asterisk character (*) appears on the active tab in the IDE. Save your application after each change you make. Click File, Save All to update all the components in your solution.

Click File, Save to update the selected item in the solution. The asterisk disappears when you have saved your changes.

The form now appears in the Windows Form Designer window, and the form's properties are visible in the Properties window.

To Set the Properties for the Form:

1. In the **Name** row of the **Properties** window, select **Form.vb** and type `frmAbout` as the new name for the form.
2. Set the remaining properties for the form as listed in Table 1.4. To set a property, select the current property in the Properties row and either select or type the new value. Some properties, such as the **FormBorderStyle** property, have a drop-down list from which you make a selection. Other properties, such as the **Size** property, require you to enter the property setting by clicking the property row and typing a value.

Adding Additional Controls to the Form and Setting Control Properties:

1. Move the pointer over the Toolbox tab on the left edge of the Windows Form Designer. The Toolbox appears.
2. Click the pushpin in the Toolbox tool window to turn off Auto Hide for the window.
3. Point to the Label tool and click to activate the tool. Move the pointer over the form. Notice that the pointer turns to a cross hair, indicating that the tool is active.

4. Click below the text in the form's title bar and drag the pointer to the approximate location shown in Figure 1.39.

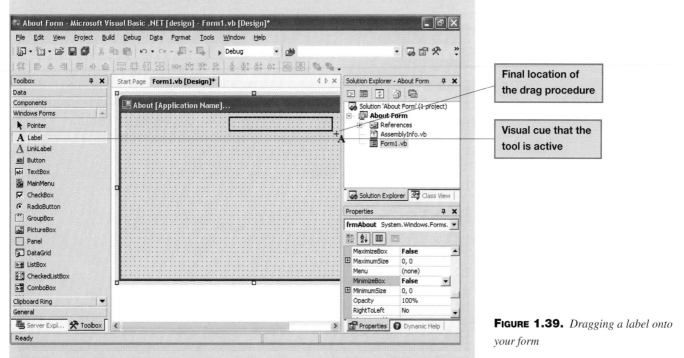

Final location of the drag procedure

Visual cue that the tool is active

FIGURE 1.39. *Dragging a label onto your form*

5. Using the settings listed in Table 1.4, set the properties for the label control you just created. To set the **Font** property, click the **Font** row in the **Properties** pane. When the row is active, an ellipsis button appears to the right of the row. If you click this button, the Font dialog box appears, and you can then specify the font properties. Alternatively, you can click the expand button, which appears as a plus sign to the left of the Font property row. The left image in Figure 1.40 shows the Font property row before expanding the Font properties. The right image shows the expanded Font properties after changing the default size to 9.75.

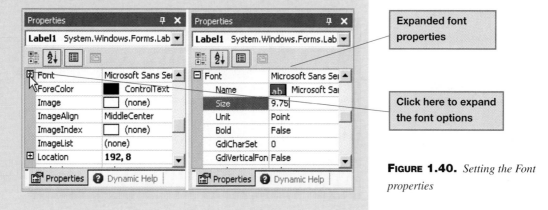

Expanded font properties

Click here to expand the font options

FIGURE 1.40. *Setting the Font properties*

6. Click the **PictureBox** tool in the Toolbox and drag a picture box to the approximate location shown on your form design document. After setting the Name property to `picLogo`, click the **Image** property. The Open dialog box appears. Navigate to the About Form folder. Click the *AboutLogo.bmp* filename to select the file, and then click **Open**, as shown in Figure 1.41.

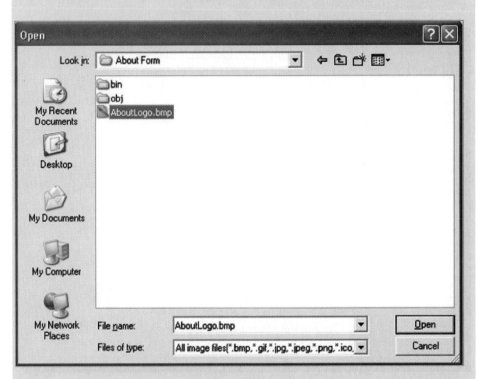

FIGURE 1.41. *Adding an image file to a picture box*

The logo now appears in the picture box. Click the PictureBox control and resize it as necessary.

7. Click the **TextBox** tool and drag a text box control onto the form as shown in Figure 1.42 .

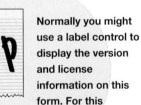

Normally you might use a label control to display the version and license information on this form. For this project you will use a text box control, because a text box has a multiline property for displaying more than one line of text in the control.

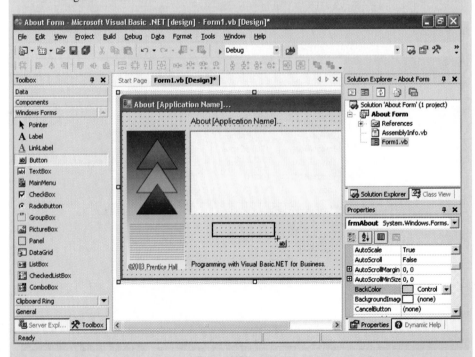

FIGURE 1.42. *About logo appearing in picture box*

8. Size and position the control as shown in your mock-up design document in Figure 1.36.

9. Set the properties specified in Table 1.4. To delete the **Text** property, select the text and press the ⬚Del⬚ key. After you select another property or click somewhere else, the default text in the box will disappear.

10. Add an additional label control to the bottom of the form for the copyright information. Set the properties as specified.

11. Click the **Button** tool and drag a button onto the form. When you set the Text property for the button, use the ampersand symbol (&) as specified in Table 1.4.

12. Create the two remaining button controls and set their properties. After you have added these controls, click the pushpin on the Toolbox tool window to set the window to Auto Hide.

13. Resize and reposition the controls on the form as necessary to make your form match the one shown in Figure 1.35.

14. Click the **Save All** button to save your changes.

Now that the form's user interface is complete, you are ready to write the code that will give the form its functionality.

Write the Code

The About form contains three buttons, each of which will respond to a Click event. The code that handles each event will reside in a procedure. As you write the code to handle the Click events, you will add comments as internal documentation.

To Write Code to Handle the Form's Click Events:

1. Press the ⬚F7⬚ key to open the Code Editor. The Code Editor window opens, and a tab for the Code Editor appears in the IDE.

2. The insertion point will be at the top of the Code Editor. Type an apostrophe character (') to indicate you are entering a comment.

3. Make sure the Num Lock key is on. Then hold down ⬚Alt⬚ and press 0169 on the numeric keypad to add a copyright symbol at the beginning of the comment.

4. Type 2003 Prentice Hall and press ⬚↵Enter⬚. On the next line, type By [Enter your name] and press ⬚↵Enter⬚. On the third line, type 'Created/Revised: [Enter the date] and press ⬚↵Enter⬚. For the fourth line, type 'About Form and press ⬚↵Enter⬚. The code will appear as shown in Figure 1.43.

Tip Placing the ampersand symbol before a character designates an *access key*, which is the key you can press while holding down the ⬚Alt⬚ key as a keyboard shortcut to evoke the button's procedure.

Tip When you save your changes, the asterisk symbol no longer appears on the Form Designer window tab in the IDE. This indicates that all changes to the form have been saved.

Tip You can also open the Code Editor by double-clicking a control.

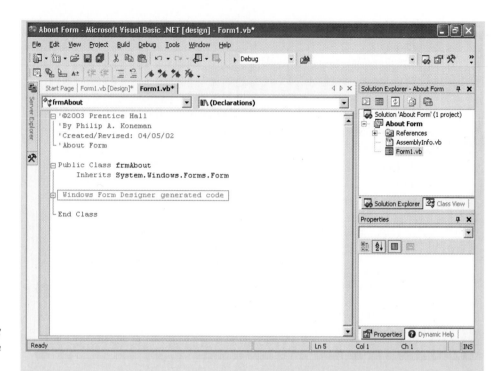

FIGURE 1.43. *Code Editor displaying the code for the About form application*

5. The Code Editor has two drop-down lists near the top of the window. The left list is the ***Class Name list***, and the right list is the ***Method Name list***. You can use these lists in the Code Editor to select a control and a method or action for the control. Click the **Class Name** list and select **btnVersionInfo**, as shown in Figure 1.44.

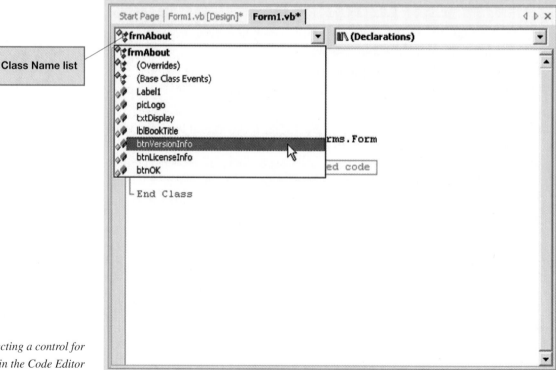

FIGURE 1.44. *Selecting a control for the About form in the Code Editor*

6. Click the **Method Name** list and select **Click** as shown in Figure 1.45. The Code Editor defines a procedure that will handle the click event for the **btnVersionInfo** control. You will write code for the event inside this procedure.

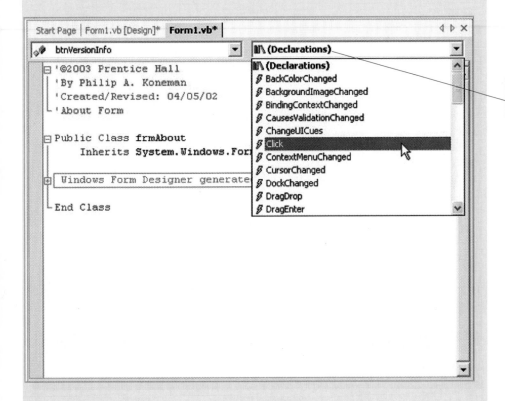

FIGURE **1.45.** *Selecting a method for a control in the Code Editor*

7. Type 'Change the Text property of the txtDisplay text box to display program version information and press ⏎Enter. This adds a remark to the code as internal documentation.

8. Place the insertion point at the beginning of the blank line between the **Private Sub** and **End Sub** statements. Type the assignment statement txtDisplay.Text = "[Application Name]" & vbCrLf & vbCrLf & "Version 0.100.0000"

    You are also adding two carriage returns, represented by **vbCrLf**, so a blank line appears in the *txtDisplay* control.

9. Click the **Class Name** list and select the **cmdLicenseInfo** object in the list.

10. Click the **Method Name** list and select the **Click** method.

11. Type 'Change the Text property of the txtDisplay text box to display license information and press ⏎Enter. Now type txtDisplay.Text = "License Information" & vbCrLf & vbCrLf & "Please refer to the license agreement accompanying this product for licensing information."

12. Select the **cmdOK Class Name** in the list and the **Click** method in the **Method Name** list. Type 'Close the current form and press ⏎Enter. Now type Me.Close. Visual Studio automatically adds open and close parentheses to the statement after you move to another line in the Code Editor. This statement will hide the form when the OK button is clicked.

When you write code to assign a value to a specific property, you are setting the properties at run time.

13. Before running your application, check the code carefully. The procedures that handle the Click events should appear as shown in Figure 1.46.

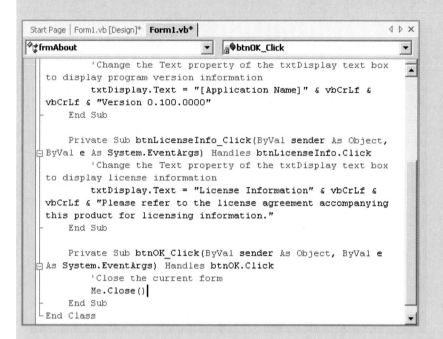

```
'Change the Text property of the txtDisplay text box
to display program version information
      txtDisplay.Text = "[Application Name]" & vbCrLf &
vbCrLf & "Version 0.100.0000"
    End Sub

    Private Sub btnLicenseInfo_Click(ByVal sender As Object,
ByVal e As System.EventArgs) Handles btnLicenseInfo.Click
      'Change the Text property of the txtDisplay text box
to display license information
      txtDisplay.Text = "License Information" & vbCrLf &
vbCrLf & "Please refer to the license agreement accompanying
this product for licensing information."
    End Sub

    Private Sub btnOK_Click(ByVal sender As Object, ByVal e
As System.EventArgs) Handles btnOK.Click
      'Close the current form
      Me.Close()
    End Sub
End Class
```

FIGURE 1.46. *Code Editor showing event procedures for the About form*

 If your code does not wrap in the Code Editor, you need to change the options for the Visual Studio.NET Code Editor. You can do this by clicking Tools, Options and selecting the Text Editor folder in the Options list. Make sure your settings match those shown in Figure 1.47.

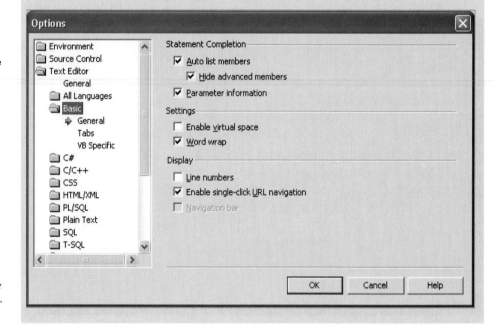

FIGURE 1.47. *Setting options for the Visual Studio.NET Code Editor*

14. Because you changed the name of the form, you need to set **frmAbout** as the startup form for the project. In the Solution Explorer, right-click the **About Form** solution and choose **Properties**. The About Form Property Pages dialog box opens.

15. Click the **Startup object:** list and choose **frmAbout**, as shown in Figure 1.48. Then click **OK**.

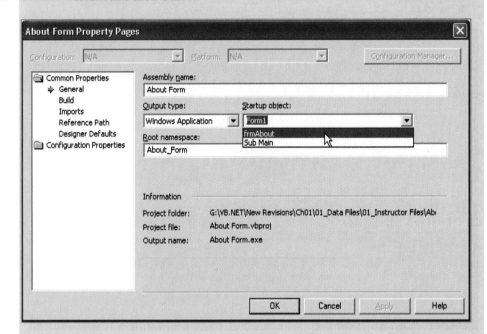

FIGURE 1.48. *Changing the About Form Property Pages*

16. Save your changes.

When you have finished writing the code, you can run the application and test its functionality.

Run the Application

You are ready to run the application and test its functionality.

To Run the Application:

1. Click the **Start** button to run the application. Visual Studio switches to run time and displays the application as it appears when running. Any properties you have assigned to controls, such as the **TabIndex** property of the buttons, will take effect now. Additional windows appear at the bottom of the screen that display the status of the project during run time.

To test your application, do the following:

Is this Text property of the label set at design time or run time?

2. Press the `Tab⇄` key multiple times to verify that the tab index property is set for the three buttons. Pressing `Tab⇄` should change the focus to each of the buttons in order.

3. Click the **Version Information** button and verify that the version information appears in the text box.

4. Click the **License Information** button and verify that the text explaining how to obtain license information appears in the text box.

5. Click the **OK** button. The form no longer displays on the screen, but Visual Studio.NET is still in run time.

6. Click the **Stop Debugging** button to exit run time and return to design time.
   If your application is running properly, save any changes you have made.

You may close the project and exit Visual Studio.NET if you are finished working for now, or proceed to the End of Chapter exercises if you intend to keep working.

Closing a Project and exiting Visual Studio.NET

Now that you've had a chance to work within the Visual Studio.NET IDE, you can close your VB.NET project and exit Visual Studio.

To close a project and exit Visual Studio:

1. Click **File**, **Close Solution**. This closes the current solution and its projects.

2. Click **File**, **Exit**, as shown in Figure 1.49. This closes Visual Studio.

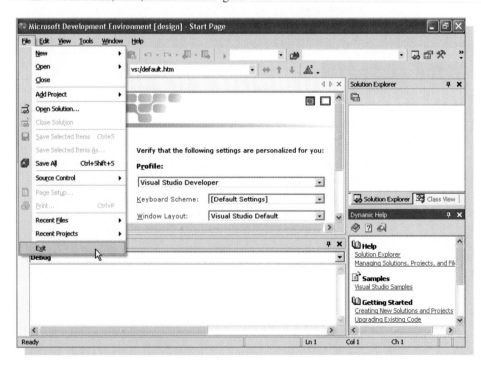

FIGURE 1.49. *Exiting Visual Studio.NET*

Summary

- Programmers use a development tool such as Visual Studio.NET to write computer programs that run in Microsoft Windows. Visual Basic.NET is one of the languages used to create Visual Studio.NET solutions.

- Microsoft Visual Studio.NET is a development tool for creating Windows and Web applications. You can use the Integrated Development Environment (IDE) to create, debug, and distribute application programs.

- You launch Visual Studio.NET by clicking the Start menu, navigating to the shortcut for Visual Studio.NET, and selecting Microsoft Visual Studio.NET.

- You use the profiles available on the Start Page to customize the IDE. You can also use a variety of features to change how tool windows appear on the screen. The IDE enables you to create the solutions, projects, and items that make up your Visual Studio.NET application. The IDE contains common development components such as the Form window, the Properties window, the Solution Explorer, and the Toolbox.

- A Visual Basic.NET solution contains at least one project, and a project includes one or more forms that contain controls. Controls on a form provide a user interface for obtaining data and handling events.

- You create a Visual Basic.NET project by first creating a Visual Studio solution and then using a project template to add one or more projects to the solution.

- Visual Studio.NET has a powerful online help system you can use to get answers to your development questions. You can also use the help system in the IDE to connect to the Web for greatly expanding the number of help topics that are available.

- Objects are Visual Basic components that provide functionality to an application. Objects have attributes called properties and perform actions called methods. Objects also have events, which trigger program instructions.

- The Toolbox contains the tools you need to add controls to a form at design time.

- When you create a Visual Basic.NET application by using the Windows Form Designer, you are working in design time. When you launch an application, it is in run time.

- Visual Studio.NET is an event-driven development environment. In contrast to procedural programs that run in a specific sequence, event-driven programs contain code routines that respond to specific actions, called events.

- To develop a Visual Basic.NET application you follow a process of planning the application, designing the user interface, writing the code, and running and testing the application.

- To revise an existing project, open the project and add the controls to the form that define the user interface. You can use the Toolbox to add controls to a form and the Properties window to change the properties of the form and its controls.

- You can set properties of controls at design time or run time. You set the property of a control at design time by using the Properties window. You can use an assignment statement to change the properties of a control at run time.

- To add functionality to applications, you use the Code Editor to write the program statements that handle specific events such as clicking a button. You can display statements in the Code Editor using Wrap mode, so that the statements are visible in the Code pane. The Code Editor also includes drop-down lists for selecting the objects and methods for the code.

- To preserve a Visual Studio.NET solution, save the solution before you run it.

- When you finish working with your projects, you can close the solution and exit Visual Studio.NET.

Key Terms

access key

ampersand symbol

applications

AutoHide

bug

button

Class Name list

code

Code Editor

command prompt

comments

computer program

concatenation

controls

debug mode

debugging

design time

development environment

development tool

dockable

document window

documentation

event

event-driven language

external documentation

files

graphical user interface (GUI)

integrated development environment (IDE)

interface

internal documentation

keyword

label

method

Method Name list

Modified-Hungarian Notation

Name property

object

procedure

profile

programming language

projects

pseudocode

pushpin

remark

run time

solution

syntax

testing

text box

text property

text string

tool window

Toolbox

user interface

view

Web application

Web Forms pages

Windows application

Windows Form Designer

Study Questions

Multiple-Choice Questions

1. Which of the languages listed below is not available in Visual Studio.NET?
   a. Visual C++
   b. Visual Basic
   c. Visual C#
   d. Visual HTML
   e. All of the above are available in Visual Studio.NET

2. Which of the following is an example of a Tool Window?
   a. Code Editor
   b. Form Designer
   c. Properties Window
   d. A & B
   e. A & C

3. Which of the following is the most definitive feature of an event-driven programming environment?
   a. Buttons for user input
   b. Routines that perform calculations
   c. Results that display on the screen
   d. Text as the primary user interface
   e. Program execution that varies based on user choices

4. During which step of program development do you identify and name the application's controls?
   a. Plan the application
   b. Design the user interface
   c. Write the code
   d. A & B
   e. A & C

5. Which interface element do you use to add controls to a form?
   a. Solution Explorer
   b. Code Editor
   c. Project Window
   d. Toolbox
   e. Properties Window

6. Which of the following statements is true concerning a Visual Basic.NET project?
   a. A project is defined by its properties and methods.
   b. A project contains at least one solution.
   c. You can use the Toolbox to add controls to a solution.
   d. A project will normally contain at least one form.
   e. A form will usually contain at least one solution.

7. Which property is required for all controls?
   a. Text
   b. File
   c. TabIndex
   d. Font
   e. Name

8. Which object name does not follow the Modified Hungarian naming convention?
   a. ButtonOpenForm
   b. cmdExit
   c. txtLastName
   d. lblInfo
   e. picImage

9. What can you use to change the properties of a control at run time?
   a. An event
   b. A method
   c. An assignment statement
   d. The ampersand (&) character
   e. Concatenation

10. Which Window do you use to name the controls added to a form?
    a. Code Editor
    b. Form Designer
    c. Toolbox
    d. Properties Window
    e. Solution Explorer

True/False Questions

1. A Visual Basic project requires at least one form.

2. An object is characterized by its attributes, called methods.

3. You cannot set control properties at run time.

4. You can use the Toolbox to add a form to a project.

5. You can use a text box to display information on the screen.

Short Answer Questions

1. What is the integrated development environment (IDE)? What key components of the IDE support your application development efforts?

2. Where should you enter program comments in the Code Editor?

3. How do procedural and event-driven programming approaches differ?

4. What are the four steps for designing Visual Basic applications?

5. How do text box controls differ from button controls?

Guided Exercises

Creating a Mileage Conversion Application

Many businesses have offices in locations around the world. For business travelers who use rental cars, a mileage conversion calculator is helpful when filling out expense reports. Figure 1.50 shows the application interface.

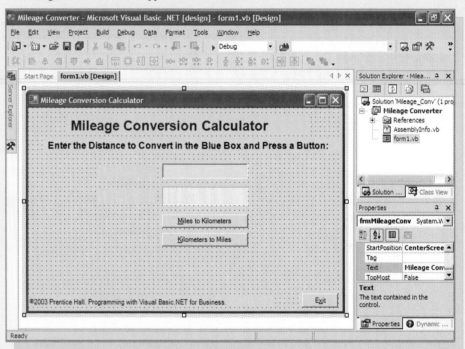

FIGURE 1.50. *Interface for the Mileage Conversion application*

Create a new Visual Basic.NET project named **Mileage Converter**. Set the Name property of Form1 to **frmMileageConv**, and using the Solution Explorer, set the Startup object for the project to **frmMileageConv**. Using Figure 1.50 as a guide, create a table listing the appropriate control properties to set at design time. Use the sample code below to write the code for the **btnMilesToKilometers** click event, which converts miles to kilometers. The conversion factors are:

$$\text{Miles to Kilometers} = \text{Miles} * 1.609$$
$$\text{Kilometers to Miles} = \text{Kilometers} * 0.621$$

```
Private Sub btnMilesToKilometers_Click(ByVal sender As
    System.Object, ByVal e As System.EventArgs) Handles
    btnMilesToKilometers.Click
  lblResult.Text = Val(txtDistance.Text) * 1.609
  lblScale1.Text = "Miles"
  lblScale2.Text = "Kilometers"
End Sub
```

Creating a Temperature Conversion Web Form

In this exercise, you will create a Web version of the Temperature Conversion application introduced earlier. To complete this exercise, you must have the ASP.NET Web Application project template that is used to create an ASP.NET Web application on a computer that has Internet Information Services (IIS) version 5.0 or later installed.

The application is similar to the Windows application version of the Temperature Calculator that is located in the *Examples* folder for this chapter. You might want to review this application before creating the Web version. Figure 1.51 shows the interface for the Web application.

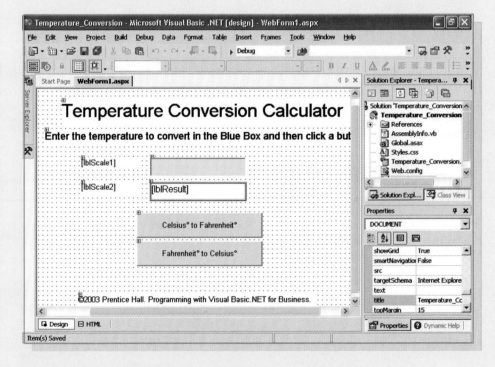

FIGURE 1.51. *Interface for the Temperature conversion Web application*

To Create a Temperature Conversion Web Form:

Launch Visual Studio.NET if it is not already running.

1. Click **File**, **New**, **Project**. Create a new Asp.NET Web Application named `Temperature_Conversion`. Notice that Visual Studio will choose the location.
2. Rename **WebForm1.aspx** as `Temperature_Converter.aspx`.
3. Enter `Temperature_Conversion.aspx` as the Title property of the form.
4. Create the Web controls shown in Figure 1.51. The Web form consists of label, text box, and button controls. Choose the font properties that suit your preference. Use this figure as a guide in the placement and naming of the objects.
5. Enter the code shown below to add internal documentation to the project, and to perform the temperature conversions.

To enter the degrees symbol, turn on the Num Lock key, hold down the Alt key, and press 0176 on the numeric keypad.

```
'©2003 Prentice Hall
'By [Enter your name here…]
'Created/Revised: [Enter the date here…]
'Temperature Conversion Web Form
Private Sub btnCelsiusToFahrenheit_Click(ByVal sender As
        System.Object, ByVal e As System.EventArgs) Handles
        btnCelsiusToFahrenheit.Click
    lblResult.Text = (9 / 5) * Val(txtTemp.Text) + 32
    lblScale1.Text = "Celsius°"
    lblScale2.Text = "Fahrenheit°"
  End Sub
Private Sub btnFahrenheitToCelsius_Click(ByVal sender As
        System.Object, ByVal e As System.EventArgs) Handles
        btnFahrenheitToCelsius.Click
    lblResult.Text = (5 / 9) * (Val(txtTemp.Text) - 32)
    lblScale1.Text = "Fahrenheit°"
    lblScale2.Text = "Celsius°"
  End Sub
```

6. Save your changes and run the application. Enter a value to convert, and click the appropriate button. The application will appear in your Web browser.

7. Close your Web browser, and make any necessary changes to the application.

8. Save your changes, and close the solution.

Case Studies

Modifying the About Form Application

The *About* form application you created in this chapter does not contain information about the development team for a specific application. Create a copy of the entire folder containing this solution. Rename the folder About Form Exercise. Modify the form, so that it contains a button for displaying information about the individuals who developed the application. Test the functionality of the form, and save your changes.

Creating a Visual Basic Splash Screen

Most applications written for the Windows environment include a splash screen, which is the form that appears when a program first runs. Create a project named Splash Screen that consists of one form with the **BorderStyle** property set to **FixedDialog**, with no controls in the Title bar. Add the *AboutLogo.bmp* image to the form, and a Label that displays information about the application. Because a splash screen normally only appears for a few seconds, you do not need any controls for closing or hiding the form, and there will be no user events to handle. Run the application to see how the form will appear, and save the changes you make to the solution.

Using Variables, Constants, and Functions in Calculations

D o you remember when your teacher explained the concepts of variables, constants, and functions when you were learning math? As you learned algebra, working with variables, constants, and functions became commonplace as you used equations to solve problems. Variables allow you to substitute values in equations; constants store values that are used multiple times in calculations, such as a sales tax rate; and functions allow you to solve complex equations for a range of values. Whatever your field of study, the equations and formulas you use require you to work with variables, constants, and functions frequently.

In the same way that variables, constants, and functions allow you to substitute values in mathematics, programmers use variables, constants, and functions to simplify code and hold values in computer memory so the values are available for later use. When variables and constants are used, the values required for calculations are available while the application is running, and the amount of memory required can be optimized. In this chapter you will learn how to write program statements that use variables, constants, and functions to simplify code and use less memory.

Performance Objectives

At the conclusion of this chapter, you will be able to:

■ Explain why you use variables and constants in applications, and differentiate the values stored in variables and constants from values stored in controls.

■ List the data types available in Visual Basic.NET.

■ Describe naming conventions for variables and constants.

■ Define variable scope.

■ Declare variables and constants.

■ Use the InputBox function for user input.

■ Use the ComboBox control for obtaining user input.

■ Use the Val function to convert text input to numeric values.

■ Perform calculations using variables and constants.

■ Format the results of calculations for display.

Using Data Stored in Controls to Perform Calculations

In Chapter 1 you learned how to store a value in the property of a control and change the property at design time and run time with the *About* form example. When you click either the *Version Information* or the *License Information* button, the Text property of the *txtDisplay* Text box changes and displays a message. The button click event for these buttons handles the code that assigns a text string to the Text property of the text box. In this example, the click event merely changes the property of a control. But what if you want to perform a calculation by using the data stored in a control? It is possible in some applications to use data stored in the properties of controls to perform calculations. Let's look at a couple of examples.

You can create applications that perform calculations by using data stored in the property of a control. For example, you might want to perform a calculation with the numeric values a user enters into a text box. Figure 2.1 shows the interface for the Simple Math Application included in your data files:

FIGURE 2.1. *Interface for the Simple Math application*

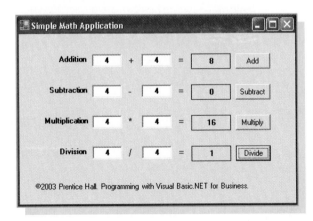

The interface for this application consists of eight text box controls for obtaining user input and four buttons for performing four simple math operations. As you learned in Chapter 1, numbers entered into a control such as a text box are interpreted as characters unless they are converted to numeric values. The application in this example uses the **Val** function to convert the numbers entered as text into numeric values that can be used in the calculations. The lines of code that respond to the click event for each button are as follows:

Addition

```
lblAddition.Text = Val(txtValue1.Text) + Val(txtValue2.Text)
```

Subtraction

```
lblSubtraction.Text = Val(txtValue3.Text) - Val(txtValue4.Text)
```

Multiplication

```
lblMultiplication.Text = Val(txtValue5.Text) *
  Val(txtValue6.Text)
```

Division

```
lblDivision.Text = Val(txtValue7.Text) / Val(txtValue8.Text)
```

Each of these code statements is an expression that uses an assignment statement to assign the result of the calculation to the Text property of a label.

Now let's look at another example. You might want an application to calculate several values, such as the state and local taxes on a retail sale, and add the results together to calculate the total tax and the total amount of sale. The application needs to retain the individual values to print a sales receipt that lists each individual tax value, the total sale amount. Figure 2.2 shows the interface for an application that uses the sale amount entered by the user to calculate the state tax, local tax, total tax, and total sale amount. This application is also included in your data files.

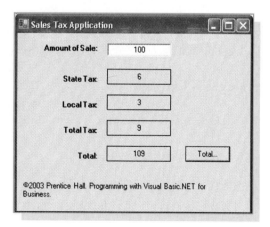

FIGURE 2.2. *Interface for the Sales Tax application*

Like the previous example, the application uses the **Val** function to convert the sale amount entered as text to a numeric value, performs the appropriate calculations, and uses an assignment statement to display the results in the Text property of the labels appearing on the form. The code statements that respond to the click event for the Total button are as follows:

```
lblStateTax.Text = Val(txtSaleAmount.Text) * 0.06
lblLocalTax.Text = Val(txtSaleAmount.Text) * 0.03
lblTotalTax.Text = (Val(txtSaleAmount.Text) * 0.06) +
  (Val(txtSaleAmount.Text) * 0.03)
lblTotal.Text = Val(txtSaleAmount.Text) + Val(lblStateTax.Text)
  + Val(lblLocalTax.Text)
```

These are two simple examples of performing calculations by using values stored in the properties of controls. As your applications become more complex, using values stored in the properties of controls is cumbersome. In addition, the values the application calculates are available only when the calculation is performed and are not retained in memory. Therefore, other applications cannot use or access those values. Let's now learn a better way to perform calculations in your applications so that the values are retained in memory and available to other applications.

Using Variables in Calculations

Using variables is a fundamental programming skill. You can greatly simplify your application's code by using variables.

WHAT ARE VARIABLES?

Variables store values that can change and be retrieved while the application is running. Unlike a control, a variable does not have properties or respond to events. A variable has a name (the word you use to refer to the value the variable contains) and a *data type* (which determines the kind of data the variable can store). You can use assignment statements to perform calculations and assign the result to a variable, as shown in the following examples:

Variable Used in an Expression	Value Stored in Memory
SaleAmount = 100	The value 100 is assigned to the SaleAmount variable.
StateTax = SaleAmount * .06	The StateTax variable is calculated as 6% of the sale amount.
LocalTax = SaleAmount * .03	The LocalTax variable is calculated as 3% of the sale amount.
TotalTax = StateTax + LocalTax	The TotalTax variable is calculated as the sum of the StateTax and LocalTax variables.
TotalSale = SaleAmount + TotalTax	The TotalSale variable is calculated as the sum of the SaleAmount and TotalTax variables.

Figure 2.3 demonstrates the values stored in memory for this example.

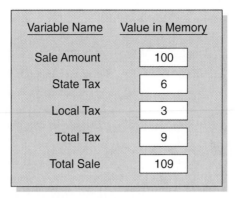

FIGURE 2.3. *Using Variables to store values in memory*

In contrast to the values stored in controls, values stored as variables are retained in memory and available at any time while a program is running. This simplifies the code for performing complex calculations, because the expressions refer to the variables and not to the Text property of controls. Now that you understand why you use variables to perform calculations, let's look more closely at what you need to do to use variables in your application's code.

Using Variables in Code

To use variables effectively, you need to understand more about how to use variables efficiently. Whether the variables you declare contain text, numbers, or some other value, understanding data types will help you select the most appropriate variables for your applications, thereby preserving memory and writing code that runs as efficiently as possible. Good programming requires that you understand the types of data you can store in variables and how to name and declare variables.

VARIABLE DATA TYPES

All variables have a data type, which refers to what kind of data the variable can hold and how the data is stored in the computer's memory. Because each data type has different memory requirements, you can conserve computer memory and have your application run faster by carefully selecting the most appropriate data type for the kind of data your application needs to store. Table 2.1 lists the data types for variables in Visual Basic.NET.

Table 2.1: Visual Basic.NET data types

Data Type	Description of the Kind of Data Stored in the Variable	Amount of Memory Used
Boolean	True or False.	2 bytes
Byte	A single ASCII character (ASCII code 0-255).	1 byte
Char	Unicode characters from 0-65535.	2 bytes
Date	Date in an eight-character format: 01/01/2003.	8 bytes
Decimal	Decimal values with up to 28 places to the right of the decimal point.	16 bytes Replaces the *Currency* data type in previous versions of Visual Basic.

Table 2.1: *(continued)*

Data Type	Description of the Kind of Data Stored in the Variable	Amount of Memory Used
Double	Double-precision floating-point numbers with 14 digits of accuracy. Values range from 1.79769313486231E+308 to -4.94065645841247E-324 for negative values, 4.94065645841247E-324 to 1.79769313486231E+308 for positive values.	8 bytes
Integer	Whole numbers ranging from -2,147,483,648 to 2,147,483,647.	4 bytes
Long	Whole numbers ranging from -9,223,372,036,854,775,808 to 9,223,372,036,854,775,807.	8 bytes
Object	Any type can be stored in an Object variable, as can references to other application objects.	4 bytes This is the default type if no type is assigned.
Short	Whole numbers ranging from -32,768 to 32,767.	2 bytes
Single	Single-precision floating-point numbers with six digits of accuracy. Values range from -3.402823E+38 to -1.401298E-45 for negative values, 1.401298E-45 to 3.402823E+38 for positive values.	4 bytes
String	Alphanumeric data; letters, digits, and other characters. "Adam Smith" is an example of a text string.	0 to 2 billion characters
User-Defined Data Type	Structured data.	Size depends on the data definition.

So how do you determine the appropriate data type to use in your applications? If you are processing text or need to store a text string in a variable, use the **String** data type. If your application needs to perform calculations between dates, use the ***Date data type***. If the variable holds data that requires only a simple Yes or No value, use the ***Boolean data type***.

For numeric data that do not include dates, such as 100 items in stock, a tax rate of 5%, gross pay of $1500, or a number expressed as an exponent (such as 3.2×10^{23}), the choice of the appropriate data type requires more consideration. To reduce the amount of memory required by your application and thereby increase program efficiency, you should select the data type with the least memory requirements. Table 2.1 shows that the **Integer**, **Long**, and **Short** data types all store whole number (non-decimal) values. Because these data types store only whole numbers, they are called ***integral data types***. Of the integral types, the Integer type is the most efficient. Therefore, if you need to store a value that will be used in calculations, such as the number of items in stock or the term of a loan, use the Integer data type.

For performing calculations, integral data types are more efficient than non-integral data types. ***Non-integral data types*** represent numbers with both integer and fractional parts. **Decimal**, **Single**, and **Double** are all non-integral data types. The ***Single and Double data types*** store ***floating-point numbers***, which are expressed as a power of 10 and therefore have an exponent, represented by an *E*. You can use these types to store numbers that are either extremely small (a number with a negative exponent, such as the thickness of a gold plating measured in microns) or extremely large (a number with a positive exponent, such as the national debt). The value of the exponent expresses the power of 10 by which the number is multiplied, for positive exponents, or divided, for negative exponents. Thus, 2.7E4 is the same as 2.7 times 10 to the 4th power, or 2.7 with the decimal point moved four spaces to the right, or 27 followed by three zeros (27000). 2.7E-4 is the same as 2.7 with the decimal point moved four places to the left or 27 preceded by a decimal point and three zeros (.00027).

The **Decimal data type** stores numbers with a fixed decimal point and therefore requires less memory and, in some cases, provides more accuracy. Floating-point (Single and Double) numbers have larger ranges than Decimal numbers but can be subject to rounding errors. Thus, if you use floating-point numbers in calculations, very small rounding errors may occur. The errors are too small to be of any significance unless you are working with complex monetary calculations. If your application makes complex calculations using money, use the Decimal data type.

Choosing the right data type for the data your applications store in variables is important. Table 2.2 lists the recommended data types for various kinds of data.

Tip For simple calculations involving money, such as calculating the value of inventory or a monthly loan payment, some programmers use the Single data type and others use the Decimal data type. This book uses the Decimal data type for all monetary calculations.

Table 2.2: Recommended data types for specific data elements

Data to Store	Recommended Data Type and Example
Employee names and addresses	String William Smith, 100 Main Street, San Francisco, CA, 90027
Number of inventory items in stock	Integer 21 100 10000
Employment status (employed/not employed)	Boolean Yes or No; 0 or -1
Speed of light	Double 2.99 10^8 meters per second
Age of a person, in years	Short 12 40
Population of a major metropolitan city	Integer 157000
Gross pay for a pay period	Decimal 2526.41
Net 30 payment due	Date 12/01/2003
Term of a loan, in months	Integer 360
Total sale amount	Decimal 360.27
Local sales tax rate	Single .065
The constant *pi*	Single 3.141592
World population	Long 5,800,000,000 (5.8 billion)

In addition to choosing a data type, you must choose a name for your variable. Let's learn how to name variables in Visual Basic.NET.

NAMING VARIABLES

Most programmers prefer descriptive names that tell the purpose of a variable and the kind of data it contains. Therefore, a standard or rule for naming variables is to begin with three characters indicating the data type and let the remainder specify the variable's purpose. For example, a variable for storing the number of units might be named *intQuantity*, where *int* indicates the data type (Integer) and *Quantity* is a descriptive name for the values the variable holds (number of units).

Because most names are constructed by joining together several words, Microsoft recommends using mixed-case formatting to simplify reading variable names and using expressive names that make sense to the human reader. The first three characters appear in lowercase, with the remaining part of the variable name appearing as descriptive words that begin with an uppercase letter. If the descriptive name includes more than one word, the first character of each word is capitalized (this is known as *Pascal-case*). Table 2.3 lists the three-character designation for each data type and an example of how to apply the Pascal-case naming to variables.

Table 2.3: Three-character identifiers for data types in variable names

Data type	Prefix	Example of a Named Variable
Boolean	bln	blnEmploymentStatus
Decimal	dec	decTotalInventory
Date (Time)	dtm	dtmNet30
Double	dbl	dblSpeedOfLight
Integer	int	intQuantity
Long	lng	lngPopulation
Object	obj	objCurrent
Single	sng	sngSalesTax
String	str	strAddress

As with object names, variable names must begin with an alphabetic character, a digit, or an underscore. In the following examples of variable names, see if you can identify the data type and purpose for each variable, based on the variable name:

shtLoanTerm

sngInterestRate

shtSalesTax

strAddress

sngHighestScore

intQuantity

sngBattingAverage

intPopulation

dtmDateOfBirth

decGrossPay

How did you do? The following list shows the data type and purpose for each variable:

Recommended Variable Name	Data Type	Purpose
shtLoanTerm	Short	The term of a loan
sngInterestRate	Single	The interest rate for a loan, savings account, or credit card
shtSalesTax	Short	The sales tax
strAddress	String	A recipient's street address
sngHighestScore	Single	The value for the highest score obtained
intQuantity	Integer	The quantity of items
sngBattingAverage	Single	The batting average of a baseball player
intPopulation	Integer	The count of citizens in a city or state
dtmDateOfBirth	Date	A person's date of birth
decGrossPay	Decimal	The gross pay for an employee

Here are some examples of poor variable names. Each name fails to indicate the data type, and the names are either too long or do not clearly identify the value being stored.

Recommended Variable Name	Examples of Poor Variable Names
shtLoanTerm	loanterm LT Term
sngInterestRate	Interest int INT Rate IR
shtSalesTax	tax SalesTax
strAddress	Addr StreetAddress
sngHighestScore	score highestscore
intQuantity	Quan Units InStock
sngBattingAverage	average AVG
intPopulation	pop Citizens POPULATION
dtmDateOfBirth	birthday DOB
decTotalInventory	total TotInv Inv

Now that you know how to choose a data type and name for a variable, let's look at how to specify a variable's data type and name in your application's code.

DECLARING VARIABLES

Before you can refer to a variable in your code and assign a value to it, you must first declare (or create) the variable by using a ***declaration statement***, which is code that names the variable, specifies the data type, and (optionally) assigns a value to the variable. The syntax for declaring a variable by using a declaration statement is

```
Accessibility VariableName As [DataType] = [InitialValue]
```

Accessibility: Defines what procedures have access to the value stored in the variable. The **Dim** and **Private** keywords are commonly used to describe accessibility.

VariableName: The name you assign the variable, by which you refer to the variable in a statement.

DataType: The data type of the variable.

InitialValue: Assigns a value to the variable when it is declared.

Notice that DataType and InitialValue are in brackets in the declaration statement. The brackets indicate that these parts of the declaration statement are optional, meaning you don't have to assign a data type or initial value. However, if you do not assign a data type to a variable, Visual Basic.NET sets the default type as **Object**. If you do not assign an initial value to a variable, Visual Basic.NET sets a default value (also called the initial value) that depends on the data type of the variable. The following table shows how Visual Basic.NET automatically sets the initial value of variables based on their data type.

Data Type of the Variable	Automatically set to
All numeric data types (Decimal, Double, Integer, Long, Short, Single)	The number 0
Boolean	False
Date	12:00 AM January 1, 0001
Object, String	Nothing (no data)

From Table 2.3, take the variable *decTotalInventory*, which you've already named and given a data type. Let's revisit the general syntax for the declaration statement for a variable:

```
Dim decTotalInventory As [Data Type] = [Initial Value]
```

The completed declaration statement for your *decTotalInventory* variable would be:

```
Dim decTotalInventory As Decimal
```

When you declare a variable, it is available for use but contains the default value until you explicitly assign a value to the variable by using an assignment statement. Here's an example:

```
Dim decTotalInventory as Decimal
decTotalInventory = 1527.95
```

Following are additional examples of statements that declare variables:

Declaration Statement	Description
`Dim shtLoanTerm As Short`	Declares the variable LoanTerm and specifies the data type as Short.
`Dim decGrossPay As Decimal`	Declares the variable GrossPay and specifies the data type as Decimal.
`Dim shtLoanTerm As Short = 30`	Declares the variable LoanTerm, specifies the data type as Short, and assigns an initial value of 30.
`Dim intPopulation As Integer`	Declares an Integer variable for Population. Because no initial value is assigned to the variable, Visual Basic.NET automatically sets it to 0.
`Dim intCounter As Integer = 1`	Declares an Integer variable for Counter and assigns the initial value 1 to the variable.
`Dim sngHighScore As Single`	Declares a variable for storing the highest score and specifies Single as the data type.
`Dim strLastName As String = "Smith"`	Declares a string variable for LastName and sets the initial value "Smith" to the string.

You can include more than one variable declaration in a single statement by separating the variable declarations with a comma (,). Here are examples of declaring more than one variable in a single statement:

Declaration Statement	Description
`Private decPrincipal, decPayment As Decimal`	Declares two variables of the decimal type.
`Dim intQuantity As Integer = 120, decPrice as Decimal = 25, decTotalInventory as Decimal = intQuantity * decPrice`	Declares three variables: an integer variable for storing the quantity of an item, a decimal variable for the item's price, and a decimal variable for the inventory value of the item. The third variable is assigned a value that is the product of the first two variables.
`Dim shtLoanTerm As Short = 360, sngLoanRate as Single = .045`	Declares a short variable with a value of 360 and a single variable with a value of .045.

Implicit and Explicit Variable Declaration

Visual Basic.NET supports two ways of declaring variables in your applications. *Explicit variable declaration* means you must explicitly declare a variable by using the *Dim* or other valid declaration statement before you can refer to the variable in code. *Implicit variable declaration* means you do not need to declare a variable but can simply include a statement in the code that makes a reference to the variable. Consider the following examples:

```
Dim decTotalInventory As Decimal
decTotalInventory = 1527.95
```

The *decTotalInventory* variable is explicitly declared before it is assigned a value. Now consider the following statements:

```
Option Explicit Off
lblResult.Text = decTotalInventory
```

Tip

By default, the properties for a Visual Basic project set Option Explicit to True (or On), thereby forcing explicit variable declaration. I recommend that you do not include the Option Explicit Off statement in your code. Explicit variable declaration is one method of minimizing errors in your applications.

This example uses the ***Option Explicit statement*** to turn off explicit variable declaration and enable implicit variable declaration. The Option Explicit statement appears at the end of the General Declarations section of your code as it appears in the Code Editor, and the statements for declaring the variable and assigning its value to a control property would appear in a procedure. If you enable implicit variable declaration by using the Option Explicit Off statement, Visual Basic.NET declares the variable automatically when the statement that includes the reference to the variable is run.

Changing the Value of a Variable

In addition to assigning a value to a variable after it's declared, you can also change the value by using an assignment statement. Consider the following examples:

Changing the Value of a Decimal Variable

```
Dim decTotalInventory as Decimal
decTotalInventory = 1527.95   'Sets the value of the variable
decTotalInventory = 2000.21   'Changes the value of the variable
decTotalInventory = decTotalInventory + 1000 'Changes the value
   to 3000.21
```

Changing the Value of a String Variable

```
Dim strLastName as String   'Declares a string variable
strLastName = "Bill"   'Assigns the text string "Bill" to the
   value of the variable
strLastName = strLastName & " Smith"   'Changes the text string
   to "Bill Smith"
```

Changing the Value of a Numeric Variable

```
Dim sngFees as Single = .05  'Declares a single variable and
   assigns a value
sngFees = .07  'Changes the value of the sngFees variable
```

VARIABLE SCOPE

Variables are always declared in code statements you write in the Code Editor. Variable declarations must specify the accessibility of the variable. The *accessibility* specifies which program statements will have access to the value stored in the variable. The accessibility of the variable is also called *variable scope*. Will the variable be accessible to only one procedure or to any procedure within a form? If your variable is declared within a procedure and will be available only to that procedure, it is a *local variable* and has *procedure scope*. If you decide you want to make your variable accessible to any procedure within a form, it is a *module-level (or form-level) variable* and has *module scope*. In the declaration statement syntax, you use the *Dim keyword* to declare a variable as a local variable. To declare a variable as a module-level variable, you use the *Private keyword*.

Let's look at an example of declaring local and module-level variables. The following code examples are contained in the *Variable Scope* solution included with your data files. The interface for this solution contains two buttons and two labels. Clicking the buttons declares a variable and displays the results in one of the labels on the form. This solution demonstrates the difference between local and form-level variables. You would not create an application like this for business users, other than for demonstration.

Declaring a Local Variable

You can declare a local variable by including the Dim keyword and variable declaration statement in the procedure that will use the variable. Here are the statements that declare a local string variable within a procedure that handles the click event for a button:

```
Private Sub btnLocalVariable_Click(ByVal sender As
   System.Object, ByVal e As System.EventArgs) Handles
   btnLocalVariable.Click
      Dim strTextMessage As String
      strTextMessage = "This is an example of a local
         variable with procedure scope."
      lblResult.Text = strTextMessage
   End Sub
```

The Dim keyword indicates a local variable with procedure scope. Because the variable is declared within a procedure, only this procedure has access to the variable. The procedure assigns a text string to the variable and then uses an assignment statement to display the variable data in the Text property of a label control. Figure 2.4 shows the result that appears when you click the **Declare a Local Variable** button:

FIGURE 2.4. *Declaring a local variable*

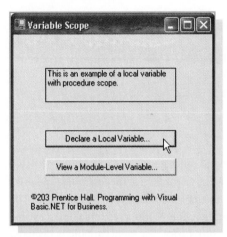

Declaring a Module-Level Variable

Now let's see how to declare a module-level variable. The declaration statement for the variable is not contained within a procedure but is declared in the General Declarations section of the Code Editor for a module. Consider the following statements:

```
'Declare a module-level variable with module scope
    Private mintUnitsInStock As Integer

    Private Sub btnModuleVariable_Click(ByVal sender As
      System.Object, ByVal e As System.EventArgs) Handles
      btnModuleVariable.Click
        mintUnitsInStock = 125
        lblResult.Text = "Number of Units in Stock: " &
          mintUnitsInStock
    End Sub
```

The statement uses the Private keyword to declare an integer variable. Because the variable is declared as a module-level variable, it is available to any procedure that references it. Many programmers add a lower-case "m" to the name of a module-level variable, to distinguish it from a local variable. The statement that handles the click event for the *btnModuleVariable* button assigns the value of 125 to the variable and then displays a text string and the variable data in the Text property of the *lblResult* control. Figure 2.5 shows the result of clicking the **View a Module-Level Variable** button:

FIGURE 2.5. *Declaring a Module-level variable*

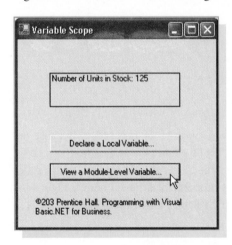

Figure 2.6 shows how the code for this module-level variable appears in the Code Editor window.

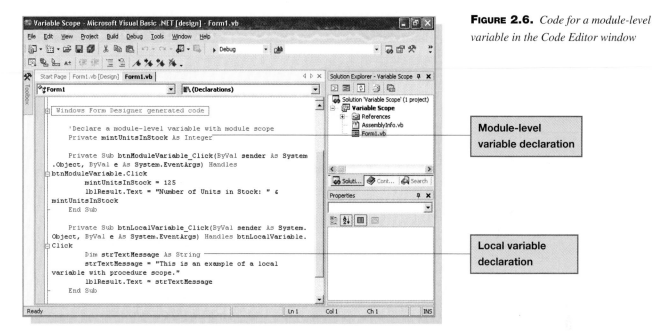

FIGURE 2.6. *Code for a module-level variable in the Code Editor window*

Let's review the code statements. The Private keyword indicates a module-level variable. Notice that the declaration statement appears immediately after the code that is generated by the Windows Form Designer in the general declarations area of the Code Editor.

This variable has module scope because it is available to any procedure contained in the form.

Now that you understand how to declare variables, let's learn how to use constants to perform simple and complex calculations and simplify your code.

Using Constants in Calculations

The code you write for your applications will sometimes contain constant values that reappear, such as the value *pi* or the current sales tax rate. You can improve your code and make it easier to maintain by using constants.

WHAT ARE CONSTANTS?

Constants store values, specified at design time, that remain the same (or constant) and cannot change while the application is running. You can use constants to add meaningful names instead of numbers in expressions that perform calculations. This simplifies your program code, making it easier to read. Although constants resemble variables, you cannot modify a constant or assign a new value to it as you can to a variable.

Like a variable, a constant has a name and a data type. A constant can be any of the following data types: Boolean, Byte, Char, DateTime, Decimal, Double, Integer, Long, Short, Single, or String. Consider the following examples:

Tip

You will recall from Chapter 1 that Visual Studio adds code to the Code Editor when you add controls to a form. It is important that you do not modify the code contained in the Windows Form Designer-generated code region of the Code Editor, which appears when you click the plus sign (+) next to this code region.

Constant Used in an Expression	Value Stored in Memory
StateTaxRate = .06	The value .06 is assigned to the StateTaxRate constant.
LocalTaxRate = .03	The value .03 is assigned to the LocalTaxRate constant.
SaleAmount = 100	The value 100 is assigned to the SaleAmount variable.
StateTax = SaleAmount * StateTaxRate	The StateTax variable is calculated as 6% of the sale amount, using the StateTaxRate constant.
LocalTax = SaleAmount * LocalTaxRate	The LocalTax variable is calculated as 3% of the sale amount, using the LocalTaxRate constant.
TotalTax = StateTax + LocalTax	The TotalTax variable is calculated as the sum of the StateTax and LocalTax variables.
TotalSale= SaleAmount + TotalTax	The TotalSale variable is calculated as the sum of the SaleAmount and TotalTax variables.

Figure 2.7 shows how you can use constants in calculations. The expression uses the values stored in the StateTaxRate and LocalTaxRate constants to determine the state and local tax values, which are stored in the StateTax and LocalTax variables.

FIGURE 2.7. *Using variables and constants in calculations*

Constant Name	Constant Value	Variable Name	Value in Memory
		Sale Amount	100
State Tax Rate	.06	State Tax	6
Local Tax Rate	.03	Local Tax	3
		Total Tax	9
		Total Sale	109

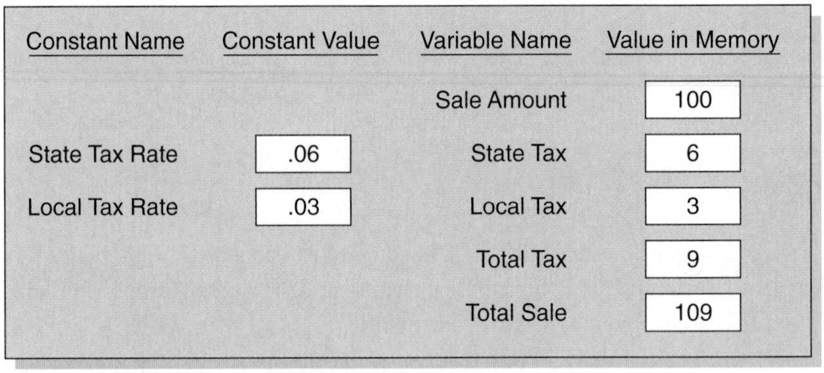

The data type for a constant is optional. If you do not assign a data type, Visual Basic.NET assigns a data type based on the expression.

NAMING CONSTANTS

You can use the same naming conventions for constants as for variables. Add the three-character *con* designation before a named constant to indicate that the declaration is for a constant, not a variable. Here are a few examples of naming constants:

conPi	Stores the value 3.14
conTaxRate	Stores a sales tax rate
conCompanyName	Stores the name of a company

DECLARING CONSTANTS

As with variables, you can declare a constant within a procedure or in the general declarations section of a form. If Option Explicit is turned on, constants must be declared with an explicit data type, using the *As* keyword.

When you declare a constant, it must be preceded by the **Const keyword**. The syntax for declaring a constant is as follows:

```
Const Constant Name As [Data Type] = Expression
```

The data type for a constant is optional. If you do not assign a data type, Visual Basic.NET assigns a data type based on the expression. For example, if you declare a constant for the number 10.5 but do not declare a data type, Visual Basic.NET assigns the type as Double, even though Single would be more efficient. To ensure the most efficient data type possible, you should include a data type when you declare constants. The following are examples of how to declare constants and assign a value to the constant:

```
Const conPi As Single = 3.1415927
Const conTaxRate As Decimal = 0.745
Const conCompanyAddress As String = "155 South Broadway Street"
Const conLoanTerm As Integer = 30
```

You can declare a module-level constant in the General Declarations section of the code. To make the constant accessible to all the form's procedures, add the Private keyword before the Const keyword. Each of the following declared constants is available to all the procedures for a form:

```
Private Const conTaxRate As Single = .075
Private Const conCompanyName As String = "ACME Enterprises, Inc."
Private Const conLoanTerm As Single = 30
```

Declaring Local Constants and Variables

Now that you understand how to declare constants and variables, let's look at an example of an application that uses local variables and constants to calculate and display sales tax information. The interface for the *Variables and Constants* solution (included in your data files) is shown in Figure 2.8. The values displayed are calculated from a sale in the amount of $1000.

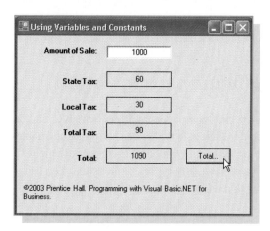

FIGURE 2.8. *Interface for Variables and Constants solution*

Now let's look at the code that provides the application its functionality. The statements are contained in a procedure that handles a button click event:

```
Private Sub btnTotal_Click(ByVal sender As System.Object, ByVal
    e As System.EventArgs) Handles btnTotal.Click

        'Declare constants for the State and Local tax rates
        Const conStateTax As Single = 0.06
        Const conLocalTax As Single = 0.03

        'Declare variables for calculations
        Dim decSaleAmount As Decimal
        Dim decStateTax As Decimal
        Dim decLocalTax As Decimal

        'Perform calculations
        decSaleAmount = Val(txtSaleAmount.Text)
        decStateTax = decSaleAmount * conStateTax
        decLocalTax = decSaleAmount * conLocalTax

        'Display results
        lblStateTax.Text = decStateTax
        lblLocalTax.Text = decLocalTax
        lblTotalTax.Text = decStateTax + decLocalTax
        lblTotal.Text = decSaleAmount + Val(lblTotalTax.Text)

    End Sub
```

Convert all variables using Val function (handwritten annotation)

Why are the variables for calculating the taxes in this procedure declared as the Decimal data type?

The procedure contains declaration statements for two constants and three variables. The input for the application is the sale amount entered in the text box on the form. The **Val** function, which you learned about in Chapter 1, converts the text value to a numeric value that can be used in the calculations. The procedure uses the constants for determining the state and local tax and stores these values in the appropriate variables. The procedure then uses a series of assignment statements to display the sales data in the labels on the form. Note that the last statement adds the value contained in a variable with the converted total tax value displayed in a label.

As you can see, variables and constants provide more flexibility than control properties for storing the values required in your application. Now that you understand how to declare and use variables and constants, let's explore other methods for obtaining user input.

Obtaining User Input

Now that you understand how variables and constants simplify calculations, you need to think about how the data assigned to variables is input into an application. The examples shown throughout this chapter use the text box control for obtaining user input, so the user actually types or enters text. You can use other controls, such as a combo box, to obtain user input.

THE COMBOBOX CONTROL

You can use the ***ComboBox control*** in your applications to display data in a drop-down combo box that allows the user to select from a list. A combo box control has two parts.

The top part is a text box where the user can enter a value. The bottom part is a list box that displays a list of items from which the user can make a selection. Figure 2.9 displays a combo box control used to select a value from 1 to 5. This form is in the *ComboBox Example* solution included in your data files.

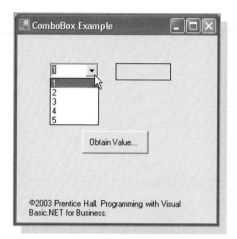

FIGURE 2.9. *Using a combo box to select a value*

You add items to a combo box at design time by adding entries to the **Item collection**. Alternatively, you can add items to the Item collection at run time by using the **Items.Add** method. Follow these steps to add items to a combo box collection at design time:

To add items to a combo box:

1. Select the combo box in the Form Designer.

2. In the **Properties** window, click the **Item** row.

3. Click the Ellipsis button to expand the Item collection, as shown in Figure 2.10.

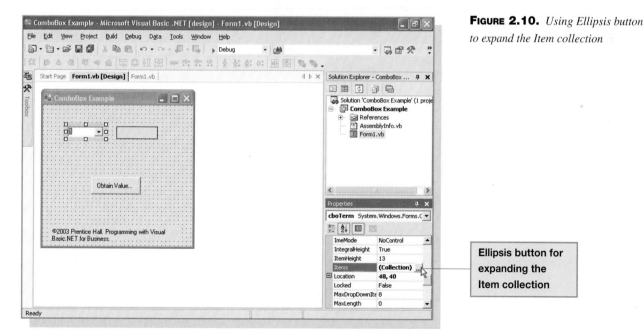

FIGURE 2.10. *Using Ellipsis button to expand the Item collection*

4. The *String Collection Editor* shown in Figure 2.11 opens. You can use this editor to enter the values you want to appear in the list. Enter one item per line. Click **OK** when you have entered all the items.

FIGURE 2.11. *String Collection Editor*

Once you have added items to the combo box, you can set the Text property to display a specific value. In this case, we set the Text property to 1 so that when the combo box is displayed, the default value of 1 appears in the list.

Assigning a Combo Box Selection to a Variable

Now let's look at how to assign the selected value in a combo box to a variable. Figure 2.12 shows the results of selecting the last item in the combo box and then clicking the **Obtain Value** button.

FIGURE 2.12. *Assigning a combo box selection to a variable*

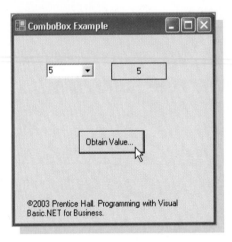

Here's the code used to obtain the value in the combo box, assign it to a variable, and then assign the variable to the Text property of a label control:

```
Private Sub btnObtainValue_Click(ByVal sender As System.Object,
   ByVal e As System.EventArgs) Handles btnObtainValue.Click
       Dim intTerm As Integer
       intTerm = Val(cboTerm.Text)
       lblResult.Text = intTerm
    End Sub
```

As you can see, the procedure contains a declaration statement for a local integer variable and uses the **Val** function to convert the selected item in the combo box and assign it to the variable. The variable value is then assigned to the Text property of a label control for display.

Combo boxes provide the flexibility of a text box control for user input, combined with the capability to provide the user with a list of predefined choices. Now let's explore how to use a function to obtain user input.

What is the scope of the variable declared in this procedure?

Using Functions in Calculations

Programmers use functions to simplify program code statements. A *function* is a procedure that returns a value. When you use a function in a program, you include one or more *arguments*, which are the values supplied to the function. All functions follow a specific syntax. You will recall from Chapter 1 that the syntax for a function includes the name of the function and one or more arguments.

There are two kinds of functions you can use in your programs. An *implicit function* is a predefined procedure that is a part of Visual Basic.NET. A programmer creates a *user-defined function* to perform an action and return a result. You will learn about user-defined functions in Chapter 7.

The **Val** function is an example of an implicit function. You have already used the **Val** function to convert text data to numbers for calculations. The syntax for the **Val** function includes the *Val keyword* and the text to convert (in parentheses), as in the following example:

```
Val(lblTotalTax.Text)
```

Visual Basic.NET includes many intrinsic functions that you can include in your applications. Some of the more common functions you will use in this book are listed in Table 2.4.

Table 2.4: Common Visual Basic.NET functions

Function	Purpose
Val	Returns the numbers contained in a string as a numeric value of appropriate type.
Format	Returns a string formatted according to instructions contained in a format expression.
InputBox	Displays a prompt in a dialog box, waits for the user to input text or click a button, and then returns a string containing the contents of the text box.
MsgBox	Displays a message in a dialog box, waits for the user to click a button, and then returns an integer indicating which button the user clicked.
IPmt	Returns the interest payment for a given period.
Pmt	Returns the payment for a given period.
PPmt	Returns the principal payment for a given period.

USING THE INPUTBOX FUNCTION TO OBTAIN USER INPUT

The InputBox function is very useful for gathering user input and assigning the input directly to a variable. The **InputBox function** displays a prompt in a dialog box, waits for the user to input text or click a button, and then returns a string containing the contents of the text box. The general syntax for the InputBox function is

```
Variable value = InputBox(Prompt, [Title], [Default
    Response])
```

Figure 2.13 shows an example of an input box appearing at run time. This input box includes a title, a prompt, and an input area.

FIGURE 2.13. *Input box at run time*

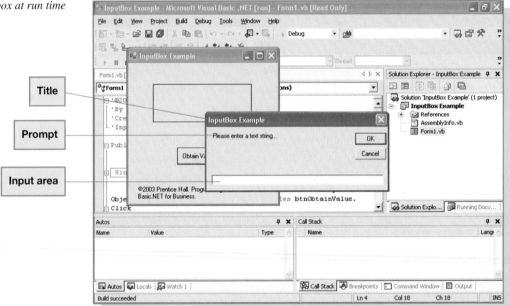

In this example, the input box appears when a user clicks the **Obtain Input** button. The text entered into the input box is assigned to a string variable, and then the value of the variable is assigned to the Text property of a label control. Figure 2.14 displays the result of entering *Programming with Visual Basic.NET* into the input box and clicking the **OK** button.

FIGURE 2.14. *Entering data in an input box*

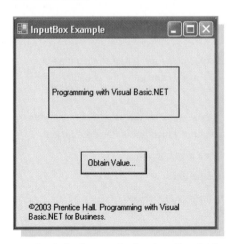

Let's look at code that handles the button click procedure:

```
Private Sub btnObtainValue_Click(ByVal sender As System.Object,
     ByVal e As System.EventArgs) Handles btnObtainValue.Click
        Dim strMessage As String
        strMessage = InputBox("Please enter a text string...",
          "InputBox Example")
        lblResult.Text = strMessage
   End Sub
```

Here is the statement that assigns the return value entered into the input box to the variable:

```
strMessage = InputBox("Please enter a text string...", "InputBox
  Example")
```

This function uses two arguments, separated by a comma. The first argument defines the message for the prompt. The second argument defines the text that appears in the label of the input box. Here are some additional examples for using the **InputBox** function for obtaining user input. Use the **Val** function to assign the return value to a numeric variable. Use an additional comma when you include the **DefaultResponse** argument but no title.

```
strLastName = InputBox("Last Name")
strAddress = InputBox("Please enter your address. . . ","Address")
intAge = Val(InputBox("Please enter your age as a whole number..
  . "))
sngRate = Val(InputBox("Please enter the annual interest
  rate,"Annual Interest Rate,".075"))
sngTerm = Val(InputBox("Please enter the loan term in
  months...",,"360")
```

Using the Val Function to Convert Text Entries to Numeric Data

When you use text boxes, combo boxes, or the **InputBox** function to obtain user input, the text of the captured value text box is of the string data type. Before you can use any numeric values entered into a text box in calculations, you must convert the data from string data to numeric data. There are multiple functions you can use to accomplish this.

THE VAL FUNCTION

In Chapter 1 you learned about the **Val** function, which you can use to convert a text string to a numeric value. The general syntax of the function is as follows:

```
Variable value = Val(argument)
```

The expression includes one required argument: the text to convert to a numeric value. Consider the following example, which you can view when you open the *Val Function Example* solution included in your data files:

Does the Val Function Example procedure use variables or values stored in the properties of controls to obtain the data used in the calculation?

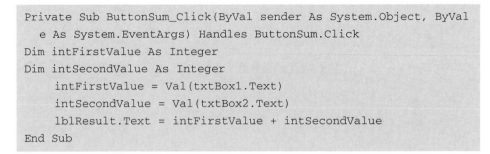

```
Private Sub ButtonSum_Click(ByVal sender As System.Object, ByVal
   e As System.EventArgs) Handles ButtonSum.Click
Dim intFirstValue As Integer
Dim intSecondValue As Integer
     intFirstValue = Val(txtBox1.Text)
     intSecondValue = Val(txtBox2.Text)
     lblResult.Text = intFirstValue + intSecondValue
End Sub
```

This example declares two local variables and then converts the text string in each text box to a numeric value by using the **Val** function. The converted values are assigned to the *firstValue* and *secondValue* variables, which are then summed, and the result is assigned to the Text property of the *lblResult* label. Figure 2.15 displays the result of summing two instances of the value 500.

Figure 2.15. *Summing two instances of a value*

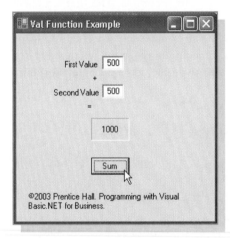

Here's another example of the **Val** function, from the *Temperature Conversion* application shown in Chapter 1:

```
Private Sub btnCelsiusToFahrenheit_Click(ByVal sender As
   System.Object, ByVal e As System.EventArgs) Handles
   btnCelsiusToFahrenheit.Click
        lblResult.Text = (9 / 5) * Val(txtTemp.Text) + 32
        lblScale1.Text = "Celsius°"
        lblScale2.Text = "Fahrenheit°"
    End Sub
```

This code example handles a button click event to convert degrees Celsius to degrees Fahrenheit. The expression **lblResult.Text = (9 / 5) * Val(txtTemp.Text) + 32** is an assignment statement that sets the Text property of the *lblResult* label to the result of the calculation. The calculation converts the value entered into the *txtTemp* text box to the selected scale (Fahrenheit or Celsius). The **Val** function is required to convert a number entered as a string to a number that can be used in a calculation.

Operator Precedence

Many of the expressions you create to perform calculations will contain both functions and operators. An ***operator*** is a character or combination of characters that accomplishes a specific computation. Visual Basic.NET supports six different kinds of operators: arithmetic, assignment, comparison, concatenation, logical, and miscellaneous.

When you use the **Val** function to convert text data to numeric values, you need to remember that the **Val** function will not convert any additional characters once it has encountered a character it does not recognize as a number. Therefore, it is important to validate the data you convert. You will learn how to perform data validation in Chapter 3.

When several operations occur in an expression, each part is evaluated and resolved in a predetermined order called *operator precedence*. Understanding operator precedence is important for creating expressions that produce the results you want. Table 2.5 lists the arithmetic operators that Visual Basic.NET supports.

Table 2.5: Visual Basic.NET arithmetic operators

Operator	Purpose
^ - Exponentiation	Raises a number to the power of another number.
* - Multiplication	Multiplies two numbers.
/ - Division	Divides two numbers and returns a floating-point result.
**** - Integer Division	Divides two numbers and returns an integer result.
Mod – Modulus arithmetic	Divides two numbers and returns only the remainder.
+ - Addition, concatenation	Adds two numbers. Also used to concatenate two strings.
− - Subtraction	Yields the difference between two numbers or indicates the negative value of a numeric expression.
+ - String concatenation	Combines two strings using a plus symbol (+).
& - String concatenation	Combines two strings using the ampersand (&) symbol.

When multiplication and division occur together in the same expression, each operation is evaluated as it occurs from left to right. When addition and subtraction occur together in the same expression, each operation is evaluated in order of appearance from left to right. You can use parentheses to override the order of precedence and force some parts of an expression to be evaluated before others. When you use parentheses, operations within parentheses are always performed before those outside. Expressions occurring with parentheses are performed according to operator precedence (multiplication, division, addition, subtraction).

> **Tip**
> The string concatenation operators (+) and (&) are not arithmetic operators, but in precedence, they follow all arithmetic operators and precede all comparison operators.

Formatting Results for Output

When you perform calculations, it is often desirable to format the results. Unformatted results may display more decimal places than required and, for monetary units, will not include a currency symbol unless they are formatted as currency. For example, consider the sales output shown in Figure 2.16, which calculates the taxes and total due for a sale in the amount of $997.25.

FIGURE 2.16. *Sales Tax application*

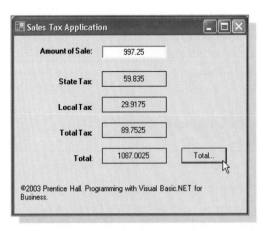

You can use the ***Format function*** to return a string that is formatted according to the instructions specified by the function. The general syntax for the expression is

```
Format(expression, [style])
```

The required *expression* can be any valid expression, such as text, or the value stored in a variable. The optional *style* is a valid format name or constant that specifies how the expression will be formatted. The format name can use a predefined format, such as the **Currency keyword** for formatting results in currency format. **Fixed** and **Percent** are other examples of predefined formats. Table 2.6 lists common predefined number formats and the characters to use when you are creating user-defined formats.

Table 2.6: Predefined and user-defined number formats

Format Name or Character	Description
General Number, G, or g	Displays number with no thousands separator.
Currency, C, or c	Displays number with thousands separator, if appropriate; displays two digits to the right of the decimal separator.
Fixed, F, or f	Displays at least one digit to the left and two digits to the right of the decimal separator.
Standard, N, or n	Displays number with thousands separator; displays at least one digit to the left and two digits to the right of the decimal separator.
Percent, P, or p	Displays number multiplied by 100 with a percent sign (%) appended to the right; always displays two digits to the right of the decimal separator.
Scientific, E, or e	Uses standard scientific notation.
D or d	Displays number as a string that contains the value of the number in decimal (base 10) format. This option is supported for integral types (Byte, Short, Integer, Long) only.
X or x	Displays number as a string that contains the value of the number in hexadecimal (base 16) format. This option is supported for integral types (Byte, Short, Integer, Long) only.
Yes/No	Displays No if number is 0; otherwise, displays Yes.

Table 2.6: (continued)

Format Name or Character	Description
True/False	Displays False if number is 0; otherwise, displays True.
On/Off	Displays Off if number is 0; otherwise, displays On.
(0)	Digit placeholder. Displays a digit or a zero.
(#)	Digit placeholder. Displays a digit or nothing.
(.)	Decimal placeholder.
(%)	Percent placeholder.
(,)	Thousands separator.

Now consider how the Format function changes the results of calculations displayed in controls. Figure 2.17 shows a modified version of the Sales Tax application, where additional labels display the effective tax rate and all results appear formatted as either Currency or Percent. In this example, the sale amount is $1000.27.

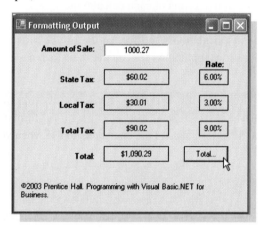

FIGURE 2.17. *Modified Sales Tax application*

Let's take a look at the code. The *Formatting Output* solution is included in your data files. Here's the procedure that declares the variables, performs the calculations, and formats the results:

```
Private Sub btnTotal_Click(ByVal sender As System.Object, ByVal
  e As System.EventArgs) Handles btnTotal.Click

        'Declare constants for the State and Local tax rates
        Const conStateTax As Single = 0.06
        Const conLocalTax As Single = 0.03

        'Declare variables for calculations
        Dim decSaleAmount As Decimal
        Dim decStateTax As Decimal
        Dim decLocalTax As Decimal
        Dim decTotalSale As Decimal

        'Perform calculations
        decSaleAmount = Val(txtSaleAmount.Text)
        decStateTax = decSaleAmount * conStateTax
        decLocalTax = decSaleAmount * conLocalTax
        decTotalSale = decSaleAmount + decStateTax +
          decLocalTax
```

```
      'Display results
      lblStateTax.Text = Format(decStateTax, "Currency")
      lblLocalTax.Text = Format(decLocalTax, "Currency")
      lblTotalTax.Text = Format(decStateTax + decLocalTax,
         "Currency")
      lblTotal.Text = Format(decTotalSale, "Currency")
      lblStateRate.Text = Format(conStateTax, "Percent")
      lblLocalRate.Text = Format(conLocalTax, "Percent")
      lblTotalRate.Text = Format((conStateTax + conLocalTax),
         "Percent")
   End Sub
```

If you compare this code with the code statements for the same procedure in the *Sales Tax Application* solution shown earlier, you will notice that this routine declares an additional variable for storing the total sale amount and uses the Format function to format the results of each calculation.

Now that you know how to declare variables and constants, obtain user input, perform calculations, and format the results of calculations for display, you are ready to create an application for calculating a loan payment.

☞ HANDS-ON PROGRAMMING EXAMPLE

The Loan Payment Application

Whether obtaining a student loan, purchasing a car, or buying a home, most people borrow money from a lending institution at some point. Whenever the Federal Reserve Board lowers interest rates, an increased number of people refinance an existing home loan, making applications that calculate a loan payment quite popular. The application you will create is targeted to students purchasing a car, but if you enter the appropriate values for the loan term and interest rate, it will accommodate any loan scenario. For this example, two upfront expenses are incurred: an origination fee of $200 and half of one point, which is 0.005% of the loan amount. Figure 2.18 shows the monthly payment and origination fees for a loan in the amount of $5,500, paid back over 4 years at an annual rate of 4.75%.

FIGURE 2.18. *Interface for Loan Payment Calculator*

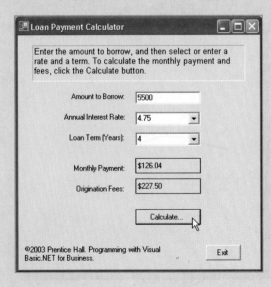

Plan the Application

The first step in planning an application is determining the inputs and outputs. This application uses three values to calculate the monthly payment on a loan and two constants to calculate the loan origination fees. The inputs and outputs are as follows:

Inputs	Outputs
Principal	Monthly payment
Term (in years)	Origination fees
Annual interest rate	

The following equation uses the principal, rate, and term to calculate the monthly payment. To calculate the monthly payment for a loan, you can use the following equation. The *rate* is the annual interest rate divided by 12 pay periods a year, and the *term* is the term of the loan in months. The term is expressed in years, so the value is multiplied by 12 periods a year.

$$\text{Monthly Payment} = \text{Principal} * (\text{Rate} / (1 - (1 + \text{Rate}) \wedge -\text{Term}))$$

The application interface uses a minimum number of controls. Text box and combo box controls obtain user input. Table 2.7 lists the additional properties you will set at design time.

Table 2.7: *Object properties for the Loan Payment application*

Object	Property	Setting
frmLoanCalculator	Text Size StartPosition	Loan Payment Calculator 400,400 CenterScreen
lblInfo	Font Borderstyle Text	Arial, 9.75pt Fixed3D Enter the amount to borrow, and then select or enter a rate and a term. To calculate the monthly payment and fees, click the Calculate button.
lblPrincipal	Text TextAlign	Amount to Borrow: MiddleRight
lblRate	Text TextAlign	Annual Interest Rate: MiddleRight
lblTerm	Text TextAlign	Length of Loan (Years): MiddleRight
txtPrincipal	TabStop TabIndex	True 0
cboRate	Items Text TabStop TabIndex	2.50, 2.75 ,3.00 , 3.25, 3.50, 3.75, 4.00, 4.25, 4.50, 4.75, 5.00, 5.25, 5.50, 5.75, 6.00 6.00 (the default value) True 1
cboTerm	Items Text TabStop TabIndex	1,2,3,4,5 1 True 2

lblPayment	TextAlign	MiddleRight
	Text	Monthly Payment:
lblFees	TextAlign	MiddleRight
	Text	Origination Fees:
lblPaymentResult	BorderStyle	FixedSingle
	TextAlign	MiddleLeft
lblFeeResult	BorderStyle	FixedSingle
	TextAlign	MiddleLeft
btnCalculate	Text	Calculate. . .
	TabStop	True
	TabIndex	3
lblCopyright	Font	Microsoft Sans Serif, 8.25pt
	Text	©2003 Prentice Hall. Programming with Visual Basic.NET for Business.
btnExit	Text	Exit
	TabStop	True
	TabIndex	4

Draw a visual representation of the application on a blank piece of paper. Figure 2.19 shows a drawing of the user interface, with the name of each control on the form.

The *lblInfo* label displays instructions telling the user to enter a loan amount and then select a term and an interest rate, using the combo boxes on the form. Clicking the **Calculate** button performs the calculations and displays the results. If the term or the rate for the loan being calculated is not available in the combo boxes, the user can enter a new value in either of these combo boxes. After the user clicks the **Calculate** button, the loan payment and origination fees are calculated, and the results display in the *lblPaymentResult* and *lblFeeResult* labels, respectively. The pseudocode for this functionality is shown in Table 2.8.

Table 2.8: *Pseudocode for the Loan Calculator application*

Event Procedure	Action
btnCalculate_Click	1. Calculate the loan payment. 2. Calculate the up-front fees. 3. Display the results in the appropriate labels.
btnExit_Click	Terminate the application.

FIGURE 2.19. *Diagram of the user interface for the Loan Payment Calculator application*

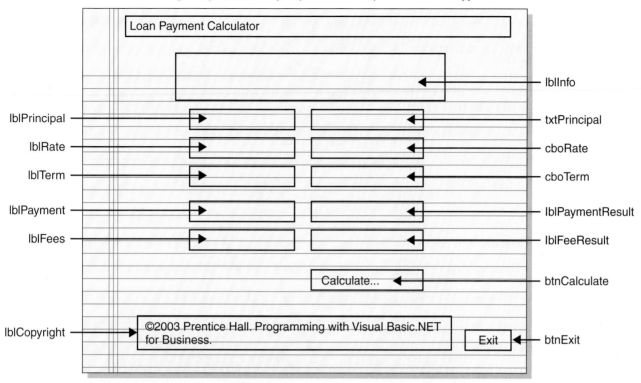

Now that you have the planning documents for the application, you are ready to begin designing the user interface in the integrated development environment (IDE).

Design the User Interface

If you have not launched Visual Studio.NET, do so now. Complete each task that follows to create your application.

To create a new project:

1. Click **File**, **New**, **Project**. Create a Windows Application named `Loan Calculator` on your hard disk or network drive and click **OK**, as shown in Figure 2.20.

FIGURE 2.20. *Creating a new project named Loan Calculator*

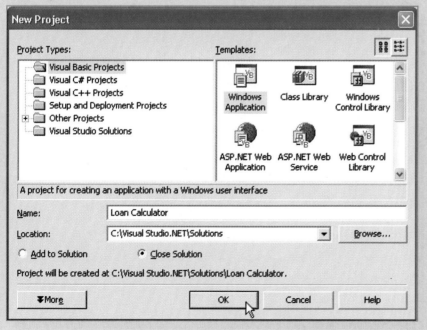

Tip

To enter the copyright symbol in the Text property of the *lblCopyright* control, turn the Num Lock key on. Then hold down the Alt key and press **0169** on the keypad. The © symbol will appear in the Text property.

FIGURE 2.21. *Using the ComboBox tool in the Toolbox*

2. If the Start Page is not visible, click **Help** and select **Show Start Page**.

3. Click **My Profile**, and set the profile to **Visual Studio Developer**. This configures your IDE so it matches the figures.

To set the form properties and add controls to the form:

1. Set the **Name** property of the form to `frmLoanCalculator`.

2. Right-click the form name and click **Display in Designer**. Set the additional form properties listed in Table 2.7.

3. Add all the controls listed in Table 2.7 to the form, except the two ComboBox controls. Place the controls in the approximate positions shown in Figure 2.18. Set the properties for each control.

4. Hover over the Toolbox and click the ComboBox tool, as shown in Figure 2.21.

Click the ComboBox tool in the Toolbox

5. Drag a **ComboBox** control onto the form in the position shown in Figure 2.22. This control will list the annual interest rates.

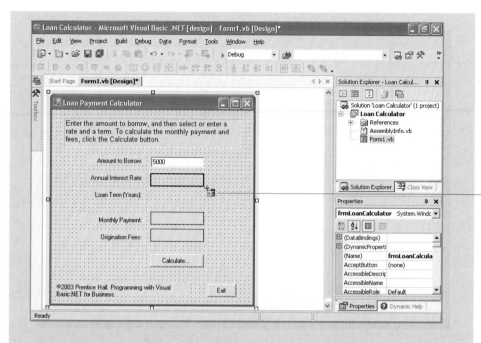

FIGURE 2.22. *Adding a combo box to the form*

Drag a **ComboBox** control onto the form in this location

6. Create another ComboBox control on the form for the loan term.
7. Click the combo box named **ComboBox1** to make it active. Click the **Items** property row, and then click the Ellipsis button.
8. The String Collection Editor appears. You can use this editor to enter the interest rates the control will display at run time. Type each rate value from 2.50 to 6.00 in the increments shown in Table 2.7. Press ⏎Enter after typing each value. When the editor contains the values shown in Figure 2.23, click **OK**.

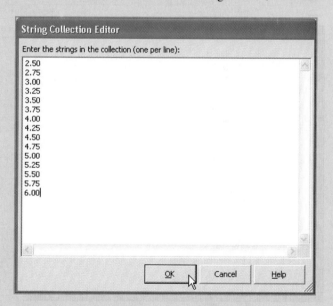

FIGURE 2.23. *Using the String Collection Editor to populate the combo box*

9. Set the **Item** property for the ComboBox2 control, and then set the remaining properties for both ComboBox controls.
10. Save your changes to the form.

You are now ready to write the code for the Loan Calculator application.

Write the Code

First you will add internal documentation to the application. You will then declare the variables and constants required for the application. Finally, you will write the statements that also handle the click events for the buttons on the form.

To add internal documentation to the application:

1. Press F7 to display the Code Editor. The insertion point appears before the Public Class statement.
2. Enter the following copyright information at the top of the Code Editor:

```
'©2003 Prentice Hall
'By [Enter your name]
'Created/Revised: [Enter the date]
'Loan Payment Calculator
```

This application requires two constants and five variables. The names and data types are listed in Table 2.9. For the constants, the value is also displayed.

Table 2.9: *Variables and constants for the Loan Calculator application*

Name	Data Type	Value
Const conOrigFee	Short	200
Const conLoanPoints	Double	.005
sngPrincipal	Single	
sngRate	Single	
intTerm	Single	
decMonthlyPayment	Decimal	
decLoanFees	Decimal	

To declare variables and constants:

1. Place the insertion point in the space below the **Inherits System.Windows.Forms.Form** statement and press ↵Enter.
2. Type Declare variables and constants as a comment and press ↵Enter.
3. Enter the declaration statement for each constant.
4. Enter the declaration statement for each variable. After you declare the constants and variables, the Code Editor should look like Figure 2.24.

How can you enter the copyright symbol (©) in the Code Editor?

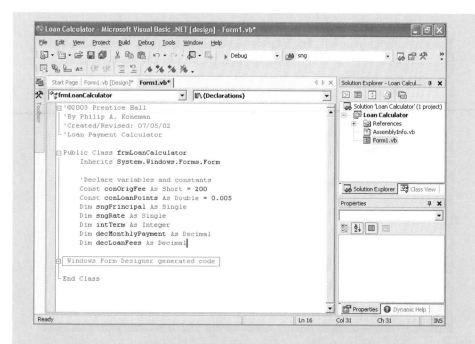

FIGURE 2.24. *Code Editor for the Loan Calculator application*

Now that you have defined the variables and constants that the application needs, you can write the subprocedures that provide the functionality.

To write code for the button click events:

1. Click the **Class Name** List in the Code Editor and select the *btnCalculate* control.
2. Click the **Method Name** list in the Code Editor and select the *Click* event.
3. Type the following code statements for the click event procedure:

```
'Assign values to the sngPrincipal, sngRate and intTerm
  variables
sngPrincipal = Val(txtPrincipal.Text)

sngRate = Val(cboRate.Text) / 100
sngRate = sngRate / 12

intTerm = Val(cboTerm.Text) * 12

'Calculate the monthly payment
decMonthlyPayment = sngPrincipal * (sngRate / (1 - (1 + sngRate)
  ^ -intTerm))

'Calculate the origination fees
decLoanFees = conOrigFee + (sngPrincipal * conLoanPoints)

'Display the monthly payment and fees
lblPaymentResult.Text = Format(decMonthlyPayment, "Currency")
lblFeeResult.Text = Format(decLoanFees, "Currency")
```

The statements include comments indicating the purpose for each statement. The procedure uses the **Val** function to convert the principal, rate, and term values from the entries in the text box and combo box controls.

Because the formula for calculating the loan payment requires the rate for a pay period (month), two statements convert the rate. The first statement divides the fractional value by 100 to express the annual interest rate as a decimal value. The next statement divides this value by 12 to express the interest rate for each pay period. The formula also requires that the loan term be expressed in payment periods, so the term expressed in years is multiplied by 12.

The monthly payment is calculated by using an assignment statement. The result of the calculation is assigned to the value of the *decMonthlyPayment* variable. The loan origination fees are calculated by using the constants for the origination fee ($200) and the loan points (one half of one percent).

After the outputs are calculated, the results are displayed in the appropriate labels on the form. The Format function formats the values as currency.

4. Select *btnExit* in the **Class Name** list and *Click* in the **Method Name** list.

5. Type `'Terminate the application` and press ⏎Enter.

6. Type `End`.

7. Save your changes.

Because you changed the name of the form, you need to set *frmLoanCalculator* as the startup form for the project.

To set the startup form:

1. Right-click the Loan Calculator solution in the Solution Explorer and select **Properties**, as shown in Figure 2.25. The *Loan Calculator Property Pages* dialog box appears.

FIGURE 2.25. *The Loan Calculator Property Pages dialog box*

2. Click the **Startup object:** list and choose **frmLoanCalculator**. Then click **OK**.

3. Save your changes.

Now that you have finished writing the code, you can run the application and test its functionality.

Run the Application

You are now ready to test the application.

To run the application:

1. Press F5 to run the application. The Visual Studio.NET compiler displays the form in Figure 2.26.

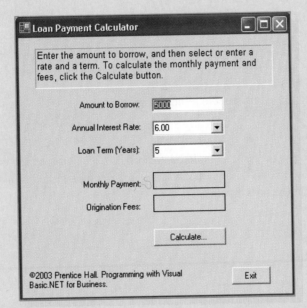

FIGURE 2.26. *Running the Loan Calculator application*

2. Enter 15000 as the loan principal.

3. Press the Tab key once and select 4.25 as the annual interest rate.

4. Press the Tab key once and select 3 as the loan term.

5. Click the **Calculate** button. Figure 2.27 displays a monthly payment of $444.53 and origination fees of $275.00.

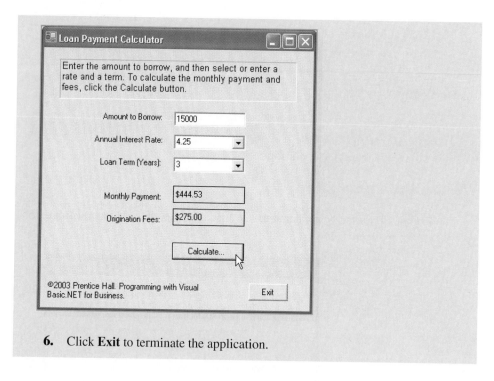

6.   Click **Exit** to terminate the application.

You have completed the Loan Calculator application. You may exit Visual Studio.NET now, or if you want to complete additional projects, close the Loan Calculator solution.

Summary

- You can use variables and constants in applications to store the values you will use in calculations. Variables retain their values throughout the execution of a program, and constants store values that remain available and do not change while the program is running.

- Visual Basic.NET supports data types you can use to store the text and numeric values you will use for variables and constants. Choose the appropriate data type for the kind of data you need. List the data types available in Visual Basic.NET.

- By following a consistent scheme for naming variables and constants, you can easily recognize the data type and scope of a variable or constant from its name.

- The placement of a variable's declaration statement determines its scope. Variables declared in a procedure have procedure scope, and variables declared in the General Declarations Section of the Code Editor have module scope.

- Declaration statements are used to declare variables and constants.

- You can use the InputBox function to obtain user input. This function displays a dialog box with a title, a prompt, and an input area.

- You can use a ComboBox control to obtain user input. A combo box has two parts: a text box for entering a unique value and a drop-down list containing a predefined list of items.

- You can use the Val function to convert text input to numeric values that can be used in calculations.

- After declaring variables and constants, you can refer to the variable or constant by name in the code expressions for performing calculations.

- You can use the Format function to format the results of calculations for display.

Key Terms

accessibility	Integer data type
arguments	integral data types
Boolean data type	local variable
Byte data type	Long data type
Char data type	module-level variable
ComboBox control	module scope
Const keyword	non-integral data types
constants	Object
Currency keyword	operator
data type	operator precedence
Date data type	Option Explicit statement
Decimal data type	Pascal case
declaration statement	Private keyword
Dim keyword	procedure scope
Double data type	Short data type
explicit variable declaration	Single data type
floating-point numbers	String data type
form-level variable	String Collection Editor
Format function	User-Defined Data Type
function	user-defined function
implicit function	Val keyword
implicit variable declaration	variable scope
InputBox function	variables

Study Questions

Multiple-Choice Questions

1. The scope of a variable determines:
   a. The number of procedures that have access to the variable.
   b. Whether or not the variable must be explicitly declared.
   c. How long the variable will remain in memory.
   d. The number of times the value of a variable can be changed.
   e. Whether the variable is a true variable or a constant.

2. Which of the following is an example of a name that is *not* recommended for variables?
   a. intCounter
   b. strFirstName
   c. decSalePrice
   d. ValueOfInventory
   e. sngConversionFactor

3. Which data type should you consider when you need to minimize memory usage and all the calculations in a procedure are based on integer values?
   a. Double
   b. Single
   c. Integer
   d. Short
   e. Long

4. Which control for obtaining user input contains predefined options that can be overridden?
   a. Label
   b. TextBox
   c. InputBox
   d. Button
   e. ComboBox

5. Which operator is used for string concatenation?
   a. #
   b. >
   c. *
   d. &
   e. \

6. If you do not specify the data type when declaring a variable, which type is used?
   a. Decimal
   b. Object
   c. String
   d. Char
   e. Short

7. Which of the following operators takes precedence over all others?
   a. +
   b. *
   c. ( )
   d. /
   e. -

8. Which of the following is not a function?
   a. InputBox
   b. decPayment
   c. Val
   d. Format
   e. Pmt

9. Which function will accept "C", "c", or "currency" as a valid argument?
   a. InputBox
   b. Click
   c. Val
   d. Format
   e. Pmt

10. Which keyword requires that all variables are declared explicitly?
    a. Val
    b. Const
    c. Option Explicit
    d. Dim
    e. Format

True/False Questions

1. Constants and variables can assume different values during program execution.

2. The InputBox property requires one argument: the prompt statement.

3. A variable that is declared in a subprocedure is available to other procedures on a form.

4. The Option Explicit statement allows for implicit variable declaration.

5. The Val function is required when you are assigning to a numeric variable user input obtained by using an InputBox.

Short Answer Questions

1. How do variables and constants differ?

2. What is an optional argument for a function? Give at least one example.

3. Why is understanding operator precedence important when you are performing calculations with formulas and expressions?

4. When might you consider using a combo box to obtain user input?

5. What is variable scope, and how do you declare a local variable?

Guided Exercises

Adding an About form to the Loan Payment application

In Chapter 1 you created a generic *About* form that can be added to any application. In this exercise, you will modify the *Loan Calculator* application to include an *About* form for display. Follow these steps to complete this task.

1. Make a copy of the *About Form* folder for the Hands-On Programming Example solution you created in Chapter 1.
2. Make a copy of the *Loan Calculator* folder for the Hands-On Programming Example solution you created in this chapter.
3. Rename the *Loan Calculator* folder as `Loan Calculator Exercise`.
4. Open the *Loan Calculator* solution from this folder.
5. Click the Project menu, and click **Add Existing Item**.
6. Navigate to the copy of the *About Form* folder you created in step 1.
7. Select the *frmAbout.vb* file and click **Open**, as shown in Figure 2.28.

Make sure you navigate to this folder when opening the solution file.

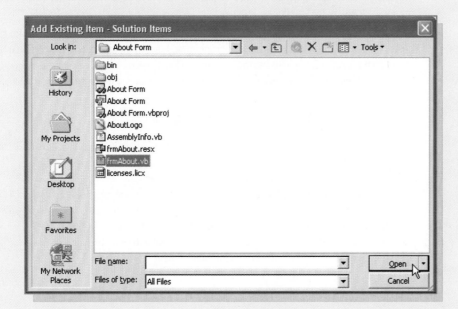

FIGURE 2.28. *Adding the existing item to a solution*

8. Right-click on the *About.vb* file in the Solution Explorer, and select **View Designer**.

9. Change the Text property of the form and the Text property of the **lblTitle** control to read About Loan Calculator.

10. Open the Code Editor. Change the reference to the application name to Loan Calculator, and change the Version Number to 1.001.0001.

11. Save your changes and close the *About Form* solution.

12. Display Form1 in the Form Designer. Add a button control just above the **Exit** button. Name the button btnAbout, and set the text of the button to About. . . . Add the following code to the button's click event:

```
Dim ShowForm As frmAbout = New frmAbout()
ShowForm.ShowDialog()
```

13. Save your changes.

14. Run the Loan Calculator application, and click the **About** button to display the About form.

15. Click the Version Information and License Information buttons to test the functionality of the form.

16. Click the **Close** button on the *About* form to hide it. Click the **Exit** button to close the Loan Calculator application when you finish viewing the *About* form.

Using the Visual Studio Debugger

As hard as you try, writing programs that do not contain errors is difficult. The errors in your programs are usually of two types. The most obvious is a *syntax error*, which is a programming statement that is incorrect. Syntax errors are almost always caught by the compiler or interpreter, which displays an error message informing you of the problem. In Visual Studio.NET, these error messages appear in the Output window.

Semantic errors are more subtle. A *semantic error* occurs when the syntax of your code is correct but the meaning is not what you intended. Because the construction obeys the language rules, semantic errors are not caught by the compiler when you run the application. As an example, if a variable does not contain the correct data, the result will be incorrect output. In this case, a semantic error leads to a *logic error* because the program includes logic that generates incorrect results. The way to detect logic errors is by testing your program, manually or automatically, and verifying that the output is what you expected. Testing should be an integral part of your software development process. Unfortunately, although testing can show you that the output of your program is incorrect, it usually does not indicate where the problem originates.

You can debug your application by using the Visual Studio.NET debugger, a powerful tool for observing the run-time behavior of your program and determining the location of semantic errors. In this exercise, you will use the debugger to locate two semantic errors in a version of the Loan Calculator application by reviewing the values contained in the program's variables.

To use the Visual Studio.NET debugger:

1. Copy the *Loan Calculator Debug* folder and all its contents from the Start folder to your hard disk or network drive.

2. Open the *Loan Calculator* solution file in this folder.

3. Press F5 to run the application. Enter 15000 as the loan principal and select **4.25** as the rate and **3 years** as the term. After you click the **Calculate** button, write down the results you obtain, and compare these to the results shown in Figure 2.27.

4. Press the F7 key to display the code for the application. Close any other windows that may be open in the development environment.

5. Scroll through the code in the Code Editor. When you reach the **sngRate = sngRate / 120** assignment statement, click this statement to select it. Then right-click and select **Insert Breakpoint**, as shown in Figure 2.29.

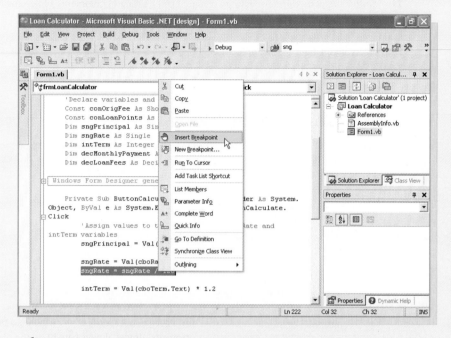

FIGURE 2.29. *Inserting a breakpoint in code*

6. A breakpoint is indicated by dark red highlighting. When you run the application, it will pause when the breakpoint is reached.
7. Scroll down the code and select the assignment statement that assigns the results of the calculation to the **lblPaymentResult.Text** property. Insert a breakpoint here.
8. Press F5 to run the application. Enter 15000 as the loan principal and select **4.25** as the rate and **3 years** as the term.
9. Click the **Calculate** button. The program runs, but when the first breakpoint is reached, the Code Editor highlights the line containing the breakpoint. Move the insertion point over any of the variables above the breakpoint to display the current value of the variable is displayed, as shown in Figure 2.30.

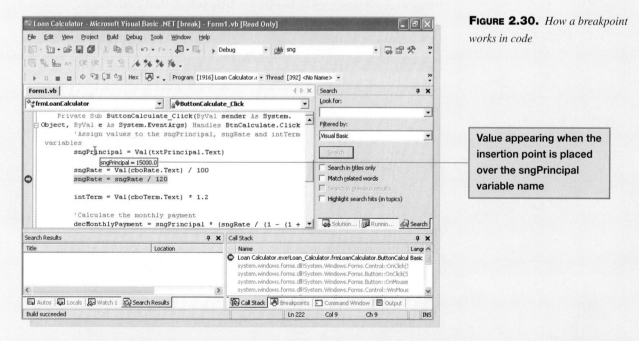

FIGURE 2.30. *How a breakpoint works in code*

Value appearing when the insertion point is placed over the sngPrincipal variable name

10. Click the **Continue** button. When the next breakpoint is highlighted, look over the values, stop program execution, and see if you can find the statements that are in error.

11. Modify the code to remove the two logic errors, and add comments indicating the changes you made.

12. Click the **Debug** menu and choose **Clear All Breakpoints**.

13. Save your changes to the application.

Case Studies

Using Variables to Perform Mileage Conversions

In Chapter 1 you reviewed an application for performing mileage conversions. In this Case Study you will create an application that performs the same calculations by using variables, constants, and functions. Recall that the conversion factors are as follows:

$$\text{Miles to Kilometers} = \text{Miles} * 1.609$$

$$\text{Kilometers to Miles} = \text{Kilometers} * 0.621$$

Your application will use the following constants and variables:

Constants	Variables
conMtoK As Single = 1.609	sngDistance As Single
conKtoM As Single = .621	sngConversion As Single

Add two buttons to the form for determining the kind of conversion to perform and a label for displaying the results. Use the InputBox function with each button to obtain the *sngDistance* value and the **Val** function to convert the text entry to a number. Display the results in the Label, and add text to indicate the kind of conversion performed.

Creating a Payroll Application

All businesses, whether large corporations or sole proprietorships, must pay tax on the income their employees earn. Create a project that calculates the gross pay, taxes, and net pay for any hourly wage and weekly hours. Use the following variables and constants:

Constants	Variables
conFederalTax – 15%	sngHourlyWage
conStateTax = 8%	intWeeklyHours
conFica = 6.2%	decGrossPay
conMediCare =1.45%	decTotalTaxes
	decNetPay

Create controls for obtaining user input, performing the calculation, and reporting the results.

Processing Decisions

L ife is full of decisions. Think of your typical day and the number of things you do based on the decisions you make. We make decisions each day that depend on specific conditions we may face. For example, your weekend plans might depend on the weather: If it rains on Saturday, you will spend the day at the museum, but if it is sunny, you will take a walk in a nearby park. Or perhaps you make decisions about your route to work based on the overall traffic flow. If the highway is at a standstill, you take your favorite scenic route, but if the traffic is moving at a steady pace on the highway, you follow the preferred route because it takes less time. As you can see, decisions are based on comparing conditions and taking a certain course of action.

As humans, we don't have the time (or the energy) to compare millions of conditions and courses of action in our daily decisions. Because computers can process millions of instructions every second, they are perfect for running business applications that process information for which the conditions producing the results will vary. In this chapter, you will learn how to write program statements that process information in response to conditions.

Performance Objectives

At the conclusion of this chapter, you will be able to:

- List the three kinds of programming structures.
- List three decision statements that are examples of decision structures.
- Use If statements to test for conditions.
- Add relational operators to decision statements.
- Create flowcharts to model decisions.
- Create nested If statements.
- Display messages onscreen with the MsgBox function.
- Validate user input.
- Compare text strings.
- Use the UCase and LCase functions with text strings.
- Use logical operators.
- Write procedures that use the Select Case decision statement.

Using Programming Structures

When you create applications with Visual Basic, you write code using program statements that tell the computer exactly what to do. A *programming structure* is the sequence in which the program statements are executed at run time. Programmers use programming structures to organize code. Program statements are organized in one of three ways: by using a **sequence structure**, a **decision structure**, or a **repetition structure**.

If your code executes program statements in order, you are using the *sequence structure*. All of the code you wrote in Chapters 1 and 2 to handle various click events used the sequence structure because the program statements are executed in sequence once the button is clicked. Sequence structures are the simplest programming structures.

A *decision structure* is a programming structure that makes a comparison between program statements. Based on the result of that comparison, the program executes statements in a certain order. If the result of the comparison is true (or yes), one statement executes, but if the result of the comparison is false (or no), an alternative statement executes. Thus the result of the comparison determines which path the program takes. Figure 3.1 demonstrates a comparison to determine the appropriate course of action and the kind of logic handled by a decision structure.

FIGURE 3.1. *Decision structure logic*

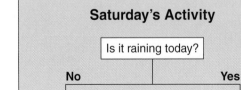

Saturday's Activity

Is it raining today?

No — Take a walk at the park

Yes — Visit the museum

If your program repeats the execution of a series of program statements, you are using a *repetition structure*. You will learn how to use repetition structures in Chapter 4. Decision structures and repetition structures are fundamental to more complex programs because business applications often require a program to analyze conditions or complete an operation a specific number of times. In this chapter, you will learn how to use decision structures in your applications.

Using Decision Structures

How do you include decision structures in your programs? By phrasing the conditions in terms of a question, you can determine the appropriate course of action. For example, credit card companies use decision structures to determine if a transaction, such as the purchase of an item, is valid. The condition for testing is phrased as a question:

Does the available credit limit exceed the amount of the sale?

When you purchase an item by using your credit card, the transaction is completed only if you do not exceed your available credit limit. A computer program that processes a transaction requires two things: the purchase amount and your available credit. The program statements will compare the two values. If the purchase amount does not exceed the available credit, the transaction is completed, but if the purchase amount exceeds the available credit, the transaction is refused. Figure 3.2 models this decision.

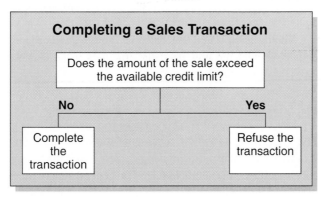

FIGURE 3.2. *Decision structure for completing a sales transaction*

How can you write program statements to respond to conditions that vary? In programming, a **condition** is an expression that uses a relational operator (such as =) to compare two statements and determine if the comparison is true or false. Such a comparison is called a **logical test**. A logical test is contained within a decision structure.

Visual Basic.NET uses a **decision statement** for handling decision structures. You can use a decision statement to test whether a condition is true or false, to test a series of conditions, to make a selection when a condition is true, or to run a series of statements if an exception occurs in testing a condition. Table 3.1 lists the decision statements supported in Visual Basic.NET.

Table 3.1: Decision statements supported in Visual Basic.NET

Decision Statement	Usage
If…Then	Executes a logical test. If the text evaluates to True, a course of action is taken.
If…Then…Else	Executes a specific statement or series of statements depending on the Boolean value of a condition. The condition usually results from a comparison of two values, but the condition can be any expression that evaluates to a True or False value. If the logical test evaluates to False, an alternative action is taken.
Select…Case	Compares the same expression to several different values. The Select statement evaluates a single expression only once and uses it for every comparison. Once the test evaluates to True, the case is applied.
Try…Catch…Finally	Used to handle exceptions—unexpected conditions encountered when an application is running, such as trying to save a file to a drive where no disk is present or trying to print to a printer that is out of paper. This statement allows you to execute a series of statements if an exception occurs while your code is running. If an exception occurs, the code is said to throw the exception, and you catch it with the appropriate Catch statement. You will learn about using the Try…Catch…Finally statement for error and exception handling in Chapter 5.

The decision statements listed in Table 3.1 are ordered from simple to more difficult. To understand how decision structures make decisions by comparing data, let's take a look at a simple example.

USING THE IF…THEN STATEMENT

The *If…Then statement* represents the simplest kind of decision structure. An If…Then statement performs a logical test, and if the test evaluates to True, the program code specifies what action to take. The general syntax for the If…Then statement is

```
If condition Then
    statements
End If
```

The statement begins with *If* and ends with *End If*. The word *Then* must appear after the condition.

Assume that a city wants to encourage its citizens to make purchases greater than $1,000. The standard sales tax rate is 7%. If the amount of a sale is less than or equal to $1,000, the standard tax rate applies to the sale, but if the sale amount is greater than $1,000, the tax rate is 5%. You can phrase this decision as a question, as follows:

Is the amount of the sale greater than $1,000?

Yes: Tax rate is 5%

No: Tax rate is 7%

The If…Then decision structure is a simplified form of the If…Then…Else structure, which you will learn about later in this chapter.

Figure 3.3 models this decision.

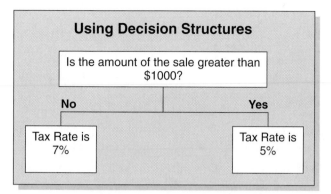

FIGURE 3.3. *Decision structure for determining tax rate on a sale*

Now let's see how you can implement this decision in a Visual Basic.NET application. Figure 3.4 shows the interface of a simple application to determine the tax rate on a sale. This code is from the *If Structure* solution included in your data files.

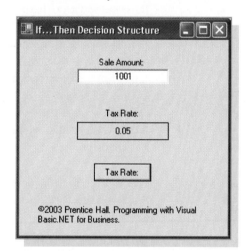

FIGURE 3.4. *Interface for Tax Rate application*

The form contains a text box for entering the sale amount and a button for displaying the tax rate. The code statements that handle the button click event follow. For clarity, the If…Then statement appears in bold.

```
Private Sub btnTaxRate_Click(ByVal sender As System.Object,
  ByVal e As System.EventArgs) Handles btnTaxRate.Click
    Dim sngTaxRate As Single
    sngTaxRate = 0.07

    If Val(txtSaleAmount.Text) > 1000 Then
        sngTaxRate = 0.05
    End If

    lblTaxRate.Text = sngTaxRate
End Sub
```

The procedure contains a declaration statement for a variable to store the tax rate, and then assigns the standard tax rate of 7% to the variable.

The If…Then statement uses the **Val** function to convert the sale amount from a text string to a numeric value, and then compares this value with 1000. If the sale amount is greater than 1000, the test evaluates to True and the decision structure assigns a new value, 5%, to the variable. If the test evaluates to False, the statement ends, and the value of 7% is retained by the variable.

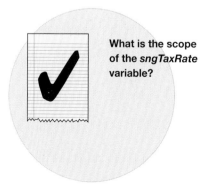

What is the scope of the *sngTaxRate* variable?

Decision statements conduct a logical test by comparing numeric or string values. The logical test uses relational operators for making the comparison.

Using Relational Operators for Comparisons

When completing a logical test, Visual Basic.NET uses at least one *relational operator* to compare conditions. The test generates a ***Boolean value***, which Visual Basic.NET assigns to a Boolean variable. A Boolean variable stores a 16-bit (2-byte) number that assumes one of two values, True or False. In the previous example, the logical test uses the greater than symbol (>) to determine if the amount of the sale exceeds 1000. Visual Basic.NET uses the relational operators shown in Table 3.2.

Table 3.2: Visual Basic relational operators

Relational Operator	Test	Example
=	Tests whether the two operands are equal	txtLastName.Text = "Smith"
<>	Tests whether the two operands are not equal	Val(txtLoanAmount.Text)<>0
<	Tests whether the first operand is less than the second operand	Val(txtLoanAmount.Text)<250000
>	Tests whether the first operand is greater than the second operand	Val(txt401K.Text)>100000
<=	Tests whether the first operand is less than or equal to the second operand	SngConversionResult<=300
>=	Tests whether the first operand is greater than or equal to the second operand	decGrossPay>=500

Here are some additional examples of using relational operators to make comparisons between data.

Relational Operator	Logical Test	Example
=	Equal to	strPassword = "127Bx9"
<>	not equal to	txtPassword.Text <> strPassword
<	less than	decTaxableIncome < 25000
>	greater than	decSaleAmount > 0
<=	less than or equal to	Val(txtUnitsInStock.Text) <= 100
>=	greater than or equal to	intReorderPoint >= intUnits

How do you determine which operators to use? This depends on the conditions you wish to test. As your program requirements become more complex, you can represent the decisions graphically. Programmers use flowcharting to represent decisions graphically and for mapping out or modeling decision statements.

Using Flowcharts to Model Decision Statements

As you learn to plan and design computer programs, you will learn new techniques for planning program structures. You have learned how to use pseudocode to model the code requirements for a program at a high level. *Flowcharting* is a modeling technique for planning the flow of a program's code to handle decision statements. A *flowchart* is a drawing that uses standardized symbols to model the steps required to handle decision statements. Table 3.3 displays common flowchart symbols.

Table 3.3: Flowchart symbols commonly used to model decision statements

Flowchart Symbol	Symbol Name	Symbol Usage
	Process	Models a program task such as declaring variables, assigning values, or performing calculations
	Decision	Models a decision for selection or repetition
	Preparation	Models the values associated with loops that will execute a set number of times.
	Data	Models input tasks, such as obtaining a value from the user, and output tasks, such as displaying the results of a calculation
	Terminator	Models the beginning (start) and end (stop) of a flowchart
	Connector	Connects flowlines in a flowchart
	Disk storage	Models data retrieved from a database for use in a decision statement or results stored in a database

A flowchart uses *flowlines* to connect the symbols and model the flow of a decision process. Let's look at two simple examples of flowcharting decision statements.

USING FLOWCHARTS TO MODEL A SIMPLE DECISION STATEMENT

To demonstrate how flowcharts model decision statements, let's return to the earlier example. The standard tax rate of 7% is assigned to a variable. The If…Then statement evaluates the amount of the sale and determines the applicable tax rate. If the test evaluates to True, the tax rate is changed to 5%. Figure 3.5 shows how a flowchart models this decision.

FIGURE 3.5. *How a flowchart models a decision*

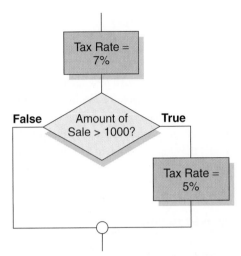

Let's look at another example. Many businesses have computerized point-of-sale (POS) systems that keep track of the number of items in inventory as inventory is sold. Inventory items have a reorder point; when the number of items in stock falls to the reorder point, the item must be reordered. Assume the reorder point for an item is 125 units. Figure 3.6 displays the interface for an application that flags inventory for reorder.

FIGURE 3.6. *Interface for Inventory Reorder application*

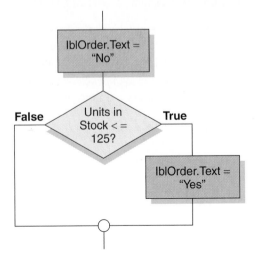

You can model this decision by using a flowchart. Figure 3.7 displays a flowchart modeling a decision for determining whether an item has reached its reorder point.

FIGURE 3.7. *Flowchart to determine reorder point for an item*

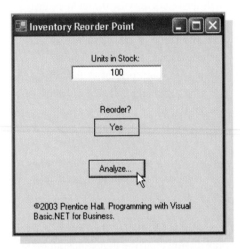

The flowchart shows that two relational operators will perform this logical test. The outcome of the test will determine the text string assigned to the label appearing on the form. As with the previous example, one event procedure includes the code statements for performing the test and determining the outcome:

```
Private Sub btnTaxRate_Click(ByVal sender As System.Object,
    ByVal e As System.EventArgs) Handles btnAnalyze.Click


        lblOrder.Text = "No"

        If Val(txtUnits.Text) <= 125 Then
            lblOrder.Text = "Yes"
        End If
    End Sub
```

The default setting for the *lblOrder.Text* string is "No". If the test evaluates to True, the decision statement changes the text string to "Yes".

As you can see, flowcharting is helpful for modeling decision statements. When you design applications that incorporate decision structures, include flowcharts in the documents you use to plan and design your applications.

Now that you understand why you would include decision structures in an application and you know how to use flowcharts to model decision statements, we will look at various ways you can use other decision statements in your applications.

Using If…Then…Else Decision Statements

The If…Then decision structure introduced earlier is a shortened form of the If…Then…Else statement. You can use an ***If…Then…Else statement*** to test for a condition and specify one option if the test evaluates to True and another if it evaluates to False. The general syntax for the If…Then…Else statement is

```
If condition Then
    statements
Else
    elsestatements
End If
```

The statement begins with *If* and ends with *End If*. The word *Then* must appear after the first condition. Let's see how to use the If…Then…Else structure to determine the appropriate tax rate for a sale. Because the statement will test a condition and specify a path for both a True and a False result, there is no need to set a default value for the tax rate variable. Figure 3.8 models this decision.

Compare the flowchart in Figure 3.8 with the flowchart in Figure 3.5. How do the decision statements represented by these two flowcharts differ?

FIGURE 3.8. *Flowchart to determine tax rate on a sale*

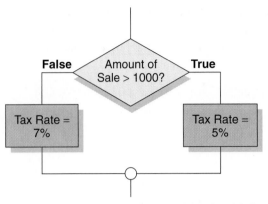

The code that handles this decision is as follows:

```
If Val(txtSaleAmount.Text) > 1000 Then
        sngTaxRate = 0.05
    Else
        sngTaxRate = 0.07
End If
```

NESTED DECISION STRUCTURES

At times you will need to use decision statements to test more than two conditions. A common method for doing so is to place a decision structure within another decision structure. Decision structures with If statements that contain additional If statements are called ***nested If statements***.

Using Nested If Statements to Test for More than Two Conditions

Nested If statements allow you to test for multiple conditions. Consider the following example:

A company assigns employee job levels based on salary. Individuals who earn $25,000 or less annually are *Administrative* employees. Employees earning more than $75,000 annually are *Senior Managers*. All other employees are *Managers*. Figure 3.9 shows a flowchart that models this decision statement as a nested If structure.

FIGURE 3.9. *Flowchart for nested If structure*

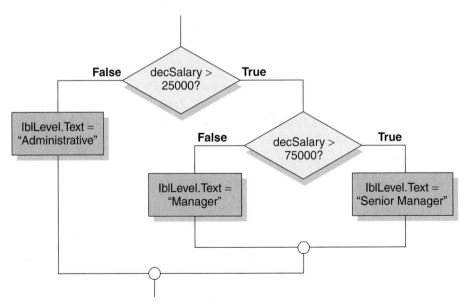

The code to implement this decision structure is as follows:

```
If decSalary > 25000 Then
    If decSalary > 75000 Then
        lblLevel.Text = "Senior Manager"
    Else
        lblLevel.Text = "Manager"
    End If
    Else
        lblLevel.Text = "Administrative"
End If
```

This code is from the *Nested If Structure* solution included in your data files. The first If statement evaluates the annual salary. If the value is less than or equal to 25,000, the test evaluates to False and the *Administrative* string is assigned to the text property of the label. If the value is greater than 25,000, the test evaluates to True and the second decision structure then determines if the annual salary is greater than 75,000. If this nested test evaluates to True, the string *Senior Manager* is assigned to the label. If the nested test evaluates to False, the *Manager* string is assigned to the label.

You can add as many nested If statements to a decision structure as are required. If the structure contains too many nested statements, however, it can become difficult to follow and the result might not be what was intended.

Using If...ElseIf...Else Statements to Test for More than Two Conditions

As an alternative to nested If statements, you can test multiple conditions by using the *If...ElseIf...Else* statement. To create this structure, add one or more **ElseIf** statements to **If...Then...Else** to test additional conditions if the first condition is **False**. The general syntax for the **If...ElseIf...Else** structure is as follows:

```
If condition Then
    statements
ElseIf elseifcondition Then
    elseifstatements
Else
    elsestatements
End If
```

For example, assume that employees earn an annual bonus that is a percentage of their annual salary. The amount of the bonus varies depending on the employee's performance rating. An employee with a performance rating lower than 1 does not receive a bonus. The bonus an employee can earn is shown here.

Rating	Bonus
3	10%
2	7.5%
1	5%

Figure 3.10 displays a flowchart modeling this decision structure.

FIGURE 3.10. *Flowchart for determining employee bonus*

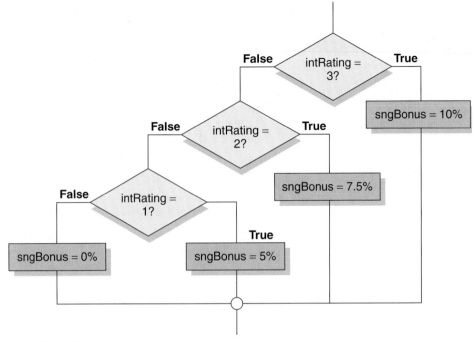

The following code statements compute a payroll bonus based on performance ratings. The statement following the Else statement runs only if the condition in each If and ElseIf statement evaluates to False.

```
If intRating = 3 Then
    sngBonus = 0.1
        ElseIf intRating = 2 Then
            sngBonus = 0.075
        ElseIf intRating = 1 Then
            sngBonus = 0.05
    Else
        sngBonus = 0
End If
```

This code is from the *Nested If Elseif Structure* solution included in your data files. Visual Basic.NET tests the conditions in the order they appear in the If...Then...Else statement. Figure 3.11 shows the bonus amount the procedure calculates for an employee earning an annual salary of $38,000 with a performance rating of 2.

FIGURE 3.11. *Interface for Employee Bonus application*

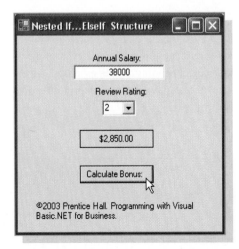

As you can see, the If decision structure is useful for determining the appropriate sequence of programming actions depending on specific conditions in your applications.

How do you know what action a procedure takes when encountering a specific condition? By displaying a message box on the screen, you can display a message for the user that provides information while an application is running.

Displaying Messages for Verifying Decisions

Many applications you are familiar with display onscreen messages to verify the decisions users make. For example, if you attempt to save a Microsoft Word document by using the name of a file in the same directory, you receive a warning message and the option to continue the procedure. Or if you inadvertently click **File**, **Exit**, a message appears giving you the option of either quitting the program or canceling the exit procedure. Windows applications use message boxes to display messages onscreen.

You can use the *MsgBox function* to display messages on the screen. A *message box* displays a message, a caption in the title bar of the dialog box, one or more command buttons, and an optional icon. Figure 3.12 identifies each part of a message box.

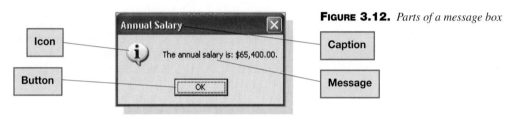

FIGURE 3.12. *Parts of a message box*

The **MsgBox** function accepts up to three arguments. The general syntax for the function is

```
MsgBox "Prompt" [, Buttons] [,"Title"]
```

Prompt: The message appearing in the dialog box displayed on the screen. A prompt is required.

Buttons: The buttons and icon appearing in the message box. Buttons are optional.

Title: The caption appearing in the title bar of the message box. A title is optional. If a title is omitted, the name of the project appears in the title bar of the message box.

The Buttons argument accepts either a numeric value or an enumeration keyword to set the display options for the buttons and icons. An *enumeration* is a symbolic name for a set of values. Table 3.4 lists the enumeration values you can use to customize the appearance of a message box.

Table 3.4: MsgBox-style enumeration values

Group	Enumeration	Value	Description
Buttons	OKOnly	0	Displays OK button only.
	OKCancel	1	Displays OK and Cancel buttons.
	AbortRetryIgnore	2	Displays Abort, Retry, and Ignore buttons.
	YesNoCancel	3	Displays Yes, No, and Cancel buttons.
	YesNo	4	Displays Yes and No buttons.
	RetryCancel	5	Displays Retry and Cancel buttons.
Icon Style	Critical	16	Displays Critical Message icon.
	Question	32	Displays Warning Query icon.
	Exclamation	48	Displays Warning Message icon.
	Information	64	Displays Information Message icon.
Default	DefaultButton1	0	First button is default.
	DefaultButton2	256	Second button is default.
	DefaultButton3	512	Third button is default.
Modality	ApplicationModal	0	Application is modal. The user must respond to the message box before continuing work in the current application.
	SystemModal	4096	System is modal. All applications are suspended until the user responds to the message box.
Window settings	MsgBoxSetForeground	65536	Specifies the message box window as the foreground window.
	MsgBoxRight	524288	Text is right-aligned.
	MsgBoxRtlReading	1048576	Specifies text should appear as right-to-left reading on Hebrew and Arabic systems.

These enumeration values are listed in groups of values. Values in the first group (values 0–5) describe the number and type of buttons displayed in the dialog box. The second group (16, 32, 48, and 64) describes the icon style. The third group (0, 256, and 512) determines which button is the default. The fourth group (0, 4096) determines the modality of the message box. The fifth group (65536, 524288, and 1048576) specifies whether or not the message box window is the foreground window and sets the alignment and direction of the text.

You can combine enumeration values to customize a message box, but you can use only one value from each group. To combine values, enter a value for the Buttons argument that is the sum of the individual enumeration values. For example, an integer value of *524324* will display a message box with both an OK and a Cancel button, a question icon, and text that is right-aligned. The integer value is the sum of the enumeration values, as shown:

Enumeration	Value
YesNo	4
Question icon	32
MsgBoxRight	524288
	524324

The following declaration will display the message box shown in Figure 3.13:

```
MsgBox ("Yes or No?",524324, "Clarification Required!")
```

FIGURE 3.13. *Message box example*

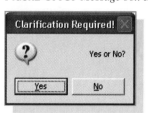

You can declare variables to store the Prompt, Buttons, and Title arguments to simplify your code. For example, the following code statements will display the message box shown in Figure 3.13:

```
Dim strPrompt As String
Dim intButtons As Integer
Dim strTitle As String

strPrompt = "Yes or No?"
intButtons = 524322
strTitle = "Clarification Required!"

MsgBox(strPrompt, intButtons, strTitle)
```

Here are some examples of statements that use the **MsgBox** function to display messages onscreen. To view the code for each example, open the *MsgBox Function* solution included with your data files.

1. This statement displays a simple message with a message, an OK button, and the project name as a title.

```
MsgBox ("Please enter a number!")
```

2. In this example, the style of the message box depends on whether text is entered into the text box.

```
If txtEntry.Text = "" Then
    MsgBox("Please enter a text string.", MsgBoxStyle.Critical,
    "Missing Data")
        Else
    MsgBox("The entry is: " & txtEntry.Text,
    MsgBoxStyle.Information, "Text Entry")
End If
```

3. This statement displays a message, the Retry and Cancel buttons, the Question icon, and a title.

```
MsgBox("Please enter the annual salary as a decimal value.", 37,
  "Enter the annual salary")
```

Tip

When you include buttons in a message box, the **MsgBox** function waits for the user to click a button and then returns an integer that indicates which button the user clicked. You can use these integer values in decision statements to handle the response.

4. These statements display the message box shown in Figure 3.12.

```
decAnnualSalary = 65400
MsgBox("The annual salary is: " & Format(decAnnualSalary,
  "Currency") & ".", MsgBoxStyle.Information, "Annual Salary")
```

5. These statements display the message box shown in Figure 3.13.

```
Dim strPrompt As String
Dim intButtons As Integer
Dim strTitle As String

strPrompt = "Yes or No?"
intButtons = 524322
strTitle = "Clarification Required!"

MsgBox(strPrompt, intButtons, strTitle)
```

6. These statements display a message box with a concatenated prompt, the Information button style, and a caption. Note that the *strPrompt* variable is assigned a concatenated text string made up of text string and variable data.

```
Dim intUnitsInStock As Integer
Dim decUnitPrice As Decimal
Dim decUnitValue As Decimal
Dim strDescription As String

Dim strPrompt As String
Dim intButtons As Integer
Dim strTitle As String

intUnitsInStock = 12
decUnitPrice = 11.98
strDescription = "Standard Computer Mouse"
decUnitValue = intUnitsInStock * decUnitPrice

strPrompt = "Item Description: " & strDescription _
& vbCrLf & "Units in Stock: " & intUnitsInStock _
& vbCrLf & "Inventory Value: " & Format(decUnitValue, "C")

intButtons = 64

strTitle = "Inventory Value"

MsgBox(strPrompt, intButtons, strTitle)
```

Now that you are familiar with using the **MsgBox** function in conjunction with decision structures, let's see how to add functionality to an application's Exit button.

Using an If Statement and the MsgBox function to Handle the Event for Exiting an Application

Most applications display a dialog box for verifying an event that may lose data, such as exiting the application or saving a file with the same filename. You can use an If statement to handle the procedure for exiting an application. The statement displays the message box shown in Figure 3.14. Clicking **Yes** terminates the application; clicking **No** ends the procedure and returns to the application.

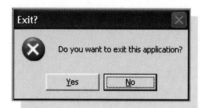

FIGURE 3.14. *Message box for exiting an application*

The code for the event is as follows:

```
Private Sub btnExit_Click(ByVal sender As System.Object, ByVal e
    As System.EventArgs) Handles btnExit.Click
Dim intResponse As Integer
intResponse = MsgBox("Do you really want to exit this
    application?", 276, "Exit?")
    If intResponse = 6 Then
        End
    End If
End Sub
```

When a user clicks a button contained in a message box, the procedure returns an integer that indicates which button was clicked. Table 3.5 lists the return values supported in Visual Basic.NET.

Table 3.5: Message box return values

Button	Value
OK	1
Cancel	2
Abort	3
Retry	4
Ignore	5
Yes	6
No	7

The procedure for the Exit button begins by declaring an integer variable, *intResponse*. An assignment statement assigns to this variable the value returned by the

Why does the **MsgBox** function use a value of 276 for the button's argument? What will the combination of the values 4, 16, and 256 display in the message box?

4: Displays the Yes and No buttons

16: Displays the Critical icon

256: Sets the second button (No, in this case) as the default

With the No button as the default, the user must click the Yes button and not simply press ⏎Enter to exit the application.

The procedure for
this Exit button is
included in the
MsgBox Function
solution included
with your data files.
You can use this
procedure for all the applications
you create.

message box, which according to Table 3.5 will be either the value 6 (assigned by clicking **Yes**) or 7 (assigned by clicking **No**).

The next code statement uses an If decision structure to evaluate the integer value assigned to the *intResponse* variable. If the value is 6, the application ends. If the value is anything other than 6, the procedure ends. Figure 3.15 shows a flowchart modeling this decision structure.

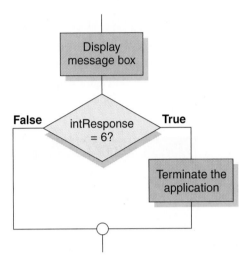

FIGURE 3.15. *Flowchart for Exit button procedure*

This example shows how to use an If statement in conjunction with a message box for verifying user choices. Let's see how to use If statements with other Visual Basic.NET controls for obtaining user input.

Using If Statements with Check Boxes and Radio Buttons

Visual Basic.NET includes a number of controls you can use to obtain user input and specify conditions. For example, assume that your company requires you to renew your benefits each year. The company has an application running on your desktop for making your selections. The amount deducted from each paycheck for your benefits varies depending on your job level and the benefits you select. Before calculating your payroll deduction, the application confirms your selections. Figure 3.16 shows the interface for this application, which is in the *Check Box and Radio Box Controls* solution included with your data files.

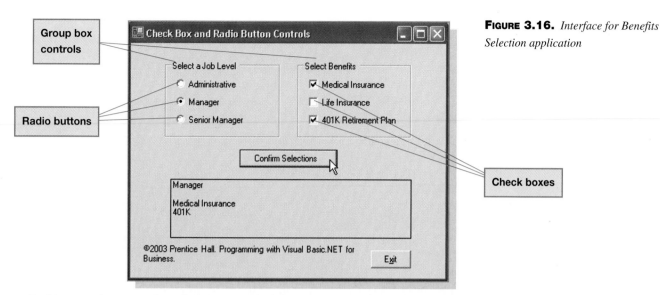

FIGURE 3.16. *Interface for Benefits Selection application*

In this example a user selected *Manager* as the job level, and the *Medical* and *401K* benefits.

RADIO BUTTON AND GROUP BOX CONTROLS

A *radio button* is a control for selecting one option from a list of possible options. You can use a *group box* control to assign a set of radio buttons to a group. Defining radio buttons as a group presents the user with a set of choices from which only one can be chosen. When a radio button control in the group is clicked, its *checked property* is set to True.

Notice that you can select only one radio button at run time when you run the *Check Box and Radio Button Controls* solution.

THE CHECK BOX CONTROL

A check box is a control you can use to indicate whether a specific condition is on or off. You can use check box controls in groups to display multiple choices from which the user can make multiple selections. Check box controls often appear within a group box so they appear as a group. Unlike radio buttons, however, multiple check boxes can be selected in the group. When the user clicks a check box at run time, a check mark appears in the box and its checked property is set to True.

Now let's see how to use If statements to obtain user input from check box and radio button controls. The code for the application shown in Figure 3.16 is as follows:

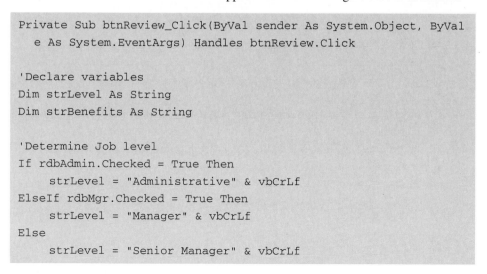

```
Private Sub btnReview_Click(ByVal sender As System.Object, ByVal
    e As System.EventArgs) Handles btnReview.Click

'Declare variables
Dim strLevel As String
Dim strBenefits As String

'Determine Job level
If rdbAdmin.Checked = True Then
    strLevel = "Administrative" & vbCrLf
ElseIf rdbMgr.Checked = True Then
    strLevel = "Manager" & vbCrLf
Else
    strLevel = "Senior Manager" & vbCrLf
```

```
End If

'Determine selected benefits
If chkMedical.Checked = True Then
    strBenefits = vbCrLf & "Medical Insurance"
End If

If chkLife.Checked = True Then
    strBenefits = strBenefits & vbCrLf & "Life Insurance"
End If

If chk401K.Checked = True Then
    strBenefits = strBenefits & vbCrLf & "401K"
End If

'Display results
lblMessage.Text = strLevel & strBenefits
End Sub
```

As you can see, all the functionality is contained in one event procedure. The procedure declares two string variables for containing the job level and benefits text strings that are displayed in the label on the form. The procedure uses an **If...ElseIf...Else** decision statement to determine the job level. Figure 3.17 models this decision.

FIGURE 3.17. *Flowchart for determining job level*

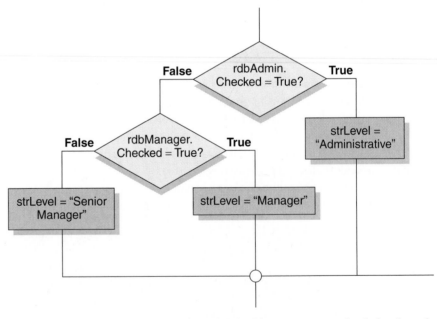

The procedure then uses a series of three If statements to check for the selected benefits. If the first test evaluates to True, a text string is assigned to the *strBenefits* variable. If the next test evaluates to True, the procedure appends a text string to the *strBenefits* variable by assigning a value consisting of its current value and the new value. If the last test evaluates to True, an additional text string is appended to the variable. Figure 3.18 models this decision structure.

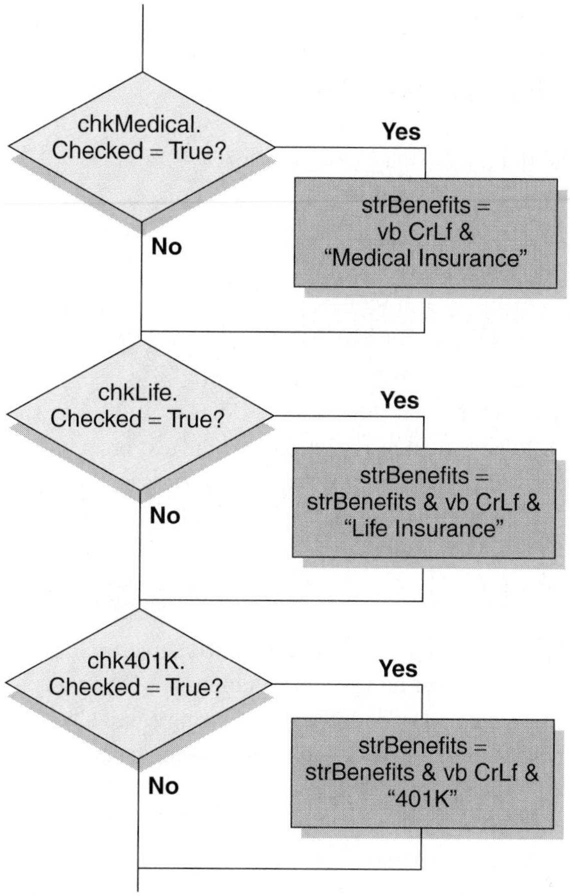

FIGURE 3.18. *Flowchart for determining benefits selection*

The results are then assigned to the Text property of the *lblResults* text box.

As you can see, radio button, check box, and group box controls are useful for obtaining user input. By using the appropriate decision structure, you can assign user selections to variables or control properties. Now let's see how to use decision structures to validate information obtained from text box and combo box controls.

Using Decision Statements for Data Validation

In the examples you have used that obtain user input from text box, input box, and combo box controls, we have assumed that the data is entered correctly. However, it is possible to inadvertently enter text where a number is required, which can produce unintended results. You may have heard the phrase "*Garbage in, garbage out.*" Because computer output depends on the quality of the data the user supplies, programmers need to check the values entered in Windows forms to make sure the data is appropriate for its intended use.

The process of checking data entered into a program is called *data validation*. You can use If statements to display a message if data is required and none has been supplied or to check to make sure numbers have been entered when the data will be used in calculations.

CHECKING FOR A REQUIRED VALUE

A common data validation task is checking to make sure users input required data. You can use a simple If…then…Else statement to check for required data. If the data has been supplied, the program continues. You can use a message box to inform users that required data is missing. Consider the following example, which checks to make sure users have entered their annual salary:

```
If txtData.Text <> "" Then
        MsgBox("You entered: " & txtData.Text,
           MsgBoxStyle.Information, "Data is Valid")
     Else
        MsgBox("Data is required. Please try again.",
           MsgBoxStyle.Critical, "Invalid Data")
     End If
```

How would you model this decision using a flowchart?

The logical test determines if the text box contains an empty string (represented by " "). If the test evaluates to True, a message box asks the user to enter data. If the test evaluates to False, a message box informs the user that the data is valid.

CHECKING FOR NUMERIC VALUES

You have used the **Val** function to convert data entered into a text box to a numeric value that can be used in calculations. However, if the **Val** function encounters an empty text sting, it converts the string to a value of zero. Therefore, it is important to validate numeric data before performing calculations.

Visual Basic.NET includes a function designed to determine if data entered into a control is a numeric value. The *IsNumeric function* checks a text string and determines if it can be evaluated as a number. If the string is evaluated as a number, the function returns a Boolean value of True. Otherwise, the function returns False. The function requires one argument: the expression to evaluate. The general syntax for the function is

```
IsNumeric(expression)
```

Consider the following procedure:

```
If IsNumeric(txtData.Text) = False Then
        MsgBox("A numeric value is required. Please try
           again.",
        MsgBoxStyle.Critical, "Invalid Data")
     Else
        MsgBox("You entered: " & txtData.Text,
           MsgBoxStyle.Information, "Data is Valid")
     End If
```

This procedure uses an If...Then...Else statement to check the data entered into a text box. If nothing is entered, or if an expression containing characters is entered, the function returns False. A numeric value or a decimal value returns a Boolean result of True. Here are some additional examples of the Boolean value returned when using the **IsNumeric** function to evaluate the value of the *txtData.Text* string:

Expression	Return Value
txtData.Text = "123"	True
txtData.Text = "123.01"	True
txtData.Text = "$1000"	False
txtData.Text = "Zero"	False
txtData.Text = "$100,000"	False
txtData.Text = "123 Dollars"	False

CHECKING FOR REQUIRED DATA

There are other occasions where you might need to verify that a text string is a numeric value within a specific range. For example, assume that your employer allows you up to 160 hours of vacation time annually. You enter your vacation hours in a text box. You can use a nested If statement to check for a numeric value and then verify that the value is less than or equal to 160 hours. Consider the following procedure:

```
If IsNumeric(txtData.Text) = True Then
    If Val(txtData.Text) <= 160 Then
        MsgBox("The vacation hours you entered are valid.",
        MsgBoxStyle.Information, "Vacation Hours are Valid")
    Else
        MsgBox("Vacation hours may not exceed 120 per year.
            Please enter a new value.", MsgBoxStyle.Critical,
            "Vacation Hours are Invalid")
    End If
    Else
    MsgBox("A value is required. Please try again.",
        MsgBoxStyle.Exclamation, "Required Value Missing")
End If
```

Each of these procedures in contained in the *Data Validation* solution in your data files. Now let's learn how to use If statements to compare text strings to one another.

Using If Statements with Text Strings

At times you will need to make comparisons between text strings. You can compare the contents of text variables, text values enclosed in quotation marks (known as *text literals*), or the contents of text boxes. String comparisons are useful in database applications, such as when validating user input or sorting string data.

When you compare text strings for data validation or sorting, the order is determined by each character's ASCII value. *ASCII (American Standard Code for Information Interchange)* is a standard designation of characters and symbols shared among computer systems. Table 3.6 lists the ASCII values from 32 to 127, which include numbers, special characters, and the uppercase and lowercase characters contained in many text strings.

Table 3.6: ASCII values from 32 to 127

ASCII Value	ASCII Character	ASCII Value	ASCII Character	ASCII Value	ASCII Character
32	{space}	64	@	96	'
33	!	65	A	97	a
34	"	66	B	98	b
35	#	67	C	99	c
36	$	68	D	100	d
37	%	69	E	101	e
38	&	70	F	102	f
39	'	71	G	103	g
40	(	72	H	104	h
41	)	73	I	105	i
42	*	74	J	106	j
43	+	75	K	107	k
44	,	76	L	108	l
45	-	77	M	109	m
46	.	78	N	110	n
47	/	79	O	111	o
48	0	80	P	112	p
49	1	81	Q	113	q
50	2	82	R	114	r
51	3	83	S	115	s
52	4	84	T	116	t
53	5	85	U	117	u
54	6	86	V	118	v
55	7	87	W	119	w
56	8	88	X	120	x
57	9	89	Y	121	y
58	:	90	Z	122	z
59	;	91	[	123	{
60	<	92	\	124		
61	=	93	]	125	}
62	>	94	^	126	~
63	?	95	_	127	DEL

COMPARING TEXT STRINGS

When you compare text strings, comparisons are made from left to right, beginning with the first character of the string. When two characters being compared are unequal, the comparison is terminated and the character with the higher ASCII value is determined to be greater. For example, an uppercase *A* (ASCII value of 65) has a lower ASCII value than a lowercase *a* (ASCII value of 97). So when sorting or comparing text, uppercase letters come before lowercase letters, while numbers, special symbols, and most punctuation marks appear before letters. Figure 3.19 shows the interface for the *String Comparison* solution included in your data files.

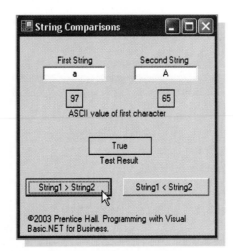

FIGURE 3.19. *Interface for String Comparison application*

Here are additional examples of string comparisons:

Value 1	ASCII Value of First Character	Value 2	ASCII Value of Second Character	Value1 > Value2?
Z	122	A	65	True
+1	43	−1	45	False
A	65	Z	90	False
A	65	?	63	True
Faith	70	Faithful	70	False
Missouri	77	Mississippi	77	True
0	48	-1	45	True
100	49	98	57	False

As you can see, numbers are treated as text. When you need to compare numbers obtained in a text box, always use the **Val** function to convert the string values to numeric values. You can use the *Text Comparisons* solution contained in your data files to see the results of comparing other text strings.

USING THE UCASE AND LCASE FUNCTIONS WITH TEXT STRINGS

When you are comparing text strings, the case of the characters is important because uppercase characters have lower ASCII values than lowercase characters. Visual Basic.NET includes two functions that are useful when manipulating or comparing text strings or text literals; the LCase and the UCase functions. The *UCase function* converts all values from lowercase to uppercase. For example, if you're using a Visual Basic form for entering records into a database, you can use the **LCase** function to convert a state entered as *co* to *CO*. This allows data entry personnel to avoid having to use the ⟨◆Shift⟩ key when entering or editing records. The *LCase function* is similar and converts uppercase values to lowercase. The functions require one argument: the text string to convert. The general syntax for the functions is as follows:

```
LCase(string)
UCase(string)
```

Figure 3.20 shows the result of using the **UCase** function to convert the text string contained in the *txtData* text box and displaying the converted value in the *lblResult* label.

FIGURE 3.20. *Using the UCase function*

Here are some additional examples of how the **LCase** and **UCase** functions convert the text string contained in the *txtData* text box:

Value in txtData.Text	LCase(txtData.Text)	UCase(txtData.Text)
Mr. Tibbs	mr. tibbs	MR. TIBBS
Az	az	AZ
Vt	vt	VT
Visual Basic.NET	visual basic.net	VISUAL BASIC.NET
strLastName	strlastname	STRLASTNAME

You can use the *UCase and LCase* solution included in your data files to see the results of other conversions.

Now that you understand how Visual Basic.NET compares text strings, let's see how to use logical operators to test for more than one condition.

Using Logical Operators with If Statements

At times, you need to test for multiple conditions in a single statement. You can use logical operators to join multiple conditions into one condition called a ***compound condition***. The most common ***logical operators*** are listed in Table 3.7.

Table 3.7: Logical operators

Logical Operator	Purpose
And	Performs a logical conjunction on two Boolean expressions. If both conditions are True, the compound condition is True.
Or	Performs a logical disjunction on two Boolean expressions. If both conditions are True, the compound condition is True. If either condition is True, the compound condition is True.
Not	Performs a logical negation on two Boolean expressions. The condition is reversed so that a True condition evaluates to False and a False condition evaluates to True.

Let's say a company determines that to qualify for a bonus, an employee must be employed for at least 12 months and earn at least $25,000 annually. Your data files include a solution named *Logical Operators*. The interface includes buttons that demonstrate how logical operators work. Figure 3.21 shows the result obtained for a salary of $24,000 and employment of 24 months.

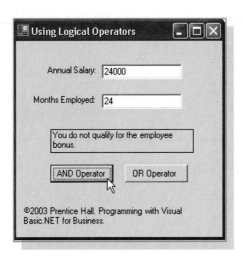

FIGURE 3.21. *Using the And logical operator*

The code for the **And Operator** button is as follows:

```
If IsNumeric(txtSalary.Text) = False Or
  IsNumeric(txtMonths.Text) = False Then
    MsgBox("You must enter the annual salary and months employed
      as a number. Please try again.", MsgBoxStyle.Critical,
      "Invalid Entry")
    ElseIf Val(txtSalary.Text) >= 25000 And Val(txtMonths.Text)
      >= 12 Then
        lblResult.Text = "You qualify for the employee bonus."
    Else
    lblResult.Text = "You do not qualify for the employee
      bonus."
End If
```

The procedure uses the *Or* operator to perform data validation: if either entry is not a number, a message box appears. The procedure then uses the *And* operator to perform the logical test, and the results are displayed in the *lblResult* label.

Now let's change the conditions for earning a bonus. If an employee earns an annual salary of at least $25,000 *or* has been employed for at least 18 months, the employee qualifies for the annual bonus. Figure 3.22 displays the result obtained for an employee earning $22,000 annually who has been employed for 21 months.

Figure 3.22. *Using the Or logical operator*

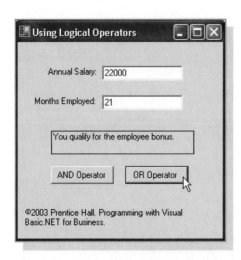

The code for the **Or Operator** button is as follows:

```
If IsNumeric(txtSalary.Text) = False Or
   IsNumeric(txtMonths.Text) = False Then
     MsgBox("You must enter the annual salary and months employed
        as a number.Please try again.", MsgBoxStyle.Critical,
        "Invalid Entry")
         ElseIf Val(txtSalary.Text) >= 25000 Or
            Val(txtMonths.Text) >= 18 Then
            lblResult.Text = "You qualify for the employee bonus."
     Else
     lblResult.Text = "You do not qualify for the employee
        bonus."
End If
```

This procedure uses the same statement to perform data validation. The *Or* operator performs the logical test and displays the results in the label.

As you can see, If statements are useful for making decisions and taking alternative courses of action based on conditions. If statements are also useful for performing data validation and comparing text strings. When combined with logical operators, If statements can test multiple conditions in compound statements.

Now that you understand how to use If statements in decision structures, let's look at how to use the Select Case decision statement.

Using the Select Case Decision Statement

The conditions you need to test sometimes become complex and require nested If statements. Although you can nest as many levels of *If* statements as your application requires, nesting too deeply makes code hard to model, write, and manage. The **Select…Case statement** is a good alternative to nested If statements when you need to test a single variable or expression for multiple values. The Select…Case structure is simpler and uses more concise code than nested If structures for testing one value against multiple conditions.

Select…Case statements compare an expression or a value to a **case block**, which is the set of cases that may apply. A **case** is an individual condition that is being tested. The syntax for the **Select…Case** decision structure is

```
Select [ Case ] expression
    [ Case expressionlist
        [ statements ] ]
    [ Case Else
        [ elsestatements ] ]
End Select
```

USING SELECT...CASE STATEMENTS

Earlier we looked at an example of determining the percentage of an employee's bonus, which varies depending on the employee's performance rating. We used an **If...ElseIf...Else** statement to determine the applicable bonus percentage:

```
If intRating = 3 Then
    sngBonus = 0.1
ElseIf intRating = 2 Then
    sngBonus = 0.075
ElseIf intRating = 1 Then
    sngBonus = 0.05
Else
    sngBonus = 0
End If
```

Suppose that the employer changes the employee review process and uses a new review form. The new form uses a 10-point scale, not a 3-point scale. However, the bonus percentages remain the same and are applied as follows:

Performance Rating	Bonus Percentage
0	No Bonus
1 to 3	5%
4 to 7	7.5%
8 to 10	10%

Coding this solution by using nested If statements and logical operators is more complex than using the Select...Case statement. Figure 3.23 shows the calculation for an employee with an annual salary of $65,000 and a performance rating of 7.

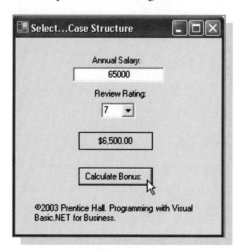

FIGURE 3.23. *Using the Select...Case statement*

Here's the code for the procedure that calculates the bonus. The Select...Case statement appears in bold:

```
Dim decSalary, decBonusPay As Decimal
Dim sngBonus As Single
Dim intRating As Integer

decSalary = Val(txtSalary.Text)
intRating = Val(cboReview.Text)

Select Case intRating
    Case Is < 1
        sngBonus = 0
    Case 1 To 3
        sngBonus = 0.05
    Case 4 To 6
        sngBonus = 0.075
    Case Is > 6
        sngBonus = 0.1
End Select

decBonusPay = decSalary * sngBonus
lblBonus.Text = (Format(decBonusPay, "Currency"))
```

As you can see, the code is concise and easy to read. The Select...Case statement determines the appropriate bonus rate based on the range of the performance rating value.

USING A SELECT...CASE STATEMENT WITH RADIO BUTTONS

You can also use a Select...Case statement to determine which radio button in a group is selected. Figure 3.24 displays a form for specifying a salary range and then verifying the selected range. This example is from the *Select Case Radio Buttons* solution included in your data files.

FIGURE 3.24. *Using the Select...Case statement with radio buttons*

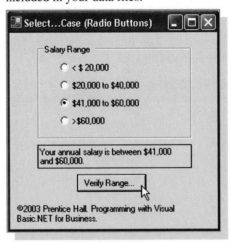

Here's the code for the Select...Case statement:

```
Select Case mintIndex
    Case 0
        lblResult.Text = "Your annual salary is less than
            $20,000."
```

```
    Case 1
        lblResult.Text = "Your annual salary is between $20,000
            and $40,000."
    Case 2
        lblResult.Text = "Your annual salary is between $41,000
            and $60,000."
    Case 3
        lblResult.Text = "Your annual salary is greater than
            $60,000."
End Select
```

The procedure uses the value of a variable named *mintIndex* to determine which button is selected. This is a module-level variable that contains the index value of the selected radio button. Each radio button has a click event that assigns a value of 0 to 3 to the variable. Once a value is assigned, the case structure returns the index for the selected button and uses this to determine the message to display.

As you can see, If...Then, If...Then...Else, and Select...Case statements allow you to add a great deal of functionality to the applications you create. How do you determine which statement to use? Keep in mind the principle that the simplest solution is usually the best solution, use your variables wisely, and make every attempt to streamline your code.

☞ HANDS-ON PROGRAMMING EXAMPLE

Modifying the Loan Payment Application

In Chapter 2 you created a simple loan payment application for determining the loan payment and associated fees for obtaining a loan. That application is targeted to students purchasing a car, and had the following up-front expenses; an origination fee of $200 and an additional fee of half of one point.

In this example you will modify how the up-front fees are calculated. Borrowers have the opportunity to reduce the up-front fees associated with the loan. One option is to choose a different type of vehicle for purchase. The lending institution has partnered with the leading automotive companies to negotiate a discount for more economical vehicles. There is an origination fee of 4.5% of the loan amount for sport utility vehicles (SUVs), 4% for trucks, 2.5 % for wagons, and 2% for sedans. In addition, the lending institution is offering an origination fee discount of 1.5% for borrowers with at least one active account at the institution. Therefore, the potential up-front fees range from 4.5% (for borrowers purchasing an SUV who do not have a current account) to 0.5% (for borrowers purchasing a sedan who currently have an account). Figure 3.25 shows the monthly payment and origination fees for a loan of $21,000, paid back over four years at an annual rate of 4.75%, for the purchase of an SUV by a customer with an existing account.

The principle that the simplest solution is the best solution can be traced to William of Ockham, who lived in Surrey, England, at the end of the thirteenth century. He is known for formulating the principle known as "Ockham's Razor," also known as the *Law of Economy*. William was an empiricist who believed that all knowledge is based on experience. When applied to matters of scientific investigation, the Law of Economy states that the simplest explanation is the best, and it is futile to develop complex hypotheses when a simple one will suffice.

We can apply the Law of Economy to programming. When developing applications, write code as concisely as possible, and use the most direct solution to a problem.

FIGURE 3.25. *Interface for loan payment calculator*

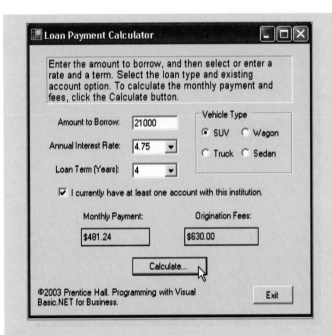

Plan the Application

The first step in planning an application is determining the inputs and outputs. You will modify a version of the *Loan Calculator* application from Chapter 2 for this example. This application uses three values to calculate the monthly payment on a loan and the data from the automobile type and existing account discount to calculate the loan origination fees. The inputs and outputs are as follows:

Inputs	Outputs
Principal	Monthly payment
Term (in years)	Origination fees
Annual interest rate	
Automobile type	
Existing account discount	

The application uses the same formula as in Chapter 2 to calculate the loan payment. The application interface includes the controls you created in Chapter 2, as well as a check box, a group box, and four radio buttons. Table 3.8 lists the new controls and their properties.

Table 3.8: *Object properties for Loan Payment application*

Object	Property	Setting
grpAutoType	Text	Vehicle Type
chkMultipleAccounts	Text	I currently have at least one account with this institution.
	TabStop	True
	TabIndex	7
rdbSUV	Text	SUV
	TabStop	True
	TabIndex	3
	Checked	True
rdbTruck	Text	Truck
	TabStop	True
	TabIndex	4
rdbWagon	Text	Wagon
	TabStop	True
	TabIndex	5
rdbSedan	Text	Sedan
	TabStop	True
	TabIndex	6

Draw a visual representation of the application on a blank piece of paper. Figure 3.26 shows a drawing of the user interface and the name of each control on the form.

FIGURE 3.26. *Diagram of user interface for Loan Payment Calculator application*

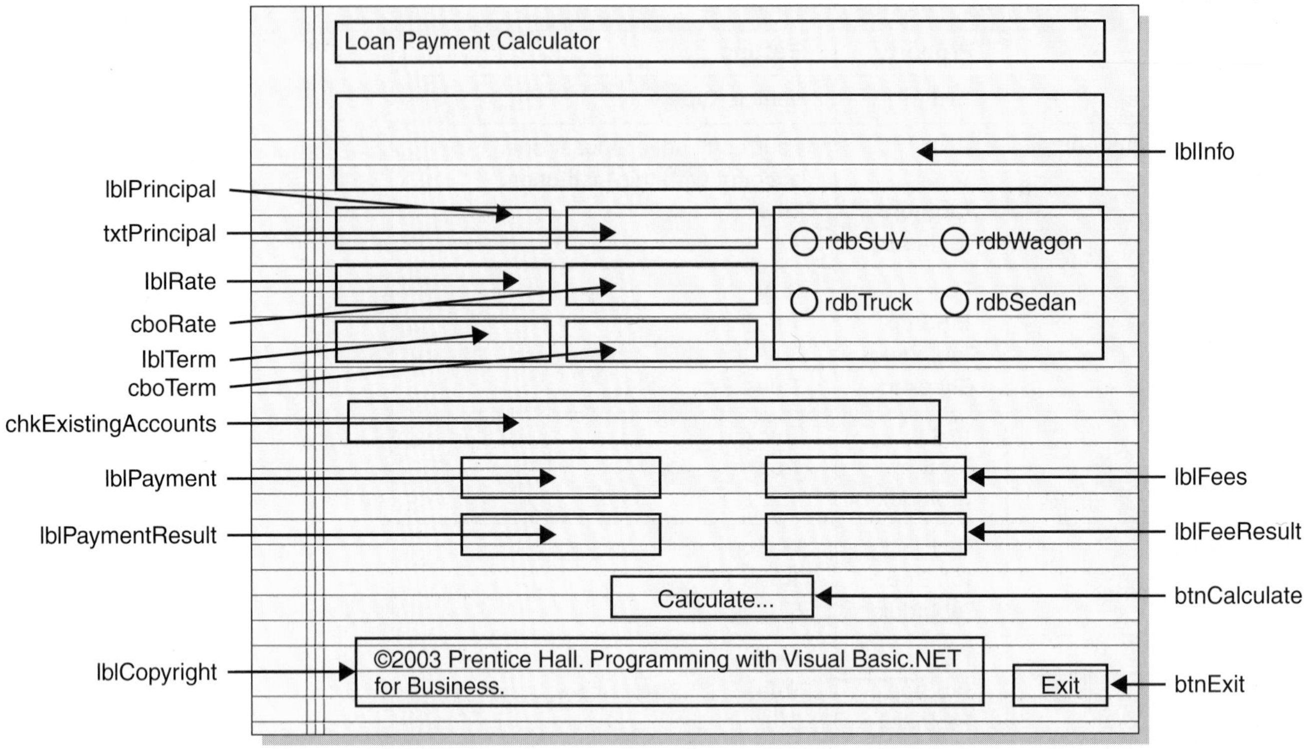

The *lblInfo* label displays instructions telling the user to enter a loan amount, term, and rate and to specify the multiple accounts option and the vehicle type. The check box for indicating multiple accounts is not checked by default, and the default vehicle type is the SUV (the highest rate). Clicking the *Calculate* button performs the calculations and displays the results. If the term or the rate for the loan being calculated is not available in the combo boxes, the user can enter a new value in either of these combo boxes. After the user clicks the *Calculate* button, the loan payment and origination fees are calculated, and the results display in the *lblPaymentResult* and *lblFeeResult* labels, respectively. The pseudocode for this functionality is shown in Table 3.9.

Table 3.9: *Pseudocode for modified Loan Calculator application*

Event Procedure	Action
btnCalculate_Click	1. Calculate the loan payment. 2. Calculate the up-front fees. 3. Display the results in the appropriate labels.
btnExit_Click	1. Display a message box verifying the intent to end the application. 2. Terminate the application.

Figure 3.27 displays a flowchart modeling the procedure for calculating the payment and displaying the results.

Now that you have the planning documents for the application, you are ready to begin designing the user interface in the integrated development environment (IDE).

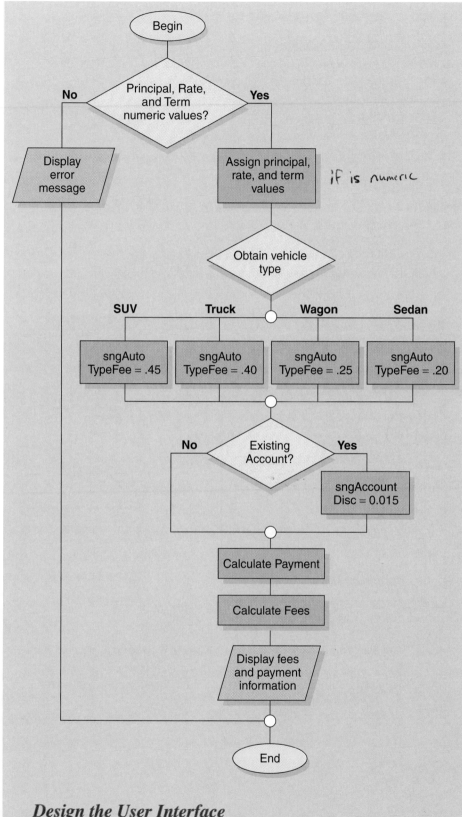

FIGURE 3.27. *Flowchart for calculating payment procedure*

Design the User Interface

Create a copy of the *Modified Loan Calculator* solution that is included with your data files. If you have not started Visual Studio.NET, do so now, and set the Profile to Visual Studio Developer.

To open an existing solution:

1. Click **File**, **Open Solution**.
2. Navigate to the *Modified Loan Calculator* folder you copied previously.
3. Open the folder and double-click the *Modified Loan Calculator.sln* file to open the solution.
4. Right-click the *Form1.vb* form in the Solution Explorer and choose **View Designer**.

You are now ready to modify the user interface by adding the controls listed in Table 3.8.

To add a group box, radio buttons, and a check box control to the form:

1. Click the Toolbox button to display the Toolbox.
2. Click the GroupBox tool and drag a group box control onto the form in the position shown in Figure 3.28.

FIGURE 3.28. *Adding a group box control to the form*

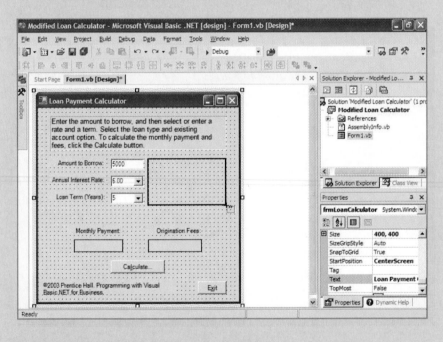

3. Change the **Name** property of the group box to `grpAutoType`, the Text property to `Vehicle Type`, and the TabIndex property to `0`.
4. Click the RadioButton tool in the Toolbox and drag a radio button onto the form, as shown in Figure 3.29.

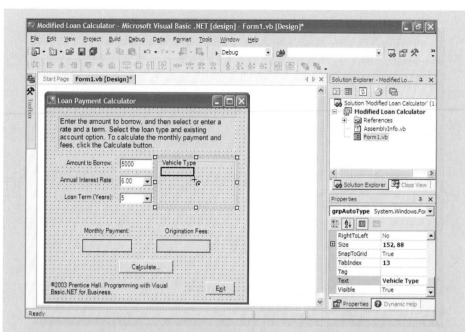

FIGURE 3.29. *Adding a radio button control to the form*

5. Use the same method to create three additional radio button controls in the group box. You should now have four radio button controls in the group box.

6. Change the Name and Text properties of each radio button control, per the specifications in Table 3.8. Change the checked property of the *rdbSUV* control to **True**. Resize and reposition the controls as necessary.

7. Click the CheckBox tool in the Toolbox and drag a check box control onto the form, as shown in Figure 3.30.

When adding radio button controls to a group box, create the group box first and then create the controls in the group box. This way, only one control can be selected at run time.

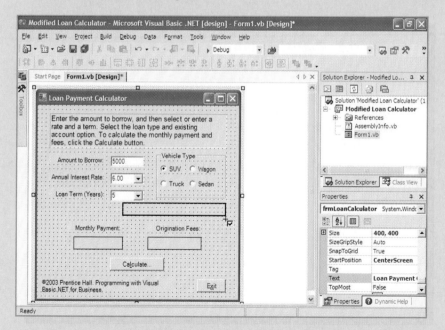

FIGURE 3.30. *Adding a check box control to the form*

8. Set the properties for this control as specified in Table 3.8. Resize the control as necessary.

9. Save your changes.

You are now ready to write the code for the *Modified Loan Calculator* application.

Write the Code

First you will add internal documentation to the application. You will then declare a module-level variable to store the index value for the selected radio button. Finally, you will write the statements that also handle the click events for the buttons on the form.

To add internal documentation to the application:

1. Press [F7] to display the Code Editor. The insertion point appears before the Public Class statement.
2. Enter the following copyright information at the top of the Code window:

```
'©2003 Prentice Hall
'By [Enter your name]
'Created/Revised: [Enter the date]
'Modified Loan Payment Calculator
```

To declare a module-level variable:

Tip

Do you remember how to enter the copyright symbol (©) in the Code Editor? Hold down the [Alt] key and press 0169 on the numeric keypad.

1. Place the insertion point in the space below the **Inherits System.Windows.Forms.Form** statement and press [↵Enter].
2. Type `'Declare the index variable for the vehicle type selection` as a comment and press [↵Enter].
3. Type `Dim mintIndex As Integer` to declare the variable, and press [↵Enter].

Now that you have declared the module-level variable required by the application, you are ready to write the code for the decision statement modeled in Figure 3.27.

To define a click event for each radio button:

1. Double-click the *rdbSUV* radio button.
2. Add the following statement for the button's **CheckChanged** event:

```
mintIndex = 0
```

3. Use the same procedure to add the following statements to the **CheckChanged** event for the remaining radio buttons:

   rdbTruck

```
mintIndex=1
```

rdbWagon
mintIndex=2
rdbSedan
mintIndex=3

You are now ready to write the code for the *btnCalculate* click procedure.

To write the procedure for the *btnCalculate* click event:

1. Double-click the *btnCalculate* button in the Form Designer to add code for the click event procedure.
2. Type the following statements to declare the variables used by the procedure:

```
'Declare variables
    Dim sngPrincipal As Single
    Dim sngRate As Single
    Dim intTerm As Integer
    Dim decMonthlyPayment As Decimal
    Dim decLoanFees As Decimal
    Dim sngAccountDisc As Single
    Dim sngAutoTypeFee As Single
```

3. Enter the following decision structure to perform data validation, assign text data to the variables, calculate the monthly payment and origination fees, and display the results:

```
'Perform data validation
    If IsNumeric(txtPrincipal.Text) = False Or
      IsNumeric(cboRate.Text) = False Or
      IsNumeric(cboTerm.Text) = False Then
        MsgBox("The loan principal, annual interest rate, and
          term must all be numeric values. Please check these
          values and try again.", MsgBoxStyle.Critical,
          "Invalid Data")
    Else
        'Assign values to the sngPrincipal, sngRate and intTerm
          variables
        sngPrincipal = Val(txtPrincipal.Text)
        sngRate = Val(cboRate.Text) / 100
        sngRate = sngRate / 12
        intTerm = Val(cboTerm.Text) * 12
        'Determine Automobile Type and assign appropriate
          points
        Select Case mintIndex
            Case Is = 0
                sngAutoTypeFee = 0.045
```

```
        Case Is = 1
            sngAutoTypeFee = 0.04
        Case Is = 2
            sngAutoTypeFee = 0.025
        Case Is = 3
            sngAutoTypeFee = 0.02
    End Select

    'Determine if the Multiple account discount applies
    If chkMultipleAccounts.Checked = True Then
        sngAccountDisc = 0.015
    End If
    'Calculate the monthly payment
    decMonthlyPayment = sngPrincipal * (sngRate / (1 - (1 +
        sngRate) ^ -intTerm))
    'Calculate the origination fees
    decLoanFees = (sngPrincipal * sngAutoTypeFee) -
        (sngPrincipal * sngAccountDisc)

    'Display the monthly payment and fees
    lblPaymentResult.Text = Format(decMonthlyPayment,
        "Currency")
    lblFeeResult.Text = Format(decLoanFees, "Currency")
End If
```

4.   Click **Save All** to save the solution.

You are now ready to add code to handle the *btnExit* click event.

To use an If Statement to code the Exit button's event procedure:

1.   Double-click the *btnExit* button in the Form Designer.
2.   Type the following statements for the procedure:

```
Dim intResponse As Integer
intResponse = MsgBox("Do you really want to exit this
    application?", 276, "Exit?")
If intResponse = 6 Then
    End
End If
```

3.   Click **Save All** to update the solution.

Run the Application

You are now ready to run the application to test its functionality.

To run the application:

1.   Press F5 to run the application.
2.   Enter 15000 as the loan principal.

3. Press the ⌨Tab⇄ key once and select **4.25** as the annual interest rate.

4. Press the ⌨Tab⇄ key once and select **3** as the loan term.

5. Select the radio button for the Truck vehicle type.

6. Check the box for existing accounts.

7. Click the **Calculate** button. Figure 3.31 displays a monthly payment of $444.53 and origination fees of $375.00.

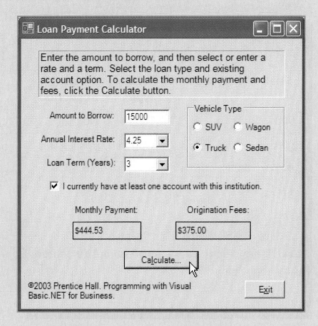

FIGURE 3.31. *Testing the Loan Payment Calculator application's Calculate button*

8. Click **Exit**. Figure 3.32 shows the message box that appears.

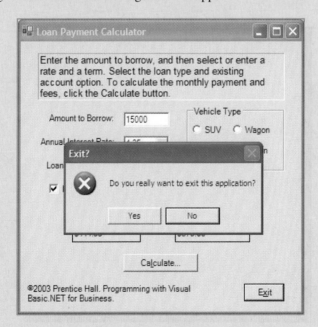

FIGURE 3.32. *Testing the Loan Payment Calculator application's Exit button*

9. Click **No** to return to the application.

10. Type abc as the loan principal and click the Calculate button. Figure 3.33 shows the data validation message that appears.

FIGURE 3.33. *Testing the Loan Payment Calculator application's data validation*

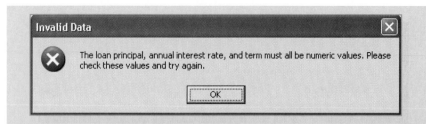

11. Using the results shown here as a guide, calculate additional loan scenarios and check the results you obtain.

Principal	Rate	Term	Vehicle Type	Existing Accounts?	Monthly Payment	Origination Fees
$24,000	6%	5	Sedan	No	$463.99	$480.00
$38,000	5.5%	4	Wagon	Yes	$883.75	$380.00
$42,000	3.25%	5	SUV	No	$759.36	$1,890.00

You have completed the Loan Payment Calculator application. You may exit Visual Studio.NET now, or if you want to complete additional projects, close the Loan Calculator application.

Summary

Visual Basic.NET code statements are organized as one of three programming structures: sequence structures, decision structures, and repetition structures.

● The If…Then, If…Else…ElseIf, and Select…Case statements are examples of decision structures.

● You can use If statements to test for a single condition or multiple conditions. The results of the comparison determine which actions are taken by the program.

● Relational operators are used to compare data. The most common relational operators are Equals (=), Less Than (<), Greater Than (>), Not Equal (<>), Greater Than or Equal To (>=), and Less Than or Equal To (<=).

● Flowcharting is a useful method for representing decision statements visually. Flowcharts are often included in the design documents for applications.

● When you add an If statement within another If statement, you are creating a nested If statement. You can use nested If statements to test for multiple conditions.

● The MsgBox function is used to display messages on the screen. A message box includes a message (called a prompt), an optional style (including buttons and icons), and an optional title that appears as the caption of the message box.

● When you use text box and combo box controls to obtain user input, it is important to check the values that are used in calculations. You can use If statements to perform data validation.

● You can use relational operators to compare text strings. Letters, numbers, and characters all have an associated ASCII value that Visual Basic.NET uses for comparing strings for operations such as sorting.

● The UCase and LCase functions convert text into all lowercase (LCase) or all uppercase (UCase) values.

● You can use logical operators (And, Or, Not) to create compound conditions that test for multiple conditions in one statement.

● When you need to compare a single value or expression against numerous conditions, the Select…Case statement is a better choice than nested If statements.

Key Terms

ASCII (American Standard Code for Information Interchange)

Boolean value

case

case block

check box

checked property

compound condition

condition

data validation

decision statement

decision structure

enumeration

flowchart

flowcharting

flowlines

group box

If…ElseIf…Else statement

If…Then statement

If…Then…Else statement

IsNumeric function

LCase function

logical operator

logical test

message box

MsgBox function

nested If statements

programming structure

radio button

relational operator

Select…Case statement

sequence structure

text literals

UCase function

Study Questions

Multiple-Choice Questions

1. Which property for a radio button control determines which control has been selected?
   - a. Name
   - b. TabIndex
   - c. TabStop
   - d. Checked
   - e. Text

2. Which structure is best for performing a simple logical test?
   - a. If...Then
   - b. Select...Case
   - c. If...Then...Else
   - d. The sequence structure
   - e. If...ElseIf...Else

3. How many distinct values can a Boolean variable assume?
   - a. One
   - b. Two
   - c. Three
   - d. Four
   - e. Eight

4. Which of the following ASCII characters has the lowest value?
   - a. Z
   - b. 0
   - c. &
   - d. 1
   - e. a

5. Which of the following controls is included within a group box control so that only one option can be selected?
   - a. Button
   - b. Check box
   - c. Text box
   - d. Label
   - e. Radio button

6. Which of the following parameters is required by the MsgBox function?
   - a. Title
   - b. Button
   - c. Prompt
   - d. A and B
   - e. A and C

7. A nested If statement will always conclude with which statement?
   - a. If
   - b. Else
   - c. ElseIf
   - d. End
   - e. End If

8. Which of the following statements is best for testing a single value against multiple conditions?
   - a. If...Then...Else
   - b. If...ElseIf...Else
   - c. Select...Case
   - d. Val
   - e. IsNumeric

9. Which flowcharting symbol models a decision?
   - a. Rectangle
   - b. Circle
   - c. Parallelogram
   - d. Oval
   - e. Diamond

10. If the Val function is used in conjunction with a text box for validating a numeric value converted to a numeric variable and an empty text string is entered, what is the result of the conversion?
    - a. A
    - b. The space character
    - c. 1
    - d. 0
    - e. -1

True/False Questions

1. An If statement requires the Then keyword.

2. The Select...Case structure can test for multiple decision paths.

3. You can nest If statements to conduct a series of logical tests.

4. Flowcharting is of little value for modeling decision statements.

5. When multiple check box controls are added to a group box control, only one control in the group can be checked.

Short Answer Questions

1. How can you use an If statement to perform data validation?

2. How do radio buttons differ from check boxes? When might you use one rather than the other?

3. How does flowcharting assist in modeling decision structures?

4. What is a message box? List a common use for a message box.

5. What is a group box, and how is one used in conjunction with a selection structure?

Guided Exercises

Adding a Decision Statement to a Mileage Reimbursement Form

If you completed the Guided Exercises for Chapter 1, you created a Mileage Conversion application for converting miles to kilometers, and vice versa. Although this application generates the intended results, you can improve its design by implementing a decision structure. By adding a group box with two radio buttons specifying the kind of conversion to perform, you can redesign the form so that it contains only one button for performing the calculation. When you finish this exercise, the Mileage Reimbursement Form will appear as shown in Figure 3.34.

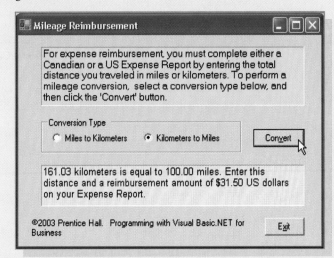

FIGURE 3.34. *Mileage reimbursement form*

Follow these steps to revise the application.

1. Open the *Mileage Reimbursement* solution in the *Mileage Reimbursement* folder on your student data disk.

2. Create the following controls and set the properties as listed. Use Figure 3.34 as a guide for placing the controls on the form.

Object	Property	Setting
grpConvType	Text	Conversion Type
rdbMtoK	Text	Miles to Kilometers
	TabStop, TabIndex	True, 0
	Checked	True (this is the default)
rdbKtoM	Text	Kilometers to Miles
	TabStop, TabIndex	True, 1
btnConvert	Text	Con&vert
	TabStop, TabIndex	True, 2
btnExit	Text	E&xit
	TabStop, TabIndex	True, 3

3. Type the following code for the procedure that handles the *Convert* button's click event:

```
'Obtain the distance traveled
    sngDistance = Val(InputBox("Enter the distance you
      traveled…"))

    'Perform data validation and the appropriate conversion
    If sngDistance <= 0 Then
        MsgBox("The distance you entered is invalid; please try
          again.", MsgBoxStyle.Critical, "Invalid Distance")
    ElseIf rdbMtoK.Checked = True Then
        sngResult = sngDistance * 1.609
        decReimbursement = sngResult * CanadaRate
        lblResult.Text = sngDistance & " miles is equal to " &
            Format(sngResult, "fixed") & " kilometers. Enter this
            distance and a reimbursement amount of " &
            Format(decReimbursement, "Currency") & " dollars
            Canadian on your Expense Report."
    Else
        sngResult = sngDistance * 0.621
        decReimbursement = sngResult * USRate
        lblResult.Text = sngDistance & " kilometers is equal to
            " & Format(sngResult, "fixed") & " miles. Enter this
            distance and a reimbursement amount of " &
            Format(decReimbursement, "Currency") & " US dollars
            on your Expense Report."
    End If
```

4. Add statements to the click event procedure for the *btnExit* control.

5. Save the solution.

6. Run the application and verify its functionality. Revise the application if necessary.

7. Close the solution.

Creating an Application to Calculate Shipping Costs

Mail order companies and Web-based businesses usually provide customers with a variety of shipping options. Depending on how quickly customers need their merchandise, most companies can ship priority next day—for a fee. In this exercise you will create an application that uses a Select…Case statement to determine which shipping option is selected and report the total amount for the sale and shipping. The shipping rates are as follows:

Standard Ground	$2.25 + 1% of the sale amount
Second Day	$5.95 + 2% of the sale amount
Next Day	$9.95 + 3% of the sale amount
Priority	$14.95 + 5% of the sale amount

The application uses the following inputs to generate these outputs:

Inputs	Outputs
Amount of sale	Shipping cost
Shipping option	Order total

Figure 3.35 shows the interface for the application.

FIGURE 3.35. *Interface for Shipping Fees application*

Follow these steps to create the application.

1. Create a new project named `Shipping Fees`.

2. Add the following controls to the form and set the properties as listed. Use Figure 3.35 as a guide for placing the controls on the form.

Object	Property	Setting
Form1	Text	Shipping Fees
	Size	300, 300
	StartPosition	CenterScreen
txtSaleAmount	Text	
	TabStop	Yes
	TabIndex	0
lblSaleAmount	Text	Sale Amount:
	TextAlign	MiddleRight
grpMethod	Text	Shipping Method
rdbGround	Text	Ground
	Checked	True
	TabStop; TabIndex	True, 1
rdb2ndDay	Text	2nd Day Air
	TabStop; TabIndex	True, 2
	Checked	True
rdbNextDay	Text	Next Day Air
	TabStop; TabIndex	True, 3
rdbPriority	Text	Priority Air
	TabStop; TabIndex	True, 4

Object	Property	Setting
lblResult	Text	
	BorderStyle	FixedSingle
	TextAlign	MiddleCenter
btnCalculate	Text	C&alculate
	TabStop, TabIndex	True, 5
btnExit	Name	E&xit
	TabStop, TabIndex	True, 6
lblCopyright	Text	©2003 Prentice Hall. Programming with Visual Basic.NET for Business.

3. Declare the following module-level variable:

```
Dim mintIndex As Integer
```

4. Type the following code for the procedure that handles the *Calculate* button's click event:

```
Dim decSaleAmount, decShippingFee, decTotalAmount As Decimal

    decSaleAmount = Val(txtSaleAmount.Text)

    If decSaleAmount <= False Then
        MsgBox("The sale amount you entered is invalid; please
            try again.", MsgBoxStyle.Critical, "Invalid Amount")

    Else
        Select Case mintIndex
            Case Is = 0
                decShippingFee = 2.25 + (decSaleAmount * 0.01)
            Case Is = 1
                decShippingFee = 5.95 + (decSaleAmount * 0.02)
            Case Is = 2
                decShippingFee = 9.95 + (decSaleAmount * 0.03)
            Case Is = 3
                decShippingFee = 14.95 + (decSaleAmount *
                    0.05)
        End Select
        decTotalAmount = decSaleAmount + decShippingFee
        lblResult.Text = "Sale Amount: " &
            Format(decSaleAmount, "Currency") & vbCrLf & _
            "Shipping Fee: " & Format(decShippingFee, "Currency")
            & vbCrLf & _ "Order Total: " & Format(decTotalAmount,
            "Currency")
    End If
```

5. Add the following statement to the **CheckChanged** event for the radio buttons:
rdbGround

```
mintIndex = 0
```

rdb2ndDay

```
mintIndex = 1
```

rdbNextDay

```
mintIndex = 2
```

rdbPriority

```
mintIndex = 3
```

6. Add statements to the click event procedure for the *btnExit* control.

7. Save the solution.

8. Run the application and verify its functionality. Revise the application if necessary.

9. Close the solution.

Case Studies

Modifying the Payroll Application

In this exercise, you will modify the Payroll application you created in Chapter 2. Create a copy of the entire folder containing this solution, and open the *Payroll Calculator* solution in Visual Studio.NET. Modify the application as follows:

1. Add a check box to the form, indicating that the pay is tax exempt. If this button is checked, no taxes are calculated or deducted.

2. Add data validation for all entries.

3. Add an If statement to the *Exit* button.

Save your changes, and test the application. When you finish, close the solution.

Adding Decision Statements to a Temperature Conversion Application

In Chapter 1 you learned how to create an application that converts temperatures between the Celsius and Fahrenheit scales. Now create a Windows application named `Temperature Converter` for performing temperature conversions. The formulas for calculating the conversion are as follows:

Celsius to Fahrenheit: (9/5) C + 32

Fahrenheit to Celsius: 5/9 (F – 32)

1. Add a text box for entering the temperature to convert, and validate this entry as numeric data.

2. Add a group box and two radio button controls so users can specify what kind of conversion to perform. Set the default as the Fahrenheit-to-Celsius conversion.

3. Add two buttons to the form: one for performing the calculation and one for exiting the application. Use an If statement to verify the user's intent to exit.

4. Display the result of the conversion in a message box, formatted to two decimal places.

Save your changes, and test the application. When you finish, close the solution.

Using Looping Structures and Lists

Repetition is a part of life. Think of the tasks you perform on a daily basis that require repetitive processes. You repeat the same processes to complete school-related tasks such as going to class, studying, completing assignments, and taking tests or work-related tasks such as calling a list of customers, updating database records, or managing a project. To get through these repetitive processes more quickly, people establish routines that allow us to efficiently complete simple and complex tasks.

In a similar way, computers quickly and accurately process repetitive tasks with programmed routines. In this chapter you will learn how to write program statements with Visual Basic.NET to perform repetitive tasks in your applications.

Performance Objectives

At the conclusion of this chapter, you will be able to:

■ Explain how repetition structures and looping structures process tasks in applications.

■ Use the For…Next, Do…Loop, and For…Each…Next statements.

■ Create and manage lists by using the ListBox control.

■ Create lists by using looping structures.

■ Populate a list box at run time by using looping structures.

Introducing Repetition Structures

As you learned in Chapter 3, decision structures and repetition structures are fundamental to complex programs. If a business application requires a program to analyze conditions, programmers use decision structures. To complete an operation a specific number of times while a certain condition is true or until a condition is true, programmers use repetition structures. A *repetition structure* repeats the execution of a series of program statements. The repetition structures supported by Visual Basic include:

■ For…Next

■ For Each…Next

■ Do…Loop

■ While

To see how repetition structures work, let's look at how to use the For…Next statement, which is one of the easiest repetition structures to understand.

Although Visual Basic.NET continues to support the While statement for loops, most programmers prefer using the Do…Loop statement.

Using For…Next Statements

The *For…Next statement* repeats a statement or procedure a specific number of times. The process of repeating a procedure until a condition is met is called *looping*. The procedure or set of statements that is repeated is called a *loop*. As the computer processes the statements, one execution of the loop is an *iteration*. When you use looping, the statements repeat until the condition is true, until the condition is false, or a specified number of times. The syntax of a For…Next statement is as follows:

```
For Counter = Start Value To End Value [Step Step Value]
    Loop statement(s)
Next [ Counter ]
```

The For…Next statement requires a *counter variable*, specified by *Counter*, which is a variable used to count the number of times the loop repeats. The *Counter* increases or decreases in value during each repetition of the loop. An *increment* is an increase in the counter; a *decrement* is a decrease in the counter. *Start Value* is the initial value of the counter. The counter begins incrementing at this value. *End Value* is the final value of the counter. When the counter reaches this value, the loop ends. ***Step Value*** is the amount by which the counter is incremented each cycle of the loop.

Let's look at two simple examples. The following table shows two examples of a For…Next loop: one for incrementing and one for decrementing.

Increase (increment)	**Decrease (decrement)**
```Dim intCounter As Integer```	```Dim intCounter As Integer```
```For intCounter = 1 To 5```	```For intCounter = 5 To 1```
```Step 1```	```Step -1```
```Next```	```Next```
Start Value = 1	Start Value = 5
End Value = 5	End Value = 1
Step Value = 1	Step Value = -1
Loop Results= 1,2,3,4,5	Loop Results = 5,4,3,2,1

The counter variable is usually declared as an integer data type, because it must be a numeric data type that supports the greater than ($>$), less than ($<$), and addition ($+$) operators. When using a For…Next statement, the iteration values for Start Value, End Value, and Step Value are expressions that must evaluate to the same data type as the counter. The step value, which is optional, can be positive or negative. If it is omitted, Visual Basic.NET supplies a default value of 1.

You can use flowcharts to model the iterations of a For…Next loop. Figure 4.1 models the statement for a simple loop.

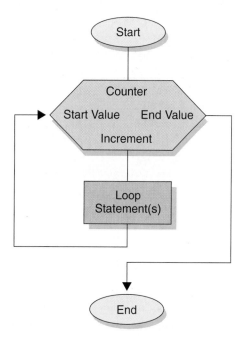

FIGURE 4.1. *Flowchart modeling a simple loop statement*

The flowchart uses the preparation symbol (hexagon) to model a For…Next loop. The flowchart symbol includes the counter, the start value, the end value, and the increment value.

Now let's look at a number of examples of loops. Your data files include a solution named *For Next*. This application is an example of a computer program that does not solve a business problem but rather contains controls that demonstrate programming principles. The form contains buttons with event procedures that run a number of loops and display the results onscreen. The interface is shown in Figure 4.2.

FIGURE 4.2. *Interface of the*
For...Next application

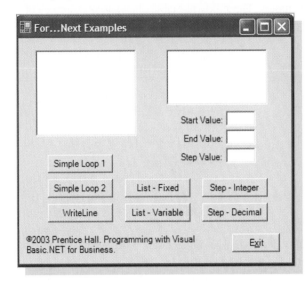

Here's an example that displays the results of a loop as a message. The following statements will execute a loop that declares a counter variable and displays the value of the counter in a message box each iteration of the loop. In this example, the loop performs three iterations.

```
Dim intCounter as Integer = 1
For intCounter = 1 to 3
MsgBox(intCounter)
Next
```

This procedure declares the *intCounter* variable and assigns 1 as its value. During each iteration, the value of *intCounter* is displayed. After three iterations, the loop ends. Figure 4.3 shows the message that appears during the second iteration of the loop.

FIGURE 4.3. *Message during loop's*
second iteration

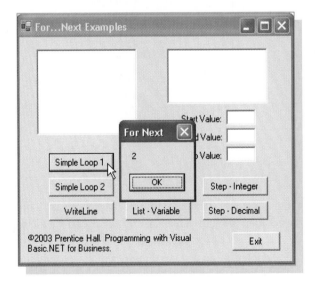

You can also use loops to obtain user input and display the results onscreen. In the next example, an event procedure displays an input box on the screen, requesting a text string. When text is entered, a message box displays the entry. This is repeated three times. Here's the code:

To see how this works, open the *For_Next* solution included with your data files and click the *Simple Loop1* button.

```
Dim intCounter As Integer
Dim strEntry As String


For intCounter = 1 To 3
    strEntry = InputBox("Please enter a text string.")
    MsgBox("You entered: " & strEntry, MsgBoxStyle.Information,
       "Entry")
Next
```

The procedure declares two variables: *intCounter* for the counter variable and *strEntry* for the text entered in the Input box. The *startvalue* is 1, and the *endvalue* is 3. Because a *stepvalue* is not included, the default step of 1 will be used. The procedure displays an Input box and assigns the entry to the *strEntry* variable. A message box appears and displays the current value on the *strEntry* variable. This is repeated three times.

DISPLAYING THE RESULTS OF A REPETITION STATEMENT

In the first example, a message box displays the value of the *intCounter* variable during each iteration of the loop. Although this demonstrates how the If…Then statement works, using this method to display results is impractical for loops that execute more than just a few iterations. Let's look at two additional ways to display the results of a loop.

One option you can use to display the output a repetition structure generates is to use the Visual Studio.NET Debug method. The debugging tools are available at run time when you are developing your applications. For example, you can use the **Debug.WriteLine statement** in your loop to test the results of the loop before finalizing your code. This statement displays the output of the loop in the Output window that appears on the screen when you run an application from the Visual Studio.NET integrated development environment (IDE). The statement requires one argument: the value or text string to write to the Output window.

Let's modify the statements shown earlier by substituting a **Debug.WriteLine** statement for the statement that displays the results in a message box. This substitution will display results in the Output window. Here are the code statements that handle the click event for the *Simple Loop 2* button:

```
Dim intCounter as Integer = 1
For intCounter = 1 to 3
Debug.Writeline(intCounter)
Next
```

Figure 4.4 shows the value of the *intCounter* variable shown in the Output window after each iteration.

FIGURE 4.4. *Output window showing value of the intCounter variable after each iteration*

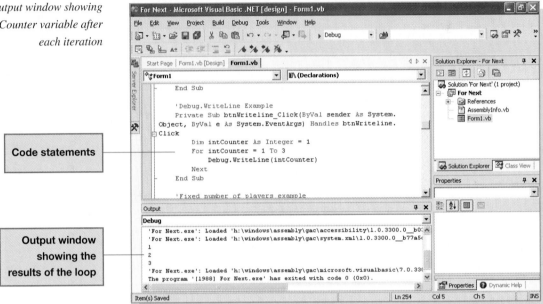

Here is another method for displaying the results of a loop. Assume you are creating a game application and want to capture the names of four players. You can still use an Input box to obtain the names, but displaying the names one at a time in a message box in a gaming application is impractical. It is more practical to list the names in a control such as a text box so the names are always visible at run time. Here's the code that handles the *List – Fixed* button's click event:

```
Dim intCounter As Integer
Dim strName As String


For intCounter = 1 To 4
    strName = strName & InputBox("Please enter a player…") &
        vbCrLf
    txtList1.Text = strName
Next
```

The procedure declares two variables: the counter variable and a variable that holds the name to be entered in the Input box during each iteration of the loop. There are two loop statements. The first statement assigns to the *strName* variable the current name appended to the name supplied during each iteration. By also concatenating a return character (vbCrLf), each name appears on a new line in the text box. The second statement in the loop displays the current value of the *strName* variable in the Text property of the *txtList1* Text box. Figure 4.5 displays the result of clicking the *List - Fixed* button and entering names. The figure shows the names that have been entered after completing the second iteration of the loop.

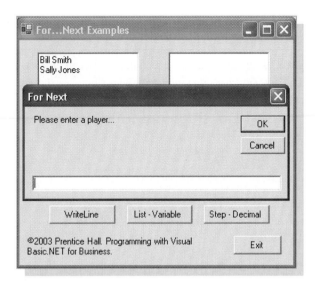

FIGURE 4.5. *Result of clicking List-Fixed button*

Now let's consider another example. The number of players participating in a game will vary. You can modify the previous procedure by obtaining the number of players and setting this value to the *endvalue* of the loop. Consider this procedure that handles the click event for the *List – Variable* button:

```
Dim intCounter, intEndValue As Integer
Dim strName As String

intEndValue = Val(InputBox("How many players?"))

If intEndValue <= 0 Then
    MsgBox("The number of players must be an integer. Please try
        again.",
    MsgBoxStyle.Critical, "Invalid Number of Players")
    Else
        For intCounter = 1 To intEndValue
            strName = strName & InputBox("Please enter a
                player…") & vbCrLf
            txtList1.Text = strName
        Next
End If
```

This procedure declares two integer variables: the first as a counter and the second to store the *endvalue*. After assigning the data obtained from an Input box to the *intEndValue* variable, the procedure uses an If statement to perform data validation. If the value entered into the Input box is less than or equal to zero, a message box appears. Remember that an empty string (" ") or a non-numeric character will return a value of zero. For positive values, the procedure executes the loop, using the *intEndValue* variable to determine the number of iterations.

Each of these examples omits the optional step value. Let's see how you can use a step value to change how the loop increments.

INCREMENTING AND DECREMENTING THE COUNTER VARIABLE

At times the step value specified in a For…Next loop will be a value other than 1. Using the *Step keyword*, you can increment (increase the value) or decrement (decrease the value) the counter by the value you specify. In the example shown earlier, the increment values were 1 and -1, respectively. Now consider the following procedure:

```
Dim intCounter, intStart, intEnd, intStep As Integer
Dim strText As String

intStart = Val(txtStart.Text)
intEnd = Val(txtEnd.Text)
intStep = Val(txtStep.Text)

For intCounter = intStart To intEnd Step intStep
    strText = strText & intCounter & vbCrLf
    txtList2.Text = strText
Next
```

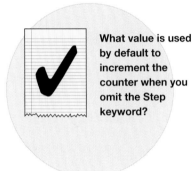

What value is used by default to increment the counter when you omit the Step keyword?

This procedure, which handles the click event for the *Step – Integer* button, obtains the start value, end value, and step value for the loop structure from three text boxes on the form. These values are used to set the starting value, the ending value, and the step value.

The code is similar to the examples you have already seen. The main difference is that this procedure uses the Step keyword to specify the value by which to increment the counter.

Figure 4.6 displays the result of the loop when the start value is 2, the end value is 10, and the step value is 2. In this case, the loop will make five iterations.

FIGURE 4.6. *Result of a loop making five iterations*

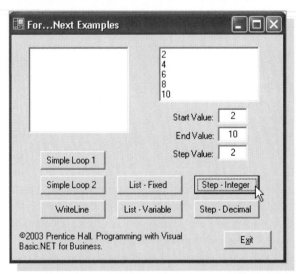

What if you need to create a list of decimal rather than integer values? You can use a decimal for the step value, but the step and counter values must use a data type that can accept decimal values. Consider the following statements from the *Step-Decimal* button:

```
Dim intStart, intEnd As Integer
Dim sngCounter, sngStep As Single
Dim strText As String

intStart = Val(txtStart.Text)
```

```
intEnd = Val(txtEnd.Text)
sngStep = Val(txtStep.Text)
For sngCounter = intStart To intEnd Step sngStep
    strText = strText & sngCounter & vbCrLf
    txtList2.Text = strText
Next
```

The *sngCounter* and *sngStep* variables are declared as Single, which accepts decimal values. Figure 4.7 displays the result of the loop for a start value of 1, an end value of 3, and a step value of 0.5. Because the step value is 0.5, the loop will make five iterations.

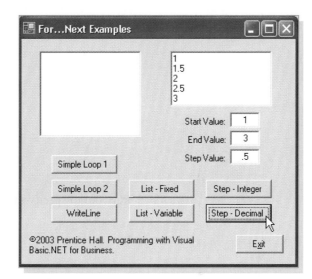

FIGURE 4.7. *Result of a loop making five iterations*

ENDLESS LOOPS

As you create For…Next loops, it is important to consider under what conditions a loop will never reach the end value. For example, you could inadvertently add a statement that resets the counter, as in the following code statements from the previous example, where the statement appearing in bold has been added.

```
Dim strName as String, intCounter as Integer
For intCounter = 1 To 4
    strName = strName & InputBox("Please enter a player…") &
        vbCrLf
intCounter = 1
    txtList1.Text = strName
Next
```

This loop will never reach the end value, and therefore the loop will never end. Avoid introducing an **endless loop** (also called an infinite loop) into your programs; this is considered a poor programming practice.

As you can see, For…Next loops are useful for generating lists of values when you know the starting, ending, and step values. One practical application of the For…Next statement is to populate controls such as combo boxes with a set of values.

Now let's learn about another statement you can use to create loops.

An endless loop is also called an infinite loop. To exit an endless loop, press the Ctrl and Break keys simultaneously.

Later in this chapter you will learn how to use a loop to populate combo box and list box controls with values.

Using Do...Loop Statements

For...Next loops are a good choice when you know the ending value for a loop and therefore how many iterations the loop will require. Sometimes, however, you do not know in advance when a loop will end because the loop will continue until a certain condition is met. Do...Loops are a good choice when you do not know in advance how many times you need to execute the statements in the loop. You can use a ***Do...Loop statement*** to create a loop that executes a block of statements *while a condition is true* or *until a condition is satisfied*. The Do...Loop statements execute a series of statements an indefinite number of times, depending on the Boolean value of the condition. The Do...Loop differs from the For...Next structure in that the Do...Loop statements can be repeated either while the condition is True or until it becomes True. In either case, you do not define an end value for the loop.

The general syntax for the Do...Loop is:

```
Do [While | Until ] condition
    [ statements ]
Loop
Or
Do
    [ statements ]
Do [While | Until ] condition
```

In this statement, the pipe character (|) indicates that you can use either the **While** or the **Until** keyword in your code.

REPEATING STATEMENTS IN A DO...LOOP WHILE A CONDITION IS TRUE

You can use the ***While keyword*** in a Do...Loop to repeat the iterations of the loop while the condition is true. There are two ways to use the While keyword to check the condition: by specifying the condition before entering the loop or by checking for the condition after the loop runs. Because the loop performs a test to check for the condition, specifying the condition before entering the loop uses a ***PreTest*** to test for the condition, and testing the condition after entering the loop uses a ***PostTest*** to check the condition. In either case, looping continues *while* the condition remains True. The syntax for each option is as follows:

```
Do While (condition)
    Statements in loop
Loop
Or
Do
    Statements in loop
Loop While (condition)
```

Figure 4.8 shows a flowchart modeling these two methods for using the While statement in a Do...Loop and provides a coding example of each method.

Tip

To run these procedures, open the *Do Loop* solution contained in your data files, run the application, and click the *Do While PreTest* and *Do While PostTest* buttons.

Testing a Condition at the Beginning of a Loop

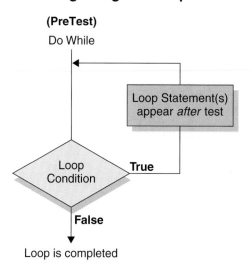

Testing a Condition at the End of a Loop

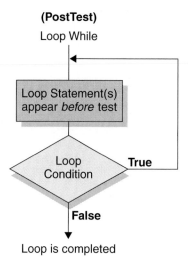

FIGURE 4.8. *Flowchart for using the While statement in a Do...Loop*

Syntax

```
Do While (condition)
    Statement(s) in loop
Loop
```

Example

```
Dim intCounter as Integer=1
Do While intCounter <=10
    Debug.Writeline(intCounter)
    intCounter = intCounter +1
Loop
```

Syntax

```
Do
    Statement(s) in loop
Loop While (condition)
```

Example

```
Dim intCounter as Integer=1
Do
    Debug.Writeline(intCounter)
    intCounter = intCounter +1
Loop While intCounter <=10
```

REPEATING STATEMENTS IN A DO...LOOP UNTIL A CONDITION IS TRUE

You can use the ***Until keyword*** in a Do...Loop to repeat the iterations of the loop *until* the specified condition evaluates to True. The structure is nearly identical to using the While keyword, and you can check the condition before you enter the loop by using a PreTest or after the loop has run at least once by using a PostTest. In either case, looping continues *until* the condition evaluates to True, which is the same as saying that the loop continues while the condition is false. The syntax for each option is shown here:

```
Do Until (condition)
    Statements in loop
Loop
Or
Do
    Statements in loop
Loop Until (condition)
```

Figure 4.9 shows a flowchart modeling these two methods for using the Until statement in a Do...Loop and provides a coding example of each method.

Figure 4.9. *Flowchart for using the Until statement in a Do...Loop*

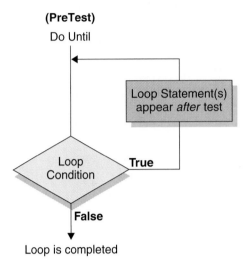

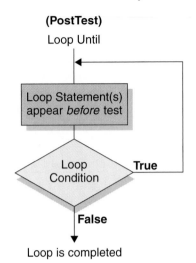

Testing a Condition at the Beginning of a Loop

(PreTest)
Do Until

Testing a Condition at the End of a Loop

(PostTest)
Loop Until

Syntax

```
Do Until (condition)
    Statement(s) in loop
Loop
```

Syntax

```
Do
    Statement(s) in loop
Loop Until (condition)
```

Example

```
Dim intCounter as Integer=1
Do until intCounter >10
    Debug.Writeline (intCounter)
    intCounter + =1
Loop
```

Example

```
Dim intCounter as Integer=1
Do
    Debug.Writeline (intCounter)
    intCounter + =1
Loop Until intCounter >10
```

In the coding example, notice the following statement for incrementing the counter variable:

```
intCounter += 1
```

The statement tells Visual Basic.NET to increment the variable by a positive value of 1 (using the + character). This statement is equivalent to:

```
intCounter = intCounter +1
```

You can use either method to increment a counter variable. You can also use this method to increment the value of one variable by the value of another variable, as in the following example, which keeps a running total of individual expense amounts:

```
decTotal += decExpense
```

EXITING A DO...LOOP BEFORE A CONDITION IS TRUE

When you use repetition structures, it is considered good coding practice to provide a single entry and exit point for the code statements. At times, however, you might need to exit a loop before a condition is met. For example, if your loop requires data input, you might need to exit the loop if a user enters data that does not meet a data validation requirement. Visual Basic.NET supports the ***Exit Loop statement*** for this purpose.

Assume you are creating a simple application that will allow you to enter up to 50 individual expense items to obtain a total for the expense report you submit each month. The statements that accomplish this are shown here:

```
Dim intCounter As Integer, decExpense As Decimal, decTotal As
   Decimal
While intCounter <= 50
    decExpense = Val(InputBox("Please enter an expense amount,
      or ENTER to quit…"))
    If IsNumeric(decExpense) = True And decExpense > 0 Then
        decTotal += decExpense
        intCounter += 1
        txtList.Text = "Expense Subtotal: " & Format(decTotal,
          "Currency")
    Else
        txtList.Text = "Total Expenses: " & Format(decTotal,
          "Currency")
        Exit While
    End If
End While
```

If you follow the logic of the code, you will see that the loop continues while the counter variable is less than or equal to 50. The loop obtains a value from the user that is validated to be a positive, numeric value. If the user enters a value less than zero, presses the ⏎Enter key, or does not make an entry, the validation test fails and the loop exits. Figure 4.10 displays the Input box for entering an expense during each iteration of the loop.

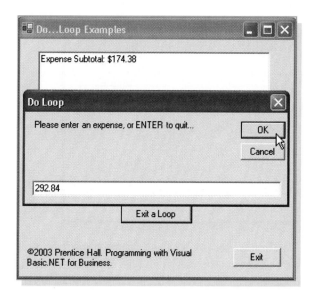

FIGURE 4.10. *Input box for entering an expense*

When the user enters a negative value or presses ⏎Enter, the loop ends and the total expenses are displayed, as shown in Figure 4.11.

FIGURE 4.11. *Total expenses*

As you can see, For...Next and Do...Loop statements are useful for processing repetitive tasks in your applications. Repetition structures are also useful for working with lists of data. Let's explore some of the ways looping statements support managing lists in Visual Basic.NET.

Working with Lists

Many applications provide users with a list of options from which to make a data selection. The Visual Basic.NET ComboBox and ListBox controls support this requirement. You learned how to use combo boxes in Chapter 2. A ***ListBox control*** is similar to a ComboBox except that a list box does not include a text box for entering a new value. List box and combo box controls have similar behaviors. Figure 4.12 shows the visual differences between these two controls.

FIGURE 4.12. *Comparing a ListBox control to a ComboBox control*

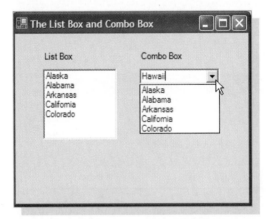

How do you know which control to use? Consider using a combo box when you want to present the user with a list of suggested choices but also want to allow a new value to be entered. Use a list box when you want to limit input to what is on the list or want to allow multiple selections. As you learned in Chapter 2, a combo box contains a text box field so choices not on the list can be typed in.

The interface design can help in determining which control to use. Combo boxes save space on a form, because the full list is not displayed until the user clicks the down arrow. A list box always displays the entire list.

Figure 4.13 displays a form containing a text box, a combo box, and two list boxes. This form is contained in the *ListBox Example* solution with your data files.

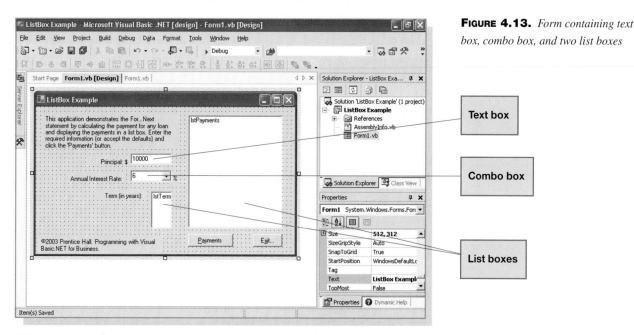

FIGURE 4.13. *Form containing text box, combo box, and two list boxes*

USING THE WINDOWS FORMS LISTBOX CONTROL

List boxes are appropriate for providing data-input options to the user as well as for displaying data on a form. Like a combo box, a list box has an ***Item property***, which defines the items in the list. The item property defines a collection of items, and in this case the ***collection*** is an ordered set of items that can be referred to as a unit. Each item in the collection defining the item list has an ***index***, which is an expression that specifies the position of a member of the collection. The first item in a list has an index of 0, the next item an index of 1, and the index value is incremented by 1 for each item in the list. As with a combo box, you can add items to the item collection of a list box at design time or at run time. A list box also has a ***SelectionMode property*** that specifies what items in the list can be selected. The settings for this property are *None*, *One*, *MultiSingle*, and *MultiExtended*. Setting the MultiSingle and MultiExtended properties to True allows multiple items in the list to be selected.

Adding Items to a ListBox or ComboBox Control at Design Time

You can easily add items to the item property of a ListBox or ComboBox control at design time by using the Windows Forms Designer and displaying the properties for the control. The *ListBox Example* solution in your data files contains the form shown in Figure 4.13. You can add, change, or remove items for the list collection at design time by using the ***String Collection Editor***, which is a tool for manipulating the items in a collection. You learned about the String Collection Editor in Chapter 2. The same editor assigns items to the collection for a List box at design time.

Using Looping Structures to Add Items to a ListBox or ComboBox Control at Run Time

Although you can add items to a control with a list at design time, you can also use looping structures in conjunction with the ***Items.Add method*** to add items to a collection at run time. This can be useful if you expect the elements in the list to change based

Visual Basic.NET also includes the *CheckedListBox control*, which displays a check mark next to items in the list. Checked list boxes can only have one item or none selected. The selected item appears highlighted on the form and is not the same as a checked item.

The ComboBox, ListBox, and CheckedListBox controls all use the String Collection Editor for adding items to the collection at design time.

on the selections users make while an application is running. If you want to use this method, however, you need to determine which procedure will *populate* the control that will contain the list (add the list items to it). You can use the ***Form load method*** of a Visual Basic.NET Windows form to specify any actions you wish to accomplish when the form is loaded into memory at run time.

The following code is from the Form Load event for the form contained in the *ListBox Example* solution.

```
Private Sub Form1_Load(ByVal sender As Object, ByVal e As
   System.EventArgs) Handles MyBase.Load
'Populate a combo box with the loan rates
Dim decRateIncrement As Decimal
     For decRateIncrement = 3 To 12 Step 0.25
     cboRate.Items.Add(decRateIncrement)
     Next

     'Populate a list box with the term values
     Dim intTermIncrement As Integer
        For intTermIncrement = 3 To 7
        lstTerm.Items.Add(intTermIncrement)
        Next
     lstTerm.SetSelected(2, True)
End Sub
```

The procedure contains two loops: one that populates a combo box with the loan rates and one that populates a list box with the available loan terms.

The For…Next loop that populates the combo box uses a start value of 3, an end value of 12, and a step value of .25 to populate the combo box with loan rates. When the counter reaches 12, the list is fully populated. When you run the application and click the drop-down button on the combo box control, the interest rates begin with 3 and increment by one quarter of a percentage point until 12 is reached.

The For…Next loop that populates the list box with the available loan terms uses a start value of 3 and an end value of 7. The step value is omitted, so it will default to 1. After the list is populated, the ***SetSelected method*** selects the item in the list with an index of 2. This way, a default value is selected when the application runs.

Visual Basic.NET uses zero-based indexes, meaning that the first item in a list has an index of 0. Which term does the SetSelected method set as the default?

SELECTING ITEMS IN A LIST

After a list box or combo box is populated, you need a way to select an item in the list. Combo boxes have a Text property; list boxes do not. When a user clicks an item in a combo box at run time, the Text property is set to the text of the item. Each item in a list box has an Index property that specifies the item's order in the list. You can reference this property code to determine what to do with a selected item.

The results of selecting an item in a list depend on the purpose of the list. As you will learn in Chapter 6, you can bind a list box control to a data source, and you can browse data in a database by using the control to enter new data or to edit existing data. You can also use a list box to perform an action using an item in the list. In the *ListBox Example* solution, the Term list box is populated at run time and the selected item in the Term list box is used as the term variable in the payment calculation. The code for the button click event is as follows:

```
Select Case lstTerm.SelectedIndex
    Case 0
        intTerm = 3
    Case 1
        intTerm = 4
    Case 2
        intTerm = 5
    Case 3
        intTerm = 6
    Case 4
        intTerm = 7
End Select
```

A select case statement sets the value of the *intTerm* variable depending on which item in the list the user selects. The default is set to 5 Years during Form load, so if the user does not make a selection, a term of 5 is used in the payment calculation.

USING THE LISTBOX CONTROL FOR DISPLAYING FORMATTED LISTS

You can also use a list box on a form to display output to the user. This is useful when a looping structure generates information during each iteration of the loop and you need to display all this information to the user. Consider the loan payment information in Figure 4.14.

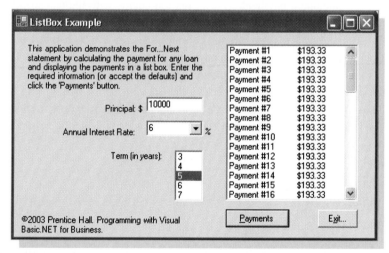

FIGURE 4.14. *List box example for loan payment*

The list includes the payment number, with the payment amount formatted as currency. The following segment of code from the Payment button's click procedure calculates the payment and displays the payment number and payment amount for each iteration the loop completes:

```
'Clear the List box
lstPayments.Items.Clear()

'Use the For…Next structure to calculate the payment and display
  the loan payments

Dim intCounter As Integer
```

```
For intCounter = 1 To intTerm * 12
    lstPayments.Items.Add("Payment #" & intCounter & vbTab &
        Format(Pmt(sngRate/ 12, intTerm * 12, -decPrincipal),
        "Currency"))

Next
```

The first statement uses the ***Clear method*** to clear any information currently in the *lstPayments* list box. This is necessary in case the user analyzes more than one loan scenario. The contents of the list are cleared before the payment information is added to the collection. The For...Next statement sets the starting value of the loop to 1 and the ending value as the term of the loan, which is expressed in years multiplied by 12 so each monthly payment will be displayed.

The statement that calculates the loan payment for display uses the Pmt function. The ***Pmt function***, one of the many intrinsic ***financial functions*** available in Visual Basic.NET, requires the rate, term, and principal as arguments. The principal is the present value of the loan and is entered as a negative value. Here is a code statement for calculating a loan payment:

```
Pmt(sngRate / 12, intTerm * 12, -decPrincipal)
```

The Rate is expressed as a monthly percentage (annual interest rate divided by 12 months), and the Term is stated in months (term in years multiplied by 12 months).

> **Tip** Other useful financial functions include the PPmt function, which calculates the portion of a loan payment that applies toward the principal, and the IPmt function, which calculates the portion of a loan payment that applies to the loan interest.

The **Items.Add** method adds the information included in parentheses to the list box. This expression concatenates a text string with the value of the counter variable and the calculated payment. The expression begins with the test string "***Payment #*** " followed by the value of the counter variable, which represents the payment number. In this example, ***vbTab*** is an internal constant that adds a tab character between the payment number and the calculated payment. The statement then uses the Format function to format the result of the calculation as currency, as specified by the **Currency** parameter. The SelectionMode property of the *lstPayments* list box is set to **None** so that no items in the list can be selected, because this list box is used only for displaying results. The results concatenated during each loop and added to each line of the list box are:

Text	intCounter	vbTab	Pmt
Payment #	1	vbTab	$199.33
Payment#	2	vbTab	$199.33
And so on…			

Open the *ListBox Example* solution and run the application, using different values for the principal, interest, and term. Notice that the list box displays a vertical scroll bar because the number of payments exceeds the number of items the control can display.

As you can see, looping structures and lists are useful for adding functionality to your Visual Basic.NET applications, setting the initial values of items in a collection and displaying results as a list. Now let's learn about one additional looping structure you can use to work with lists and collections.

Using the For...Each...Next Statement

Visual Studio.NET includes a looping statement for working with items in a collection. A collection is a group of individual objects treated as one unit. Earlier you worked with the items in a list box and combo box; these are one kind of collection. There are many other kinds of collections in Visual Basic.NET. For example, the controls on a form belong to a collection. The data an application generates as it performs calculations can be assigned to a collection. The computer system itself includes data about the computer hardware and software that is stored in a collection.

The ***For…Each…Next statement*** is similar to the For…Next statement, but it executes the statements in the loop for each element in a collection. This statement is more complex than a For…Next statement, because it references a collection. The general syntax is

You will learn more about collections in Chapter 8.

```
For Each element In collection
    Statements
Next [element]
```

Element is a special kind of a variable called an ***object variable*** for working with a group or collection. An object variable keeps track of each item or object contained in a collection. For each iteration of the loop, Visual Basic sets the value of *element* to one of the elements in the collection and executes the statements contained in the structure. After all the elements in the collection have been assigned to *element*, the For Each loop terminates and control passes to the statement following the **Next** statement.

Here's an example. Assume you want to toggle between hiding and displaying a series of text boxes that appear on a form. The following code statements use a nested loop structure to determine the type of control and, for text box controls, the current visible state.

```
'Declare object variables
Dim objControl As Control
Dim objTextBox As TextBox

For Each objControl In Controls
    If TypeOf objControl Is TextBox Then
        objTextBox = objControl
        If objTextBox.Visible = True Then
            objTextBox.Visible = False
        Else
            objTextBox.Visible = True
        End If
    End If
Next
```

The procedure declares two variables: one to reference each control on the form and another to reference each text box as it is processed by the loop. The statement begins with the *For Each* clause and ends with the *Next* clause. The element is a control on the form, represented by the *objControl* variable. The first If statement within the loop determines whether the current control is a text box. If this statement evaluates to True, the inner loop determines the Visible property of the text box. If the text box is currently visible, it becomes hidden; if the text box is currently hidden, it becomes visible. The loop processes each control on the form and, for each text box, toggles the Visible property to show or hide the control. Figure 4.15 displays the interface from the *For…Each…Next Example* solution with the text boxes displayed.

FIGURE **4.15.** *Text boxes in the For...Each...Next example*

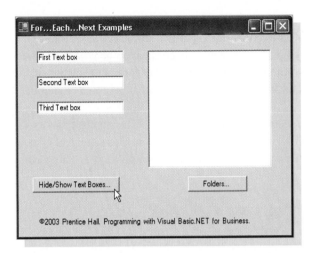

Now let's look at a more complex example. The list of folders on a particular disk drive is an example of a collection. Figure 4.16 shows the folders available on Drive G of a computer system.

FIGURE **4.16.** *Folders in the For...Each...Next example*

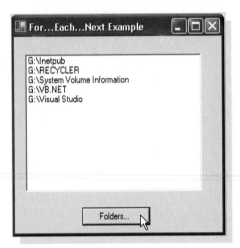

This collection is the list of subdirectories in the root directory of the drive. This is an example of information Visual Basic.NET can obtain from the system and return as a collection. Here is an example of the code that generates this list:

```
'Declare variables
Dim strLetter As String
Dim folders() As DirectoryInfo

Clear the List box
lstDir.Items.Clear()

'Obtain a drive letter
strLetter = InputBox("Please enter a drive letter…") folders =
    New DirectoryInfo(strLetter & ":\").GetDirectories
Dim folder As DirectoryInfo
For Each folder In folders
    lstDir.Items.Add(folder.FullName)
Next
```

The procedure takes advantage of the **DirectoryInfo class** in Visual Studio.NET that is used to obtain information about folders on a computer drive. To use this class, you declare a variable named *folders* that makes this class available to your application.

A string variable stores the letter of the drive for which you want to obtain a list of folders. The *folder* variable is an instance of the Folders class, so it is possible to obtain the list of folders for the drive the user specifies at run time. The list of folders is assigned to the *Folder* variable, which is the element variable for working with the elements in the collection.

The For…Each…Next statement uses a loop to add each directory name as an item in the *lstDir* list box.

Open the *For Each Next Example* solution and run the application. Click the *Folders* button and enter a valid drive letter. The list box will display the folders found on the drive.

Although For…Each…Next statements are more complex than For…Next statements, they are useful for processing collections, as the examples shown here demonstrate.

At this point you might not understand the concept of a class. You will learn more about classes in Chapter 9.

☞ HANDS-ON PROGRAMMING EXAMPLE

Creating a loan amortization schedule using looping structures

Many people consider real estate to be a sound investment. Although the value of a real estate investment fluctuates over time, real estate tends to increase in value. So how long does it take to earn a return on a real estate investment? Tax considerations aside, this depends on how the property was acquired. If you paid cash for a house, the value you realize at the time of sale is equal to the value of the home and its surrounding property. For those unable to pay cash for a home, the outstanding balance on the mortgage determines the gain or loss that is realized at the time of sale.

When you pay back a loan, only a portion of the monthly payment applies to the outstanding balance; the remainder applies to the accrued loan interest. The percentage of the payment applied to the loan principal versus that applied to the loan interest changes as you pay down the loan. A bank or lending institution will provide a schedule of plan payments called an amortization schedule. To *amortize* is to spread out—thus, an amortization schedule shows how the principal and interest payments are spread out over the term of the loan. Figure 4.17 shows an amortization schedule for a loan of $50,000 at an interest rate of 8%, paid over a term of 25 years.

FIGURE 4.17. *Interface for loan amortization schedule*

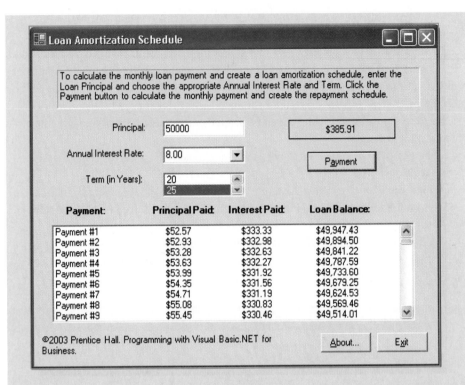

The Visual Basic.NET application for creating an amortization schedule supports the following conditions:

1. The loan amount must be at least $50,000 but no more than $200,000.
2. The loan term must be 10, 15, 20, 25, or 30 years.
3. The annual interest rate may vary from 3% to 8%, in increments of one-quarter of a percent.
4. If the loan principal, term, and annual interest rate are not specified, the defaults are $50,000, 25 years, and 8%, respectively.

Plan the Application

The first step in planning the application is to determine the inputs and outputs. This application is similar to the loan payment calculators you have created in previous chapters, except that you will use three financial functions to calculate the monthly payment, the principal payment, and the interest payment. The monthly payment will remain the same for the duration of the loan. The amount of the principal and interest payments vary each month, but the sum of these two payments always equals the monthly payment. The **Pmt** function calculates the monthly payment, the ***PPmt function*** calculates the principal payment, and the ***IPmt function*** calculates the interest payment. The amortization schedule displays payment information for each monthly payment. The schedule displays the following information:

The payment number

The principal payment

The interest payment

The loan balance

The inputs and outputs are as follows:

Inputs	Outputs
Principal	Payment number
Interest rate	Principal payment
Term	Interest payment
	Loan Balance

The loan principal is obtained from a text box, so you need to validate the principal. The interest rate is obtained from a combo box, so you also need to validate this entry. The loan term is selected from a list box, and the values are added to the collection when the form loads at run time. The form contains three buttons: one to calculate and display the loan amortization data, one to display an *About* form, and one to exit the application. Table 4.1 lists the objects and properties for the application.

Table 4.1: *Objects and properties for the Amortization Schedule application*

Object	Property	Setting
Form1	Text Size StartPosition	Loan Amortization Schedule 525, 425 CenterScreen
lblInfo	Text TextAlign BorderStyle	To calculate the monthly loan payment and create a loan amortization schedule, enter the Loan Principal and choose the appropriate Annual Interest Rate and Term. Click the Payment button to calculate the monthly payment and create the repayment schedule. MiddleLeft Fixed3D
lblPrincipal	Text TextAlign	Principal: MiddleRight
lblRate	Text TextAlign	Rate: MiddleRight
lblTerm	Text TextAlign	Term (in Years): MiddleRight
txtPrincipal	Text TextAlign BorderStyle TabStop TabIndex	50000 MiddleCenter FixedSingle True 0
lblPayment	Text Font.Bold	Payment: True
lblPPayment	Text Font.Bold	Principal Paid: True

lblIPayment	Text Font.Bold	Interest Paid: True
lblBalance	Text Font.Bold	Loan Balance: True
btnPayment	Text TabStop TabIndex	P&ayment True 3
lblMonthlyPayment	Text BorderStyle TextAlign	 FixedSingle MiddleCenter
lblCopyright	Text	©2003 Prentice Hall. Programming with Visual Basic.NET for Business.
btnAbout	Text TabStop TabIndex	&About… Yes 4
btnExit	Text TabStop TabIndex	E&xit Yes 5
cboRate	Text TabStop TabIndex	8.00 True 1
lstTerm	TabStop TabIndex	True 2
lstSchedule	SelectionMode	None

Draw a visual representation of the application on a blank piece of paper. Figure 4.18 shows a drawing of the user interface and the name of each control on the form.

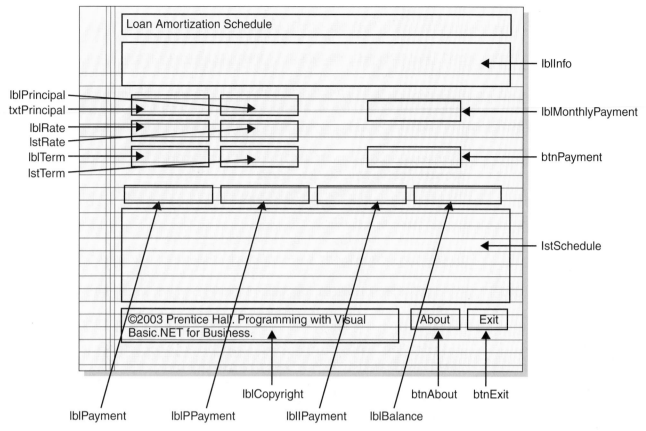

FIGURE 4.18. *Diagram of the user interface for the loan amortization schedule*

The application requires users to input the loan principal and then choose a loan rate and loan term. The default text for the *txtPayment* text box is 50000. If a rate and term are not selected from the list, the defaults of 8% annual interest and 30-year term are used for the calculation. The pseudocode for this functionality is shown in Table 4.2.

Table 4.2: *Pseudocode for the Loan Amortization Schedule application*

Event Procedure	Action
Form_Load	Populate the Rate and Term List boxes.
btnPayment_Click	1. Declare variables. 2. Perform data validation. 3. Calculate the monthly payment. 4. Declare variables for the amortization schedule. 5. Use a loop to populate the list box with the amortization schedule data.
btnAbout_Click	Display the *About* form.
btnExit_Click	1. Verify user intent to terminate application. 2. Cancel or terminate.

Design the User Interface

Now that you have created the planning documents for the application, you are ready to begin designing the user interface. If you have not launched Visual Studio.NET, do so now, and set the Profile to Visual Studio Developer. You will begin by creating the project, setting the form properties, and adding the About form to the project. You will then add the controls to the form and set the control properties.

To create the Loan Amortization project and add the About form to the project:

1. Create a new Visual Basic Windows Application project named Loan Amortization.
2. Set the properties for Form1 as specified in Table 4.1.
3. Click **Project**, **Add Existing Item**. Navigate to the *Start* folder for this project and locate the *frmAbout.vb* form in the *About Form* folder. Click **Open**. The form is added to the Solution Explorer.
4. Click **Save All** to save your changes.

To add the text box, label, and button controls to the form and set the control properties:

1. Using Figure 4.18 as a guide, add the text box, label, and button controls to the form, and set the control properties as specified.
2. Save your changes. The controls should look similar to the controls in Figure 4.19.

FIGURE 4.19. *Positioning controls on the form*

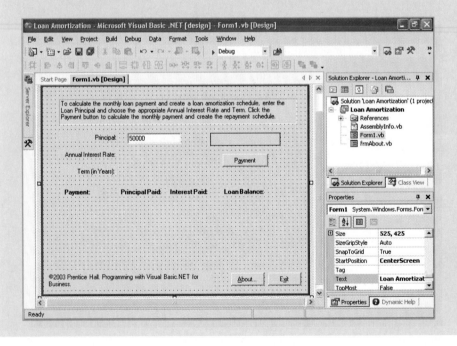

To add combo and list box controls to the form:

1. Add a combo box to the right of the *lblRate* label. Set the properties for the combo box as specified in Table 4.1.

2. Move the pointer over the Toolbox tab at the left side of the Form Design window and select the **ListBox** tool, as shown in Figure 4.20.

FIGURE 4.20. *Selecting the ListBox tool from the Toolbox*

3. Drag a list box onto the form in the position shown in Figure 4.21.

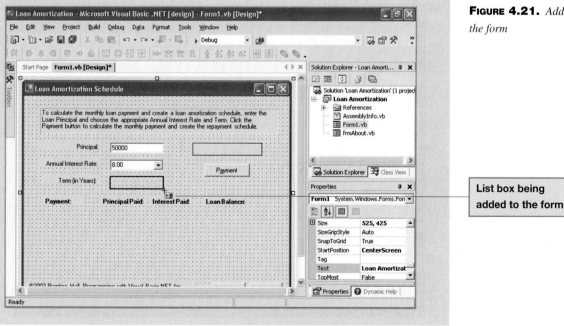

FIGURE 4.21. *Adding a ListBox to the form*

List box being added to the form

4. Change the **Name** property of the list box to `lstTerm`. Set the **TabStop** and **TabIndex** properties as specified in Table 4.1.

5. Add a list box to the form for the amortization schedule information. Change the **Name** property to `lstSchedule` and the SelectionMode property to `None`.

6. Save your changes. The form now includes the controls shown in Figure 4.22.

FIGURE 4.22. *Form with all controls in place*

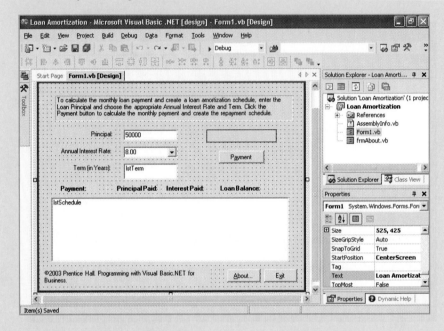

You are now ready to write the code for the Loan Amortization application.

Write the Code

First you will add copyright information and then enter the code statements for the Form Load event. After you finish the application by writing the procedures for the button click events, you will be ready to test the application.

To write the code:

1. Press F7 to display the Code Editor. If the Windows-generated designer code region is expanded, collapse it.

2. Using the format you learned in Chapter 2, add copyright information at the top of the Code Editor.

3. Click the **Class Name** list and select **Base Class Events**. Then click the **Method Name** list and select **Load**, as shown in Figure 4.23.

Here's the copyright statement:

```
'©2003
 Prentice Hall
 'By [Enter
   your name]
'Created/Revised: [Enter
    the date]
'Loan Amortization
    Application
```

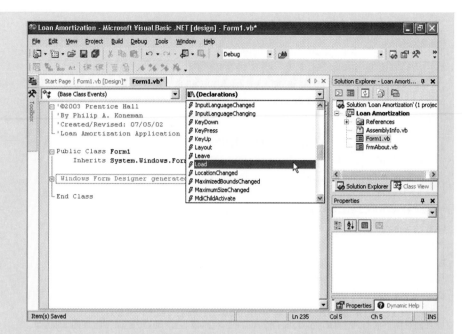

FIGURE 4.23. *Selecting the Load method*

4. Place the insertion point below the Private Sub statement and type the following:

```
'Populate the Rate Combo box
Dim sngCounter As Single
For sngCounter = 3 To 8 Step 0.25
    cboRate.Items.Add(Format(sngCounter, "Fixed"))
Next


'Populate the Term List box
Dim intCounter As Integer
intCounter = 10

Do Until intCounter = 35
    lstTerm.Items.Add(intCounter)
    intCounter += 5
Loop

'Set the 4th item in the list as the default term
lstTerm.SetSelected(3, True)
```

The procedure for the Form Load event uses a For…Next statement to populate the *cboRate* combo box. The starting value is 3, the ending value is 8, and the step value is 0.25. A Do…Loop statement populates the *lstTerm* List box. Note that the increment value for the *intCounter* variable is 5.

5. Click the **Save All** button to update the solution. You are now ready to write the code to calculate the monthly payment and generate the loan repayment schedule.

Notice that the cboRate.Items.Add statement uses the Format function to create a predefined format. The "Fixed," "f," and "F" format setting displays two digits to the right of the decimal. This way, all interest rate values will be formatted the same.

To write a procedure to handle the btnPayment click event:

Most of the functionality for this application is performed by the code that handles the click event for the *btnPayment* control. As you can see in Table 4.2, this procedure will validate data, perform calculations, and populate the *lstSchedule* control with the amortization schedule data.

1. Click the **Form1.vb** Tab in the IDE to display the Form Designer window.
2. Double-click the *btnPayment* button to create an event procedure.
3. Type the following code statements for the procedure:

```
'Declare variables for calculating the loan payment
Dim sngPrincipal, sngRate As Single
Dim intTerm As Integer
Dim decPayment As Decimal
'Perform data validation
If IsNumeric(txtPrincipal.Text) = False Or
  Val(txtPrincipal.Text) < 50000 Or Val(txtPrincipal.Text) >
  200000 Then
    MsgBox("The loan principal must be a number at least 50000
      and not greater than 200000. Please try again.",
      MsgBoxStyle.Critical, "Invalid Data")
Else
    If IsNumeric(cboRate.Text) = False Or Val(cboRate.Text) < 3
      Or Val(cboRate.Text) > 8 Then
MsgBox("The loan term must be a positive decimal value between 3
  and 8. Please try again.", MsgBoxStyle.Critical, "Invalid
  Data")
    Else
'Assign values to the sngPrincipal, sngRate and intTerm
  variables
sngPrincipal = Val(txtPrincipal.Text)
sngRate = Val(cboRate.Text) / 100
sngRate = sngRate / 12
intTerm = Val(lstTerm.Text) * 12

'Calculate the monthly payment and display the result, formatted
  as Currency
decPayment = Pmt(sngRate, intTerm, -sngPrincipal)
lblMonthlyPayment.Text = Format(decPayment, "Currency")

'Declare local variables
Dim decPpmt As Decimal
Dim decIPmt As Decimal
Dim decBalance As Decimal
Dim intPayment As Integer

'Initialize the loan beginning balance
decBalance = sngPrincipal

'Clear the listbox of any prior items
lstSchedule.Items.Clear()
```

```
'Generate the amortization schedule
For intPayment = 1 To intTerm
     'Calculate the interest payment and principal payment
     decPpmt = PPmt(sngRate, intPayment, intTerm, -sngPrincipal)

     decIPmt = IPmt(sngRate, intPayment, intTerm, -sngPrincipal)
     decBalance = decBalance - decPpmt

     'Populate the list box with the schedule
     lstSchedule.Items.Add _
     ("Payment #" & intPayment & vbTab & vbTab & _
     Format(decPpmt, "c") & vbTab & vbTab & _
     Format(decIPmt, "c") & vbTab & vbTab & _
     Format(decBalance, "c"))
Next
     End If
End If
```

4. Click the **Save All** button to update the solution.

This procedure is relatively complex. Review each statement, and read the remarks explaining what each statement block accomplishes.

The data validation for the loan principal and loan rate values is performed by using a nested IF structure. The first validation test is for the loan principal. If the entry fails validation, an error message is displayed. If the loan principal passes the validation test, the nested If statement validates the loan rate. If the loan rate validation fails, a message box is displayed. If the rate passes data validation, the procedure continues to the variable assignment and payment calculations.

The monthly payment is calculated by using the **Pmt** function. The statements that calculate the principal and interest payments use the **PPmt** and **IPmt** financial functions.

A loop populates the *lstSchedule* List box with loan payment information. The loop statements declare three variables to hold the principal payment (**decPpmt**), interest payment (**decIpmt**), and outstanding balance (**decBalance**) values that are performed during each iteration of the loop.

The statement that adds items to the list box control adds the payment number (using the counter variable *intPayment*), the interest payment, the principal payment, and the loan balance for each payment period. To make the code more readable, the routine uses the ***continuation character***. This character—the underscore (_) followed by the space character—makes the code easier to read in the Code Editor.

Now that you have written the code to calculate the monthly payment and create the amortization schedule, you are ready to write the code for the **About** and **Exit** buttons.

To write code procedures for the About and Exit buttons:

1. Switch to the Form Designer and double-click the *btnAbout* button.

2. Type the following code statements:

```
Dim ShowForm As frmAbout = New frmAbout()
ShowForm.ShowDialog()
```

3. Switch to the Form Designer, double-click the *btnExit* button, and type the following statements:

```
Dim intResponse As Integer
intResponse = MsgBox("Do you really want to exit this
   application?", 276, "Exit?")
     If intResponse = 6 Then
          End
     End If
```

4. Click the **Save All** button to update the solution.

Run the Application

You are now ready to run the Loan Amortization application and test its functionality.

To run the application:

1. Click the Start button or press the F5 key to run the application. Tab through the controls to verify the correct **TabIndex** setting for each control.
2. Tab into the text box for entering the loan principal, and type 100 as the amount.
3. Click the **Payment** button. The message shown in Figure 4.24 appears.

FIGURE 4.24. *Testing the Payment button for data validation*

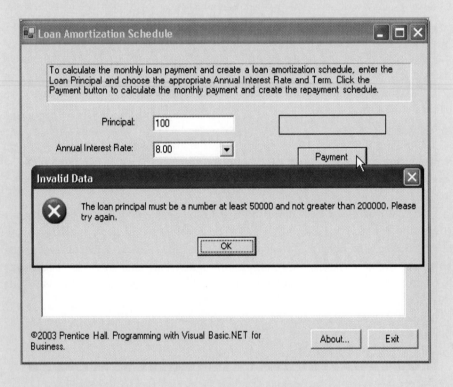

4. Click **OK**. Enter 100000 for the loan amount and enter 12 as the loan rate.
5. Click the **Payment** button. The message shown in Figure 4.25 appears.

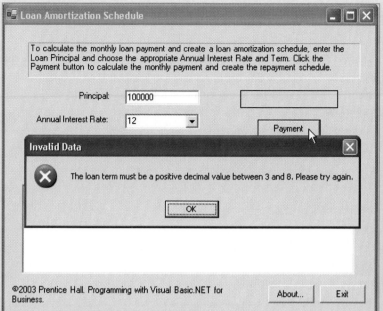

FIGURE 4.25. *Testing the Payment button for data validation*

6. Click **OK**. Type 75000 as the loan principal, select 5.00 as the rate, and select 20 as the term. Click the **Payment** button.

7. Scroll to the last item in the Schedule List box. Your values should match those shown in Figure 4.26.

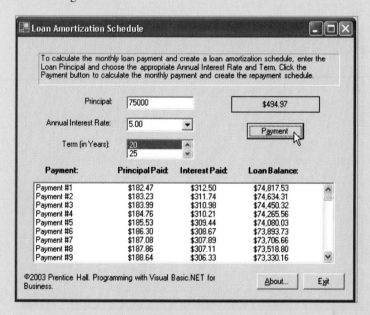

FIGURE 4.26. *Testing the Schedule list box*

8. Click the **About** button to verify that the *About* form displays.

9. Click the **Exit** button to verify the functionality of the procedure.

10. Click **File**, **Close Solution** when you finish testing the application.

Summary

- The For...Next statement executes a loop a specific number of times. This statement requires a counter variable, and the loop continues until the counter reaches a specific value.

- You can use a Do...Loop to execute a series of statements an indefinite number of times. This is a good choice when you want a loop to continue while a condition is true or until a condition is met.

- Use the While keyword in a Do...Loop to repeat the statements as long as a condition is true.

- Use the Until keyword in a Do...Loop to repeat the statements until a condition is met.

- A list box control displays lists on the screen from which users can select one or more items. You can also use a list box to display data that processed as a list.

- You can use the String Collection Editor at design time to add items to a list for a list box or combo box.

- To add items to a list box at run time, use the Items.Add method in your code.

- The Index property of an item in a list is set to True when the item has been selected.

- You can use looping statements to populate a list at run time.

- The For...Each...Next statement performs actions on the items in a collection.

Key Terms

Clear method	iteration
collection	ListBox control
continuation character	loop
counter variable	looping
Debug.WriteLine statement	object variable
decrement	Pmt function
Directory Info class	populate
Do...Loop statement	PostTest
End value	PPmt function
endless loop	PreTest
Exit Loop statement	repetition structure
financial functions	SelectionMode property
For...Each...Next statement	SetSelected method
For...Next statement	Start Value
Form load method	Step keyword
increment	Step Value
index	String Collection Editor
IPmt function	Until keyword
Item property	vbTab
Items.Add method	While keyword

Study Questions

Multiple-Choice Questions

1. Which looping structure executes a block of code a set number of times?
   a. Do...While
   b. For...Next
   c. Select...Case
   d. Do...Until
   e. If...Then

2. Which of the following is not a valid Step increment?
   a. 0
   b. 1
   c. 100
   d. -1
   e. 2

3. Which interface tool adds items to a collection at design time?
   a. Code Editor
   b. Toolbox
   c. String Collection Editor
   d. Solution Explorer
   e. Menu bar

4. Which data type would not work as a counter variable?
   a. String
   b. Single
   c. Integer
   d. Boolean
   e. A and D

5. Which of the following keywords is not used in a looping structure?
   a. For
   b. Select
   c. While
   d. Next
   e. Do

6. One complete pass through a looping structure is called a(n):
   a. Execution
   b. Cycle
   c. Revolution
   d. Iteration
   e. Bound

7. Which keyword is used to move out of a loop before the condition is met?
   a. Pre
   b. End
   c. Post
   d. Exit
   e. Stop

8. Which of the following predefined formats displays the results of a calculation as currency?
   a. "$$.$$"
   b. "F"
   c. "C"
   d. "f"
   e. "$"

9. Which of the following is the continuation character?
   a. Ampersand (&)
   b. Currency ($)
   c. Asterisk (*)
   d. Apostrophe (')
   e. Underscore (_)

10. Which structure populates a list at run time?
    a. Do...While
    b. For...Next
    c. Select...Case
    d. Do...Until
    e. If...Then

True/False Questions

1. You can add items to a list box control at run time but not at design time.

2. You can execute a block of statements a set number of times by using a Do...While statement.

3. Including the continuation character in code simplifies reading and interpreting complex statements.

4. The For...Each...Next statement is useful for working with collections.

5. The While keyword repeats the statements in a loop until a condition is true.

Short Answer Questions

1. What is the Index property of a list box item, and how is it used?

2. How can you add items to a list box collection at run time?

3. How does the For…Next structure differ from the Do…While structure?

4. How can you clear the item collection for a list box at run time?

5. How does a list box differ from a combo box? When would you use one over the other?

Guided Exercises

Creating a Mileage Conversion Table

In previous chapters you created the formulas for converting mileage between miles and kilometers. In this exercise, you will create an application for displaying a table of mileage conversion values. The application has a simple interface: a group box for specifying the type of conversion, a list box for displaying the conversion table, and a button to perform the conversion. Clicking the **Convert** button displays two input boxes for the range of values to convert. The application interface is shown in Figure 4.27.

FIGURE 4.27. *Interface for Mileage Conversion application*

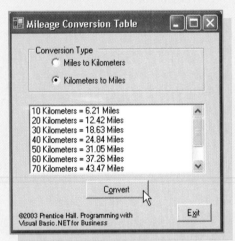

To create this application, complete the following steps:

1. In Visual Studio.NET, click **File**, **New Project**. Create a new Windows Application named `Mileage Conversion Table`.

2. Change the Text property of the form to `Mileage Conversion Table`.

3. Create a group box in the upper left portion of the form. Add two radio buttons to the group box. Change the Text properties to match Figure 4.27. Set the **Checked** property of the first radio button control to `True`.

4. Create a list box below the group box. Set the **TabStop** property of the listbox to `False`.

5. Add a button control to the bottom of the form. Change the Name property to `btnConvert` and the **Text** property to C&onvert.

6. Add an Exit button to the form. Change the **Text** property to E&xit. Add code to the button's click event to terminate the application after verifying the user's intent to exit.

7. Add the following code to the *btnConvert* click event:

```
Dim intLow As Integer
Dim strInput As String
strInput = (InputBox("Please enter the first distance to include
    in the table"))

If IsNumeric(strInput) = False Then
    MsgBox("The distance you entered is invalid!. Please try
        again.", MsgBoxStyle.Critical, "Invalid Distance!")
Else
    intLow = Val(strInput)
    Dim intHigh As Integer
    strInput = (InputBox("Please enter the second distance to
        include in the table"))
    If IsNumeric(strInput) = False Then
        MsgBox("The distance you entered is invalid!. Please
            try again.", MsgBoxStyle.Critical, "Invalid
            Distance!")
    Else
        intHigh = Val(strInput)
        lstTable.Items.Clear()

        Select Case grpConversion.Focus
            Case rdbMtoK.Checked
                Dim intCounter As Integer
                For intCounter = intLow To intHigh Step 10
                    lstTable.Items.Add(intCounter & " Miles =
                        " & (Format((intCounter * 1.609), "f") &
                        " Kilometers"))
                Next
            Case rdbKtoM.Checked
                Dim intCounter As Integer
                For intCounter = intLow To intHigh Step 10
                    lstTable.Items.Add(intCounter & "
                        Kilometers = " & (Format((intCounter *
                        0.621), "f")) & " Miles")
                Next
        End Select
    End If
End If
```

8. Save the application.

9. Run the application to verify that the formulas are performing the calculations correctly. Use the values shown in Figure 4.27 to test your application.

10. Save any updates and close the solution.

Creating a Payroll Application for Multiple Employees

In previous chapters, you created and modified a payroll application for calculating an employee's gross pay, taxes, and net pay depending on the employee's hourly wage and the hours worked during the period. In this exercise, you will create a similar application that will allow you to perform payroll calculations for multiple employees and display the results in a list box. The user is prompted to enter the number of employees for whom to create a payroll record. Figure 4.28 shows the application interface with payroll data for three employees.

FIGURE 4.28. *Interface for Payroll application*

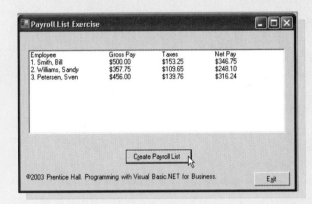

To create this application, complete the following steps:

1. In Visual Studio.NET, click **File**, **New Project**. Create a new Windows Application named `Payroll List`.

2. Change the Text property of the form to `Payroll List Exercise`.

3. Create a list box on the form. Change the TabStop property to `False`.

4. Create a button on the form that will handle the event for entering all data and creating the employee list. Change the Name property to `btnPayroll` and the Text property of the button to `C&reate Payroll List`.

5. Add an additional button for exiting the application. Change the Text property to `E&xit`. Add code to the click event for this button to terminate the application, after verifying the user's intent to exit.

6. Add the following code to the click event for the *btnPayroll* control:

```
        'Declare variables and constants

Const federalTax As Single = 0.15
Const stateTax As Single = 0.08
Const fica As Single = 0.062
Const medicare As Single = 0.0145

Dim strName As String        'Last Name, First Name
Dim sngWage As Single          'Employee's hourly wage
Dim intHours As Integer        'Hours worked
Dim intCount As Integer          'The number of employees
Dim decGrossPay As Decimal    'Result of calculation
Dim decTaxes As Decimal   'Result of calculation
Dim decNetPay As Decimal       'Result of calculation

intCount = Val(InputBox("Enter the number of employee records to
   create"))
```

```
        If intCount < 1 Then
            MsgBox("You must create a record for at least one
                employee. Try again.", MsgBoxStyle.Critical, "Invalid
                number!")
        Else
            'Add headings to the list box
            lstPayroll.Items.Add("Employee" & vbTab & vbTab &
                "Gross Pay" & vbTab & "Taxes" & vbTab & vbTab & "Net
                Pay")

            'Loop to obtain employee data and create the payroll
                list
            Dim intCounter As Integer
            For intCounter = 1 To intCount

                'Obtain data - for simplicity, there is no data
                    validation!
                strName = InputBox("Enter the last and first name
                    for employee " & intCount)
                sngWage = Val(InputBox("Enter the employee hourly
                    wage for employee  & intCount))
                intHours = Val(InputBox("Enter the hours worked by
                    employee " & intCount))

                'Perform calculations
                decGrossPay = intHours * sngWage
                decTaxes = (decGrossPay * federalTax) +
                    (decGrossPay * stateTax) + (decGrossPay * fica)
                    + (decGrossPay * medicare)
                decNetPay = decGrossPay - decTaxes
                lstPayroll.Items.Add(intCount & ". " & strName &
                    vbTab & vbTab & Format(decGrossPay, "c") & vbTab
                    & vbTab & Format(decTaxes, "c") & vbTab & vbTab
                    & Format(decNetPay, "c"))
            Next
        End If
End Sub
        End If
```

7. Save the changes to your application.

8. Run the application and test its functionality.

9. Save any change you make to the solution.

10. Close the solution.

Case Studies

Calculating the Value of Inventory

Retail companies determine the total value of their inventory by adding together the values of all inventory items they have in stock. Create an application that uses a looping structure for entering the value of an inventory item in an input box, displaying the item in a text box, and then dis-

This application does not validate the payroll data as it is entered. How would you change the code statements to perform data validation?

playing the total for all items entered. You will need to provide a way of exiting out of the loop after all items have been entered. Name the project Inventory Value. Figure 4.29 displays the interface for the application.

FIGURE 4.29. *Interface for Inventory Value application*

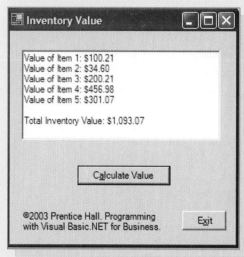

When you finish creating the application, test it by using the values shown in Figure 4.29. Save any changes you make after revising the application.

Creating a Temperature Conversion Table

In Chapter 1 you learned how to create an application that converts temperatures between the Celsius and Fahrenheit scales. In this case study you will create a similar application, except that this application creates a table of temperature conversion values. Create a Windows application named Temperature Conversion Table for performing temperature conversions. The formulas for calculating the conversion are as follows:

$$\text{Celsius to Fahrenheit: } (9/5)\ C + 32$$

$$\text{Fahrenheit to Celsius: } 5/9\ (F - 32)$$

1. Obtain the temperature to convert using an input box and validate the entry as numeric data.

2. Add a group box and two radio button controls for the user to specify what kind of conversion to perform. Set the default as the Fahrenheit to Celsius conversion.

3. Add two buttons to the form: one for performing the calculation and one for exiting the application. Use an If statement to verify the user's intent to exit.

4. Add a procedure to the *btnConvert* button that prompts the user for the first and last temperatures to include in the table. Increment the values listed in the table by 1 degree.

5. Display the table results, formatted to 2 decimal places, in the *lstResults* list box.

Save your changes and test the application. When you finish, close the solution.

File Access, Dialog Boxes, Error Handling, and Menus

In Chapter 1 you learned about the Input, Processing, Output, and Storage (IPOS) cycle that defines what computer programs do. The programs you have created obtain user input, use the input to process a result, and display the results of processing as output on the screen. Another powerful capability of computers, however, is storing information in a data file and accessing this data at a later time.

Programs for opening and saving files usually include interface elements besides buttons and input boxes for performing actions and making selections. For example, Microsoft Word includes commands on the **File** menu for opening and saving files. When you open a file, a dialog box for specifying the file's name, location, and file type appears on the screen. Although you can create your own forms as dialog boxes and add the controls for opening and saving files, Visual Basic.NET includes predefined dialog boxes for performing these tasks. When you add menus to your application that display predefined dialog boxes for actions such as opening and saving files, the interface for your application is simple to use and follows the standards for programs designed to run on the Microsoft Windows operating system. In this chapter you will learn how to work with data files, handle errors associated with data files, and refine the look of your applications by adding menus to the program interface.

Performance Objectives

At the conclusion of this chapter, you will be able to:

- Describe how program files differ from data files.
- Explain how sequential files differ from random files.
- Read and write sequential data.
- Create a record structure and a user-defined data type, and read and write random data.
- Write procedures to handle file input and output exceptions by using the Try… Catch… Finally statement.
- Add predefined dialog boxes to a form by using common dialog controls.
- Use the RichTextBox control to create and store formatted text.
- Add menus to a form by using the MainMenu control.
- Add a context menu to a form by using the ContextMenu control.

Data File Basics

Computers use two kinds of files. The computer uses ***program files*** to run and support programs. Files with an *.exe* extension (executable files) are examples of program files. Program files include the computer's operating system (Windows 2000, Windows NT, or Windows XP, for example) and all the applications the computer supports, such as Microsoft Word (Word.exe), Microsoft Excel (Excel.exe), and Microsoft Internet Explorer (IExplore.exe). The Windows Start button lists the programs that are available on a computer, and the **Start** menu contains shortcuts to these program files.

The files you have created for your Visual Studio.NET programs are compiled into executable files. During design, every Visual Studio solution includes a Bin folder that contains an executable file for a specific Visual Studio.NET solution. When you run a program to test it, the executable is created. After you finish designing a program, you can use a Setup and Deployment project to create the program executables that can be installed and run on a computer.

 **To learn how to create a Setup and Deployment project, see Appendix A.**

To save something you create when using an application, you first create a ***data file***. The kind of data you save depends on the program you are using. The papers you write while using Word are stored as one kind of data file; the class schedule you create in Excel is another kind of data file; and the e-mail message you save for reference is yet another kind of data file. Microsoft Word documents have a .doc file extension, indicating that they are data files created in Word. Microsoft Excel workbooks have an .xls file extension, indicating that they are data files created in Excel. E-mail messages are often stored as simple text files and have a .txt file extension.

Why are data files important? Obtaining input by using the keyboard and producing output on the screen are basic capabilities of any computer program. An example is the *Hello World* application you created in Chapter 1; the application responds to events generated by the user but does not save the text for later use. Often the programs you use need to use data that already exists. For example, if you need to modify and then print an employee memo regarding bonuses that your manager gave to you on a floppy disk, you need to open the file from within a program, make changes, save the changes, and then print the memo. A basic feature of most programs is the capability for obtaining input from a file stored on disk and saving new or updated information to a data file. A program *reads a file* to obtain input and *writes to a file* to save output to disk. Reading data from and writing data to files is called **file input/output**, or **file I/O** for short. How the program accesses (reads and writes) the data depends on the file type, which describes what kind of data the file contains. Visual Basic.NET allows your applications to access three file types: sequential, random, and binary. In this chapter you will learn about sequential and random file access. Binary files are complex and beyond the scope of this text.

Sequential File Access

Sequential file access is the best choice when you're working with files consisting only of text, like the files created with a typical text editor such as Notepad or WordPad. Text editors are useful for creating and editing text files that can be read by any computer, regardless of the operating system. Web developers use text editors to write HTML documents for the Web. As the name implies, sequential files contain text data consisting of a series of characters, one after another in sequence. The data for the file is a continuous stream of characters. As an analogy, think of watching a movie stored on a VHS tape. As you view the movie, the information from the tape is retrieved in sequential order. Before you can watch the last scene, you must first move the tape through the preceding scenes. In the same way, a sequential data file reads and writes all the text as a continuous stream of data. Figure 5.1demonstrates how a program reads and writes sequential files.

FIGURE 5.1. *How a program reads and writes sequential files*

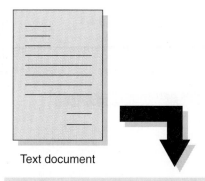

Text document

To: All employees From: Bill Smith, CEO Re: Employee Bonuses...

Text document as a stream of characters

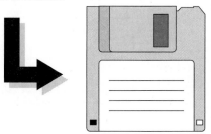

Text stream is written to and read from disk sequentially

READING AND WRITING DATA BY USING SEQUENTIAL FILE ACCESS

To read and write data by using sequential file access, you must first open the file so it is available for use. When the file is open, you can either read the contents of the file into the application or write data from your program to the file. You can use one of three modes to access (read or write) the data in the file: *input mode* for reading data from a file and *output mode* or *append mode* for writing data to the file. The output mode overwrites the existing file; the append mode appends data to the end of the file. When your program finishes reading or writing data, you must close the file. Following are the steps for reading text from and writing text to sequential files:

Reading Data	Writing Data
1. Open the file.	1. Open the file.
2. Read text from the file.	2. Write text to the file.
3. Close the file.	3. Close the file.

Visual Basic.NET includes internal functions for reading and writing data files. The *FileOpen function* provides a simple method for opening a sequential file to input, output, or append data. You can use this function in your code statements that read and write sequential data. The general syntax of this function is

```
FileOpen(Filenumber, Filename, Mode)
```

- *Filenumber*: An integer assigned to the file while it is open
- *FileName*: The name of the file to open
- *Mode*: How the file will be accessed (input, output, or append)

Let's look at a simple example of using the **FileOpen** function to open a sequential data file. Figure 5.2 displays a form that contains text box, label, and menu controls.

FIGURE 5.2. *Menu item for opening data files*

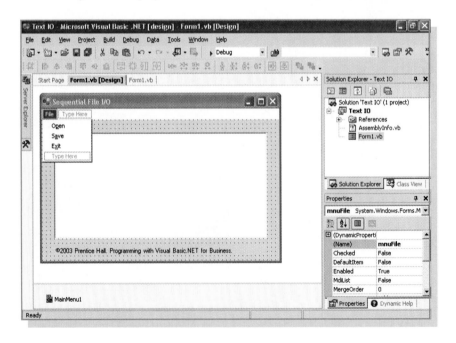

The menu contains items for opening and saving a file and for exiting the application. The text box displays the text to be read from a file or the text to be written to the file. Figure 5.3 displays the text in the *MyFile.txt* file included with your data files.

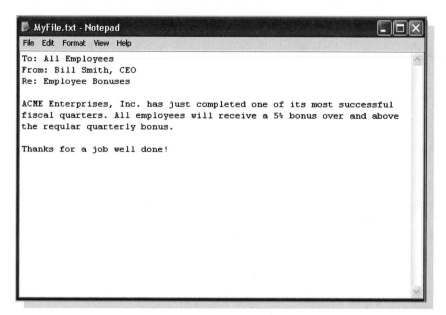

 The form in Figure 5.2 includes a MainMenu control that adds a menu to the top of the form. Menus are a common interface feature in programs that run on computers with the Microsoft Windows operating system. You will learn how to use the MainMenu control to add menus to forms later in this chapter.

FIGURE 5.3. *Contents of the* MyFile.txt *file displayed in Windows Notepad*

When the user selects **Open** from the **File** menu, the text is read into the text box and appears as shown in Figure 5.4.

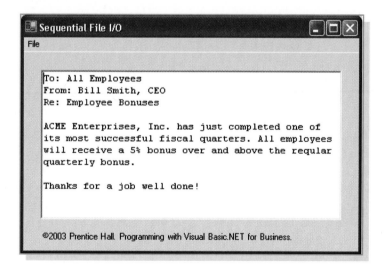

FIGURE 5.4. *Contents of the* MyFile.txt *file displayed in a TextBox control*

The procedure for opening the file to generate the result shown in Figure 5.4 handles the click event for the **File**, **Open** menu item. The procedure is as follows:

 This example works only if the *MyFile.txt* file is in the root directory of a floppy disk in Drive A: when the application is run.

```
Private Sub mnuFileOpen_Click(ByVal sender As System.Object,
    ByVal e As System.EventArgs) Handles mnuFileOpen.Click
    FileOpen(1, "A:\MyFile.txt", OpenMode.Input)
    txtFile.Text = InputString(1, LOF(1))
    FileClose(1)
End Sub
```

You may view the code for this example by opening the *Sequential Files* solution in the *Text IO* folder included with your data files.

In the previous procedure, the file is assigned a file number of 1 when opened. The mode is input, so data is read from the file to the text box on the form. The Filename parameter includes the path and name of the file. The **FileOpen** function uses two other functions to open the file for reading: the **InputString function** and the **Length of File (LOF) function**. The *InputString function* reads a series of characters (called a character string) from a text file. The InputString function has two required parameters: the number assigned to the file and the number of characters contained in the file.

Because a text file will vary in length, how can you determine ahead of time the number of characters the file contains? This is what the LOF (Length of File) function is designed to do. The *LOF function* obtains the number of characters contained in a file that has been opened by using the **FileOpen** function. The previous code example contains the following:

```
txtFile.Text = InputString(1, LOF(1))
```

Notice that this is an assignment statement. The statement uses the **InputString** function to read a string of characters from the open file into the Text property of the *txtFile* text box. The **LOF** function determines the number of characters to read. After the characters are read into the text box, the file is closed.

The statement for writing data from the text box control to the data file is similar to the procedure for reading data from the file. The code statements that handle the click event for the **File**, **Save** menu item are as follows:

```
Private Sub mnuFileSave_Click(ByVal sender As System.Object,
    ByVal e As System.EventArgs) Handles mnuFileSave.Click
        FileOpen(1, "a:\MySavedFile.txt", OpenMode.Output)
        Print(1, txtFile.Text)
        FileClose(1)
    End Sub
```

This routine uses another predefined function for working with sequential data. The *Print function* writes each character in the text box to the *MySavedFile.txt* text file. In this example, the **Print** function uses two parameters: the number of the file opened for output and the expression to write to the file. The expression for this example is the **Text** property of the *txtFile* control. As with the previous procedure, the **FileOpen** function specifies the filename and path of the file to which the text is written. When your program finishes reading or writing data, you must close the file. The event procedure uses the *FileClose function* to close the file opened for output.

Now that you have learned a simple method for reading and writing sequential data, let's learn how to use random file access to read from and write to data files.

Random File Access

As you learned in the section on data files, sequential file access is the best choice when the data in a file consists of lines of text. For files in which the data is divided into a series of fields and records, such as an employee's name and address, *random file access* is the best choice. A *field* is a single data element in a record. Examples of fields are an employee's last name, the part number for an item, or the title of a CD in your music collection. A *record* is a collection of fields that distinguish one item in the data file from another. Figure 5.5 shows the structure for a data file. In this example, the data file stores employee names, addresses, and pay rates. Each record contains the same nine fields of data.

Employee ID	Last Name	First Name	Address	City	State	Zip Code	Telephone	Pay Rate
121121122	Carr	Laura	9575 Summit Road	Eagle	CO	80012	(719) 344-9087	$15.00
221323131	Bailey	Charles	211 Shrine Pass Crt.	East Vail	CO	80996	(719) 344-2010	$18.00
223343232	Holmes	Philip	48533 Piney Crk. Dr.	Beaver Crk.	CO	80921	(719) 374-8923	$30.00
722121313	Jackson	Rebecca	10054 Ruler Court	Vail	CO	80997	(719) 344-2070	$21.00
732313111	Lindsey	Mark	14419 Brooke Road	Avon	CO	80933	(719) 444-3221	$12.00
841412121	Sanchez	Maria	101 Main Street	West Vail	CO	80978	(719) 377-2366	$18.00

Fields

Records

FIGURE 5.5. *Data file consisting of nine fields and six records*

In a random access file, each field and record has a fixed length. Because all records occupy the same amount of space on disk, any record in the file can be accessed directly. In the way that a sequential data file is like viewing a movie on a VHS tape, a random access file is more like a DVD disc, where you can jump to any scene of the movie without viewing the scenes that precede it. Just as a DVD refers to each scene of the movie by using a number, the records in a data file are numbered, beginning with record number 1 and incrementing by a value of 1 until all the records are identified. In a random file you can read any record, modify it, and write it back to the file without accessing any of the other records. Figure 5.6 demonstrates how a program reads and writes data to a random access file.

FIGURE 5.6. *How a program reads and writes to a random access file*

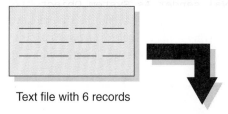

Text file with 6 records

Text file as fixed-length records

121121122	Carr	Laura	9575 Summit Road	Eagle	CO	80012	(719) 344-9087	$15.00
221323131	**Bailey**	**Charles**	**211 Shrine Pass Crt.**	**East Vail**	**CO**	**80996**	**(719) 344-2010**	**$18.00**
223343232	Holmes	Philip	48533 Piney Crk. Dr.	Beaver Crk.	CO	80921	(719) 374-8923	$30.00
722121313	Jackson	Rebecca	10054 Ruler Court	Vail	CO	80997	(719) 344-2070	$21.00
732313111	Lindsey	Mark	14419 Brooke Road	Avon	CO	80933	(719) 444-3221	$12.00
841412121	Sanchez	Maria	101 Main Street	West Vail	CO	80978	(719) 377-2366	$18.00

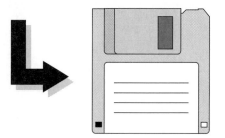

Second record read, modified, and written to disk

The steps for reading records from or writing records to a random access file are as follows:

Reading and Writing Records

1. Create a record structure.
2. Declare a structure variable of the type defined in the record structure.
3. Open the data file containing the records.
4. Read one or more records from the file, or write one or more records to the file.
5. Close the file.

Because a random access file requires that all records have the same length, you need a way to define the structure for the records. To accomplish this, you create a record structure—a user-defined data type that defines the structure for the variable that refers to each record. Because the records in a random access file are all the same length and therefore have a consistent format, the data is referred to as ***structured data***. In Visual Basic.NET, you create a user-defined data type as the record structure for storing structured data.

CREATING A USER-DEFINED DATA TYPE RECORD STRUCTURE

A ***user-defined data type (UDT)*** is a special kind of a variable that contains one or more variables for defining the structure for each record in a file. The record structure is declared by using a structure statement that consists of the **Structure** and **End Structure** keywords. Contained within the keywords are the individual variables called ***field variables*** that determine what kind of data is contained within the structure. You can define a record structure by using the following syntax, where *StructureName* is the name of the record structure, and one or more field variables are declared within the structure:

```
Structure StructureName
        Field variable declarations
End Structure
```

For example, an Employee data file might contain a user-defined data type named *Employee*:

```
Structure Employee
        Public intNumber As Integer
        <VBFixedString(9)> Public strEmpID As String
        <VBFixedString(20)> Public strLastName As String
        <VBFixedString(15)> Public strFirstName As String
        <VBFixedString(35)> Public strAddress As String
        <VBFixedString(15)> Public strCity As String
        <VBFixedString(2)> Public strState As String
        <VBFixedString(5)> Public strZipCode As String
        <VBFixedString(14)> Public strHomePhone As String
        Public sngPayRate As Single
    End Structure
```

The **Structure keyword** begins the record definition, and the field variables are declared before the **End Structure keyword**. Field variables declared with any data type other than String are assigned a length, depending on the field data type:

Data Type	Length
Boolean, Char, Short	2 bytes
Integer, Single	4 bytes
Double, Long, Date/Time	8 bytes
Decimal	16 bytes

When you declare a String field variable you must assign a length, because all records must be the same length in a random access file. In this example, the *strEmployeeID* field variable is assigned a length of 9 characters, and the *strLastName* field variable is assigned a length of 20 characters.

DECLARING A STRUCTURE VARIABLE

After declaring the structure, you can declare a variable, called a **structure variable**, with the data type of the structure. Because the structure itself can contain members with differing data types, the variable that refers to the structure has the structure as a data type. You can name a structure variable with a three-character prefix of *udt*. When you refer to this variable in your code, you have access to each of the members contained within the structure. Here's an example of how to declare a variable based on a structure:

```
Dim udtEmployees As Employee
```

After you have defined the structure, you can refer to the entire record variable in your code statements by its name, such as udtInventory in our example. To refer to the field variables in your code, you must reference the structure name and the field name, separated by a period, as follows:

```
udtEmployees.strEmpID = txtEmpID.Text
udtEmployees.strLastName = txtLastName.Text
udtEmployees.strFirstName = txtFirstName.Text
```

Figure 5.7 shows the code for declaring the structure and declaring three form-level variables. The *udtEmployees* variable is a structure variable. The *intCurrentRecord* and *intTotalStructure* variables hold the values assigned to the record counters.

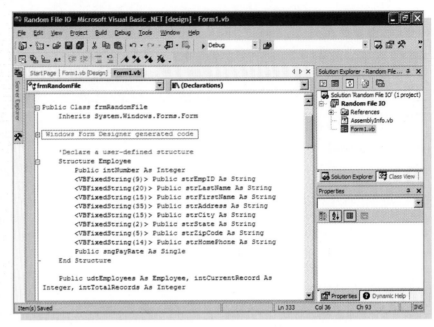

How do you determine the length of each record? One method is to count the number of characters assigned to the structure. For the data structure explained previously, the length is:

intNumber	4 bytes
strEmpID	9 bytes
strLastName	20 bytes
strFirstName	15 bytes
strAddress	35 bytes
strCity	15 bytes
strState	2 bytes
strZipCode	5 bytes
strHomePhone	14 bytes
sngPayRate	4 bytes
	123 bytes total

You can also use the ***Len function*** to determine the record length for the structure variable. The **Len** function displays a number representing the number of characters in a string or the number of bytes stored in a variable. The **Len** function requires one parameter: an expression for the object containing the text string or for the variable to be counted. For example, this statement determines the length of the *udtEmployees* structure variable:

```
Len(udtEmployees)
```

You can use the **Len** function in your code statements. Consider the following statement:

```
MsgBox("The length of the variable in bytes is: " &
    Len(udtEmployees), MsgBoxStyle.Information, "Using the Len
    function")
```

When contained in a procedure where the *udtEmployees* variable has been declared, this statement will display the message box shown in Figure 5.8.

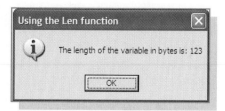

FIGURE 5.8. *Message box displaying the length of the* udtEmployees *structure variable*

OPENING A RANDOM ACCESS FILE

Before you can read the records in a random access file or write data to a random access file, you must first open the file. You can use the **FileOpen** function, as follows:

```
FileOpen(1, "a:\Employees.txt", OpenMode.Random,
  OpenAccess.ReadWrite, OpenShare.Shared, Len(udtEmployees))
```

This statement uses all the parameters for the **FileOpen** function. In addition to the parameters you learned about for using this function to open a sequential access file, the following optional parameters are included:

Share	Specifies the operations restricted on the open file by other processes: Shared, Lock Read, Lock Write, and Lock Read Write. Defaults to Shared.
RecordLength	Number identifying the file. Can be any value between 1 and 32,767 (bytes). For files opened for random access, this value is the record length. For sequential files, this value is the number of characters.

READING RECORDS FROM A RANDOM ACCESS FILE

Now let's look at an example. Figure 5.9 shows a form that displays the first of three records in the *Employees.txt* random access file included with your data files.

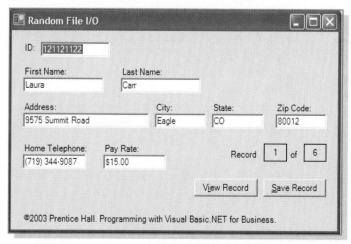

FIGURE 5.9. *Form for displaying records in a random access file*

The form is from the *Random File IO* solution included with your data files. The Form_Load event initializes the form by opening the *Inventory.txt* file and displaying the first record. There are two buttons on the form: one for displaying another record in the file and one for creating a new record or updating an existing record. To display another record, click the **View Record** button and enter a number between 1 and 6. For example, clicking the **View Record** button and entering a value of 3 in the input box displays the third record in the file, as shown in Figure 5.10.

FIGURE 5.10. *Displaying a specific record in a file*

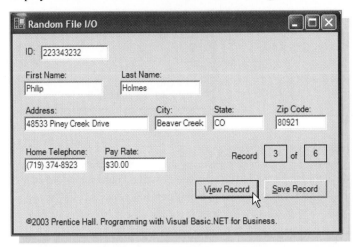

Here's the code for the button's click event:

```
Private Sub btnViewRecord_Click(ByVal sender As System.Object,
  ByVal e As System.EventArgs) Handles btnViewRecord.Click
    'Determine the record to view
    intCurrentRecord = Val(InputBox("Which record number do you
      want to view?"))

    'Validate user input
    If intCurrentRecord > intTotalRecords Then
        MsgBox("This record number does not exist. Please try
          again.", MsgBoxStyle.Critical, "Invalid record
          number")
    Else
        'Open the file and read fields into the text boxes on
          the form
        FileOpen(1, "a:\Employees.txt", OpenMode.Random,
          OpenAccess.ReadWrite, OpenShare.Shared,
          Len(udtEmployees))
        FileGet(1, udtEmployees, intCurrentRecord)
        FileClose(1)
        txtEmpID.Text = udtEmployees.strEmpID
        txtLastName.Text = udtEmployees.strLastName
        txtFirstName.Text = udtEmployees.strFirstName
        txtAddress.Text = udtEmployees.strAddress
        txtCity.Text = udtEmployees.strCity
        txtState.Text = udtEmployees.strState
        txtZipCode.Text = udtEmployees.strZipCode
        txtHomePhone.Text = udtEmployees.strHomePhone
        txtPayRate.Text = Format(udtEmployees.sngPayRate, "c")

        'Update Record Counters
        lblCurrentRecord.Text = udtEmployees.intNumber
        lblTotalRecords.Text = intTotalRecords
    End If
End Sub
```

The procedure begins by displaying an input box and assigning the value entered into the *intCurrentRecord* variable. An If… Then… Else statement then determines if the entry is valid. If the number is less than or equal to the total number of records displayed on the form's counter, the procedure opens the file and reads the record of the record number with the same value as the *intCurrentRecord* value. After the procedure closes the file, the text boxes on the form are filled with the contents of the field variables. Finally, the record counters are updated. If the number entered into the input box text box is greater than the total number of records, an error message appears.

WRITING RECORDS TO A RANDOM ACCESS FILE

Writing a record to a random access file reverses the process of reading a record from the file. In the example shown here, you can add a new record to the file by entering information in the text boxes on the form and then clicking the **Save Record** button. Figure 5.11 shows the entry for what will be the seventh record in the file.

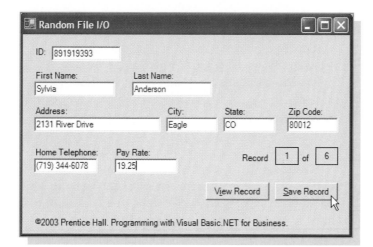

FIGURE 5.11. *Form displaying data entered for a new record*

Clicking the **Save Record** button displays a message box for specifying whether to save this as a new record or as an edit to an existing record. The procedure then writes the record to the *Employees.txt* file and updates the record counters. Figure 5.12 shows the form after the new record has been saved to the file.

Notice that the record counter indicates that the form is currently displaying the first of six records. This means the Save Record button has not yet been clicked.

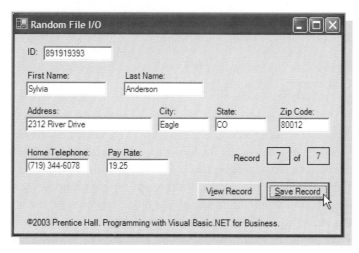

FIGURE 5.12. *Form displaying a new record that has been written to the file*

Here's the code for the button's click event:

```
Private Sub btnSaveRecord_Click(ByVal sender As System.Object,
  ByVal e As System.EventArgs) Handles btnSaveRecord.Click
    'Determine the save procedure - add a new record or edit the
      current record
    Dim intResponse As Integer
    intResponse = MsgBox("Are you adding a new record or editing
      the current record? Click 'Yes' to add a new record, 'No'
      to make changes to the current record, or 'Cancel' to
      cancel this procedure.", MsgBoxStyle.YesNoCancel, "Edit
      or Create a Record")
    If intResponse = 6 Then
        intCurrentRecord = Val(lblTotalRecords.Text) + 1
    Else
        intCurrentRecord = Val(lblCurrentRecord.Text)
    End If

    'Obtain record data to write
    udtEmployees.intNumber = intCurrentRecord
    udtEmployees.strEmpID = txtEmpID.Text
    udtEmployees.strLastName = txtLastName.Text
    udtEmployees.strFirstName = txtFirstName.Text
    udtEmployees.strAddress = txtAddress.Text
    udtEmployees.strCity = txtCity.Text
    udtEmployees.strState = txtState.Text
    udtEmployees.strZipCode = txtZipCode.Text
    udtEmployees.strHomePhone = txtHomePhone.Text
    udtEmployees.sngPayRate = Val(txtPayRate.Text)

    'Open the file and write the record
    FileOpen(1, "a:\Employees.txt", OpenMode.Random,
      OpenAccess.ReadWrite, OpenShare.Shared, Len(udtEmployees))
    FilePut(1, udtEmployees, intCurrentRecord)
    intTotalRecords = LOF(1) / Len(udtEmployees)
    FileClose(1)

    'Update Record Counters
    lblCurrentRecord.Text = intCurrentRecord
    lblTotalRecords.Text = intTotalRecords
End Sub
```

The procedure begins by determining whether the record to save is a new record or edits to an existing record. If the text boxes contain data for a new record and the user clicks the **Yes** button, the *intCurrentRecord* variable is incremented by 1 so the new record has a record number that is one more than the total number of records. If the user clicks **No**, the record number is set to the current record so the procedure can update information for the current record. The procedure then assigns the text entries in the text box controls on the form to the field variables of the *udtInventory* structure variable. The data file is opened for random access, and the procedure writes the record to the file. The value of the *intTotalRecords* variable is recalculated by dividing the length of the file by the length of each record to determine the total number of records. The record counters are then updated as necessary.

As you can see, sequential and random file access methods are useful for reading data into a program from a data file or writing data from a program to a data file. Depending on the kind of data your program uses, either sequential or random access will be the best choice.

As you develop programs for reading from and writing to data files, certain errors might happen. If you attempt to write text to a file on an unformatted disk, a run-time error will occur. Let's learn how to anticipate and handle file input and output (I/O) errors.

Processing I/O Errors by Using Exceptions

As you create applications with Visual Basic.NET, you need to be aware of the actions that cause an application to fail and generate an error. The following kinds of errors are common in Visual Basic.NET. *Compile errors* are errors in the program code that prevent the application from running. You can use the Visual Basic.NET debugging tools to isolate and correct compile errors. *Logic errors* occur in formulas or calculations; the application runs, but it produces inaccurate information. Careful program planning and design can assist in eliminating logic errors.

Run-time errors cause an application to halt when it is running. Run-time errors can result from attempting to perform impossible calculations, such as dividing by zero. For file input and output, run-time errors are usually associated with referencing an invalid drive letter, attempting to read to or write from a file that does not exist, or trying to read from or write to a floppy disk when the drive is empty.

Your programs must be able to uniformly handle any errors that occur during run time. In Visual Basic.NET, an *exception* is any error condition or unexpected behavior that occurs in a procedure during run time. If a procedure raises an error, it is said to "throw an exception."

In Chapter 3 you learned about decision structures. The Try… Catch… Finally statement is designed to handle the exceptions thrown by an error.

USING THE TRY… CATCH… FINALLY STATEMENT TO HANDLE I/O EXCEPTIONS

As an example of handling file I/O errors, let's look at the program that reads data from a sequential file. A common run-time error is attempting to open a file when a disk is not in the drive. Here's a procedure that attempts to open a file and read the text sequentially.

```
FileOpen(1, "A:\MyFile.txt", OpenMode.Input)
txtFile.Text = InputString(1, LOF(1))
FileClose(1)
```

If a file named *MyFile.txt* does not exist on drive A, or if a disk is not in the drive, the error message shown in Figure 5.13 will appear when you attempt to read the file.

FIGURE 5.13. *Error message indicating a run-time error*

In this case, Visual Basic.NET throws an exception to indicate the error, meaning that the application has encountered an exception not handled in the application's code.

Because there are no code statements to handle the exception, the error message states that the exception is unhandled.

Visual Basic.NET supports ***structured exception handling***, which is a method for creating applications that catch and handle exceptions. Structured exception handling refers to the code structures you write to detect and respond to exceptions raised by errors. In Visual Basic.NET, the Try… Catch… Finally statement uses a decision structure to handle a thrown exception. The following procedure is from the *Exception Handling* solution included with your data files:

```
Private Sub mnuFileOpen_Click(ByVal sender As System.Object,
  ByVal e As System.EventArgs) Handles mnuFileOpen.Click
    Try
        FileOpen(1, "A:\MyFile.txt", OpenMode.Input)
        txtFile.Text = InputString(1, LOF(1))
    Catch Err As System.IO.IOException
        MsgBox("The file does not exist or a disk is not in the
            drive. Please place a disk containing the file
            'MyFile.txt' in Drive A: and try again.",
            MsgBoxStyle.Critical, "File Error!")
    Finally
        FileClose(1)
    End Try
End Sub
```

The **Try** statement attempts to open the file and read its contents into the text box. The **Catch** statement handles an exception that is thrown and displays an error message. If the **Try** statement is successful in reading the file, the **Finally** statement executes and closes the file. Figure 5.14 shows the message that appears when a disk is not in the drive and the exception is handled.

FIGURE 5.14. *Message box for handling an exception*

If the user clicks **OK**, places a disk with the file in the drive, and clicks **File**, **Open**, the file opens without error.

Now that you know how to handle file I/O errors, let's look at other methods for opening and saving files.

In the examples shown so far for opening files for reading and writing data, the code statements refer to the name and file location of the data file referenced in the procedure. This works if you need to open only a single file for access and the location of the file never changes. If you need to open more than one file for access or the location of a file changes, you can include predefined dialog boxes for opening and saving files in your programs.

Visual Basic.NET also supports the On Error statement for error handling, which is the message supported in previous versions of Visual Basic. To learn how to use the On Error statement to handle errors, complete the *On Error* case study at the end of this chapter.

Adding Common Dialog Boxes to Windows Forms

Windows applications almost always include dialog boxes for obtaining user information. A ***dialog box*** is a window that appears on the screen and presents users with one or more options. You can create your own dialog boxes by creating a form with a **Borderstyle** property of **FixedDialog** and then adding the appropriate controls to the form.

You can also take advantage of the common dialog boxes included in Visual Basic.NET and easily add these to your applications. A ***common dialog box*** is a predefined dialog box for performing useful functions such as opening and saving files, changing fonts, or printing. You add a ***common dialog control*** to a Windows form to display a common dialog box. When you add a common dialog control to a form, the functionality for completing the task is contained in the control. There are specific advantages to using common dialog controls in your programs. First, program development is simpler, because the functionality for the dialog boxes has already been created and you do not need to write this code. Second, the dialog boxes have a layout and include controls that are consistent with other programs that run in the Windows operating system. Finally, predefined dialog boxes allow you to reuse program components that have been created previously and preconfigured.

Common dialog controls are available on the Windows Forms tab in the Toolbox. Table 5.1 lists the predefined Visual Basic.NET dialog box controls you can add to your applications.

Table 5.1: Predefined dialog controls in Visual Basic.NET

Control Name	What the Control Does
ColorDialog	Allows users to select a color from a palette in a predefined dialog box or add custom colors to the color palette.
FontDialog	Lists the fonts that are currently installed on the system. Useful for changing the text property of text box and rich text box controls.
OpenFileDialog	Allows users to open files for reading by using a preconfigured dialog box.
PageSetupDialog	Sets page details for printing via a preconfigured dialog box.
PrintDialog	Selects a printer, chooses the pages to print, and determines other print-related settings.
PrintPreviewDialog	Displays a document as it will appear when it is printed.
SaveFileDialog	Allows users to open files for writing by using a preconfigured dialog box.

By using standard Windows dialog boxes in your applications, you provide basic functionality familiar to users. Let's look at the three commonly used predefined dialog boxes and how to add them to Windows forms.

USING THE OPENFILEDIALOG CONTROL

The ***OpenFileDialog*** control displays a dialog box on the screen for browsing and opening files. This control uses the ***StreamReader object*** to read a stream of characters sequentially from a file. To open a file by using the OpenFileDialog control, you must first declare a StreamReader object variable. The StreamReader object derives its functionality from the ***System.IO namespace***, which includes classes that provide an access layer for reading and writing to I/O devices such as drives and printers.

Let's look at an example. Figure 5.15 shows a Windows form for opening and saving sequential text files. This solution is in the *FileStreamIO* folder included with your data files.

To use the System.IO classes, you must include the following statement at the beginning of your code:
`Imports System.IO`

FIGURE 5.15. *Form for opening and saving sequential files*

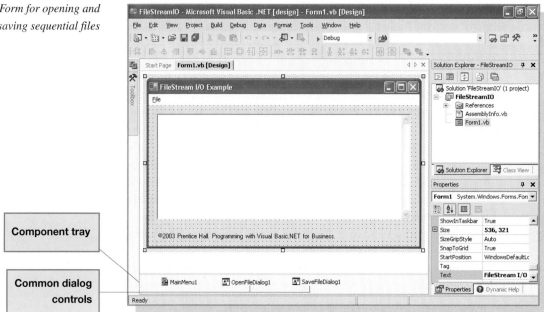

Component tray

Common dialog controls

The procedures for opening and saving data files are contained in the **File** menu. Notice that the *OpenFileDialog1* and *SaveFileDialog1* controls do not appear on the form but below the form in an area of the IDE called the ***component tray***. This area of the Windows Form Designer displays controls that do not appear at run time but need to be available at design time for setting their properties. For example, the component tray shown in Figure 5.15 contains three common dialog controls.

The **File** menu contains the **Open** menu item for opening files. Clicking **File**, **Open** displays the dialog box in Figure 5.16.

FIGURE 5.16. *Common dialog box for opening a file*

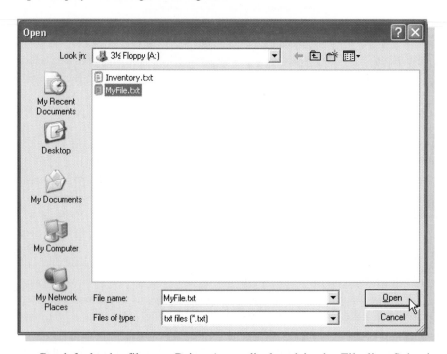

By default, the files on Drive A are displayed in the File list. Selecting the *MyFile.txt* file and clicking **Open** reads the contents of the text file into the text box on the screen, as shown in Figure 5.17.

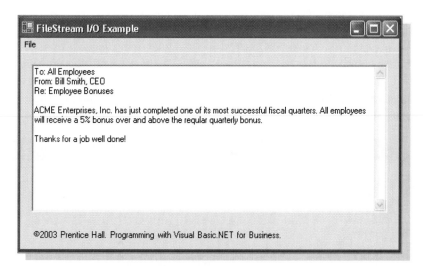

FIGURE 5.17. *Contents of a text file displayed in a text box*

Let's look at the code for displaying the dialog box.

```
Private Sub mnuFileOpen_Click(ByVal sender As System.Object,
    ByVal e As System.EventArgs) Handles mnuFileOpen.Click


'Set drive and file type defaults
OpenFileDialog1().Filter = "txt files (*.txt)|*.txt"
OpenFileDialog1().InitialDirectory = "A:\"


'Open the selected file
    If OpenFileDialog1().ShowDialog() = DialogResult().OK Then
        Dim strStream As Stream
        strStream = OpenFileDialog1().OpenFile()
        Dim strReader As New StreamReader(strStream)
        txtFile.Text = strReader.ReadToEnd()
        txtFile.SelectionLength = 0
        strReader.Close()
    End If
End Sub
```

The procedure handles the click event for the *mnuFileOpen* menu item. The first statement sets the Filter property for the *OpenFileDialog1* control, so that only text files are displayed.

The StreamReader object has methods for handling the events the user generates by interacting with the controls displayed in the FileOpen dialog box. The procedure uses an If statement to display the dialog box. The ***ShowDialog method*** displays the dialog box. The DialogResult enumeration verifies that a file has been selected in the dialog box. The IF structure determines the file name selected in the **File Name:** text box. The procedure then declares two variables: one for the stream to read (*myStream*) and one for the stream reader object (*strReader*) that reads the stream contained in the *myStream* variable.

The ***ReadToEnd method*** reads the entire contents of the stream and assigns all characters in the stream to the text property of the *txtFile* text box. Setting the SelectionLength property of the text box to zero moves the cursor, placing it at the beginning of the text entry. The last statement in the procedure uses the ***Close method*** to close the stream reader and the file it opened.

For more information about the methods supported by the StreamReader object, search for *StreamReader* in the Help system and open the *StreamReader Members* topic.

USING THE SAVEFILEDIALOG CONTROL

Saving data from a text box to a text file is similar to reading text from a file. To write information to a file by using the SaveFileDialog control, the procedure uses the StreamWriter object variable. The solution shown in the preceding figures has a menu item for saving files. Figure 5.18 shows the dialog box that appears when a user clicks **File**, **Save As**.

FIGURE 5.18. *Common dialog box for saving files*

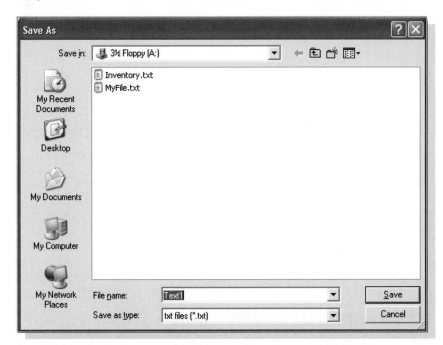

Now let's look at the code for the *mnuFileSaveAs* click event:

```
Private Sub mnuFileSaveAs_Click(ByVal sender As System.Object,
  ByVal e As System.EventArgs) Handles mnuFileSaveAs.Click
'Set drive, file type, and default file name
SaveFileDialog1.Filter = "txt files (*.txt)|*.txt"
SaveFileDialog1.OverwritePrompt = True
SaveFileDialog1.FileName = "Text1"

'Declare a variable for the file name
Dim strFileName As String

'Save the filestream to a text file
    If SaveFileDialog1.ShowDialog() = DialogResult.OK Then
        strFileName = SaveFileDialog1.FileName

        Dim myStream As New FileStream(strFileName,
          OpenMode.Output)
        Dim strWriter As New StreamWriter(myStream)
        strWriter.Write(txtFile.Text)
        strWriter.Close()
    End If
End Sub
```

The first three statements set the defaults for the *SaveFileDialog1* object. The **Filter** property displays text files. The **OverWritePrompt** property uses a Boolean value to determine if the file already exists. If the Boolean value is True, a message appears, warning that the existing file will be overwritten. The third statement uses the **FileName** property to set a default file name of *Text1*. This default file name will appear whenever the **Save As** menu item is selected.

The If… Then block for the procedure is similar to the block of statements used for a StreamReader object. The ***StreamWriter object*** writes a stream of characters to a file opened in output or append mode. As in the previous example, the procedure declares two variables: one for the stream to write (*myStream*) and one for the stream writer object (*strWriter*) variable. The StreamWriter object uses the ***Write method*** to write the contents of the *txtFile* text box to the open file. After the contents are written to the file, the Close method closes the StreamWriter object and the text file.

As you can see, using common dialog controls for reading and writing data provides significant advantages. Now let's explore the common dialog control for changing the font in a program.

USING THE FONTDIALOG CONTROL

Another useful predefined dialog box in Visual Basic.NET is the ***FontDialog control***, which displays a dialog box with a list of the fonts currently installed on the system. This dialog box is useful for displaying formatted text in controls on a form. Figure 5.19 displays a form with a **Font** menu item for displaying a Font dialog box.

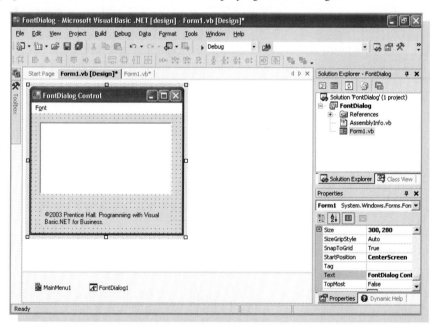

FIGURE 5.19. *Form for changing the font settings*

This form is from the *FontDialog* solution included with your data files. Now let's see the dialog box the control displays. Figure 5.20 shows the dialog box that appears after you click the **Font** menu.

Figure 5.20. *The Font common dialog box*

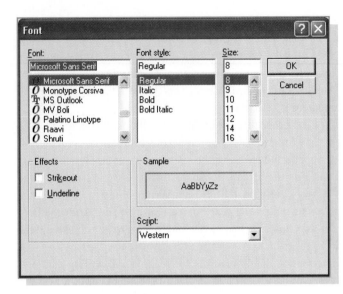

The code for changing the font property of the text box is as follows:

```
Private Sub MenuItemFont_Click(ByVal sender As System.Object,
  ByVal e As System.EventArgs) Handles mnuFont.Click
    If FontDialog1.ShowDialog() <> DialogResult.Cancel Then
        txtText.Font = FontDialog1.Font
    End If
End Sub
```

The routine uses an If… Then block to verify that the **Cancel** button has not been selected and then assigns the selected font to the **Font** property of the text box control.

As you can see, the code for changing the Font property of a text box control at run time is very simple, because the common dialog control does most of the work. In this example, the font changes are not written to the file, because plain text files (also called ASCII files) do not contain information regarding font attributes. To save font settings, you need to use a RichTextBox control, which is described later in this chapter.

EXCEPTIONS AND COMMON DIALOG CONTROLS

One advantage of using predefined dialog boxes in your applications is that much of the error handling occurs behind the scenes. Consider the following procedure:

```
Private Sub mnuFileOpen_Click(ByVal sender As System.Object,
  ByVal e As System.EventArgs) Handles mnuFileOpen.Click

'Set drive and file type defaults
OpenFileDialog1().Filter = "txt files (*.txt)|*.txt"
OpenFileDialog1().InitialDirectory = "A:\"

'Open the selected file
    If OpenFileDialog1().ShowDialog() = DialogResult().OK Then
        Dim strStream As Stream
```

```
        strStream = OpenFileDialog1().OpenFile()
        Dim strReader As New StreamReader(strStream)
        txtFile.Text = strReader.ReadToEnd()
        txtFile.SelectionLength = 0
        strReader.Close()
    End If
End Sub
```

This code should look familiar; it is from the *FileStreamIO* solution. The procedure uses an **OpenFileDialog control** for specifying the file to open. If a disk is not in the drive, the message shown in Figure 5.21 appears.

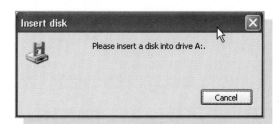

FIGURE 5.21. *Error message generated by a common dialog control*

If you place a disk in the drive, the procedure continues. If you click **Cancel**, the default directory changes to the system default, and the procedure continues.

Now that you have learned how to use common dialog controls for reading and writing simple text data, let's learn how to read and write formatted text.

Using the RichTextBox Control for Reading and Writing Formatted Text

Visual Basic.NET includes a control for reading, writing, and displaying formatted text. The ***RichTextBox control*** is typically used to provide text manipulation and display features similar to word processing applications such as Microsoft Word. It can also be used to create and edit Rich Text Format (RTF) files. ***Rich Text Format (RTF)*** is a file format that adds codes, or ***tags*** (also called tokens), to plain text to change the way the text appears. Microsoft Word and other applications support the RTF markup language. Here's an example of the first few lines of a file with the RTF markups that indicate how the data is displayed:

```
{\rtf1\ansi\ansicpg1252\deff0\deflang1033\deflangfe1033{\fonttbl
  {\f0\fscript\fprq2\fcharset0 Comic Sans
  MS;}{\f1\fnil\fcharset0 Trebuchet MS;}}
{\colortbl;\red51\green51\blue153;\red0\green128\blue0;}
\viewkind4\uc1\pard\cf1\b\f0\fs20\'a92003 Prentice Hall\par
Programming with Visual Basic.NET for Business\par
Chapter 5: File Access, Dialog Boxes, Error Handling, and

Menus\par \cf0\b0\par
This is an example of a Rich Text Format (RTF) document.}
```

Figure 5.22 shows a form with a RichTextBox control displaying RTF text. This solution is in the *RichText IO* folder included with your data files.

FIGURE 5.22. *Form with a RichTextBox control*

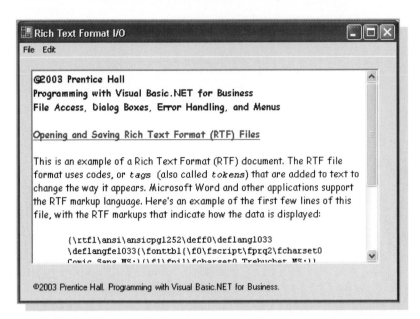

When naming a rich text box control, add the *rtxt* four-character designation to the control name to differentiate the control from a text box control. You can use the RichTextBox control in conjunction with the OpenFileDialog and SaveFileDialog controls to read and write RTF files. You can set the Filter method to display RTF files and then use the LoadFile method to read the contents of an RTF file. Here's the code for reading text from an RTF file into a RichTextBox control:

```
Private Sub mnuFileOpen_Click(ByVal sender As System.Object,
   ByVal e As System.EventArgs) Handles mnuFileOpen.Click
OpenFileDialog1().Filter = "RTF files (*.rtf)|*.rtf"
OpenFileDialog1().InitialDirectory = "A:\"

    If OpenFileDialog1().ShowDialog() = DialogResult().OK Then
        rtxtFile.LoadFile(OpenFileDialog1.FileName,
        RichTextBoxStreamType.RichText)
    End If
End Sub
```

This procedure is similar to the procedure shown earlier for reading text from a plain ASCII file. The Filter property displays only RTF files in the file list, and the next statement sets the initial directory to drive A. The IF structure determines the file name selected in the **File Name:** text box. After you select a file and click the **Open** menu item, the control uses the LoadFile method to load a rich text stream into the control.

As you can see, reading an RTF file into a rich text box control is virtually identical to reading a text file into a text box control. Both tasks use sequential file access to read a file stream from a data file and assign the file stream to the Text property of the appropriate control. The data in the control does differ; text box controls display plain text, and rich text box controls display RTF data.

Now let's look at the code for writing text entered into a rich text box control to an RTF data file. Here's the code for the *mnuFileSaveAs* menu item:

What kind of file access does this procedure use?

```
Private Sub mnuFileSaveAs_Click(ByVal sender As System.Object,
     ByVal e As System.EventArgs) Handles mnuFileSaveAs.Click
SaveFileDialog1.Filter = "RTF Files|*.rtf"
SaveFileDialog1.OverwritePrompt = True
SaveFileDialog1.FileName = "RichText1"

    If SaveFileDialog1.ShowDialog() = DialogResult.OK Then
        rtxtFile.SaveFile(SaveFileDialog1.FileName,
            RichTextBoxStreamType.RichText)
    End If
End Sub
```

In this example, the file is written in RTF format. The Filter property sets the default file type to RTF. When a file is selected and the File, **Save As** menu item is clicked, the procedure uses the *SaveFile method* to write a rich text stream to the file.

Now that you know how to read and write RTF data, let's see how to change the font attributes of the text contained in a rich text box control.

CHANGING FONT ATTRIBUTES IN A RICHTEXTBOX CONTROL

Rich text displays font attributes such as the font, font style, size, color, and effects. Figure 5.23 shows the Font dialog box that appears after the user clicks the **Edit**, **Font** menu item.

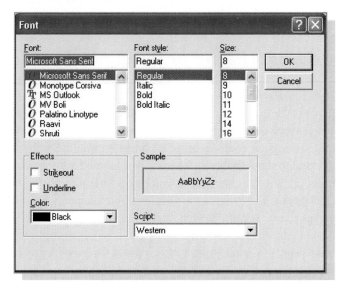

FIGURE 5.23. *Font dialog box for changing the font attributes in a rich text box control*

The following code handles the mnuEditFont click event:

```
Private Sub mnuEditFont_Click(ByVal sender As System.Object,
  ByVal e As System.EventArgs) Handles mnuEditFont.Click

    FontDialog1.ShowColor = True

    If FontDialog1.ShowDialog() <> DialogResult.Cancel Then
        rtxtFile.SelectionFont = FontDialog1.Font
        rtxtFile.SelectionColor = FontDialog1.Color
    End If
  End Sub
```

Figure 5.24 shows the result of changing the Font attributes for the text contained in a rich text box control. For this example, we opened the *RichText.rtf* file included with your data files, selected all the text, and set the font to Tahoma, 14 point, Maroon.

FIGURE 5.24. *Changing the font attributes in a rich text box control*

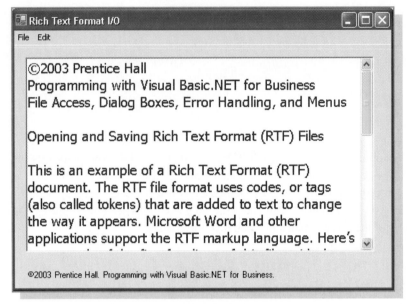

If you write this text to an RTF data file, the formats are retained.

Now that you know how to read and write plain text and RTF data and how to use common dialog controls to simplify and standardize the design of your programs, you can make your application even easier to use by adding menus.

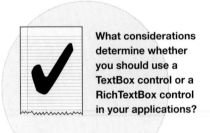

What considerations determine whether you should use a TextBox control or a RichTextBox control in your applications?

Adding Menus to Windows Forms

How you design your Visual Basic.NET applications with the Windows Form Designer impacts the usability of your applications. A computer screen is a relatively small design space for presenting your application's interface to users. *Interface design* refers to designing the components of a computer program with which a user will interact. The design should adhere to specific design standards, be visually appealing, and make using the program intuitive. Menus are a vital part of the user interface in Windows applications. The Windows applications you frequently use contain a menu bar, and the menus follow specific design standards. For example, the File menu is normally the menu farthest to the left at the top of the screen. If an application includes a Help menu, it is usually the menu farthest to the right at the top of the screen. A *menu* is a graphical element that contains associated commands. A menu holds *menu items* that are grouped by a common theme—for example, File commands such as Open, Save As, and Exit. Figure 5.25 shows a File menu with three menu items.

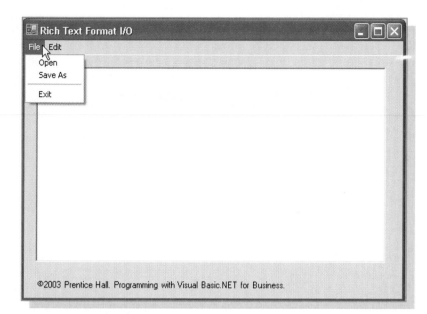

FIGURE 5.25. *A File menu containing three menu items*

As your applications become more advanced and complex, you will want to group related commands in menus. Let's look at how to create and add menus to Windows forms with a simple three-step process.

Creating and Adding Menus to Windows Forms

In Visual Basic.NET, you create a menu on a Windows form by adding a *MainMenu control* to the form. After adding this control, you can create one or more menu items at design time. Visual Studio.NET includes a tool called the *Menu Designer* that you use to create menus. Creating menus with the Menu Designer is a three-step process:

1. Add a MainMenu control to a form.
2. Add menu items to the MainMenu control.
3. Write code to handle each menu item's MenuItem.Click event.

Let's look at each of these steps in more detail.

ADDING A MAINMENU OBJECT TO A FORM

The *RichText IO* solution shown in Figure 5.25 contains a MainMenu control, a File menu with three menu items, and an Edit menu with one menu item. None of the applications in previous chapters contained menus.

The **MainMenu control** is the container for the menus and menu items on a form. The MainMenu control is available as a tool in the Toolbox. To add a menu to a form, select the tool and drag a main menu onto the form, as shown in Figure 5.26. By default, the control is named MainMenu1.

FIGURE 5.26. *Adding a MainMenu control to a form*

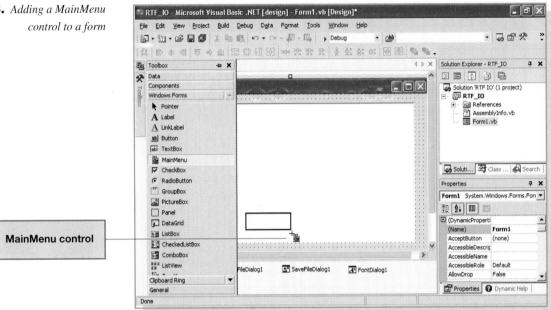

The MainMenu object does not appear on the form but below the form in the component tray. Notice that the component tray shown in Figure 5.26 contains three common dialog controls. These are not visible when the application is running but have properties that can be set at design time.

After you add the MainMenu control to the form, click the **Menu** property row for the form and select **MainMenu1** from the list. This sets the MainMenu control as the menu for the form.

USING THE MAINMENU CONTROL

After you add a MainMenu control to a form, you can add menu items to the MainMenu control by typing in the areas marked "Type Here." Figure 5.27 shows a menu item added to the MainMenu control.

FIGURE 5.27. *Adding a menu item to the MainMenu control*

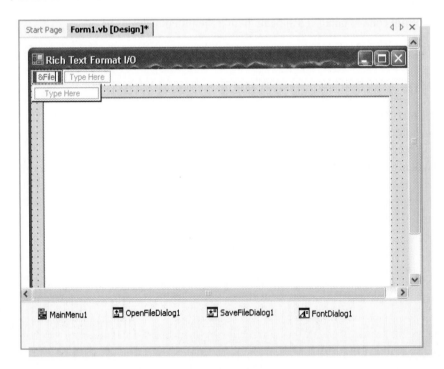

In this example, one menu item, File, has been added. You can use the ampersand character (&) with menu items just as you do with buttons to identify the accelerator key for the menu. Once you have added an item, you can add additional submenu items under that existing item or create another menu item at the same menu item level.

As you add menu items to the MainMenu control, Visual Basic.NET gives each menu item a default name of MenuItem1, MenuItem2, and so forth. To change a menu item's default name, select the menu item and change its name property. Precede the names of menu items with the three-character *mnu* designation. A File-menu item's name would be *mnuFile*. As you add submenu items under an existing menu item, start the submenu item's name with the *mnu* designation followed by the name of the parent (original) menu item and the new submenu item's name. For example, in the **File** menu, the **Open** submenu item's name would be *mnuFileOpen*. This application contains the following two menu items and four submenu items:

mnuFile   mnuEdit

mnuFileOpen   mnuEditFont

mnuFileSaveAs

mnuFileExit

You can add a separator line between groups of menu items. ***Separator lines*** organize the menu items contained in a menu. The **File** menu shown in Figure 5.25 contains a separator line before the **Exit** menu item. To add a separator line above a menu item, click the MainMenu control in the component tray, select the menu item, right-click, and select **Insert Separator**. Figure 5.28 shows a separator line being added above the **Exit** menu item in the Rich Text Format IO solution.

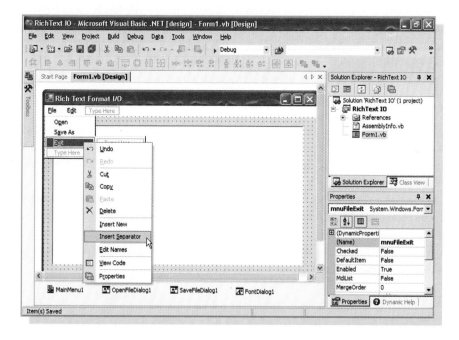

FIGURE 5.28. *Adding a separator line above a menu item*

WRITING CODE TO HANDLE MENU-ITEM CLICK EVENTS

The final step in adding menus to a Windows form is writing the code to handle the menu-item click events. You can access the click event for a menu item in the same way that you access the click event for any other object belonging to a form: by double-clicking the object. Figure 5.29 displays the code for the click event handled by the mnuFileOpen click event, which will display a common dialog box that filters RTF files.

FIGURE 5.29. *Code for the mnuFileOpen click event*

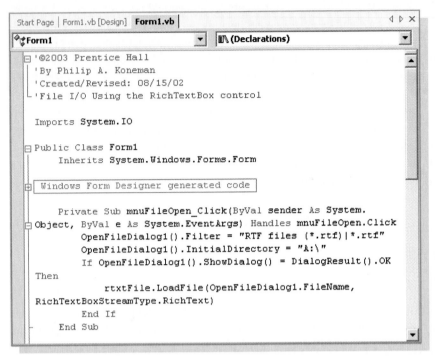

```
Start Page | Form1.vb [Design]  Form1.vb                                    ◁ ▷ ×
Form1                              ▼    (Declarations)                         ▼

   '©2003 Prentice Hall
   'By Philip A. Koneman
   'Created/Revised: 08/15/02
   'File I/O Using the RichTextBox control

   Imports System.IO

   Public Class Form1
       Inherits System.Windows.Forms.Form

   Windows Form Designer generated code

       Private Sub mnuFileOpen_Click(ByVal sender As System.
   Object, ByVal e As System.EventArgs) Handles mnuFileOpen.Click
           OpenFileDialog1().Filter = "RTF files (*.rtf)|*.rtf"
           OpenFileDialog1().InitialDirectory = "A:\"
           If OpenFileDialog1().ShowDialog() = DialogResult().OK
   Then
               rtxtFile.LoadFile(OpenFileDialog1.FileName,
   RichTextBoxStreamType.RichText)
           End If
       End Sub
```

Each menu item has properties you can set at design time or run time. You can disable a menu item when an application initially starts by setting the **Enabled** property to False. For example, if an application contains a File menu with both Save and Save As menu items, the Save As menu should be disabled until a file has been saved by using the Save menu. Or, for menus that allow users to make selections that change the application's interface options, you can add a check mark for the default settings by setting the **Checked** property of these menu items to **True**.

ADDING A CONTEXT MENU TO A FORM

Most Windows applications include context menus as a shortcut for performing common tasks. A context menu is a menu that appears when you right-click over a control. Visual Basic.NET includes the ***ContextMenu control*** for creating context menus.

To add a context menu to a form, you must first add a ContextMenu control to the form. A ContextMenu control is similar to a MainMenu control; when you add a ContextMenu control to a form, it appears in the component tray. You can add menu items to a context menu by using the Menu Designer. Figure 5.30 displays the menu items for a context menu control.

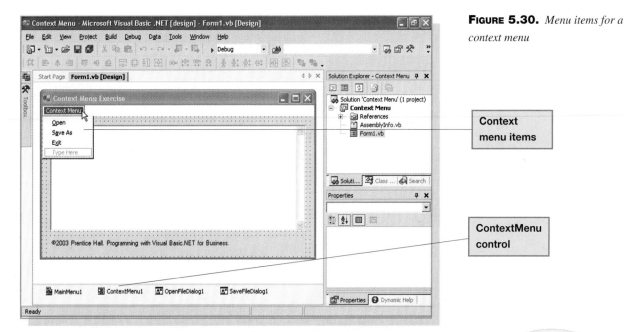

FIGURE 5.30. *Menu items for a context menu*

To use a context menu on a form, the ContextMenu property for the form must display the name of the ContextMenu control. This sets the context menu displayed on the form.

Now that you have learned about accessing data in files, handling exceptions, and adding common dialog controls and menus to your forms, let's go through an example that applies each of these concepts in a single application.

Although the context menu appears at the top of the form at design time, the context menu will appear at the location where the user right-clicks the form at run time.

☞ HANDS-ON PROGRAMMING EXAMPLE

Creating a Text Editor application

Many business applications include a text editor for creating and revising text data. As a professional, you might need to use a text editor to revise an HTML document, create an initialization file, or write custom files for printing a batch of receipts. Windows includes Notepad as the standard text editor of choice and also includes WordPad, with which you can create RTF files. The application you will create is a text editor for reading and writing simple text as well as RTF text. Figure 5.31 displays the interface for the *Enhanced Text Editor* application.

FIGURE 5.31. *The Enhanced Text Editor application*

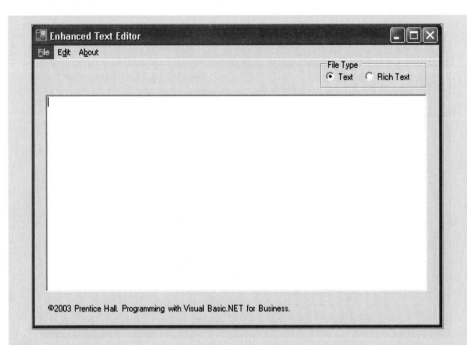

The Enhanced Text Editor supports the following functionality:

1. Reads and writes both ASCII and RTF files.
2. Contains a group box control with radio buttons for specifying the file type (ASCII or RTF format).
3. Has a MainMenu control with menu items for all functionality: reading and writing files, changing font attributes, displaying an About form, and exiting the application.

Plan the Application

The first step in planning an application is determining the inputs and outputs. The Enhanced Text Editor is designed for creating, opening, modifying, and saving text and Rich Text files. The inputs and outputs are as follows:

Inputs	Outputs
Text (entered on the keyboard)	Text files
Text (read from a file)	RTF files

The application uses the OpenFileDialog, SaveFileDialog, and FontDialog common dialog controls. A MainMenu control contains three menu items: File, Edit, and About. The File menu contains three submenu items: Open, Save As, and Exit. The Edit menu contains one submenu item: Font. The About menu item displays the About form. Table 5.2 lists the controls and properties of the form.

Table 5.2: *Objects and properties for the Enhanced Text Editor application*

Object	Property	Setting
Form1	Text StartPosition Size Menu	Enhanced Text Editor CenterScreen 585, 400 MainMenu1
MainMenu	Name	MenuItem1
mnuFile	Text	&File
mnuFileOpen	Text	O&pen
mnuFileSaveAs	Text	S&ave As
mnuFileExit	Text	E&xit
mnuEdit	Text	E&dit
mnuEditFont	Text	F&ont
mnuAbout	Text	A&bout
OpenFileDialog	Name	OpenFileDialog1
SaveFileDialog	Name	SaveFileDialog1
FontDialog	Name	FontDialog1
rtxtFile	Text	
grpFileType	Text	File Type
rdbText	Text Checked TabStop TabIndex	Text True True 0
rdbButtonRTF	Text TabStop TabIndex	Rich Text True 1
lblCopyright	Text	©2003 Prentice Hall. Programming with Visual Basic.NET for Business.

Draw a visual representation of the application on a blank piece of paper. Figure 5.32 shows a drawing of the user interface and the name of each control on the form.

FIGURE 5.32.

Interface for the Enhanced Text Editor application

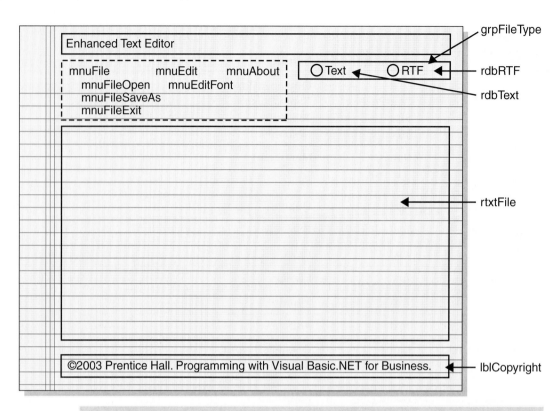

The form's primary features are the menu items and the rich text box for working with text. The radio buttons for specifying the file type determine if the file to be opened for reading and writing contains ASCII text or RTF text. The pseudocode for this functionality is shown in Table 5.3.

Table 5.3: *Pseudocode for the Enhanced Text Editor application*

Event Procedure	Action
mnuFileOpen_Click	1. Determine the file type. 2. Use the ShowDialog method to display the Open dialog box. 3. Open a filestream as text or RTF. 4. Read the filestream into the RichTextBox control.
mnuFileSaveAs_Click	1. Determine the file type. 2. Use the ShowDialog method to display the Save As dialog box. 3. Open a filestream as text or RTF. 4. Write the filestream into file opened for output.
mnuFileExit_Click	1. Verify user intent to terminate application. 2. Cancel or terminate.
mnuEditFont_Click	1. Use the ShowDialog method to display the Font dialog box. 2. Set the text property of the selected text to the font selected in the Font dialog box.
mnuAbout_Click	Display the About form.

Now that you have created the planning documents for the application, you are ready to begin designing the user interface.

Design the User Interface

If you have not launched Visual Studio.NET, do so now and set the Profile to Visual Studio Developer. Create a new Visual Basic.NET Windows Application project named `Enhanced Text Editor`. Set the properties for the form as listed in Table 5.2. Complete each of the following tasks to create the application.

To add controls to the form:

1. Use the Toolbox to add a MainMenu control to the form. Accept *MainMenu1* as the name for this control.
2. Create the menu items and settings listed in Table 5.2. Right-click the *mnuFileExit* menu item and select **Insert Separator**, as shown in Figure 5.33, to add a separator line between the **Save As** and **Exit** menu items.

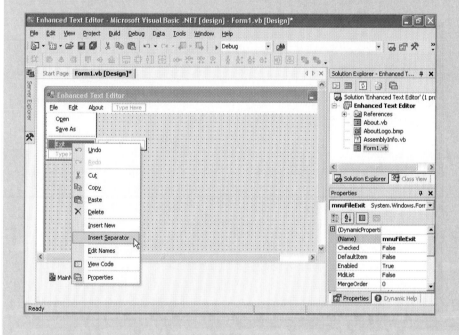

FIGURE 5.33. *Adding a separator to the MainMenu1 control*

3. Click the lower scroll button on the Windows Forms tab in the Toolbox until the OpenFileDialog, SaveFileDialog, and FontDialog controls are visible.
4. Drag an OpenFileDialog control onto the form, as shown in Figure 5.34. Repeat the procedure to add SaveFileDialog and FontDialog controls to the form.

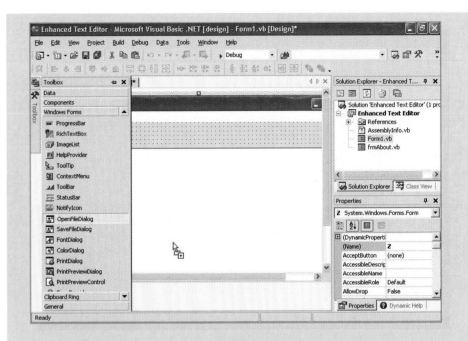

5. Add a GroupBox control to the form and add two RadioButton controls inside the group box. Set the properties for these controls as specified in Table 5.2.

6. Add a RichTextBox control to the form. Name the control `rtxtFile` and delete the default setting for the Text property.

7. Add a Label control to the lower left corner of the form. Set the properties as specified in Table 5.2.

8. Click **Project**, **Add Existing Item**. Navigate to the folder containing your data files for this project and locate the *frmAbout.vb* form in the *About Form* folder. Click **Open**. The form is added to the Solution Explorer.

9. Click the **Save All** button to save your project.

Now that the interface design for the Enhanced Text Editor application is complete, you are ready to write the code providing the functionality.

Write the Code

Your first task is to add comments to the Code Editor and then import the System IO namespace. You will then create procedures for opening a file, saving a file, exiting the application, changing the font properties, and displaying the About form.

To add comments and import the System IO namespace:

1. Press F7 to display the Code Editor. If the Windows Form Designer generated code region is expanded, collapse it.

2. Place the insertion point at the beginning of the Code Editor.

3. Type the following code:

```
'©2003 Prentice Hall
'By [Enter your name]
'Created/Revised: [Enter the date]
'Enhanced Text Editor Application

Imports System.IO
```

To create a procedure that handles the mnuFileOpen_Click event:

1. Click the **Class Name drop-down** list and select *mnuFileOpen* from the list.
2. Click the **Method Name** list and select **Click**.
3. Type the following code for the procedure:

```
'Determine if File Type is Text
If rdbText.Checked = True Then


    'Set the default font, if a text file is opened after an RTF
     file has been loaded
    rtxtFile.Font = New Font("Courier New", 10,
      FontStyle.Regular)
    rtxtFile.SelectionColor = Color.Black


    'Open a text file and read contents into the rich text box
    OpenFileDialog1().Filter = "txt files (*.txt)|*.txt"
    OpenFileDialog1().InitialDirectory = "A:\"


    If OpenFileDialog1().ShowDialog() = DialogResult().OK Then
        Dim myStream As Stream
        myStream = OpenFileDialog1().OpenFile()
        Dim strReader As New StreamReader(myStream)
        rtxtFile().Text = strReader.ReadToEnd()
        rtxtFile().SelectionLength = 0
        strReader.Close()
    End If


Else
    'Open an RTF file and read contents into the rich text box
    OpenFileDialog1().Filter = "RTF files (*.rtf)|*.rtf"
    OpenFileDialog1().InitialDirectory = "A:\"


    If OpenFileDialog1().ShowDialog() = DialogResult().OK Then
        rtxtFile.LoadFile(OpenFileDialog1.FileName,
          RichTextBoxStreamType.RichText)
    End If
End If
```

To create a procedure that handles the mnuFileSaveAs_Click event:

1. Click the **Class Name drop-down** list and select *mnuFileSaveAs* from the list.
2. Click the **Method Name** list and select **Click**.
3. Type the following code for the procedure:

```
'Determine if File Type is Text
If rdbText.Checked = True Then


    'Open a text file for writing
    OpenFileDialog1().Filter = "txt files (*.txt)|*.txt"
```

```
            OpenFileDialog1().InitialDirectory = "A:\"
        If OpenFileDialog1().ShowDialog() = DialogResult().OK Then
            Dim myStream As Stream
            myStream = OpenFileDialog1().OpenFile()
            Dim strReader As New StreamReader(myStream)
            rtxtFile().Text = strReader.ReadToEnd()
            rtxtFile().SelectionLength = 0
            strReader.Close()
        End If

Else

        'Open an RTF file for writing
        SaveFileDialog1.Filter = "RTF Files|*.rtf"
        SaveFileDialog1.OverwritePrompt = True
        SaveFileDialog1.FileName = "RichText1"


    If SaveFileDialog1.ShowDialog() = DialogResult.OK Then
        rtxtFile.SaveFile(SaveFileDialog1.FileName,
            RichTextBoxStreamType.RichText)
    End If
End If
```

4. Save your changes.

Now that you have added procedures for reading and writing text and rich text data, you are ready to write the procedure for changing the font attributes in response to the MenuItemFont_Click event.

To create a procedure that handles the mnuEditFont_Click event:

1. Click the **Class Name drop-down** list and select *mnuEditFont* from the list.
2. Click the **Method Name** list and select **Click**.
3. Type the following code for the procedure:

```
FontDialog1.ShowColor = True

If FontDialog1.ShowDialog() <> DialogResult.Cancel Then
    rtxtFile.SelectionFont = FontDialog1.Font
    rtxtFile.SelectionColor = FontDialog1.Color
End If
```

To create a procedure that handles the MenuItemAbout_Click event:

1. Click the **Class Name drop-down** list and select *mnuAbout* from the list.
2. Click the **Method Name** list and select **Click**.
3. Type the following code for the procedure:

```
Dim ShowForm As frmAbout = New frmAbout()
ShowForm.ShowDialog()
```

To create a procedure that handles the mnuFileExit_Click event:

1. Click the **Class Name drop-down** list and select *mnuFileExit* from the list.
2. Click the **Method Name** list and select **Click**.
3. Type the following code for the procedure:

```
Dim intResponse As Integer
intResponse = MsgBox("Do you really want to exit this
   application?", 276, "Exit?")
If intResponse = 6 Then
     End
End If
```

Run the Application

You are now ready to run the Enhanced Text Editor application and test its functionality.

To run the application:

1. Click the Start button or press the F5 key to run the application.
2. Click **File**, **Open**. Text is the default file type and Drive A: is the default drive. Select the *MyText.txt* file and click **Open**.
3. The file is displayed as shown in Figure 5.35.

If your file list is different, navigate to the folder that contains the data files for this chapter.

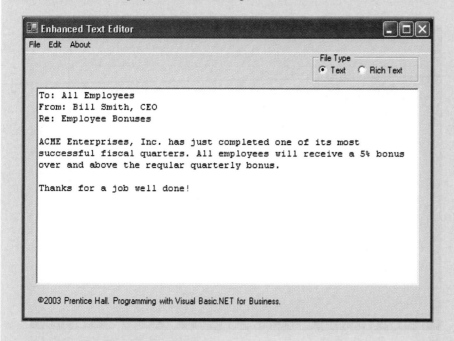

FIGURE 5.35. *Enhanced Text Editor displaying a plain text file*

4. Click the **Rich Text** radio button.
5. Click **File**, **Open**. Select the *EmployeeMemo.rtf* file and click **Open**. The form now looks like Figure 5.36.

FIGURE 5.36. *Enhanced Text Editor displaying a plain text file*

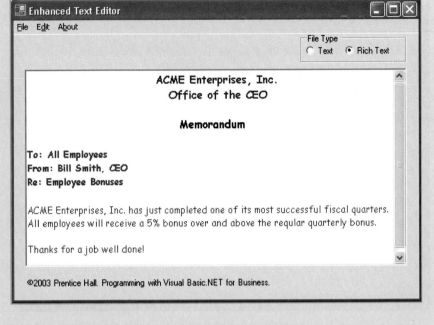

6. Click **About** and then click the **License Information** button in the *About* form. The application displays the *About* form shown in Figure 5.37.

FIGURE 5.37. *About form and license information for the Enhanced Text Editor application*

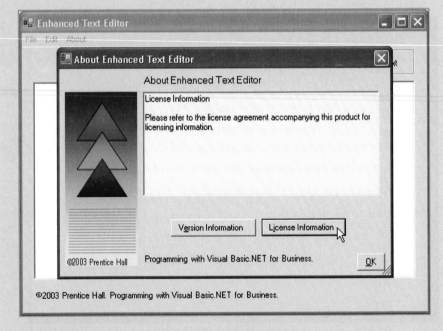

7. Select a portion of the text in the application and click **Edit**, **Font**. Apply different font styles to test this functionality.
8. Modify the file and save it with a different name to test the functionality of the **File**, **Save As** menu item.
9. If you make changes to the project, click the **Save All** button to save your changes.
10. Close the solution.

Summary

- Computers use two kinds of files. Program files are the applications that run on the computer. Data files store information for later use.

- Visual Basic.NET supports three kinds of file access: sequential, random, and binary. Sequential files store information as a continuous stream of information. Random files store information in fixed-length fields and records.

- You can use the FileOpen statement in a procedure to read data from a file opened in Input mode or to write data to a sequential file opened in Output or Append mode. Visual Basic.NET reads and writes a sequential file as a continuous stream of data.

- To read and write random access data, you must first declare a structure and then declare a structure variable with a data type of the structure. The structure defines the fields that comprise each record. The FileOpen command reads and writes individual records in the file.

- You can simplify your programs by adding common dialog controls to fulfill common tasks such as opening files (OpenFile Dialog), saving files (SaveFileDialog), and changing fonts (FontDialog).

- Programs that read and write data may produce run-time errors when there are problems opening a file. You can use the Try… Catch… Finally decision statement to handle exceptions that are thrown from run-time errors associated with file input and output.

- Visual Basic.NET supports the Rich Text Format (RTF) for displaying formatted text. You can use the rich text box control in your programs to read, write, and modify formatted Rich Text Format files.

- You can use the MainMenu control to add menus to a form. To add a menu, you add a MainMenu control to the form, add menu items to the menu by using the Menu Editor, and then write code statements to handle the menu events.

- You can use the ContextMenu control to add context menus to a form. A context menu will appear wherever the user right-clicks the form. You add a ContextMenu control to the form, define the menu items by using the Menu Editor, and then write code statements to handle the menu events.

Key Terms

append mode	input mode
Close method	InputString function
common dialog box	Interface design
common dialog control	Len function
compile errors	Length of File (LOF) function
component tray	logic errors
ContextMenu control	MainMenu control
data files	menu
dialog box	Menu Designer
End Structure keyword	menu items
exception	OpenFileDialog
field	output mode
field variables	Print function
FileClose function	program files
file input/output	random file access
file I/O	ReadToEnd method
FileOpen function	record
FontDialog control	Rich Text Format (RTF)

RichTextBox control

run-time errors

SaveFile method

Separator lines

sequential file access

ShowDialog Method

StreamReader object

StreamWriter object

Structure keyword

structure variable

structured data

structured exception handling

System.IO namespace

tags (tokens)

Try… Catch… Finally statement

user-defined data type (UDT)

Write method

Study Questions

Multiple-Choice Questions

1. Which control displays text containing tags that specify the text formats?
   a. TextBox
   b. Label
   c. FontDialog
   d. RichTextBox
   e. FileSaveDialog

2. Which of the following are *not* valid modes for the FileOpen statement?
   a. Input
   b. Structured
   c. Output
   d. Append
   e. None of these are valid.

3. Which statement is required before you can take advantage of the functionality provided by an OpenFileDialog or a SaveFileDialog control?
   a. Try… Catch… Finally
   b. FileClose
   c. Imports System.IO
   d. InputStream
   e. FileOpen

4. Which required argument is an integer value to specify the file opened for input?
   a. Mode
   b. FileNumber
   c. FileStream
   d. FileName
   e. InputStream

5. Which property determines whether the user is warned if a file opened for output already exists?
   a. FileOpen
   b. Filter
   c. Mode
   d. FileStream
   e. OverWriteMode

6. Which method must be included in a procedure before a SaveFileDialog control can be displayed?
   a. Visible
   b. SaveFileDialog
   c. Mode
   d. ShowDialog
   e. StreamWriter

7. Which property of a form must have a value other than None before a menu can be displayed?
   a. Enabled
   b. Text
   c. MenuItem
   d. Menu
   e. Visible

8. Which property determines what kinds of files to display in a dialog box?
   a. Mode
   b. Filter
   c. Visible
   d. Text
   e. LOF

9. Which function determines the number of characters contained in a file opened for input?
   a. InputStream
   b. FileOpen
   c. LOF
   d. FileClose
   e. LoadFile

10. Which control supports a list of program options when you right-click somewhere on a form or control?
    a. FileOpenDialog
    b. ContextMenu
    c. FontDialog
    d. SaveFileDialog
    e. MainMenu

True/False Questions

1. The FileOpenDialog is a common dialog control in Visual Studio.NET.

2. You can use the MainMenu control to display menu items on a form.

3. You can use the Try... Catch... Finally statement to handle errors associated with file input and output.

4. When you use the FileOpen command, you can open a file in any of five modes.

5. The System.IO namespace does not include a generic layer for file input and output functions.

Short Answer Questions

1. How does sequential file access differ from random file access?

2. What are the advantages of using predefined dialog box controls in your application?

3. What is the FileOpen statement, and how does its functionality differ from the OpenFileDialog and SaveFileDialog controls?

4. What is a menu item, and how does it differ from a MainMenu control?

5. When should you use a RichTextBox control rather than a TextBox control in your applications?

Guided Exercises

Adding a Menu to the Mileage Reimbursement Application

In Chapter 3 you created a Mileage Reimbursement application for converting distance expressed in miles and kilometers for mileage reimbursement. Currently, there are three buttons on the form for performing the conversion and exiting the application. In this exercise you will modify a version of this application by adding a MainMenu control to the form and writing procedures to handle the click events for the menu items. The menus have the following structure:

```
C&onvert    E&xit
    &Miles to Kilometers
    &Kilometers to Miles
```

The menu items have the following names:

```
mnuConvert
mnuConvertMtoK
mnuConvertKtoM
mnuExit
```

The application interface is shown in Figure 5.38.

FIGURE 5.38. *The Updated Mileage Reimbursement application*

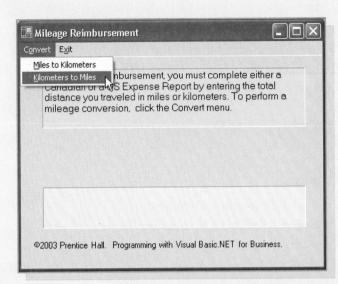

To create this application, complete the following steps:

1. Open the *Updated Mileage Reimbursement* solution included in your data files.

2. Add a MainMenu control to the form. Delete the buttons from the form.

3. Create the menu items described previously.

4. Enter the following code statements in the procedure that handles the *mnuConvertMtoK* click event:

```
'Obtain the distance traveled
sngDistance = Val(InputBox("Enter the distance you traveled… "))


'Perform data validation and the appropriate conversion
If sngDistance <= 0 Then
    MsgBox("The distance you entered is invalid; please try
        again.", MsgBoxStyle.Critical, "Invalid Distance")
Else
    sngResult = sngDistance * 1.609
    decReimbursement = sngResult * CanadaRate
    lblResult.Text = sngDistance & " miles is equal to " &
        Format(sngResult, "fixed") & " kilometers. Enter this
        distance and a reimbursement amount of " &
        Format(decReimbursement, "Currency") & " dollars Canadian
        on your Expense Report."
End If
```

5. Enter the following code statements in the procedure that handles the *mnuConvertKtoM* click event:

```
'Obtain the distance traveled
sngDistance = Val(InputBox("Enter the distance you traveled… "))

'Perform data validation and the appropriate conversion
If sngDistance <= 0 Then
    MsgBox("The distance you entered is invalid; please try
        again.", MsgBoxStyle.Critical, "Invalid Distance")
Else
sngResult = sngDistance * 0.621
```

```
decReimbursement = sngResult * USRate
lblResult.Text = sngDistance & " kilometers is equal to " &
    Format(sngResult, "fixed") & " miles. Enter this distance
    and a reimbursement amount of " &
    Format(decReimbursement, "Currency") & " US dollars on
    your Expense Report."
End If
```

6. Write a procedure to exit the application. This procedure should verify the user's intent to exit before terminating the application.

7. Save your changes.

8. Run the program and test its functionality. For verification purposes, 100 kilometers is equal to 62.1 miles.

Creating an Employee Address Book application

In this chapter you learned how to create a user-defined data type for storing records in a random access data file. In this exercise you will create a contact database that stores employee name and salary information.

The application is called **Employee Address Book**. It contains the following menus:

&Records   E&xit
               &Open Record
               &Save Record

You need to declare the following data structure:

```
Structure Employee
    Public intNumber As Integer
    <VBFixedString(20)> Public strLastName As String
    <VBFixedString(15)> Public strFirstName As String
    Public sngHourlyWage As Single
End Structure
```

The application interface is shown in Figure 5.39.

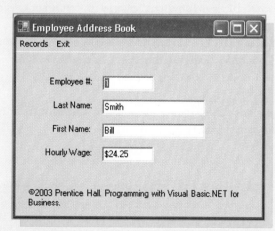

FIGURE 5.39. *The Employee Address Book application*

To create this application, complete the following steps:

1. Copy the *Addressbook.txt* file to a floppy disk.

2. Create a new Visual Basic Windows application project named `Address Book`.

3. Declare the data structure described earlier.

4. Add text box and label controls to the form for storing the Employee Number, Last Name, First Name, and Hourly Wage fields.

5. Add a MainMenu control to the form. Add the menu items listed earlier.

6. Declare the following form-level variables:

```
Public udtEmployee As Employee
Dim intTotalRecords, intCounter As Integer
```

7. Enter the following statements in the procedure that handles the menu item for opening a record:

```
intCounter = Val(txtNumber.Text)

If intCounter <= intTotalRecords Then
    FileOpen(1, "a:\AddressBook.txt", OpenMode.Random,
      OpenAccess.ReadWrite, OpenShare.Shared, Len(udtEmployee))
    FileGet(1, udtEmployee, intCounter)
    FileClose(1)

    txtNumber.Text = udtEmployee.intNumber
    txtLastName.Text = udtEmployee.strLastName
    txtFirstName.Text = udtEmployee.strFirstName
    txtHourlyWage.Text = udtEmployee.sngHourlyWage

Else
    MsgBox("This record number does not exist. Please try
      again.", MsgBoxStyle.Critical, "Invalid record number")
End If
```

8. Enter the following statements in the procedure that handles the menu item for saving a record:

```
intCounter = Val(txtNumber.Text)
udtEmployee.intNumber = txtNumber.Text
udtEmployee.strLastName = txtLastName.Text
udtEmployee.strFirstName = txtFirstName.Text
udtEmployee.sngHourlyWage = txtHourlyWage.Text

FileOpen(1, "a:\AddressBook.txt", OpenMode.Random,
  OpenAccess.ReadWrite, OpenShare.Shared, Len(udtEmployee))
FilePut(1, udtEmployee, intCounter)

intTotalRecords = LOF(1) / Len(udtEmployee)
FileClose(1)
```

9. Add the following procedure for the Form_Load event:

```
FileOpen(1, "a:\AddressBook.txt", OpenMode.Random,
  OpenAccess.ReadWrite, OpenShare.Shared, Len(udtEmployee))
FileGet(1, udtEmployee, 1)
intTotalRecords = LOF(1) / Len(udtEmployee)
```

```
FileClose(1)
txtNumber.Text = udtEmployee.intNumber
txtLastName.Text = udtEmployee.strLastName
txtFirstName.Text = udtEmployee.strFirstName
txtHourlyWage.Text = udtEmployee.sngHourlyWage
```

10. Create a procedure that handles the mnuExit click event.

11. Save your changes. Test your application.

Case Studies

Adding a Context Menu to a Control

As you learned in this chapter, context menus provide another way to make menu commands available on a form. In this case study, you will open a solution and modify it by adding a context menu with three menu items. The context menu items will provide the same functionality as the main menu items that appear on the form. When you finish, the application will display the context menu shown in Figure 5.40 when the user right-clicks over the form.

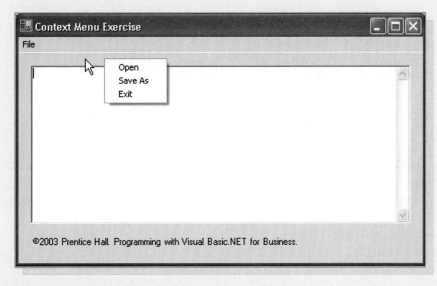

FIGURE 5.40. *A context menu on a form*

To add a context menu to a control:

1. Open the *Context Menu.sln* file in the *Context Menu* folder included with your data files.

2. Display the Toolbox.

3. Create the following context menu controls and set the properties as listed.

Object	Property	Setting
ContextMenu1		
cmnuFileOpen	Text	Open
cmnuFileSaveAs	Text	Save As
cmnuFileExit	Text	Exit

4. Set the **ContextMenu** property of the *txtFile* text box control to **ContextMenu1**.
5. Use copy and paste in the Code Editor to replicate the code from the mnuFileOpen_Click procedure for the *cmnuFileOpen_*Click procedure.
6. Replicate the code from the *mnuFileSaveAs_*Click procedure for the *cmnuFileSaveAs_*Click procedure.
7. Replicate the code from the *mnuFileExit_*Click procedure for the *cmnuFileExit_Click* procedure.
8. Save and run your application. Right-click over the text box and test the functionality of the context menu items.
9. Close the solution.

Using the On Error Statement for Error Handling

In this chapter you learned how to use the Try… Catch… Finally statement to handle file I/O exceptions thrown when an error occurs. For compatibility with previous releases, Visual Basic.NET also supports the On Error statement for handling errors. In this case study, you will learn how to use the On Error statement to handle a file input error.

Open the *On Error* solution contained in the *On Error* folder included with your data files. Replace the existing code for the *mnuFileOpen_Click* procedure with the following code:

```
Private Sub mnuFileOpen_Click(ByVal sender As System.Object,
  ByVal e As System.EventArgs) Handles MenuItemOpen.Click
'Use the On Error statement to trap file I/O errors
On Error Goto ErrorHandler
FileOpen(1, "A:\MyFile.txt", OpenMode.Input)
txtFile.Text = InputString(1, LOF(1))
Exit Sub
FileClose(1)


ErrorHandler:
'Display an error message
MsgBox("'The file does not exist or a disk is not in the drive.
  Please place a disk containing the file 'MyFile.txt' in Drive
  A: and try again.", MsgBoxStyle.Critical, "File Error!")
'Close the file
FileClose(1)
End Sub
```

After modifying the project, save your changes and test the application. The procedure works as follows: If an error is encountered, program execution branches to the lines of code contained in the ErrorHandler routine, and the procedure is exited. If no error occurs, program execution continues after the Exit Sub statement, and the file is closed.

Connecting to Databases With ADO.NET

Businesses store all kinds of information in data files, and it is not uncommon for these data files to be independent of one another. Employee information is kept in one file, strategic and tactical planning documents are kept in other files, and information about customer orders and inventory are also stored separately. To maintain accurate records and store data efficiently, most businesses use databases. A database is simply a collection of related information stored in a file. A random access file is a simple database, but as a database, a random access file has limitations. There is no security on a text file, and the fields and records can be viewed with a text editor. Random access files work fine for programs running on a single computer, but they are not a good choice for programs that support multiple users. Finally, even though random access files allow programs to read and write fields and record data, some programs need to relate fields contained in separate data structures to one another.

To overcome the limitations of random access files, more sophisticated business applications use a database such as Microsoft Access or Microsoft SQL server behind the scenes to provide information to the user. Using the Web to check the balance in your savings account is an example of connecting to a database. To gain account information, you initiate a secure connection and provide user credentials, and a database presents your account information, using a Web page interface. In addition, the account information is structured as fields and records, so information such as account number, last name, and account balance can be easily reported and updated. In this chapter, you will learn how to use a technology called ADO.NET to connect a Visual Basic.NET program to a database.

Performance Objectives

At the conclusion of this chapter, you will be able to:

- Explain basic database concepts.
- Describe the features and capabilities of ADO.NET.
- Use ADO.NET to connect to a database.
- Create data connections, data adapters, and datasets by using the Server Explorer.
- Populate a dataset with records from a database.
- Display database records in a Visual Basic.NET application by using the DataGrid control.
- Bind controls to an ADO.NET data source.
- Add buttons to a Visual Basic.NET form to navigate among records and use the Position property of a dataset to display records.
- Add records to and delete records from a database.

Database Concepts

Before learning how to connect to a database by using ADO.NET, let's cover basic database concepts. Businesses store all kinds of information on computers, and people in different departments have information that is specific to their line of work. But what good is a bunch of data scattered on different computers and in many places throughout an organization? Someone or something must organize all this data. A *database* is a collection of related information organized on a computer. A random access file is an example of a simple database that contains only fields and records. The contacts list that stores the names, addresses, and telephone numbers in your e-mail program is an example of a database that contains fields and records. Businesses work with so much data that a powerful program for organizing all of an organization's data in one place is required. A *database management system (DBMS)* is a computer application for managing databases and pulling together data to generate reports and make decisions. A database created with a DBMS consists of one or more files that include forms, tables, specific views of tables called queries, and reports for displaying, filtering, and printing database records. Figure 6.1 shows how a database management system combines business data so it can be managed effectively and used efficiently.

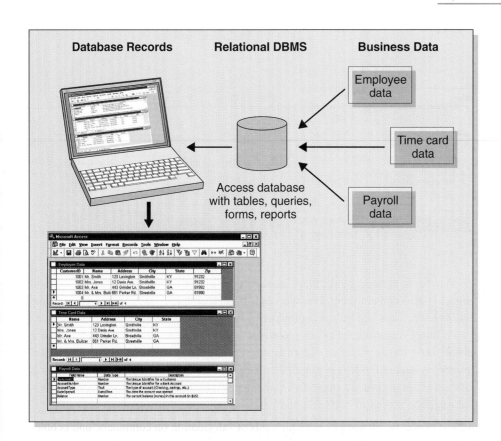

For daily operations, many businesses use databases based on the relational model. The random access file introduced in Chapter 5 stores one kind of information—employee data—that might be required by a business. Here's the data contained in the *Employees.txt* file:

1	121121122	Carr	Laura	9575 Summit Drive	Eagle	CO	80012	(719) 344-9087	$15.00
2	221323131	Bailey	Charles	211 Shrine Pass Court	East Vail	CO	80996	(719) 344-2010	$18.00
3	223343232	Holmes	Philip	48533 Piney Creek Drive	Beaver Creek	CO	80921	(719) 374-8923	$30.00
4	722121313	Jackson	Rebecca	10054 Ruler Court	Vail	CO	80997	(719) 344-2070	$21.00
5	732313111	Lindsey	Mark	14419 Brooke Road	Avon	CO	80933	(719) 444-3221	$12.00
6	841412121	Sanchez	Maria	101 Main Street	West Vail	CO	80978	(719) 377-2366	$18.00

Clearly, other files contain information that is pertinent to how a business manages its employees. The relational model splits data into separate row and column storage areas called **tables**. Each table is made up of fields and records. A **field** is a single data element in a record. As you learned in Chapter 5, examples of fields are an employee's last name, the part number for an item, or the title of a CD in your music collection. A **record** is a collection of fields that distinguish one item in the data file from another. Figure 6.2 shows a report consisting of nine fields and six records that lists employee information.

Employee Address List

ID	Last Name	First Name	Address	City	State	Zip Code	Phone	Pay Rate
121121122	Carr	Laura	9575 Summit Road	Eagle	CO	80012	(719) 344-9087	$15.00
221323131	Bailey	Charles	211 Shrine Pass Crt.	East Vail	CO	80996	(719) 344-2010	$18.00
223343232	Holmes	Philip	48533 Piney Crk. Dr.	Beaver Crk.	CO	80921	(719) 374-8923	$30.00
722121313	Jackson	Rebecca	10054 Ruler Court	Vail	CO	80997	(719) 344-2070	$21.0
732313111	Lindsey	Mark	14419 Brooke Road	Avon	CO	80933	(719) 444-3221	$
841412121	Sanchez	Maria	101 Main St.	West Vail	CO	80978	(719) 377-2366	

FIGURE 6.2. *Report from an employee database consisting of nine fields and six records*

Databases created by database management systems store fields and records in tables but also contain other database objects, such as forms and reports, for entering and editing records and for generating useful information in reports.

At times you will need to link records in one table to records in another table, such as when a customer places an order for an inventory item. A ***relational database management system (RDBMS)*** is a computer application that manages a database in which different kinds of data are stored in separate tables. In an RDBMS, employee information might be stored in one table and employee time-card records in a second table. Microsoft Access and SQL 2000 are examples of relational database management systems for creating databases. Visual Basic.NET applications can read records from and write records to the tables created with a RDBMS. Figure 6.3 displays two tables in a Microsoft Access database: one containing employee records and one containing related employee time-card data.

FIGURE 6.3. *A relational database with two tables*

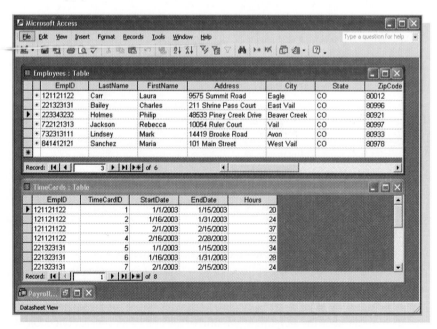

In Figure 6.3, the Employees table uses Social Security numbers to uniquely identify each employee. A field that uniquely identifies a record is called a ***primary key.*** The TimeCards table does not repeat the name and address information for each employee. The time-card records do, however, include the Employee ID. Dividing the data into separate tables minimizes repetition of information in the database. Suppose each time-card record contained all the address information for an employee. Not only would the name and address information be repeated in the table, but if the data needed to be changed—for example, if an employee moved or married and changed her last name— you would need to update the records in multiple places. Relational databases are designed to minimize the information that must be repeated in multiple records. The tables shown in Figure 6.3 can be related to one another by using the common field *EmpID*. Figure 6.4 shows the relationship that exists between these tables.

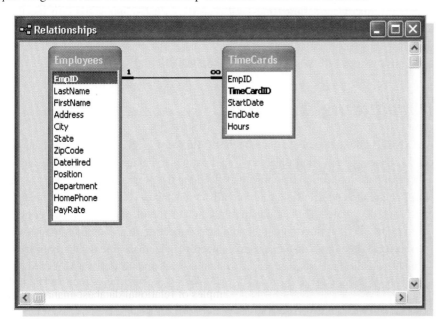

FIGURE 6.4. *A relationship between two tables using the* EmpID *field*

The relationship between these tables is a ***parent-child relationship*** (also called a ***one-to-many relationship***). One-to-many means that for one employee, multiple (many) time cards might exist. The employee name and address information is in one table, so if the employee data changes, it is updated in one place. The tables are related by using the EmpID field. This field is the primary key in the Employees table. The field in the child table that links information to the parent table is called the ***foreign key***. Because the tables are related by the Employee ID (EmpID) fields, data from both tables can be displayed on a form like the one in Figure 6.5.

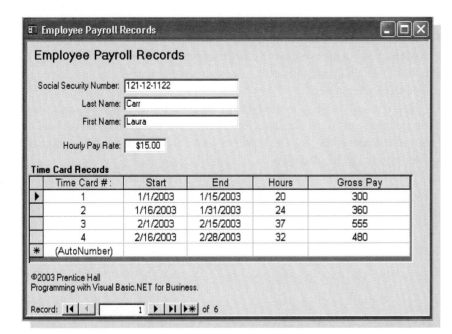

FIGURE 6.5. *A form displaying data from two related tables*

The EmpID is a unique value (meaning it appears only once) in the Employees table, but is a repeating value (meaning it appears more than once) in the TimeCards table. In this example, the Employees table uses EmpID as the primary key. Because all individuals have a unique Social Security number, many databases use an employee's Social Security number as the primary key value. The Time Cards table uses the EmpID field as a foreign key. The keys allow the form shown in Figure 6.5 to relate Laura Carr's four time-card records with her name data on the Payroll form.

Now that you have an understanding of basic database concepts, let's learn how ADO.NET works with Visual Basic.NET applications and a database.

Introducing ADO.NET

ADO.NET is the data access component of Microsoft's .NET framework that enables you to connect your Visual Basic.NET applications to databases. ADO.NET consists of a series of data connection components you add to the programs you create so your programs can read and write fields and records in a database. ADO.NET was created with multi-user, distributed applications in mind, in which multiple users have a copy of the program installed on their computers but are connecting to a database on a network or Web server. When more than one user connects to a database, the database must be able to handle all the requests it receives to display and update fields and records. If too many people connect at the same time, performance slows down. ADO.NET is designed to improve database performance.

ADO.NET AND DISCONNECTED DATA

Previous technologies for connecting to a database required you to establish a connection that remained active the entire time the program was running. With ADO.NET, a Visual Basic.NET program that interacts with the records in a database is not connected to the database. When the program first connects to the database, it makes a copy of the records. This copy of the database is called a ***dataset.*** Once the fields and records are in the dataset, the program closes the database and then closes the connection to the database. The dataset is not connected to the database; hence, the term "disconnected dataset." Whenever the program makes changes to a field or record, the dataset reconnects to the database, makes these changes, and then closes the connection. Because the data connection is active only when changes are made, multiple users accessing records in the same database can work more efficiently by not connecting simultaneously and tying up limited resources.

How does ADO.NET do this? The connection to the database is established by using managed providers. The managed provider you use depends on the kind of database you are connecting to. The managed provider supplies the connection and data adapter required by the database.

The ADO.NET disconnected dataset provides a flexible way of working with database records. Figure 6.6 shows how ADO.NET uses managed providers to connect to a specific database and generate a disconnected dataset.

You will learn more about managed providers, connections, and data adapters in a later section.

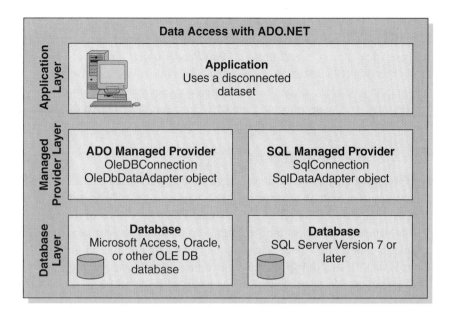

FIGURE 6.6. *A disconnected ADO.NET dataset*

ADO.NET AND XML

No discussion of ADO.NET would be complete without mentioning the role of XML for data access. ***XML (Extensible Markup Language)*** is a text-based language for storing data in a way that also describes the structure of the data. XML documents represent data in a hierarchy that differs from how relational databases store data. XML provides a consistent format for data that can be passed easily between applications and across networks and the Internet. More and more applications will use XML to communicate and share data. For this reason, Visual Studio.NET and other Microsoft products are XML-based, meaning they use XML as the format for storing data records.

Why is XML important to ADO.NET? Regardless of the managed provider you are using, the underlying fields and records in the disconnected dataset are stored as XML. Visual Studio.NET uses XML as a data storage technology because XML is optimized for sharing data across the Internet. Because XML documents contain both data and information about the structure of the data, any application that understands XML can use the data. Other applications, such as the tools in Office XP, also store data as XML. This means the Visual Basic.NET programs you create to connect to a database by using an ADO.NET managed provider will also represent the data in the database as XML so it is available to other applications.

Now let's learn more about how ADO.NET establishes a database connection.

MANAGED PROVIDERS

ADO.NET contains a set of objects called ***managed providers*** to establish and manage a connection between a Visual Basic.NET program and a database. Managed providers are used to communicate between a database (also called a *data source*) and a dataset. ADO.NET supports two primary managed providers, the ADO provider and the SQL Server provider. You use the ***ADO provider*** to connect your VB.NET programs to a variety of non-SQL databases, such as Microsoft Access and Oracle. The ***SQL Server Provider*** is used exclusively with Microsoft SQL databases.

A managed provider includes four objects for connecting to a database: the **Connection object**, the **DataAdapter object**, the **Command object**, and the

Tip

You do not need to understand XML to connect to a database. If you complete the Case Studies at the conclusion of this chapter, you will learn how to save data from a Visual Basic.NET application as XML.

DataReader object. The Connection and DataAdapter objects are required to create a disconnected dataset. The **Command object** is used to create commands telling the database what actions to perform. The **DataReader object** connects to a database and delivers read-only data that cannot be edited. This object is useful for displaying information from a database when the information does not require updating.

Because the Connection and DataAdapter objects are required to create a disconnected dataset, let's look at them in more detail.

The Connection Object

The **Connection object** connects your application to the database so you can read and write database records. A disconnected dataset needs a way to communicate changes in the dataset to the database. The specific connection object you will use depends on the kind of database that stores the fields and records used by your program. ADO.NET includes a connection object that works in conjunction with each managed provider. Your Visual Basic.NET programs use either an **OleDbConnection object** or a **SqlConnection object** to communicate with a database.

The DataAdapter Object

Once a connection object establishes a connection between your Visual Basic.NET program and a database, a **DataAdapter object** manages all communications between the program and the database. Like the connection objects, ADO.NET includes a **data adapter** for each kind of managed provider. The **OleDbDataAdapter object** is suitable for use with any non-SQL database, and the **SqlDataAdapter object** communicates with SQL databases.

Let's summarize how ADO.NET connects your Visual Basic.NET programs to an external database. ADO.NET uses a disconnected dataset to display fields and records in your application. To create a dataset, you create a data adapter and then generate a dataset.

Creating and Generating a Dataset

Now that you understand at a theoretical level how ADO.NET connects to a database, it's time to see how to create or generate a dataset. The database for this example is named *Employees.mdb* and contains one table and one form. The database stores name and address information about a company's employees. The form displaying employee records is shown in Figure 6.7.

Tip Using the Command object is beyond the scope of this book. You will use the DataReader object in the first Case Study at the end of this chapter.

Tip In this chapter you will work exclusively with Microsoft Access as the database for a dataset, so you will use the ADO provider and the *OleDbConnection* and *OleDbDataAdapter* objects.

FIGURE 6.7. *Microsoft Access database form displaying an employee record*

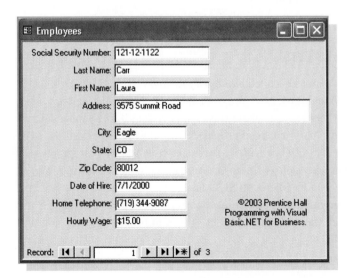

Visual Basic.NET provides two ways to create and generate a dataset: by writing lines of code to generate the data connection, data adapter, and dataset at run time or by using the Server Explorer to create these data connection components by dragging and dropping them on a form. Using the Server Explorer to create the data components requires three steps:

1. Create a data adapter.

2. Configure the data adapter.

3. Generate and fill the dataset.

Let's look at each of these steps in more detail.

CREATING A DATASET BY USING THE SERVER EXPLORER

The easiest method for creating an ADO.NET data connection is to use the Visual Studio.NET Server Explorer. The **Server Explorer** is a powerful tool in Visual Studio.Net for viewing all the resources on your system, including databases. By using the Server Explorer to create your data connection, you can use drag-and-drop methods to create the OleDbConnection and OleDbDataAdapter objects. After you put these on your form, you can generate and fill the dataset. The following steps explain how to create a data connection to the *Employees.mdb* Microsoft Access database. After you have created the data connection objects and have generated and filled the dataset, you can add controls to the form to display the database records. You can follow these steps by opening the *Simple Dataset Example(Start)* project included with your data files.

The results of the steps shown here are in the *Simple Dataset Example(Completed)* solution folder. The project for which you will create a data connection is shown in Figure 6.8.

If you want to follow these steps, copy the *Employees.mdb* database file to a floppy disk.

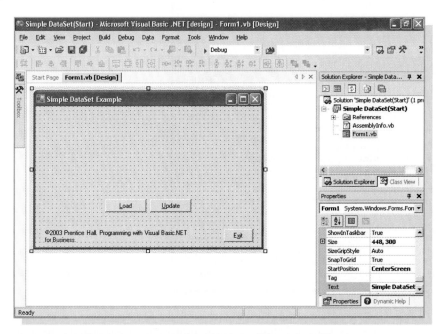

FIGURE 6.8. *Visual Basic project ready for a data connection*

To create a data connection by using the Server Explorer:

1. Hover the pointer over the Server Explorer button until the Server Explorer window opens.

2. Right-click inside the Server Explorer window and select **Add Connection**, as shown in Figure 6.9.

FIGURE 6.9. *Displaying the Server Explorer and adding a new data connection*

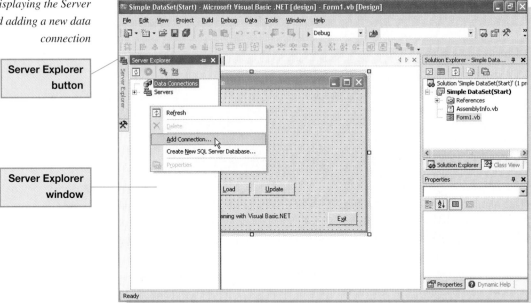

Server Explorer button

Server Explorer window

3. The Data Link Properties dialog box appears. Click the **Provider** tab. This is where you select the managed provider to use. Select **Jet 4.0 OLE DB Provider** from the list, as shown in Figure 6.10.

FIGURE 6.10. *Choosing a data provider*

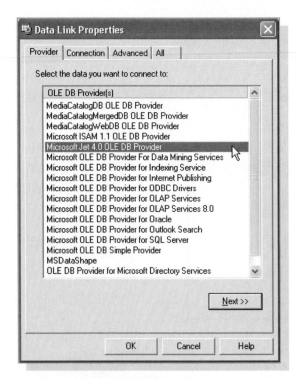

Because the Employees.mdb file is a Microsoft Access database, the Jet 4.0 OLE DB managed provider is the correct provider to use.

4. Click the **Connection** tab and then click the Ellipsis button to the right of the Database Name text box. Navigate to the *Employees.mdb* database on your disk and click Open.

5. Because this database does not contain a password, do not modify the information for logging on to the database. When your settings match those shown in Figure 6.11, click the **Test Connection** button.

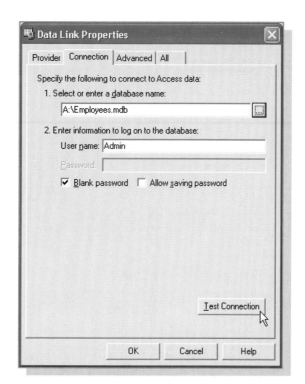

FIGURE 6.11. *Testing the data connection*

The message box in Figure 6.12 should appear.

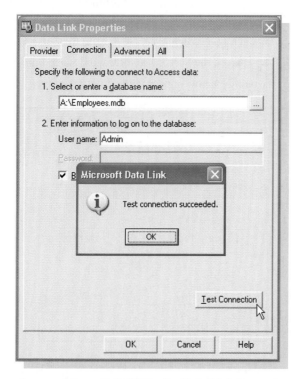

FIGURE 6.12. *Verification that the data connection is successful*

6. Click **OK** in the message box, and then click **OK** in the Data Link Properties dialog box. The Server Explorer now contains the connection you just created.

To add OleDbConnection and OleDbDataAdapter objects to the form:

1. Expand the Data Connections list in the Server Explorer window by clicking the Expand button (+) that appears just below the Data Connections icon, as shown in Figure 6.13.

FIGURE 6.13. *The Expand button for the Data Connection*

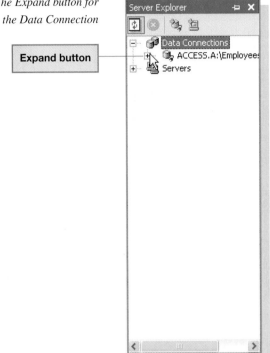

2. Click the Expand button for the *ACCESS.A:\Employees.mdb.Admin* connection, and then click the Expand button for Tables.

3. Drag the *Employees* table from the Server Explorer to your form.

4. Close the Server Explorer window and display the Toolbox.

Two objects now appear in the component tray, as shown in Figure 6.14.

FIGURE 6.14. *OleDbConnection and OleDbDataAdapter objects added to the component tray*

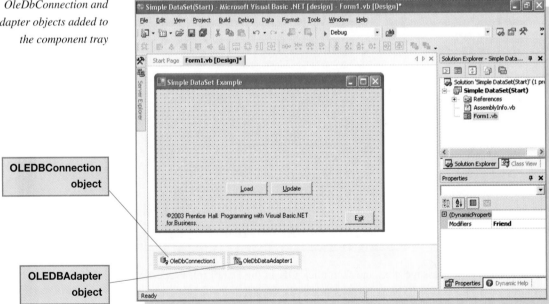

The objects added to the component tray are given the default names of *OleDbConnection1* and *OleDbDataAdapter1*, respectively. The left object is a Data Connection object, and the right object is a Data Adapter object.

You have now completed the first two steps in creating a dataset. The OleDbDataAdapter has been created and configured. The adapter also created an OleDbConnection object. You are now ready to generate the dataset.

To generate a dataset:

1. Click **Data**, **Generate dataset**, as shown in Figure 6.15. The Generate Dataset dialog box appears.

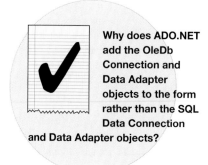

Why does ADO.NET add the OleDb Connection and Data Adapter objects to the form rather than the SQL Data Connection and Data Adapter objects?

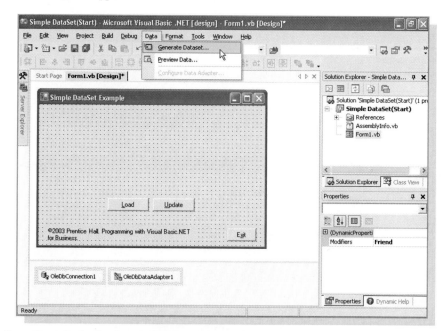

FIGURE 6.15. *Selecting the menu option to generate a dataset*

2. By default, the dataset is named *dataset1*. The dataset includes the fields from the *Employees* table specified in the SQL statement contained in the OleDbDataAdapter1 connection. When your settings match those shown in Figure 6.16, click OK.

FIGURE 6.16. *Verifying the dataset to generate*

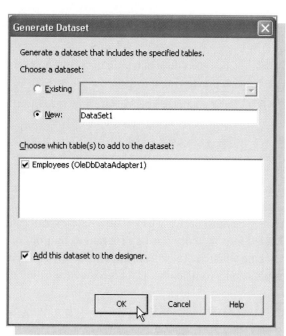

Because this is the first instance of a dataset created from the dataset1 object, Visual Basic.NET has added an additional digit (1) to the object. A dataset named dataset11 now appears in your application.

3. Click the **Data** menu, and then click **Preview Data** to open the Data Adapter Preview dialog box.

4. Click the **Fill Dataset** button in the upper left corner of the dialog box. The preview of the filled (populated) dataset is shown in Figure 6.17.

FIGURE 6.17. *Previewing the dataset*

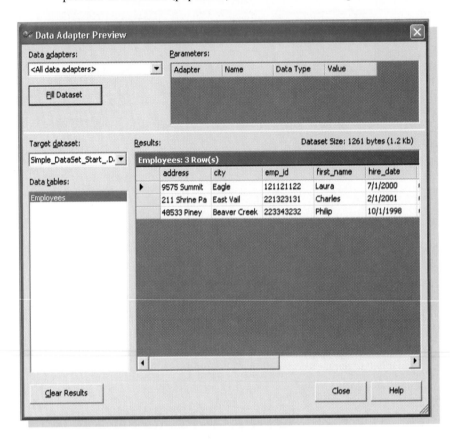

5. Click the **Close** button in the Data Adapter Preview dialog box when you finish previewing this data.

6. Save your changes. You are now ready to fill the dataset.

FILLING A DATASET

In the previous steps you previewed the data in the dataset without actually filling the dataset. After generating a dataset, you must instruct Visual Basic.NET to fill it with data. You can do this easily by using the *Fill command.* As you design your applications, you must decide when to fill a dataset with data. This can be done when a form is loaded into memory during program execution, or in response to an event, such as clicking a button. To understand how the fill command is used, let's add a button to the application's form and write a procedure for filling the dataset.

To fill the dataset:

1. Double-click the **Load** button to open the Code Editor.

2. Enter the following statement for the click event:

Notice that the columns representing the database fields appear in alphabetical order.

```
OleDbDataAdapter1.Fill(dataset11)
```

This statement uses the **Fill** method to read data from the database into the dataset.

Once you have generated and filled a dataset, you cannot view the dataset's records until you add one or more controls to the form to display the data elements. The easiest way to view records in a dataset is by adding a DataGrid control to the form.

Using the DataGrid Control

You can use the Windows Forms *DataGrid control* to display data as a series of rows and columns. The control must be bound to the dataset, meaning that the properties for the control specify which fields to display in the control. After the control is bound to a data source, the data appears in simple rows and columns, as in a spreadsheet. To display records in a dataset in a DataGrid control, do the following:

To display records in the dataset:

1. In the Toolbox, click the **DataGrid** tool, as shown in Figure 6.18.

After you execute a Fill command, the dataset disconnects from the database.

FIGURE 6.18. *The DataGrid tool*

2. Drag a DataGrid control onto the form.

3. In the Properties window, set the **DataSource** property to `DataSet11` and the **DataMember** property to the `Employees` member. The ***DataSource property*** specifies which dataset the control is bound to. If the dataset includes more than one table or query, the ***DataMember property*** specifies which table or query contains the records to display in the DataGrid. The property settings should appear as in Figure 6.19.

FIGURE 6.19. *Setting the DataSource and DataMember properties of a DataGrid control*

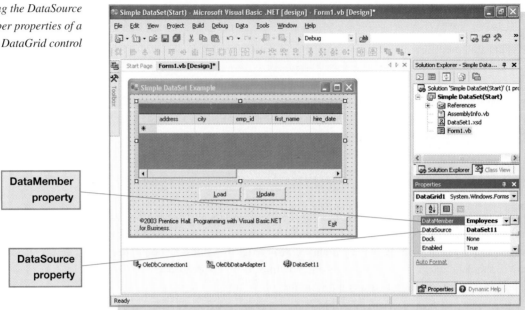

4. Run the application and click the **Load** button. The DataGrid displays the records shown in Figure 6.20.

FIGURE 6.20. *DataGrid displaying records from the* Employees *table*

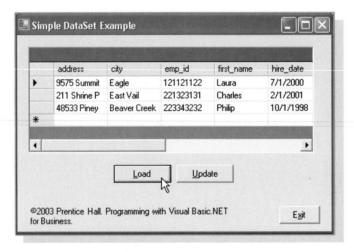

CHANGING DATA IN A DATAGRID

Viewing data from a database is an important part of building applications. But more importantly, you must be able to change the data records. All databases require updates; new records are added, obsolete records are deleted, and other records are changed. Because an ADO.NET dataset is disconnected from its data source, you first make changes to the dataset and then write these changes back to the database.

You can use the *Update command* for a data adapter to write additions, deletions, and changes back to the data source.

To update a data source with changes made to the dataset, you do the following:

To update a data source:

1. Double-click the **Update** button to open the Code Editor to display the code for this button's click event.

2. Type the following statement:

Tip

When you created the data adapter by dragging the *Employees* table from the Server Explorer to the form, ADO.NET created a Structured Query Language (SQL) statement to handle the Insert, Delete, and Update commands that are called by the Update command. These commands allow the data adapter to write changes in the dataset from the data adapter to the data source.

```
OleDbDataAdapter1.Update(dataset11)
```

3. Save your changes.

4. Run the application and click the **Load** button to load the dataset.

5. Click the row selector for the third record, as shown in Figure 6.21. The entire row is selected in the DataGrid.

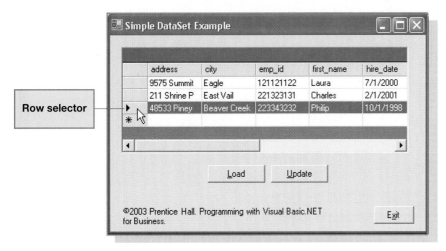

Row selector

FIGURE 6.21. *Using the row selector in a DataGrid to highlight a record*

6. Press the Del key to delete the record from the dataset.

7. Click the **Update** button. The change is written to the database.

8. Click the **Exit** button to exit the application, and choose **Yes** to exit.

9. Click **File**, **Close Solution** to close the solution.

Binding Controls to a Database

The preceding example uses the DataGrid control to demonstrate how ADO.NET uses a disconnected dataset for manipulating records and writing these changes back to the data source. Although the DataGrid is a useful control, you might not always want to display database records in a spreadsheet format. For many business applications, you might prefer a form that displays one record at a time, like the form shown in Figure 6.22.

Tip

Establishing a connection by using the Server Explorer to drag a table object to a form is one method of creating an **OleDbDataConnection, OleDbDataAdapter, and dataset. You can also use the Data tab in the Toolbox or create database objects with code. To explore the use of data controls in the Toolbox to connect to databases, complete the Exercises and Case Studies at the conclusion of this chapter.**

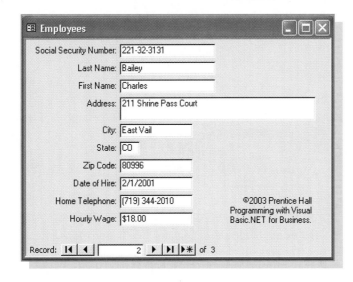

FIGURE 6.22. *Microsoft Access form displaying a database record*

You can create a form similar to this in Visual Basic.NET by adding controls such as text boxes to a form and then binding (connecting) each control to a specific field in the data adapter.

Figure 6.23 displays a form with three text boxes that are bound to a dataset. The form also contains three buttons: one to load the dataset and two (**Previous** and **Next**) for navigating among database records.

FIGURE 6.23. *Visual Basic.NET form with three text box controls bound to a data source*

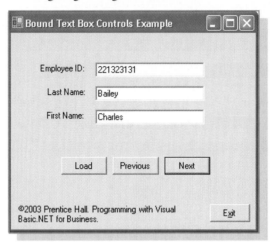

The form uses the *Employees* Data Connection, the same data connection you created in the previous example.

By dragging the *Employees* table from the Server Explorer to the form, you create the appropriate **OleDbConnection** and **OleDbDataAdapter** objects. After you generate a dataset, the fields are available for binding to specific controls.

TextBox, ComboBox, and ListBox controls all have an *Advanced DataBinding property* that can be set to a specific DataAdapter object. Figure 6.24 shows how to use the **Advanced DataBinding** dialog box available in the **Advanced** property row to bind a control to an object in the data adapter.

Tip Once you create a Data Connection, it is available to any Visual Basic.NET project.

Advanced property row

Text property

Field in the data adapter bound to the control

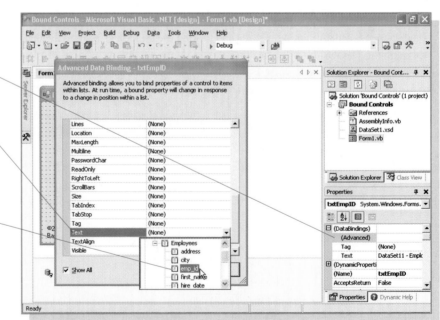

FIGURE 6.24. *Setting the AdvancedBinding property of a text box control*

The example form also contains two buttons for navigating among records in the dataset. The code for these buttons uses the *Position property* of the data-binding mechanism to make sure the objects bound to the dataset all display the same record. The records in the dataset are like rows in a table; the first record has a record index of zero, because the position is zero-based. The last record (last row in the table) has a Position property of the count of the rows minus one. The buttons on the form use the **Position** property to move through the records in the table and display the field data in the controls on the form. Following is the code for the *btnPrevious* and *btnNext* buttons used for navigating among records in the database:

ADO.NET uses a disconnected dataset. Therefore, you must write code to increment the Position property to navigate among records in a dataset.

```vb
Private Sub btnPrevious_Click(ByVal sender As System.Object, _
    ByVal e As System.EventArgs) Handles btnPrevious.Click

    Me.BindingContext(dataset11, "Employees").Position -= 1

End Sub
```

To move to the previous record in the dataset, the **Position** property is incremented by one less than the current position.

```vb
Private Sub btnNext_Click(ByVal sender As System.Object, ByVal e _
    As System.EventArgs) Handles btnNext.Click
    Me.BindingContext(dataset11, "Employees").Position += 1

End Sub
```

To move to the next record in the dataset, the **Position** property is incremented by one more than the current position.

The form in Figure 6.23 is in the *Bound Controls* solution included with your data files. If you want to see how the navigation buttons move through the dataset, run the application, click the **Load** button to load the dataset, and then click the **Next** and **Previous** buttons.

Now that you have learned the basics for establishing a data connection in ADO.NET, let's go through an example that demonstrates how to create a data connection, data adapter, and dataset.

The *Bound Controls* solution requires the data connection you created earlier in this chapter using the Server Explorer.

☛ HANDS-ON PROGRAMMING EXAMPLE

Creating an Address Book Database Application for Managing Employee Records

Businesses use a variety of databases for managing the data that is critical to the company's success. Because most databases hold more data than any individual needs for a given task, custom screen forms provide access to the components required for a specific business function. In this example you will create a Visual Basic.NET application for managing employee records in an Address Book database. Figure 6.25 displays the interface for the *Employee Address Book* application.

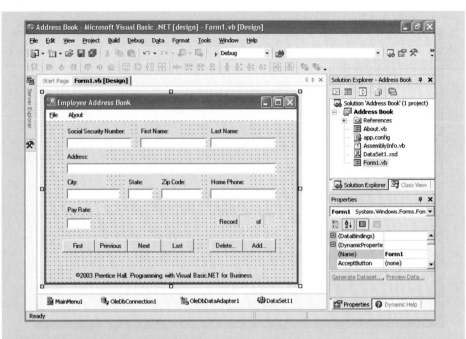

FIGURE 6.25. *Employee Address Book application*

The *Employee Address Book* application is a form bound to one table in the *Payroll.mdb* database. The address book is for managing employee records and supports the following functionality:

1. Provides access to the *Payroll.mdb* database.
2. Contains navigation buttons for moving through a dataset.
3. Includes buttons for adding and deleting records.
4. Includes record counters that display the current record number and the total number of records.
5. Prohibits users from deleting employee records if an associated time-card record exists.
6. Includes exception handling to handle exceptions thrown when opening the data source, deleting records, and adding records.

Although the requirements for this application are relatively simple, you need to create the OleDb connection, the OleDb adapter, and a dataset and then bind the controls on the form to the dataset. In addition, you need to handle exceptions for filling the dataset if the database cannot be found and for deleting employee records that have associated records in the TimeCards table.

Plan the Application

The first step in planning an application is determining the inputs and outputs. The Employee Address Book is for entering, editing, and displaying database records. The inputs and outputs are as follows:

Inputs	Outputs
Fields and records (entered on the keyboard)	Fields and records
Fields and records (read from a database)	

The Address Book application consists of one form with nine text boxes and six buttons. A MainMenu control contains two menu items: **File** and **About**. The **File** menu contains a menu item for exiting the application. The **About** menu item displays the About form. Table 6.1 lists the controls and properties your form will contain.

Table 6.1: *Objects and properties for the Address Book application*

Object	Property	Setting
Form1	Text StartPosition Size Menu	Employee Address Book CenterScreen 496, 357 MainMenu1
mnuFile	Text	&File
mnuFileExit	Text	E&xit
mnuAbout	Text	A&bout
lblEmpID	Text TextAlign	Social Security Number: MiddleLeft
lblFirstName	Text TextAlign	First Name: MiddleLeft
lblLastName	Text TextAlign	Last Name: MiddleLeft
lblAddress	Text TextAlign	Address: MiddleLeft
lblCity	Text TextAlign	City: MiddleLeft
lblState	Text TextAlign	State: MiddleLeft
lblZipCode	Text TextAlign	Zip Code: MiddleLeft
lblHomePhone	Text TextAlign	Home Phone: MiddleLeft
lblPayRate	Text TextAlign	Pay Rate: MiddleRight
lblCopyright	Text	©2003 Prentice Hall. Programming with Visual Basic.NET for Business.
lbl1	Text	Record
lbl2	Text	of
lblCurrentRecord	Text TextAlign BorderStyle	 MiddleCenter Fixed3D
lblTotalRecords	Text TextAlign BorderStyle	 MiddleCenter Fixed3D

txtEmpID	AdvancedDataBinding.Text TabStop TabIndex	Employees.EmpID True 0
txtFirstName	AdvancedDataBinding.Text TabStop TabIndex	Employees.FirstName True 2
txtLastName	AdvancedDataBinding.Text TabStop TabIndex	Employees.LastName True 1
txtAddress	AdvancedDataBinding.Text TabStop TabIndex	Employees.Address True 3
txtCity	AdvancedDataBinding.Text TabStop TabIndex	Employees.City True 4
txtState	AdvancedDataBinding.Text TabStop TabIndex	Employees.State True 5
txtZipCode	AdvancedDataBinding.Text TabStop TabIndex	Employees.ZipCode True 6
txtHomePhone	Text TabStop TabIndex	Home Phone: True 7
txtPayRate	AdvancedDataBinding.Text TabStop TabIndex	Employees.PayRate True 9
btnFirst	Text TabStop	First False
btnPrevious	Text TabStop	Previous False
btnNext	Text TabStop	Next False
btnLast	Text TabStop	Last False
btnAdd	Text TabStop	Add… False
btnDelete	Text TabStop	Delete… False

Draw a visual representation of the application on a blank piece of paper. Figure 6.26 shows a drawing of the user interface and the name of each control on the form.

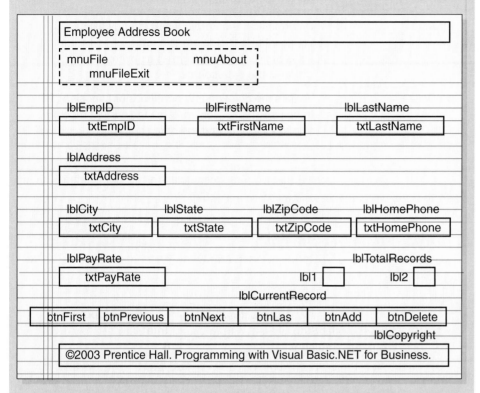

FIGURE 6.26. *Interface for the Employee Address Book application*

The form's primary features are the text boxes for displaying field data and the buttons for navigating the dataset and adding and deleting records. The pseudocode for the application's functionality is shown in Table 6.2.

Table 6.2: *Pseudocode for the Employee Address Book application*

Event Procedure	Action
mnuFile_Click	Displays one menu item: Exit
mnuFileExit_Click	1. Verifies user intent to terminate application. 2. Cancels or terminates.
mnuAbout_Click	1. Displays the About form.
btnFirst	Displays the first record in the dataset.
btnPrevious	Displays the previous record in the dataset.

btnNext	Displays the next record in the dataset.
btnLast	Displays the last record in the dataset.
btnAdd	1. Determines if the Employee ID already exists. 2. Verifies that all fields contain data. 3. Adds the data on the form as a new record. 4. Updates the data source.
btnDelete	1. Verifies the deletion and continues or cancels. 2. If the user clicks 'Yes', deletes the current record from the dataset and the data source.

Now that you have created the planning documents for the application, you are ready to begin designing the user interface in the IDE.

Design the User Interface

If you have not launched Visual Studio.NET, do so now. Perform each task that follows to complete this application.

To create a new project and solution:

1. Copy the *Payroll.mdb* database file from your data files to a floppy disk.
2. Click **File**, **New Project**.
3. In the New Project dialog box, type `Employee Address Book` as the name of the project. Set the location to the drive and folder where you store your solutions, and click **OK**.
4. Click **Project**, **Add Existing Item**. Navigate to the *frmAbout.vb* form in the *About Form* folder. Click **Open**. The form is added to the Solution Explorer.

To design the user interface:

1. Add each object listed in Table 6.1 to the form.
2. Set the object properties as specified. When you finish, your form should look like Figure 6.27.

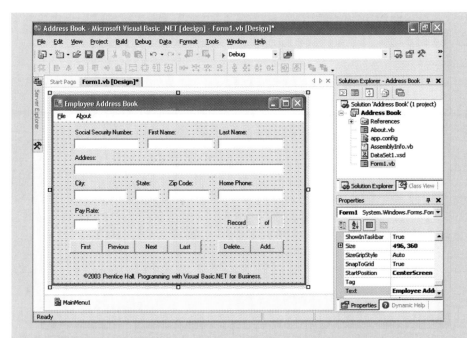

FIGURE 6.27. *Controls added to the Employee Address Book application*

3. Save your changes to the solution.

To create an OleDb connection, OleDb adapter, and dataset:

1. Click **View**, **Server Explorer**.
2. Expand the tree for the Data Connections.
3. Right-click inside the Server Explorer and choose **Add Connection**. The Data Link Properties dialog box appears.
4. Click the **Provider** tab and select **Microsoft JET 4.0 OLE DB Provider** from the list.
5. Click the **Connection** tab and navigate to the *Payroll.mdb* database on your student data disk.
6. Click the **Test Connection** button to verify that the database connection is working properly. Click **OK** in the Microsoft Data Link dialog box, and then click **OK** in the Data Link dialog box.
7. Expand the tree for the connection you just created until you can see the tables contained in the connection.
8. Drag the *Employees* table from the Server Explorer window to your form, as shown in Figure 6.28.

FIGURE 6.28. *Dragging a table from the Server Explorer to the form*

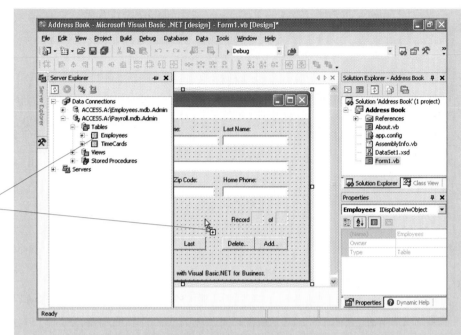

Notice that Visual Studio.NET adds the OleDbConnection1 and OleDbDataAdapter1 objects to the component tray.

9. Close the Server Explorer.

10. Save your changes.

How can you preview the records in the dataset?

Generating the Dataset

Now that you have designed the user interface and added the OleDb objects to the form, you are ready to generate the dataset.

To generate the dataset:

1. Click **Data**, **Generate Dataset**.

2. By default, Visual Studio names the dataset "DataSet1" and displays the *Employees* table. When your settings match those in Figure 6.29, click **OK**.

FIGURE 6.29. *Generating the dataset*

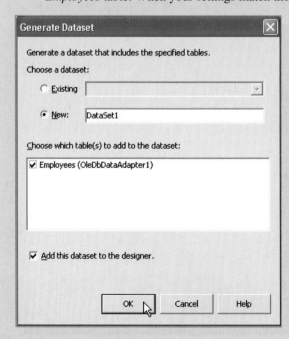

3. Save your changes.

Binding Controls to the Dataset

Now that you have generated the dataset, you can bind each of the text box controls to the appropriate field in the dataset.

To bind controls to the dataset:

1. Click the *txtEmpID* text box to select it.
2. Expand the **DataBindings** list in the Properties pane, and click the **Advanced** row. An Ellipsis button appears.
3. Click the Ellipsis button to display the Advanced Data Binding dialog box.
4. Click the **Text** row and expand the tree for the fields until the *EmpID* field is visible, as shown in Figure 6.30.

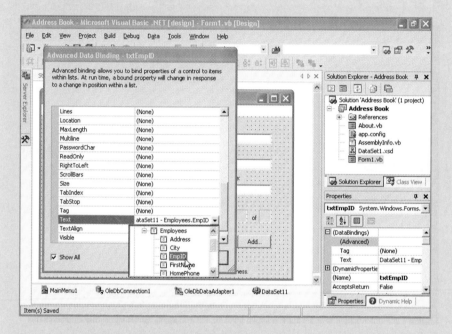

FIGURE 6.30. *Setting the Advanced DataBinding property for the* txtEmpID *control*

5. Click the *EmpID* field. The Text row now shows **dataset11 - Employees.EmpID**.
6. Click the **Close** button to close the Advanced Data Binding dialog box for the txtEmpID control.
7. Repeat steps 1–6 for the remaining text box controls on the form. Use Table 6.1 as a guide as you complete the data binding for each text box control.
8. Save your changes.

Now that the user interface for the Employee Address Book application is complete, you are ready to write the code providing the functionality.

Write the Code

Your first tasks are to add comments to the Code Editor, define variables for holding the record counters, and initialize the form. Then you will write the code that provides each button its functionality. Finally, you will write the procedures that handle the menu-item click events for exiting the application and displaying the About form.

To add comments to the application:

1. Press F7 to display the Code Editor. If the WindowsForm Designer Generated code region is expanded, collapse it.
2. Place the insertion point at the beginning of the Code Editor.
3. Type the following comments:

```
'©2003 Prentice Hall
'By [Enter your name]
'Created/Revised: [Enter the date]
'Employee Address Book Application
```

4. Place the insertion point immediately below the **Inherits System.Windows.Forms.Form** statement, and type the following:

```
'Declare variables for record counters
Dim intCurrentRecord, intTotalRecords As Integer
```

5. Save your changes.

To write the procedure that initializes the form:

1. Click the **Class Name** list in the Code Editor and select **(Base Class Events)** in the list.
2. Click the **Method Name** list and select **Click**.
3. Type the following code for the procedure:

```
Try
    'Populate the dataset
    OleDbDataAdapter1.Fill(dataset11)
Catch
    MsgBox("Database not found. Please try again.",
      MsgBoxStyle.Critical, "File Error")
    'Terminate the application
    End
Finally
    'Determine the number of records in the Dataset
    intTotalRecords = BindingContext(dataset11,
      "Employees").Count
    lblTotalRecords.Text = intTotalRecords

    'Set the current record variable (first record has an index
      of 0, so add 1)
    intCurrentRecord = BindingContext(dataset11,
      "Employees").Position + 1
    lblCurrentRecord.Text = intCurrentRecord
    OleDbDataAdapter1.Fill(dataset11)
    'Disable the First and Previous buttons
    btnFirst.Enabled = False
    btnPrevious.Enabled = False
End Try
```

In Chapter 5 you learned how to use the Try… Catch… Finally structure to handle exceptions. This procedure uses a Try… Catch… Finally statement to open the data connection and fill the dataset. If the database cannot be found, a message is displayed and the application terminates. If the database is found, the procedure fills the dataset and then determines the value for the intTotalRecords variable. Because the text box controls are bound to the dataset, the first record will be displayed on the form. Because the First and Previous buttons will not navigate to a different record, the procedure disables these buttons.

4. Save your changes.

To write procedures to navigate among records:

1. Create a procedure for the **btnFirst_Click** Event. Type the following code for the procedure:

```
Me.BindingContext(dataset11, "Employees").Position = 0

'Reset the CurrentRecord variable
intCurrentRecord = BindingContext(dataset11,
  "Employees").Position + 1
lblCurrentRecord.Text = intCurrentRecord

'Disable the First and Previous buttons
btnFirst.Enabled = False
btnPrevious.Enabled = False

'Enable the Last and Next buttons
btnLast.Enabled = True
btnNext.Enabled = True
```

2. Create a procedure for the **btnPrevious_Click** Event. Type the following code for the procedure:

```
Me.BindingContext(dataset11, "Employees").Position -= 1

'Reset the CurrentRecord variable
intCurrentRecord = BindingContext(dataset11,
  "Employees").Position + 1
lblCurrentRecord.Text = intCurrentRecord

'Determine if buttons need to be disabled
If intCurrentRecord = 1 Then
    'Disable the buttons
    btnFirst.Enabled = False
    btnPrevious.Enabled = False
End If

'Enable the Last and Next buttons
btnLast.Enabled = True
btnNext.Enabled = True
```

3. Create a procedure for the **btnNext_Click** Event. Type the following code for the procedure:

```
Me.BindingContext(dataset11, "Employees").Position += 1


'Reset the CurrentRecord variable
intCurrentRecord = BindingContext(dataset11,
   "Employees").Position + 1
lblCurrentRecord.Text = intCurrentRecord


'Determine if buttons need to be disabled
If intCurrentRecord = BindingContext(dataset11,
   "Employees").Count Then
     'Disable the buttons
     btnLast.Enabled = False
     btnNext.Enabled = False
End If


'Enable the First and Previous buttons
btnFirst.Enabled = True
btnPrevious.Enabled = True
```

4. Create a procedure for the **btnLast_Click** Event. Type the following code for
   the procedure:

```
Me.BindingContext(dataset11, "Employees").Position =
   BindingContext(dataset11, "Employees").Count - 1


'Reset the CurrentRecord variable
intCurrentRecord = BindingContext(dataset11,
   "Employees").Position + 1
lblCurrentRecord.Text = intCurrentRecord


'Disable the Last and Next buttons
btnLast.Enabled = False
btnNext.Enabled = False


'Enable the First and Previous buttons
btnFirst.Enabled = True
btnPrevious.Enabled = True
```

   Each of these procedures uses the **Position** property to display the
   appropriate field data on the form.

5. Save your changes.

To write procedures for adding and deleting records:

1. Create a procedure for the **btnAdd_Click** Event. Type the following code for
   the procedure:

```
Me.BindingContext(dataset11, "Employees").Position =
   BindingContext(dataset11, "Employees").Count - 1
'Reset the CurrentRecord variable
intCurrentRecord = BindingContext(dataset11,
   "Employees").Position + 1
lblCurrentRecord.Text = intCurrentRecord
```

```
'Disable the Last and Next buttons
btnLast.Enabled = False
btnNext.Enabled = False


'Enable the First and Previous buttons
btnFirst.Enabled = True
btnPrevious.Enabled = True
    End Sub
    Private Sub btnAdd_Click(ByVal sender As System.Object,
        ByVal e As System.EventArgs) Handles btnAdd.Click
'Declare a variable to add a row to the dataset
Dim AddRow As DataRow


'Populate the new dataset row with date on the form
AddRow = dataset11.Tables("Employees").NewRow
AddRow("EmpID") = txtEmpID.Text
AddRow("FirstName") = txtFirstName.Text
AddRow("LastName") = txtLastName.Text
AddRow("Address") = txtAddress.Text
AddRow("City") = txtCity.Text
AddRow("State") = txtState.Text
AddRow("ZipCode") = txtZipCode.Text
AddRow("HomePhone") = txtHomePhone.Text
AddRow("PayRate") = txtPayRate.Text


Try
    'Add the new row to the dataset
    dataset11.Tables("Employees").Rows.Add(AddRow)

    'Update the database
    OleDbDataAdapter1.Update(dataset11)
    MsgBox("A record has been added to the database.",
      MsgBoxStyle.Information, "Add Record")

    'Refresh the dataset
    OleDbDataAdapter1.Fill(dataset11)

    'Determine the number of records in the Dataset
    intTotalRecords = BindingContext(dataset11,
        "Employees").Count
    lblTotalRecords.Text = intTotalRecords

    'Navigate to the last record
    Me.BindingContext(dataset11, "Employees").Position =
      intTotalRecords

    'Set the current record variable
    intCurrentRecord = BindingContext(dataset11,
        "Employees").Position + 1

    lblCurrentRecord.Text = intCurrentRecord
```

```
                                'Disable the Last and Next buttons
                                btnLast.Enabled = False
                                btnNext.Enabled = False
                        Catch
                                MsgBox("Cannot save this record. The Employee ID must be
                                    unique.", MsgBoxStyle.Critical, "Save Operation Failed")
                                Exit Try
                        End Try
```

This procedure is more complex than the procedure for deleting records. The procedure declares a variable for adding a row to the dataset. The variable is populated with data from the text box controls on the form. The Try… Catch… Finally statement adds a record only if the Employee ID is unique. If an exception is thrown, a message box is displayed on the screen. Otherwise, the record is added to the data source, and the form is initialized by recalculating the record counter variables.

2. Create a procedure for the **btnDelete_Click** Event. Type the following code for the procedure:

```
'Get the current record number (using the position property)
intCurrentRecord = BindingContext(dataset11,
    "Employees").Position


If MsgBox("Delete Record? Click 'Yes' to delete, 'No' to
    cancel.", MsgBoxStyle.YesNo, "Delete Record Operation") =
    MsgBoxResult.Yes Then
        'Remove the current record from the dataset if no related
            time card records exist
        Try
BindingContext(dataset11,
    "Employees").RemoveAt(intCurrentRecord)
OleDbDataAdapter1.Update(dataset11)


'Refresh the dataset
OleDbDataAdapter1.Fill(dataset11)


'Navigate to the first record
Me.BindingContext(dataset11, "Employees").Position = 0


'Determine the number of records in the Dataset
intTotalRecords = BindingContext(dataset11, "Employees").Count
lblTotalRecords.Text = intTotalRecords


'Get the current record number (using the position property)
intCurrentRecord = BindingContext(dataset11,
    "Employees").Position + 1
lblCurrentRecord.Text = intCurrentRecord
        Catch
```

```
MsgBox("Cannot delete this record, because one or more time card
   records exist for this employee.", MsgBoxStyle.Critical,
   "Delete Operation Failed")
     End Try
Else
     MsgBox("Delete operation cancelled and record not deleted.",
       MsgBoxStyle.Information, "Record Not Deleted")
End If
```

This procedure uses the Try... Catch... Finally statement to make sure no related time-card records exist before an employee record is deleted, which would trigger an exception. The Catch statement handles this exception and displays a message box.

3. Save your changes.

You have almost finished creating the Employee Address Book application. Your last task is to write code to handle the click events for the menu items on the form.

To write procedures for handling the menu click events:

1. Click the **Class Name** drop down list and select *mnuFileExit* from the list.
2. Click the **Method Name** list and select **Click**.
3. Type the following code for the procedure:

```
Dim intResponse As Integer
   intResponse = MsgBox("Do you really want to exit this
       application?", 276, "Exit?")
   If intResponse = 6 Then
        End
End If
```

4. Click the **Class Name** drop down list and select *mnuAbout* from the list.
5. Click the **Method Name** list and select **Click**.
6. Type the following code for the procedure:

```
Dim ShowForm As AboutForm = New AboutForm()
ShowForm.ShowDialog()
```

7. Save your changes.

Run the Application

You are now ready to run the Employee Address Book application and test its functionality.

To run the application:

1. Click the **Start** button or press the [F5] key to run the application.
2. If the database is found, the form displays the first record in the database.
3. Test the navigation buttons, taking note of which buttons are hidden as you navigate through the dataset.
4. Navigate to the first record and try deleting it. Because the Time Cards table contains associated tables, you receive the error message shown in Figure 6.31.

FIGURE 6.31. *Error message that appears when a record cannot be deleted*

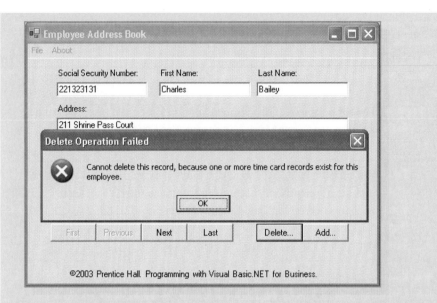

5. Click the **Add** button. Because you are attempting to add a record with an Employee ID that already exists, you receive the message shown in Figure 6.32.

FIGURE 6.32. *Error message that appears when a record cannot be added*

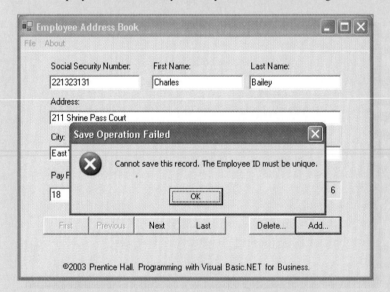

6. Enter unique values in each text box and click the **Add** button. The record is successfully added to the database. Notice that the total records counter increased by a value of 1.

7. Without navigating to another record, click the Delete button to delete this record.

8. Click the **About** menu. The About form appears.

9. Continue testing your application to check its functionality. When you finish, click **File**, **Exit**.

Summary

- A database is an organized collection of related information. A Database Management System (DBMS) is an application for creating databases consisting of tables, queries, forms, reports, and other database objects. A Relational Database Management System (RDBMS) stores database records in separate tables that can be related to one another.

- ADO.NET is a set of components in Visual Studio.NET for connecting to databases. In ADO.NET, a data connection consists of a disconnected dataset maintained through a managed provider and a data adapter. ADO.NET supports two managed providers: the SQL Server Provider for Microsoft SQL databases and the ADO Provider for all other databases.

- To connect a Visual Basic.NET application to a database, you must first create a data connection, configure the data connection, create a dataset, and then fill the dataset.

- The easiest way to create a data connection is to use the Visual Studio.NET Server Explorer.

- Once a dataset has been created, you can populate it with records from the data source by using the Fill command.

- The DataGrid control displays records in a dataset.

- To add more flexibility to your Visual Basic.NET application that displays records from a database, you can create controls that are bound to the fields in the dataset. Once you create controls bound to fields in a dataset, you can write code procedures for navigating records by using the Position property.

- To add, delete, and modify records in a database, changes in the disconnected dataset must be written to the data source.

Key Terms

ADO provider

Advanced DataBinding property

Command object

Connection object

data adapter

DataAdapter object

database

Database Management System (DBMS)

DataGrid control

DataMember property

DataReader object

dataset

DataSource property

field

Fill command

foreign key

managed providers

OleDbConnection object

OleDbDataAdapter object

one-to-many relationship

parent-child relationship

Position property

primary key

record

Relational Database Management System (RDBMS)

Server Explorer

SQL Server Provider

SqlConnection object

SqlDataAdapter object

tables

Update command

XML (Extensible Markup Language)

Study Questions

Multiple-Choice Questions

1. Which of the following is used to uniquely identify each record in a database?
   a. Instance
   b. Key
   c. Primary key
   d. Foreign key
   e. Field

2. Which object allows you to establish a connection between your application and a Microsoft Access database?
   a. OleDbConnection
   b. OleDbDataAdapter
   c. SqlConnection
   d. OleDbDataReader
   e. SqlDataAdapter

3. Which of the following is not a managed provider object?
   a. OleDbConnection
   b. SqlConnection
   c. OleDbDataAdapter
   d. Dataset
   e. SQLDatasetAdapter

4. An ADO.NET dataset is characterized as:
   a. Connected
   b. Read-only
   c. Managed
   d. Unstructured
   e. Disconnected

5. Which object extracts records from a database as read-only?
   a. OleDbDataAdapter
   b. Dataset
   c. SqlDataAdapter
   d. OleDbDataReader
   e. OleDbConnection

6. Which property of a text box causes it to display data from a dataset?
   a. Text
   b. Name
   c. AdvancedDataBinding
   d. DataSource
   e. DataMember

7. Which property can be incremented to display the next or previous record in a list?
   a. AdvancedDataBinding
   b. Position
   c. DataMember
   d. Text
   e. DataSource

8. Which method is used in ADO.NET to navigate to the next record in a dataset?
   a. Position +1
   b. MoveNext
   c. Position -1
   d. MoveLast
   e. CurrentRecord

9. Which control easily displays all the records in a dataset?
   a. ComboBox
   b. ListBox
   c. DataGrid
   d. CheckedListBox
   e. TextBox

10. Which of the following objects automatically creates a connection with a Microsoft Access database?
    a. SqlDataAdapter
    b. OleDbConnection
    c. OleDbDataAdapter
    d. SqlConnection
    e. Dataset

True/False Questions

1. ADO.NET lets you access a data source in a connected fashion.

2. ADO.NET offers two primary managed providers.

3. When you make changes to a DataGrid control's dataset, the changes are automatically made to the data source.

4. A DataGrid control displays one record in a database on a form.

5. You can bind controls to the members of a dataset by using the Advanced Binding property of the controls.

Short Answer Questions

1. What is ADO.NET, and how does it support connecting to databases?

2. What is a disconnected dataset and what are its primary advantages?

3. What methods can you use to create an OleDb data adapter and OleDb connection?

4. How does using a DataGrid control for displaying records differ from using TextBox controls for displaying field data? When might you use each method?

5. What is data binding, and how does it support viewing records and fields in a database?

Guided Exercises

Creating a Database Connection by Using Data Components

In this chapter you learned how to create a database connection by using the Server Explorer. This is one option you have for creating data components. You can also use the Data tab in the Toolbox to create OleDb connections, OleDb adapters, and datasets. In this exercise you will create a disconnected dataset by using data components. The finished application will display the records shown in Figure 6.33.

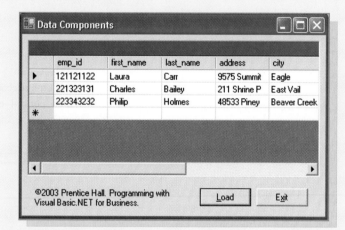

FIGURE 6.33. *Data Components form*

To create a dataset by using data components:

1. Launch Visual Studio.NET and open the *Data Components* solution included with your data files.
2. Display the Toolbox.
3. Click the **Data** tab.
4. Drag an **OleDbDataAdapter** onto the form. The Data Adapter Configuration Wizard appears.
5. Click the **Next** button.
6. Click the **New Connection** button.
7. Create a Jet 4.0 OLE DB Provider connection that connects to the *Employees.mdb* database on your student data disk.

8. Test the connection and click OK.

9. Click **Next** when you return to the Data Adapter Configuration Wizard.

10. Accept the default to use SQL statements and click **Next**.

11. Type SELECT emp_id, first_name, last_name, address, city, state, zip_code, home_phone, pay_rate FROM Employees as the SQL statement, as shown in Figure 6.34. This will select the specified fields from the Employees table. Then click **Next**.

FIGURE 6.34. *SQL statement specifying the data to load into the dataset*

12. After the data components are generated, click **Finish**.

13. Drag a dataset from the Toolbox to the form. Select the option for an untyped dataset, and click **OK.**

14. Double-click the **Load** button to open its click event. Type the following statements:

```
OleDbDataAdapter1.Fill(dataset1)
DataGrid1.DataSource = dataset1
DataGrid1.DataMember = "Employees"
```

15. Save your changes.

16. Press F5 to run the application. Click the **Load** button. The disconnected dataset is created, and the DataGrid is populated.

17. Click the **Exit** button and close the solution.

Creating a Parent-Child Relationship on a Form

In this chapter you learned how relational database systems use keys to relate data in separate tables. You can create Visual Basic.NET applications that display linked data in a parent-child relationship. In this exercise you will modify an application that will display employee records in TextBox and ListBox controls on a form and associated time-card records in a DataGrid control. In addition, the ListBox can be used to navigate among records by selecting the last name of an employee in the list. Figure 6.35 shows the form you will modify to display data from related tables in the *Payroll.mdb* database.

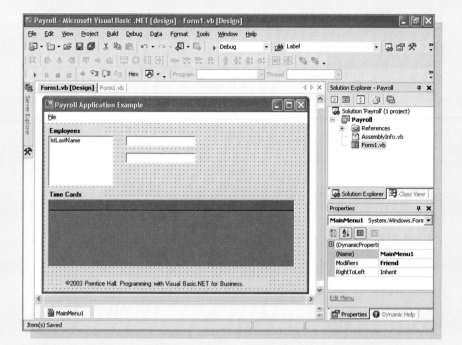

FIGURE 6.35. *Payroll Application form*

To create a database connection to multiple related tables:

1. In Visual Studio.NET, click **File**, **Open Solution** and navigate to the *Payroll* solution in your data files. Display *Form1* in the IDE.
2. Click **View**, **Server Explorer**. Expand the list for the *Payroll.mdb* data connection until both tables are visible.
3. Drag the *Employees* table from the Server Explorer onto the form to create the OleDbDataAdapter1 object.
4. Drag the *Time Cards* table from the Server Explorer onto the form to create the OleDbDataAdapter2 object. Then close the Server Explorer.
5. From the **Data** menu, choose **Generate Dataset**. Both tables are added to the dataset, which has the default name of *DataSet1*. Then click **OK**.
6. You now need to create a relationship between the tables. Double-click the *dataset1.xsd* file in the Solution Explorer.
7. From the XML Schema tab in the Toolbox, drag a Relation object onto the *Time Cards* table. The **Edit Relation** dialog box appears. Click **OK** to create the relationship shown in Figure 6.36.

FIGURE 6.36. *Editing a data relation*

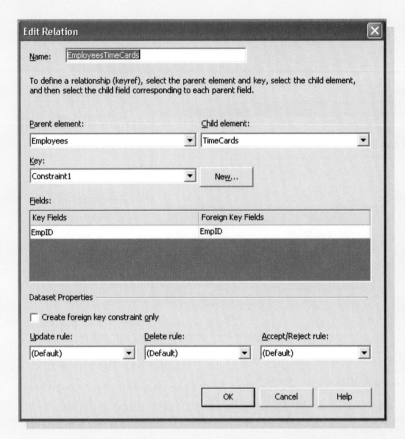

8. In the **DataSource** property of the *lstLastName* list box, select **dataset11** as the data source.

9. In the **DisplayMember** property for *lstLastName*, display the drop-down list. Select *Employees*, expand the node, and then select LastName. Set the DataSource property of the **lstLastName** list box to **dataset11**.

10. Set the **DataSource** property of the DataGrid1 data grid to **dataset11**.

11. Set the **Advanced Data Binding** Property of the text boxes on the form to the appropriate fields in the dataset.

12. Create an event procedure for the **Form1_Load** event. Type the following statements:

```
OleDbDataAdapter1.Fill(dataset11)
OleDbDataAdapter2.Fill(dataset11)
```

This populates the dataset with the appropriate data from each data adapter.

13. Save your changes.

14. Press F5 to run the application. The form should display the time-card records for Laura Carr.

15. Click **Bailey** in the list box. The data on the form changes to display the time-card records for Charles Bailey, as shown in Figure 6.37.

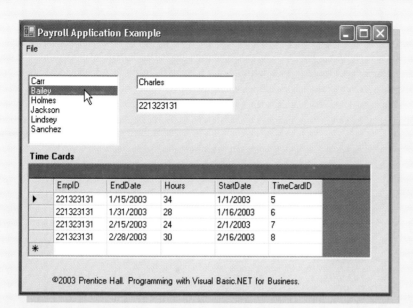

FIGURE 6.37. *Payroll Application form displaying related records in a parent-child relationship*

16. Click **File**, **Exit** to close the solution.

Case Studies

Creating a DataReader

In this chapter you learned that you can use the ADO.NET DataReader object to connect to a database to extract and display data that does not need to be changed. This is useful in situations where you want to view data from a database and use the data in your application. Figure 6.38 displays the structure of the *Products* table in the *Products.mdb* database that is included on your student data disk.

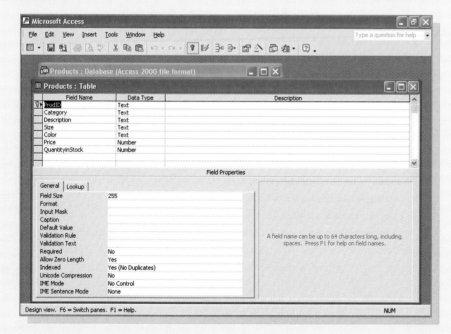

FIGURE 6.38. *Structure for the* Products *table*

Notice that the table includes numeric fields for storing the quantity of an inventory item as well as the item's price. Assume that you need to create an application to display the current value of the inventory in a list. You can calculate the value of each item by multiplying the units in stock by the price. Figure 6.39 shows a Visual Basic.NET form that displays the inventory and each item's current value. The data appearing in the list box is extracted from the Products table by using an ADO.NET DataReader. As the data is read into the list box, the quantity in stock and the price of each item are read into two variables used to calculate the value of each product.

FIGURE 6.39. *Visual Basic.NET application displaying record data in a list box*

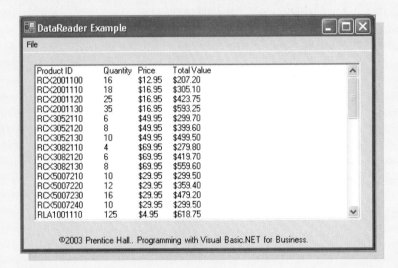

This Case Study will reinforce the concepts you learned in Chapter 4 for adding items to a list box. In this application, the items in the list box are obtained from the Products database, and the appropriate field data is used to calculate the inventory value for each product. To complete this Case Study, do the following:

To create a DataReader:

1. Copy the *Product.mdb* database file included in your data files to a floppy disk.
2. Open the *DataReader* solution included with your data files.
3. Press F7 to open the Code Editor.
4. Click the **Class Name** list in the Code Editor and select (**Base Class Events**).
5. Enter the following code for the **Form_Load** event. Make sure you enter the appropriate drive and path to the database (in this example, the *Products.mdb* database is located in the root directory of the disk in drive A).

As you type each line of code, type the line completely, allowing the statements to wrap in the Code Editor unless a Continuation character (_) is included.

```
Dim MyDataReader As OleDb.OleDbDataReader = Nothing
Dim ConnectionString As String =
  "Provider=Microsoft.Jet.OLEDB.4.0;Data source =
  a:\Products.mdb;Persist Security Info=False"
Dim MyConnection As New OleDb.OleDbConnection(ConnectionString)
Dim MyCommand As New OleDb.OleDbCommand("SELECT * FROM
  Products", MyConnection)


'Add header information to the listbox
lstData.Items.Add("Product ID" _
 & vbTab & "Quantity" & vbTab _
 & "Price" & vbTab & "Total Value")


Try
    'Open connection
    MyConnection.Open()
```

```
    MyDataReader = MyCommand.ExecuteReader
    'Declare variables to capture the quantity and price of
      each item
    Dim intQuantity As Integer
    Dim sngPrice As Single
    'Read Data into the variable
    While MyDataReader.Read()
sngPrice = Val(MyDataReader("Price"))
intQuantity = Val(MyDataReader("QuantityinStock"))

'Populate the listbox with field data and the calculated value
  for each inventory item
lstData.Items.Add(MyDataReader("ProdID") _
    & vbTab & MyDataReader("QuantityinStock") _
    & vbTab & Format(MyDataReader("Price"), "c") _
    & vbTab & Format(sngPrice * intQuantity, "c"))
    End While
Finally
    MyConnection.Close()
End Try
```

The procedure creates the DataReader object and the connection to the database. An SQL command extracts all records from the database. The DataReader extracts one record from the database at a time, uses the **Val** function to enter the *QuantityinStock* and *Price* character data into the appropriate variables, and calculates the inventory value for each item. The **Format** function formats the data for display in the list box.

6. Save your changes.

7. Run the application to test its functionality.

8. Close the solution.

Saving Database Records as XML

As you learned in this chapter, XML is now the native data format for ADO.NET datasets. Saving data as XML is useful when you want to pass the data to another application. In this case study, you will create a procedure that saves records in a dataset to an XML file. After creating the XML file, you can view its contents by using Microsoft Internet Explorer. To complete this exercise, do the following:

To save database records as XML:

1. Copy the *Products.mdb* database file to a floppy disk.

2. Open the *SaveAsXML* solution included with your data files.

3. Enter the following for the **Form_Load** event, making sure you specify the location for the *Products.mdb* database:

```
Dim DSAdapter As OleDb.OleDbDataAdapter
Dim ConnectionString As String
Dim SqlString As String

ConnectionString = "Provider = Microsoft.Jet.OLEDB.4.0;Data
   source=A:\Products.mdb;Persist Security Info=False"

SqlString = "SELECT * FROM Products"

MyData = New DataSet()
DSAdapter = New OleDb.OleDbDataAdapter(SqlString,
   ConnectionString)
DSAdapter.Fill(MyData, "Products")
DataGridData.DataSource = MyData
DataGridData.DataMember = "Products"
```

When the form is loaded, the dataset is filled, as shown in Figure 6.40.

FIGURE 6.40. *Dataset filled with records*

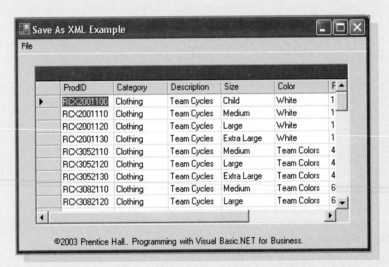

@2003 Prentice Hall.. Programming with Visual Basic.NET for Business.

4.   Enter the following code for the **mnuFileSaveAsXML_Click** event:

```
'Write data to an XML file
Dim SaveAsXML As FileStream = New FileStream("A:\Products.xml",
   FileMode.OpenOrCreate, FileAccess.Write)
Dim WriteXML As StreamWriter = New StreamWriter(SaveAsXML)
MyData.WriteXml(WriteXML)
MsgBox("All records in the database table have been written as
   XML.", MsgBoxStyle.Information, "Save AS XML")
```

5.   Save your changes.
6.   Run the application and select the **Save As XML** menu item.
7.   Navigate to the location where you saved the file, and double-click it. The XML data is displayed in Microsoft Internet Explorer, as shown in Figure 6.41.

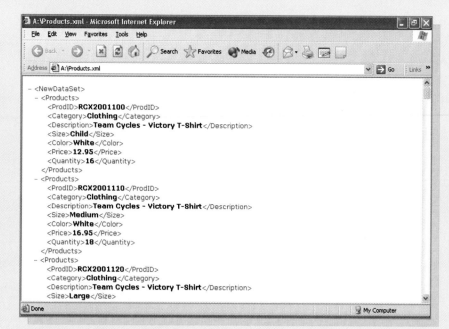

FIGURE 6.41. *XML file displayed in Microsoft Internet Explorer*

8. Close the solution.

CHAPTER 7

Using Sub Procedures, Function Procedures, and Modules

U p to this point, you have learned much of what you need to know about building applications that incorporate variables, selection structures, repetition structures, menus, dialog boxes, and data input and output. In many respects, these skills define the fundamentals of programming applications for activities in the information processing cycle: obtaining input, processing information, displaying output, and storing data for later use. Having mastered these basics, you are ready to begin learning how to make your programs more efficient by designing code that can be reused.

Visual Studio.NET supports program design that allows you to minimize the amount of code you need to write to provide functionality in your programs. For example, you might want a certain procedure to be available from both a menu and a command button. By creating general procedures and functions, you can easily run the code in the procedure from more than one control. By adding code modules to your projects, you can store procedures that can be run from any form within the solution.

Performance Objectives

At the conclusion of this chapter, you will be able to:

- Explain how programmers use procedures to write efficient applications.
- Describe how sub procedures differ from function procedures.
- Create a sub procedure.
- Perform data validation by using a sub procedure.
- Create a function procedure.
- Pass arguments to procedures, to a procedure by value, and to a procedure by reference.
- Create a sub procedure that calls a function procedure.
- Create a region for storing procedures.
- Create a module.
- Add a function procedure to a module.
- Call a procedure in a module.
- Create an application with multiple forms.

Procedures, Sub procedures and Function Procedures

The code you write to perform actions in your programs is contained in a procedure. By definition, a ***procedure*** is a series of code statements that perform specific actions. In Visual Basic.NET, there are two kinds of procedures. Sub procedures perform an action. Function procedures return a value. The code you have written since Chapter 1 consists of procedures. By understanding more about procedures, you can make your programs more efficient. Procedures allow you to

- Break your program into smaller units that perform tasks and can be called by more than one control. When a procedure accomplishes a single task, the code is easy to manage and much easier to debug.
- Efficiently manage the scope of your programs by reusing code developed in one program in other programs, with little or no modification.

Now let's learn more about using sub and function procedures in Visual Basic.NET programs.

Using Sub procedures

A ***sub procedure*** is a procedure that performs a series of actions or tasks but does not return a result. In Visual Basic.NET there are two kinds of sub procedures, event and user-defined. An ***event procedure*** belongs to a specific object or event. A ***user-defined sub procedure*** is not associated with a specific object but can be invoked, or called, by more than one object. Most of the procedures you wrote in Chapters 1 through 6 are event procedures.

DECLARING A SUB PROCEDURE

The event procedures you wrote in the preceding chapters use the same syntax that is required for declaring user-defined sub procedures. All procedures begin with the **Sub** keyword and end with **End Sub**. The syntax for all procedures is as follows:

```
[accessibility] Sub subname[(argumentlist)]
    ' Statements of the Sub procedure go here
End Sub
```

- ■ The *accessibility* of a sub procedure determines the range of procedures that can make a call to the sub procedure

- ■ The **argumentlist** refers to a list of arguments that can be sent to the sub procedure.

Now let's explore sub procedures in more detail.

DETERMINING THE ACCESSIBILITY OF A SUB PROCEDURE

You can create a procedure by including one or more code statements in the procedure declaration. How you create a sub procedure depends on the kind of access you want the procedure to have. As explained previously, the accessibility of a procedure refers to the range of other program statements that can call it. For example, if only procedures on a form need to call the procedure, you can restrict, or limit, the procedure's accessibility. To limit the accessibility of a procedure, you assign a keyword to the procedure. These keywords are optional, but if you omit the accessibility, the sub procedure will have public accessibility. Sub procedures have public accessibility by default. Table 7.1 lists the accessibility options for the procedures you will create in this chapter.

Table 7.1: Accessibility keywords for procedures

Keyword	Access
Public	Declares a procedure to be accessible from anywhere within the same project or from other projects that reference the project.
Private	Declares a procedure that is available only to the procedure in which the function is declared.
Friend	Declares a procedure to be accessible from within the same project but not from outside the project.

An example of a declaration statement for a procedure is the code contained in an **Exit** button or an **Exit** menu item. The code statements for an event procedure are contained within an event associated with the specific object. Following is an example of an event procedure you used in many of the programs in previous chapters:

```
Private Sub btnExit_Click(ByVal sender As System.Object, ByVal e
    As System.EventArgs) Handles btnExit.Click
Dim intResponse As Integer
intResponse = MsgBox("Do you really want to exit this
    application?", 276, "Exit?")
    If intResponse = 6 Then
        End
    End If
End Sub
```

This procedure identifies the event that contains the procedure; the btnExit_Click event. The **Private** keyword indicates that the procedure belongs to the click event for the *btnExit* control. No other procedure can call the click event, because it is private to this declaration procedure. The procedure declares a variable named *intResponse* for containing the result of the user input in the message box verifying the user's intent to exit or terminate the application. If the user clicks the **Yes** button, the application terminates and the procedure ends. If the user clicks the **No** button, the procedure ends without terminating the application.

CREATING USER-DEFINED PROCEDURES

You can also create user-defined sub procedures. For example, you could write a user-defined sub procedure for exiting a program. More than one control in a program can call this sub procedure. Rather than writing the procedure in two places, you write the statements in one place (the user-defined sub procedure) and then include a statement in the code for each control that can call the procedure. Calculations, manipulating text or controls, and managing database records are procedures you might want to call from various controls. Following is an example of a user-defined sub procedure:

```
Friend Sub AppExit()
Dim intResponse As Integer
intResponse = MsgBox("Do you really want to exit this
    application?", 276, "Exit?")
    If intResponse = 6 Then
        End
    End If
End Sub
```

Because an event procedure identifies the specific event that runs the procedure, from this point on we will refer to both event procedures and user-defined procedures as sub procedures.

This sub procedure is almost identical to the event procedure shown earlier, except that it does not name a specific event that runs the procedure. The procedure is named *AppExit*. The guidelines for naming procedures are to use a noun that describes the action performed by the procedure. If the procedure requires more than one noun to describe it, combine nouns into one phrase, and capitalize the first character of each noun in the phrase. To run the code in this procedure, you must make a reference to the procedure by name (AppExit) in a code statement. A code statement that references a sub procedure is known as the calling code. The **calling code** is a statement or an expression within a statement that specifies the procedure by name; it can also be referred to as the **calling statement.** The procedure containing the calling code is sometimes referred to as the **calling procedure**. When the procedure is called, the statements in the sub procedure are run. When the procedure is finished running, the code statements following the calling procedure run.

Let's return to the previous example, in which a procedure for exiting or terminating an application can be called from multiple event handlers. The *Procedure* solution included with your data files contains the *AppExit* procedure shown earlier.

CALLING A SUB PROCEDURE

The *AppExit* procedure incorporates the code used in previous chapters for exiting an application. You have used these statements in the event handlers for button click and menu click events.

The *Procedures* solution contains three controls that can call the *AppExit* sub procedure: a command button, a menu item, and a context menu item. Because the procedure is declared with the **Friend** keyword, any event handler in the application can call the procedure, and it is therefore accessible from any other procedure within the application. Each of the following event procedures makes a call to the *AppExit* procedure:

```
Private Sub btnExit_Click(ByVal sender As System.Object, ByVal e
  As System.EventArgs) Handles btnExit.Click
    Call AppExit()
End Sub

Private Sub mnuFileExit_Click(ByVal sender As System.Object,
  ByVal e As System.EventArgs) Handles mnuFileExit.Click
    Call AppExit()
End Sub

Private Sub cmnuFileExit_Click(ByVal sender As System.Object,
  ByVal e As System.EventArgs) Handles cmnuFileExit.Click
    Call AppExit()
End Sub
```

 **Tip** When you call a procedure, you can include the **Call** statement, but this is optional. By simply referencing the name of the called procedure in the calling code, you invoke the procedure.

Figure 7.1 displays the *AppExit* sub procedure as it appears in the Code Editor.

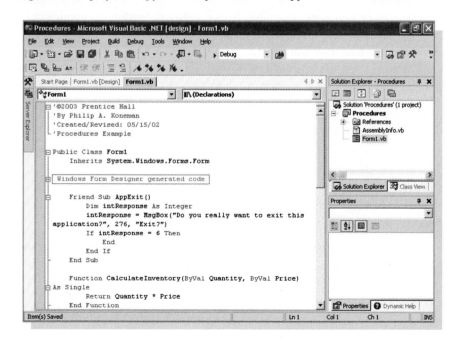

FIGURE 7.1. *The AppExit( ) sub procedure*

Figure 7.2 displays the three event procedures that make a call to the *AppExit* sub procedure.

FIGURE 7.2. *Three event procedures that call the AppExit() sub procedure (note that the Call statement is omitted)*

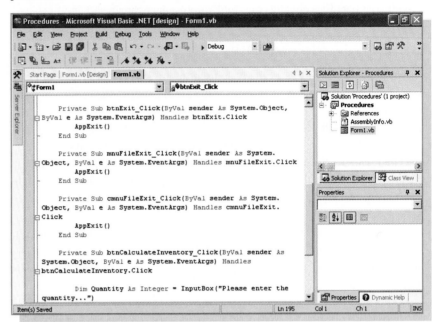

How do sub procedures reduce code and promote program efficiency? Because the *AppExit* sub procedure is written once and not replicated in the three event procedures that exit the application, program maintenance is improved. If you need to modify the routine, you modify the procedure, and each of the calling procedures runs the updated code contained in the procedure.

PASSING ARGUMENTS TO SUB PROCEDURES

At times, a sub procedure needs data to perform an action. A sub procedure can accept values that are sent to it. A value sent to a function procedure is called an ***argument***. An argument can be a constant, a variable, or an expression. Sending an argument to a procedure is called ***passing*** an argument. A procedure that accepts an argument includes a ***parameter*** that receives the argument.

For example, consider the following sub procedure, named *DisplayInfo*, which is from the *Employee Information* solution included with your data files:

```
Private Sub DisplayInfo(ByVal strFirstName, ByVal strLastName,
  ByVal decSalary)
    lblInfo.Text = "Employee Information:" & vbCrLf _
    & "First Name: " & strFirstName & vbCrLf _
    & "Last Name: " & strLastName & vbCrLf _
    & "Annual Salary: " & Format(decSalary, "Currency")
End Sub
```

This procedure receives three arguments for displaying employee information: first name, last name, and annual salary. The following calling procedure obtains these values, sends them to the *DisplayInfo* procedure, and displays them on the form shown in Figure 7.3.

Tip

Remember that the Call keyword is optional; it does not appear in the calling procedures shown in Figure 7.2.

Tip

A parameter is a variable name in a procedure, and an argument is a value sent to the function. Therefore, functions can include parameters that accept arguments.

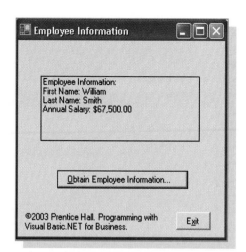

FIGURE 7.3. *Form displaying employee information*

```
Private Sub btnInfo_Click(ByVal sender As System.Object, ByVal e
    As System.EventArgs) Handles btnInfo.Click
Dim strFirstName, strLastName As String, decSalary As Decimal
    strFirstName = InputBox("Please enter the employee's first
        name...")
    strLastName = InputBox("Please enter the employee's last
        name...")
    decSalary = InputBox("Please enter the employee's annual
        salary...")
    Call DisplayInfo(strFirstName, strLastName, decSalary)
End Sub
```

Now that you know how to declare and use sub procedures, let's see how to use sub procedures to support data validation.

USING A SUB PROCEDURE TO PERFORM DATA VALIDATION

You can perform data validation by using sub procedures in your applications. In Chapter 3 you learned how to use decision structures to perform data validation. In Chapter 5 you learned how to handle exceptions in Visual Basic.NET. In this chapter, you will bring it all together by learning how to use a sub procedure for data validation that handles invalid data as an exception.

Within Visual Basic.NET controls, the *CausesValidation property* determines whether the control causes validation to be performed when the control is clicked. By default, the **CausesValidation** property for a control such as a text box is **True**. To perform validation by handling an event using the CausesValidation property, you need to write a procedure that handles the event. The form shown in Figure 7.4 requires three values obtained by the user to calculate the payment for a loan.

Notice that the code for the *DisplayInfo* procedure includes the **ByVal** keyword. You will learn about passing arguments By Value (**ByVal**) and By Reference (**ByRef**) later in this chapter.

FIGURE 7.4. *Form containing text box controls for obtaining required user input*

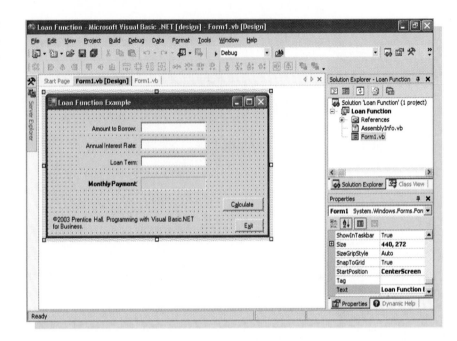

How can you validate user input? One method you can use is to include an If...Then statement to determine if a required value is entered into each text box. In the statements for the click event procedure for the button or menu item for calculating the loan payment, you would include the code statement for performing data validation. In this case, you would use one or more decision structures to determine what has been entered into the text boxes and provide user feedback if the values are zero or are not numeric.

Another method is to write a sub procedure that handles an event raised by the **CausesValidation** property. To raise an event is to trigger the event by some action, such as trying to tab out of a text box that requires a value. The sub procedures that follow handle the event that is raised when the **CausesValidation** property of the controls for obtaining the loan principal, loan rate, and loan term are set to **True**. These sub procedures are contained in the *Loan Payment* solution you will create as an Exercise at the end of this chapter.

Validating the Loan Principal

```
Private Sub txtPrincipal_Validating(ByVal sender As
  System.Object, ByVal e As
  System.ComponentModel.CancelEventArgs) Handles
  txtPrincipal.Validating
    Try
        If Val(txtPrincipal.Text) < 2000 Or
          Val(txtPrincipal.Text) > 50000 Then
            Throw New Exception()
        End If
    Catch ex As Exception
        ' Cancel the event and select the text to be corrected
          by the user
        e.Cancel = True
```

```vb
        txtPrincipal.Select(0, txtPrincipal.Text.Length)
        MsgBox("The loan amount must be a number between 2000
            and 50000.", MsgBoxStyle.Critical, "Invalid Entry!")
    End Try
End Sub
```

Validating the Loan Rate

```vb
Private Sub txtRate_Validating(ByVal sender As System.Object,
  ByVal e As System.ComponentModel.CancelEventArgs) Handles
  txtRate.Validating
    Try
        If Val(txtRate.Text) < 0.025 Or Val(txtRate.Text) >
            0.125 Then
            Throw New Exception()
        End If
    Catch ex As Exception
        ' Cancel the event and select the text to be corrected
            by the user
        e.Cancel = True
        txtRate.Select(0, txtRate.Text.Length)
        MsgBox("The loan rate must be a decimal value greater
            than zero and less than 15%.", MsgBoxStyle.Critical,
            "Invalid Entry!")
    End Try
End Sub
```

Validating the Loan Term

```vb
Private Sub txtTerm_Validating(ByVal sender As System.Object,
  ByVal e As System.ComponentModel.CancelEventArgs) Handles
  txtTerm.Validating
    Try
        If Val(txtTerm.Text) < 1 Or Val(txtTerm.Text) > 10 Then
            Throw New Exception()
        End If
    Catch ex As Exception
        ' Cancel the event and select the text to be corrected
            by the user
        e.Cancel = True
        txtTerm.Select(0, txtTerm.Text.Length)
        MsgBox("The loan term must be at least 1 and not more
            than 10.", MsgBoxStyle.Critical, "Invalid Entry!")
    End Try
End Sub
```

Each of these sub procedures performs data validation in response to the ***Validating event*** for a control. When the user tabs out of a control or selects another control on the form, an error message appears if the data validation requirements are violated. The routine that catches the exception thrown by the violation generates the error message. The validation rules are as follows:

Control	Validation Rule
txtPrincipal	The loan principal must be a value between $2,000 and $50,000.
txtRate	The annual interest rate must be a value between 2.5% and 12.5%.
txtTerm	The loan term must be at least one year but not greater than 10 years.

Each sub procedure begins with a handler that will be called if the text box is empty, contains any non-numeric characters, or contains a numeric value that violates the business rules. A Try. . . Catch. . . Finally statement determines if the rule for each control is violated. If the rule is violated, an exception is thrown and an error message is displayed to the user. Figure 7.5 displays the error message that appears when a user tabs out of the *txtPrincipal* text box without entering a value.

FIGURE 7.5. *Error message when the* txtPrincipal *text box does not contain a valid value*

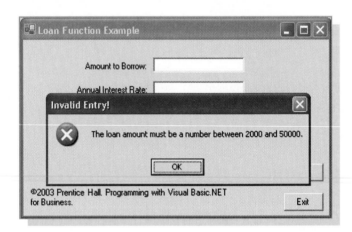

When you write even one sub procedure to handle an event raised by a Validating event, your form should contain at least one control with the **CausesValidation** property set to **False** as an exit point for the procedure. If all the controls have the **CausesValidation** property set to **True**, any action will change the focus to the object that has violated the validation rules, and the user will be unable to cancel the operation. Thus, a good strategy is to set the **CausesValidation** property of an Exit button to **False**.

Now that you understand how to use event procedures and user-defined sub procedures in your programs, let's learn how to return values to a calling procedure by using function procedures.

Using Function Procedures

A *function procedure* performs a series of actions or tasks and returns a value. A function procedure is a series of code statements enclosed by the ***Function*** and ***End Function*** statements. A function procedure is very similar to a user-defined sub procedure, except that a function procedure returns a value to the procedure that calls it. You use a function procedure when you need the procedure to perform an action and return a value. A function procedure can also accept arguments passed to it by the calling procedure. The syntax for a function procedure is as follows:

```
[accessibility] Function functionname[(argumentlist)] As
     datatype
   ' Statements of the Function procedure.
End Function
```

- The **accessibility** of a function determines the range of procedures that can make a call to the function.

- The **argumentlist** refers to a list of arguments (parameters) that can be sent to the sub procedure.

- The **datatype** of an argument specifies what kind of data the argument contains.

You call a function procedure in the same way you call a sub procedure. To call a function, a calling procedure includes a reference to the name of the function, including any arguments sent to it. By default, the accessibility of a procedure is Public so it can be called from anywhere within an application.

Now let's explore function procedures in more detail.

INTRINSIC FUNCTION PROCEDURES

Visual Basic.NET includes several predefined functions you can call from within your applications. You used a few of these in previous solutions. The **Val** function accepts a string value and returns a numeric value. The **Format** function returns a formatted string or variable to a value passed to it. The **Pmt**, **IPmt**, and **PPmt** functions accept arguments for a loan's principal, rate, and term and then return payment information. Intrinsic function procedures provide predefined functionality you can include in your applications.

CREATING USER-DEFINED FUNCTION PROCEDURES

You can create user-defined function procedures in almost the same way you create user-defined sub procedures. A function procedure begins with the **Function** keyword and ends with an **End Function** statement. Consider the following example:

```
Private Function CashBonus(ByVal sngSale) As Single
'Declare a variable for the bonus percentage
Dim sngBonus As Single

    'Determine bonus percentage based upon employee type
    If rdbHourly.Checked = True Then
        sngBonus = 0.035
    Else
        sngBonus = 0.05
    End If
    'Calculate the bonus and return the value to the calling
      procedure
    Return sngBonus * sngSale
End Function
```

Assume that the employees at a Home Electronics store earn a cash bonus for sales totaling $500 or more. The bonus is a percentage of the sale, but the percentage varies depending on whether the employee is an hourly or a salaried employee. Hourly employees earn a 3.5% bonus on sales of $500 or more, and salaried employees earn a 5% bonus on these sales. The application determines the employee's status, verifies the amount of the sale, and calculates the bonus. Using the function we just looked at, Figure 7.6 displays the calculated bonus for an hourly employee on a sale totaling $650. This calculation is performed when the user clicks the *btnCalculate* button.

FIGURE 7.6. *Bonus calculation for a sale of $650 made by an hourly employee*

The function for calculating the bonus is named *CashBonus* and is contained in the *Cash Bonus* solution included with your data files. It receives an argument for the sales amount, determines the employee type, and assigns the appropriate bonus percentage to the Bonus variable. Every function procedure has a data type, just as every variable does. The data type is specified by the **As** clause in the Function statement and determines the type of the return value.

Calling a Function Procedure and Passing a Variable to the Procedure

You can call a function procedure by using either an assignment statement or an expression. In the following example, the calling procedure obtains the sales amount from the user and performs data validation on the amount entered in an input box. If the amount of the sale is at least $500, the amount of sale is assigned to the *sngSaleAmount* variable and the function is called. Otherwise, an error message is displayed. The message box that includes the statement to call the *CashBonus* function passes the SaleAmount variable to the procedure. The result is returned to the calling procedure and displayed in a message box. The following calling procedure calls the *CashBonus* function:

```
Private Sub btnCalculate_Click(ByVal sender As System.Object,
  ByVal e As System.EventArgs) Handles btnCalculate.Click
'Declare a variable for the sale amount
Dim sngSaleAmount As Single

'Obtain the sale amount
sngSaleAmount = Val(InputBox("Please enter the amount of the
  sale", "Enter Sale Amount"))

'Perform data validation
    If sngSaleAmount <= 500 Then
        MsgBox("The amount of the sales must be at least $500
            to qualify for a bonus. Please try again.",
            MsgBoxStyle.Exclamation, "Invalid Sales Amount")
    Else
```

```
       MsgBox(Format(CashBonus(sngSaleAmount), "Currency"),
          MsgBoxStyle.Information, "Employee Bonus")
      End If
'Call the CashBonus procedure, sending the Sale Amount as an
  argument
CashBonus(sngSaleAmount)
End Sub
```

The calling statement is:

```
CashBonus(sngSaleAmount)
```

Let's explore the code. The calling procedure calls the *CashBonus* function procedure, which requires a single argument (*sngSale*) for the amount of the sale. The calling procedure passes the value of the *sngSaleAmount* variable to the procedure, which returns the calculate value to the calling statement. Notice that the name of the passed variable does not need to be the same as the argument name in the procedure. Figure 7.7 shows how the calling function passes the *sngSaleAmount* variable to the *sngSale* argument of the *CashBonus* procedure.

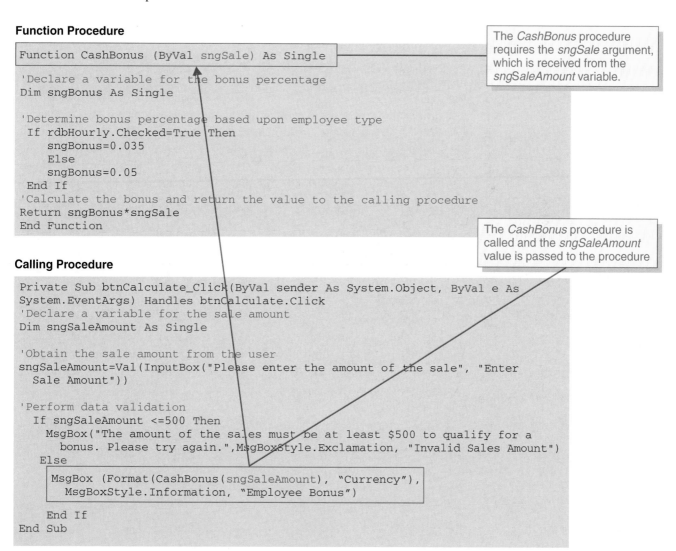

Function Procedure

```
Function CashBonus (ByVal sngSale) As Single

'Declare a variable for the bonus percentage
Dim sngBonus As Single

'Determine bonus percentage based upon employee type
 If rdbHourly.Checked=True Then
    sngBonus=0.035
    Else
    sngBonus=0.05
 End If
'Calculate the bonus and return the value to the calling procedure
Return sngBonus*sngSale
End Function
```

> The *CashBonus* procedure requires the *sngSale* argument, which is received from the *sngSaleAmount* variable.

> The *CashBonus* procedure is called and the *sngSaleAmount* value is passed to the procedure

Calling Procedure

```
Private Sub btnCalculate_Click(ByVal sender As System.Object, ByVal e As
System.EventArgs) Handles btnCalculate.Click
'Declare a variable for the sale amount
Dim sngSaleAmount As Single

'Obtain the sale amount from the user
sngSaleAmount=Val(InputBox("Please enter the amount of the sale", "Enter
  Sale Amount"))

'Perform data validation
 If sngSaleAmount <=500 Then
    MsgBox("The amount of the sales must be at least $500 to qualify for a
      bonus. Please try again.",MsgBoxStyle.Exclamation, "Invalid Sales Amount")
   Else
    MsgBox (Format(CashBonus(sngSaleAmount), "Currency"),
       MsgBoxStyle.Information, "Employee Bonus")

    End If
End Sub
```

FIGURE 7.7. *Calling procedure sending a value to a function procedure*

In the code shown in Figure 7.7, is the bonus amount displayed in the message box formatted?

You can format the result of the function by using the predefined Format function you used previously. You will recall that the Format function requires two arguments: the expression to format and a valid style. In this case, the expression will be the result of the *CashBonus* function. The style can be "C", "c", or "Currency". Any of these style parameters will display the result with the thousands separator, two digits to the right of the decimal separator, and a currency symbol.

To format the function result, make changes to the calling procedure. The following statement is the code for the btnCalculate_Click event. In addition, the Information symbol is displayed, and the title bar of the message box contains a text string.

```
MsgBox(Format(CashBonus(sngSaleAmount), "Currency"),
   MsgBoxStyle.Information, "Employee Bonus")
```

This calling procedure formats the result as currency.

Passing More Than One Variable to a Procedure

In the preceding example, you passed one variable to the procedure. Let's look at an application that passes two variables to a function procedure. Let's say you need to calculate the value of the inventory for a specific item. The value of an inventory item is calculated as the number of items in stock multiplied by the price of the item. This can be represented by a simple formula:

```
Inventory Value = Units in Stock * Price
```

The function you create to calculate inventory values will receive two arguments: the units in stock and the price of the item. The calling procedure will obtain the units in stock and the item price from the user and then pass these parameters to the function procedure. In your data files, the *Procedures* solution contains a function named *CalculateInventory*. The code for the function is as follows:

```
Private Function CalculateInventory(ByVal intQuantity, ByVal
   sngPrice) As Single
      Return intQuantity * sngPrice
End Function
```

This function uses the ***Return statement*** to return the results of the calculation to the calling procedure.

The calling procedure declares two variables for the quantity in stock and the item price and then uses two consecutive **Input** function statements to validate the user entries and assign values to the variables. After obtaining these values, the function calculates the inventory value and displays the result in a message box. Following is the calling procedure:

```
Private Sub btnCalculateInventory_Click(ByVal sender As
   System.Object, ByVal e As System.EventArgs) Handles
   btnCalculateInventory.Click
      Dim intQuantity As Integer, sngPrice As Single
intQuantity = Val(InputBox("Please enter the quantity in stock.
   .."))
   If intQuantity <= 0 Then
```

```
        MsgBox("The quantity must be greater than zero. Please
            try again.", MsgBoxStyle.Critical, "Invalid
            Quantity")
        Else
        sngPrice = Val(InputBox("Please enter the retail price
            for this item. . ."))
        If sngPrice <= 0 Then
            MsgBox("The price must be greater than zero.
                Please try again.", MsgBoxStyle.Critical,
                "Invalid Price")
            Else
            MsgBox(Format(CalculateInventory(sngPrice,
                intQuantity), "Currency"),
                MsgBoxStyle.Information, "Inventory Value")
        End If
    End If
End Sub
```

When you run the application and enter 120 units of an item selling for $7.99, the result is shown in Figure 7.8.

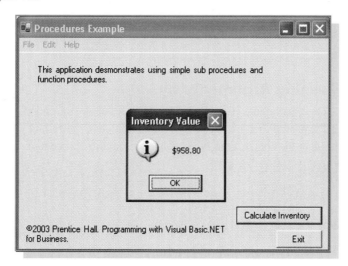

FIGURE 7.8. *Inventory value as calculated by the* InventoryValue *function*

PASSING ARGUMENTS BYVAL AND BYREF

In Visual Basic.NET, you can pass an argument to a procedure by value or by reference. Passing an argument by value means the called procedure cannot modify the contents of the variable element in the calling code underlying the argument. Passing an argument by reference allows the called procedure to modify the contents in the same way that the calling code itself can.

You can specify how an argument is passed to a procedure by passing the variable to the procedure by value or by reference. You can use the **ByVal** or **ByRef** keyword when referencing the argument in the function procedure to determine how the function uses the variable. If you require the variable in the calling procedure to keep its value and not be changed by the function, use the *ByVal keyword* when passing the variable to the procedure. If, however, the procedure must change the value of the variable it receives before returning a value, use the *ByRef keyword*.

When you pass a variable to a procedure by value, you are passing the current value of the variable, so it cannot be changed by the function receiving the variable. When you pass a variable by reference, you pass the variable's reference in memory, which gives the called procedure access to the variable itself. For example, you might use a variable as a counter and require the called procedure to increment its value. Or the opposite might be the case; the variable passed to the called procedure might need to remain a fixed value, such as the gross pay for an employee.

The following examples demonstrate how the **ByVal** and **ByRef** keywords affect the value of a variable that belongs to the calling procedure. Your data files include a solution named *Passing Arguments*. Figure 7.9 shows the interface for this application.

FIGURE 7.9. *Interface for the* Passing Arguments *solution*

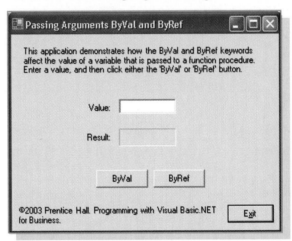

Passing Arguments by Value

When a variable is passed to a procedure by value, the called procedure can modify the value passed to it, but the value of the variable in the calling procedure will not change. Look at the code for the *IncrementByVal* function procedure:

```
Private Function IncrementByVal(ByVal intValue)
    intValue = intValue + 10
    Return intValue
End Function
```

The function procedure receives the *intValue* variable, attempts to change the value, and returns the updated value to the calling procedure. Now look at the code for the calling procedure:

```
Private Sub btnByVal_Click(ByVal sender As System.Object, ByVal
    e As System.EventArgs) Handles btnByVal.Click
Dim intValue As Integer
    intValue = Val(txtValue.Text)
    lblResult.Text = IncrementByVal(intValue)
    MsgBox(intValue)
End Sub
```

The calling procedure assigns the user entry from a text box to the *intValue* variable. The *IncrementByVal* procedure is called, and the result is assigned to the text property of a label. After receiving the return value, the calling procedure displays the value of the *intValue* variable in a message box. If you enter 200 in the text box and click the **ByVal** button, the procedure returns 210 as the return value and displays 210 in the label on the form. The message box, however, displays 200. Although the return value has been changed, the variable is unchanged, as Figure 7.10 shows.

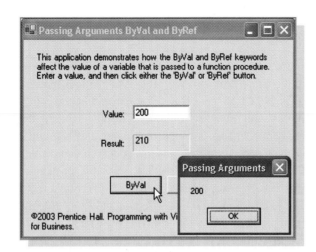

FIGURE 7.10. *Passing a variable to a procedure by value*

Passing Arguments by Reference

Now look at the code for a function procedure that uses the ByRef keyword:

```
Private Function IncrementByVal(ByRef intValue)
    intValue = intValue + 10
    Return intValue
End Function
```

This function is identical to the *IncrementByVal* function, except that it uses the ByRef keyword. Now look at the code for a calling procedure that calls this function:

```
Private Sub btnByRef_Click(ByVal sender As System.Object, ByVal
  e As System.EventArgs) Handles btnByRef.Click
Dim intValue As Integer
    intValue = Val(txtValue.Text)
    lblResult.Text = IncrementByRef(intValue)
    MsgBox(intValue)
End Sub
```

The calling procedure is also identical to the IncrementByVal calling procedure, except it calls the *ByRef* function. When you enter 200 in the text box and click the **ByRef** button, the procedure returns 210 and the value of the underlying variable is also changed to 210, as Figure 7.11 shows.

In Visual Basic.NET, parameters are passed **ByVal** by default for variables. References to classes, interfaces, and arrays are passed **ByRef** by default. You will learn about passing array parameters in Chapter 8.

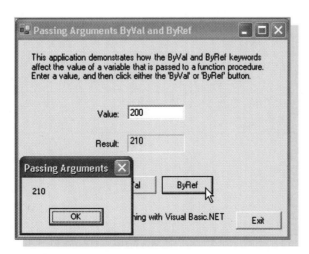

FIGURE 7.11. *Passing a variable to a procedure by reference*

ORGANIZING PROCEDURES BY USING THE #REGION STATEMENT

When you create sub- and function procedures, you might want to organize your code in the Code Editor so that it is easier to manage. You already know that the Visual Basic.NET IDE has a feature for expanding and collapsing code segments in the Code Editor, with tree view controls for displaying and hiding the code contained within the segments. You can add code to a segment by creating a code region. A *region* is an area of the Code Editor that contains code you can display or hide by expanding and collapsing the region. Code regions are useful for maintaining the Code Editor and therefore making code easier to manage. You create a region by entering one or more code blocks enclosed within the ***#Region*** and ***#End Region*** statements. Here is an example from the *Payroll* solution you will create later in this chapter. The code region is named *Procedures*.

```
#Region "Procedures"
Function CalculatePay(ByVal Hours, ByVal PayRate)
    sngGrossPay = Hours * PayRate
    sngTotalTaxes = (sngGrossPay * fedTax) + (sngGrossPay *
        stateTax) + (sngGrossPay * localTax)
    sngNetPay = sngGrossPay - sngTotalTaxes
    Return sngNetPay
End Function
Friend Sub AppExit()
    Dim intResponse As Integer
    intResponse = MsgBox("Do you really want to exit this
        application?", 276, "Exit?")
    If intResponse = 6 Then
        End
    End If
End Sub
#End Region
```

Notice that the statement defining a region begins and ends with the pound sign (#) character.

Once the procedure is contained within a region, you can collapse the entire region in the Code Editor by clicking the minus sign (-) next to the name of the region. Figure 7.12 displays the Code Editor with the code region collapsed.

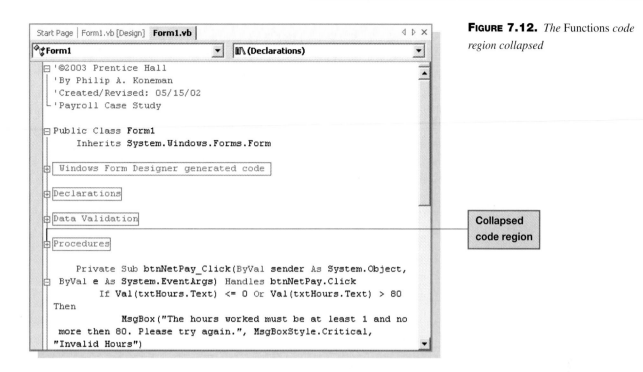

FIGURE 7.12. *The* Functions *code region collapsed*

Collapsed code region

Figure 7.13 shows the code region expanded. To expand a region, click the plus sign (+) next to the region name.

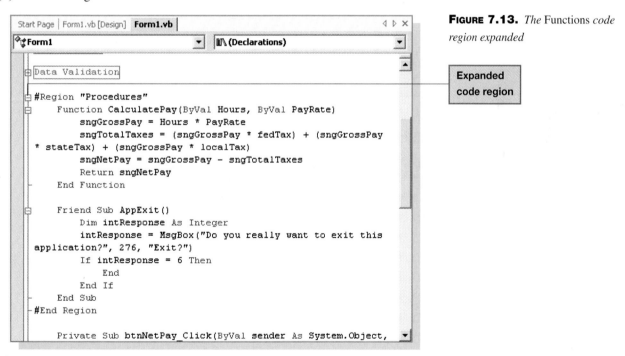

FIGURE 7.13. *The* Functions *code region expanded*

Expanded code region

You have learned how to streamline your code by using functions and procedures. You can further manage and organize your applications by creating modules.

Using Modules and Multiple Forms in Windows Applications

A *module* is a component you can add to a project that provides a simple way of organizing functions and other program elements, such as variables, that are used anywhere (globally) in a solution. A module contains code but no controls or other interface elements such as forms and controls. You can add a module to a project by using code or by using the IDE. To add a module to your project by using the IDE, choose **Project**, **Add Module**, as shown in Figure 7.14.

FIGURE 7.14. *Adding a module to a project*

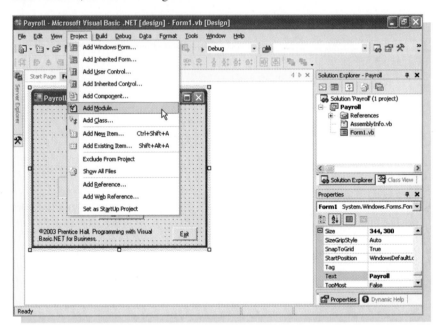

When the **Add New Item** dialog box appears, select **Module** in the Templates: pane and click **Open**, as shown in Figure 7.15.

FIGURE 7.15. *Selecting a module template*

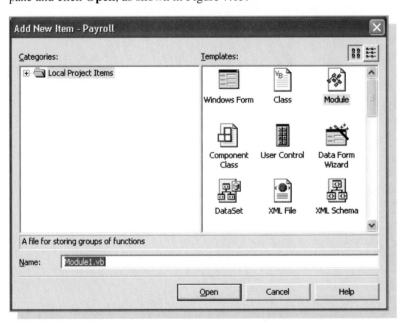

The Code Editor displays the statements to declare and end the module, and the Solution Explorer now includes the *Module1.vb* file. You can enter the module statements directly in the Code Editor. You can declare a module as **Public** and make its data and functions available to procedures outside the module. By default, modules have **Friend** access.

USING MODULES

After you add a module to a project, you can use it to store code statements and procedures that are used by other objects in the project. Your data files include a solution named *Using Modules* that contains the forms and the module shown in Figure 7.16.

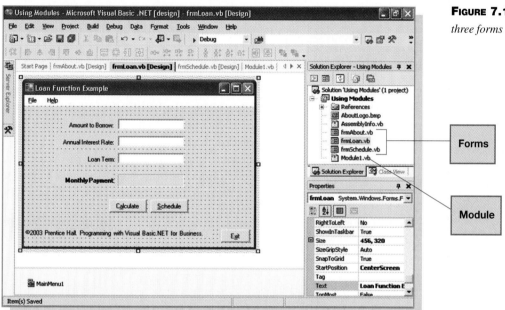

FIGURE 7.16. *Solution containing three forms and one module*

A module contains only program code. The code in this module is grouped by regions. Figure 7.17 shows the first two regions in the module.

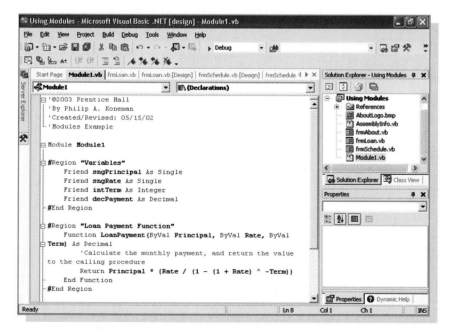

FIGURE 7.17. *Two code regions in the* Module1 *module*

The first region declares variables that will be available to other objects in the solution. Notice that each variable is declared with **Friend** access.

The next region includes a function for calculating the monthly payment for a loan. The function has three arguments, *Principal*, *Rate*, and *Term*, and therefore accepts three values from the calling procedure.

The arguments are passed by value, so the function will not be able to modify the values stored in the variables holding the values passed to the procedure. Here's the function procedure for calculating the monthly payment:

Notice that the arguments for the function do not require the same names as the variables passed to the function.

```
Function LoanPayment(ByVal Principal, ByVal Rate, ByVal Term) As
    Decimal
'Calculate the monthly payment, and return the value to the
    calling procedure
    Return Principal * (Rate / (1 - (1 + Rate) ^ -Term))
End Function
```

The function calculates the loan payment by using the values passed to it and returns the payment to the calling procedure. The formula for calculating the monthly payment uses each of the three arguments passed to it. The return value is a decimal value, because the procedure is declared as a Decimal data type.

Now let's look at a calling procedure that calls the function and passes the arguments to it. The calling procedure is an event procedure that handles the click event for the *btnCalculate* button appearing on the *frmLoan* form. The event procedure is as follows:

To calculate the monthly payment for a loan, you can either use the intrinsic Pmt function, or create an expression using this formula:
Payment = Principal * (Rate / (1 - (1 + Rate) ^ -Term)).

```
Private Sub btnCalculate_Click(ByVal sender As System.Object,
    ByVal e As System.EventArgs) Handles btnCalculate.Click
    'Assign values to variables
    sngPrincipal = Val(txtPrincipal.Text)
    sngRate = Val(txtRate.Text) / 12
    intTerm = Val(txtTerm.Text) * 12
    'Call the loan function and assign the return value to a
        variable
    decPayment = LoanPayment(sngPrincipal, sngRate, intTerm)
    lblMonthlyPayment.Text = Format(decPayment, "currency")
    btnSchedule.Enabled = True
End Sub
```

The procedure begins by assigning the values stored in three text boxes to the *sngPrincipal*, *sngRate*, and *intTerm* variables.

The procedure then calls the *LoanPayment* function and assigns the return value to the *decPayment* variable. The calling procedure passes the values of the *sngPrincipal*, *sngRate*, and *intTerm* variables to the function.

Notice that the procedure does not validate the data. This is because the three text boxes have their **CausesValidation** property set to True, and an event procedure for each control validates the user input.

The last statement in the procedure sets the Enabled property of the *btnSchedule* button to True. The Form_Load event disables this button until the monthly payment is calculated.

Now let's see how the function works. Figure 7.18 displays the monthly payment for a loan of $6,000 at 6%, paid back over 4 years.

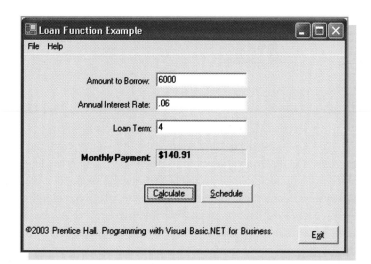

FIGURE 7.18. *Return value from the LoanPayment function*

The event procedure for the *btnSchedule* button calls a sub procedure that calculates the principal and interest payments for each month and creates a simple schedule listing these payments and the loan balance. The calling procedure is as follows:

```
Private Sub btnSchedule_Click(ByVal sender As System.Object,
  ByVal e As System.EventArgs) Handles btnSchedule.Click
    Call CreateSchedule()
End Sub
```

Now let's look at the sub procedure that creates the payment schedule. This procedure is contained in the *Module1* module:

```
Sub CreateSchedule()
    Dim objSchedule As frmSchedule = New frmSchedule()
    Dim intPayment As Integer
    Dim decLoanPpmt As Decimal
    Dim decLoanIPmt As Decimal
    Dim decLoanBalance As Decimal
    'Initialize the loan beginning balance
    decLoanBalance = sngPrincipal
    'Clear the listbox of any prior items
    objSchedule.lstSchedule.Items.Clear()
    'Generate the repayment schedule
    For intPayment = 1 To intTerm
        'Calculate the interest payment and principal payment
        decLoanPpmt = PPmt(sngRate, intPayment, intTerm, -
          sngPrincipal)
        decLoanIPmt = IPmt(sngRate, intPayment, intTerm, -
          sngPrincipal)
        decLoanBalance = decLoanBalance - decLoanPpmt
        'Populate the list box with the payments
        objSchedule.lstSchedule.Items.Add _
        ("Payment #" & intPayment & vbTab & _
        Format(decLoanPpmt, "c") & vbTab & _
```

```
              Format(decLoanIPmt, "c") & vbTab & _
              Format(decLoanBalance, "c"))
      Next intPayment
      'Display the form as modal
      objSchedule.ShowDialog()
End Sub
```

The *CreateSchedule* procedure uses the values contained in the *sngPrincipal*, *sngRate*, and *intTerm* variables in its calculation. The procedure also declares the variables it needs to store the principal and interest payments, the loan balance, and the *intPayment* counter variable used to populate a list box with the schedule. In addition, the procedure declares an object variable that creates an instance of the *frmSchedule* form, because the loan payment schedule appears on another form. Figure 7.19 displays the loan repayment schedule.

FIGURE 7.19. *Form displaying the loan repayment schedule*

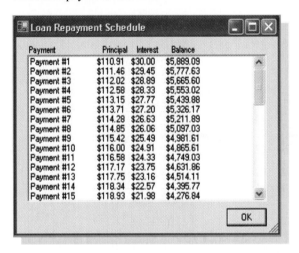

As you can see, sub procedures, function procedures, and modules help you simplify your application by breaking complex code into manageable units. You can organize procedures by using the #Region statement or by adding a module to your project and storing the called procedures in the module.

Now let's look at another example of a solution that contains a module, procedures, and multiple forms.

If you scroll to the bottom of the loan repayment schedule, the loan balance is zero after payment number 48.

☞ HANDS-ON PROGRAMMING EXAMPLE

Creating a Multiform Savings Analysis Application

A foundational principle in finance is the time value of money. Simply stated, money invested in an account that earns interest will increase in value over time, and the longer you have to invest, the more your investment will grow. You can calculate the value of an investment by using the intrinsic Visual Basic.NET *FV function*, which includes five parameters:

```
Future Value = FV(Interest/12, Term*12, -Additions,
Initial Deposit, Pay Type)
```

Where *Additions* are monthly contributions, the *Initial Deposit* is the amount deposited when the account is opened, and *Pay Type* indicates whether additional deposits are made at the beginning or the end of the month.

Figure 7.20 shows a Microsoft Excel workbook that calculates the future value of money in a savings account after one year.

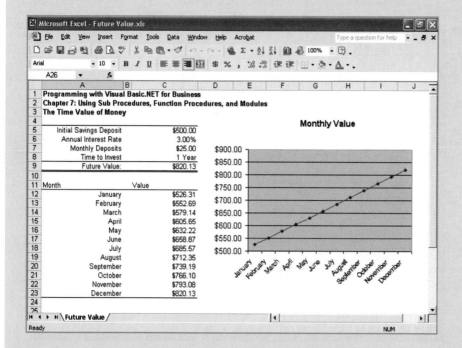

FIGURE 7.20. *The future value of money in a savings account*

As a student, you might have one or more student loans. Let's say you need to begin repaying your loan in three years. Before the payments begin, you are looking for a safe investment to help you save for the loan payments you will make. Your bank offers 1-, 2-, and 3-year Certificate of Deposit (CD) accounts that require a minimum investment of $500 and pay 4%, 5%, and 6% interest, respectively. You also have the option of making monthly deposits to the account, but you must determine the monthly amount at the time you open the account. You have decided to write a Visual Basic.NET application to explore various savings scenarios. In addition to simply calculating what your investment will be worth when the account reaches maturity, you are also interested in the monthly increase.

This exercise will teach you how to create a multiform application from the ground up and will demonstrate how to use a module for storing procedures. Your solution will consist of three forms: a Savings Plan, a Monthly Savings Report, and an About form. The solution will also contain one module for the procedures. Figure 7.21 shows the Savings Plan form, which appears when you run the application.

FIGURE 7.21. *The Savings Plan form*

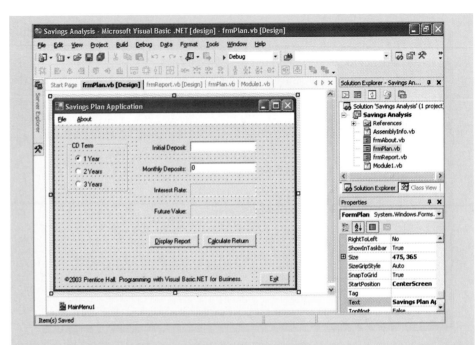

The application calculates the future value of money in a CD account, according to the following conditions:

1. A deposit of at least $500 is required to open the account.
2. The account will mature in 1, 2, or 3 years.
3. The annual interest rate depends on the CD term: 1 year, 4%; 2 years, 5%; 3 years, 6%.
4. Interest is compounded monthly.
5. You can make monthly deposits to your CD, but you must specify the monthly deposit amount when you open the account.

Plan the Application

The first step in planning an application is determining the inputs and outputs. The Savings Analysis application obtains user input and calculates the future value of an investment. The inputs and outputs are as follows:

Inputs	Outputs
Initial deposit	Future value
Monthly deposits	Schedule of monthly value
Interest rate	
Investment term	

The Savings Analysis application consists of three forms: the *Savings Plan* form for information about the account, the *Monthly Savings Report* form to list the value of the account on a monthly basis, and the *About* form, which provides information about the application.

Draw a visual representation of the forms on a blank piece of paper. Figure 7.22 displays a drawing of the user interface and the name of each control on the Savings Plan and Monthly Savings Report forms.

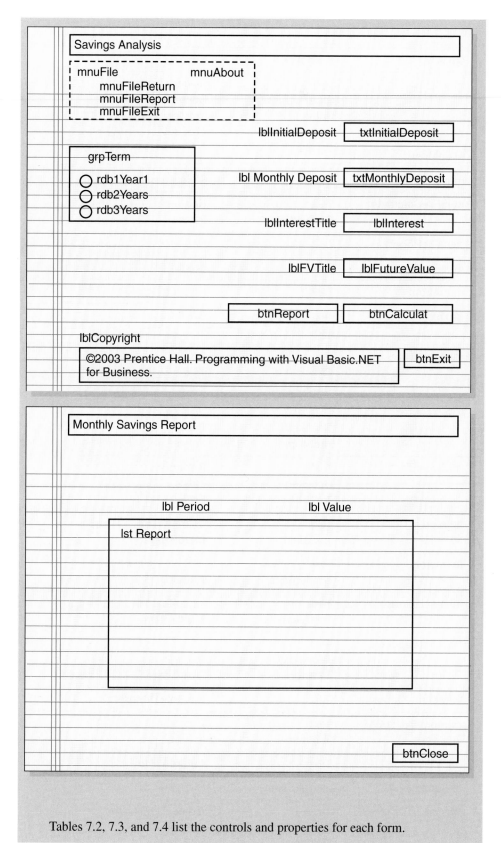

FIGURE 7.22. *The* frmPlan *form*

Tables 7.2, 7.3, and 7.4 list the controls and properties for each form.

Table 7.2: *Objects and properties for the* Savings Plan *form*

Object	Property	Setting
frmPlan	Text StartPosition Name Size	Savings Analysis CenterScreen frmPlan 475, 365
MainMenu1		
mnuFile	Text	&File
mnuFileCalculate	Text Enabled	Re&turn False
mnuFileReport	Text	Re&port
mnuFileExit	Text	E&xit
mnuAbout	Text	&About
grpTerm	Text TabIndex	CD Term 3
rdb1Year	Text Checked TabStop	1 Year True False
rdb2Years	Text Checked TabStop	2 Years False False
rdb3Years	Text Checked TabStop	3 Years False False
lblInterestTitle	Text TextAlign	Interest Rate: MiddleRight
lblInterest	Text BorderStyle	 Fixed3D
lblInitialDeposit	Text TextAlign	Initial Deposit: MiddleRight
txtInitialDeposit	Text TabIndex TabStop	 0 True
lblMonthlyDeposit	Text	Monthly Deposit
txtMonthlyDeposit	Text TabIndex	0 1
lblFVTitle	Text	Future Value
lblFutureValue	BorderStyle	Fixed3D
btnCalculate	Text Enabled TabStop	&Calculate Return False False

btnReport	Text TabStop	&Display Report False
btnExit	Text TabStop CausesValidation	E&xit False False
lblCopyright	Text	©2003 Prentice Hall. Programming with Visual Basic.NET for Business.

Table 7.3: *Objects and properties for the* Monthly Savings Report *form*

Object	Property	Setting
frmReport	Text StartPosition Size	Monthly Savings Report CenterScreen 375, 300
lstReport	TabStop	False
lblPeriod	Text	Period:
lblValue	Text	Current Value:
btnClose	Text TabStop TabIndex	&Close True 0

Table 7.4: *Objects and properties for the* About *form*

Object	Property	Setting
frmAbout	Text StartPosition	About Savings Plan CenterScreen
lblTitle	Text	About Savings Analysis

The application first displays the Savings Plan form. After selecting the term for the CD, the user can specify a monthly deposit option. The **Calculate Return** button or **Return** menu item calculates the return on the investment at the maturity date. These controls are disabled until the user enters an investment amount in the *txtInitialDeposit* text box. Once the data is validated and the future value is calculated, the Report button and menu item are activated. Clicking either of these calculates the monthly change in value and creates a report in a list box control on the Monthly Savings Report form.

The routine for calculating the future value and creating the monthly report are contained in a module. Data validation for the opening deposit and monthly additions are performed by using sub procedures that handle the **Validating** event for these controls. The pseudocode for the application's functionality is shown in Table 7.5.

Table 7.5: *Pseudocode for the Savings Analysis application*

Form or File	Event Procedure	Action
frmPlan	mnuFileReturn_Click	1. Call the Calculate sub procedure. 2. Display formatted results. 3. Activate the mnuFileReport and btnReport controls.
	mnuFileReport_Click	Call the CreateReport sub procedure.
	mnuFileExit_Click	Call the ExitApp sub procedure.
	mnuAbout_Click	Display the About form.
	btnCalculate_Click	1. Call the Calculate () procedure. 2. Display formatted results. 3. Activate the mnuFileReport and btnReport controls.
	TextPrincipal_Validating	Display a validation message if validation fails.
	txtMonthlyDeposit_ Validating	1. Set the Enabled property of the mnuFileReturn and btnCalculate controls to True. 2. Validate the monthly deposit amount. 3. Display a validation message if validation fails, and set the Enabled property of the mnuFileReturn and btnCalculate controls to False.
frmReport	btnOK_Click	Close the FormReport form.
	Calculate sub procedure	1. Obtain account values. 2. Call the CalculateValue function procedure. 3. Display the return value, formatted as currency.
Module1	CalculateReturn function procedure	1. Calculate future value. 2. Return results to the calling procedure.
	CreateReport sub procedure	1. Calculate the monthly account value. 2. Populate the list box with formatted report data. 3. Display the FormReport form.
	AppExit sub procedure	1. Verify user intent to terminate application. 2. Cancel or terminate.

Now that you have created the planning documents for the application, you are ready to begin designing the user interface in the IDE.

Design the User Interface

If you have not launched Visual Studio.NET, do so now. Perform each task that follows to complete this application.

To create a new project and solution:

1. Click **File**, **New**, **Project**.
2. Navigate to the drive and folder where you will save your project. Type `Savings Analysis` as the Project Name and click **OK**.
3. Right-click the *Form1.vb* form in the Solution Explorer and rename the form as `frmPlan.vb`. Set *frmPlan.vb* as the Startup object.
4. Display the properties for the form. Set the Name, Text, Size, and StartPosition properties as specified in Table 7.2.
5. Click **Project**, **Add New Item**.
6. Select **Windows Form** as the template type, type `frmReport.vb` as the form name, and click **Open**, as shown in Figure 7.23.

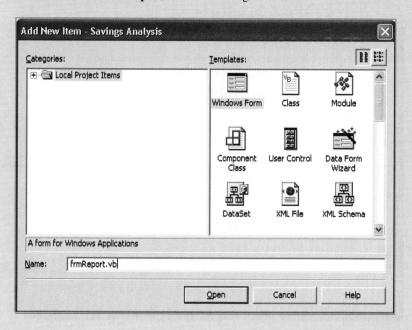

FIGURE 7.23. *Adding the frmReport form to the solution*

7. Set the Text, Size, and StartPosition for the form as specified in Table 7.3.
8. Click **Project**, **Add Module**. Accept the defaults shown in Figure 7.24 and click **Open**.

FIGURE 7.24. *Adding a module to the solution*

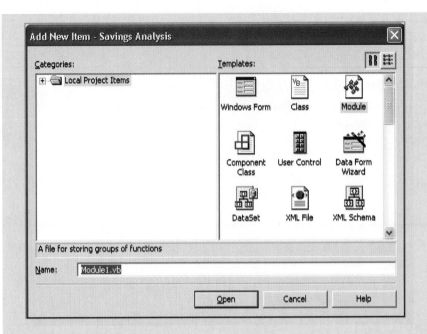

9. Right-click the *Savings Analysis* project in the Solution Explorer and select **Properties**.
10. The **Savings Analysis Property Pages** dialog box appears. Select *frmPlan* as the Startup Object and click **OK**.
11. Click **Project, Add Existing Item**. The **Add Existing Item** dialog box appears.
12. Navigate to the location containing the data files for this project. Select the *About.vb* file and click **Open**.
13. Right-click the *frmPlan.vb* form in the Solution Explorer and select **View Designer**.
14. Click **File, Save All**. Your solution now contains three forms and one module.

To add controls to the frmPlan form and set control properties:

1. Using Figure 7.21 as a guide, display the Toolbox and add the controls listed in Table 7.2 to the *frmPlan* form. Set the control properties as specified.
2. Save your changes.

To add controls to the frmReport form and set control properties:

1. Use the Form Designer to display the *frmReport.vb* form.
2. Display the Toolbox if necessary. Using Figure 7.22 as a guide, add the controls listed in Table 7.3 to the frmReport form.
3. Close the Toolbox and set the control properties as specified.
4. Save your changes. The form should look like Figure 7.25.

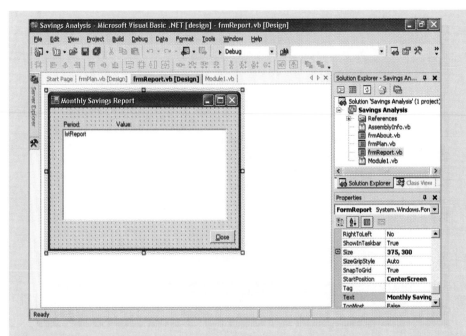

FIGURE 7.25. *The frmReport form*

Now that the interface design for the Savings Analysis application is complete, you are ready to write the code providing the functionality.

Write the Code

Let's begin by creating the procedures that will be contained on the *Module1.vb* file. The code for the module will declare variables, contain a function procedure for calculating the future value of the account, contain a sub procedure for creating the monthly investment report, and contain a sub procedure for exiting the application. Each of the module's procedures will be called by both button and menu item controls.

To add code to the project's module:

1. Right-click the *Module1.vb* file in the Solution Explorer and choose **View Code**.
2. Place the insertion point at the beginning of the Code Editor, and type the following comments:

```
'©2003 Prentice Hall
'By [Enter your name]
'Created/Revised: [Enter the date]
Savings Analysis Application
```

3. Place the insertion point below the module declaration statement and press ↵Enter twice. Type the following statements to define the region for declaring variables:

```
#Region "Declare Variables"
    Friend sngInitialDeposit As Single
    Friend sngMonthlyDeposit As Single
    Friend sngRate As Single
    Friend intTerm As Integer
#End Region
```

4. Place the Insertion Point below the Declare Variables region and press ⏎Enter twice. Type the following statements:

```
#Region "Sub Procedure to Exit"
    Friend Sub AppExit()
        Dim intResponse As Integer
        intResponse = MsgBox("Do you really want to exit this
            application?", 276, "Exit?")
        If intResponse = 6 Then
            End
        End If
    End Sub
#End Region
```

Why are these variables declared with **Friend** access?

FIGURE 7.26. *Code region for variable declarations*

When you finish, the Code Editor should look like Figure 7.26.

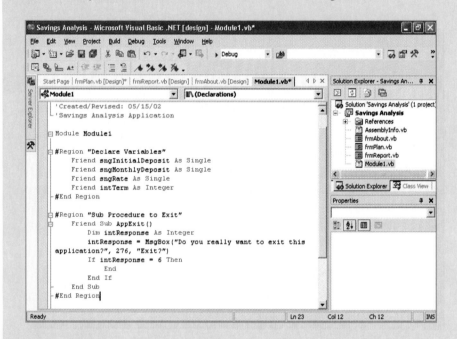

5. Collapse the two regions you just created. Press ⏎Enter twice and type the following statements:

```
#Region "Calculate Value Function"
    Function CalculateValue(ByVal Rate, ByVal Term, ByVal
        MonthlyDeposit, ByVal InitialDeposit)
    'Calculate the value at maturity, and return the value to
        the calling procedure
    Return FV(Rate / 12, Term * 12, -MonthlyDeposit, -
        InitialDeposit, DueDate.BegOfPeriod)
    End Function
#End Region
```

This function procedure calculates the future value of the account at maturity. The calling procedure sends four values to the *CalculateValue* procedure (Rate, Term, MonthlyDeposit, InitialDeposit).

6. Collapse the Calculate Value function region and press ⏎Enter twice. Type the following statements:

The **FV** function has five parameters. Four arguments are passed from the calling procedure. The fifth, which specifies whether the additional deposits are made at the beginning or the end of the month, uses one of two keywords: DueDate.BegOfPeriod or DueDate.EndOfPeriod.

```
#Region "Monthly Report"
  Sub CreateReport()
    'Declare variables required by the procedure
    Dim Report As frmReport = New frmReport()
    Dim intMonth As Integer
    Dim sngStartValue As Single
    Dim sngPeriodValue As Single

    'Clear the listbox of any prior items
    Report.lstReport.Items.Clear()

    'Set the initial start value
    sngStartValue = sngInitialDeposit + sngMonthlyDeposit

    'Generate the monthly value schedule
    For intMonth = 1 To intTerm * 12

        'Calculate the Monthly Value
        sngPeriodValue = sngStartValue + _
        ((sngStartValue) * (sngRate / 12))

        'Populate the list box with the monthly value
        Report.lstReport.Items.Add _
        ("Month #" & intMonth & vbTab & _
        Format(sngPeriodValue, "Currency"))
        sngStartValue = sngPeriodValue + sngMonthlyDeposit
    Next intMonth

    'Display the form as modal
    Report.ShowDialog()
  End Sub
#End Region
```

Enter the code statements carefully to avoid errors. This sub procedure declares an object variable to create an instance of the *frmReport* form. The procedure then declares the local variables required to generate the monthly value report. The procedure clears the list box in the event that a report has already been generated. The procedure then calculates the monthly value for each month until the account reaches maturity. These values are added to the list box on the form.

7. Save your changes.

You are now ready to add code to the *frmPlan* form. The code performs data validation by handling the event raised by the *txtDeposit* and *txtAddition* **CausesValidation** property settings, which are both set to **True**. The form also contains a sub procedure

You learned about the **ShowDialog** method in Chapter 2. What does this method do? The **ShowDialog** method displays the About form as a modal form. This means the user must close this form before interacting with any other objects in the application.

for obtaining user input, setting the account values, and calling the function procedure for calculating the future value. The click events for the menu items and buttons on the form make calls to the appropriate sub procedures for calculating the future value, creating the monthly schedule, and exiting the application.

To add code to the frmPlan form:

1. Right-click the *frmPlan.vb* file in the Solution Explorer and choose **View Code**.
2. Place the insertion point at the beginning of the Code Editor, and type the following comments:

```
'©2003 Prentice Hall
'By [Enter your name]
'Created/Revised: [Enter the date]
Savings Analysis Application
```

3. Place the insertion point below the Windows Form Designer generated code region, and enter the following statements to perform data validation and enable the *mnuFileReturn* and *btnCalculate* controls:

```
#Region "Data Validation"
'Validate the initial deposit
    Private Sub TextPrincipal_Validating(ByVal sender As
        System.Object, ByVal e As
        System.ComponentModel.CancelEventArgs) Handles
        txtInitialDeposit.Validating
        Try
                If Val(txtInitialDeposit.Text) <= 0 Then
                    Throw New Exception()
                End If
        Catch ex As Exception
            ' Cancel the event and select the text to be
              corrected by the user
            e.Cancel = True
            txtInitialDeposit.Select(0,
                txtInitialDeposit.Text.Length)
            MsgBox("The initial deposit must be a positive
                number.", MsgBoxStyle.Critical, "Invalid
                Entry!")
        End Try
    End Sub


'Validate the monthly deposit
    Private Sub txtMonthlyDeposit_Validating(ByVal sender As
        System.Object, ByVal e As
        System.ComponentModel.CancelEventArgs) Handles
        txtMonthlyDeposit.Validating
        mnuFileReturn.Enabled = True
        btnCalculate.Enabled = True
        Try
```

```
            If Val(txtMonthlyDeposit.Text) < 0 Then
                Throw New Exception()
            End If
        Catch ex As Exception
            ' Cancel the event and select the text to be
              corrected by the user
            e.Cancel = True
            txtMonthlyDeposit.Select(0,
                txtMonthlyDeposit.Text.Length)
            MsgBox("The monthly deposit amount must be a
                positive number.", MsgBoxStyle.Critical,
                "Invalid Entry!")
            mnuFileReturn.Enabled = False
            btnCalculate.Enabled = False
        End Try
    End Sub
#End Region
```

4. Place the insertion point below the region you just created. Type the following statements to define the *Calculate* sub procedure:

```
Region "Calculate"
    Private Sub Calculate()
        'Obtain account values
        sngInitialDeposit = Val(txtInitialDeposit.Text)
        sngMonthlyDeposit = Val(txtMonthlyDeposit.Text)

        If rdb1Year.Checked = True Then
            intTerm = 1
            sngRate = 0.03
            lblInterest.Text = "3%"
        ElseIf rdb2Years.Checked = True Then
            intTerm = 2
            sngRate = 0.04
            lblInterest.Text = "4%"
        Else
            intTerm = 3
            sngRate = 0.05
            lblInterest.Text = "5%"
        End If

        'Call the CalculateValue function and assign the return
          value to the text property of the lblFutureValue
          label
        lblFutureValue.Text = Format(CalculateValue(sngRate,
          intTerm, sngMonthlyDeposit, sngInitialDeposit),
          "Currency")

        'Enable controls to create the monthly value report
```

```
                btnReport.Enabled = True
                mnuFileReport.Enabled = True
         End Sub
#End Region
```

This region contains the sub procedure that obtains the user input, determines the appropriate term and rate values, and calls the *CalculateValue* function procedure. The return value is formatted and displayed in a label on the form. You are now ready to create the procedures for the button and menu click events that calculate the return, create the report, and exit the application.

5. Place the insertion point below the last region you created. Select the *btnCalculate* object in the **Class Name** list and the click event in the **Method Name** list. Type the following statement within the procedure:

```
Call Calculate()
```

This event procedure calls the *Calculate* sub procedure, which performs the data validation and calls the *CalculateValue* function procedure.

6. Create an event procedure for the *mnuFileReturn* menu item and type the following statement within the procedure:

```
Call Calculate()
```

Tip

The menu item performs the same action as the *btnCalculate* button. Therefore the procedure requires only one statement.

7. Create an event procedure for the *btnReport* button. Type the following statement within the procedure:

```
Call CreateReport()
```

8. Create a click procedure for the *mnuFileReport* menu item. Type the following calling statement within the procedure:

```
Call CreateReport()
```

9. Create a click event for the *btnExit* control. Type the following statement within the procedure:

```
Call AppExit()
```

10. Create a click event for the *mnuFileExit* menu item. Type the following calling statement within the procedure:

```
Call AppExit()
```

11. Create a click event for the *mnuAbout* control. Type the following statements within the procedure:

```
Dim ShowForm As frmAbout = New frmAbout()
ShowForm.ShowDialog()
```

12. Save your changes.

You are almost ready to test the application. First, however, you need to add an event procedure to the *frmReport* form to close the form.

To add code to the frmReport form:

1. Right-click on the *frmReport.vb* file in the Solution Explorer and choose **View Code**.

2. Place the insertion point at the beginning of the Code Editor, and type the following comments:

```
'©2003 Prentice Hall
'By [Enter your name]
'Created/Revised: [Enter the date]
Savings Analysis Application
```

3. Create a click event for the *btnOK* control. Type the following statement inside the procedure:

```
Me.Close()
```

4. Save your changes.

Run the Application

You are now ready to run the Savings Analysis application and test its functionality.

To run the application:

1. Click the **Start** button or press the [F5] key to run the application.

2. Press the [Tab⇆] key once. When you attempt to exit the *txtInitialDeposit* control, the error message shown in Figure 7.27 appears.

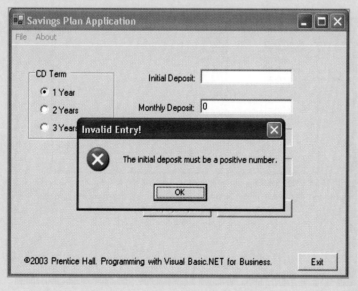

FIGURE 7.27. *Error message when data validation for initial deposit value fails*

3. Click **OK**. Correct the entry by typing 500 as the initial deposit amount
4. Press Tab⇆ once and type 25 as the monthly addition.
5. Press Tab⇆ again and click the **Calculate Return** button. The value of the account at maturity is calculated, the interest rate is displayed, the formatted result appears on the form, and the button to display the monthly report is enabled, as shown in Figure 7.28.

FIGURE 7.28. *Calculated return on a deposit with monthly additions*

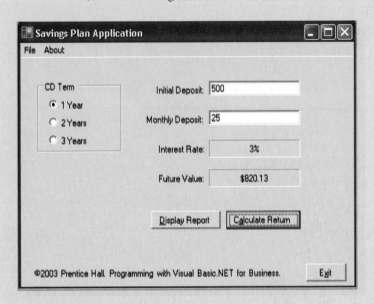

6. Click the **Display Report** button. The monthly report form appears, as shown in Figure 7.29. Compare your values with the ones shown here.

FIGURE 7.29. *Report of the monthly values until maturity*

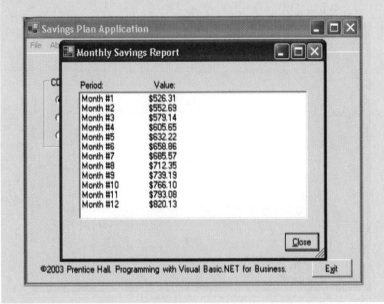

7. Click the **Close** button to close the report.

8. Click the **About** menu. The *About* form appears. Click **OK** to close the *About* form.

9. Test the exit procedures by using both the menu and the **Exit** button.

10. After exiting the application, run it again and click **File**, **Return**. You will receive an error message because you did not enter an initial deposit amount.

11. Try other savings scenarios, and verify that the application is working correctly.

12. When you finish, exit the application, and close the solution.

You can open the *Future Value.xls* Excel workbook on your student data disk and change the values in cells C5 through C8 to verify the values your application produces.

Summary

- Programmers use sub procedures, function procedures, and modules to organize and simplify the code for Visual Basic.NET programs.

- Visual Basic.NET supports two kinds of procedures. Sub procedures perform an action. Function procedures perform an action and return a value. Sub procedures are of two types, event procedures and user-defined procedures. Function procedures are of two types, intrinsic functions and user-defined functions.

- To create a sub procedure, use the Sub statement, give the procedure a name, include the code statements for the procedure, and end the procedure with the End Sub statement.

- You can write procedures that perform data validation by handling an event raised by the CausesValidation property of a control with this property set to True.

- To create a function procedure, use the Function statement, give the procedure a name, include the code statements for the procedure, and end the procedure with the End Function statement.

- Procedures (sub procedures and function procedures) often contain parameters. You can pass an argument to a parameter by reference or by value. To pass the value of a variable to a procedure by value so that the underlying value cannot be changed, use the ByVal keyword. To pass the value of a variable to a procedure by reference so that the underlying value can be changed, use the ByRef keyword.

- A procedure is called by another procedure by referencing the name of the called procedure in a calling statement contained in the calling procedure.

- You can use code regions to organize your program code. To create a region, enter one or more code statements enclosed within the # Region and End Region statements.

- Modules are Visual Basic.NET objects that contain code but no objects or controls. You can organize and simplify your code by adding variable declarations, sub procedures, and function procedures to modules. To create a module, click the Project menu and add a module to the solution.

- To add a function procedure to a module, type the statement that defines the function procedure. By default, modules have Friend access so any sub procedures or function procedures can be called by any procedure in the solution.

- To call a procedure in a module, include a statement that calls the procedure by name and passes any arguments to the parameters for the procedure.

- To create an application with multiple forms, use the Project menu to add one or more additional forms to the solution. Define one form as the Startup form, and write a procedure to display the other forms as appropriate.

Key Terms

#End Region statement	function procedure
#Region statement	Function statement
accessibility	FV function
argument	module
ByRef keyword	parameter
ByVal keyword	passing
call	Private
calling code	procedure
calling procedure	Public
calling statement	region
CausesValidation property	Return statement
End function	Sub keyword
End Region	Sub procedure
End sub	user-defined sub procedure
event procedure	Validating event
Friend	

Study Questions

Multiple-Choice Questions

1. How many arguments are required by a function procedure?
   - a. 0
   - b. 1
   - c. 2
   - d. 3
   - e. 4

2. Which statement is true regarding procedures?
   - a. A function procedure performs an action without returning a value.
   - b. The procedure making a call is the called procedure.
   - c. A function procedure returns a value to the calling procedure.
   - d. A function procedure can accept parameters that are passed to it.
   - e. A sub procedure does not return a value to the calling procedure.

3. Consider the following statement:
   ```
   Return
     CalculateBonus(EmpType,
     AnnualSalary)
   ```
   How many arguments are passed to this procedure?
   - a. 0
   - b. 1
   - c. 2
   - d. 3
   - e. 4

4. Which of the following is an intrinsic function in Visual Basic.NET?
   - a. CalcBonus (Pay, Sales)
   - b. Pmt(Principal, Rate, Term)
   - c. NextRec()
   - d. PN (v, R, T)
   - e. AppExit()

5. Which keyword limits the accessibility of a function to the procedure in which it is defined?
   - a. Sub
   - b. Friend
   - c. Public
   - d. Call
   - e. Private

6. The following function calculates net pay:
   ```
   Function NetPay(GrossPay,
     FederalTaxes, StateTaxes,
     LocalTaxes)
   GrossPay-
     (FederalTaxes+StateTaxes+
     LocalTaxes)
   End Function
   ```
   For sngPay = 800 and sngFed = 75, and sngState =20, sngLocal =10, what value is returned to a calling procedure that calls this function?
   - a. 855
   - b. 905
   - c. 695
   - d. 705
   - e. 895

7. What is the name of the line of code that makes a call to a procedure?
   - a. Called procedure
   - b. Called statement
   - c. Calling statement
   - d. Calling procedure
   - e. Return value

8. Which of the following is not a valid name for a sub procedure?
   - a. Sub AppExit ()
   - b. Function TotalPay (Hours, Wage)
   - c. Sub NewRecord()
   - d. Pmt(Principal, Rate, Term)
   - e. Function AppExit

9. Which character precedes the Region keyword for defining a region?
   - a. '
   - b. ?
   - c. /
   - d. &
   - e. #

10. Which statement is false regarding modules?
    - a. A module can contain variable declarations.
    - b. A project can include more than one module.
    - c. A module can contain function procedures and sub procedures.
    - d. A module can contain menu items.
    - e. A module requires a name.

True/False Questions

1. A module is a Visual Studio.NET object you can use to organize your procedures in a single location.

2. A sub procedure performs an action without returning a value to the calling procedure.

3. A procedure cannot make a call to another procedure.

4. The #Region and End Region statements simplify the code within a procedure.

5. If you want to change the underlying variable in a called procedure, pass the argument by reference.

Short Answer Questions

1. Explain how a module can be used to simplify your program code.

2. How do a calling statement and a called procedure differ?

3. How do you format the results returned by a function procedure as currency?

4. When might you pass an argument to a procedure by reference?

5. What is the primary difference between a sub procedure and a function procedure?

Guided Exercises

Adding Procedures to a Database Application

In Chapter 6 you learned how to create a disconnected dataset that binds controls on a form to database fields. You created a Visual Basic.NET project for entering and editing employee records. In this exercise you will modify a version of the Address Book application so that it includes menu and context menu items for navigating among records. Figure 7.30 shows the interface for the application.

FIGURE 7.30. *Interface for the Address Book application*

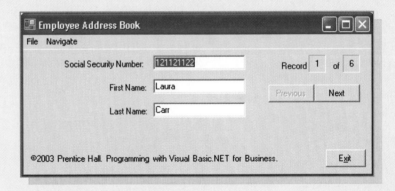

You will complete the following tasks:

1. Add menu items to the *MainMenu1* control for moving to the next and previous records.

2. Add a Context Menu to the form with menu items for moving to the next and previous records.

3. Add functions to the application for moving among records and exiting the application: **SubPrevious()**, **SubNext()**, and **AppExit()**.

4. Add calling procedures to evoke the subfunctions.

To modify the Address Book application:

1. Launch Visual Studio.NET and open the *Address Book.sln* file in the *Address Book* folder included with your data files.

2. Copy the *Employee.mdb* database file from your data files folder to a floppy disk, or modify the *OleDbDataAdapter1* data adapter to specify the location of the database.

3. Display the Toolbox.

4. Add the controls listed in Table 7.6 to the form. Set the **ContextMenu** property of the form as specified.

Table 7.6: Objects and properties for the *Address Book* application

Object	Property	Setting
mnuNavigate	Text	&Navigate
mnuNavigatePrevious	Text	&Previous Record
mnuNavigateNext	Text	Ne&xt Record
ContextMenu1		
cmnuPrevious	Text	Previous

5. Create a region and name it `Procedures`. Add the following procedures to the region:

```
Friend Sub NextRecord()
    Me.BindingContext(DataSet11, "Employees").Position += 1
    'Reset the CurrentRecord variable
    intCurrentRecord = BindingContext(DataSet11,
        "Employees").Position + 1
    lblCurrentRecord.Text = intCurrentRecord
    'Determine if controls need to be disabled
    If intCurrentRecord = BindingContext(DataSet11,
        "Employees").Count Then
            'Disable the controls
            btnNext.Enabled = False
            mnuNavigateNext.Enabled = False
            cmnuNext.Enabled = False
    End If
    'Enable the Previous controls
    btnPrevious.Enabled = True
    mnuNavigatePrevious.Enabled = True
```

```
        cmnuPrevious.Enabled = True
End Sub


Friend Sub PreviousRecord()
     Me.BindingContext(DataSet11, "Employees").Position -= 1
     'Reset the CurrentRecord variable
     intCurrentRecord = BindingContext(DataSet11,
        "Employees").Position + 1
     lblCurrentRecord.Text = intCurrentRecord
     'Determine if controls need to be disabled
     If intCurrentRecord = 1 Then
           'Disable the controls
           btnPrevious.Enabled = False
           mnuNavigatePrevious.Enabled = False
           cmnuPrevious.Enabled = False
     End If
     'Enable the Next controls
     btnNext.Enabled = True
     mnuNavigateNext.Enabled = True
     cmnuNext.Enabled = True
End Sub


Friend Sub AppExit()
     Dim intResponse As Integer
     intResponse = MsgBox("Do you really want to exit this
        application?", 276, "Exit?")
     If intResponse = 6 Then
           End
     End If
End Sub
```

6. Add three calling procedures to call the three record navigation functions you just created. For the record navigation functions, three event procedures (Menu, Context Menu, and Button) will call each function.

7. Save your application.

8. Run the application and test the functionality of the procedures you created.

9. Close the solution.

Creating a User-Defined Function Procedure for Calculating a Loan Payment

In Chapter 4 you learned how to use the predefined Pmt function to calculate the payment on a loan. In this exercise you will create your own function procedure for calculating a loan payment. This function will receive three arguments: the loan principal, interest rate, and term. The calling procedure will perform data validation on the user input before calling the function procedure. The application will support the following business rules:

1. The loan principal must be a value between $2,000 and $50,000.

2. The annual interest rate must be a value between 2.5% and 12.5%.

3. The loan term must be at least one year but not greater than 10 years.

Assume you are considering an auto loan with a principal of $14,000, an annual interest rate of 7.5%, and a term of 4 years. The calculated payment is shown in Figure 7.31.

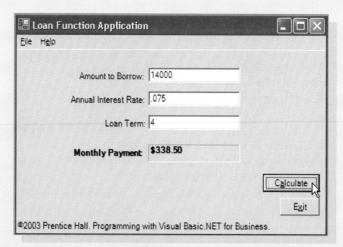

FIGURE 7.31. *Payment calculation*

To create the function procedure, you need to know how to calculate a loan payment. When the term and rate are expressed in payment periods (the years multiplied by 12 months per year for the term and the annual interest divided by 12 months per year), you can calculate a monthly payment as follows:

$$\text{Monthly Payment} = \text{Loan Principal}(\text{Interest}/1-(1+\text{Interest})^{\wedge}-\text{Periods})$$

Where

Loan Principal = Amount to borrow

Interest = Annual Rate / 12 months

Period = Loan term in years, multiplied by 12 months/year

To create a loan application with a user-defined function procedure:

1. Click **File**, **New**, **Project**. Name the project `Loan Function`.
2. Add the controls in Table 7.7 to the form, and set the properties as specified.

Table 7.7: Objects and properties for the *Loan Function* application

Object	Property	Setting
Form1	Text	Loan Function Application
MainMenu1		
mnuFile	Text	&File
mnuFileCalculate	Text	C&alculate
mnuFileExit	Text	E&xit
lblPrincipal	Text	Amount to Borrow:
lblRate	Text	Annual Interest Rate:
lblTerm	Text	Loan Term:
lblPayment	Text	Monthly Payment:
lblMonthlyPayment	Text	
btnCalculate	Text	C&alculate
btnExit	Text	E&xit
lblCopyright	Text	©2003 Prentice Hall. Programming with Visual Basic.NET for Business.

3. Display the Code Editor. Add comments explaining the purpose of the application.

4. Declare three variables immediately below the Inherits statement for the class:

```
Friend sngPrincipal As Single
Friend sngRate As Single
Friend intTerm As Integer
```

5. Create a region named Data Validation and add the following statements:

```
Private Sub txtPrincipal_Validating(ByVal sender As
    System.Object, ByVal e As
    System.ComponentModel.CancelEventArgs) Handles
    txtPrincipal.Validating
        Try
            If Val(txtPrincipal.Text) < 2000 Or
                Val(txtPrincipal.Text) > 50000 Then
                    Throw New Exception()
            End If
        Catch ex As Exception
            ' Cancel the event and select the text to be corrected
              by the user
            e.Cancel = True
            txtPrincipal.Select(0, txtPrincipal.Text.Length)
            MsgBox("The loan amount must be a number between 2000
                and 50000.", MsgBoxStyle.Critical, "Invalid Entry!")
        End Try
End Sub


Private Sub txtRate_Validating(ByVal sender As System.Object,
    ByVal e As System.ComponentModel.CancelEventArgs) Handles
    txtRate.Validating
        Try
            If Val(txtRate.Text) < 0.025 Or Val(txtRate.Text) >
                0.125 Then
                    Throw New Exception()
            End If
        Catch ex As Exception
            ' Cancel the event and select the text to be corrected
              by the user
            e.Cancel = True
            txtRate.Select(0, txtRate.Text.Length)
            MsgBox("The loan rate must be a decimal value greater
                than zero and less than 15%.", MsgBoxStyle.Critical,
                "Invalid Entry!")
        End Try
End Sub


Private Sub txtTerm_Validating(ByVal sender As System.Object,
    ByVal e As System.ComponentModel.CancelEventArgs) Handles
    txtTerm.Validating
```

```
    Try
        If Val(txtTerm.Text) < 1 Or Val(txtTerm.Text) > 10 Then
            Throw New Exception()
        End If
    Catch ex As Exception
        'Cancel the event and select the text to be corrected
          by the user
        e.Cancel = True
        txtTerm.Select(0, txtTerm.Text.Length)
        MsgBox("The loan term must be at least 1 and not more
            than 10.", MsgBoxStyle.Critical, "Invalid Entry!")
    End Try
End Sub
```

6. Create a region named `Procedures` and add the following statements:

```
Sub CalculatePayment()
    'Assign values to variables
    sngPrincipal = Val(txtPrincipal.Text)
        sngRate = Val(txtRate.Text) / 12
        intTerm = Val(txtTerm.Text) * 12

    'Call the LoanPayment function
    lblMonthlyPayment.Text = Format(LoanPayment(sngPrincipal,
        sngRate, intTerm), "Currency")
End Sub

Function LoanPayment(ByVal Principal, ByVal Rate, ByVal Term) As
  Decimal
    'Calculate the monthly payment, and return the value to the
      calling procedure
    Return Principal * (Rate / (1 - (1 + Rate) ^ -Term))
End Function

Friend Sub AppExit()
    Dim intResponse As Integer
    intResponse = MsgBox("Do you really want to exit this
      application?", 276, "Exit?")
    If intResponse = 6 Then
        End
    End If
End Sub
```

7. Create the following calling procedures:

```
Private Sub btnCalculate_Click(ByVal sender As System.Object,
  ByVal e As System.EventArgs) Handles btnCalculate.Click
    CalculatePayment()
End Sub
Private Sub mnuFileCalculate_Click(ByVal sender As
  System.Object, ByVal e As System.EventArgs) Handles
  mnuFileCalculate.Click
```

```
        CalculatePayment()
End Sub
Private Sub btnExit_Click(ByVal sender As System.Object, ByVal e
   As System.EventArgs) Handles btnExit.Click
     AppExit()
End Sub
Private Sub mnuFileExit_Click(ByVal sender As System.Object,
   ByVal e As System.EventArgs) Handles mnuFileExit.Click
     AppExit()
End Sub
```

8. Save your changes.

9. Run the application and test the functionality. Close the solution when you are finished.

Case Studies

Creating a function procedure to calculate the future value of an investment

In the Hands-on Programming Example for this chapter, you used the Future Value (FV) function to calculate the value of a savings account at maturity. You can create a user-defined function for calculating the future value of an investment by using the following formula:

$$\text{Future Value} = \text{Present Value } (1 + \text{Interest per Period})^{\text{Periods}}$$

Create a project named `Future Value Function`. Create a form for obtaining the amount of the investment, the annual interest rate, and the term of the investment. Use combo boxes for the rate and the term, and populate the controls with rates in half-percent increments from 2% to 8% and terms from 2 to 10 years. Create a function procedure that will receive the three arguments. Add a button control that calls the function procedure, and validate the entries using validation procedures. Format the result as currency. Run the application to test its functionality. Verify the accuracy of your application by using the *Future Value.xls* workbook included with your files.

Creating a function procedure for converting mileage

In Chapter 2 you created an application that performs mileage conversions. Now create a project named `Mileage` that converts miles to kilometers or kilometers to miles. Obtain user input by using the InputBox function. Perform data validation before performing the calculation. The formulas you need are:

$$\text{Kilometers} = \text{Miles} * 1.609$$

$$\text{Miles} = \text{Kilometers} * 0.621$$

Create two controls that call the function procedure. Format the result of the conversion, using the "G" style ("G" is for General Number). Test your application after creating it.

Creating a function procedure for performing a temperature conversion

In Chapter 2 you created an application that performs a temperature conversion from Fahrenheit to Celsius and vice versa. Now create a project named `Temperatures` that performs these conversions by using two separate functions. Use a text box to obtain user input. Perform data validation before performing a calculation. The formulas you need are:

$$C = 5/9 \ (F - 32)$$

$$F = (9/5) \ C + 32$$

Create two controls that call the function procedure. Test your application after creating it.

Creating a payroll application

In Chapter 3 you created a Payroll Calculator that determines the gross pay, taxes, and net pay, given an employee's hourly wage and hours worked. Create a Windows Form application named `Payroll` that obtains an employee's hourly wage and total hours for the pay period. Use the following constants to determine the taxes withheld:

Federal Tax – 15%

State Tax – 8%

Local Tax – 3%

Create a function that calculates the gross pay, total taxes, and net pay. Run the application and test its functionality. Close the solution when you finish.

Using Arrays, Structures, and Collections

In previous chapters, you have worked with data in a variety of ways. Text boxes, combo boxes, list boxes, and input boxes are effective ways of obtaining user input and storing a single value in a variable. Random access files provide a method for storing data records in a user-defined structure and reading fields from the structure into the text property of a control or the value of a variable. ADO.NET provides more sophisticated ways of working with fields and records stored in external databases.

Some programs require more efficient methods for working with lists of data in memory or with multiple variables. When you need to efficiently work with a list of values in memory, multiple data types, or multiple values, you need to know about arrays, structures, and collections. In this chapter you will learn how to use an array to store multiple values in a single variable, use a structure to store related pieces of information in a variable, and use an array list to store a collection of items in memory.

Performance Objectives

At the conclusion of this chapter, you will be able to:

- Explain how to manipulate data by using arrays, structures, and collections
- Declare a single-dimension array
- Store data in an array
- Reference elements in an array
- Add data to an array at run time
- Declare a multidimensional array
- Use dynamic arrays
- Populate an array by reading data from a disk file
- Declare a structure
- Create and use a structure variable
- Use the ArrayList to create a collection

Using Arrays

Programmers commonly create software with the ability to hold lists of data. The Visual Basic.NET environment provides a variety of methods for storing the data your applications require. Think of these methods as providing containers for your data. Variables are one type of container. The value of a variable is assigned at run time, and the contents of the variable can change during program execution. List boxes and combo boxes are containers that hold multiple values in a list. The items in the list are a collection that can be assigned at design time by using the Collection editor or at run time by modifying existing items in the list or adding new items.

Recall the Amortization Schedule solution you created in Chapter 4. The solution uses variables, combo boxes, and a list box as containers for data. To generate the amortization schedule, you created a looping structure that calculated the principal payment, interest payment, and loan balance. The structure added the payment number and these values to a list box to create the schedule. Figure 8.1 shows the schedule displayed in a list box.

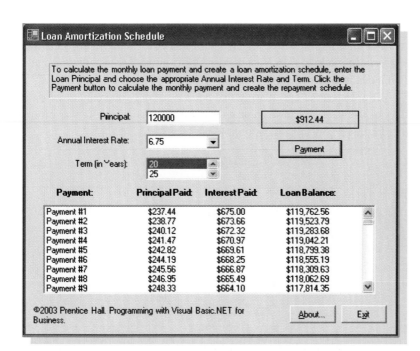

FIGURE 8.1. *The Amortization Schedule solution from Chapter 4*

The list box holds a list of data created by a code procedure. After the principal and interest payment values are calculated, they are added to the list box but are not held as variables in memory. Because a list box contains only text, the information for each payment is joined (or *concatenated*) and the resulting string is added to the list. The size of the list is dynamic, meaning that its size is not determined at design time but varies at run time depending on the loan term. However, if you wanted to reuse any of the individual principal or interest payment values in another calculation, you could not do so.

Now envision an application that generates the loan repayment information and stores the information as rows and columns in memory. The values in memory for the first 10 payments would include the information shown in Figure 8.2.

Payment Number	Principal Paid	Interest Paid	Loan Balance
1	237.44	675.00	119762.56
2	238.77	673.66	119523.79
3	240.12	672.32	119283.68
4	241.47	670.97	119042.21
5	242.82	669.61	118799.38
6	244.19	668.25	118555.19
7	245.56	666.87	118309.63
8	246.95	665.49	118062.69
9	248.33	664.10	117814.35
10	249.73	662.71	117564.62

FIGURE 8.2. *Representing loan repayment data as rows and columns*

If you could store the data this way in memory, you would be able to extract any value out of memory by referencing its row and column location. This is what arrays do. When you need to store multiple values in memory, use an array as a container for holding the data. An **array** is a special kind of variable that can hold multiple values. Each value in the array is called an **element.** Each of the numbers in Figure 8.2 is an element if you conceptualize this table as an array stored in memory. Each element in the array is identified by an *index*. The index identifying each element in an array is also referred to as the *subscript* for the element. For this reason, arrays are also known as *subscripted variables*. In Visual Basic.NET, arrays are *zero-based*, meaning that the first index is always zero.

Now conceptualize an array that consists of only one column of data, such as the days of the week. Because an array is a variable, let's name this array *strDays*. Figure 8.3 illustrates how this array might look.

FIGURE 8.3. *An array with seven elements, with index values from 0 to 6*

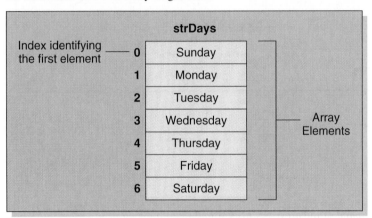

Think of an array as a table or grid stored in memory. You can use assignment statements and looping structures to add items to the cells in the grid. An array has a *size* to determine how many rows the array contains. In addition to having a size, an array also has a *dimension*. The dimensionality of an array refers to the number of columns in the array. Think of the dimension of an array as expressing the number of rows and columns in the array. An array with one column is a *single-dimension array,* like the array shown in Figure 8.3. An array consisting of rows and multiple columns is called a *multidimensional array.* A simple multidimensional array consists of rows and columns. This is an example of a *two-dimensional array*. You can also create arrays on three or more dimensions. Think of a two-dimensional array as a grid on a piece of paper. Multidimensional arrays can also contain columns in other dimensions. For example, a three-dimensional array is like a cube. Obviously, referencing the elements in a three-dimensional array is more complex than working with data in a two-dimensional array.

Now let's learn how to create a single-dimension array.

In this chapter, you will learn how to work with single-dimension and two-dimensional arrays.

DECLARING A SINGLE-DIMENSION ARRAY

An array contains multiple variables accessed through indices corresponding in a one-to-one fashion to the order of the variables in the array. For example, consider the following statements for declaring a variable and assigning a value:

```
Dim strDay as String
strDay = "Monday"
```

The first statement declares a string variable for storing the name of a specific day of the week. The second statement assigns a text string to the variable. The value of the variable will not change unless a code statement performs another assignment. However, the variable can hold only one value at a time.

Declaring an array is similar to declaring a variable, except that the declaration statement includes the size of the array. The general syntax for declaring an array is:

```
Dim ArrayName (size) As Datatype
```

Just as with variables, the accessibility of an array is determined by which keyword you use to declare it (Dim, Public, Protected, Friend, Protected Friend, or Private). If you declare the array within a procedure, you must use the Dim keyword, and the array's accessibility will be private to the procedure.

The array declaration statement must include parentheses, because these declare the variable as an array and not a scalar variable. A *scalar variable* consists of a single element. An array is a variable with a declared size, so an array is also called an *array variable*. When you declare the size for the array, the array is a *static array*, meaning that its size will not change. If you do not know the intended size of the array when you declare it, simply include a set of parentheses without declaring the size. The array will then be a *dynamic array*, meaning its size can change during run time. You will learn how to work with dynamic arrays later in this chapter.

An array declaration specifies a data type, and all its elements must be of type declared. If you declare an array as an *Object data type*, the elements can contain different kinds of data (such as a mixture of string and numeric types). You can also declare an array to store the values in a user-defined data type that includes multiple data types.

The recommended naming conventions for arrays are the same as those for variables; that is, the name of the array begins with a three-character designation of its data type, followed by a description of the kind of data the array contains. Just as with variables, the name of an array uses camel casing, where the first word in the variable name appears in lowercase and each additional word begins with an uppercase letter. Consider the following statement:

```
Dim strWeekDays(6)As String
```

This statement declares an array with a size of 7. Why is the size of this array 7 and not 6? The first element in the array has an index of 0, making a total of seven elements in the array: 0,1,2,3,4,5,6. When you declare an array, the number of elements in the array will always be one more than the size in the array declaration statement.

Table 8.1 lists a few examples of statements that declare single-dimension arrays.

Table 8.1: Declaring single-dimension arrays

Declaration	Usage
Dim strWeekDays(6)	7 elements, Object data type, Private accessibility
Dim strWeekDays(6) As String	7 elements, String data type, Private accessibility
Friend strMonths(11) As String	12 elements, String data type, Friend accessibility
Dim intCounter( ) As Integer	Dynamic size, Integer data type, Private accessibility
Public sngExamScores(99)	100 elements, single data type, public accessibility

Storing Data in an Array

When you first declare an array, you set its size, but it does not contain any data. To add values to the array, you must specify the index for the element that will contain the values. Programmers talk of "initializing" or "populating" an array. In Chapter 4 you learned how to use a For. . . Next loop to populate the items in a list box or combo box. In this chapter, you will learn a variety of methods for initializing and populating lists of related information.

For example, the following statement assigns a text string to the second element in the array:

```
strWeekDays(1)= "Tuesday"
```

When you assign a value to an element in an array, other elements in the array are unaffected by this assignment. Each element is independent of the others. You can assign a value to any of the elements, but you do not have to assign a value to all elements. Consider the following statements that define an array for listing the typical workdays in a week:

```
Dim strWeekDays (6)
strWeekDays (1)= "Monday"
strWeekDays (2)= "Tuesday"
strWeekDays (3)= "Wednesday"
strWeekDays (4)= "Thursday"
strWeekDays (5)= "Friday"
```

The *strWeekDays* array consists of seven elements with indices ranging from 0 to 6. Five of these elements list the five work days. The first element represents Sunday, the first day of the week. The last element represents Saturday, the last day of the week. Therefore, five of the seven elements contain a value representing one of the five work days. Figure 8.4 compares the value stored in a scalar variable to values stored in an array.

FIGURE 8.4. *Comparing a value stored in a scalar variable to values stored in an array*

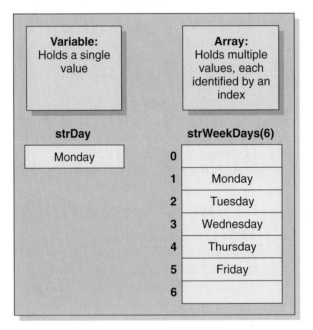

Referencing Elements in an Array

After you declare an array and fill one or more of its elements with data, you can use the contents of the array in your applications. Think of how you have used the values stored in variables in your code. Once a variable has been declared and assigned a value, you can use that value by referencing the name of the variable. The same is true for arrays, except that because the individual values are referenced by an index, you must reference the name of the array and an index value to use the value in the array. The following application is included in the *Simple Array* solution in your data files. Figure 8.5 displays a simple Windows form that declares an array, initializes some of its elements, and then displays a specific element.

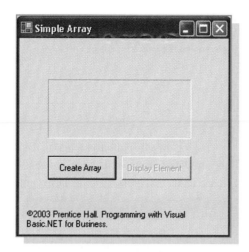

FIGURE 8.5. *Form for displaying elements in an array*

The array is declared with **Friend** access so it is available to all procedures on the form. Clicking the **Create Array** button runs the following procedure:

```
Private Sub btnCreate_Click(ByVal sender As System.Object, ByVal
  e As System.EventArgs) Handles btnCreate.Click
        strWeekDays(0) = "Sunday"
        strWeekDays(1) = "Monday"
        strWeekDays(2) = "Tuesday"
        strWeekDays(3) = "Wednesday"
        strWeekDays(4) = "Thursday"
        strWeekDays(5) = "Friday"
        strWeekDays(6) = "Saturday"

    'Enable to button to display the array
    btnDisplay.Enabled = True
End Sub
```

Clicking the button populates the array with the names of the days of the week.

You can reference any element in the array by using its index number. For example, the following assignment statement displays the first element in the array in a label control:

```
lblResult.Text = strWeekDays(0)
```

A statement like this is fine if you know ahead of time which element you want to reference. However, you will often need to provide users with the option of selecting a specific array element. Consider the following procedure:

```
Private Sub btnDisplay_Click(ByVal sender As System.Object,
  ByVal e As System.EventArgs) Handles btnDisplay.Click
        Dim arrayIndex As Integer
        arrayIndex = InputBox("Enter the index of the element
          to display. . .", "Enter element index")
        lblResult.Text = strWeekDays(arrayIndex)
End Sub
```

The first statement in the procedure declares an integer variable to store the number for the element to retrieve. The second statement assigns the user input obtained with an input box to this value. Clicking the **Create Array** button populates the array. Clicking the **Display Element** button displays an input box for user input. The input box is shown in Figure 8.6. In this example, 4 is the array element to display.

FIGURE 8.6. *Specifying the array element to display*

FIGURE 8.6. *Specifying the array element to display*

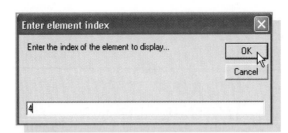

Clicking the **OK** button assigns 4 to the index variable. This value is passed to the array as the array index number in the assignment statement. The fifth element in the array is then assigned to the text property of the label control on the form. Figure 8.7 displays this result.

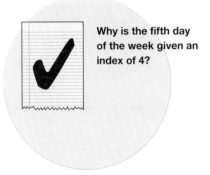

Why is the fifth day of the week given an index of 4?

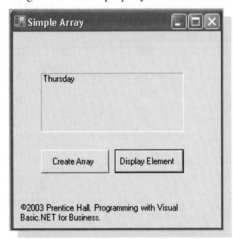

FIGURE 8.7. *Displaying the value for array index 4*

Working with Zero-Based Arrays

Working with zero-based arrays can be confusing, particularly if the array is large, such as an array for storing expenses for any day of the year. In such a case, you would need 365 elements in the array, and the size would be declared as (364). Whenever you wanted to reference a specific day of the year, the reference would be one less than the day you want to display, to account for the fact that January 1 has an index of zero.

You can get around this issue by declaring an array with a size that is one more than your application requires and then not use the first element in the array. For example, declaring an array with a size of (365) actually creates 366 elements, with the first element indexed as zero. You can assign values to elements 1 through 365 and refer to each element by its associated index. Consider the following code statements, which are contained in the *Simple Array Modified* solution included with your data files:

```
Friend strWeekDays(7) As String

Private Sub btnCreate_Click(ByVal sender As System.Object, ByVal
    e As System.EventArgs) Handles btnCreate.Click
    strWeekDays(1) = "Sunday"
    strWeekDays(2) = "Monday"
    strWeekDays(3) = "Tuesday"
    strWeekDays(4) = "Wednesday"
    strWeekDays(5) = "Thursday"
    strWeekDays(6) = "Friday"
    strWeekDays(7) = "Saturday"


    'Enable to button to display the array
    btnDisplay.Enabled = True
End Sub
```

The declaration statement sets up an array with eight elements. The btnCreate_Click event populates elements 1 through 8 with the days of the week. Figure 8.8 compares two methods for declaring an array to store the days of the week.

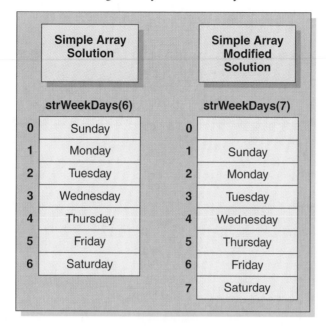

Simple Array Solution

strWeekDays(6)

0	Sunday
1	Monday
2	Tuesday
3	Wednesday
4	Thursday
5	Friday
6	Saturday

Simple Array Modified Solution

strWeekDays(7)

0	
1	Sunday
2	Monday
3	Tuesday
4	Wednesday
5	Thursday
6	Friday
7	Saturday

Tip

Declaring an array with elements you do not intend to use works for simple arrays. For more complex arrays that read data from a file, you should avoid declaring elements you do not intend to use. Therefore, familiarize yourself with referencing elements in zero-based arrays.

FIGURE 8.8. *Declaring an array with one additional element*

ADDING DATA TO AN ARRAY AT RUN TIME

Although you sometimes need to populate an array or a list at design time, there will also be many times when you will add items to a list or an array at run time. The loan amortization schedule shown earlier is an example: the list box control was populated at run time with the loan payment data calculated after defining the specific loan scenario.

Using the example of creating an array to store the days of the week, suppose you want to create an application for tracking your mileage during the week, which can be reimbursed as a business expense. Figure 8.9 shows a Windows form for entering mileage and calculating the total mileage for the week. This form is contained in the *Weekly Mileage* solution in your data files.

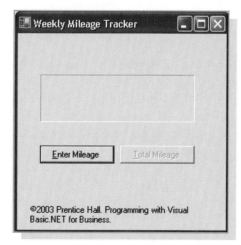

FIGURE 8.9. *Form for entering weekly mileage*

The code for the application includes the following array declaration statement:

```
Friend sngMileage(6) As Single
```

The array has **Friend** access so any procedure in the assembly can use its elements. The array contains seven elements of the Integer data type. Clicking the **Enter Mileage** button displays two input boxes, one for entering the day of the week and one for entering the mileage that day. You may click the **Enter Mileage** button as many times as you wish to enter the mileage for a specific day or to change a value in the array. Clicking the **Total Mileage** button totals all elements in the array. Following is the code for each button's click event:

```
Private Sub btnEnterMileage_Click(ByVal sender As System.Object,
  ByVal e As System.EventArgs) Handles btnEnterMileage.Click

    'Declare variables required by the procedure
    Dim intDay As Integer
    Dim sngMiles As Integer

    'Obtain input
    intDay = InputBox("Which day?", "Enter the day as a value 0
      through 6")
    sngMiles = InputBox("How many miles did you travel on day "
      & intDay & " ?", "Enter daily mileage")

    'Display verification message
    sngMileage(intDay) = sngMiles
    MsgBox("On Day " & intDay & " you traveled " & sngMiles & "
      miles.", MsgBoxStyle.OKOnly, "Mileage")

    'Enable to button to display the array
    btnTotalMileage.Enabled = True
End Sub
```

Two variables hold the values for the day index and the daily mileage. These values are used to assign the mileage to an element in the array. Each time the mileage for a day is entered, a message box verifies the entry.

Following is the event procedure that uses the values in the array to total the weekly mileage:

```
Private Sub btnTotalMileage_Click(ByVal sender As Object, ByVal
  e As System.EventArgs) Handles btnTotalMileage.Click

    'Declare variables required by the procedure
    Dim sngTotalMiles As Integer
    Dim intCounter As Integer

    'Initialize the total miles before looping through the array
    sngTotalMiles = 0

    'Step through the array and sum the mileage
    For intCounter = 0 To 6
        sngTotalMiles = sngTotalMiles + sngMileage(intCounter)
    Next intCounter

    'Display results
    lblResult.Text = "You traveled a total of " & sngTotalMiles
      & " miles this week."
End Sub
```

Tip

Notice how the messages for user input and verification use string concatenation to combine text strings with the variables in constructing each message.

This procedure declares two variables, one as a counter for a loop and one to hold the accumulated mileage. The variable to hold the mileage is initialized to zero before looping through the array. The loop structure adds mileage for an element in the array to the *sngTotalMiles* variable.

Assume you drove 30 miles on Monday (Day 1), 150 miles on Thursday (Day 4), and 50 miles on Saturday (Day 6). Figure 8.10 shows how these values will be stored in the *sngMileage* array.

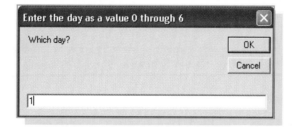

		intMiles(6)
Sunday	0	
Monday	1	30
Tuesday	2	
Wednesday	3	
Thursday	4	150
Friday	5	
Saturday	6	50

FIGURE 8.10. *Values stored in the* sngMileage *array*

Make sure you type 1 and not Monday. The procedure needs the index value for the day, not the name of the day. To simplify the example, the procedure does not validate the index values, so entering a value less than zero or greater than the size of the array generates a run time error.

To enter the mileage, you click the **Enter Miles** button to display the input box for the *intDay* assignment. To enter a value for Monday, you enter 1 as the day of the week, as shown in Figure 8.11, and click OK.

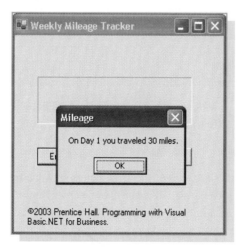

FIGURE 8.11. *Entering an index value of* 1 *for* Monday

After entering 30 in the input box for the *intMiles* assignment and 1 for the *intDay* assignment, you will see the verification message in Figure 8.12.

FIGURE 8.12. *Verification of the mileage for Day 1 (Monday)*

If you run the application, enter the remaining values, and click the Total Mileage button, the label on the form will display 230 miles, as shown in Figure 8.13.

FIGURE 8.13. *Label displaying the total miles for the week*

Now that you know how to declare and use a single-dimension array, let's learn how to declare and use arrays with more than one dimension.

DECLARING A TWO-DIMENSIONAL ARRAY

Recall that a multidimensional array has multiple rows and columns. Let's look at an example of declaring a two-dimensional array.

Suppose you want to track the miles you drive each month on a weekly basis. You can declare a multidimensional array to store these values. The array shown earlier will accept daily mileage for one week. By declaring more dimensions, you can store your daily mileage for the entire month. Figure 8.14 shows how you might construct this array.

FIGURE 8.14. *Two-dimensional array for storing monthly mileage*

		Week 1 0	Week 2 1	Week 3 2	Week 4 3	Week 5 4
Sunday	0					
Monday	1	35	36	38	34	
Tuesday	2					
Wednesday	3		22		20	
Thursday	4					
Friday	5	45		42		
Saturday	6					

The array has 7 elements and 5 dimensions, for a total of 35 storage areas. The syntax for declaring a multidimensional array is

```
Dim ArrayName (size,dimension) As Dat
```

You can declare a two-dimensional array that holds data of different types by setting the data type to Object.

The size of the array determines the number of array elements, and the dimension of the array determines how many columns the grid will contain. In Visual Studio.NET, the number of dimensions an array contains is called the *rank* of the array. You can retrieve the rank property of an array after it has been declared. The interface for the Monthly Mileage application is almost identical to the Weekly Mileage form shown in Figure 8.9.

Now consider the following code statement contained in the *Monthly Mileage* solution included with your data files:

```
Friend sngMileage(6, 4) As Single
```

This statement declares an array of 7 elements and 5 dimensions. The code for adding mileage to the array is more complex, because the array has more than one column. Therefore, an extra variable, named *intWeek*, is required for the additional columns.

```
Private Sub btnEnterMileage_Click(ByVal sender As System.Object,
   ByVal e As System.EventArgs) Handles btnEnterMileage.Click
      'Declare variables required by the procedure
      Dim intDay As Integer
      Dim intWeek As Integer
      Dim sngMiles As Single

      'Obtain input
      intDay = InputBox("Which day?", "Enter the day as a value 0
         through 6")
      intWeek = InputBox("Which week?", "Enter the week as a value
         from 0 to 4")
      sngMiles = InputBox("How many miles did you travel this day
         (round to a whole number)?", "Enter daily mileage")

      'Display verification message
      intMileage(intDay, intWeek) = sngMiles
      MsgBox("On Day " & intDay & " of week " & intWeek & " you
         traveled " & sngMiles & " miles.", MsgBoxStyle.OKOnly,
         "Mileage")

      'Enable to button to display the array
      btnTotalMileage.Enabled = True
End Sub
```

The procedure uses three input boxes for obtaining the day, the week, and the miles traveled. The *intDay* and *intWeek* variables are passed to the array when the mileage is assigned to an element. Passing these variables ensures that the value is stored in the correct element in the array.

Calculating the mileage for the month is also more complex for a two-dimensional array than for a single-dimension array. Review the following procedure:

```
Private Sub btnTotalMileage_Click(ByVal sender As Object, ByVal
   e As System.EventArgs) Handles btnTotalMileage.Click
      Dim sngTotalMiles As Single
      Dim intCounter As Integer
      'Initialize the total miles before looping through the array
      sngTotalMiles = 0

      'Step through the array and sum the mileage
      For intCounter = 0 To 6
      sngTotalMiles = sngTotalMiles + intMileage(intCounter, 0) +
         intMileage(intCounter, 1) + intMileage(intCounter, 2) +
         intMileage(intCounter, 3) + intMileage(intCounter, 4)
      Next intCounter

      'Display results
```

```
        lblResult.Text = "You traveled a total of " & sngTotalMiles
            & " miles this month."
End Sub
```

The procedure is similar to the procedure for calculating the weekly mileage discussed earlier. The looping structure is different; as the procedure loops through the array, it checks for values in all elements simultaneously by adding together the values in all elements across all dimensions. Figure 8.14 lists values for mileage during an entire month.

If you run the application, enter the mileage shown in Figure 8.14, and click the Total Mileage button, you will see a result of 272, as shown in Figure 8.15.

FIGURE 8.15. *Label displaying the total miles for the month*

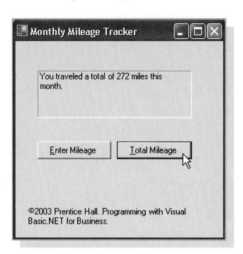

Now look at another example. A computer training center can accommodate up to 10 students in a computer lab. The computers are arranged in two rows, and each computer is assigned a number. As students register for a training class, the student is assigned to a computer. You can use a two-dimensional array to store student names as each student is assigned to a computer in the lab. The *Computer Lab Attendees* solution included with your data files has a form for assigning students to a computer and displaying the current assignment of any computer in the lab. Figure 8.16 represents a two-dimensional array for assigning students to computers and displays the form for making the computer assignments.

Visual Representation of a two-dimensional array for assigning students to computers

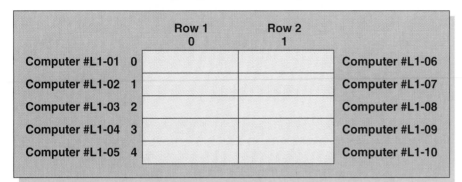

	Row 1 / 0	Row 2 / 1	
Computer #L1-01 0			Computer #L1-06
Computer #L1-02 1			Computer #L1-07
Computer #L1-03 2			Computer #L1-08
Computer #L1-04 3			Computer #L1-09
Computer #L1-05 4			Computer #L1-10

FIGURE 8.16. *Two-dimensional array for assigning students to computers, and the form for assigning students to computers*

Application interface for the Computer Lab Attendees solution

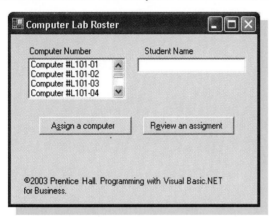

The program creates a two-dimensional array to store the student names, as follows:

```
Friend strComputer(0, 4) As String
```

Now look at the event procedure for assigning students to a computer. Here's the code for the *btnAssign* click event:

How many elements are contained in this array?

```
Private Sub btnAssign_Click(ByVal sender As System.Object, ByVal
  e As System.EventArgs) Handles btnAssign.Click

    Select Case lstComputerNumber.SelectedIndex
        Case 0
            If strComputer(0, 0) = "" Then
                strComputer(0, 0) = txtName.Text
            End If
        Case 1
            If strComputer(0, 1) = "" Then
                strComputer(0, 1) = txtName.Text
            End If
        Case 2
            If strComputer(0, 2) = "" Then
                strComputer(0, 2) = txtName.Text
            End If
```

```
        Case 3
            If strComputer(0, 3) = "" Then
                strComputer(0, 3) = txtName.Text
            End If
        Case 4
            If strComputer(0, 4) = "" Then
                strComputer(0, 4) = txtName.Text
            End If
        Case 5
            If strComputer(1, 0) = "" Then
                strComputer(1, 0) = txtName.Text
            End If
        Case 6
            If strComputer(1, 1) = "" Then
                strComputer(1, 1) = txtName.Text
            End If
        Case 7
            If strComputer(1, 2) = "" Then
                strComputer(1, 2) = txtName.Text
            End If
        Case 8
            If strComputer(1, 3) = "" Then
                strComputer(1, 3) = txtName.Text
            End If
        Case 9
            If strComputer(1, 4) = "" Then
                strComputer(1, 4) = txtName.Text
            End If
    End Select
End Sub
```

The procedure uses a Select. . . Case statement to determine if a computer is currently available; if so, the procedure assigns the name in the text box to the array. Notice that each Select. . . Case statement includes the indices for the array element.

Now let's look at the procedure for determining who is assigned to a computer. The code for the *btnReview* click event is as follows:

```
Private Sub btnReview_Click(ByVal sender As System.Object, ByVal
    e As System.EventArgs) Handles btnReview.Click
    Select Case lstComputerNumber.SelectedIndex
        Case 0
            If strComputer(0, 0) = "" Then
                MsgBox("This computer is not assigned.",
                    MsgBoxStyle.Information, "Computer is
                    available")
            Else
                MsgBox("Computer L101-01 is assigned to: " &
                    strComputer(0, 0), MsgBoxStyle.Information,
                    "Computer not available")
```

```
            End If
    Case 1
        If strComputer(0, 1) = "" Then
            MsgBox("This computer is not assigned.",
                MsgBoxStyle.Information, "Computer is
                available")
        Else
            MsgBox("Computer L101-02 is assigned to: " &
                strComputer(0, 1), MsgBoxStyle.Information,
                "Computer not available")
        End If
    Case 2
        If strComputer(0, 2) = "" Then
            MsgBox("This computer is not assigned.",
                MsgBoxStyle.Information, "Computer is
                available")
        Else
            MsgBox("Computer L101-03 is assigned to: " &
                strComputer(0, 2), MsgBoxStyle.Information,
                "Computer not available")
        End If
    Case 3
        If strComputer(0, 3) = "" Then
            MsgBox("This computer is not assigned.",
                MsgBoxStyle.Information, "Computer is
                available")
        Else
            MsgBox("Computer L101-04 is assigned to: " &
                strComputer(0, 3), MsgBoxStyle.Information,
                "Computer not available")
        End If
    Case 4
        If strComputer(0, 4) = "" Then
            MsgBox("This computer is not assigned.",
                MsgBoxStyle.Information, "Computer is
                available")
        Else
            MsgBox("Computer L101-05 is assigned to: " &
                strComputer(0, 4), MsgBoxStyle.Information,
                "Computer not available")
        End If
    Case 5
        If strComputer(1, 0) = "" Then
            MsgBox("This computer is not assigned.",
                MsgBoxStyle.Information, "Computer is
                available")
        Else
            MsgBox("Computer L101-06 is assigned to: " &
                strComputer(1, 0), MsgBoxStyle.Information,
                "Computer not available")
        End If
```

```
            Case 6
                If strComputer(1, 1) = "" Then
                    MsgBox("This computer is not assigned.",
                        MsgBoxStyle.Information, "Computer is
                        available")
                Else
                    MsgBox("Computer L101-07 is assigned to: " &
                        strComputer(1, 1), MsgBoxStyle.Information,
                        "Computer not available")
                End If
            Case 7
                If strComputer(1, 2) = "" Then
                    MsgBox("This computer is not assigned.",
                        MsgBoxStyle.Information, "Computer is
                        available")
                Else
                    MsgBox("Computer L101-08 is assigned to: " &
                        strComputer(1, 2), MsgBoxStyle.Information,
                        "Computer not available")
                End If
            Case 8
                If strComputer(1, 3) = "" Then
                    MsgBox("This computer is not assigned.",
                        MsgBoxStyle.Information, "Computer is
                        available")
                Else
                    MsgBox("Computer L101-09 is assigned to: " &
                        strComputer(1, 3), MsgBoxStyle.Information,
                        "Computer not available")
                End If
            Case 9
                If strComputer(1, 4) = "" Then
                MsgBox("This computer is not assigned.",
                   MsgBoxStyle.Information, "Computer is
                   available")
                Else
                MsgBox("Computer L101-10 is assigned to: " &
                   strComputer(1, 4), MsgBoxStyle.Information,
                   "Computer not available")
                End If
        End Select
    End Sub
End Sub
```

To assign a student to a computer, you select the computer in the list box, enter a name in the text box, and click the **Assign a computer** button. If the computer has already been assigned, a message box appears. Figure 8.17 shows the message indicating that computer #L101-03 has been assigned.

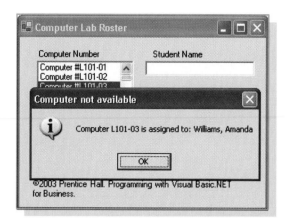

FIGURE 8.17. *Message indicating that a computer is assigned*

USING DYNAMIC ARRAYS

At times you will want to use an array in your application but will not know at design time the size of the array. In Chapter 7 you created an application for determining the future value of a CD account. You will use a similar application here to explain how to declare and use dynamic arrays.

The size and dimensions of a dynamic array can change at run time. You can declare an array as dynamic by omitting the size in the array declaration. Here's an example:

```
Friend sngFutureValue() As Single
```

This array has **Friend** access so it will be available to any procedure in the solution to which it belongs. The data type is single, and the size can be changed.

Using the ReDim Statement and the Preserve Keyword

Once you declare an array as dynamic, you need to use the **ReDim statement** to resize the array. ReDim is short for "redimension." When you redimension an array, you change its size. If the array contains values you want to retain while resizing it, you can use the Preserve keyword. The **Preserve keyword** retains the current data in the array as the array is resized. This is useful when you are using looping structures to populate an array, as you will see shortly.

Determining the Bounds of an Array at Run Time

When you work with dynamic arrays, you might need to determine the size of the array. The **bounds** of an array describe its size. The bounds express the lower and upper values of the indices for the array elements. Visual Basic.NET includes two keywords for determining the bounds of an array: the **Lbound keyword** for the lower bound and the **Ubound keyword** for the upper bound.

Dynamic arrays have an upper bound determined at run time. The **UBound** keyword is useful for obtaining the size of a dynamic array after it has been redimensioned.

Now that you have a basic understanding of dynamic arrays, let's view an example of how to use the **ReDim** statement and the **Preserve** and **UBound** keywords with a dynamic array. Figure 8.18 shows a simple Windows form for determining the future value of a savings account. This form is contained in the *Future Value* solution included with your data files. The figure shows how to create an array of return values for a deposit of $1,000 for a term of 3 years. The interest rate for the Certificate of Deposit is 5%.

FIGURE 8.18. *Form for calculating the value of a Certificate of Deposit at maturity*

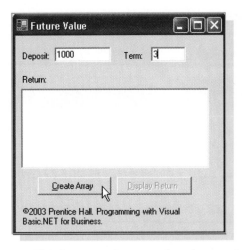

The form contains a text box for entering the amount of the initial deposit, a text box for indicating the term of the account (in years), and a list box for displaying the future value information. The form includes the array declaration statement shown earlier in this chapter. The **Create Array** button event procedure determines the number of months the account will be held, resizes the array, and populates each array element with the monthly increase in value. After the array is populated, the total increase in value is displayed in a message box. Following is the code for the button's click event:

```
Private Sub btnArray_Click(ByVal sender As System.Object, ByVal
  e As System.EventArgs) Handles btnArray.Click
    'Declare variables required by the procedure
    Dim intCounter As Integer
    Dim sngRate As Single
    Dim intTerm As Integer
    Dim sngStartValue As Single
    Dim sngPresentValue As Single

    'Set the initial start values
    sngRate = 0.05
    intTerm = Val(txtTerm.Text)
    sngStartValue = Val(txtDeposit.Text)

    'Calculate monthly increase in value and populate the array
    For intCounter = 0 To (intTerm * 12) - 1

        'Calculate the Monthly Value
        sngPresentValue = sngStartValue + ((sngStartValue) *
          (sngRate / 12))

        'Populate the current array element
        ReDim Preserve sngFutureValue(intCounter)
        sngFutureValue(intCounter) = sngPresentValue
        sngStartValue = sngPresentValue
    Next intCounter
```

```
    'Determine the size of the array to obtain present value
    Dim intSize As Integer
    intSize = (UBound(sngFutureValue))
    MsgBox("The value of this account after " & intSize + 1 & "
      months is " & (Format(sngFutureValue(intSize),
      "Currency")) & ".")

    'Enable to button to display the return
    btnReturn.Enabled = True
End Sub
```

The procedure is similar to the procedure you created in Chapter 7 for performing a future value calculation. The difference is that the values are stored in an array rather than being added to a list box. The procedure declares five variables that are private to the procedure: *intCounter* is a counter variable for the looping structure, *sngRate* stores the interest rate, *intTerm* stores the term of the account supplied by the user, and *sngStartValue* and *sngPresentValue* store the values for determining the monthly increase. The rate, term, and initial deposit values are initialized before the loop resizes and populates the array.

The procedure uses a For. . . Next statement to resize and populate the array. Because the loop will use the indices of the array and the array is zero-based, the procedure determines the number of loop iterations as follows:

```
For intCounter = 0 To (intTerm * 12) - 1
```

The calculation for each monthly increase in value is the present value multiplied by the interest rate for the period. These values are used to populate the array:

```
For intCounter = 0 To (intTerm * 12) - 1

    'Calculate the Monthly Value
    sngPresentValue = sngStartValue + ((sngStartValue) *
      (sngRate / 12))

    'Populate the current array element
    ReDim Preserve sngFutureValue(intCounter)
    sngFutureValue(intCounter) = sngPresentValue
    sngStartValue = sngPresentValue
Next intCounter
```

Each iteration of the loop calculates the successive monthly increase. The ReDim statement resizes the array by adding one element per iteration. The Preserve keyword preserves the values in the array as elements are added to it. Finally, after the monthly increase has stored the appropriate array element, the starting value for the next loop is set to the increased value.

How do we know the array has been populated? The procedure determines the upper bound of the array, retrieves the value stored in the last element, and displays this value in a message box as a concatenated and formatted text string:

```
'Determine the size of the array to obtain present value
        Dim intSize As Integer
        intSize = (UBound(sngFutureValue))
        MsgBox("The value of this account after " & intSize + 1
            & " months is " & (Format(sngFutureValue(intSize),
            "Currency")) & ".")
```

The form also contains a button for verifying the monthly increase for each month. This button extracts each element from the array, concatenates the value with a text string, and adds the information to a list box. Figure 8.19 shows the return for a deposit of $1,000 for a term of 3 years.

FIGURE 8.19. *Populating a list box with values in an array*

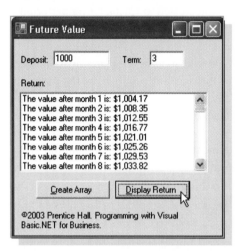

POPULATING AN ARRAY BY READING A DISK FILE

At times you might need to populate an array by using data from a text file. For example, many businesses spend money training their employees. Acme Wireless offers a three-day New Employee Hire training class every month. A maximum of 10 employees can attend a training session. As a measure of class effectiveness, each employee is given a written test after completing the class. The scores on these exams are tabulated, and the high score, low score, and average score are reported. Figure 8.20 displays a form for calculating these scores.

FIGURE 8.20. *Form for reading data from a text file into an array*

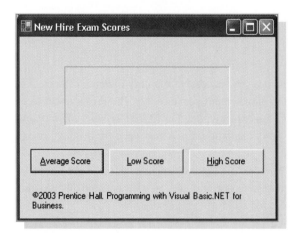

The form is in the *Scores* solution included with your data files. To run this program, you need a copy of the *Scores.txt* file on a floppy disk. Figure 8.21 shows the scores contained in the text file.

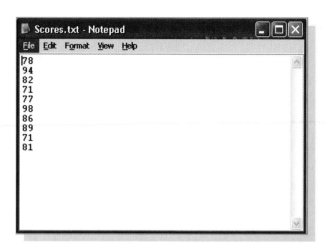

FIGURE 8.21. *Scores in the* Scores.txt *file*

Now let's look at the code for reading data from a text file into an array. The form contains the following declaration statement for a dynamic array:

```
Friend intScores() As Integer
```

In Chapter 5 you learned how to open files for input. When the form for the *Scores* solution is loaded at run time, a Form Load event opens the text file, resizes the array, reads the first score into the first element of the array, and loops through this procedure until all scores are read. Here's the code:

```
Private Sub Form1_Load(ByVal sender As Object, ByVal e As
   System.EventArgs) Handles MyBase.Load
     'Declare counter variable
     Dim intCounter As Integer
     FileOpen(1, "a:\Scores.txt", OpenMode.Input)
     Do While Not EOF(1)
          ReDim Preserve intScores(intCounter)
          Input(1, intScores(intCounter))
          intCounter = intCounter + 1
     Loop
     FileClose(1)
End Sub
```

The variable *intCounter* is declared as a counter variable. The loop continues until all scores are read into the array. The array is resized during each loop, and the **Preserve** keyword preserves the values read during previous iterations. When you run the application, the scores are loaded into the array.

Now let's see how the average score is calculated. The procedure is almost identical to the For. . . Next loop you used to determine the monthly increase in the *Future Value* example. Here's the procedure for the *btnAverage* click event:

```
Private Sub btnAverage_Click(ByVal sender As Object, ByVal e As
   System.EventArgs) Handles btnAverage.Click
     'Declare variables used by the procedure
     Dim intCounter As Integer
     Dim sngAvgScore As Single
     'Initialize the average score value
     sngAvgScore = 0
     For intCounter = 0 To UBound(intScores)
          sngAvgScore = sngAvgScore + intScores(intCounter)
```

```
                Next intCounter
                sngAvgScore = sngAvgScore / intScores.Length
                lblResult.Text = "The average score is: " & sngAvgScore
End Sub
```

The procedure declares two variables, a counter variable and a variable for storing the average score. After initializing the average score variable to zero, the procedure uses a loop to add each score to the average score variable. Notice that the procedure uses the **UBound** keyword to determine the index of the last element in the array. The scores are added together during each iteration of the loop. After the loop is complete, the scores have been added up but the average has not yet been calculated. Arrays have a *Length property* that returns the size of the array as an integer value. This value corresponds to the total number of scores in the array. The following statement divides the accumulated score by the total number of scores to calculate the average:

```
sngAvgScore = sngAvgScore / intScores.Length
```

Finally, the average is displayed in the result label as a concatenated string by using the following statement:

```
lblResult.Text = "The average score is: " & sngAvgScore
```

Figure 8.22 displays the average of the scores from the text file shown in Figure 8.21.

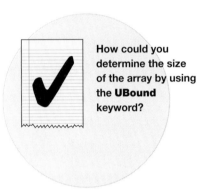

How could you determine the size of the array by using the **UBound** keyword?

FIGURE 8.22. *Displaying the average score*

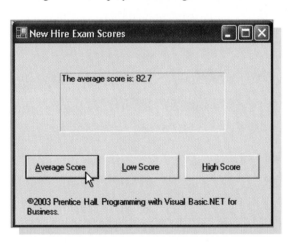

Now let's see how the low and high scores are determined. This is actually quite simple, because Visual Basic.NET includes a *sort method* that sorts the elements in a one-dimensional array. You can use the following statement to sort the contents of the array of scores:

```
Array.Sort(intScores)
```

When the scores are sorted, the low score is contained in the first element of the array and the high score in the last element. The first element always has an index of zero. You can determine the last element by using the **UBound** keyword. Once you obtain these values, you can display them in a text string as the text property of the *lblResult* label on the form. The following procedures return the low and high scores, respectively.

Obtaining the Low Score

```
Private Sub btnMinScore_Click(ByVal sender As System.Object,
  ByVal e As System.EventArgs) Handles btnMinScore.Click
  Array.Sort(intScores)
    lblResult.Text = "The lowest score is: " & intScores(0)
End Sub
```

Obtaining the High Score

```
Private Sub btnMaxScore_Click(ByVal sender As System.Object,
  ByVal e As System.EventArgs) Handles btnMaxScore.Click
  Array.Sort(intScores)
    lblResult.Text = "The highest score is: " &
      intScores(UBound(intScores))
End Sub
```

Arrays provide one method for storing related information in memory. Sometimes, however, you will need to combine data of different types in one variable. Although you can declare a multidimensional array as an **Object** data type and include multiple data types in the array, a structure might be a more effective method for manipulating related data.

Using Structures with Arrays

In Chapter 5 you learned how to create structures and declare a structure variable for storing multiple data types in one variable. Structures are useful when you want a single variable to hold several related pieces of information. For example, you might want to keep an employee's identification number, name, and wage together as a unit. You could declare multiple variables to accomplish this, or you could define a structure and use it for a single employee variable. The advantage of the structure is seen when you have many employees and therefore many variables to store each employee's information. You can add the data from a structure into an array if the array is declared by using the **Object** data type.

DECLARING STRUCTURES

As you learned in Chapter 5, declaring a structure is similar to declaring a variable. A structure declaration begins with the **Structure** statement, and ends with the **End Structure** statement. When you declare a structure, at least one member of the structure is required between the declaration statements. The advantage of a structure is that the members can be of any data type. Consider the following example from the *Employee Structure* solution included with your data files:

```
Structure Employee
    <VBFixedString(11)> Public strEmployeeID As String
    <VBFixedString(15)> Public strLastName As String
    <VBFixedString(10)> Public strFirstName As String
    Public sngWage As Single
End Structure
```

When you declare a structure, you can specify its accessibility by using the **Public**, **Friend**, or **Private** keyword. By default, a structure is **Public**. If you use the **Dim** statement without any keywords, the accessibility defaults to **Public**. This example uses **VBFixedString** to define the size of the structure elements of the String data type.

DECLARING STRUCTURE VARIABLES

After you create a structure, you can declare a variable that uses the structure. Here is an example of how to declare a structure variable that uses the data type based on the *Employee* structure:

```
Friend strEmployees As Employee
```

This statement declares a variable named *Employees* that is based on the *Employee* structure (which is a user-defined data type). The variable is now available for use. After declaring the structure variable, you can declare an array of the **Object** data type that can use the data in a structure variable. The following array declaration statement is from the *Employee Structure* solution:

```
Friend objEmployeesArray(0) As Object
```

Now let's see how to add records to the *Employee* structure and use the structure to populate an array of the **Object** data type. Figure 8.23 displays the form contained in the *Employee Structure* solution for adding fields to a structure and populating an array with these values.

FIGURE 8.23. *Form for adding data from a structure variable to an array*

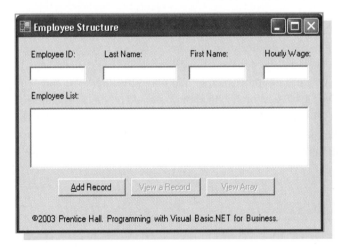

The form has text boxes for entering record information and buttons for adding a record to the array, displaying one element in the array, and displaying all the records in the array. Now let's look at the event procedures for accomplishing these tasks.

```
Private Sub btnAddData_Click(ByVal sender As System.Object,
   ByVal e As System.EventArgs) Handles btnAddRecord.Click

      'Add fields to the structure variable
      strEmployees.strEmployeeID = txtID.Text
      strEmployees.strLastName = txtLastName.Text
      strEmployees.strFirstName = txtFirstName.Text
      strEmployees.sngWage = Val(txtWage.Text)
```

```
'Determine size of the array
Dim intSize As Integer
intSize = UBound(objEmployeesArray)

'Redimension the array and add new data
ReDim Preserve objEmployeesArray(intSize + 1)
objEmployeesArray(intSize) = strEmployees.strEmployeeID &
    vbTab _
& strEmployees.strLastName & vbTab &
    strEmployees.strFirstName & vbTab _
& strEmployees.sngWage

'Verify the record added to the array
MsgBox("The following record has been added to the array:" &
    vbCrLf &
objEmployeesArray(intSize), MsgBoxStyle.Information, "Record
    added")

'Clear the text boxes
txtID.Text = ""
txtLastName.Text = ""
txtFirstName.Text = ""
txtWage.Text = ""

'Enable buttons
btnViewArray.Enabled = True
btnViewRecord.Enabled = True
End Sub
```

This procedure assigns data from the text boxes to the structure variable, determines the current size of the array, resizes the array, and adds the data from the structure variable to the array. A message box verifies the data that is added to the array. Figure 8.24 shows the verification message that appears when a record is added from the structure to the array.

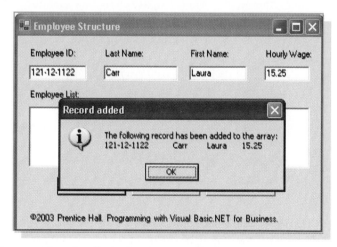

FIGURE 8.24. *Message verifying the record added to the array*

Now let's look at the procedure for displaying the contents of the array.

```
Private Sub btnViewArray_Click(ByVal sender As System.Object,
  ByVal e As System.EventArgs) Handles btnViewArray.Click
    Dim intCounter As Integer
    Dim intSize As Integer
    intSize = UBound(objEmployeesArray) - 1

    'Clear the list box
    lstEmployees.Items.Clear()

    'Populate the list box with records from the array
    For intCounter = 0 To intSize
        lstEmployees.Items.Add(objEmployeesArray(intCounter))
    Next intCounter
End Sub
```

This procedure determines the size of the array by using the **UBound** method. It then clears the list of any previous data and uses a loop to add each element in the array as an item in the list box. Figure 8.25 shows the result of clicking the **View Array** button.

FIGURE 8.25. *Displaying the contents of the array*

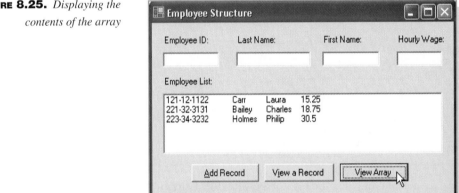

Now let's look at the procedure for displaying one element in the array.

```
Private Sub btnViewRecord_Click(ByVal sender As System.Object,
  ByVal e As System.EventArgs) Handles btnViewRecord.Click
    Dim intSize, intRecord As Integer

    intSize = UBound(objEmployeesArray)
    intRecord = InputBox("Number of Records: " & intSize &
      vbCrLf & "Please
    enter a number for the record you want to view.")
    MsgBox("Record " & intRecord & vbCrLf &
      objEmployeesArray(intRecord - 1),
    MsgBoxStyle.Information, "Employee Record")
End Sub
```

This procedure determines the size of the array and also declares a variable, *intRecord*, to store the index value of the specific record to display. An assignment statement assigns the number entered into an input box to the value of this variable. Figure 8.26 displays the input box for entering the index number. Note that the text for the message uses the *intSize* variable to display the total number of records in the array.

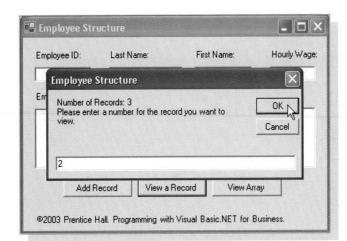

FIGURE 8.26. *Message requesting the record number to display*

Why does the reference to the *intSize* variable subtract 1 from this value when it displays the size of the array?

Figure 8.26 shows a value of 2 entered as the record to display. The procedure uses this value, less 1, as the index value for the element to display. A message box concatenates a text string with the variable element to display the contents of the array. Figure 8.27 shows the contents of the second element in the array.

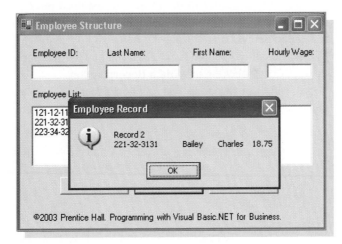

FIGURE 8.27. *Displaying one element in the array*

Tip

The data is structured in the array so that it can be written to a tab-delimited data file. Working with the data in array as opposed to reading and writing individual records minimizes file input and output (I/O).

Now that you know how to use structures and arrays, let's explore another way of working with a collection of data in memory.

Using an ArrayList to Create a Collection

Visual Basic.NET supports numerous ways for creating lists of related items. In Chapter 4 you learned how to use the **String Collection Editor** to add items to the collection defining the members of a list box or combo box. You are familiar with the concept of a collection because the items in a list box or combo box are one kind of collection. A collection is similar in concept to an array, in that a *collection* contains a list of items that can be manipulated at run time.

The **ArrayList** is another kind of collection you can use to create an array of items that can easily be manipulated. An *ArrayList* is a sophisticated type of array with some significant differences. For one, the capacity of an ArrayList is changed dynamically as items are added to the collection. You can also add or remove a range of elements from an ArrayList rather than working with one element at a time. Unlike an array, an ArrayList has only one dimension. Let's see how to use an ArrayList to easily create a collection of employee records. Figure 8.28 shows a form from the *Employee Collection* solution:

FIGURE 8.28. *Form for creating a collection of employee records by using an ArrayList*

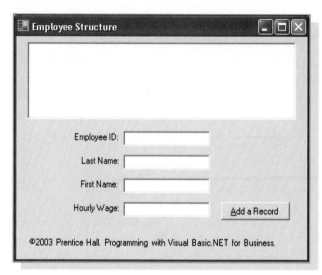

This form is similar to the form you just used to create a structure. The form includes a list box control and uses an ArrayList to store items in the collection. The items in the ArrayList are displayed in the list box control at the top of the form each time a new employee record is entered by adding the appropriate information in the text box controls and clicking the **Add a Record** button.

Let's look at the code that implements this functionality. The form uses an Employees structure variable based on the following structure:

```
Structure Employee
    <VBFixedString(11)> Public strEmployeeID As String
    <VBFixedString(15)> Public strLastName As String
    <VBFixedString(10)> Public strFirstName As String
    Public sngPayRate As Single

    Public Overrides Function ToString() As String
        Return strEmployeeID & vbTab & strLastName & vbTab &
            strFirstName & vbTab & Format(sngPayRate, "Currency")
    End Function
End Structure
```

The structure includes a function (ToString) that displays the collection items as text. The ArrayList and an object variable for the structure are declared as follows:

```
Friend EmpArray As New ArrayList()
Friend strEmployee As Employee
```

The form also includes a function for defining a new employee record. The code for the function is as follows:

```
Public Function CreateEmployee(ByVal strEmployee) As Employee
    'Create new employee
    EmpArray.Add(strEmployee)
    lstEmployees.Items.Add(strEmployee)
    Return strEmployee
End Function
```

The function includes one parameter to receive the employee structure passed to it as an argument. The parameter creates a new customer record and adds it to the ArrayList and displays the record in the list box.

The form contains a button for adding records to the ArrayList. Here is the code defining the button's click event:

```
Private Sub btnAddRecord_Click(ByVal sender As System.Object,
  ByVal e As System.EventArgs) Handles btnAddRecord.Click
    'Obtain field data
    strEmployee.strEmployeeID = txtID.Text
    strEmployee.strLastName = txtLastName.Text
    strEmployee.strFirstName = txtFirstName.Text
    strEmployee.sngPayRate = Val(txtPayRate.Text)

    'Call the CreateEmployee function
    Call CreateEmployee(strEmployee)

    'Clear the text boxes
    txtID.Text = ""
    txtLastName.Text = ""
    txtFirstName.Text = ""
    txtPayRate.Text = ""
End Sub
```

The procedure obtains values for the employee ID, last name, first name, and hourly wage by using the text boxes on the form. After obtaining these values, the procedure calls the *CreateEmployee* function, which adds the record to the ArrayList and displays the list in the list box. Figure 8.29 shows two records that have been added to the ArrayList, with a third record ready to be added as well.

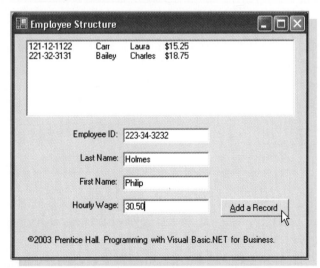

FIGURE 8.29. *Records added to an ArrayList and displayed in a list box*

Now that you have learned about using arrays, structures, and collections for manipulating lists of data, how do you decide which option to use when you need to create and manipulate lists of data in your applications? Here are a few guidelines for selecting among these options:

■ Use an array when the data in the array is of the same data type and the items in the array do not need to be revised after the array had been created and populated.

■ Use structures when you want to store data of multiple types in a variable. Once you define a structure, you can declare a structure variable based on the structure. You can then add members to the structure variable by referencing the variable name and the member element.

■ Use a collection such as an ArrayList when you are working with a single-dimension, dynamic set of items that will need to change frequently.

☞ HANDS-ON PROGRAMMING EXAMPLE

Using a Two-Dimensional Array to Create a Loan Repayment Schedule

In this chapter you learned that arrays are a good choice when you need to work with a collection of data in which the elements are of the same data type. In previous chapters you have created more than one application for creating a loan repayment schedule. In this example, you will learn how to add loan repayment data to a multidimensional array and use the array to report the payment information for any payment in the schedule.

Most people purchase a car sometime in their life. Although some prefer purchasing vehicles with cash, automobile dealers have a variety of financing options available for those wanting to make payments over time. Figure 8.30 shows the Auto Loan Calculator you will create for determining the monthly payments on a car loan.

FIGURE 8.30. *The Auto Loan Calculator application*

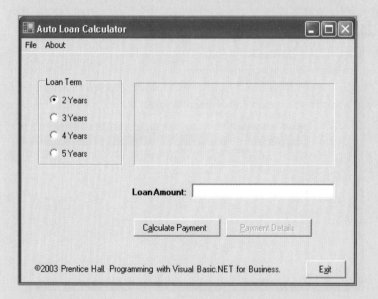

Financing options usually have limitations regarding the annual interest rate and the amount of time you can take to pay back the loan. In this case, loan calculations are limited as follows:

1. The loan amount must be at least $4,000 but not more than $45,000.
2. The loan term must be at least 2 years but not more than 5 years.
3. The annual interest rate depends on the term: 2 years, 4%; 3 years, 4.5%; 4 years, 5.5%; 5 years, 6%.

The form contains a text box and four radio buttons for obtaining user input. To calculate the loan payment, enter the loan amount as text, select a loan term, and click either the **Calculate Payment** button or the **Calculate Payment** menu item. Figure 8.31 shows the loan payment for a $12,000 loan paid back over 3 years.

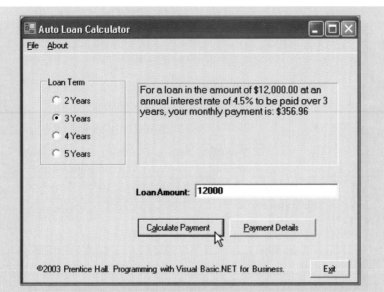

FIGURE 8.31. *Calculating the monthly payment*

The form also contains a button and a menu item for retrieving the details of any loan payment. These details include the amount of the payment that applies to the loan principal, the amount of the payment that applies to the loan interest, and the outstanding balance. Figure 8.32 shows the details for payment number 20.

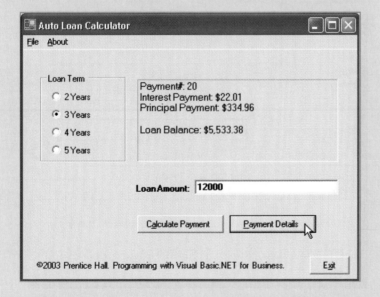

FIGURE 8.32. *Payment details for payment number 20*

This application takes advantage of what you have learned in previous chapters. After you plan the application and design the user interface, we'll take a look at the code that gives the application its functionality.

Plan the Application

The first step in planning an application is determining the inputs and outputs. The Auto Loan Calculator application obtains user input to calculate the monthly payment for a loan and then uses an array to store the details about each monthly payment. The inputs and outputs are as follows:

Inputs	Outputs
Loan principal	Monthly payment
Annual interest	Array containing monthly payment details
Loan term	Report listing payment details for a specific payment

The Auto Loan Calculator application consists of two forms: *frmLoan* and *frmAbout*. Draw a visual representation of the form on a blank piece of paper. Figure 8.33 displays a drawing of the user interface and the name of each control on the Auto Loan Calculator form.

FIGURE 8.33. *The frmLoan form*

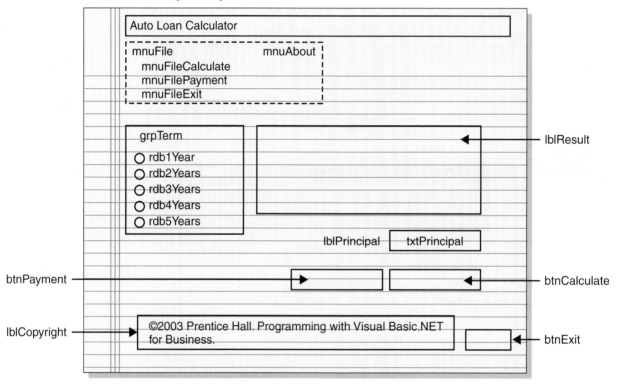

Table 8.2 lists the controls and properties for the *frmLoan* form.

Table 8.2: *Objects and properties for the Auto Loan form*

Object	Property	Setting
frmLoan	Text StartPosition Size	Auto Loan Calculator CenterScreen 475, 365
MainMenu1		
mnuFile	Text	&File
mnuFileCalculate	Text	&Calculate Payment
mnuFilePayment	Text Enabled	&Payment Details False
mnuFileExit	Text	E&xit
mnuAbout	Text	&About
grpTerm	Text TabIndex	Loan Term 1
rdbYear1	Text Checked	1 Year True
rdb2Years	Text Checked	2 Years False
rdb3Years	Text Checked	3 Years False
rdb4Years	Text Checked	4 Years False
rdb5Years	Text Checked BorderStyle	5 Years False Fixed3D
lblPrincipal	Text TextAlign Font Style	Loan Amount: MiddleRight Bold
txtPrincipal	Text TabIndex Font Style CausesValidation	 0 Bold True
lblResult	BorderStyle Text	Fixed3D
btnCalculate	Text	&Calculate Payment
btnPayment	Text TabIndex	&Payment Details 2
btnExit	Text TabIndex CausesValidation	E&xit 3 False
lblCopyright	Text	©2003 Prentice Hall. Programming with Visual Basic.NET for Business.

The routines for calculating the loan payment and obtaining payment information are contained in procedures. The pseudocode for the application's functionality is shown in Table 8.3.

Table 8.3: *Pseudocode for the Auto Loan Calculator*

Event Procedure	Action
mnuFileCalculate_Click	Calls the Calculate sub procedure.
mnuFilePayment_Click	Calls the CreateReport sub procedure.
mnuFileExit_Click	Calls the ExitApp sub procedure.
mnuAbout_Click	Displays the About form.
btnCalculate_Click	Calls the Calculate sub procedure.
btnPayment_Click	Calls the CreateReport sub procedure.
btnExit_Click	Calls the AppExit sub procedure.
btnOK_Click	Closes the frmAbout form.
txtPrincipal_Validating	Performs data validation on the loan principal.
Calculate sub procedure	1. Obtains the loan principal, term, and rate values. 2. Calls the CalculatePayment function procedure.
CalculatePayment Function procedure	1. Calculates the loan payment. 2. Declares and populates the sngSchedule array. 3. Returns the loan payment to the calling procedure.
CreateReport Sub procedure	1. Obtains a payment index. 2. Obtains payment information from the sngSchedule array. 3. Displays the payment information.

Now that you have created the planning documents for the application, you are ready to design the user interface in the integrated development environment (IDE).

Design the User Interface

Now you can begin designing the user interface. If you have not launched Visual Studio.NET, do so now. Perform each task that follows to complete this application.

To create a new project and solution:

1. Click **File, New Project**.
2. Navigate to the drive and folder where you will save your project. Type `Auto Loan` as the Project Name and click **OK**.

3. Right-click the *Form1.vb* form in the Solution Explorer and rename the form as `frmLoan.vb`.
4. Display the properties for the form. Set the **Name**, **Text**, **Size**, and **StartPosition** properties as specified in Table 8.2.
5. Right-click the *Auto Loan* project in the Solution Explorer and select **Properties**.
6. The **Auto Loan Property Pages** dialog box appears. Select frmLoan as the Startup Object and click **OK**.
7. Click **Project**, **Add Existing Item**. The **Add Existing Item** dialog box appears.
8. Navigate to the location of the data files for this chapter. Select the *About.vb* file and click **Open**.
9. Right-click the *frmPlan.vb* form in the Solution Explorer and select **View Designer**.
10. Click **File**, **Save All**. Your project now contains two forms.

To add controls to the *frmLoan* form and set control properties:

1. Using Figure 8.30 as a guide, display the Toolbox and add the controls listed in Table 8.2 to the *frmLoan* form.
2. Set the control properties as specified.
3. Save your changes.

Now that the interface design for the Auto Loan Calculator application is complete, you are ready to write the code providing the functionality.

Write the Code

The form uses two sub procedures and one function procedure. One sub procedure is for exiting the application. The other sub procedure and the function procedure are used to calculate the loan payment, create an array of loan payment values, and display the loan payment information.

Let's begin by declaring the variables that need to be accessible by the procedures on the form.

To declare variables with Friend access:

1. Right-click on the *frmLoan.vb* file in the Solution Explorer and choose **View Code**.
2. Place the insertion point at the beginning of the Code Editor, and type the following comments:

```
'©2003 Prentice Hall
'By [Enter your name]
'Created/Revised: [Enter the date]
'Auto Loan Calculator
```

3. Place the insertion point immediately below the Inherits System.Windows.Forms.Form statement, press ↵Enter, and type the following declaration statements:

```
'Declare variables
Friend sngPrincipal As Single
Friend sngRate As Single
Friend intTerm As Integer


'Declare array
Friend sngSchedule(59, 2) As Single
```

Notice that the array is declared with 59 elements (60 rows). This is the maximum number of rows required for a loan term of 5 years (5 multiplied by 12 is 60, or 59 zero-based elements).

4. Place the insertion point below the region for the Windows Designer Generated Code. Type `#Region "Procedures"` and press ⏎Enter. This statement declares a region where you will enter the procedures for the application. Press ⏎Enter twice. Type `#End Region` and press ⏎Enter again. The code should match Figure 8.34.

FIGURE 8.34. *Code displayed in the Code Editor*

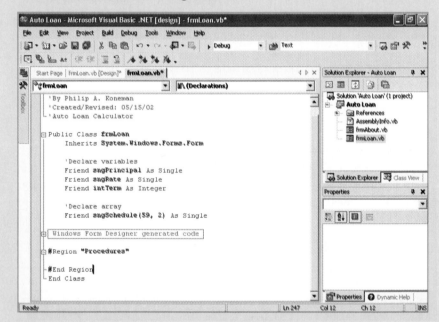

5. Save your changes.

To calculate the loan payment, the user supplies a loan principal amount in the *txtPrincipal* text box. You can use the **CausesValidation** property to raise an event if the user does not supply a principal amount before trying to calculate the loan payment.

To validate the loan principal:

1. Right-click on the *frmLoan.vb* file in the Solution Explorer and choose **View Code**.

2. Click the **Class Name** list in the Code Editor and select *txtPrincipal*.

3. Click the **Method Name** list in the Code Editor and select **Validating**.

4. Type the following statements for the procedure:

```
Try

    If Val(txtPrincipal.Text) < 4000 Or Val(txtPrincipal.Text) >
    45000 Then

        Throw New Exception()

    End If
```

```
Catch ex As Exception
    ' Cancel the event and select the text to be corrected by
      the user()
    e.Cancel = True
    txtPrincipal.Select(0, txtPrincipal.Text.Length)
    MsgBox("The loan amount must be at least 4000 but not
        greater than 45000. Please try again.",
        MsgBoxStyle.Critical, "Invalid Entry!")
End Try
```

5. Save your changes.

You are now ready to write the code for the Calculate sub procedure.

To write the code for the Calculate sub procedure:

1. Place the insertion point at the top of the Procedures region you created previously.

2. Type the following statements:

```
Sub Calculate()
    sngPrincipal = Val(txtPrincipal.Text)

    'Obtain term and rate
    If rdb2Years.Checked = True Then
        intTerm = 2
        sngRate = 0.04
    ElseIf rdb3Years.Checked = True Then
        intTerm = 3
        sngRate = 0.045
    ElseIf rdb4Years.Checked = True Then
        intTerm = 4
        sngRate = 0.055
    Else
        intTerm = 5
        sngRate = 0.06
    End If

    lblResult.Text = "For a loan in the amount of " & _
        Format(sngPrincipal, "Currency") & _
        " at an annual interest rate of " & _
        sngRate * 100 & "% to be paid over " & _
        intTerm & " years, your monthly payment is: " & _
        Format(CalculatePayment(sngPrincipal), "Currency")

    'Enable controls to create the monthly value report
    btnPayment.Enabled = True
    mnuFilePayment.Enabled = True
End Sub
```

This procedure begins by obtaining the values for the loan principal, loan term, and loan rate. The principal is validated by the procedure you already created. The values for the rate and term depend on which radio button is selected for the term.

The procedure then displays the loan payment information. Notice that the procedure calls the **CalculatePayment** function, which returns the loan payment to this procedure.

After displaying the loan payment, the procedure enables the button and menu item for displaying the payment information.

You are now ready to write the code for the **CalculatePayment** function procedure.

To write the code for the CalculatePayment function procedure:

1. Place the insertion point below the code for the Calculate sub procedure and press ⏎Enter.
2. Type the following statements:

```
Function CalculatePayment(ByVal Principal)
    'Calculate monthly payment, and create and populate an array
      of repayment
    values
    Dim sngPmt As Single
    Dim sngPpmt As Single
    Dim sngIPmt As Single
    Dim sngBalance As Single

    Dim intCounter As Integer
    Dim intSize As Integer
    intSize = (intTerm * 12)

    'Calculate the monthly payment
    sngPmt = Pmt(sngRate / 12, intTerm * 12, -Principal)

    'Calculate payment and initialize loan balance
    sngBalance = sngPrincipal

    'Redimension the array
    ReDim sngSchedule(intSize, 2)

    'Populate array
    For intCounter = 1 To intSize
        sngIPmt = IPmt(sngRate / 12, intCounter, intTerm * 12,
          -Principal)
        sngPpmt = PPmt(sngRate / 12, intCounter, intTerm * 12,
          -Principal)
        sngBalance = sngBalance - sngPpmt
        sngSchedule(intCounter - 1, 0) = sngIPmt
        sngSchedule(intCounter - 1, 1) = sngPpmt
        sngSchedule(intCounter - 1, 2) = sngBalance
    Next intCounter

    'Return the monthly payment to the calling procedure
    Return sngPmt
End Function
```

3. Save your changes.

This procedure declares the local variables required to calculate the loan payment and populate the array. The procedure uses the **Pmt** function to calculate the monthly payment and the **PPmt** and **IPmt** functions to calculate the principal and interest payments.

Notice that the array is resized to the minimum size required by the loan term. Then the array is populated with the interest payment, principal payment, and loan balance values for each monthly payment.

You are now ready to write the sub procedure for generating a report of a specific monthly payment.

To write the code for the CreateReport sub procedure:

1. Place the insertion point below the code for the **CalculatePayment** function procedure and press ⏎Enter.

2. Type the following statements:

```
Sub CreateReport()
    Dim intCounter, intSize As Integer
    intSize = UBound(sngSchedule)
    'Display payment information for the specified payment
    intCounter = InputBox("Which Payment?")

    If intCounter > 0 And intCounter <= intSize Then
        lblResult.Text = "Payment#: " & intCounter & vbCrLf & _
        "Interest Payment: " & _
        Format(sngSchedule(intCounter - 1, 0), "Currency") & _
            vbCrLf & "Principal Payment: " & _
            Format(sngSchedule(intCounter - 1, 1), "Currency") & _
            vbCrLf & vbCrLf & "Loan Balance: " & _
            Format(sngSchedule(intCounter - 1, 2), "Currency")
    Else
        MsgBox("The loan payment number must not exceed " & _
            intSize & ". Please try again.", _
            MsgBoxStyle.Critical, "Invalid Entry!")
    End If
End Sub
```

3. Save your changes.

This procedure declares two variables for obtaining the index value from the array. An input box requests the payment number to display. An If statement verifies that the payment number is within the range of the array and then extracts the interest payment, principal payment, and loan balance values from the array. These are combined with the payment number and displayed in the text property of the *lblResult* label.

You are now ready to create the procedure for exiting the application.

To create the *AppExit* sub procedure:

1. Place the insertion point below the *CreateReport* sub procedure and press ⏎Enter twice.

2. Type the following statements:

Tip

Notice that the array index for the rows is 1 less than the value of the counter variable. This is because the counter variable begins with a value of 1, but the array is zero-based.

```
Dim intResponse As Integer
    intResponse = MsgBox("Do you really want to exit this
      application?", 276, "Exit?")
   If intResponse = 6 Then
        End
   End If
```

3. Save your changes.

Now that you have created the procedures the application will use, you are ready to write the event procedures for calling the procedures. The interface contains three buttons and four menu items. You will therefore need to write seven event procedures. This is not as difficult as it sounds. With the exception of the mnuAbout_click event, the event procedures require only one line of code.

To create event procedures:

1. Place the insertion point below the *Procedures* region you created.
2. Use the **Class Name** and **Method Name** drop-down lists in the Code Editor to create the following procedures:

```
Private Sub btnCalculate_Click(ByVal sender As System.Object,
   ByVal e As System.EventArgs) Handles btnCalculate.Click
        Calculate()
   End Sub

    Private Sub mnuFileCalculate_Click(ByVal sender As
       System.Object, ByVal e As System.EventArgs) Handles
       mnuFileCalculate.Click
        Calculate()
    End Sub

    Private Sub btnPayment_Click(ByVal sender As System.Object,
       ByVal e As System.EventArgs) Handles btnPayment.Click
        CreateReport()
    End Sub

    Private Sub mnuFilePayment_Click(ByVal sender As
       System.Object, ByVal e As System.EventArgs) Handles
       mnuFilePayment.Click
        CreateReport()
    End Sub

    Private Sub btnExit_Click(ByVal sender As System.Object,
       ByVal e As System.EventArgs) Handles btnExit.Click
        AppExit()
    End Sub

    Private Sub mnuFileExit_Click(ByVal sender As System.Object,
       ByVal e As System.EventArgs) Handles mnuFileExit.Click
        AppExit()
    End Sub
```

```
Private Sub mnuAbout_Click(ByVal sender As System.Object,
    ByVal e As System.EventArgs) Handles mnuAbout.Click
        Dim ShowForm As frmAbout = New frmAbout()
        ShowForm.ShowDialog()
End Sub
```

Six of the event procedures include only a calling statement. The seventh procedure is familiar to you, because you have used it in most of the applications you have created.

3. Save your changes.

Run the Application

You are now ready to run the Auto Loan Calculator and test its functionality.

To run the application:

1. Click the **Start** button or press the F5 key to run the application.
2. Click the **Calculate Payment** button. The error message shown in Figure 8.35 appears.
3. Click **OK** to close the message box.

FIGURE 8.35. *Error message that appears when the loan principal fails validation*

4. Type 15000 as the loan amount.
5. Select the option for a 4-year term.
6. Click the **Calculate Payment** button, as shown in Figure 8.36. A monthly payment of $348.85 is displayed.

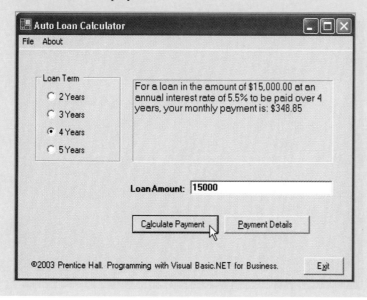

FIGURE 8.36. *Loan payment information*

7. Click **File**, **Calculate Payment**. Verify that the payment, rate, and term do not change.

8. Change the term to 5 years and the loan amount to 12,000. Using the Calculate Payment button or the Calculate Payment menu item, the payment should be $231.99.

9. Click the **Payment Details** button. Type 100 as the payment number and click **OK**. The error message shown in Figure 8.37 appears. Using the same values, verify the functionality of the **Payment Details** menu item.

FIGURE 8.37. *Error message when the loan payment number is outside the bounds of the array*

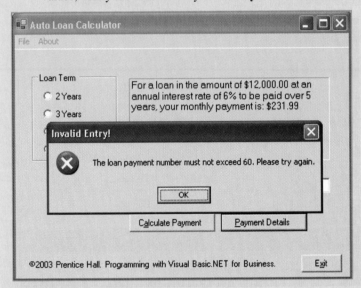

10. Check the functionality of the **About** menu item, the **Exit** button, and the **Exit** menu item.

11. Make any corrections to your application, and save your changes. Close the solution when you finish.

Summary

- In Visual Basic.NET you can manipulate data by using arrays, structures, and collections. Arrays are variables that can store more than one value. To declare an array, use a declaration statement, name the array, and specify the size and dimensionality of the array. A structure is a variable that holds multiple data types. You can use a structure to populate an array with data of different types if the array is declared with the Object data type. A collection is a list of items that can easily be manipulated at run time. An ArrayList is a special kind of array that creates a collection.

- You can declare a static, single-dimension array by declaring the array name and size. To declare a dynamic single-dimension array, declare the array name without a size specified in the required parentheses.

- To store data in an array, use a declaration statement that references the array name and the index for the element that contains the data you need. To retrieve values from an array, reference the array name and the element's index.

- In Visual Basic.NET, arrays are zero-based. You can access the elements in an array by referencing the element's position in the array. For a single-dimension array, reference the element by using the index number. For a two-dimensional array, reference the element by using its column and row index.

- You can add data to an array at run time by using a looping structure or by reading data from a file. After values are stored in an array, they are available to procedures that can access the array.

- To create a multidimensional array, declare the array name and the size and dimension of the array. Common multidimensional arrays include two-dimensional arrays, which consist of multiple rows and columns.

- Dynamic arrays provide flexibility when the size and rank of the array is determined at run time. To declare a dynamic array, do not include a size in the declaration. You can resize an array at run time by using the ReDim keyword. To resize the array and keep the existing data, use the Preserve keyword.

- You can populate a dynamic array at run time by reading data from a random access file into the array. Use the FileOpen command to open a file and read its contents into the array. The ReDim keyword resizes the array until the end of the file is reached, and the Preserve keyword preserves the existing data as new rows are added to the array.

- Structures are useful when a variable must contain multiple elements of varying data types. To declare a structure, use the Structure and End Structure keywords and define the structure members within this declaration.

- To use a structure, you must declare a structure variable that is based on the defined structure.

- You can use an ArrayList collection to work with lists that dynamically change at run time. An ArrayList is a special kind of array that is dynamically resized at run time, contains only a single dimension, and can accept multiple values simultaneously. To create an ArrayList, define a structure and use the ToString function to convert data in the structure to string data. Then declare a structure variable of the ArrayList type.

Key Terms

array	Lbound keyword
array variable	length property
ArrayList	multidimensional array
bounds	Object data type
collection	Preserve keyword
dimension	rank
dynamic array	ReDim statement
element	scalar variable
index	single-dimension array

size

sort method

static array

subscript

subscripted variables

two-dimensional array

Ubound keyword

zero-based

Study Questions

Multiple-Choice Questions

1. An array is declared as follows:
   ```
   Dim strName(5)
   ```
   How many elements are in this array?
   a. 0
   b. 2
   c. 4
   d. 5
   e. 6

2. Which declaration declares an array in a procedure where the accessibility of the elements is private to that procedure?
   a. Private
   b. Friend
   c. Shared
   d. Dim
   e. Public

3. You declare an array as follows:
   ```
   intExamScores (24) As
   Integer
   ```
   The first and last elements have indices of:
   a. 0, 0
   b. 0, 23
   c. 0, 1
   d. 1, 25
   e. 1, 1

4. In Visual Basic.NET, the Lbound keyword always returns a value of:
   a. 0
   b. The size of the array -1
   c. 1
   d. The size of the array +1
   e. The value of UBound -1

5. Which of the following best defines a dynamic, multidimensional array with access to all procedures in an assembly?
   a. Dim intScores( )
   b. Public strEmail(99)
   c. Friend intScores(,)
   d. Dim intTestScores(100,2)
   e. Friend sngGrades(99)

6. Which keyword, property, or method determines the size of an array?
   a. UBound
   b. ReDim
   c. Lbound
   d. Preserve
   e. Length

7. Which keyword, property, or method retains the values of an array when it is resized?
   a. UBound
   b. ReDim
   c. Lbound
   d. Preserve
   e. Length

8. Which of the following is the most compelling reason to consider using a collection rather than an array?
   a. The related data is of a single data type.
   b. The number of related elements will change significantly at run time.
   c. The related data is of multiple data types.
   d. You need to perform calculations using the related items.
   e. The related data must be sorted.

9. An array is declared as follows:
   ```
   Dim strTaxRate(4,5)
   ```
   How many elements are in this array?
   a. 9
   b. 20
   c. 16
   d. 25
   e. 30

10. Which statement is false concerning structures?
    a. A structure can contain data of only a single data type.
    b. A structure can be used without an explicit declaration.
    c. You declare a structure with the Structure and End Structure keywords.
    d. A structure can contain data of multiple data types.
    e. A structure can accept string and numeric values.

True/False Questions

1. You can declare an array in Visual Basic.NET so that the first element will have an index of 1.

2. If you declare an array without defining the size inside the parentheses, the array is dynamic.

3. If you resize an array by using the ReDim statement, the contents of the array are preserved.

4. Before you can declare a structure variable, you must define the structure.

5. A collection such as an ArrayList can be dynamically changed at run time.

Short Answer Questions

1. What is a zero-based array?

2. How does a static array differ from a dynamic array? When would you consider using one rather than the other?

3. How do you declare a static array? How do you declare a dynamic array?

4. What is the difference between a structure and a structured variable?

5. What considerations might make an ArrayList a better choice than an array?

Guided Exercises

Tracking Employee New-Hire Training Effectiveness

Because arrays are variables, you can declare more than one array for use in your applications. Acme Wireless has seen great results from the three-day new hire training program they recently implemented. To demonstrate the effectiveness of the program, each of the 15 employees attending a session will be given a written test before taking the class, and a second test 8 weeks after completing the class. You want to store employee scores on these two tests by using two different arrays to calculate the low score, average score, and high score for both tests. Figure 8.38 shows the application you will create for summarizing the test scores.

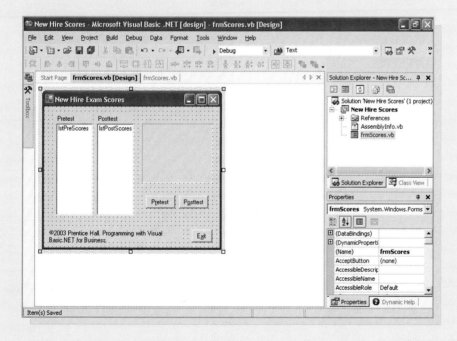

FIGURE 8.38. *Form for comparing pre- and posttest scores for new employees*

You will complete the following tasks:

1. Create the user interface.

2. Declare an array for each set of test scores.

3. Create the procedures for populating the arrays, sorting the arrays, and calculating the average score for each test.

4. Display the score results.

To create this application, complete the following steps:

To create the New Hire Scores application:

1. Copy the *PreScores.txt* and *PostScore.txt* files from your data files folder to a floppy disk.

2. Launch Visual Studio.NET.

3. Click **File**, **New Project**. Create a project named New Hire Scores.

4. Use the Solution Explorer to change the name of the form to frmScores. Set the properties of the project to display *frmScores*.

5. Display the Toolbox.

To design the user interface:

1. Using Figure 8.38 as a guide, add the controls and set the properties listed in Table 8.4.

Table 8.4: Objects and properties for the New Hire Scores form

Object	Property	Setting
FrmScores	Text	New Hire Exam Scores
	StartPosition	CenterScreen
	Size	350, 300
lstPreScores	TabStop	False
lstPostScores	TabStop	False
lblPreScores	Text	Pretest
lblPostScores	Text	Posttest
lblResults	Text	
	BorderStyle	Fixed3D
lblCopyright	Text	©2003 Prentice Hall. Programming with Visual Basic.NET for Business.
btnPreTest	Text	P&retest
	TabStop	True
	TabIndex	0
btnPostTest	Text	P&ostTest
	TabStop	True
	TabIndex	1
btnExit	Text	E&xit
	TabStop	True
	TabIndex	2

2. Open the Code Editor and add comments at the beginning of the form's code defining the author, date created, and purpose.

3. Declare the following arrays immediately below the Windows Form Designer generated code region:

```
Friend intPreScores() As Integer
Friend intPostScores() As Integer
```

4. Create the following event procedure for the btnPreTest_Click event:

```
Private Sub btnPretest_Click(ByVal sender As Object, ByVal e As
   System.EventArgs) Handles btnPretest.Click

    'Open file, read data, populate array and list box
    Dim intCounter As Integer
    lstPreScores.Items.Clear()
    FileOpen(1, "A:\PreScores.txt", OpenMode.Input)
    Do While Not EOF(1)
        ReDim Preserve intPreScores(intCounter)
        Input(1, intPreScores(intCounter))
        lstPreScores.Items.Add(intPreScores(intCounter))
        intCounter = intCounter + 1
    Loop
    FileClose(1)

    'Calculate the average score
    Array.Sort(intPreScores)
    Dim sngAvgScore As Single
    sngAvgScore = 0
    For intCounter = 0 To UBound(intPreScores)
        sngAvgScore = sngAvgScore + intPreScores(intCounter)
    Next intCounter
    sngAvgScore = sngAvgScore / intPreScores.Length

    'Display results
    lblResults.Text = "Pretest Score Results" & vbCrLf &
       vbCrLf & "Average Score: " & sngAvgScore & vbCrLf & "Low
       Score: " & intPreScores(0) & vbCrLf & "High Score: " &
       intPreScores(UBound(intPreScores))
End Sub
```

5. Create the following event procedure for the btnPosttest_Click event

```
Private Sub btnPosttest_Click(ByVal sender As Object, ByVal e As
    System.EventArgs) Handles btnPosttest.Click

    'Open file, read data, populate array and list box
    Dim intCounter As Integer
    lstPostScores.Items.Clear()
    FileOpen(1, "A:\PostScores.txt", OpenMode.Input)
    Do While Not EOF(1)
        ReDim Preserve intPostScores(intCounter)
        Input(1, intPostScores(intCounter))
        lstPostScores.Items.Add(intPostScores(intCounter))
        intCounter = intCounter + 1
    Loop
    FileClose(1)

    'Calculate the average score
    Array.Sort(intPostScores)
    Dim sngAvgScore As Single
    sngAvgScore = 0
    For intCounter = 0 To UBound(intPreScores)
        sngAvgScore = sngAvgScore + intPostScores(intCounter)
    Next intCounter
    sngAvgScore = sngAvgScore / intPostScores.Length
    'Display results
    lblResults.Text = "Posttest Score Results" & vbCrLf &
        vbCrLf & "Average Score: " & sngAvgScore & vbCrLf & "Low
        Score: " & intPostScores(0) & vbCrLf & "High Score: " &
        intPostScores(UBound(intPostScores))
End Sub
```

6. Add statements to define the event procedure for the btnExit_Click event.

7. Save your changes.

8. Run the application and test its functionality.

9. Close the solution.

Tracking Business Expenses for an entire Fiscal Quarter

In this chapter you saw an example of an application that tracks expenses for a week by using a single-dimension array. In this Exercise you will create a multidimensional array for tracking business expenses for an entire fiscal quarter, such as January through March. Your array will have 31 rows and 4 columns. You will use a list box to select a month and day before entering an expense. Figure 8.39 shows a Windows form for entering and totaling these expenses.

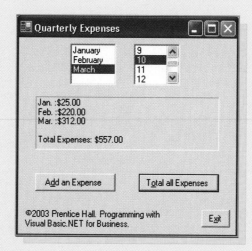

FIGURE 8.39. *Form for entering and totaling quarterly expenses*

You will complete the following tasks:

1. Create the user interface.

2. Declare a multidimensional array for storing the quarterly expenses.

3. Create a procedure for adding expenses and verifying the expenses.

4. Create a procedure for summarizing expenses by month and by quarter. To create this application, complete the following steps:

To create the Quarterly Expenses application:

1. Launch Visual Studio.NET.

2. Click **File**, **New**, **Project**. Create a project named `Quarterly Expenses`.

3. Use the Solution Explorer to change the name of the form to `frmExpenses`. Set the properties of the project to display *frmExpenses*.

4. Display the Toolbox.

To design the user interface:

1. Using Figure 8.39 as a guide, add the controls and set the properties listed in Table 8.5.

Table 8.5: Objects and properties for the Quarterly Expenses form

Object	Property	Setting
frmExpenses	Text	Quarterly Expenses
	StartPosition	CenterScreen
	Size	312, 300
lstMonth	TabStop	False
	Items (Collection)	January, February, March
lstDay	TabStop	True
	TabIndex	0
	Items (Collection)	1,2,3,4,5,6,7,8,9,10,11,12,13,14,15, 16,17,18,19,21,21,22,23,24,25,26,27, 29,30,31
lblResult	Text	
	BorderStyle	Fixed3D
lblCopyright	Text	©2003 Prentice Hall. Programming with Visual Basic.NET for Business.

btnAdd	Text	A&dd an Expense
	TabStop	True
	TabIndex	1
btnTotal	Text	T&otal all Expenses
	TabStop	True
	TabIndex	2
btnExit	Text	E&xit
	TabStop	True
	TabIndex	3

2. Open the Code Editor and add comments at the beginning of the form's code defining the author, date created, and purpose.

3. Declare the following arrays immediately below the Windows Form Designer generated code region:

```
Friend sngExpenses(30, 3) As Single
```

4. Create the following form_Load event:

```
Private Sub frmExpenses_Load(ByVal sender As Object, ByVal e As
    System.EventArgs) Handles MyBase.Load
        'Set defaults, in case no day and month are selected
        lstMonth.SelectedIndex = 0
        lstDay.SelectedIndex = 0
    End Sub
```

5. Create the following event procedure for the btnAdd_Click event:

```
Private Sub btnAdd_Click(ByVal sender As Object, ByVal e As
    System.EventArgs) Handles btnAdd.Click
    Dim intCol As Integer
    Dim intRow As Integer
    Dim sngAmount As Single

    sngAmount = Val(InputBox("Please enter an expense as a
        decimal value."))
    intCol = lstMonth.SelectedIndex
    intRow = lstDay.SelectedIndex
    sngExpenses(intRow, intCol) = sngAmount
    MsgBox("You entered " & sngExpenses(intRow, intCol) & " as
        an expense.")
End Sub
```

6. Create the following procedure for the btnTotal_Click event:

```
Private Sub btnTotal_Click(ByVal sender As System.Object, ByVal
  e As System.EventArgs) Handles btnTotal.Click
    Dim intCounter As Integer
    Dim sngJan As Single
    Dim sngFeb As Single
    Dim sngMar As Single
    sngJan = 0
    sngFeb = 0
    sngMar = 0
    'Total all expenses for January
    For intCounter = 0 To 30
        sngJan = sngJan + sngExpenses(intCounter, 0)
    Next

    'Total all expenses for February
    intCounter = 0
    For intCounter = 0 To 30
        sngFeb = sngFeb + sngExpenses(intCounter, 1)
    Next

    'Total all expenses for March
    intCounter = 0
    For intCounter = 0 To 30
        sngMar = sngMar + sngExpenses(intCounter, 2)
    Next

    'Display results
    lblResult.Text = "Jan. :" & Format(sngJan, "Currency") &
        vbCrLf & "Feb. :" & Format(sngFeb, "Currency") & vbCrLf &
        "Mar. :" & Format(sngMar, "Currency") & vbCrLf & vbCrLf &
        "Total Expenses: " & Format(sngJan + sngFeb + sngMar,
        "Currency")
End Sub
```

7. Add statements to define the event procedure for the btnExit_Click event.
8. Save your changes.
9. Run the application and test its functionality.
10. Close the solution.

Case Studies

Creating an array for tracking your CD collection

If you are the typical consumer, you have more compact discs (CDs) in your music collection than you can manage. In this Exercise you will create a Windows form with dynamic array for organizing your CDs. The array will store the following information:

CD Title

Musical Category

Artist

Create a Windows Form project named CD Collection. Add text box controls for entering the information for each CD. Add a list box to the form that displays the entire CD collection.

Creating a payroll application

In Chapter 7 you created a Windows Form application named *Payroll* for calculating an employee's gross pay, taxes, and net pay. Create an application named `Payroll Array` that stores payroll data for multiple employees. Use the following constants to determine the taxes withheld:

Federal Tax: 15%

State Tax: 8%

Local Tax: 3%

Assume that you have no more than 10 employees. The array will store the employee's Social Security number, last and first names, hourly wage, and hours worked. From these, your application can calculate the gross pay, taxes withheld, and net pay. Display the Employee ID, Gross Pay, Total Taxes, and Net Pay in a list box for all employees in the array. Run the application and test its functionality. Close the solution when you finish.

CHAPTER 9

Object-Oriented Programming with Visual Basic.NET

Objects are central to programming today. Object-oriented programming is considered the programming approach of choice, because objects that can be reused and configured for specific purposes make programming more efficient. In this chapter, you will learn about object-oriented programming (OOP) and the capabilities in Visual Basic.NET for working with objects.

Performance Objectives

At the conclusion of this chapter, you will be able to:

■ Describe how object-oriented programming simplifies program development by building objects that can be used to create new objects with similar characteristics.

■ Create classes to encapsulate functionality that is exposed to objects instantiated from the class.

■ Store information in objects by using fields and properties.

■ Create and call class methods.

■ Create a derived class that inherits properties and methods from a base class.

■ Use overrides to override a method in a base class.

Object-Oriented Programming

Object-oriented programming (OOP) emphasizes working with objects and building programs by defining categories of objects that share common characteristics. We will use the concept of a computer to explain object-oriented concepts.

When you think of a computer in general terms, certain characteristics come to mind. Computers are electronic devices that have various components that support the input, processing, output, and storage (IPOS) cycle. Computers have a keyboard and a mouse for input, a screen or monitor for output, and a hard disk for storage, and a processor. All objects have characteristics that differentiate one object from another. These characteristics identify the category to which an object belongs. Keyboards, screens, monitors, processors, and hard disks are the core set of characteristics that define an object as a computer. You might own other electronic devices, such as a cell phone or a calculator, with unique characteristics that differentiate them from your computer. Electronic devices have some characteristics in common, but are different objects. For example, a calculator has a keypad for input, a display for output, and a processor, but not a hard disk for storage. A calculator performs calculations, but it is not a personal computer. You can differentiate a calculator and other devices that perform calculations from a personal computer by listing the characteristics of each object. Think of the devices you see at an electronics store: some are cell phones, others are calculators, some might be personal digital assistants, and some are personal computers. Each specific object you see belongs to a category of electronic devices. Computers are one category, calculators another, and so on.

Because Visual Basic.NET is an object-oriented language, let's learn more about objects and classes, two fundamental concepts in object-oriented programming.

OBJECTS AND CLASSES

Almost everything you do in Visual Basic.NET requires you to use objects. In the same way that you could classify every object in the world as belonging to a category by defining the critical characteristics of the object, every object in an application also belongs to a category and is differentiated by the characteristics of the category. In Visual Basic.NET, an ***object*** is anything in your application that defines the application's interface or provides its functionality. Objects include forms, controls, modules, data connections, structures, and menus. In object-oriented terms, the set of characteristics differentiating one category from another is called a class. Classes and objects are related to one another, and some people even use these terms interchangeably. Generally speaking, a **class** is a generic representation of something. In our previous example, the classes of computers and cell phones are generic representations of objects people use.

Think of the distinction between objects and classes this way: If you ask three friends to describe the critical characteristics of a computer, and you summarize their descriptions, you will arrive at a list of characteristics that describe any computer. From this list of characteristics you can conceptualize a computer without reference to a specific computer. Your concept is abstract (generic) and encompasses all the characteristics necessary for any specific computer you can think of. An object is a specific occurrence of a class called an **instance** of the class. Because an object is an *instance* of a class, the act of creating a specific object is called **instantiation.** A class instance possesses all the critical characteristics of the class. For example, an instance of the computer class must contain the characteristics we've mentioned: keyboard, screen, processor, hard drive, and so on. The computer you use to create Visual Basic.NET solutions is an instance of the computer class.

Now let's consider an object in Visual Basic.NET. A button control has certain characteristics that differentiate it from a text box control. The button class is an abstract concept that includes the characteristics that make a button what it is. A button as an *object* is a specific instance of a button you create on a form. The Toolbox contains a tool for the button class; when you add a button to a form, you are instantiating a button object. Figure 9.1 represents this distinction.

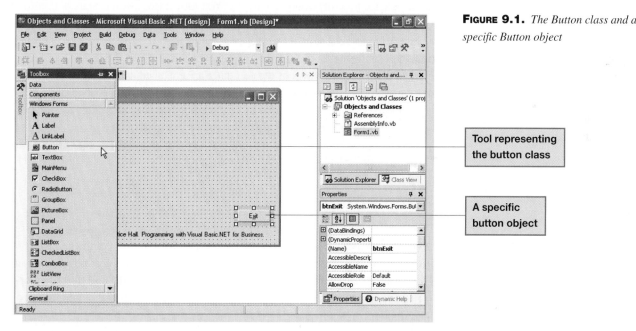

FIGURE 9.1. *The Button class and a specific Button object*

Tool representing the button class

A specific button object

OBJECT PROPERTIES AND METHODS

Now let's explore this button in more detail. The **Button** class defines the functionality that is available to any button in a program. The button named *btnExit* is an instantiated object that gets its functionality from the **Button** class. Visual Basic.NET objects have properties and methods. The object has certain attributes: its characteristics and behaviors. As you learned in Chapter 1, a **property** is a characteristic of an object, and properties can be set at design time or at run time. In Visual Basic.NET, a behavior is an action, called a **method**, that the object supports. The button object we're talking about has a name property, *btnExit*, that differentiates it from other buttons that might appear on the form. A button object derives its methods from the class to which it belongs. For example, the **Button** class in Visual Basic.NET has a **Show** method, which displays the button on the form. The action the method performs is to set the **Visible** property of the button to **True**. The **Show** method is defined for the **Button** class, so any button you create is able to use the **Show** method. This means you do not have to define this functionality in your applications. You can take advantage of the properties and methods that have been defined for the class.

ENCAPSULATION AND ABSTRACTION

Two concepts essential to object-oriented programming are abstraction and encapsulation. The concept of *encapsulation* is relatively simple. To encapsulate is to enclose something, as with a capsule. In object-oriented programming, this means the characteristics and behaviors of an object are wrapped up in a self-contained unit. The object is like a black box that hides its functionality from any object that uses it. To use the functionality encapsulated in an object, you do not need to understand exactly how the object performs the action. Abstraction is related to encapsulation. *Abstraction* refers to hiding from the user the internal details of an object. The encapsulated object uses abstraction to hide details from the user that are irrelevant from the user's perspective or could inadvertently be changed by the user. The characteristics and behaviors of an object that are visible to the user are said to be *exposed*.

Let's return to the analogy of a computer to demonstrate encapsulation and abstraction. To use your computer to create Visual Basic.NET solutions, you do not need to know exactly how the computer works. You turn it on, use the Start button to launch Visual Studio.NET, and create your solutions. To make the computer work, you do not need to know exactly how it receives commands from the keyboard, processes information, stores information in memory, presents information on the screen, and stores your work to disk. The workings of the computer are encapsulated within your computer, so as long as you know how to turn it on and how to launch and use its programs, you are able to do your work. The workings of the computer are encapsulated and abstracted, and the objects you need for using the computer are exposed.

Now that you understand more about objects and classes, let's look at another example of using a class.

USING CLASSES

When you create a program, you use classes developed by others or classes you develop. The .NET framework contains a vast collection of predefined classes you can use to instantiate objects. In our earlier example, the button object obtains its functionality from the predefined **Button** class that is a part of the .NET framework. The **Button** class provides properties and methods to any instantiated button. Now consider the following procedure:

```
Private Sub btnDisplayTitle_Click(ByVal sender As System.Object,
  ByVal e As System.EventArgs) Handles btnDisplayTitle.Click
    Dim msgBox As MessageBox
    msgBox.Show("Programming with Visual Basic.NET for
      Business")
End Sub
```

This is another example of using the properties and methods of a class. In this case, *msgBox* is declared as an instance of the **MessageBox** class that is a part of the .NET Framework. The **MessageBox** class also includes the **Show** method, so this functionality is available to the instance of the object the code creates. Developing a program that uses a message box is simplified because you do not have to create the logic behind the **Show** method. The **MessageBox** class encapsulates the logic of the **Show** method and exposes the method to us. Any procedure that declares an instance of the **MessageBox** class has the same methods exposed to it. Therefore, we are reusing the functionality of the **Show** method.

In some respects, the concepts of encapsulation, abstraction, and exposure are similar to calling a function. The logic for performing a task such as a calculation is contained in the function, which is called by a calling procedure. The function performs the action and returns the result to the calling procedure. The calling procedure merely receives the result; it does not need to know how the function performs the action. In the same way, controls derive functionality from classes that expose properties and methods to the objects instantiated from them. How is this so? The .NET framework consists of a hierarchy of classes. Consider a common control for Windows and Web forms: the text box. A text box on a Windows form derives its functionality (properties and methods) from a class called **System.Windows.Forms.TextBox.** The .NET framework also supports instantiating objects for Web clients, and these objects derive their functionality from the **System.Web.UI** classes. A text box on a Web form derives its functionality from the **System.Web.UI.WebControls.TextBox** class. Figure 9.2 shows how these classes support the instantiated controls.

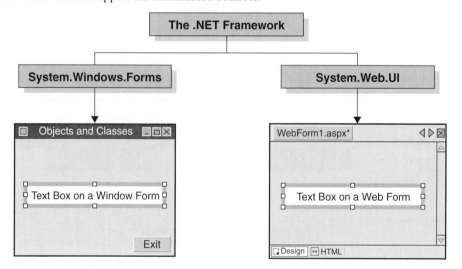

FIGURE 9.2. *How objects derive functionality from classes*

Remember that a primary goal of object-oriented programming is to simplify program development by making objects reusable. The properties and methods exposed by a class to an object are available for use once the object is instantiated.

What if a predefined class in Visual Basic.NET does not provide the functionality you need? Let's learn how object-oriented programming makes it easy to reuse and modify existing objects.

Reusability of objects and code is not only a central focus of object-oriented programming but a good practice in procedural programming as well. Visual Studio.NET supports numerous ways of reusing code and objects. Functions and procedures minimize redundant code. Instantiating objects from classes minimizes the code required to implement functionality.

INHERITANCE AND POLYMORPHISM

Although previous releases of Visual Basic provide support for classes and objects, these releases were not truly object-oriented. This is because previous versions lacked one or more qualities essential to object-oriented programming. True object-oriented programming requires objects to support three features: encapsulation, inheritance, and polymorphism.

We've already learned about encapsulation and abstraction, so now let's learn how inheritance and polymorphism extend the usability of classes and objects. ***Inheritance*** describes the ability to create new classes based on an existing class. To understand this concept, let's return to our example of the computer class. As you know, there are different kinds of computers; desktop computers and laptop computers are two examples. Both categories of computers share common characteristics: a keyboard and a mouse or touchpad for input, a monitor or a screen for output, a hard drive for storage, and a processor. There are also distinct differences between these categories of computers. A desktop computer typically has a monitor with a cathode ray tube (CRT), and a laptop has a flat screen that uses liquid crystal technology. A desktop computer typically has a relatively large case and is not portable, but a laptop computer has a small footprint, weighs a few pounds, and is portable. Both computers have a hard disk, but the drive on a desktop is often of the 5.25- or 3.5-inch format while the hard disk on a laptop has a footprint that is smaller than a 3X5 card, at about 2.25 by 3.5 inches.

Let's say we define a class called **Computer**. This class has properties such as input devices, output devices, a processor, and random-access and long-term memory (RAM and a hard disk). The computer class also has methods, such as receiving input, processing information, displaying output, and reading and writing files. But you might be interested in extending the properties and methods from the computer class to more specific categories of computers, such as laptop and desktop computers. Therefore, we define two new classes, one named **Laptop Computer** and another named **Desktop Computer**. Figure 9.3 demonstrates how we derive two classes from the **Computer** class. Any instance of a computer will belong to either the **Laptop Computer** or the **Desktop Computer** class.

FIGURE 9.3. *How derived classes inherit functionality from a base class*

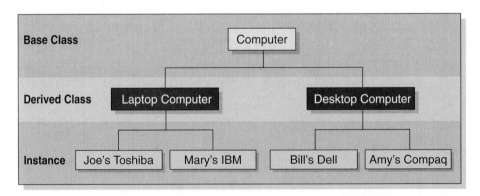

Both the **Laptop Computer** and **Desktop Computer** classes inherit properties and methods from the **Computer** class, which is the base class. A ***base class*** is the class from which a new class inherits its functionality. The new class is called a ***derived class*** because it inherits all the properties and methods and events of the base class and can be customized with additional properties and methods. In this example, both Laptop Computer and Desktop Computer are examples of a derived class, because they obtain, or derive, their functionality from the Computer base class. You could also create additional classes from the Desktop class, such as **Small Desktop**, **Mid Tower**, and **Large Tower**. These would also be derived classes.

Does this sound complicated? The good news is that you have already been using inheritance in your programs. The ***Inherits keyword*** designates the base class from which the derived class inherits its functionality. Every project you have created by using Visual Basic.NET declares a derived class. If you create a new Windows Form application, Visual Basic.NET will create a class named Form1 that inherits from the **System.Windows.Forms.Form** class, and the following statements will appear in the Code for the form:

```
Public Class Form1
     Inherits System.Windows.Forms.Form
#Region " Windows Form Designer generated code "
End Class
```

You don't have to do anything to create this code; it is created automatically when you create a new Windows application project. The first statement declares a class named Form1 that inherits all the functionality from the Form class that is a part of the .NET framework System class.

We can now return to the question we began answering before describing encapsulation and inheritance: What if the .NET framework does not include the functionality you need? Polymorphism is the answer.

Polymorphism is essential to object-oriented programming because it allows you to use items with the same names, no matter what type of object is in use at the moment. Polymorphism literally means "many forms." This quality of object-oriented programs means you can create multiple classes that can be used interchangeably, even though each class implements the same properties or methods in different ways. For example, given a base class of **Computer**, polymorphism enables you to define different **DisplayOutput** methods for any number of derived classes. The **DisplayOutput** method of a derived class named **Laptop computer** with the property of **LCD Display** might be completely different from the **DisplayOutput** method for an object of the **Desktop Computer** class that has a **CRT Display** property.

Now that you are familiar with the basic concepts of object-oriented programming, let's see how easy it is to create classes in Visual Basic.NET.

Creating Classes

At times, a predefined class in the .NET Framework might not provide the functionality you need. If this is the case, you can create your own classes and then declare objects based on these classes. You define a class by using the *Class statement*, providing a name for the class, entering the code statements that define the class, and completing the class declaration with the *End Class* statement. The syntax for declaring a class is as follows:

```
Class (name)
    Inherits (classname)
    statements
End Class
```

The name of the class is required. The guidelines for naming classes are the same as for naming procedures. Use a noun that describes the class, such as *Computer*. If the class name requires more than one noun to describe it, combine the nouns into one phrase and capitalize the first character of each noun in the phrase. If a class inherits from another class, use the Inherits keyword followed by the name of the class it inherits from only one other class. For example, **LaptopComputer** could be a class that inherits from the **Computer** class. Here's an example:

```
Class LaptopComputer
    Inherits Computer
    [additional statements here]
End Class
```

> **You will learn about class inheritance later in this chapter.**

Remember that the purpose of a class is to provide functionality that you can easily include in your programs. When you create a new class, think about the object-oriented characteristics and behaviors the class will expose. The *characteristics* of a class are defined by using either fields or properties. The *behaviors* of a class, which are its methods, are determined by using a sub procedure or a function procedure. Now let's learn how to define the characteristics of a class by using fields and properties.

Using Fields and Properties to Add Information to Objects

The characteristics of a class are stored in an object that is created (instantiated) from the class. You can use either fields or properties to store information in an object. Fields and properties are declared differently within a class. A **Field** is a public variable that is exposed by a class. To store information in a class by using fields, you simply declare the variables defining the fields. Properties use a **property procedure** to get or set the properties of an object.

STORING INFORMATION IN OBJECTS BY USING FIELDS

Let's look at an example. Assume you want to create a class that displays a shipping label using address information. The class can be used in any application with name and address data. The class displays the shipping label by using fields. In this case, we'll add the class to the Address Book application shown in Figure 9.4, which is contained in the *Field Example* solution in your data files.

FIGURE 9.4. *Address Book interface for previewing a shipping label*

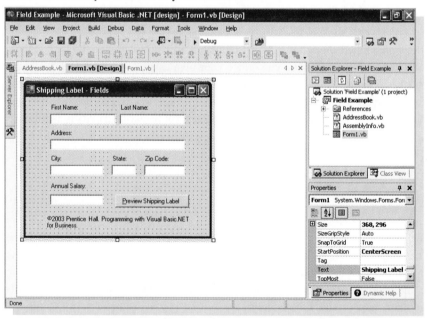

You can add a field to the class declaration by using public variables. After adding a field to a class, you can assign a value to the field for any object that is an instance of the class. In this example, the class named *AddressBook* contains the following statements that declare the class and the fields by using variables:

```
Class AddressBook
    'Declare public variables to store information
    Public strLastName As String
    Public strFirstName As String
    Public strAddress As String
    Public strCity As String
    Public strState As String
    Public strZipCode As String
    Public sngAnnualSalary As Single

    Friend Sub DisplayLabel()
        'Display the mailing label in a message box
        MsgBox("Ship To:" & vbCrLf & strFirstName & " " &
            strLastName & vbCrLf & strAddress & vbCrLf & strCity
            & " " & strState & " " & strZipCode,
            MsgBoxStyle.Information, "Shipping Label")
    End Sub
End Class
```

Everything contained within the **Class** and **End Class** statements is a part of the class declaration. In addition, this class contains a sub procedure for displaying the information assigned to the fields as a preview of the shipping label.

Once you have declared a class and fields, you need to create an instance of the class to use its fields. The following statement creates an instance of the *AddressBook* class:

You will learn how to define and call methods later in this chapter.

```
Dim myAddressBook As AddressBook = New AddressBook()
```

Now that the class has been instantiated, you can assign values to the fields in the *myAddressBook* object in a similar way to assigning a value to a variable. The following code statements declare an instance of the class and then assign the text in the text boxes on the form shown in Figure 9.4 into the fields declared in the class.

```
'Assign text values to class field variables
myAddressBook.strLastName = txtLastName.Text
myAddressBook.strFirstName = txtFirstName.Text
myAddressBook.strAddress = txtAddress.Text
myAddressBook.strCity = txtCity.Text
myAddressBook.strState = txtState.Text
myAddressBook.strZipCode = txtZipCode.Text
```

Notice that each assignment statement references both the name of the object (*myAddressBook*) and the field name.

Now that you know how to store information in objects by using fields, let's look at an example of how to store the shipping label information by using property procedures.

STORING INFORMATION IN OBJECTS BY USING PROPERTIES

You can use properties to store information in objects. To store information in a property, you create a property procedure, which is a series of Visual Basic code statements that acts on a custom property of a class.

Storing information in a property requires a local variable within the class to store the property value. After declaring the variable, you can declare the property. Declaring a property is similar to declaring a variable; to declare a property, you use the **Property** keyword to declare the property name and then declare the data type that the property stores and returns. To protect the property values from direct modification, declare the local variable storing the property as **Private**.

To store a value for the property, you use a *Set property procedure*. This procedure begins with the *Set statement*, includes the assignment statement, and concludes with *End Set*. To retrieve a value from a property, use the *Get property procedure*. A Get Property procedure begins with the *Get statement* and ends with *End Get*. You must specify whether the value stored in the property can be obtained and also changed. If a procedure can only obtain the property, it is read-only. If a procedure can obtain the property and also change it, the property is read-write. You can use the Get and Set statements to define the read-write status of the property. If you declare a property procedure that includes both the **Get** and **Set** procedures, the default setting is called a read-write property. If a property procedure contains only a Get procedure or a Set procedure, you need to declare whether it is ReadOnly or WriteOnly. As explained previously, a *ReadOnly property* can be read, but its value cannot be set. A *WriteOnly property* can be assigned, but its value cannot be read. To protect the property values from direct modification, declare property variables as **Private**.

The following example declares property variables and then declares the properties, using the **Get** and **Set** procedures to manipulate the property values. This code is contained in the *AddressBook* class in the *Property Example* solution in your data files:

```
Class AddressBook
    'Declare property variables to store information
    Private strLastName As String
    Private strFirstName As String
    Private strAddress As String
    Private strCity As String
    Private strState As String
    Private strZipCode As String
    Private sngAnnualSalary As Single


    'Declare property procedures
    Public Property LastName() As String
        Get
            Return strLastName
        End Get
        Set(ByVal Value As String)
            strLastName = Value
        End Set
    End Property


    Public Property FirstName() As String
        Get
            Return strFirstName
        End Get
        Set(ByVal Value As String)
            strFirstName = Value
        End Set
    End Property
```

```
    Public Property Address() As String
        Get
            Return strAddress
        End Get
        Set(ByVal Value As String)
            strAddress = Value
        End Set
    End Property

    Public Property City() As String
        Get
            Return strCity
        End Get
        Set(ByVal Value As String)
            strCity = Value
        End Set
    End Property

    Public Property State() As String
        Get
            Return strState
        End Get
        Set(ByVal Value As String)
            strState = Value
        End Set
    End Property

    Public Property ZipCode() As String
        Get
            Return strZipCode
        End Get
        Set(ByVal Value As String)
            strZipCode = Value
        End Set
    End Property

    Friend Sub DisplayLabel()
        'Display the mailing label in a message box
        MsgBox("Ship To:" & vbCrLf & strFirstName & " " &
            strLastName & vbCrLf & strAddress & vbCrLf & strCity
            & " " & strState & " " & strZipCode,
            MsgBoxStyle.Information, "Shipping Label")
    End Sub
End Class
```

In this code example, each property variable is declared as **Private**. Each property procedure is declared as **Public**, because the properties will be exposed to any object requesting the property. The **Get** property procedure is called like a function and retrieves the value in the property variable. The **Set** property procedure stores its result in the property variable. To summarize, the property procedure declares the property, the property variable stores the value for the property, and the Get and Set procedures store and retrieve the value stored in a property.

USING FIELDS VERSUS PROPERTIES TO STORE INFORMATION IN AN OBJECT

Because you can use both fields and properties to store information in an object, how do you know which option to use? Fields are simply public variables that a class exposes, but properties use property procedures to control how values are set or returned. If the information is of the String data type and does not need to be validated, use a field. Fields are a good choice for the shipping label because the text in the label does not require validation. But if the information needs to be controlled as read-only or write-only, or if validation is required by the class before storing information in the object, use a property procedure.

Now that you know how use fields and properties to declare classes and store information in the instantiated objects a class supports, let's learn how to use methods with objects.

Class Methods

Methods represent actions that an object can perform. For example, the *myAddressBook* object could have a **DisplayLabel** method for displaying a shipping label using information in the Address Book.

CREATING AND CALLING CLASS METHODS

You are now used to working with forms and procedures, but how can you call a method that belongs to a class? You must first create an instance of the object class. To create an instance of an object, declare a variable with the appropriate scope and then assign the object to the variable. Consider the following statement:

```
Dim myAddressBook As AddressBook = New AddressBook()
```

This statement declares an object named **myAddressBook** that derives its functionality from the **AddressBook** class. This statement is contained in the code for the Form1 class, so when the form is instantiated at run time, the *myAddressBook* object is created.

This statement creates an instance of the object. In essence, the statement is saying "let myAddressBook refer to an object that is an instance of the AddressBook class."

You create class methods by adding procedures—either subroutines or sub functions—to your class. After you create a method, any procedure that has access to the method can call the method. The following code, which is contained in both the *Field Example* and *Property Example* solutions, displays a preview of the shipping label by using data in the Address Book:

```
Friend Sub DisplayLabel()
    'Display the mailing label in a message box
    MsgBox("Ship To:" & vbCrLf & strFirstName & " " &
        strLastName & vbCrLf & strAddress & vbCrLf & strCity & "
        " & strState & " " & strZipCode, MsgBoxStyle.Information,
        "Shipping Label")
End Sub
```

You will recognize the sub procedure for this method, because it is a part of the class declarations shown earlier. This method is very simple. After name and address information is stored in an object (using either fields or properties), the method uses the information in the object to display the information as it will appear in a shipping label. The method is part of the class declaration, so it is exposed to any object created from the class.

Because the **DisplayLabel** procedure is contained in the **AddressBook** class, you must instantiate an object based on the class to expose the functionality of the procedure. Recall that the following statement, which appears in the general declarations of the code for the Form1 form in the *Field Example* solution, will declare an object named *myAddressBook*, which is based on the **AddressBook** class:

```
Dim myAddressBook As AddressBook = New AddressBook()
```

To use the method, you need to create a calling procedure that calls the method. The following event procedure validates the information in each text box and then calls the DisplayLabel procedure:

```
Private Sub btnLabel_Click(ByVal sender As System.Object, ByVal
  e As System.EventArgs) Handles btnLabel.Click

    'Validate that name and address information has been entered
    If txtLastName.Text <> "" _
    And txtFirstName.Text <> "" _
    And txtAddress.Text <> "" _
    And txtCity.Text <> "" _
    And txtState.Text <> "" _
    And txtZipCode.Text <> "" Then

        'Assign text values to class field variables
        myAddressBook.strLastName = txtLastName.Text
        myAddressBook.strFirstName = txtFirstName.Text
        myAddressBook.strAddress = txtAddress.Text
        myAddressBook.strCity = txtCity.Text
        myAddressBook.strState = txtState.Text
        myAddressBook.strZipCode = txtZipCode.Text

        Call myAddressBook.DisplayLabel()
    Else
        MsgBox("All address information is required to display
          a mailing label. Please try again.",
          MsgBoxStyle.Critical, "Invalid Employee Record!")
    End If
End Sub
```

This procedure uses an If. . . Then. . . Else statement to make sure each text box on the form contains text. If all the text boxes for name and address information contain text, the text string in each text box is assigned to the appropriate field in the *myAddressBook* object. Once the fields contain data, a call is made to the **DisplayLabel** procedure. Notice that to assign text to the fields and to call the procedure, the name of the object (*myAddressBook*) is required in each statement.

Now let's see what the shipping label looks like. Figure 9.5 displays name, address, and annual salary information for an employee.

FIGURE 9.5. *Address Book information for an employee*

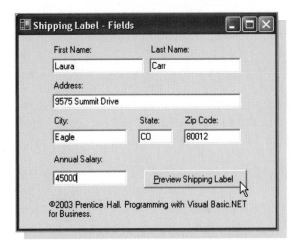

To preview the name and address information as a shipping label, click the **Preview Shipping Label** button. Figure 9.6 shows the message box that displays the shipping label information.

FIGURE 9.6. *Shipping Label generated by the DisplayLabel procedure*

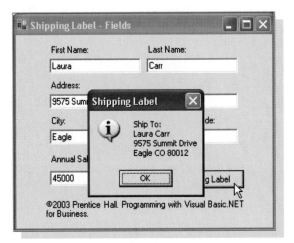

As you can see, creating classes, storing information in objects instantiated from classes, and calling class methods is relatively simple. Creating derived classes that inherit the functionality of a base class extends the power of object-oriented programming. Let's learn more about derived classes and inheritance.

Using Inheritance to Create a Derived Class

Inheritance simplifies program development by enabling derived classes to inherit the fields, properties, and methods of a base class. In this example, let's assume that a business pays executives and managers bonuses that are calculated differently. All employees receive a bonus that is 2.5% of the employee's annual salary. Managers receive an additional bonus of 1.5% percent of the manager's annual salary, plus an additional 1% bonus for each employee the manager manages, up to 10 employees. Executives receive an additional bonus that is 7.5% of the executive's annual salary, plus an additional 0.5 % for each manager in the executive's department within the company. Figure

9.7 displays the bonus for William Smith, who earns an annual salary of $67,000 and manages three employees.

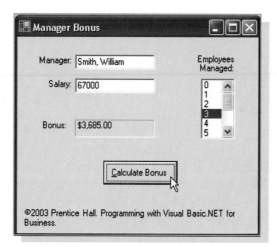

FIGURE 9.7. *Bonus for a manager earning $67,000 annually who manages three employees*

How can you use object-oriented principles to create classes for paying the bonuses? By declaring a class named *Bonus* that calculates the bonus as 2.5% of the employee's annual salary, you can account for the standard bonus. You can also declare two additional classes, one for managers (*ManagerBonus*) and one for executives (*ExecutiveBonus*), that inherit the functionality of the Bonus class but add to the functionality to calculate the appropriate bonus. Figure 9.8 shows the Bonus class and two derived classes.

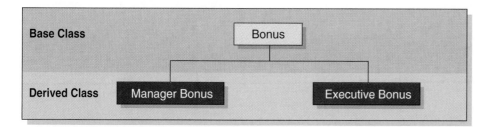

FIGURE 9.8. *A base class with two derived classes*

To demonstrate inheritance, let's work with two classes, the **Bonus** class, and the **ManagerBonus** class. The **ManagerBonus** is a derived class that inherits the properties, fields, and methods of the **Bonus** class. Because a manager's bonus has an additional component that is used to calculate the total bonus, we will declare a property in the **ManagerBonus** class to hold information about how many employees a manager manages. The *Inheritance Example* solution included with your data files declares the two classes. Here is the code that declares the **Bonus** class:

```
Public Class Bonus
    'Declare public variables to store field values
    Public strEmployee As String
    Public sngSalary As Single
    Public sngBonusRate As Single

    'Declare a property variable to store the Bonus property
    Private sngBonus As Single

    'Declare property procedure for the Bonus property
    Public ReadOnly Property Bonus() As Single
```

```
            Get
                sngBonus = (sngSalary * sngBonusRate)
                Return sngBonus
            End Get
        End Property
        Public Overridable Function sngCalculateBonus()
            Return Bonus
        End Function
End Class
```

Why does this class declare only one field?

As you can see, the class declaration includes three Public variables for storing information in fields, a property variable for storing the manager bonus, and a read-only property procedure for getting the property value. By using a read-only property to store the bonus, only the bonus is exposed to the procedure that obtains the value of the employee bonus. A function procedure obtains the value of the read-only property, **Bonus**.

Now let's look at the code for the **ManagerBonus** class:

```
Public Class ManagerBonus
    Inherits Bonus

    'Declare a public variable to store the number of employees
      in a field
    Public intEmployeesManaged As Integer

    'Declare a property variable to store the Manager Bonus
    Private sngManagerBonus As Single

    'Declare property procedure for the ManagerBonus property
    Public ReadOnly Property ManagerBonus() As Single
        Get
            sngManagerBonus = (sngSalary * sngBonusRate) +
                (sngSalary * (0.01 * intEmployeesManaged))
            Return sngManagerBonus
        End Get
    End Property
    Public Overrides Function sngCalculateBonus()
        Return ManagerBonus()
    End Function
End Class
```

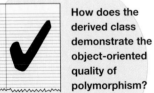

How does the derived class demonstrate the object-oriented quality of polymorphism?

The **ManagerBonus** uses a field to store the number of employees managed and a read-only property to store the manager bonus. The *sngCalculateBonus* function procedure obtains the value stored in the read-only **ManagerBonus** property.

The class declares only one field to store the number of employees, because it inherits the other fields from the base class. The class is declared with the Inherits keyword, which specifies that this class will inherit the properties and methods contained in the **Bonus** class.

Figure 9.9 shows how the **ManagerBonus** derived class inherits the properties from the **Bonus** base class. The arrows represent those elements that are inherited. The highlighted field in the derived class represents the additional property that is declared in the **ManagerBonus** class.

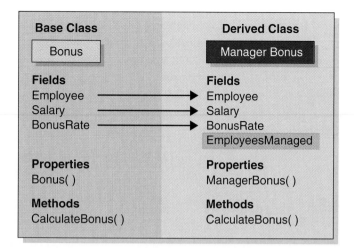

FIGURE 9.9. *Fields, properties, and methods inherited by a derived class*

OVERRIDING METHODS

As you explore the sngCalculateBonus function procedure in the two classes just described, notice that the function in the **Bonus** class uses the *Overridable keyword*, and the same function in the **ManagerBonus** class uses the *Overrides keyword*. Recall from our discussion of object-oriented programming that polymorphism literally means "many forms." In other words, if a method in a base class does not fit the requirements of the same methods in a derived class, you can create a new method with the same name that performs different actions. Visual Basic.NET supports polymorphism by providing *overrides*. You can override a method in the base class by using the Overridable keyword to declare it. You can then declare the same method in the derived class, with different functionality, if the derived class declares the method by using the Overrides keyword. This means that the function as declared in the Bonus class can be overridden so that when an object based on the **ManagerBonus** class needs to calculate the bonus, it can call a function with the same name.

Now let's see how the application calculates a bonus. Suppose that William Samuels earns $54,000 annually as a manager and manages four employees. We expect his bonus to be calculated as follows:

Base bonus = $1350 ($54,000 × 2.5%)

Additional bonus = $2160 ($54,000 × (4 × 1%))

Total bonus = $3,510

☞ HANDS-ON PROGRAMMING EXAMPLE

Using Object-oriented Programming to Calculate Employee Payroll

Creating classes and then extending the functionality of common classes can simplify program development. In this Exercise you will create a base class for storing employee information and calculating payroll taxes. You will then extend the functionality of this class to two derived classes.

Many companies have multiple categories for employees. The company pays some employees hourly, while others earn an annual salary. Some employees are eligible to participate in a company-sponsored retirement plan, but other employees might not meet the qualifications for participation. The program calculates payroll data for employees as follows:

Hourly Employees

1. Gross Pay is calculated as total hours for the period multiplied by the pay rate.
2. Pay rate must be at least $6.25 but not greater than $25.
3. Hours worked may not exceed 80.
4. Union fees are 1.5% of gross income.
5. Federal tax is 15% of gross pay.
6. FICA and Medicare tax is 13.5% of gross income.
7. State Tax is 4% of gross income.

Salaried Employees

1. Gross Pay is calculated as the annual salary divided by 26 (the number of pay periods per year).
2. Annual salary must be at least $50,000 but not greater than $150,000.
3. A deduction of 5% of gross pay before taxes is contributed to the company 401K retirement plan.
4. Federal tax is 15% of gross pay.
5. FICA and Medicare tax is 13.5% of gross income.
6. State tax is 4% of gross income.
7. Federal tax is 15% of gross pay.

The program contains a single form for obtaining employee information and displaying the appropriate payroll information. Figure 9.10 shows the gross pay, union fee, total taxes, and net pay for an hourly employee.

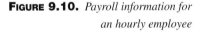

FIGURE 9.10. *Payroll information for an hourly employee*

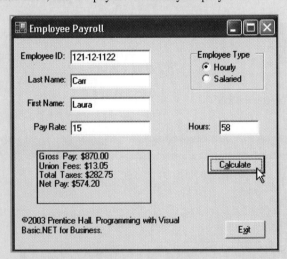

For salaried employees, the hourly pay rate and hours worked do not apply. The form obtains the annual salary for salaried employees. Figure 9.11 shows the gross pay, 401K deduction, total taxes, and net pay for a salaried employee.

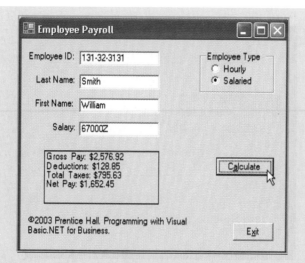

FIGURE 9.11. *Payroll information for a salaried employee*

Plan the Application

The first step in planning an application is determining the inputs and outputs. The Payroll application obtains user input and calculates the payroll information for hourly and salaried employees. The inputs and outputs are as follows:

Inputs	Outputs
Employee information	Gross Pay
Annual Salary or Hourly Pay Rate	Union Fees (Hourly employees only)
Hours Worked (Hourly employees only)	401K Deduction (Salaried employees only)
Employee Type	Taxable Income (Salaried employees only)
Total Taxes	
Net Pay	

To calculate payroll for hourly and salaried employees, the solution contains one form (for obtaining employee data and displaying payroll information) and three classes. The base class, named **Employee**, stores employee information, tax-rate constants, gross pay, total taxes, and net pay. This data is stored in fields. The form implements a method for calculating the net pay by using an overridable sub procedure named *CalculatePayroll*.

The Employees class is the base class from which the **HourlyEmployee** and **SalariedEmployee** classes derive their functionality. Each derived class inherits the constants, fields, and methods from the **Employee** class, but the derived classes also add the constants and fields necessary to calculate the payroll information. The derived classes also override the *CalculatePayroll* procedure and add the functionality required by the employee type. Figure 9.12 shows the constants, fields, and methods for the **Employee** base class and the **HourlyEmployee** and **SalariedEmployee** derived classes. The additional constants and fields required by the derived classes are highlighted.

FIGURE 9.12. *Constants, fields, and methods for the base class and derived classes*

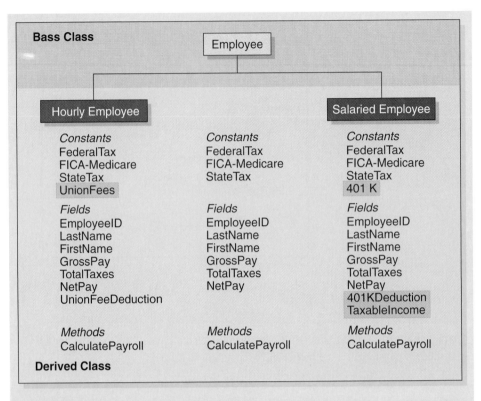

The application uses one form to obtain employee data and display the appropriate payroll information. A group box contains radio buttons for selecting the employee type. Clicking a radio button in the group box changes the interface. When the **Hourly** radio button is checked, the label for the pay rate displays Pay Rate: and the Hours label and text box are visible. When the **Salaried** radio button is checked, the label for the pay rate displays Salary: and the Hours label and text box are hidden. Figure 9.13 displays the form, and the Solution Explorer shows the three classes contained in the solution.

FIGURE 9.13. *Program interface for the Payroll application*

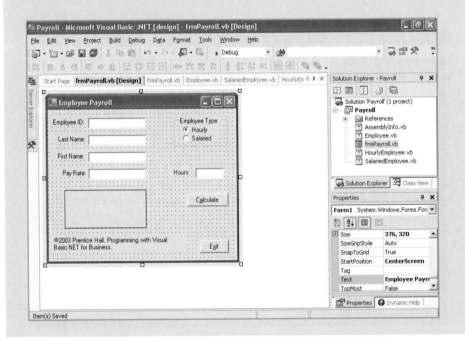

Table 9.1 lists the objects and properties for the *frmPayroll* form. For all properties not listed here, accept the defaults.

Table 9.1: *Objects and properties for the Payroll form*

Object Name	Property	Setting
frmPayroll.vb	Size StartPosition Text	376, 320 CenterScreen Employee Payroll
lblEmployeeID	Text TextAlign	Employee ID: MiddleRight
txtEmployeeID	Text TabStop TabIndex	 True 0
lblLastName	Text TextAlign	Last Name: MiddleRight
txtLastName	Text TabStop TabIndex	 True 1
lblFirstName	Text TextAlign	First Name: MiddleRight
txtFirstName	Text TabStop TabIndex	 True 2
grpEmployeeType	Text TabStop TabIndex	Employee Type True 3
rdbHourly	Text Checked	Hourly True
rdbSalaried	Text Checked	Salaried False
lblPayRate	Text TextAlign TabStop TabIndex	Pay Rate: MiddleRight True 4
txtPayRate	Text	
lblHours	Text TextAlign	Hours: MiddleRight
txtHours	Text TabStop TabIndex	 True 5
lblResult	Text BorderStyle	 Fixed3D

btnCalculate	Text	C&alculate
	TabStop	True
	TabIndex	6
btnExit	Text	E&xit
	TabStop	True
	TabIndex	7
lblCopyright	Text	©2003 Prentice Hall. Programming with Visual Basic.NET for Business.

Draw a visual representation of the form on a blank piece of paper. Figure 9.14 shows a drawing of the Payroll form and its controls.

FIGURE 9.14. *The Payroll form*

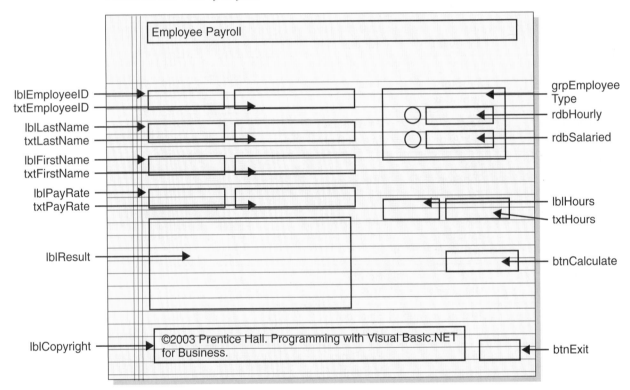

Now let's look at the design for the classes the application requires. The **Employee** base class includes the constants and properties shown in Table 9.2.

Table 9.2: *Constants and fields for the Employee base class*

Constant or Field	Name	Accessibility	Data Type
Federal Tax Rate	conFederalTax = 0.15	Public	Single
FICA / Medicare Tax Rate	conFICAMedicare = 0.135	Public	Single
State Tax Rate	conStateTax = 0.04	Public	Single
Employee ID	strEmployeeID	Public	String
Last Name	strLastName	Public	String
First Name	strFirstName	Public	String
Gross Pay	sngGrossPay	Public	Single
Total Taxes	sngTotalTaxes	Public	Single
Net Pay	sngNetPay	Public	Single

Table 9.3 lists the additional constants and fields for the **HourlyEmployee** derived class.

Table 9.3: *HourlyEmployee constants and fields*

Constant or Field	Name	Accessibility	Data Type
Union Fees	conUnionFees = 0.015	Private	Single
Union Fees Deduction	sngUnionFeeDeduction	Public	Single

Table 9.4 lists the additional constants and fields for the **SalariedEmployee** derived class.

Table 9.4: *SalariedEmployee constants and fields*

Constant or Field	Name	Accessibility	Data Type
401K Deduction Percentage	con401K	Private	Single
401K Deduction Amount	sng401KDeduction	Public	Single
Taxable Income	sngTaxableIncome	Public	Single

The routines for determining the employee type, calculating the employee payroll information, and exiting the application are contained in procedures. The pseudocode for the application's functionality is shown in Table 9.5.

Table 9.5: *Pseudocode for the Payroll application*

Event Procedure	Action
ToggleSettings sub procedure	1. Determines whether the **Hourly** or **Salaried** radio button is checked. 2. Changes the form interface to display the appropriate text boxes for pay rate, hours, and salary information.
rdbHourly_CheckedChanged event	Calls the *ToggleSettings* sub procedure.
rdbSalaried_CheckedChanged event	Calls the *ToggleSettings* sub procedure.
Sub CalculatePayroll (Employee Class)	Overridable 1. Calculates the total taxes. 2. Calculates net pay.
Sub CalculatePayroll (HourlyEmployee Class)	Overrides 1. Calculates the union fee deduction. 2. Calculates the total taxes. 3. Calculates net pay.
Sub CalculatePayroll (SalariedEmployee Class)	Overrides 1. Calculates the 401K deduction. 2. Calculates the taxable income. 3. Calculates the total taxes. 4. Calculates net pay.

btnCalculate_Click event	1. Determines if the **Hourly** or **Salaried** radio button is checked.
	2. Calls the appropriate procedure:
	  a. CalculateHourly
	  b. CalculateSalaried

CalculateHourly sub procedure	1. Performs data validation on the pay rate and hours worked values. 2. Creates an instance of the **HourlyEmployee** class. 3. Calculates the gross pay. 4. Calls the myHourlyEmployee.CalculatePayroll sub procedure. 5. Displays the payroll information in the lblResult label.
CalculateSalaried Sub procedure	1. Performs data validation on the annual salary value. 2. Creates an instance of the **SalariedEmployee** class. 3. Calculates the gross pay. 4. Calls the mySalariedEmployee.CalculatePayroll sub procedure. 5. Displays the payroll information in the lblResult label.

Now that you have created the planning documents for the application, you are ready to begin designing the user interface in the integrated development environment (IDE).

Design the User Interface

If you have not launched Visual Studio.NET, do so now. Perform each task that follows to complete this application.

To create a new project and solution:

1. Click **File**, **New Project**.
2. Navigate to the drive and folder where you will save your project. Type `Payroll` as the Project Name and click **OK**.
3. Right-click the *Form1.vb* form in the Solution Explorer and rename the form as `frmPayroll.vb`.
4. Display the properties for the form. Set the **Name**, **Text**, **Size**, and **StartPosition** properties as specified in Table 9.1.
5. Right-click the *Payroll* project in the Solution Explorer and select **Properties**.
6. The **Payroll Property Pages** dialog box appears. Select *frmPayroll* as the Startup Object and click OK.
7. Click **Project, Add Class**, as shown in Figure 9.15.

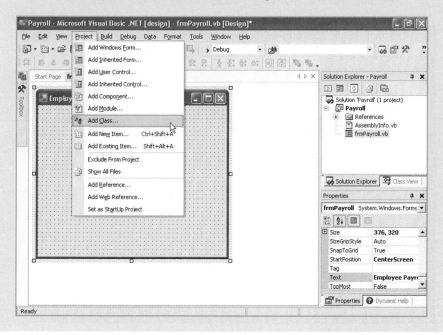

FIGURE 9.15. *Adding a class to a project*

8. The **Add New Item** dialog box appears. Name the class `Employee.vb` and click **Open**, as shown in Figure 9.16.

FIGURE 9.16. *Naming a class*

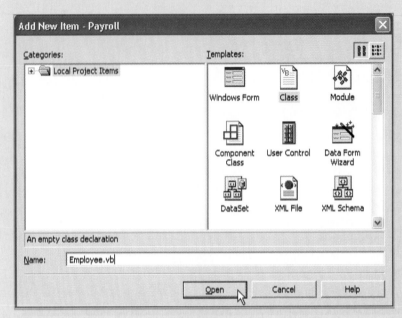

9. Repeat the procedure for adding a class to the project, and add the `SalariedEmployee.vb` and `HourlyEmployee.vb` classes.
10. Display the *frmPayroll* form in the Form Designer.
11. Using Figure 9.14 as a guide, add the controls listed in Table 9.1 to the form and set the control properties.
12. Save your changes.

Now that the interface design for the Payroll application is complete, you are ready to write the code providing the functionality.

Write the Code

The project uses three classes to provide functionality to the application. Let's begin by writing the code statements for the **Employee** class.

To write the code for the Employee class:

1. Display the Code Editor for the **Employee** class.
2. Place the insertion point at the beginning of the Code Editor and type the following comments.

```
'©2003 Prentice Hall
'By [Enter your name here...]
'Created/Revised: [Enter the date here...]
'Employee Base Class
```

3. Place the insertion point just below the **Public Class Employee** declaration statement, and type the following code:

```
'Declare Constants
    Public Const conFederalTax As Single = 0.15
    Public Const conFICAMedicare As Single = 0.135
    Public Const conStateTax As Single = 0.04
```

```
'Declare public variables for fields
Public strEmployeeID As String
Public strLastName As String
Public strFirstName As String
Public sngGrossPay As Single
Public sngTotalTaxes As Single
Public sngNetPay As Single
```

These statements declare the field variables and the constants required to calculate the total taxes.

4. Press ⏎Enter twice and type the following statement for the *CalculatePayroll* sub procedure:

```
Public Overridable Sub CalculatePayroll()
     sngTotalTaxes = (sngGrossPay * conFederalTax) +
       (sngGrossPay * conFICAMedicare) + (sngGrossPay *
       conStateTax)
     sngNetPay = sngGrossPay - sngNetPay
  End Sub
```

The procedure uses the values that will be stored in the object fields to calculate the total taxes and the net pay. The **Overridable** keyword indicates that this procedure can be overridden by the derived classes that will use a procedure of the same name to calculate the payroll for hourly and salaried employees.

5. Save your changes.

You are now ready to write the code statements for the **HourlyEmployee** class.

To write the code for the HourlyEmployee class:

1. Display the Code Editor for the **HourlyEmployee** class.
2. Place the insertion point at the beginning of the Code Editor and type the following comments.

```
'©2003 Prentice Hall
'By [Enter your name here…]
'Created/Revised: [Enter the date here…]
'HourlyEmployee Derived Class
```

3. Place the insertion point just below the **Public Class HourlyEmployee** declaration statement, and type the following code:

```
Inherits Employee
   Private Const conUnionFees As Single = 0.015
   Public sngUnionFeeDeduction As Single
   Public Overrides Sub CalculatePayroll()
       sngUnionFeeDeduction = sngGrossPay * conUnionFees
         sngTotalTaxes = (sngGrossPay * conFederalTax) +
         (sngGrossPay * conFICAMedicare) + (sngGrossPay *
         conStateTax)
       sngNetPay = sngGrossPay - sngTotalTaxes -
         sngUnionFeeDeduction
   End Sub
```

The **Inherits** keyword indicates that this derived class inherits the constants, fields, and methods from the **Employee** base class. The procedure declares a constant for the union fee percentage and a variable for the *sngUnionDeduction* field for storing the union fee deducted from the gross pay. The *CalculatePayroll* sub procedure uses the **Overrides** keyword to override the sub procedure of the same name in the base class.

4. Save your changes.

You are now ready to write the code statements for the **SalariedEmployee** class.

To write the code for the SalariedEmployee class:

1. Display the Code Editor for the **SalariedEmployee** class.
2. Place the insertion point at the beginning of the Code Editor and type the following comments.

```
'©2003 Prentice Hall
'By [Enter your name here…]
'Created/Revised: [Enter the date here…]
'SalariedEmployee Derived Class
```

3. Place the insertion point just below the **Public Class SalariedEmployee** declaration statement, and type the following code:

```
Inherits Employee

    Private Const con401K As Single = 0.05
    Public sng401KDeduction As Single
    Public sngTaxableIncome As Single

    Public Overrides Sub CalculatePayroll()
        sng401KDeduction = sngGrossPay * con401K
        sngTaxableIncome = sngGrossPay - sng401KDeduction
        sngTotalTaxes = (sngTaxableIncome * conFederalTax) +
            (sngTaxableIncome * conFICAMedicare) +
            (sngTaxableIncome * conStateTax)
        sngNetPay = sngTaxableIncome - sngTotalTaxes
    End Sub
```

As with the **HourlyEmployee** derived class, the **Inherits** keyword indicates that the **SalariedEmployee** derived class inherits constants, fields, and methods from the **Employee** base class. The procedure declares a constant for the 401K deduction percentage and variables for the *sng401KDeduction* and *sngTaxableIncome* fields. The *CalculatePayroll* sub procedure in this class also uses the **Overrides** keyword to override the sub procedure of the same name in the base class.

4. Save your changes.

The class declarations are complete. You are now ready to write the procedures for the *frmPayroll* form. Let's begin by writing the sub procedure for changing the user interface based on the employee type and the event procedures that will call this procedure.

To write the ToggleSettings sub procedure and the event procedures to call the procedure:

1. Display the Code Editor for the *frmPayroll* form.
2. Place the insertion point at the beginning of the Code Editor and type the following comments:

```
'©2003 Prentice Hall
'By [Enter your name here...]
'Created/Revised: [Enter the date here...]
'Employee Payroll
```

3. Place the insertion point just below the **Windows Form Designer generated code** region. Create a code region for the procedures that change the interface based on the employee type as follows: Type #Region "Toggle Interface Settings, press ←Enter twice, and type #End Region.
4. Place the insertion point inside the region you just created and type the following code statements to define the procedure:

```
Private Sub ToggleSettings()
    If rdbHourly.Checked = True Then
        lblPayRate.Text = "Pay Rate:"
        lblHours.Visible = True
        txtHours.Visible = True
    Else
        lblPayRate.Text = "Salary:"
        lblHours.Visible = False
        txtHours.Visible = False
    End If
End Sub
```

This is a very simple procedure. It uses a decision structure to determine which radio button is currently selected and changes the form interface accordingly.

5. Press ←Enter twice.
6. Use the **Class Name** and **Method Name** lists in the Code Editor to create a **CheckChanged** event for the *rdbHourly* radio button. The procedure includes the following statements:

```
Private Sub rdbHourly_CheckedChanged(ByVal sender As
  System.Object, ByVal e As System.EventArgs) Handles
  rdbHourly.CheckedChanged
    Call ToggleSettings()
End Sub
```

This is also a simple procedure. It determines the current checked property of the radio button and calls the *ToggleSettings* procedure.

7. Use the **Class Name** and **Method Name** lists in the Code Window to create a **CheckChanged** event for the *rdbSalaried* radio button. The procedure includes the following statements:

```
Private Sub rdbSalaried_CheckedChanged(ByVal sender As
  System.Object, ByVal e As System.EventArgs) Handles
  rdbSalaried.CheckedChanged
        Call ToggleSettings()
End Sub
```

8. Save your changes.

Now let's create the sub procedures that calculate the hourly and salaried employee payroll information.

To create the sub procedures for calculating payroll:

1. Create a code region named Procedures for Calculating Payroll.

2. Place the insertion point inside the region you just created. Type the following statements for the *CalculateHourly* sub procedure:

```
Private Sub CalculateHourly()
    If Val(txtPayRate.Text) >= 6.25 And Val(txtPayRate.Text) <=
    25 Then
        If Val(txtHours.Text) > 0 And Val(txtHours.Text) <= 80
        Then

            Dim myHourlyEmployee As HourlyEmployee = New
              HourlyEmployee()
            myHourlyEmployee.sngGrossPay = Val(txtPayRate.Text)
              * Val(txtHours.Text)
            Call myHourlyEmployee.CalculatePayroll()
            lblResult.Text = "Gross Pay: " & vbTab &
              Format(myHourlyEmployee.sngGrossPay, "C") _
              & vbCrLf & "Union Fees: " & vbTab &
              Format(myHourlyEmployee.sngUnionFeeDeduction,
              "C") _
              & vbCrLf & "Total Taxes: " & vbTab &
              Format(myHourlyEmployee.sngTotalTaxes, "'C") &
              vbCrLf & "Net Pay: " & vbTab &
              Format(myHourlyEmployee.sngNetPay, "C")
        Else
            MsgBox("The hours worked must be at least 1 and not
              more than 80. Please try again.",
              MsgBoxStyle.Critical, "Invalid Hours"')
        End If
    Else
        MsgBox("The hourly pay rate must be at least 6.25 but
          not more than 25. Please try again.",
          MsgBoxStyle.Critical, "Invalid Pay Rate")
    End If
End Sub
```

The procedure begins with a nested If statement that validates both the pay rate and the hours worked values entered into the text boxes on the form. If the validation test passes, the procedure declares an instance of the **HourlyEmployee** class, calculates the gross pay by using the values in the text boxes on the form, and assigns the gross pay amount to the *sngGrossPay* field. The procedure then calls the *CalculatePayroll* function that defines the method for the class. The results of the calculations are formatted and displayed in the *lblResult* label. If the validation fails, a message box displays an error message.

3. Press ⏎Enter twice and type the following statements for the *CalculateSalaried* sub procedure:

```
Private Sub CalculateSalaried()
    If Val(txtPayRate.Text) >= 50000 And Val(txtPayRate.Text) <=
    150000 Then

        Dim mySalariedEmployee As SalariedEmployee = New
          SalariedEmployee()

        mySalariedEmployee.sngGrossPay = Val(txtPayRate.Text) /
          26
        Call mySalariedEmployee.CalculatePayroll()
        lblResult.Text = "Gross Pay: " & vbTab &
          Format(mySalariedEmployee.sngGrossPay, "C") _
          & vbCrLf & "Deductions: " & vbTab &
          Format(mySalariedEmployee.sng401KDeduction, "C") _
          & vbCrLf & "Total Taxes: " & vbTab &
          Format(mySalariedEmployee.sngTotalTaxes, "C") &
          vbCrLf & "Net Pay: " & vbTab &
          Format(mySalariedEmployee.sngNetPay, "C")
    Else
        MsgBox("The annual salary must be at least 50000 but
          not more than 150000. Please try again.",
          MsgBoxStyle.Critical, "Invalid Annual Salary")
    End If
End Sub
```

This procedure uses an If statement to validate the annual salary. If the validation passes, the procedure declares an instance of the **SalariedEmployee** class, calculates the gross pay by using the values in the text box on the form, and assigns the gross pay amount to the *sngGrossPay* field. The procedure then calls the *CalculatePayroll* function that defines the method for the class. The results of the calculations are formatted and displayed in the *lblResult* label. If the validation fails, a message box displays an error message.

4. Save your changes.

Now that you have defined the sub procedures for calculating payroll for hourly and salaried employees, you are ready to write the event procedures for the *btnCalculate* and *btnExit* buttons.

To write the event procedure for the *btnCalculate* and *btnExit* buttons:

1. Use the **Class Name** and **Method Name** lists in the Code Editor to create a click event for the *btnCalculate* button.
2. Type the following code statements for the procedure:

```
If rdbHourly.Checked = True Then
    Call CalculateHourly()
        Else
    Call CalculateSalaried()
End If
```

This is a very simple procedure. It determines whether the *rdbHourly* radio button is checked, and if so, it calls the *CalculateHourly* sub procedure. If the *rdbHourly* radio button is not checked, the procedure calls the *CalculateSalaried* sub procedure.

3. Use the **Class Name** and **Method Name** lists in the Code Editor to create a click event for the *btnExit* button.

4. Type the following code statements for the procedure:

```
Dim intResponse As Integer
    intResponse = MsgBox("Do you really want to exit this
        application?", 276, "Exit?")
    If intResponse = 6 Then
        End
    End If
```

5. Save your changes.

Run the Application

You are now ready to run the Payroll application and test its functionality.

To run the application:

1. Click the Start button or press the [F5] key to run the application.

2. Click the **Calculate** button. Because the text box for the pay rate is empty, the error message shown in Figure 9.17 appears.

FIGURE 9.17. *Error message that appears when the Pay Rate data validation fails*

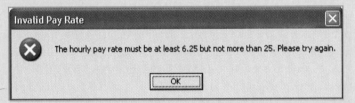

Invalid Pay Rate

The hourly pay rate must be at least 6.25 but not more than 25. Please try again.

OK

3. Click **OK** to remove the error message. Type 8 in the **Pay Rate** text box, and click the **Calculate** button. The pay rate is validated, but because the **Hours** text box is empty, the error message shown in Figure 9.18 appears.

FIGURE 9.18. *Error message that appears when the Hours data validation fails*

Invalid Hours

The hours worked must be at least 1 and not more than 80. Please try again.

OK

4. Click **OK**. Type 111-22-3333 as the **Employee ID**, Adams as the **Last Name**, Sally as the **First Name**, 24.25 as the **Pay Rate**, and 67 as the **Hours**. Click the **Calculate** button. Your results should match the results shown in Figure 9.19.

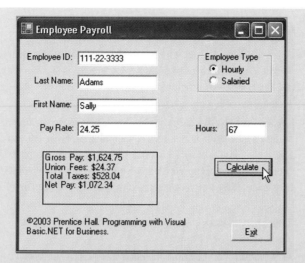

FIGURE 9.19. *Payroll calculation for Sally Adams*

5. Click the **Salaried** radio button, and then click the **Calculate** button. The message shown in Figure 9.20 is displayed.

FIGURE 9.20. *Error message that appears when the Annual Salary data validation fails*

6. Click **OK**. Change the annual salary to 64000 and click **Calculate**. Now your results should match the results shown in Figure 9.21.

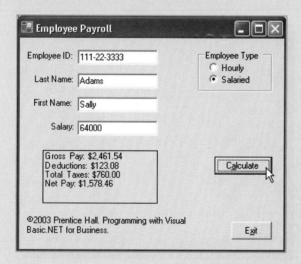

FIGURE 9.21. *Payroll calculation for Sally Adams*

7. Test the functionality of the *btnExit* button. Make any modifications to your solution that are necessary.
8. Save your changes.
9. Close the solution.

Summary

- Object-oriented programming emphasizes objects as abstractions of things in the world. Objects have characteristics known as properties and behaviors known as methods. The goal of object-oriented programming is to develop objects whose properties and methods can be extended to other objects based on them.

- Visual Basic.NET is a true object-oriented language because it supports the qualities of encapsulation, abstraction, inheritance, and polymorphism. An object's properties and methods can be hidden or abstracted from other objects through encapsulation and made available to other objects by being exposed. Through polymorphism, the methods and properties of a base class are inherited by a derived class, and the derived class can modify these properties and methods.

- In object-oriented programming, all objects can be characterized as belonging to a class of objects. The class defines the structure of the object, and each object is a realization, or instantiation, of the class.

- All Visual Basic.NET objects derive from either predefined classes that are part of the .NET framework or from user-defined classes. You can create a user-defined class by adding a class declaration to a project. You can then add class properties and methods as code statements in the class declaration.

- You can store information in objects by using fields and properties. To store information in an object by using fields, you declare a variable to hold the field information. To store information in an object by using properties, you must declare property procedures.

- Methods are any action that a class performs. You can create a class method by adding either a sub procedure or a function procedure to a class. To use a method, a procedure must contain a calling procedure that calls the method.

- A derived class inherits the properties and methods of a base class when the declaration includes the Inherits keyword.

- You can declare a class method as overridable. A derived class with a method declared with the Overrides keyword can implement unique functionality.

Key Terms

abstraction

base class

class

Class statement

derived class

encapsulation

End Class

End Get

End Set

exposed

field

Get property procedure

Get statement

inheritance

Inherits keyword

instance

instantiation

method

object

object-oriented programming (OOP)

Overridable keyword

override

Overrides keyword

polymorphism

property

property procedure

ReadOnly property

Set property procedure

Set statement

WriteOnly property

Study Questions

Multiple-choice questions

1. Which quality of object-oriented programs refers to a class as a self-contained unit with characteristics and behaviors?
   a. Abstraction
   b. Polymorphism
   c. Encapsulation
   d. Inheritance
   e. Exposure

2. Which quality of object-oriented programs refers to the derivation of behaviors from one class to another?
   a. Abstraction
   b. Polymorphism
   c. Encapsulation
   d. Inheritance
   e. Exposure

3. Which object-oriented feature is now implemented in Visual Basic.NET?
   a. Abstraction
   b. Polymorphism
   c. Encapsulation
   d. Inheritance
   e. Exposure

4. A declaration contains the Overrides keyword. What is being declared?
   a. Property procedure
   b. Base class
   c. Constructor
   d. Method
   e. Derived class

5. A property variable is declared as:
   a. Private
   b. Friend
   c. Public
   d. Protected
   e. Protected Friend

6. Which of the following property declarations can be inherited?
   a. Private LastName as String
   b. Public PayRate as Single
   c. Friend HoursWorked as Integer
   d. A and B
   e. B and C

7. What kind of procedure uses the Set keyword?
   a. Property
   b. Constructor
   c. Method
   d. Function
   e. Derived

8. How many property procedures does Visual Basic.NET support?
   a. One
   b. Two
   c. Three
   d. Four
   e. Five

9. Which of the following statements is false regarding inheritance?
   a. A derived class inherits procedures from one and only one base class.
   b. A base class cannot inherit properties and methods from a derived class.
   c. A property is exposed to a derived class only if it is declared as Friend or Public.
   d. The Inherits keyword specifies that a derived class inherits properties and methods from a base class.
   e. A method in the base class declared with the Overrides keyword can override a method in the derived class.

10. An application declares a derived class that overrides a method of the base class. This capability is most related to which object-oriented concept?
    a. Encapsulation
    b. Abstraction
    c. Polymorphism
    d. Inheritance
    e. Constructors

True/False Questions

1. In object-oriented terms, a derived class obtains its functionality from a base class.

2. You can assign information to objects by using fields or property procedures.

3. By default, a property procedure declared with the Set statement is read/write.

4. A base class can override the properties of a derived class.

5. A derived class can inherit its functionality from more than one base class.

Short Answer Questions

1. How does a base class differ from a derived class?

2. How do the qualities of abstraction and encapsulation relate to one another?

3. A class contains three properties. When would you declare the variables for these properties with Friend or Public accessibility?

4. How do overrides support polymorphism?

5. When should you consider using properties rather than methods to store information in an object?

Guided Exercises

Creating a Class for Calculating the Wholesale Value of an Inventory Item

Businesses that store inventory need to know the value of specific inventory items. Create a Windows application for calculating the wholesale value of an inventory item. Wholesale value is the cost of the item multiplied by the number of items in stock. Your project will contain one form for defining the application interface, and a class named WholesaleInventory. The interface will appear as shown in Figure 9.22.

FIGURE 9.22. *The Wholesale Inventory application*

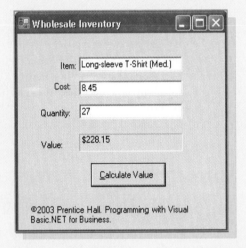

To create the Wholesale Inventory Windows Form application:

1. Launch Visual Studio.NET if it is not already running.
2. Click **File**, **New Project**. Create a new Windows Form application named `Wholesale Inventory`.
3. Using Figure 9.22 as a guide, add the appropriate controls to the form.
4. Add comments in the Code Editor that document the purpose for the application.
5. Add a class named `WholesaleInventory` to the application.
6. Refer to the code shown throughout this chapter to write your procedures. The **WholesaleInventory** class will include the following properties:

   Item

   Cost

   Quantity

7. Save your changes.
8. Run and test your application.
9. Enter the item cost and quantity shown in Figure 9.22 to test your application.
10. Save any modifications, and close your solution when you finish.

Creating a Derived Class for Calculating the Retail Value of an Inventory Item

In this Exercise you will create a Windows Form application that calculates the retail value of an inventory item. Your project will include one form defining the application interface and two classes: the **WholesaleInventory** class you created in the previous exercise as the base class and a derived class named **RetailInventory**. This application will contain an additional text box for entering the retail mark-up of the item as a decimal value. The method for calculating the inventory value will be overridden to take into account the marked-up price. You can calculate the retail value from the wholesale cost and quantity as follows:

```
Retail Value = (Wholesale Cost X Quantity X Markup)
```

The interface will look like Figure 9.23.

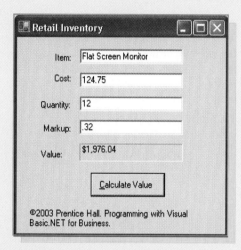

FIGURE 9.23. *The Retail Inventory application*

To create the Retail Inventory Windows Form application:

1. Launch Visual Studio.NET if it is not already running.
2. Click **File**, **New Project**. Create a new Windows Form application named `Retail Inventory`.
3. Import the **InventoryValue** class from the *Wholesale Inventory* solution.
4. Using Figure 9.23 as a guide, add the appropriate controls to the form.
5. Add comments in the Code Editor that document the purpose for the application.
6. Add a class named `RetailInventory` to the application. This is the derived class.
7. Refer to the code shown throughout this chapter to write your procedures, and inherit the appropriate elements from the **WholesaleInventory** class.
8. Save your changes.
9. Run and test your application.
10. Enter the item cost and quantity shown in Figure 9.23 to test your application.
11. Save any modifications, and close your solution when you finish.

Case Studies

Creating a Class for Calculating the Amount of a Sale for a New Vehicle

Retail businesses collect taxes on the items they sell. Car dealerships collect state sales tax and, depending on where the business is located, sometimes local taxes as well. Create a Visual

Basic.NET solution named New Auto Sale that consists of a form for entering a description of the car to be sold, the purchase price, and the total sales tax, using the following calculations:

State sales tax: 8% of the purchase price

Local Sales tax: 3% of the purchase price

The application uses a class named **NewAuto** that includes fields and properties for storing the vehicle description and price. The vehicle description and price are stored in fields; all other values are stored in properties. Calculate the state tax, local tax and total tax. Return the details about the vehicle, price, total taxes, and total sale in a label on the form.

Creating a Derived Class for Calculating the Amount of a Sale for a Used Vehicle

Assume that the car dealership in the previous case study also sells used cars. The tax rate is the same, but the sale price of a used vehicle includes a 1.5% detail charge that does not incur tax. Create a Visual Basic.NET solution named Used Auto Sale that imports the **NewAuto** class and creates a derived class named **UsedAuto** that calculates and displays the charges for a used car.

Creating Distributed Web Applications by Using ASP.NET

The vision for the .NET framework is to enable information sharing, regardless of application, operating system, or device. Geography is not the factor in business it used to be for accessing the data and services you need. Checking your e-mail and schedule appointments from your desktop computer at work, a computer terminal at the local Internet Café, your cell phone as you board a plane, or your handheld planner while you are riding in a taxi on the way to meet a customer are all examples of how information technology is undergoing a transformation so that many kinds of devices can access and share information.

You can use the Visual Studio.NET framework to develop not only desktop applications but also Web applications, Web services, and mobile services. With Visual Basic.NET, you can create applications that leverage the power of the World Wide Web. This includes everything from a traditional Website that serves HTML pages to fully featured business applications that run on the Internet and exchange data by using XML. With the increased capabilities of today's Web servers, the increasing speed of Internet connections, and the familiarity of the Web browser as an essential computing tool, there will be an even greater emphasis on Web applications in the .NET framework. In this chapter, you will learn how to create Web applications that can run on any computer that has a Web browser and an Internet connection.

Performance Objectives

At the conclusion of this chapter, you will be able to:

- Describe the key benefits of using ASP.NET for Web Forms applications.
- Explain how client-side and code-behind scripting differ.
- Add controls to a Web Forms project by using Design layout, and view the HTML for controls by using HTML layout.
- Explain how HTML controls, HTML Server controls, and Web Server controls differ and when to use each kind of control.
- Create a Visual Basic.NET Web Forms project.
- Use data-validation controls in Web Forms projects.
- Use ADO.NET objects to bind Web Server controls to a data source.

Why Use ASP.NET?

In Chapter 1 you learned how Windows applications and Web forms differ. A ***Windows application*** is a program designed to run on a desktop computer in the Microsoft Windows environment; it includes the graphical interface supported by the Windows operating system. A ***Web application*** includes Web Forms pages that have a Web interface; it runs from a Web server and displays the user interface in a Web browser. Traditionally, the tools for developing Windows applications and Web applications were different and did not integrate well with one another. For example, if you developed a Website by using Microsoft FrontPage, you could not change the site by using Microsoft Visual Studio Version 6.

In recent years, the technologies for developing Web pages have progressed until rather than simply presenting content users can view in a Web browser, Web applications are interactive. For example, if you go to the Website for your bank and you have an Internet account, you can view the balance in your savings and checking accounts and also transfer money from one account to another.

At this point you have done enough programming to know that developing a Web page that authenticates a user, accesses the account records from a database, and interacts with the database by creating a record for the account transfer requires program code. A recent technology for providing program code for interaction in Web pages is Microsoft's Active Server Pages (ASP) technology. Although ASP solves the problem of providing interactivity in Web pages for the average programmer, the knowledge and skills required to write a Web application have little in common with those needed to do traditional Windows application development.

ASP.NET, Microsoft's new technology for Web development, is part of the .NET framework. ASP.NET lets you build interactive Web pages by using the same visual tools you use to create Windows applications. This means the knowledge and skills for developing Web applications and Windows applications are the same. In Visual Basic.NET, you can create Web applications by using the same Integrated Development Environment (IDE) you use to develop Windows applications. A Visual Studio Web application is built around ASP.NET. This new ***ASP.NET*** platform includes both the objects and controls you create at design time and the code that executes at run time from a Web server. Because ASP.NET is part of the .NET framework, your ASP.NET Web projects have access to the full range of features available in the Visual Studio development environment.

ASP.NET SYSTEM REQUIREMENTS

ASP.NET Web applications run on a Web server configured with Microsoft Internet Information Services (IIS). You can create ASP.NET applications when Visual Studio.NET is running on Windows 98, Windows Me, and Windows XP Professional with the .NET framework installed on your computer. To create and run Web Forms projects on these platforms by using ASP.NET, you must have Internet Information Services (IIS) version 5.0 or later.

If you have Windows 2000 Server or Windows NT 4.0 on your computer, IIS is installed automatically and no further configuration is required.

Now that you understand the advantages of using ASP.NET for developing Web content, let's review the basics of designing applications for the Web.

WEB DESIGN BASICS: DESIGNING WEB PAGES BY USING HTML

Web pages are often static documents that provide information but do not provide any real-time interaction with the user. The most basic kind of Web page consists of a simple text document available on the Internet. This represents a simple *client-server computing model*, where the document is posted on a *Web server*—that is, a server that contains Web documents available to anyone with Internet access. The computer that requests a Web page from the server is called the *client*, and in the case of Internet or distributed computing, the client computer must have a Web browser installed. A *Web browser* is application software that interprets the contents of a Web page and displays the page onscreen. This simple client-server model for distributed computing is shown in Figure 10.1.

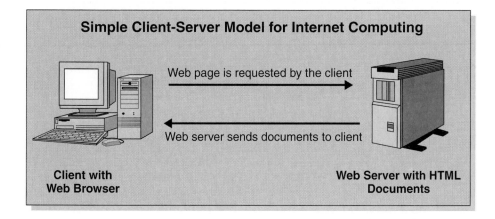

FIGURE 10.1. *A simple client-server model for Internet computing*

To appreciate the power of ASP.NET for creating interactive applications, let's take a look at how to develop simple Web pages. You can write simple Web documents that include both text and graphics by using a text editor like the one you created in Chapter 5. A *Web document* (also called a Web page) is a simple text document that contains the information to display and instructions for displaying it. The documents posted on the Web server are written in a format that the client's Web browser will understand. The Web document consists of ASCII text for the information to display and additional elements called "tags" that mark up the text and define how to display it. The Web browser uses these tags to interpret and display the document. The tags are written by using a *markup language*, which defines the standards for what each tag must include. The most common markup language is **HTML**, which stands for ***Hypertext Markup Language***. The tags are enclosed in brackets consisting of the less-than and greater-than symbols (< and >). You can create HTML Web pages in any application that saves text in ASCII format. If you want to create a simple Web document, enter the following text in Notepad or the text editor you created in Chapter 5.

```
<HTML>
    <BODY>
        <H1>Simple Web Page Example</H1>
        This is an example of a very simple Web page consisting
            of text and a graphic. The text elements are enclosed
            with tags that tell the Web browser how to display
            the information.
    <BR>
            <H3>©2003 Prentice Hall</H3>
            <HR>
            <H3>Programming with Visual Basic.NET for
                Business</H3>
            <img SRC="VSLogo.gif">
            <H3>Simple Web Page Example</H3>
            <HR>
    </BODY>
</HTML>
```

The file contains text that will display and the markup tags indicating how the browser should format each line of text and display the image (the *VSLogo.gif* file). Figure 10.2 shows how the file appears in the text editor you created in Chapter 5.

FIGURE 10.2. *Creating an HTML document by using the Enhanced Text Editor*

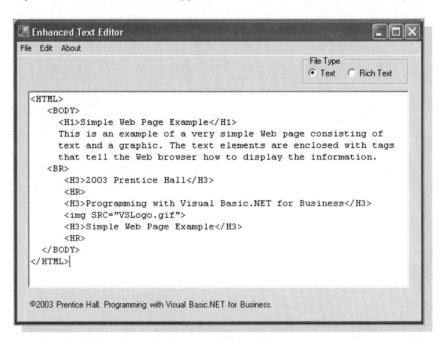

If you save this text file with an .htm file extension, Windows will recognize it as an HTML document. When you open the file by using My Computer or the Windows Explorer, Windows will launch your default Web browser, and the file will appear as shown in Figure 10.3.

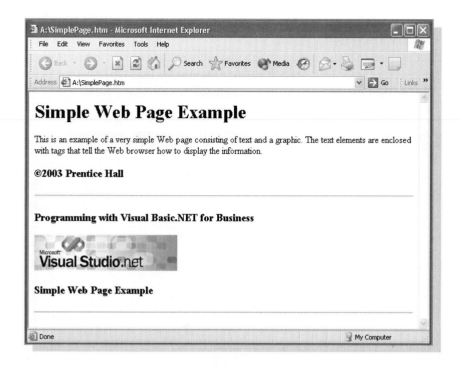

FIGURE 10.3. *Simple HTML document as it appears in a Web browser*

As you can see, creating static Web pages is easy if you know the HTML tags to add to a document. But what about Web pages that respond to user commands? Let's learn how to add interactivity to Web pages.

ADDING INTERACTIVITY TO WEB PAGES BY USING ASP.NET

Displaying text and images as static Web pages is appropriate for some information, but many businesses and organizations need to give users a way to interact with the information that is available on the Web. Interactivity requires code. There are two ways to handle code and scripting in Web pages: *client-side* and *code-behind.* Some technologies preceding ASP.NET use ***client-side scripting***. This means the code that defines the interactivity for a Web page is either embedded in the HTML or contained in a separate program downloaded with the page and run by the browser.

When the programming code is separated from the user interface, it is called ***code-behind scripting***. "Code-behind" means the HTML and controls that define the Web Form interface are contained in a separate file from the code statements that provide the functionality. The two files are compiled at run time and form a single unit. The code behind the interface runs from the Web server. ASP.NET supports code-behind scripting.

Visual Studio.NET supports ASP.NET, so you can create your Web applications by using the same development environment you use to create Windows Forms applications. Visual Studio.NET contains all the tools to quickly build Web Forms applications. You use the tools in the IDE to create the interface for the Web page by dropping controls onto a Web form. In Visual Studio.NET, ***Web Forms pages*** are programmable Web pages that make up the user interface for your Web application. You then use Visual Basic.NET to write the code that provides functionality to the application. The interface and the code remain separate.

Web Forms pages present the page interface to the user regardless of the browser they use and provide interactivity by running code on the Web server. Thus, the Web applications you create will include a combination of HTML for defining the interface and code-behind program statements to provide the Web application with its functionality and interactivity.

Consider a simple interactive Hello World! Web page created in Visual Basic.NET and shown in Figure 10.4. At run time, the form displays in a Web browser. Clicking the button on the form changes the Text property of the label that is located just above the button.

FIGURE 10.4. *Hello World! Web Forms project at run time*

Now let's look at designing the interface for the page in the IDE. Figure 10.5 shows the Web Forms project at design time.

FIGURE 10.5. *Hello World! Web Forms project at design time*

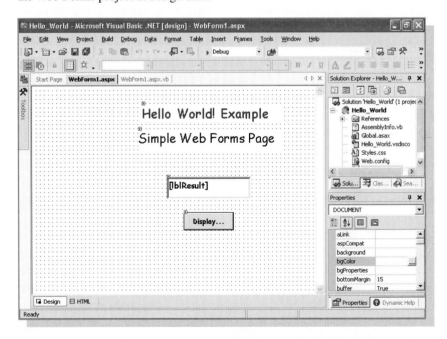

As with any Web page, if you right-click in the browser and select View Source, you can open the HTML comprising the page in a text editor. You can also open the Web Forms file (the file ending in .aspx) to view the HTML code that defines the user interface for the page. Notice that the Designer for a Web Forms project has two tabs at the bottom of the screen. The leftmost tab, **Design**, shows the visual controls that define the page. The controls, such as labels and buttons in this example, are available in the Toolbox. There is also an **HTML** tab in the Designer. Clicking this tab displays the HTML tags that define the page. Figure 10.6 shows the HTML code that defines the interface for the Hello World! Web Forms project.

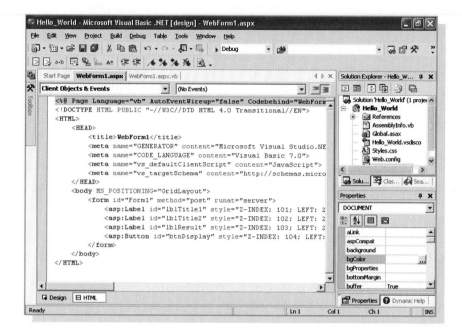

FIGURE 10.6. *HTML text defining the Hello World! Web Forms interface*

The HTML text in Figure 10.6 includes the ***Runat attribute*** tag. The RunAt="server" attribute tells the Web server that the code behind the controls is to be handled on the Web server. The HTML text defines the user interface. Note that the HTML text does not include any code that provides functionality for the program. The program code is contained in another file, ending in *.aspx.vb*. Let's take a look at the program code that provides the functionality for the Hello World! application. When you view the program code for the project, the IDE displays the code shown in Figure 10.7.

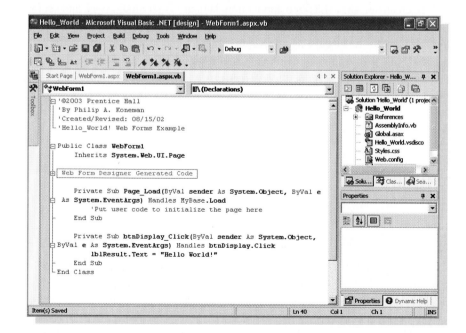

FIGURE 10.7. *Program code for the Hello World! Web Forms project*

This code should be familiar to you; it includes a simple assignment statement that handles the click event for the button:

```
Private Sub btnDisplay_Click(ByVal sender As System.Object,
  ByVal e As System.EventArgs) Handles btnDisplay.Click
  lblResult.Text = "Hello World!"
End Sub
```

Web server controls that incorporate code-behind scripting is one feature that distinguishes ASP.NET from earlier Web technologies. Understanding the concept of code-behind in Visual Basic.NET provides a glimpse into ASP.NET. To summarize, ASP.NET has the following features:

- ASP.NET Web Forms pages are not text-based, so you cannot create and edit them in a text editor. Although you can view the HTML used to create the user interface, you cannot edit the program code in an HTML editor.
- When you develop an ASP.NET solution, you write the code in the Visual Studio.NET IDE. It is much easier to develop reusable code routines when you use code-behind technology.
- In ASP.NET Web forms, the code behind the interface that provides the functionality is contained in a separate file.
- In ASP.NET Web Forms projects, the client application downloaded to the Web browser contains only the interface.

Now that you understand the concept of code-behind scripting, let's see how to create an ASP.NET Web application.

Creating an ASP.NET Web Forms Project

In Chapter 1 you learned how to create an application for performing a temperature conversion, much like the applications that are available on Websites such as www.weather.com. Now you will create a Web Forms version of the temperature conversion application as an introduction to ASP.NET Web Application projects.

To create an ASP.NET Web application, launch Visual Studio.NET and set the profile to Visual Studio Developer. Then click **File**, **New Project**. In the New Project dialog box, make sure Visual Basic Projects is highlighted in the Project Types: list, click the ASP.NET Web Application template, and enter the name for the Web application. In this case, the project is named `Temperature_Conversion`. Notice that Visual Studio.NET assigns a location, as shown in Figure 10.8.

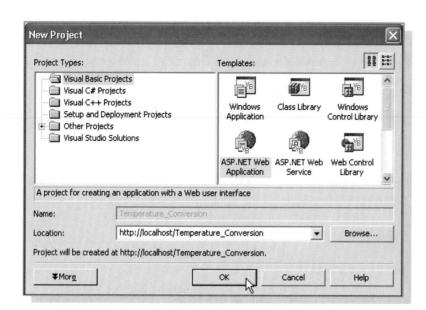

FIGURE 10.8. *Creating a new Visual Basic.NET Web Application project*

After you enter the name for the project, Visual Studio.NET displays the IDE shown in Figure 10.9.

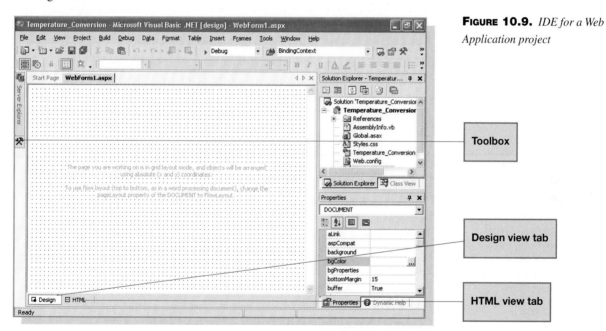

FIGURE 10.9. *IDE for a Web Application project*

The IDE for developing Web forms is almost identical to the IDE for developing Windows forms. Let's take a look at some of the differences in the IDE for Web Forms development.

THE WEB FORMS DESIGN INTERFACE

Creating a Web form in Visual Studio.NET is similar to developing a Windows form: you create the user interface and then add the code to the objects contained in the interface. Look again at Figure 10.9, which displays interface elements unique to creating Web Forms projects.

The interface in Figure 10.9 contains the two tabs you saw previously: Design and HTML. These correspond to the two views the IDE provides for creating the user interface: Design view (the default) and HTML view. In *Design view,* you add controls to the form by using the Toolbox and manipulating the controls directly on the form. *HTML view* provides access to the HTML markup that defines the user interface. Because Design view is so powerful, you might rarely need to use HTML view. However, if you are familiar with HTML, you can create your Web-page interface directly in HTML view, either by typing HTML tags directly into the editor or by dragging and dropping elements from the Toolbox and seeing their markup inserted into the document. Once the form contains a few controls, you can use HTML view to see the HTML statements that define these controls. Because the IDE does so much of the work for you as you create your Web pages, we recommend that you work primarily in Design view.

Form Layout

Another difference between the IDEs is that the IDE for Web forms uses a grid for placing the objects on the form. The Web Forms IDE also supports two modes for viewing the page layout for your forms: GridLayout (the default) and FlowLayout. When the IDE is set to *GridLayout mode*, you create your page by adding controls to the grid and manipulating their size and position, just as you do when creating a Windows form. GridLayout mode is easier to use than *FlowLayout mode*, which builds the page from top to bottom. Instead of adding controls to a grid and placing them where you want, you must develop your page in a linear fashion. For example, if you want a text box to appear at the top of the form and a button below it, you must first create the text box and then the button. If you create the button first, it will appear above the text box.

Look at Figure 10.9 again. The text in the middle of the Designer explains that the page is currently in GridLayout mode. The text also explains how to switch to FlowLayout mode.

Tip Using FlowLayout requires advanced planning, because you must create each element for your page in the order in which it should appear on the form.

Designing Web Forms applications in GridLayout is very similar to developing Windows Forms applications. We recommend GridLayout because it is easier to use and provides greater flexibility in changing the design of your page. You can switch between layouts by changing the PageLayout property for the document.

The Web form shown in Figure 10.9 is in Design view and uses the GridLayout mode. These are the default settings—the settings you will use for the Web Forms projects in this chapter.

USING CONTROLS

The Visual Studio.NET IDE includes the controls you can add to your Web forms. As with Windows Forms, the controls you can add to your forms are contained in the Toolbox; however, Web forms use some controls that are different from Windows Forms controls. The IDE currently displays the Visual Studio Developer profile, so the Toolbox is not visible. To display the Toolbox, move the pointer over the tab at the left of the Design window. Figure 10.10 shows the Toolbox for Web Forms design. Two separate tabs contain the Web Server and HTML controls you will use in designing the user interface for a Web form.

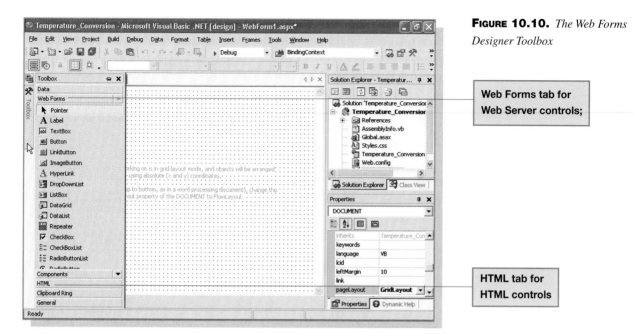

FIGURE 10.10. *The Web Forms Designer Toolbox*

The controls listed under the Web Forms tab are called **Web Server controls**. The controls listed under the HTML tab are called **HTML controls**. Figure 10.11 shows both sets of controls. Note that the screen resolution has been increased to show more of the tools listed under each tab.

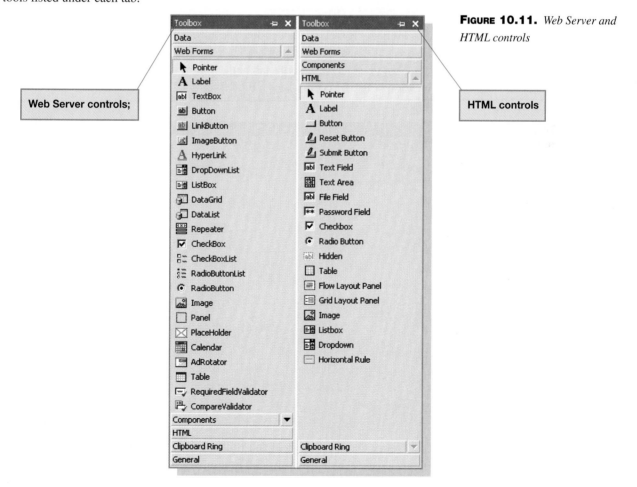

FIGURE 10.11. *Web Server and HTML controls*

ASP.NET supports both kinds of controls. To see how they differ, let's create four controls—two HTML controls and two Web Server controls—on the form for the Temperature Conversion application. Display the Toolbox, click the HTML Tab, select the Text Field tool, and add a Text Field control to the Web form, as shown in Figure 10.12.

FIGURE 10.12. *Using the HTML tab to add a Text Field control Web form*

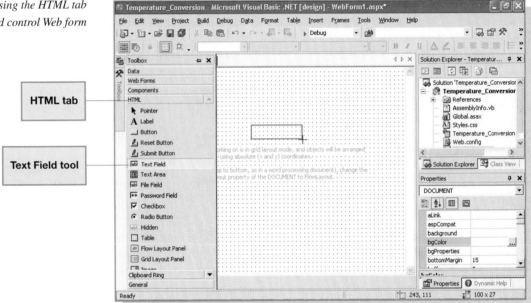

From the HTML tab, add a Button control to the form, immediately below the text field you just added to the form.

Now click the Web Forms tab in the Toolbox, and add two Web Server controls to the form: a TextBox control and a Button control. The form should now look like Figure 10.13.

FIGURE 10.13. *Web form with four controls*

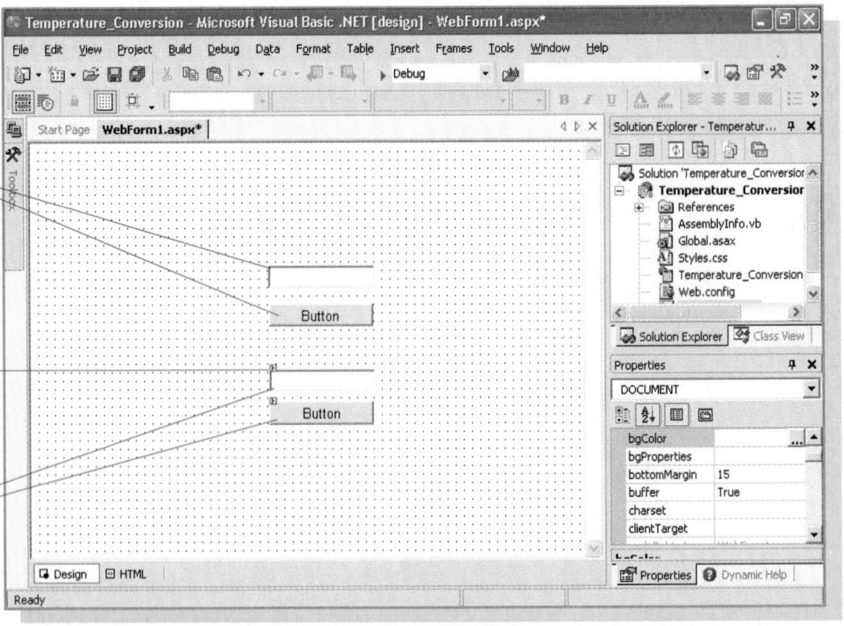

Notice that the Text Field and Button HTML controls at the top of the form look almost identical to the TextBox and Button Web Server controls below the HTML controls. The only difference is a small green marker called a **_glyph_** that appears next to the

Web Server controls. Any time you see a glyph next to a control, the glyph indicates that this is a server-based control.

Now that the form contains two sets of controls, let's see how they differ.

HTML Controls

The Text Field and Button controls you added to the top of the form are HTML controls. HTML controls should be familiar to you from surfing the Web. An *HTML control* is the kind of control you typically see on web pages; when you open a Web page with text boxes, labels, buttons, and tables, you are seeing HTML controls. These controls use tags to send data input to the server. To add functionality to these controls, you would need to add client-side code to define the actions the controls would accomplish.

You can add simple HTML controls to a Web form in two ways: by using the HTML tab in the Toolbox or by entering HTML tags and text to the form in HTML view. Consider the following example for creating an HTML control that sends a text entry in an HTML text box control to the server:

```
<INPUT TYPE="text" NAME="Temperature" VALUE="Enter the
   temperature here">
```

In this example, the Web page includes a text box for entering the temperature. The INPUT tag specifies the information to send to the Web server. The set of HTML controls is limited to a few controls that can be displayed by any browser. In addition, HTML controls are browser-based and use client-side technology; to add interactivity, you would need to write the program statements at the client side. HTML controls, therefore, are not visible to the server. Although Visual Studio.NET includes the HTML tab in the Toolbox for adding HTML controls to your Web forms, we do not recommend using them in Web forms because they are not visible to the server as programmable elements. HTML controls are client-based. The controls available in ASP.NET are code-behind and server-based.

HTML Server Controls

An *HTML Server control* is similar to its HTML control counterpart, except that its functionality is visible to the server. You can convert an HTML control to an HTML Server control by right-clicking the control and selecting Run As Server Control, as shown in Figure 10.14.

FIGURE 10.14. *Converting an HTML control to an HTML Server control*

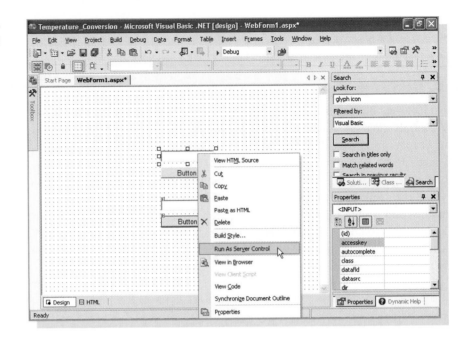

Converting an HTML control to an HTML Server control lets you use basic controls such as buttons and text boxes on your forms and also add functionality recognized by the server. When you convert a control, the Web Forms Designer adds the **RunAt="server"** attribute to the element, which alerts the server to treat the element as a control. A glyph appears on the control in Design view to indicate that the control is server-based.

Web Server Controls

The TextBox and Button controls at the bottom of the Web form are Web Server controls. A **Web Server control** is a Visual Studio.NET control available on the Web Forms tab of the Toolbox. These controls include not only form-type controls such as buttons and text boxes, but also special-purpose controls such as a calendar or a data grid. Web Server controls are **rich controls**, which means they include properties you can set to customize the look and feel of the control. Web Server controls also behave more like the controls you are used to working with in Windows forms.

From the perspective of interface design, the only difference between an HTML control and a Web Server control is the tab in the Toolbox you use to create it. As you can see from Figure 10.13, both kinds of controls look the same on the form. As noted earlier, Visual Studio.NET includes both kinds of controls, but you should use Web Server controls if you want your application to take advantage of code-behind scripting. Use the Web Forms tab in the Toolbox, and avoid using the HTML tab.

We are finished comparing HTML, HTML Server, and Web Server controls. If you are following along in Visual Studio.NET, delete all four controls from the Temperature Conversion Web Forms project.

ADDING WEB SERVER CONTROLS TO A WEB FORMS PROJECT

Now let's see how to add Web Server controls to the Temperature Conversion application and set the control properties. You will add text box, label, and button controls to the form. The Web Forms tab in the Toolbox contains these controls. You can add controls to the form by selecting a control in the Toolbox and dragging it to the form or by using the pointer to draw the control on the form. Figure 10.15 shows how the form will appear after you add the controls to it. This Web Forms project is included with your data files, and is located in the *Temperature_Conversion* folder.

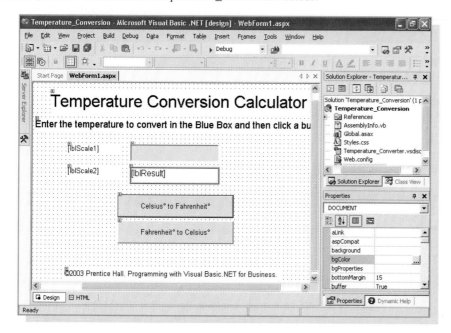

FIGURE 10.15. *Temperature Conversion Web form with Web Server controls*

You add code to the event procedure for a control in the same way you write code for Windows Forms applications: double-click the control to create a Click Event procedure and display the Code Editor. Following is the code for the conversions in this example:

Each control has a glyph. What does this indicate about the controls?

```
'Convert Celsius to Fahrenheit
    Private Sub btnCelsiusToFahrenheit_Click(ByVal sender As
        System.Object, ByVal e As System.EventArgs) Handles
    btnCelsiusToFahrenheit.Click
        'Calculate the Conversion
        lblResult.Text = (9 / 5) * Val(txtTemperature.Text) + 32
        'Add the appropriate temperature scales to the labels
        lblScale1.Text = "Celsius°"
        lblScale2.Text = "Fahrenheit°"
    End Sub

'Convert Fahrenheit to Celsius
    Private Sub btnFahrenheitToCelsius_Click(ByVal sender As
        System.Object, ByVal e As System.EventArgs) Handles
    btnFahrenheitToCelsius.Click
        lblResult.Text = (5 / 9) * (Val(txtTemperature.Text) -
        32)
        'Add the appropriate temperature scales to the labels
        lblScale1.Text = "Fahrenheit°:"
        lblScale2.Text = "Celsius°:"
```

You might notice that neither of the procedures performs data validation. The conversions are performed in the context of an assignment statement. The **Val** function converts the text value to a number that is used in the calculation. After the conversion is performed, the Text properties of the labels to the left of the *txtTemperature* and *lblResult* controls are given the appropriate values.

To be consistent with the documentation standards established in Chapter 1 for Windows applications, the following remarks appear in the Code Editor:

```
'©2003 Prentice Hall
'By Philip A. Koneman
'Created/Revised: 08/15/02
'Temperature Conversion Web Forms Application
```

To test the functionality, let's convert 100 degrees Celsius to Fahrenheit. The results are shown in Figure 10.16.

FIGURE 10.16. *Temperature Conversion Web form performing a conversion*

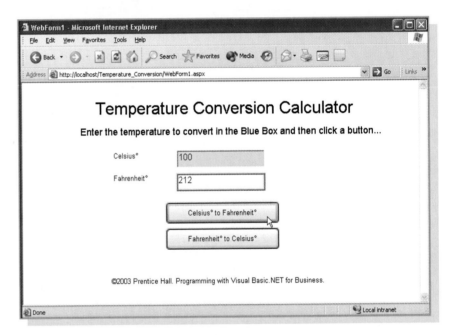

Now let's look at the HTML. The HTML statements defining the user interface are listed here:

```
<%@ Page Language="vb" AutoEventWireup="false"
    Codebehind="WebForm1.aspx.vb"
    Inherits="Temperature_Conversion.WebForm1"%>
<!DOCTYPE HTML PUBLIC "-//W3C//DTD HTML 4.0 Transitional//EN">
<HTML>
    <HEAD>
        <title>WebForm1</title>
        <meta content="Microsoft Visual Studio.NET 7.0"
          name="GENERATOR">
        <meta content="Visual Basic 7.0" name="CODE_LANGUAGE">
        <meta content="JavaScript"
          name="vs_defaultClientScript">
        <meta content="http://schemas.microsoft.com/
          intellisense/ie5" name="vs_targetSchema">
```

```
</HEAD>
<body MS_POSITIONING="GridLayout">
<form id="Form1" method="post" runat="server">

<asp:label id="lblTitle" style="Z-INDEX: 101; LEFT: 146px;
POSITION: absolute; TOP: 32px" runat="server" Width="542px"
Height="47px" Font-Names="Arial" Font-Size="X-
  Large">Temperature
Conversion Calculator</asp:label>

<asp:button id="btnFahrenheitToCelsius" style="Z-INDEX: 108;
  LEFT: 279px; POSITION: absolute; TOP: 275px"'
  runat="server" Width="'224px" Height="43px"
  Text="Fahrenheit° to Celsius°"></asp:button>

<asp:label id="lblScale2" style="Z-INDEX: 104; LEFT: 180px;
  POSITION: absolute; TOP: 173px" runat="server"
  Width="105px" Height="21px" Font-Names="Arial" Font-
  Size="X-Small"></asp:label>

<asp:label id="lblInstructions" style="Z-INDEX: 102; LEFT:
  116px; POSITION: absolute; TOP: 83px" runat="server"'
  Width="590px" Height="26px" Font-Names="Arial" Font-
  Size=Enter the temperature to convert in the Blue Box and
  thenclick a button. . . </asp:label>

<asp:label id="lblScale1" style="Z-INDEX: 103; LEFT: 180px;
  POSITION: absolute; TOP: 131px" runat="server"
  Width="107px" Height="21px" Font-Names="Arial" Font-
  Size="X-Small"></asp:label>

<asp:textbox id="txtTemperature" style="Z-INDEX: 105; LEFT:
  303px; POSITION: absolute; TOP: 130px" runat="server"
  Width="171px" Height="32px" Font-Names="Arial" Font-
  Size="Small" BackColor="#C0FFFF"></asp:textbox>

<asp:label id="lblResult"' style="Z-INDEX: 106; LEFT: 301px;
  POSITION: absolute; TOP: 172px" runat="server"
  Width="174px" Height="34px" Font-Names="Arial" Font-
  Size="Small" BorderStyle="Ridge"></asp:label>

<asp:button id="btnCelsiusToFahrenheit" style="Z-INDEX: 107;
  LEFT: 279px; POSITION: absolute; TOP: 226px"
  runat="server" Width="224px" Height="43px" Text="Celsius°
  to Fahrenheit°"></asp:button>

<asp:label id="lblCopyright" style="Z-INDEX: 109; LEFT:
  175px; POSITION: absolute; TOP: 367px" runat="server"
```

```
        Width="418px" Height="27px" Font-Names="Arial" Font-
        Size="X-Small">©2003 Prentice Hall. Programming with
        Visual Basic.NET for Business.</asp:label>
      </form>
      </body>
</HTML>
```

Each control begins with an <asp tag and has the **Runat** attribute set to the server, which specifies that the control is a Web Server control. Therefore, the application uses code-behind to run the compiled procedures that perform the conversion. When the Web page loads, the client machine contains the HTML statements that define the user interface. The program logic resides on the Web server, where the conversion procedures are run.

Click the **HTML** tab in the IDE to display the HTML for the controls. To set the text wrap for the Code Editor, click **Tools**, **Options**. Click the **Text Editor** folder to expand it, and then click the **HTML/XML** folder. Make sure the Word Wrap check box in the Options dialog box is selected, as shown in Figure 10.17.

FIGURE 10.17. *Setting the word-wrap option for the Web Forms Code Editor*

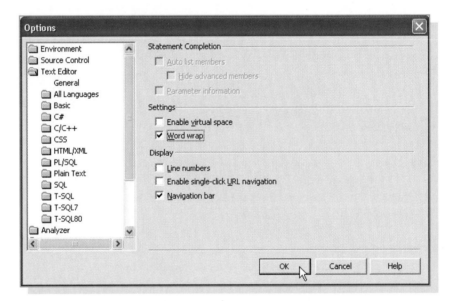

You can change the word-wrap setting any time you are viewing HTML or XML in the Code Editor so that all the code for a control or data element will display in the window. Figure 10.18 displays the HTML tag for the *lblTitle* Web control. Notice the **RunAt="server"** attribute for the control.

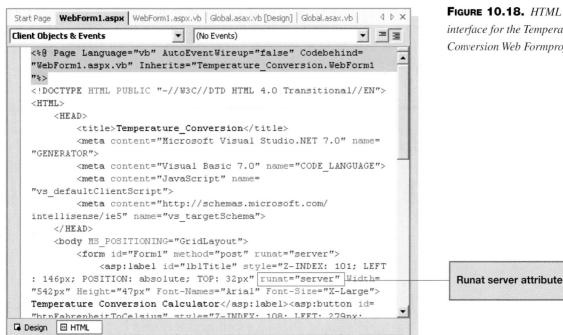

FIGURE 10.18. *HTML defining the interface for the Temperature Conversion Web Formproject*

Now that you know how to add controls to a Web form, let's think about collecting data from users. When you create a Visual Basic.NET Windows application that obtains user input, you frequently validate the data collected in text box and combo box controls. If a Web Forms project uses Web Server controls, how can you validate the data? Let's learn how to validate user input in Web Forms projects.

Validating Data in Web Forms Projects

In the preceding example, the procedures for performing the temperature conversion do not perform any data validation. As you learned previously, validating data in Windows Forms applications is a standard programming practice. It is even more critical that your Web Forms projects include data validation. Here's why. If your form is sending data to the server where a calculation will be performed, you can rely on the page to validate the data, but then the user is waiting for a response from the server to determine if the data is correct. Figure 10.19 depicts this scenario.

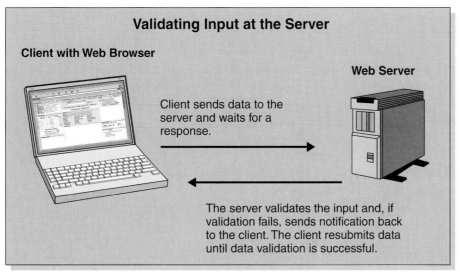

FIGURE 10.19. *Validating input at the server*

If the form is complex, or if the server is serving multiple clients simultaneously, performing data validation on the server might slow down overall performance. In addition, the client must resubmit data to the server until the data validation is successful. A better alternative is to perform data validation at the client.

VALIDATION CONTROLS

Visual Studio.NET Web Forms projects include a *validation control*. Validation controls provide an easy way to perform data validation, such as testing a value to verify that it is within a range of values. You can use data validation controls in Web Forms projects to validate user input at the client and minimize calls made to the server. Validation controls also allow you to customize the error message returned to the user. You can use validation controls in conjunction with any control that is processed by the Web Forms page, including both HTML and Web Server controls.

How does data validation using validation controls work? Figure 10.20 depicts how the client uses validation controls to validate data before sending it to the server.

FIGURE 10.20. *Using validation controls to validate input before sending a request to the server*

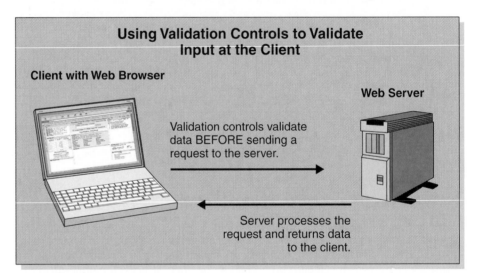

Each validation control references a Web Server control that resides somewhere on the page. When the user's input is being processed, the ASP.NET page framework passes the user's input to the appropriate validation control. The validation control then performs a test of the user input and sets a property to indicate whether or not the input passed the test. You can use a Visual Studio.NET validation control to accomplish this.

You can include multiple validation controls on a form. After all the validation controls have been called, a Page property is set. If any of the validation controls show that data validation failed, the entire page is set to an invalid status. Because validation controls include a way of returning a message to the user, the error can be corrected before the server is called to perform additional processing.

Let's see an example of how to validate data by using validation controls. Figure 10.21 displays a form with two validation controls: a **RangeValidator** control and a **RequiredFieldValidator** control. This Web Forms project, which is included with your data files, is located in the *Data_Validation* folder.

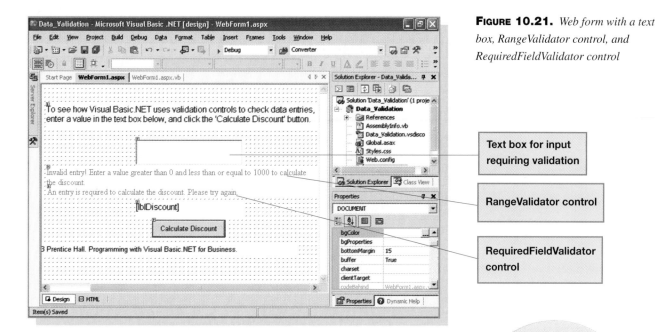

FIGURE 10.21. *Web form with a text box, RangeValidator control, and RequiredFieldValidator control*

Text box for input requiring validation

RangeValidator control

RequiredFieldValidator control

Both validation controls validate the entry in the *txtValue* text box. The control properties for the validation controls are listed in Table 10.1.

Table 10.1: Validation control properties

Control	Property	Setting
RangeValidator1	ControlToValidate	txtValue
	MinimimValue	1
	Maximum Value	1000
	Type	Double
	ErrorMessage	Invalid entry! Enter a value greater than 0 and less than or equal to 1000 to calculate the discount.
RequiredFieldValidator1	ControlToValidate	txtValue
	ErrorMessage	An entry is required to calculate the discount. Please try again.

To see how validation controls work, run the application and click the **Calculate Discount** button. Because the text box is empty, the *RequiredFieldValidator1* control displays the message shown in Figure 10.22.

To view this solution do the following:

1. Copy the *Data_Validation* folder from your data files to the *VnetPub\wwwroot* folder on your computer.

2. From the Windows Taskbar, Click **Start**, select **Run**, type *inetmgr.exe* into the Open box and click OK.

3. When IIS opens select Default Web Site in the left pane, and look for the application folder in the right pane.

4. Right-click the Data_Validation folder and select Properties.

5. Click **Create**, and then click **OK**.

You will now be able to run this solution.

FIGURE 10.22. *Data validation message raised by the RequiredFieldValidator1 control*

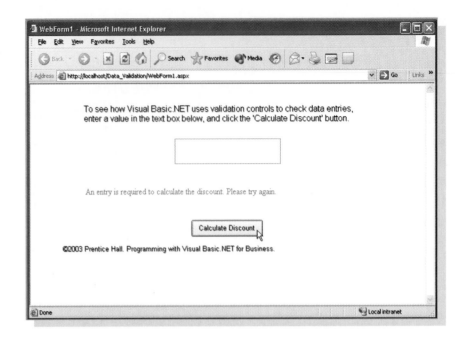

Now type `12000` in the text box and click the **Calculate Discount** button. Because the value is outside the range, the *RangeValidator1* control displays the message in Figure 10.23.

FIGURE 10.23. *Data validation message raised by the RangeValidator1 control*

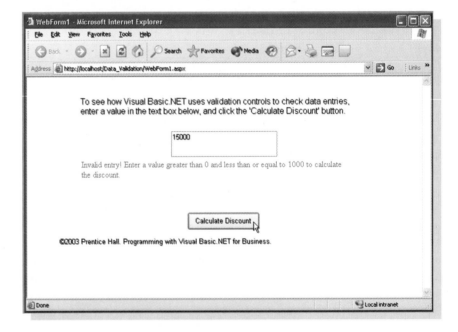

Now type `575` in the text box and click the Calculate Discount button. Because the value is within the range, the value is sent to the server to calculate the discount. Figure 10.24 displays the value returned by the server.

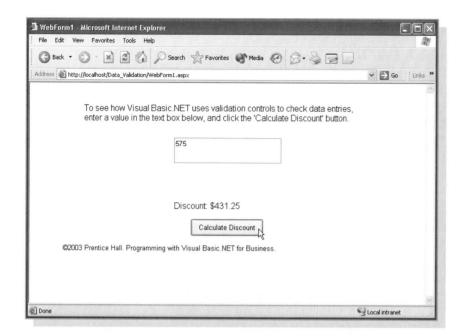

FIGURE 10.24. *Discount returned by the server to the client*

Validation controls perform data validation before sending a request to the server. After all data on the form is validated, the data is sent to the server for processing. Visual Basic.NET includes the following validation controls:

RequiredFieldValidator. Verifies that a required entry contains data.

CompareValidator. Compares an entry with a constant value or the property value of another control. Comparisons are made by using a comparison operator (less than, equal to, greater than, and other combinations).

RangeValidator. Verifies that an entry is within the specified lower and upper boundaries. The boundaries can include pairs of numbers, alphabetic characters, and dates.

RegularExpressionValidator. Verifies that an entry matches a pattern defined by a regular expression. You can use this control to check for predictable sequences of characters, such as social security numbers, e-mail addresses, telephone numbers, and postal Zip codes.

CustomValidator. You can use this control to check an entry against validation logic that you define. This type of validation supports a check against values derived at run time.

Validation controls are easy to use and configure. Because validation controls provide immediate feedback without a round trip to the server, the user's experience with the page is enhanced. You will practice adding validation controls to a Web Forms project in the first Hands-On Programming Example later in this chapter.

Now that you know how to add Web Server controls to Web forms and perform data validation, let's learn how to display database records in a Web Forms project.

Using ADO.NET Data Access Objects in Web Forms

When you think about the Websites you visit on a regular basis, there is a good chance many of them provide the information you request by pulling that information from a database. ASP.NET includes controls for pulling data from a database on the server and displaying the information in the client's Web browser. Many of the Websites you visit display data as read-only. This means users can view the data but probably do not need to update it. For example, consider the market data shown in Figure 10.25. This information is available as read-only, because viewers have no need to update it.

FIGURE 10.25. *Financial site displaying read-only data*

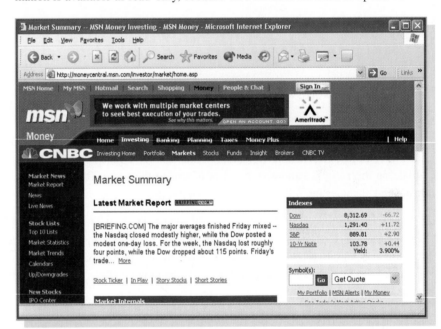

Some businesses use the Web for self-service applications. In a ***self-service application***, you can view and update data directly through the Web rather than relying on a customer service representative. If you place an order for merchandise online, you need to input personal information, such as your credit card number and expiration date, which is sent to a Web server. If you want to change your payroll deductions or number of exemptions, many large businesses provide self-service applications for you to perform these tasks online. The role of self-service applications will increase in the future.

Self-service applications require access to database records. A Web Forms project can connect to a database by using ADO.NET objects to bind Web Server controls to a database. When you create a Web Forms project in Visual Studio.NET, the Toolbox includes the same ADO.NET data components you learned about in Chapter 6. You can use these objects to connect your Web application to a database. To connect a Web Forms project to a database, you need to create a **OleDbConnection object**, a **OleDbDataAdapter object**, and a **Dataset object**.

You will recall from Chapter 6 that you can use the Server Explorer to view any existing data connections and drag the table from a data connection to a form to create an **OleDbConnection** object and an **OleDbDataAdapter** object. Once these objects appear on the form, you can generate the dataset object the same way you did in Chapter 6 when you used ADO.NET to bind controls on a Windows form to a data source.

Let's look at how to bind a control on a Web form to a database. Our Web form contains a single Web Server control: a DataGrid control with the default ID of *DataGrid1*. You will bind the Web form to an Access database.

Figure 10.26 displays our form after you drag the *Employees* table from the *Payroll* Data Connection in the Server Explorer to the form and generate the dataset. Each data access object is contained in the component tray in the Web Forms Designer. The DataGrid control can now be bound to the data source.

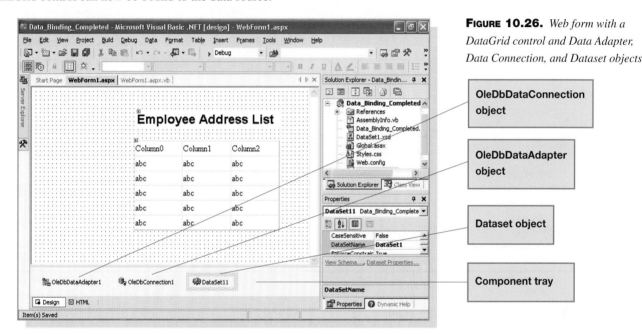

FIGURE 10.26. *Web form with a DataGrid control and Data Adapter, Data Connection, and Dataset objects*

The DataGrid does not display the names of the fields in the database as the table headings, because the control currently is unbound. To bind the control to the data source, you set the **DataSource** property to **DataSet11** and the **DataMember** property to **Employees**. If you right-click the DataGrid control, you can select the *Property Builder*, a visual tool you can use to set the display options for the data grid. In addition to setting the order of the columns, you can rename the column headings. Figure 10.27 shows the Columns tab of the Property Builder for the DataGrid control.

To follow this example, copy the *Data_Binding_Start* and *Data_Binding_ Solution* folders from your data files to the *InetPub\wwwroot* folder on your computer. You will also need to copy the *Payroll.mdb* file from your data files to a floppy disk. Finally, follow the procedure listed in the Tip on page 443 to change the properties for the solution you wish to run.

FIGURE 10.27. *Using the Property Builder to configure columns in the data grid*

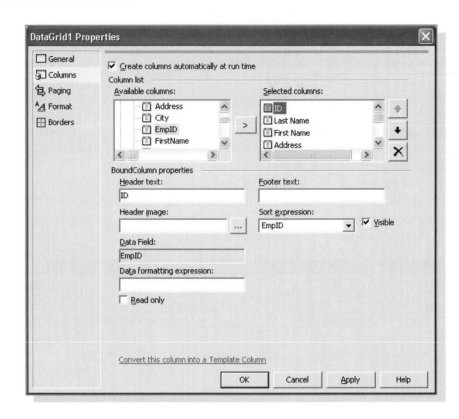

To determine which columns of data to display, make sure the option to generate columns automatically is not checked.

You can also change how the records appear by changing the AutoFormat of a DataGrid control to make the page more visually appealing. The *AutoFormat* for the control is a predefined set of formats that apply to the database fields displayed in the DataGrid control. If you right-click over the control and choose **AutoFormat**, you can select from a list of predefined AutoFormat schemes. For this example, we chose the Colorful scheme. Figure 10.28 shows how to select Auto Format from the context menu. After selecting an Auto Format, you can resize the DataGrid control as necessary.

FIGURE 10.28. *Selecting AutoFormat from the context menu*

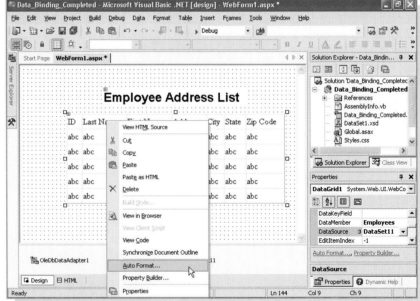

You will use code to fill the dataset and perform the data binding. A Web Forms project contains a ***Page_Load event***, which determines what happens the first time the page is loaded. We added the following statements to this event procedure:

```
Private Sub Page_Load(ByVal sender As System.Object, ByVal e As
    System.EventArgs) Handles MyBase.Load
    'Put user code to initialize the page here
    If Not (IsPostBack) Then
        OleDbDataAdapter1.Fill(DataSet11)
        DataGrid1.DataBind()
    End If
End Sub
```

The If statement uses the ***IsPostBack keyword***, which returns a value indicating whether the page is being loaded and accessed for the first time or in response to a client request being sent back to the server. When a user first requests a form, it is displayed with the data determined at design time. If the user changes some data, moves to another page, and then returns to the first page, a ***postback event*** retains the data changed by the user. The If statement fills the DataGrid with the records in the dataset only if there is no postback event.

Now that you have customized the data grid and set its properties at run time by using the Page_Load event, let's see how the records appear when the application is run. Figure 10.29 shows how the data grid appears in a Web browser.

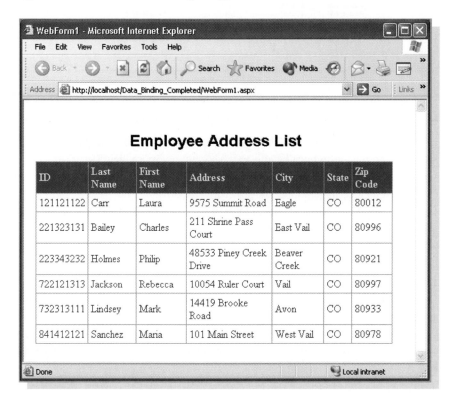

FIGURE 10.29. *Database records as they appear in a bound DataGrid control*

As you can see, it is easy to bind a rich control such as a Web Server control to a data source.

Now that you have learned the basics of creating Web Forms projects, let's complete two hands-on exercises to give you more experience creating Web forms.

☞ HANDS-ON PROGRAMMING EXAMPLE

Creating an ASP.NET Page for a Loan Amortization Schedule

As you learned in Chapter 4, the schedule of repaying a loan is known as an amortization schedule. To amortize is to *spread out*—thus an amortization schedule shows how the principal and interest payments are spread out over the term of the loan. Figure 10.30 shows a Web Forms amortization schedule for a car loan in the amount of $15,000, at an interest rate of 3.75%, paid back over 4 years.

FIGURE 10.30. *Web forms loan amortization application*

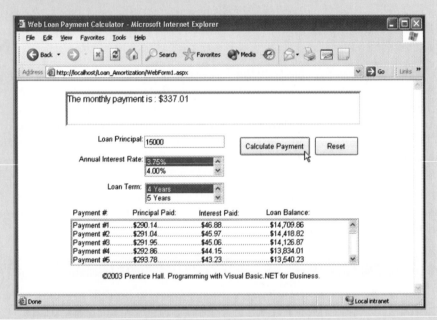

The Visual Basic.NET application generating this schedule calculates the loan payment and creates the amortization schedule according to the following conditions:

1. The loan amount must be at least $2,000 but no more than $25,000.
2. The loan term must be at least 1 year but not more than 5 years.
3. The annual interest rate will vary from 3% to 5%, at intervals of a quarter of a percentage point.
4. If the loan term and annual interest rate are not specified, the defaults are 5 years and 5%, respectively.

Plan the Application

The first step in planning the application is to determine the inputs and outputs. This application is similar to the loan amortization schedule you created in Chapter 4. The Web form contains list box controls for the interest rate and term values. The user will enter the loan amount in a text box. To validate the loan principal, add **RangeValidator** and **RequiredFieldValidator** controls to the form. The inputs and outputs are as follows:

Inputs	Outputs
Principal	Payment number
Interest rate	Principal payment
Term	Interest payment
	Loan Balance

The loan principal is obtained from a text box, so you will need to validate the principal by using Validation controls. Draw a visual representation of the application on a blank piece of paper. Figure 10.31 shows a drawing of the user interface and the name of each control on the form.

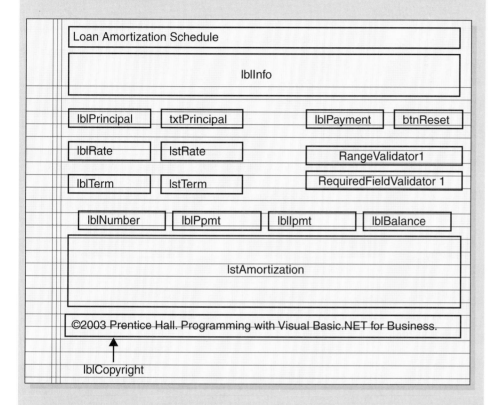

FIGURE 10.31. *Interface for the Web Loan Payment Calculator*

The application uses a looping structure to generate the amortization schedule and populate a list box with the payment information for each pay period. The loop uses the **Pmt** (payment), **PPmt** (principal payment), and **IPmt** (interest payment) functions to calculate the values for each payment period in the schedule. Change the **FontName** property of all label and text box controls to `Arial`. Table 10.2 lists the objects and properties for the application.

Table 10.2: *Objects and properties for the Amortization Schedule application*

Object Name	Property	Setting
WebForm1	Title	Web Loan Payment Calculator
lblInfo	Font Size BorderStyle	Small Inset
lblPrincipal	Text Size TabIndex	Loan Amount: X-Small 0
txtPrincipal	Text	

lblRate	Text Size	Annual Interest Rate: X-Small
lstRate	Items Collection: Text Items Collection: Value ListItem0 Selected TabIndex	3.00%, 3.25%, 3.50%, 3.75%, 4.00%, 4.25%, 4.50%, 4.75%, 5.00% .03, .0325, .035, .0375, .04, .0425, .045, .0475, .05 True 1
lblTerm	Text Size	Loan Term: X-Small
lstTerm	Items Collection: Text Items Collection: Value ListItem8 Selected TabIndex	1 Year, 2 Years, 3 Years, 4 Years, 5 Years 1,2,3,4,5 True 2
btnPayment	Text TabIndex	Calculate Payment 3
btnReset	Text TabIndex	Reset 4
RangeValidator1	ErrorMessage MaximumValue MinimumValue Type ControlToValidate	Invalid entry! Please enter a loan amount of at least 2000 but not greater than 25000. 25000 2000 Text txtPrincipal
RequiredFieldValidator	ErrorMessage ControlToValidate	Entry required! Please enter a loan amount of at least 2000 but not greater than 25000. txtPrincipal
lblNumber	Text	Payment #:
lblPPmt	Text Size	Principal Paid: X-Small
lblIPmt	Text Size	Interest Paid: X-Small
lblBalance	Text Size	Loan Balance: X-Small
lstAmortization	TabIndex	5
lblCopyright	Text Font Size	©2003 Prentice Hall. Programming with Visual Basic.NET for Business. X-Small

The application requires users to input the loan principal and choose a loan rate and loan term. If the rate and term are not selected from the lists, the calculation uses defaults of 5% annual interest and a 5-year term. Table 10.3 lists the pseudocode for specific events.

Table 10.3: *Pseudocode for the Loan Amortization Schedule application*

Event Procedure	Action
Page_Load	1. Initialize the lblInfo text. 2. Populate the Rate and Term list boxes.
btnPayment_Click	1. Validate data entry. 2. Calculate the payment, principal payment, and interest payment. 3. Populate the lstSchedule list box with the loan amortization data.

Now that you have created the planning documents for the application, you are ready to begin designing the user interface in the IDE.

Design the User Interface

If you have not launched Visual Studio.NET, do so now. Use the Start Page to set the profile to Visual Studio Developer. Perform each task that follows to complete this application.

To create a new Web Forms project:

1. Click **File**, **New, Project**. The **New Project** Dialog box appears.
2. Select **ASP.NET Web Application** as the project template and type `Loan_Amortization` as the name for the project.
3. Use the scroll bar in the Solution Explorer Tool window to display the name of the form, which is *WebForm1.aspx*.
4. Right-click the current name and select **Properties**.
5. Use the Name row to rename the form as `Loan_Amortization.aspx`.
6. Right-click inside the Design window and select **Properties** from the context menu. The DOCUMENT Property Pages dialog box appears.
7. Change the page title from *WebForm1* to `Web Loan Payment Calculator` and click **OK**.

You are now ready to create the user interface by adding the controls in Table 10.2.

To add Web Server controls to the form:

1. Move the pointer over the Toolbox icon to display it. Click the pushpin to lock the Toolbox.
2. Click the Web Forms tab. Click the Label control and drag a label to the top of the form. Set the properties as specified.
3. Add the controls for the principal, rate, and term. Set the control properties as specified in Table 10.2.
4. Select the *lstRate* control. In the Properties pane, click the **Collections** property in the **Item** row and enter the interest rate text and values in Table 10.2. When all the values are added, set the **Selected** property of the last entry to **True**, as shown in Figure 10.32. This sets 5.00% as the default value.

To set the Font properties, click the expand button in the Font properties row to display additional font properties.

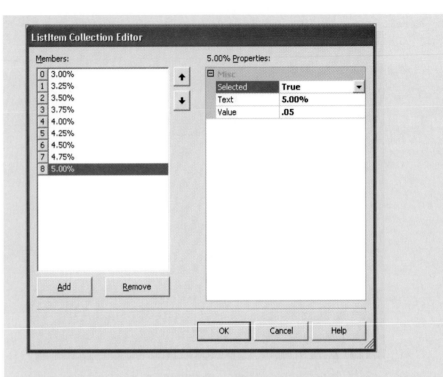

5. Add the text and value entries for the loan term. Set the default to 5 Years. The items in this collection should look like Figure 10.33.

FIGURE 10.33. *Loan term values*

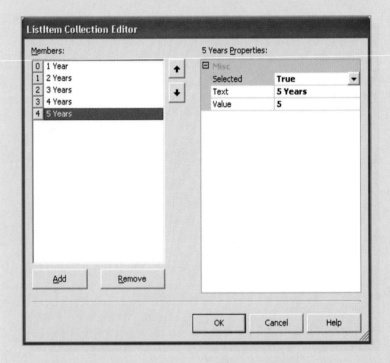

6. Add the remaining controls to the form, and set the control properties.
7. Click the **Save All** button on the Toolbar. The controls on your form should look similar to those in Figure 10.34.

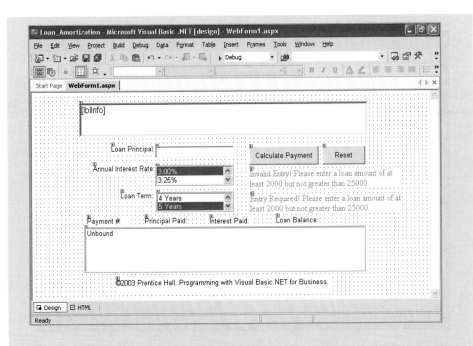

FIGURE 10.34. *Adding Web Server controls to the form*

Now that the interface design for the Amortization Schedule application is complete, you are ready to write the code providing the functionality.

Write the Code

Your first task is to add code for the events that occur when the page loads at run time. You will then add code to handle the *btnPayment* and *btnReset* click events.

To write code for the Page_Load event:

1. Press F7 to display the Code Editor. If the region displaying the **Windows Form Designer Generated Code** region is expanded, collapse it.
2. Place the insertion point at the top of the Code Window and type the following comments to document the application:

```
'©2003 Prentice Hall
'By [Enter your name here. . .]
'Created/Revised: [Enter the date here. . .]
'Web Loan Payment Calculator
```

3. Scroll down in the Code Editor until the procedure for the **Page_Load** event is visible. Enter the following statement immediately below the comment indicating where to add code to initialize the page:

```
lblInfo.Text = "'To calculate a loan payment, enter the amount
   to borrow (the principal), the annual interest rate, and the
   length of time required to repay the loan (the term). To
   create the loan repayment table schedule, click the 'Calculate
   Payment' button."
```

The code should now look like Figure 10.35.

FIGURE 10.35. *Code for the Web form*

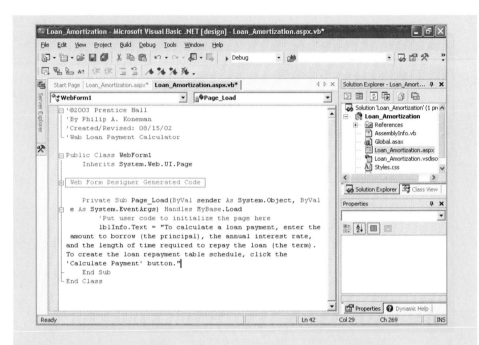

To write code for the btnPayment click event:

1. Click the **Class Name** list in the Code Editor and select the *btnPayment* control.
2. Click the **Method Name** list in the Code Editor and select the **Click** event.
3. Place the insertion point below the **Private Sub** statement and type the following statements for the procedure:

```
'Declare variables used by the procedure
Dim sngPrincipal As Single = Val(txtPrincipal.Text)
Dim sngRate As Single = Val(lstRate.SelectedItem.Value)
Dim intTerm As Integer = Val(lstTerm.SelectedItem.Value)
Dim sngPayment As Single
Dim sngPpmt As Single
Dim sngIpmt As Single
Dim sngBalance As Single
Dim intCounter As Integer

'Calculate and display the monthly payment
sngPayment = Pmt(sngRate / 12, intTerm * 12, -sngPrincipal)
lblInfo.Text = "The monthly payment is : " & _
Format(sngPayment, "Currency")

'Initialize the loan beginning balance
sngBalance = sngPrincipal

'Clear the list box of any prior items
lstAmortization.Items.Clear()

'Generate the amortization schedule
For intCounter = 1 To intTerm * 12
    sngPpmt = PPmt(sngRate / 12, intCounter, intTerm * 12, -
        sngPrincipal)
```

```
    sngIpmt = IPmt(sngRate / 12, intCounter, intTerm * 12, -
      sngPrincipal)
    sngBalance = sngBalance - sngPpmt


    'Populate the list box with the schedule
    lstAmortization.Items.Add _
    ("Payment #" & intCounter & "..........." & _
    Format(sngPpmt, "c") & "....................." & _
    Format(sngIpmt, "c") & "......................." & _
    Format(sngBalance, "c"))
Next intCounter
```

The procedure declares eight variables for calculating the loan payment and generating the amortization schedule. The statement that adds items to the list box adds the payment number (using the counter variable *intCounter*), the principal payment, the interest payment, and the loan balance for each payment period. Each calculated value is formatted as currency, and periods (.) act as dot leaders to separate the figures in the list box. The routine uses the continuation character (_) to make the code more readable.

To write code for the btnReset click event:

1. Click the **Class Name** list in the Code Editor, and select the *btnReset* control.
2. Click the **Method Name** list in the Code Editor, and select the **Click** event.
3. Place the insertion point below the Private Sub statement, and type the following statements for the procedure:

```
lblInfo.Text = "To calculate a loan payment, enter the amount to
  borrow (the principal), the annual interest rate, and the
  length of time required to repay the loan (the term). To
  create the loan repayment table schedule, click the 'Calculate
  Payment' button."

txtPrincipal.Text = ""
lstAmortization.Items.Clear()
```

4. Save your changes.

Run the Application

You are now ready to run the Loan Amortization Web Forms application and test its functionality.

To run the application:

1. Click the Start button or press the F5 key to run the application. Tab through the controls to verify the correct TabIndex setting for each control.
2. Tab into the text box for entering the loan principal, and type 100 as the amount.
3. Click the **Calculate Payment** button. The Range validation control will display an error message.
4. Type 22000 for the loan amount. Select 4.75 as the interest rate and 3 years as the term.

5. Click the **Calculate Payment** button. You should now see the loan summary information and amortization schedule shown in Figure 10.36.

FIGURE 10.36. *Calculating a loan payment*

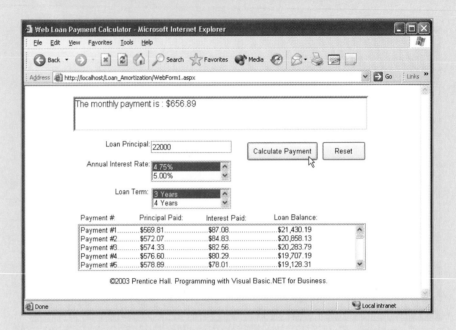

6. If your application does not run correctly, make any changes that are necessary, and save your changes.
7. Click **File**, **Close Solution** when you finish testing the application.

☞ HANDS-ON PROGRAMMING EXAMPLE

Creating an ASP.NET Page for Displaying Employee Address Book Records

You learned in Chapter 6 that businesses use a variety of databases to manage the data that is critical to their success. Because most databases hold more data than any individual needs to work with at any time, custom screen forms provide access to the data supporting business processes. With the increasing popularity of self-service applications, client-server applications that use the Web to connect to a database will become more common. In this example, you will create a Visual Basic.NET Web Forms application for viewing employee records in an Address Book database. Figure 10.37 shows how the Web Forms application appears in Internet Explorer.

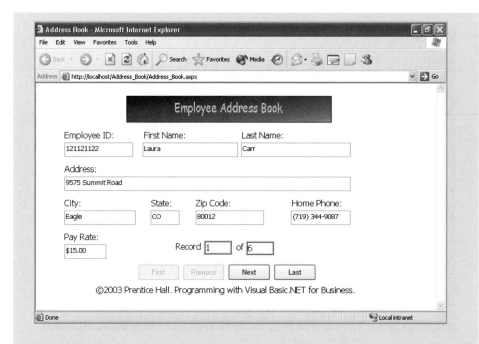

FIGURE 10.37. *The Web Employee Address Book*

The Employee Address Book Web Forms application includes controls bound to the *Employees* table in the *Payroll.mdb* database. The Web version of Address Book is for viewing employee records. This application supports the following functionality:

1. Provides access to records in the *Payroll.mdb* database.
2. Contains navigation buttons for moving through a dataset.
3. Includes record counters that display the current record number and the total number of records.

Although the requirements for this application are relatively simple, you will need to create the OleDbConnection, the OleDbDataAdapter, and a Dataset and then bind the controls on the form to the dataset. You can use the same data connection you created in Chapter 6.

Plan the Application

The Address Book application consists of one form with 14 labels, 9 text boxes, 4 buttons, and 1 image control.

Draw a visual representation of the application on a blank piece of paper. Figure 10.38 shows a drawing of the user interface and the name of each control on the form.

If you do not have a data connection established, refer to the section *"Creating a Dataset by Using the Server Explorer"* in Chapter 6.

For Web Forms applications, you can assign an image file to a control by setting the control's ImageURL property to the name of the JPEG or GIF file the control will display.

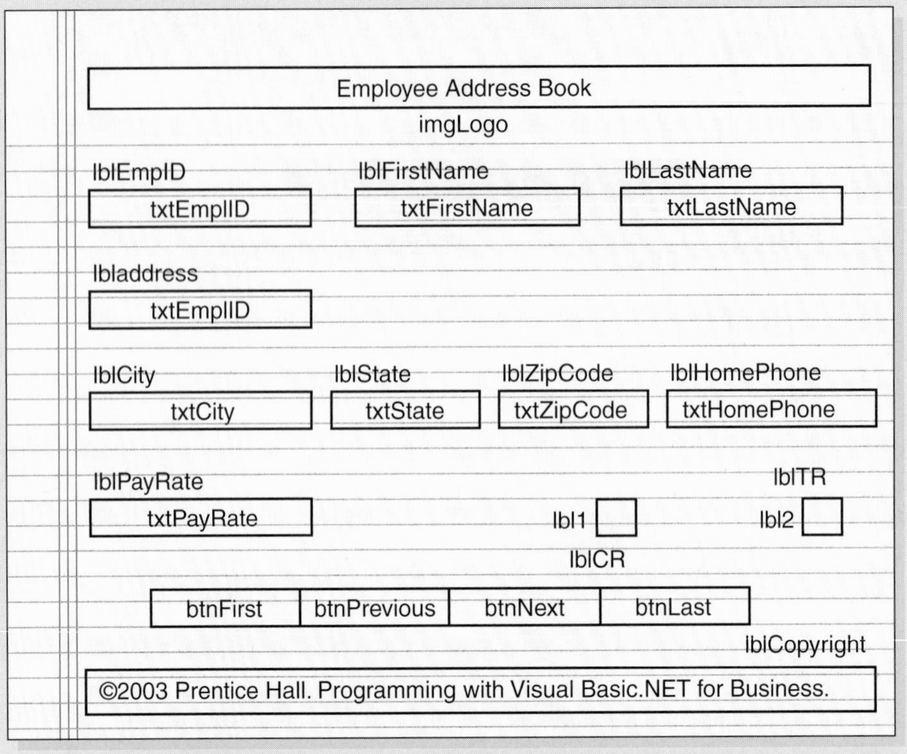

FIGURE 10.38. *Interface for the Web Forms Employee Address Book*

As you create these controls, set the **Text** property of all controls to Tahoma. Table 10.4 lists the controls and properties for the Address Book Web Forms application.

Tip

Although the DataBinder property is listed for each text box control, you will add a procedure to set the DataBinder properties at run time.

Table 10.4: *Objects and Properties for the Address Book Web Forms application*

Object	Property	Setting
imgLogo	ImageURL	AB_Logo.jpg
lblEmpID	Text	Employee ID:
lblLastName	Text	Last Name:
lblFirstName	Text	First Name:
lblAddress	Text	Address:
lblCity	Text	City:
lblState	Text	State:
lblZipCode	Text	Zip Code:
lblHomePhone	Text	Home Phone:
lblPayRate	Text	Hourly Wage:
lblCopyright	Text	©2003 Prentice Hall. Programming with Visual Basic.NET for Business.
lbl1	Text	Record
lbl2	Text	of
lblCR	Text BorderStyle	Ridge

lblTR	Text	
	BorderStyle	Ridge
txtEmpID	DataBinder	EmpID
	TabIndex	0
txtLastName	DataBinder	LastName
	TabIndex	1
txtFirstName	DataBinder	FirstName
	TabIndex	2
txtAddress	DataBinder	Address
	TabIndex	3
txtCity	DataBinder	City
	TabIndex	4
txtState	DataBinder	State
	TabIndex	5
txtZipCode	DataBinder	ZipCode
	TabIndex	6
txtHomePhone	Text	Home Phone:
	TabIndex	7
txtPayRate	DataBinder	PayRate
	TabIndex	8
btnFirst	Text	First
btnPrevious	Text	Previous
btnNext	Text	Next
btnLast	Text	Last

The form's primary features are the text boxes for displaying field data and the buttons for navigating the dataset. The pseudocode for the application's functionality is shown in Table 10.5.

Table 10.5: *Pseudocode for the Web Forms Address Book application*

Event Procedure	Action
btnFirst	Displays the first record in the dataset. Disables the *btnFirst* and *btnPrevious* controls.
btnPrevious	Displays the previous record in the dataset.
btnNext	Displays the next record in the dataset.
btnLast	Displays the last record in the dataset. Disables the btnNext and btnLast controls.

Now that you have created the planning documents for the application, you are ready to begin designing the user interface in the IDE.

Design the User Interface

If you have not launched Visual Studio.NET, do so now. Use the Start Page to set the Profile to Visual Studio Developer. Perform each task that follows to complete this application.

To create a new Web Forms project:

1. Click **File, New, Project**. The **New Project** Dialog box appears.
2. Select **ASP.NET Web Application** as the project template, and type `Address_Book` as the name for the project.
3. Use the scroll bar in the Solution Explorer Tool window to display the name of the form, which is *WebForm1.aspx*.
4. Right-click the current name and select **Properties**.
5. Use the Name row to rename the form as `Address_Book.aspx`.
6. Right-click inside the Design window, and select **Properties** from the context menu. The **DOCUMENT Property Pages** dialog box appears.
7. Change the Page title from WebForm1 to `Address Book`, and click **OK**.
8. Click **Project, Add Existing Item**. The **Add Existing Item—Address_Book** dialog box appears.
9. Navigate to the location where the data files for this chapter are stored.
10. Click the **Files of Type:** drop-down list in the dialog box, and select **Image Files**.
11. Select the *AB_Logo.jpg* image and click **Open**, as shown in Figure 10.39.

FIGURE 10.39. *Adding an image file to an ASP.NET solution*

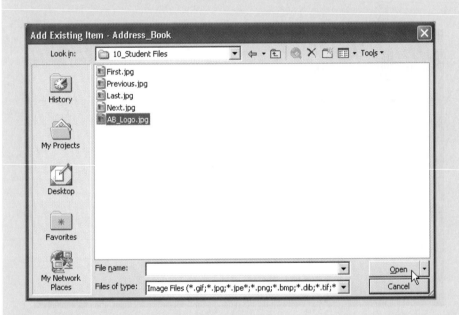

The image now appears in the Solution Explorer. You will display this image in the Image control on the form.

12. Save your changes.

You are now ready to create the user interface by adding the controls listed in Table 10.4.

To add Web Server controls to the form:

1. Move the pointer over the Toolbox icon to display it. Click the pushpin to lock the Toolbox.
2. Click the **Web Forms** tab in the Toolbox.
3. Drag an Image control from the Toolbox to the form. Set the ID of the control to `imgLogo`.
4. Click the **ImageURL** row in the Properties for this control. An ellipsis button will appear.

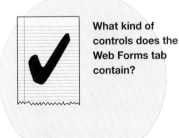

What kind of controls does the Web Forms tab contain?

5. Click the Ellipsis button to locate the image file for the control. The **Select Image** dialog box appears.

6. Select the *AB_Logo.jpg* image file and click **OK**, as shown in Figure 10.40.

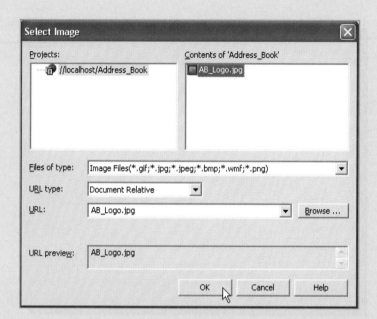

FIGURE 10.40. *Adding an existing image to the project*

7. The image is now displayed in the control. Resize the control as necessary.

8. Add each additional control in Table 10.4 to the form. Set the object properties as specified.

9. Close all tool windows currently displayed in the Web Forms Designer window.

10. Use the pointer to select all objects on the form.

11. Click **Format**, **Align** and select **To Grid**, as shown in Figure 10.41. After aligning the controls, click on an empty portion of the form to deselect the controls.

Remember to set the Font property of all controls to Tahoma.

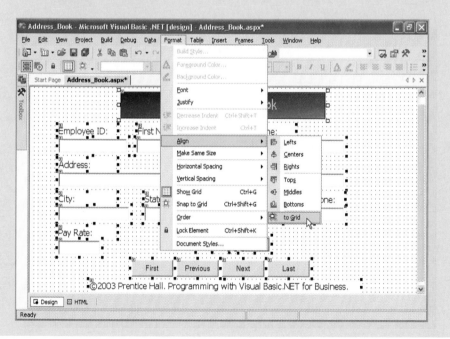

FIGURE 10.41. *Aligning the controls on the form*

12. Make any additional adjustments to the position of the controls, and then save your changes. Your form should now contain the controls shown in Figure 10.42.

FIGURE 10.42. *The Web form and its controls*

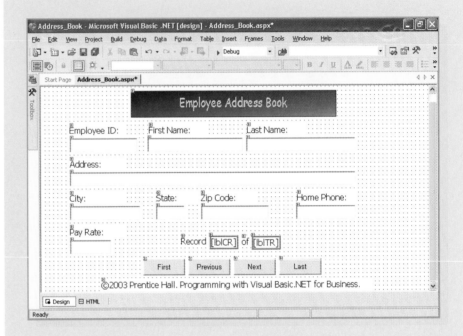

Before you can write the code that adds functionality to the application, the form requires three data objects to connect it to the back-end database: a Data Connection object, a Data Adapter object, and a Dataset object. Because the form will display records from an Access database, you will create OleDbConnection and OleDbDataAdpater objects on the form.

To create the OleDBConnection and OleDBDataAdapter objects:

1. Move the pointer over the Server Explorer tab to display the Server Explorer tool window.
2. Expand the tree for the connection, and click the *Payroll.mdb* connection.
3. Expand the list for the Tables until the *Employees* table is visible in the connection.
4. Drag the *Employees* table from the Server Explorer window to your form, as shown in Figure 10.43.

If this connection does not exist, refer to page 241 in Chapter 6 for the steps required to create a new data connection.

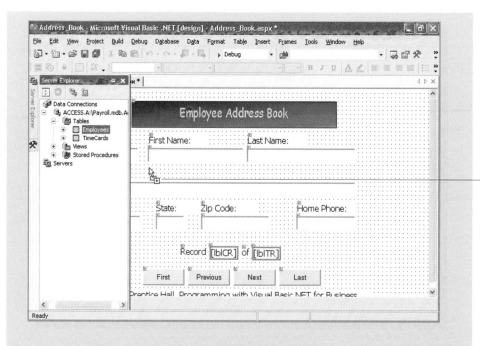

FIGURE 10.43. *Dragging a table onto the form*

Table object being dragged unto the form

Visual Studio.NET adds the **OleDbConnection1** and **OleDbDataAdapter1** objects to the form's component tray.

5. Display the Solution Explorer and Properties windows and save your changes.

To generate the dataset:

Now that the form contains the data connection and data adapter objects, you are ready to generate the dataset.

1. Click the **OleDbDataAdapter1** control in the component tray to select it.
2. Click **Data**, **Generate Dataset**. The **Generate Dataset** dialog box appears.
3. Select the option to create a new dataset, and make sure the option to add the dataset to the designer is checked.
4. Click **OK**. A new dataset named *DataSet11* is added to the component tray, as shown in Figure 10.44.

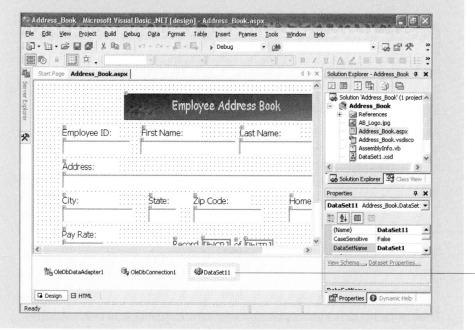

FIGURE 10.44. *The dataset appearing in the component tray*

Dataset added to the component tray

How can you preview the data in the dataset?

5. Click the **Save All** button to save your changes.

Now that the interface design for the Employee Address Book application is complete, you are ready to write the code providing the functionality.

Write the Code

Your first task is to add comments to the Code Editor and then define the procedures for loading the page and performing the data binding. Then you will write the code for navigating through the dataset by using the buttons on the form.

To add comments to the application:

1. Press F7 to display the Code Editor. If the **Web Form Designer Generated Code** region is expanded, collapse it.
2. Place the insertion point at the beginning of the Code Editor.
3. Type the following comments:

```
'©2003 Prentice Hall
'By [Enter your name]
'Created/Revised: [Enter the date]
'Employee Address Book Web Forms Application
```

4. Place the insertion point immediately below the **Inherits System.Web.UI.Page** statement, and type the following variable declarations:

```
'Declare variables used for record navigation
    Public intPosition As Integer
    Public intCurrentRecord As Integer
    Public intTotalRecords As Integer
```

To initialize the page:

1. Scroll to the bottom of the Code Editor until the statement **'Put user code to initialize the page here** is visible.
2. Type the following statements after this comment and before the End Sub statement:

```
Me.OleDbDataAdapter1.Fill(Me.DataSet11.Employees)
        Me.DataBind()

        If Me.IsPostBack Then
            Me.DataSet11 = CType(ViewState("Dataset1"),
                DataSet)
            Me.intPosition = CType(ViewState("Position"),
                Integer)
        Else
            Me.OleDbDataAdapter1.Fill(Me.DataSet11.Employees)
            ViewState("Dataset1") = Me.DataSet11
            ViewState("Position") = 0
        End If
```

```
'Set the value of the counter variable for total
  records and initialize the label
intTotalRecords = Me.DataSet11.Employees.Count
lblTotalRecords.Text = intTotalRecords
```

Notice that the first statement uses the Me keyword. The **Me keyword** behaves like an object variable referring to the current instance of a class. When a class can have more than one instance, **Me** provides a way to refer to the specific instance of the class where the code is currently executing. These statements store the dataset with the page when it is loaded and also set the value of the *intPosition* variable, which determines the current record displayed in the form. The counter variables are also initialized. You use the **Count** method to set the *intTotalRecords* value. The *intCurrentRecord* value will always be one more than the value of the **intPosition** property.

To bind controls to the dataset at run time:

1. Select (**Base Class Events**) in the Control Name drop-down list, and then select **DataBinding** in the Method Name drop-down list. Visual Studio adds an event handler to the Code Editor.
2. Type the following statements for the procedure:

```
'Declare a variable for the data row
Dim dr As DataRow
dr =
   Me.DataSet11.Employees.DefaultView(intPosition).Row

'Bind the values in the columns of the dataset to the
  text box controls
Me.txtEmpID.Text = DataBinder.Eval(dr, "EmpID")
Me.txtFirstName.Text = DataBinder.Eval(dr, "FirstName")
Me.txtLastName.Text = DataBinder.Eval(dr, "LastName")
Me.txtAddress.Text = DataBinder.Eval(dr, "Address")
Me.txtCity.Text = DataBinder.Eval(dr, "City")
Me.txtState.Text = DataBinder.Eval(dr, "State")
Me.txtZipCode.Text = DataBinder.Eval(dr, "ZipCode")
Me.txtHomePhone.Text = DataBinder.Eval(dr, "HomePhone")
Me.txtPayRate.Text = DataBinder.Eval(dr, "PayRate",
  "{0:C}")

'Set the value of the counter variable for the current
  record and initialize the label
intCurrentRecord = intPosition + 1
lblCurrentRecord.Text = intCurrentRecord

'Initialize the Enabled property of the buttons, based
  upon the current position in the dataset
If Me.intPosition = 0 Then
    btnFirst.Enabled = False
    btnPrevious.Enabled = False
Else
    btnFirst.Enabled = True
    btnPrevious.Enabled = True
End If
```

In Chapter 6 you learned how to bind control on a form to a specific data member in a data set using the DataBindings property. Web forms controls also use the DataBindings property to specify which member in a dataset the control will display. You can set the DataBindings property at design time by setting this property, or at run time by including code statements that bind the controls.

Why is the value of *intCurrentRecord* one more than the value of intPosition? The position value for the dataset is zero-based, so the number for the current record is always one more than the index value.

```
           If Me.intPosition = Me.DataSet11.Employees.Count - 1
             Then
                 btnNext.Enabled = False
                 btnLast.Enabled = False
           Else
                 btnNext.Enabled = True
                 btnLast.Enabled = True
           End If
```

The first statements declare a local variable named *dr* to store the data row value and assign the appropriate row in the dataset as its value. The next series of statements bind each text box control to the appropriate columns in the dataset, which is bound to the *Employees* table. Then the procedure determines the current record and sets the value of the counter variable to display the appropriate current record in the label on the form. The procedure concludes with two IF statements to determine the Enabled state of the navigation buttons, based on the current row in the dataset.

Now that you have written the procedures for initializing the page and binding the controls to the dataset, you are ready to write the procedures for moving through the records in the dataset.

The data binding statement for the Pay Rate field includes "{0:C}" in the statement. This formats the field as currency.

To write procedures to navigate among records:

1. Create a procedure for the **btnFirst_Click** event. Type the following code for the procedure:

```
Me.intPosition = 0
ViewState("Position") = Me.intPosition
DataBind()
```

This procedure sets the current row of the dataset to zero, the position value of the first record.

2. Create a procedure for the **btnLast_Click** event. Type the following code for the procedure:

```
Me.intPosition = intTotalRecords - 1
ViewState("Position") = Me.intPosition
DataBind()
```

Because the application views the records but does not add to the dataset, the number of records remains constant. Therefore, the procedure can use the *intTotalRecords* value, less one, to determine which record is the last record in the dataset.

3. Create a procedure for the **btnPrevious_Click** event. Type the following code for the procedure:

```
If Me.intPosition > 0 Then
    Me.intPosition -= 1
    ViewState("Position") = Me.intPosition
    DataBind()
End If
```

This procedure checks the current position to make sure the form is not currently displaying the first record. The procedure then sets the position value to one less than the current value to display the previous record in the dataset.

4. Create a procedure for the **btnNext_Click** event. Type the following code for the procedure:

```
If Me.intPosition < Me.DataSet11.Employees.Count Then
    Me.intPosition += 1
    ViewState("Position") = Me.intPosition
    DataBind()
End If
```

This procedure checks the current position to make sure the form is not currently displaying the last record. The procedure then sets the position value to one more than the current value to display the next record in the dataset.

5. Save your changes.

Run the Application

You are now ready to run the Employee Address Book application and test its functionality.

To run the application:

1. Click the Start button or press the ⌷F5⌷ key to run the application.
2. If the database is found, the form displays the first record in the database, which is the record for Laura Carr.
3. Test the **First** and **Last** navigation buttons, taking note of which buttons are hidden as you navigate through the dataset.
4. Test the **Previous** and **Next** navigation buttons, taking note of which buttons are hidden as you navigate through the dataset.
5. When you finish testing the application, close your Web browser.

Summary

- Visual Studio.NET uses ASP.NET for developing Web Forms projects. You can use the IDE to create Web forms in the same way you create Windows forms. The same visual tools for developing Windows applications are available for Web Forms projects. To create a Web Forms project, you add controls to a form and then write code to provide the program's functionality. Because Web Forms projects share the same IDE as Windows applications, you can use the same development tools for your Web Forms projects.

- Prior to ASP.NET, many Web applications used client-side scripting to add interactivity to Web pages. Client-side scripting embeds program code in the HTML that defines a page. Visual Studio.NET and the ASP.NET framework support code-behind scripting, which means that the HTML defines the interface and the code providing interactivity is stored in a different file. This simplifies program development, because the interface design and program code are independent.

- You can add controls to a form in either Design layout or HTML layout. To add a control to a form in either view, drag the control from the Toolbox to the form. In Design Layout, you can reposition and resize the control. You can switch to HTML layout to review the HTML text that defines the control.

- Visual Studio.NET supports HTML, HTML Server, and Web Server controls. HTML controls use client-side scripting to send information to the server. Although supported in Visual Studio.NET, HTML controls are not visible to the server. HTML Server controls are HTML controls that are visible to the server. You can convert an HTML control to an HTML Server control by specifying that the control should be run as a server control. Web Server controls provide the most functionality in Visual Basic.NET Web Forms projects. These are rich controls with properties for changing the appearance and functionality of the control.

- To create a Visual Basic.NET Web Forms project, you must have Internet Information Services (IIS) and the .NET framework installed on your computer. You can then create Web Forms projects in almost the same way that you create Windows form projects: by using the IDE to add controls to the form and the Code Editor to write the procedures that provide functionality to the application.

- You can use data validation controls in Web Forms projects to validate user input at the client and minimize calls made to the server.

- Web Forms projects support ADO.NET objects to bind Web Server controls to databases. You can bind Web Server controls to database fields at design time by setting the DataBindings property for the control. To bind a control at run time, use the DataBinding method in the Page Load event to bind controls to specific data rows in the data set.

Key Terms

ASP.NET	HTML controls
AutoFormat	HTML Server controls
client	HTML view
client-server computing model	Hypertext Markup Language
client-side scripting	IsPostBack keyword
code-behind scripting	Markup language
CompareValidator	Me keyword
CustomValidator	Page_Load event
Design view	postback event
FlowLayout mode	Property Builder
glyph	RangeValidator
GridLayout mode	RegularExpressionValidator
HTML	RequiredFieldValidator

rich controls

Runat attribute

self-service application

validation control

Web application

Web browser

Web document

Web Forms pages

Web server

Web Server controls

Windows application

Study Questions

Multiple-Choice Questions

1. Which of the following controls might be considered a rich control?
   a. Text box
   b. DataGrid
   c. Label
   d. ListBox
   e. Panel

2. An ASP.NET Web Forms interface is defined by using:
   a. Code-behind scripting
   b. The Windows Form Designer
   c. A Data Connection object
   d. RTF
   e. SGML

3. Which controls use code-behind scripting?
   a. HTML controls
   b. HTML Server controls
   c. Web Server controls
   d. A and B
   e. B and C

4. Which of the following Web Server controls does not have an HTML control counterpart?
   a. Text box
   b. Label
   c. DataGrid
   d. Button
   e. Table

5. Which keyword behaves like an object variable referring to the current instance of a class?
   a. Me
   b. Postback
   c. IsPostBack
   d. Position
   e. Count

6. Which of the following statements is false?
   a. A DataGrid control displays records from a dataset.
   b. A DataSet object requires a DataAdapter and a DataConnection object.
   c. Controls on a Web form can be bound to specific columns of a dataset.
   d. Web forms do not support disconnected datasets.
   e. Web forms do not support connected recordsets.

7. Which kind of control checks data on a form before it is sent to the server?
   a. Data
   b. HTML
   c. Validation
   d. Web Server
   e. Text box

8. Which of the following best describes the architecture of Visual Basic.NET Web Forms applications?
   a. Stand-alone client
   b. Client-server
   c. Client-server with processing with functionality supported by client-side scripting
   d. A and B
   e. B and C

9. Which of the following controls has a property to specify a URL?
   a. Text box
   b. DataGrid
   c. Label
   d. RangeValidator
   e. Image

10. Which property of a Web Server ListBox control determines what is displayed in the list's item collection?
    a. ID
    b. Value
    c. Text
    d. DataSource
    e. DataTextField

True/False Questions

1. You can add controls to a Web form in either Design mode or HTML mode.

2. HTML controls use code-behind scripting.

3. A validation control works in conjunction with a Web Server or HTML Server control.

4. You can add an OleDbDataAdapter to a Web form.

5. ADO.NET Data connection objects support read-only but not read-write capabilities.

Short Answer Questions

1. How do client-side and code-behind Web-development technologies differ?

2. What are three key advantages to using ASP.NET to develop your Web applications?

3. How do HTML controls, HTML Server controls, and Web Server controls differ?

4. How can you perform client-side data validation in Web Forms projects?

5. How do you bind a DataGrid Web Server control to a data source?

Guided Exercises

Creating a Mileage Conversion Web Forms Application

Many businesses have offices in locations around the world. For business travelers who use rental cars, a mileage conversion calculator is helpful when filling out expense reports. Create a Web Forms version of the Mileage Conversion application you created in Chapter 1. The completed Web Forms application is shown in Figure 10.45.

FIGURE 10.45. *The Mileage Conversion Web form*

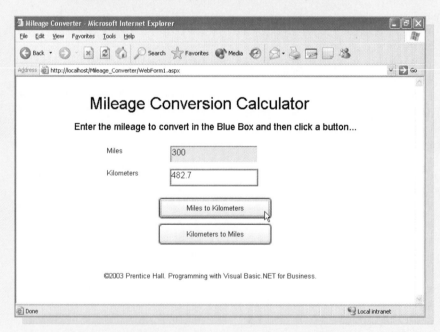

To create a Mileage Conversion Web form:

1. Launch Visual Studio.NET if it is not already running.
2. Click **File**, **New Project**. Create a new Web form named `Mileage_Conversion`. Because this is a Web Forms project, Visual Studio chooses the location.
3. Set the title of the page to `Mileage Converter`.
4. Using Figure 10.45 as a guide, add the appropriate controls to the form.
5. Add the following comments in the Code Editor:

```
'©2003 Prentice Hall
'By [Enter your name here...]
'Created/Revised: [Enter the date here...]
Mileage Conversion Web Forms Application
```

6. Using the following conversion factors, write the code for the buttons that perform the conversions:

$$Miles\ to\ Kilometers = Miles * 1.609$$

$$Kilometers\ to\ Miles = Kilometers * 0.621$$

7. Run and test the application.
8. Close your Web browser, and make any necessary changes to the application.
9. Save your changes, and close the solution.

Creating a Web Form for Displaying Inventory Records

Web forms are useful for displaying data to be viewed but not changed. In this exercise you will create a Web Forms project for viewing inventory records. The form displays records from the *Products.mdb* database that is included with the data files for this chapter. The completed Web Forms application is shown in Figure 10.46.

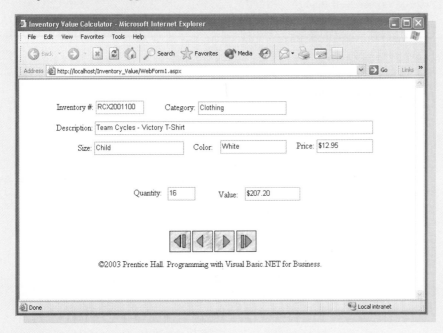

FIGURE 10.46. *Web form for viewing inventory records*

To create an Inventory Web form:

1. Launch Visual Studio.NET if it is not already running.
2. Click **File**, **New Project**. Create a new Web form named *Inventory_Value*. Set the title of the page to `Inventory Value Calculator`.
3. Using Figure 10.46 as a guide, add the following controls to the form that are bound to the related data elements:

Label	Text Box	Corresponding Field
lblID	txtID	item_id
lblCategory	txtCategory	item_category
lblDescription	txtDescription	item_description
lblColor	txtColor	item_color
lblSize	txtSize	item_size
lblPrice	txtPrice	item_price
lblQuantity	txtQuantity	item_quantity
lblValue	txtValue	Calculated quantity (item_price*item_quantity)

4. Use a Web Forms **ImageButton** control for the navigation buttons. You can use the **ImageButton** control to add a button to a Web form that contains a graphic, as shown previously in Figure 10.46. Name the buttons *imgbtnFirst*, *imgbtnPrevious*, *imgbtnNext*, and *imgbtnLast*, respectively.

5. Four image files are included with your data files, and you will assign an image to each of the ImgButton controls. The image file names are *First.jpg*, *Previous.jpg*, *Next.jpg*, and *Last.jpg*. Add each of these items to the project, and then set the **ImageURL** property of each button to display the appropriate image.

6. Use the Server Explorer to create a new data connection to the *Inventory.mdb* database.

7. Drag the *Inventory* table from the data connection to the form to create the data connection and data adapter objects.

8. Generate a dataset for the form.

9. Add the following code to the project:

Comments:

```
'©2003 Prentice Hall
'By [Enter your name here. . .]
'Created/Revised: [Enter the date here. . .]
'Inventory Value Web Forms Application
```

Variable Declaration:

```
Public intPosition As Integer
```

Page Load Event:

```
Private Sub Page_Load(ByVal sender As System.Object, ByVal e As
    System.EventArgs) Handles MyBase.Load
    Put user code to initialize the page here
            Me.OleDbDataAdapter1.Fill(Me.DataSet11.Inventory)
            Me.DataBind()
        If Me.IsPostBack Then
            Me.DataSet11 = CType(ViewState("Dataset1"),
                DataSet)
            Me.intPosition = CType(ViewState("Position"),
                Integer)
        Else
            Me.OleDbDataAdapter1.Fill(Me.DataSet11.Inventory)
            ViewState("Dataset1") = Me.DataSet11
            ViewState("Position") = 0
        End If
End Sub
```

(Base Overrides) DataBinding Event:

```vb
Private Sub Page_DataBinding(ByVal sender As Object, ByVal e As
  System.EventArgs) Handles MyBase.DataBinding
      'Declare a variable for the data row
      Dim dr As DataRow
      dr =
        Me.DataSet11.Inventory.DefaultView(intPosition).Row

      'Bind the values in the columns of the dataset to the
        text box controls
      Me.txtID.Text = DataBinder.Eval(dr, "item_id")
      Me.txtCategory.Text = DataBinder.Eval(dr,
        "item_category")
      Me.txtDescription.Text = DataBinder.Eval(dr,
        "item_description")
      Me.txtColor.Text = DataBinder.Eval(dr, "item_color")
      Me.txtSize.Text = DataBinder.Eval(dr, "item_size")
      Me.txtPrice.Text = DataBinder.Eval(dr, "item_price",
        "{0:C}")
      Me.txtQuantity.Text = DataBinder.Eval(dr,
        "item_quantity")

      'Declare variables to calculate and display the value
        of the inventory item
      Dim intQuantity As Integer
      Dim sngPrice As Single
      Me.txtValue.Text = Format(CInt(txtQuantity.Text) *
        Csng(txtPrice.Text), "Currency")
End Sub
```

Button Click Events:

```vb
Private Sub imgbtnFirst_Click(ByVal sender As Object, ByVal
  e As System.Web.UI.ImageClickEventArgs) Handles
  imgbtnFirst.Click
    Me.intPosition = 0
    ViewState("Position") = Me.intPosition
    DataBind()
End Sub

Private Sub imgbtnLast_Click(ByVal sender As Object, ByVal e
  As System.Web.UI.ImageClickEventArgs) Handles
  imgbtnLast.Click
    Me.intPosition = Me.DataSet11.Inventory.Count - 1
    ViewState("Position") = Me.intPosition
    DataBind()
End Sub
```

```
Private Sub imgbtnPrevious_Click(ByVal sender As Object,
   ByVal e As System.Web.UI.ImageClickEventArgs) Handles
   imgbtnPrevious.Click
      If Me.intPosition > 0 Then
          Me.intPosition -= 1
          ViewState("Position") = Me.intPosition
          DataBind()
      End If
End Sub

Private Sub imgbtnNext_Click(ByVal sender As Object, ByVal e
   As System.Web.UI.ImageClickEventArgs) Handles
   imgbtnNext.Click
      If Me.intPosition < Me.DataSet11.Inventory.Count Then
          Me.intPosition += 1
          ViewState("Position") = Me.intPosition
          DataBind()
      End If
End Sub
```

10. Run and test the application.

11. Close your Web browser, and make any necessary changes to the application.

12. Save your changes, and close the solution.

Case Studies

Creating a Web Form for Calculating Payroll Withholding

In Chapter 9 you created a Windows application for calculating payroll withholding. Now create a Web Forms version of the project. Name the project Payroll. Add text boxes on the form for obtaining the employee's name, hourly pay rate, payroll date, and hours worked. Return in a label on the Web form the gross pay, total taxes, other deductions, and net pay. Use the following conditions to determine taxes and withholding:

1. Gross pay is calculated as total hours for the period multiplied by the pay rate.

2. Pay rate must be at least $6.25 but not greater than $25.

3. Hours worked may not exceed 80.

4. Union fees are 1.5% of gross income.

5. Federal tax is 15% of gross pay.

6. FICA and Medicare taxes are 13.5% of gross income.

7. State tax is 4% of gross income.

Add validation controls to the form to validate the pay rate and hours worked.

Creating a Web Form for Calculating Shipping Costs

Self-service Web forms are useful for allowing customers to make decisions before completing the sale of items available on the Web. Create a Web Forms project named Shipping_Costs that calculates the total shipping costs for orders placed over the Web. The form will contain three radio buttons for three kinds of shipping: Ground, Second Day Air, and Next Day Air. The company ships to four zones in the United States: West, Midwest, East, and Alaska/Hawaii. The user selects a zone by using a list box. The fees for shipping depend on the amount of the sale and the zone, as follows:

	West (1)	Midwest (2)	East (3)	Alaska/Hawaii (4)
Ground	Amount*.04	Amount*.045	Amount*.055	Amount*.06
2nd Day	Amount*.06	Amount*.065	Amount*.85	Amount*.09
Next Day	Amount*.08	Amount*.085	Amount *.105	Amount*.125

Store the shipping rates in an array. Add validation controls to validate the amount of the sale as greater than zero and less than $1,000. Return the shipping rate in a label on the form by returning values from the array.

XML and ADO.NET

In business environments, applications need to exchange data in order to integrate with one another. Extensible Markup Language (XML) is the data format the .NET framework uses to store data. Visual Studio.NET is XML-based and uses XML as the native format for displaying and describing data. Visual Basic.NET uses XML as a technology for providing a cost-effective method for integrating data. The Internet provides the infrastructure on which the .NET framework can share information. ADO.NET is Microsoft's new technology for connecting Visual Studio.NET applications to remote data sources. In this chapter, you will learn why the .NET framework uses XML to integrate data, how to structure XML data sources by using the XML Designer, and how to use XML with ADO.NET for representing data in Visual Basic.NET applications.

Performance Objectives

At the conclusion of this chapter, you will be able to:

- Understand why using XML is important in today's business applications.
- Describe how the generalized Extensible Markup Language (XML) differs from other common specific markup languages.
- Describe the characteristics of XML.
- Create an XML file by using the XML Designer.
- Create an application that reads data from an XML file.
- Create an application that writes data to an XML file.
- Understand XML schemas, including elements, attributes, data types, and naming conventions.
- Create an XML schema from an XML file by using the XML Designer.
- Add elements to a schema.
- Associate a schema with an XML file.
- Create relationships between schemas.
- Create an application that displays data from an external XML file.

Why Use XML?

When you think of how businesses need to share information with one another and with customers on a daily basis, you can appreciate the complexity of integrating all the data necessary to support business transactions. Businesses have relationships both with customers and with suppliers. Transactions between a business and a customer, such as selling a product, are called business-to-customer (B-to-C) transactions. When a business orders its materials or supplies from other businesses (suppliers), it is called a business-to-business (B-to-B) transaction. The process of obtaining the materials required to manufacture or produce a product is known as procurement.

Assume you are a retailer needing to place an order with one or more suppliers so your products are available to customers when they request them. One way is to place your order with a supplier by using the telephone or by sending a fax order. After you fax the order, the supplier's sales or customer service representative needs to transcribe your order into the company's business processes for fulfillment. The supplier's sales representative needs to verify that the items are in stock, your credit is acceptable, and the products can be selected in the warehouse and then shipped. Many businesses procure inventory and supplies in this manner. The B-to-B transaction has a real person (the sales representative) as a key component in completing the transaction. As with any process that involves manual steps, there is potential for error. Likewise, a sales representative who receives too many orders at one time might delay your order.

Automating the sales order and fulfillment processes by using computers seems like a good solution to this scenario. However, getting to the point where your computer system can integrate with the supplier's system so you can place an order with them requires negotiation, coordination, and expense. As the number of suppliers increases, the cost of integration with every supplier might also increase. A business needs a sufficient number of orders to justify these costs. Figure 11.1 shows the challenge of integrating a computer system with the systems of multiple suppliers.

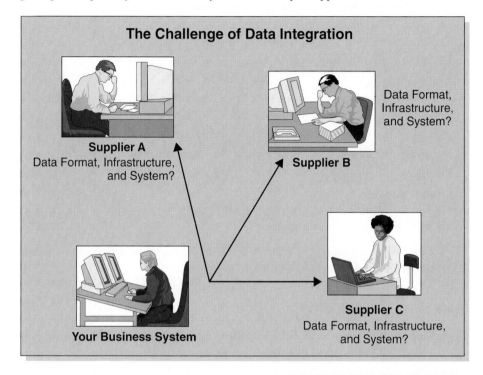

FIGURE 11.1. *Integrating B-to-B transactions*

Before the Internet, two companies doing business electronically would need a Local Area or Wide Area Network (LAN or WAN) connecting their computers to integrate data and business processes. In addition, all the computers that send transactions back and forth on the network would need a common way of representing the data and would need to use the same programs for managing sales and inventory. For a transaction to be successful, the sending computer must represent the data and instructions in a format that the receiving computer can understand.

The Internet provides a common infrastructure for the two computers to communicate, but this solves only half the problem of integration. Extensible Markup Language (XML) is the answer to the other half of this problem of how to represent the data and instructions in a common format. Figure 11.2 shows a primary goal of XML in Visual Studio.NET: to provide a data structure format that enables computers to integrate data, using the Internet as a common infrastructure.

FIGURE 11.2. *Integrating B-to-B*
transactions by using XML

FIGURE 11.2. *Integrating B-to-B transactions by using XML*

Before discussing more about the structure of XML, we will first review a few concepts related to markup languages.

MARKUP LANGUAGES

As you learned in Chapter 6, ***Extensible Markup Language (XML)*** is a tag-based language for storing data in a way that also describes the structure of the data. XML shares certain characteristics with other markup languages.

Rich Text File Markup

In Chapter 5, you learned about ***Rich Text Format (RTF)*** documents. RTF is a file format that uses markup tags to text to change the text displays. Many applications are able to interpret these tags and display the text appropriately. Figure 11.3 shows how a simple RTF document appears in the text editor you created in Chapter 5.

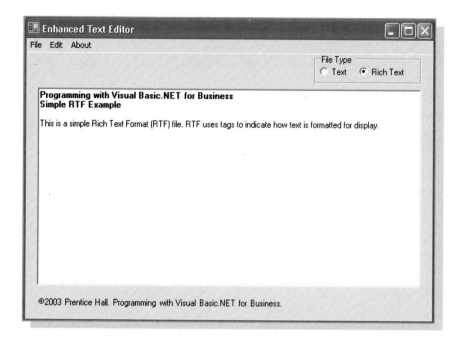

FIGURE 11.3. *RTF document as it appears in a text editor*

With most text editors, you can open an RTF document as text and see the tags that produce the formatting. The marked-up text for this document is as follows:

```
{\rtf1\ansi\ansicpg1252\deff0\deflang1033{\fonttbl{\f0\fnil\fcha
  rset0 Microsoft Sans Serif;}}
{\colortbl ;\red0\green0\blue0;}
\viewkind4\uc1\pard\cf1\b\f0\fs17 Programming with Visual
  Basic.NET for Business\par
Simple RTF Example\par
\cf0\b0\par
This is a simple Rich Text Format (RTF) file. RTF uses tags to
  indicate how text is formatted for display. \par
}
```

The tags consist of various characters that follow a specific syntax interpreted by the application used to open the file. RTF does not determine how a document is structured, but only how the text will be displayed.

Hypertext Markup Language

In Chapter 10 you learned to create a simple Web page by using ***Hypertext Markup Language (HTML)***. HTML also uses tags to define how a Web page is displayed when opened with a Web browser. Figure 11.4 shows the Web page from Chapter 10 as an example of how a Web browser displays HTML.

FIGURE 11.4. *Web browser displaying HTML*

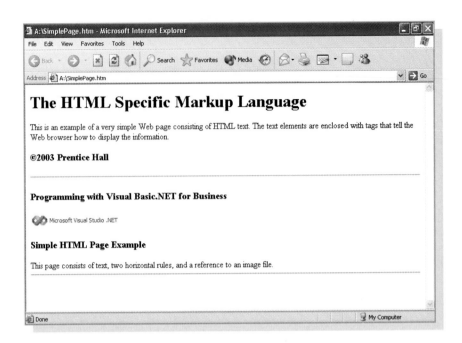

Because HTML is text that includes tags, you can view any HTML document by using a text editor. These tags tell the Web browser how to format this document. The marked up text for this document is as follows:

```
<HTML>
    <BODY>
        <H1>The HTML Specific Markup Language</H1>
        This is an example of a very simple Web page consisting
            of HTML text. The text elements are enclosed with
            tags that tell the Web browser how to display the
            information.
    <BR>
        <H3>©2003 Prentice Hall</H3>
        <HR>
        <H3>Programming with Visual Basic.NET for Business</H3>
        <IMG SRC="VSLogo.jpg" width="179" height="29">
        <H3>Simple HTML Page Example</H3>
        This page consists of text, two horizontal rules, and a
            reference to an image file.
        <HR>
    </BODY>
</HTML>
```

RTF and HTML are examples of specific markup languages. A *specific markup language* is a markup language that accomplishes a specific purpose. HTML has the purpose of formatting documents for the Web; RTF formats text. Because each language has a specific purpose, they are not interchangeable. Therefore, text that is marked with RTF tags will not display in a Web browser, which only interprets HTML. Likewise, an RTF editor will not display HTML the same way a Web browser does, but will merely display the text and the markup tags.

XML derives from another markup language called the ***Standard Generalized Markup Language (SGML)***. SGML is a ***generalized markup language***. Generalized markup languages define the structure and meaning of the text in a document without specifying how the text should be used. Generalized markup languages do not support a specific purpose and are generic enough to be used in a variety of applications. Therefore, XML is the perfect data platform on which to build data integration using the Internet as the common infrastructure.

If you are new to programming and Visual Studio.NET, you are unlikely to develop projects that perform data integration. The goal of this chapter is to expose you to XML as the data integration platform in the .NET framework. To understand the role of XML in Visual Basic programming, we will focus on creating XML components and using these components in simple applications.

Characteristics of XML

If you have worked with HTML, XML will look familiar to you. XML is a subset of SGML that is designed specifically to send data over the Internet. You create XML documents (also called files) by using tags to define the structure of data to support data exchange among computer systems. XML documents are ***self-describing***, meaning that the document contains both data and information about the data's structure. HTML and RTF contain tags that indicate how the data is displayed, without any concern for the structure of the information. XML contains tags that specify how the data is structured.

XML can also represent structured data, such as field and record information about employees. An XML file containing information for two employees might look like this:

```
<Employee>
    <lastname>Smith</lastname>
    <firstname>William</firstname>
    <payrate>20.25</payrate>
</Employee>
<Employee>
    <lastname>Severson</lastname>
    <firstname>Gloria</firstname>
    <payrate>20.5</payrate>
</Employee>
```

XML uses tags to differentiate the data contained in the file. XML terms each unique piece of information an ***element***. Elements are enclosed within a ***start-tag*** and an ***end-tag***. The start-tag is designated by the less-than symbol (<), the name of the element, and a greater than symbol (>). The end-tag uses the less-than symbol (<), the name of the element, and a forward-slash and greater-than symbol together (/>). These tags enclose each element in the file. In the preceding example, the following is designated as a *LastName* element:

```
<lastname>Smith</lastname>
```

Elements can contain other elements, as shown in the following example, which includes three elements (last name, first name, and pay rate) for one employee element:

```
<Employee>
    <lastname>Severson</lastname>
    <firstname>Gloria</firstname>
    <payrate>20.5</payrate>
</Employee>
```

XML tags define the structure of an XML document or file. You can define as many XML elements as required by your application. XML is a flexible standard that has been widely adopted. The advantage of XML is that it separates the user interface from the structured data. This separation of data from its presentation enables a system to integrate data from diverse sources. By standardizing on a specific XML data structure, a business can achieve data integration.

Now that you understand how XML represents data and the structure of data, let's learn how to create XML files by using the XML Designer.

Creating XML Files by Using the XML Designer

The Visual Studio.NET Integrated Development Environment (IDE) includes a tool called the ***XML Designer*** for working with XML files. You can use the XML Designer to create new XML files or, after adding existing XML files to a project, to view the structure and data in the file. To use the XML Designer to create an XML data file, you must first create a Visual Basic.NET project. Figure 11.5 shows the project we will use to demonstrate how to create XML files.

FIGURE 11.5. *A Visual Basic.NET project for demonstrating the XML Designer*

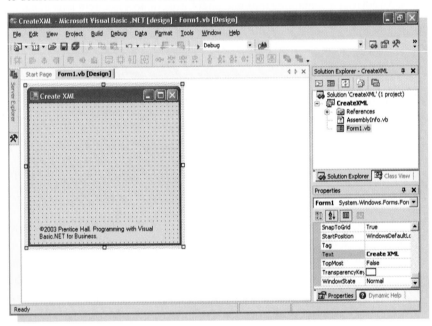

The project consists of a form that contains a label control. This project is in the *CreateXML* folder included with your data files for this chapter.

ADDING AN XML FILE TO A PROJECT

You can add an XML file to a project by clicking **File**, **New**, **File**. In the **New File** dialog box, select the **XML File** template and click **Open**, as shown in Figure 11.6.

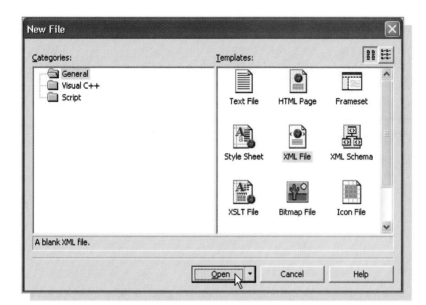

Visual Basic adds a tab named **XMLFile1** to the IDE. The following tagged text shows the XML structure and data you will add to the file. This should look familiar, because it contains the same information for two employees shown previously.

```xml
<?xml version="1.0" encoding="utf-8" ?>
<Employee>
<Employee>
    <lastname>Smith</lastname>
    <firstname>William</firstname>
    <payrate>20.25</payrate>
</Employee>
<Employee>
    <lastname>Severson</lastname>
    <firstname>Gloria</firstname>
    <payrate>20.5</payrate>
</Employee>
</Employee>
```

The XML Designer has features that assist you in creating XML files. To create a data element named *Employee*, place the insertion point below the statement that Visual Studio added to the window and type <Employee>. The IDE automatically adds the closing XML tag shown in Figure 11.7.

FIGURE 11.7. *Start and End XML tags created by the XML Designer*

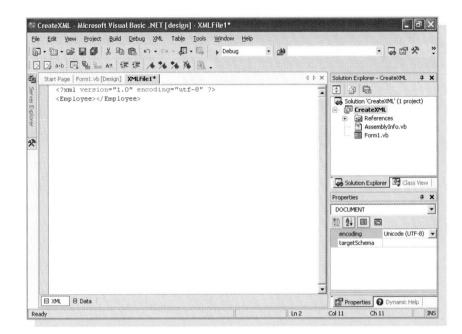

XML is case-sensitive. An element named "lastname" is different from an element named "LastName."

Press (↵Enter). Type <Employee> and press (↵Enter) again. The IDE adds the closing tag for the Employee element. Type <lastname>Smith.

Move the insertion point after the closing tag for the first name element and press (↵Enter). After you add each element for the two employees to the file, it should look like Figure 11.8.

FIGURE 11.8. *XML file displaying information for two employees*

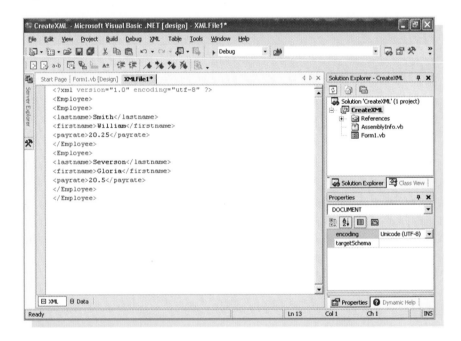

VALIDATING XML DATA

The XML Designer has a great feature for validating data you add to an XML file. Notice that two tabs appear at the bottom of the XML Designer window in the IDE. You can use *XML view* to enter the XML elements in the designer. Clicking the **Data** tab changes the Designer to *Data view*, which displays the XML data as it will appear without the tags. If the XML structure is correct, Data view will display the data in the grid shown in Figure 11.9.

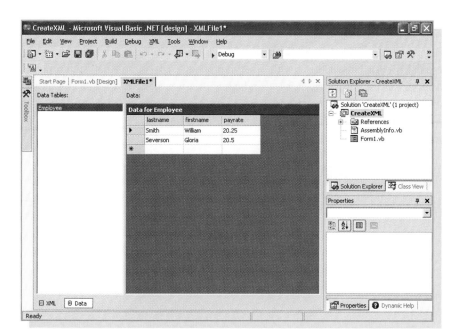

FIGURE 11.9. *Displaying a data grid in Data view*

How does the Designer validate data? If there are any inconsistencies in the structure of the XML file, a grid will not appear. For example, change the lastname element for William Smith as follows:

```
<LastName>Smith</lastname>
```

You can see that the opening tag for the element is incorrect because it contains uppercase characters and XML tags are case-specific. If you make this change to the data in XML view and then try to switch to Data view, you will receive the message in Figure 11.10.

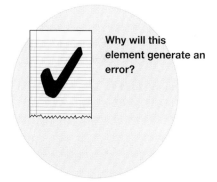

Why will this element generate an error?

FIGURE 11.10. *Message indicating an XML element contains an error*

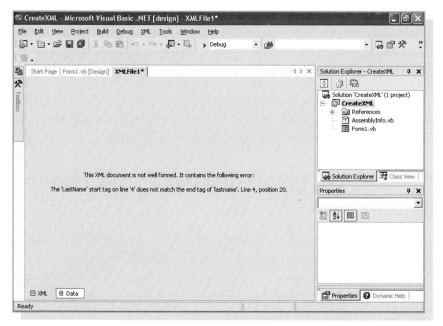

The message states that this is not a well-formed document. You will recall that an XML document contains data as well as information defining the structure of the data. A ***well-formed document*** is an XML file in which the data and the structure are consistent. One advantage of using the XML Designer for creating XML documents is that the Designer validates your XML data before you save it.

Notice the **XMLFile1** tab in Figures 11.8, 11.9, and 11.10 indicates that this file contains unsaved data.

SAVING XML DATA TO A FILE

After you have added an XML file to a Visual Basic.NET project, you can save it as an eternal file for later use. As with other components of your Visual Studio projects, an asterisk on the tab for the object indicates that you have not saved the most recent changes to the project.

To save an XML file, click **File**, **Save XMLFile1 As**. The **Save File As** dialog box in Figure 11.11 appears.

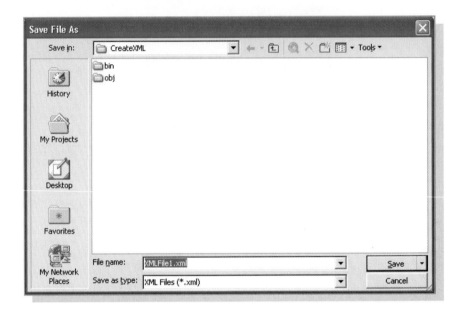

FIGURE 11.11. *Save File As dialog box for saving a file displayed in the XML Designer*

The default location for saving the file is the folder for the Visual Basic.NET project. In this example, you will save the file in the *bin* folder. The *bin* folder is the default data location for the project, and you will use this location in the next example. The default filename is the name given to the tab in the XML Designer when you added it to the project. In most cases, you will change the filename when you save it. To save this file, click the *bin* folder to open it and name the file `Employees.xml`. Then click the **Save** button.

As you can see, creating an XML file is relatively simple. Now that you know how to create XML files by using the XML Designer, we will demonstrate how to create a Visual Basic.NET application that reads data from an XML file.

Creating an Application that Reads Data from an XML File

As you will recall from Chapter 6, ADO.NET supports data access in the .NET framework. When you connect to an external database, you add Data Connection and Data Adapter objects to the project. You configure these objects so the disconnected dataset can read data from the external data source, modify the data, and write the data back to the data source. ADO.NET represents the data as XML in the dataset.

The .NET framework and ADO.NET support data from external sources in a variety of data formats. You can also use an XML file as the external source of data for your application. Figure 11.12 models the architecture for two data-access methods. The first method uses a relational database as the ADO.NET data source, and the second method uses an XML file as the ADO.NET data source.

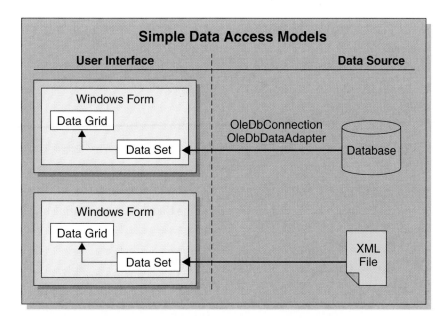

FIGURE 11.12. *Two data architectures for an ADO.NET data source*

Both methods model a Windows Form application interface that consists of a form with a dataset that populates a DataGrid control. The first method uses Data Connection and Data Adapter objects to read data into the dataset from an external Microsoft Access database. The second method reads data from an XML file into the dataset.

Reading XML data into a dataset and populating a control with this data is easy to do. The steps are as follows:

1. Create a Visual Basic project.

2. Create and save an XML data source.

3. Create the user interface.

4. Write code to create a dataset and read XML data into the dataset.

5. Populate the DataGrid control with records in the dataset.

Your data files for this chapter include a project named *XMLReader*. Figure 11.13 shows the application interface.

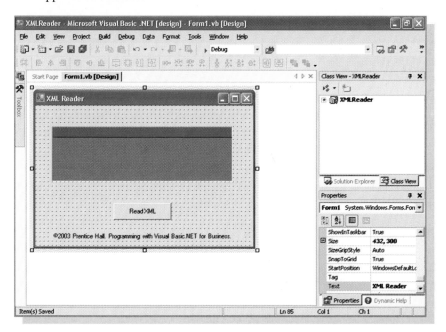

FIGURE 11.13. *A Visual Basic.NET project for reading XML data into a DataGrid control*

The user interface consists of a DataGrid control, a button, and a label that displays the copyright information. All data sources require a dataset, which you can create programmatically. The code for creating the dataset declares the dataset at the form level, so it will be available to any additional buttons you add to the application. The following code creates the dataset at run time:

```
'Declare a dataset
Dim dsEmployees As New DataSet("Employees")
```

In the declaration, *Employees* is the name of the dataset, which corresponds to the root element of the XML file (Employee). The functionality to open the XML file, read its contents into the dataset, and then populate the DataGrid control, using data from the dataset, is as follows:

```
Private Sub btnReadXML_Click(ByVal sender As System.Object,
   ByVal e As System.EventArgs) Handles btnReadXML.Click
     Dim strDirectory As String
     strDirectory = Environment.CurrentDirectory
     Dim strFile As String
     strFile = strDirectory & "\Employees.xml"
     Dim fsReadXML As New System.IO.FileStream _
         (strFile, System.IO.FileMode.Open)
     dsEmployees.ReadXml(fsReadXML)
     fsReadXML.Close()
     With DataGrid1
         .DataSource = dsEmployees
         .DataMember = "Employee"
         .CaptionText = .DataMember
     End With
End Sub
```

The code begins with variable declarations for the XML filename and location:

```
     Dim strDirectory As String
     strDirectory = Environment.CurrentDirectory
     Dim strFile As String
     strFile = strDirectory & "\Employees.xml"
```

The XML file is stored in the *bin* directory for the solution, because the **Environment.CurrentDirectory** method returns this location. When you store the file location in a string variable, the *strFile* assignment statement combines the file path with the filename (and its leading backslash character) to return the path and filename of the XML data source.

The next series of statements declares an instance of a FileStream object named *fsReadXML*:

```
     Dim fsReadXML As New System.IO.FileStream _
     (strFile, System.IO.FileMode.Open)
     dsEmployees.ReadXml(fsReadXML)
     fsReadXML.Close()
```

The statement opens the file, reads the contents into the *dsEmployees* dataset, and then closes the file. This creates the disconnected dataset and frees up the open file.

The last series of statements populates the DataGrid control with data from the dataset:

```
With DataGrid1
    .DataSource = dsEmployees
    .DataMember = "Employee"
    .CaptionText = .DataMember
End With
```

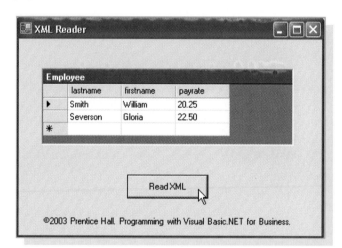

How does a disconnected dataset conserve system resources and improve working with data?

The **With. . . End With** construction allows multiple statements to refer to the DataGrid1 control. The DataSource property is set to the *dsEmployees* dataset, and the DataMember property is set to the Employee element in the XML file. The last statement sets the caption of the DataGrid1 control to the name of the DataMember property so the text string *Employee* appears. When the application is running, clicking the **Read XML** button will produce the result shown in Figure 11.14. As you can see, the data grid displays the two employee records contained in the XML file.

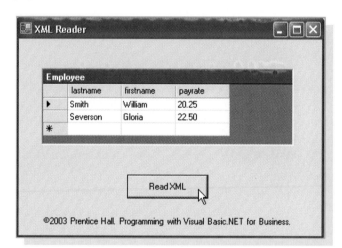

FIGURE 11.14. *A data grid displaying two employee records*

Now let's learn how to create a project that writes data from a form to an XML file.

Creating an Application that Writes Data to an XML File

Some applications, such as desktop applications that read stock quotes from the Web, use data in a read-only format. Many applications that read data from an external source need to make modifications to the data and then write the data back to the data source. You will recall from Chapter 6 that a dataset is a disconnected copy of the data residing in the external location. You learned how to write records in a dataset bound to an Access database as an XML file. We will now show you how to create an application that reads data from an XML file and writes changes to the data back to the same XML data source. Your data files for this chapter include a project named *XMLWriter*. The application interface is almost identical to the *XMLReader* application. The only difference is the addition of a second button shown in Figure 11.15 for writing changes made to the data grid back to the XML data file.

FIGURE 11.15. *A Visual Basic.NET project for writing data from a data grid to an XML file*

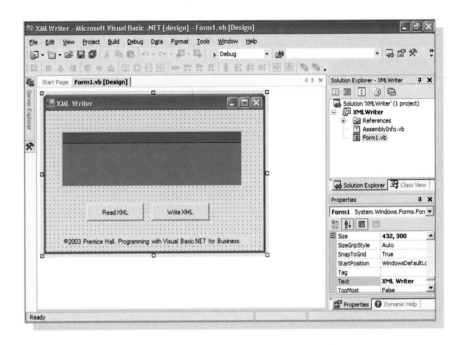

The code for updating the XML file with changes to the disconnected dataset is as follows:

```
Private Sub btnWriteXML_Click(ByVal sender As System.Object,
  ByVal e As System.EventArgs) Handles btnWriteXML.Click

    Dim strDirectory As String
    strDirectory = Environment.CurrentDirectory
    Dim strFile As String
    strFile = strDirectory & "\Employees.xml"

    Dim fsWriteXML As New System.IO.FileStream _
        (strFile, System.IO.FileMode.Truncate)
    dsEmployees.WriteXml(fsWriteXML)
    fsWriteXML.Close()
End Sub
```

The code will look familiar. The routine uses the same method for setting the file name and path as you used in the procedure that reads XML data into the dataset. The procedure for updating the XML file with changes to the dataset uses the **WriteXML** method. The **Truncate** mode for file access truncates (cuts off) the existing file if the new file is shorter. This way, the XML remains valid because remnants of the old file are gone.

```
    (strFile, System.IO.FileMode.Truncate)
    dsEmployees.WriteXml(fsWriteXML)
```

The XML file initially read into the application contains the same two employee records shown in Figure 11.14. After running the application and reading data into the dataset, we changed the last name in the first record and added a third record to the dataset, as shown in Figure 11.16.

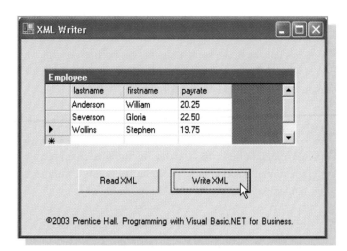

FIGURE 11.16. *Data grid displaying a new record*

To view the changes directly in the XML file, click **File**, **Open** and navigate to the *bin* folder for the project. Clicking the **Write XML** button writes the changes in the data grid to the XML file, and the changes look like Figure 11.17.

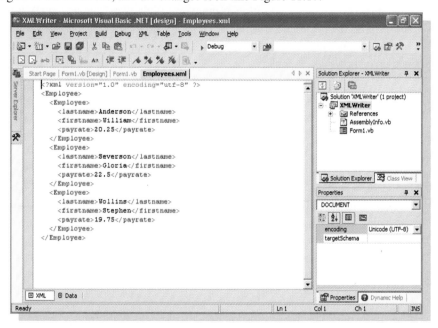

FIGURE 11.17. *XML file displaying three employee records*

Now that you understand the basics of reading and writing XML data, let's learn how Visual Studio.NET validates XML by using schemas.

XML Schemas

An ***XML schema*** is a document that defines and validates the content and structure of XML data. A schema defines and describes both the structure of data and the data using the ***XML Schema Definition Language (XSD).*** The .NET framework uses XML schemas to define the valid structure, valid data content, and valid relationships for XML data. Schemas are stored in text files with an *.xsd* extension. When you create schemas by using Visual Studio.NET, the user interface includes tabs for examining the contents of the XSD file directly.

Elements and attributes are the building blocks of XML schemas. Elements have attributes. An *attribute* of an element is like a property, providing further definition about an element in the same way that properties describe the characteristics of objects and classes. After you define a schema, you can create data types that define the valid content for the elements and attributes.

XML ELEMENTS, ATTRIBUTES, AND TYPES

An XML element describes the data it contains. A simple element definition consists of the element name and a data type. The following example shows how to define an element named payrate with a simple-type value of integer.

```
<xsd:element name="payrate" type="xsd:number" />
```

The element classifies the data, which in this case is the hourly pay rate for an employee. The *type* defines the valid content the element contains. Types can be simple or complex. Simple types include the data types you are used to using in Visual Basic.NET, such as string, decimal, and Boolean data. There are over 40 simple types built into the XML Schema definition of the World Wide Web Consortium (W3C).

In the preceding example, a valid data type for this element is Integer. The following example shows a valid instance of XML data that conforms to the *payrate* element defined in the previous example:

```
<payrate>22.25</payrate>
```

The following example shows an invalid instance of the *payrate* element:

```
<payrate>twenty-two</payrate>
```

An attribute is a named simple-type definition that cannot contain other elements. You can assign an attribute an optional default value, which must appear at the bottom of complex-type definitions. If you declare multiple attributes, the declarations may appear in any order. The following example shows how to declare an attribute named *Bonus*:

```
<xsd:element name="EmployeeInfo">
    <xsd:complexType>
        <xsd:sequence>
            <xsd:element name="SSN" type="xsd:string" />
            <xsd:element name="lastname" type="xsd:string" />
            <xsd:element name="firstname" type="xsd:string" />
            <xsd:element name="payrate" type="xsd:decimal" />
        </xsd:sequence>
        <xsd:attribute name="Bonus" type="xsd:decimal" />
    </xsd:complexType>
</xsd:element>
```

Attributes are optional, so if a specific employee is not on a bonus plan, the XML data will still be valid. An attribute is restricted to built-in (primitive) data types. The built-in data types include the following:

Data Type	The Kind of Data It Represents
string	Character strings.
Boolean	Boolean values, which are either True or False.
decimal	Arbitrary precision numbers.
float	Single-precision 32-bit floating-point numbers.
double	Double-precision 64-bit floating-point numbers.
duration	A duration of time.
dateTime	A specific instance of time.
time	An instance of time that recurs every day.
date	A calendar date.
gYearMonth	A specific Gregorian month in a specific Gregorian year. A set of one-month-long, non-periodic instances.
gYear	A Gregorian year.
gMonthDay	A specific Gregorian date that recurs, specifically, a day of the year, such as the third of May.
gDay	A Gregorian day that recurs, specifically, a day of the month, such as the fifth day of the month.
gMonth	A Gregorian month that recurs every year.
hexBinary	Arbitrary hex-encoded binary data.
base64Binary	Base64-encoded arbitrary binary data.
anyURI	A URI as defined by RFC 2396.
QName	A qualified name. A qualified name is composed of a prefix and a local name separated by a colon.
NOTATION	A NOTATION attribute type. A set of QNames.

If your application uses data stored in a user-defined data type, you can declare the elements for each field within the data type.

NAMING CONVENTIONS FOR ELEMENTS AND ATTRIBUTES

The Visual Studio.NET help system includes the following recommendations for naming elements and attributes:

- XML is case-sensitive. An element named "zipcode" differs from an element named "ZipCode."

- Element names cannot start with a number or underscore or with the letters "XML."

- Element names cannot contain spaces.

- Attribute values must always be in quotation marks.

Now that you have a basic understanding of XML, you are ready to learn to create XML schemas.

Tip

Attributes are beyond the scope of what you need to know about XML schemas to use XML data in your Visual Basic.NET applications. We provide a definition of attributes here because most information sources that define XML schemas will also define attributes.

Creating Schemas

You can create a schema from an existing XML file or by defining the schema with the XML Designer. An XML schema file begins with header information that identifies the version of XML and additional information used by the schema. The XML Designer adds this information automatically when you use the designer to create the schema.

CREATING AN XML SCHEMA FROM AN XML FILE

To create a schema from an XML file, load the file into the XML Designer. The following example uses the project located in the *XMLSchema* folder in your data files. When the XML file is loaded in the XML Designer, click **XML**, **Create Schema**, as shown in Figure 11.18.

FIGURE 11.18. *Creating a schema for an XML file*

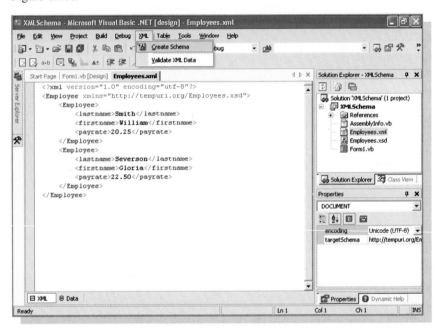

The schema file added to the solution has an *.xsd* file extension. To view the schema in the IDE, right-click the *Employees.xsd* file in the Solution Explorer and select **Open**. The XML Designer adds the schema shown in Figure 11.19 to the IDE.

FIGURE 11.19. *Viewing a schema in the IDE*

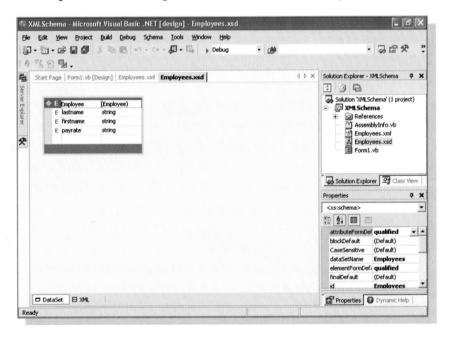

Notice that the IDE names the schema with the default name of *Employees.xsd* and that each data type is given the default of string. This is because the numeric data representing the pay types in the XML file are interpreted as text. In the next section you will learn how to change the data type for an element.

The project contains unsaved data. Click **File**, **Save All** to update the solution.

Now click the **XML** tab in the XML Designer. Figure 11.20 displays the XML statements that define the schema.

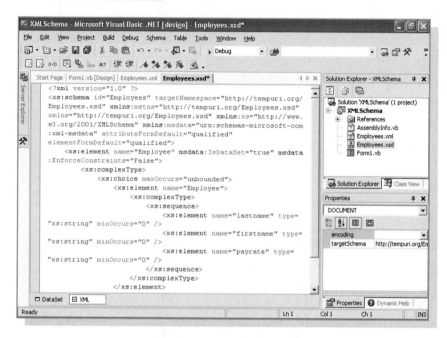

FIGURE 11.20. *XML view of the Employees.xsd schema*

Close the solution when you finish viewing the schema.

CREATING A DATASET SCHEMA BY USING THE XML DESIGNER

You can define datasets for your applications as XML schemas. By defining a dataset as a schema, you can associate the dataset with an XML file and validate the data as well-formed XML. The following example demonstrates how to create a schema and then associate an XML file with the dataset schema. After you associate the XML file with the schema, you can add data to the file by using the XML Designer. In the example that follows, you create a new Windows project named *XMLEmployees*. The Dataset schema includes elements for representing employee data.

Adding a Dataset and an XML File to the XML Designer

Create a new Visual Basic project and name it `XMLEmployees`. To add a dataset to the XML Designer, click the **Project** menu and choose **Add New Item**. Select **DataSet** in the **Templates** pane. Name the dataset `dsEmployees` and then click **Open**, as shown in Figure 11.21.

FIGURE 11.21. *Adding a Dataset schema to a project*

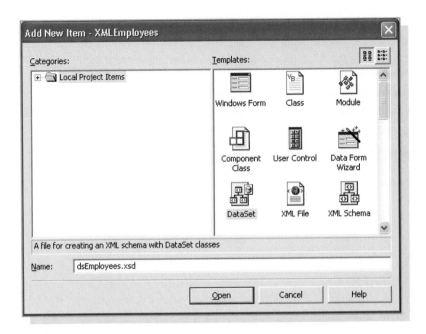

Figure 11.22 shows the dataset added to the XML Designer.

FIGURE 11.22. *DataSet schema added to the XML Designer*

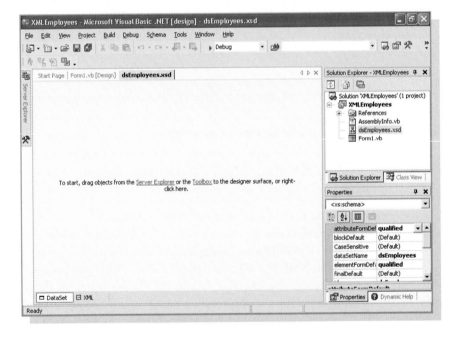

The dataset is currently empty. Notice the message appearing in the XML Designer, specifying how to proceed.

Adding Elements to the DataSet Schema

The Dataset schema requires elements to represent the data in the associated XML file. Without clicking the XML tab in the XML Designer, drag an element from the Data tab of the Toolbox to the XML Designer, as shown in Figure 11.23.

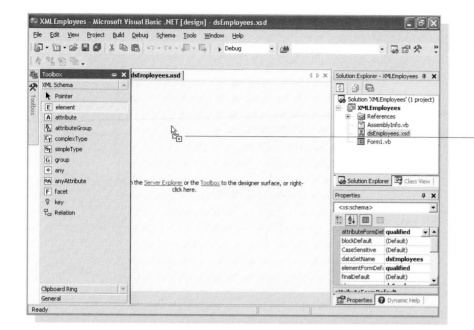

FIGURE 11.23. *Adding an element from the Toolbox to the Dataset schema*

Dragging an element to the XML Designer

The first row of the type should be selected; if it is not, click the row to select it. Rename the first row as `Employees`. Do not select a data type for this element. Press the `Tab` key three times to navigate to the next row. The elements for the dataset are listed in Table 11.1, which displays the remaining elements for this schema.

Table 11.1: Defined elements for the Employees DataSet schema

Element Choice	Name	Type
Element	ssn	String
Element	lastname	String
Element	firstname	String
Element	payrate	Decimal

To assign the **Decimal** type to the *payrate* element, click the drop-down list and choose **Decimal**, as shown in Figure 11.24.

XML supports the Decimal and not the Single type. We will use the built-in Decimal data type to represent the pay rate.

FIGURE 11.24. *Dataset schema with named elements*

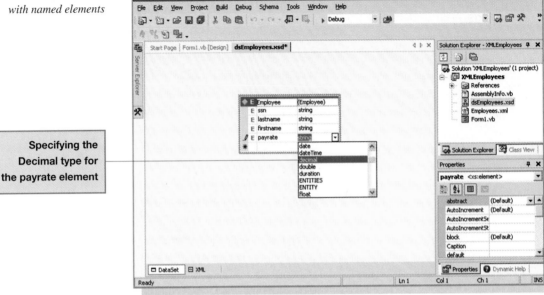

Specifying the Decimal type for the payrate element

Click **File**, **Save All** to save these changes.

Remember that schemas define the structure and content for XML data. By creating a schema to define the structure of the XML tags for your data, you ensure that the XML Designer displays each element in DataSet view. To view the tags for the schema, click the **XML** tab in the XML Designer. Figure 11.25 displays the XML Schema Definition (XSD) tags for the Dataset schema.

FIGURE 11.25. *Tags defining the Dataset schema*

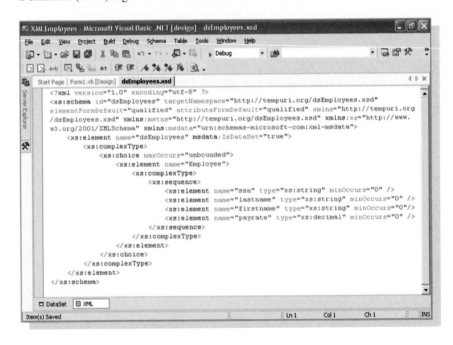

Tip

To display the tags in XML view, we closed the Solution Explorer and Properties windows in the IDE.

The schema needs an XML file to store the data this application requires. Let's now add an XML file.

Adding an XML File to the XML Designer

Click the **Project** menu and choose **Add New Item**. Select **XML File** in the **Templates** pane. Name the file Employees and click **Open**, as shown in Figure 11.26. Visual Studio adds an XML file to the Designer.

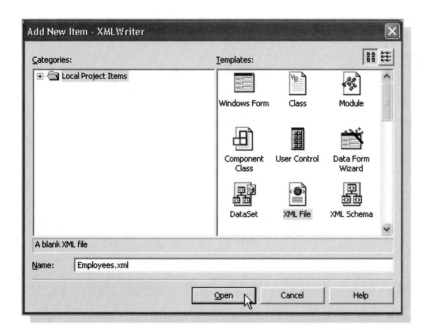

FIGURE 11.26. *Adding an XML file to the project*

Now that you have defined the data types for the schema, you need to create the data definition for the XML file.

Associating the DataSet Schema with the XML File

A data definition is a new element added to the schema that associates the schema with the XML data file. Click the **targetSchema** row in the Properties window. When the drop-down list appears, click the list and choose **http://tempuri.org/dsEmployees.xsd**, as shown in Figure 11.27. This creates an association between the schema and the XML file so that the elements represented in the schema appear in the XML file.

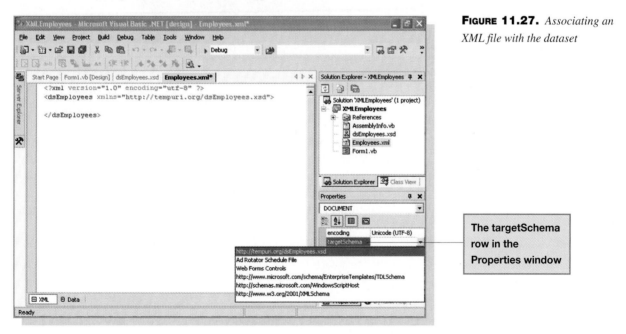

FIGURE 11.27. *Associating an XML file with the dataset*

The targetSchema row in the Properties window

Adding Data to an XML File by Using the XML Designer

Once a schema is associated with an XML file, you can use the XML Designer to add data to the file. Table 11.2 lists three employee records for the file.

Table 11.2: Employee data for the Employees XML file

ssn	lastname	firstname	Payrate
111-22-3333	Wolings	Stephen	18.25
222-33-4444	Irwin	Jill	20.5
333-44-5555	Carlsen	Anna	20.75

You can add data to the file in either Data view or XML view. If you use Data view, a grid appears in the Designer. Data view provides a visual workspace for easily entering the fields and records, and you do not have to worry about adding tags. If you use XML view, you need to add the opening tag and the data. If you use the XML Designer to enter records, it is a good idea to validate the XML before saving the file.

When you use Data view to add records to the XML file, Visual Studio maintains the validity of the data by generating well-formed XML as you enter the data. Figure 11.28 displays the records listed in Table 11.2 as they appear in Data view.

FIGURE 11.28. *Data view displaying three employee records*

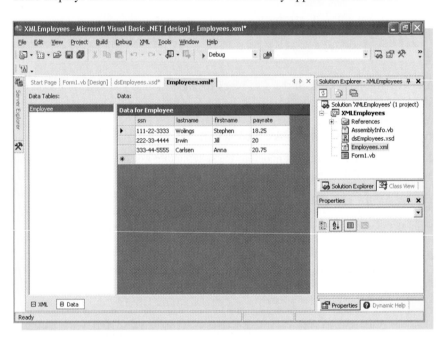

After entering the employee records, save the changes. When a schema is associated with an XML file, the XML Designer enforces the validity of the data you enter. You can view the well-formed XML data by switching to XML view. If you use XML view, you need to carefully construct the start- and end-tags in the Designer. To validate the data, click the **XML menu** and choose **Validate XML Data**. Figure 11.29 displays well-formed XML data for the three employee records shown in Table 11.2.

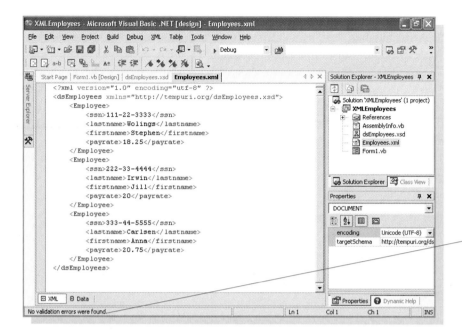

FIGURE 11.29. *XML view displaying valid and well-formed XML data*

As you can see, creating a schema and then adding well-formed XML data to the schema is a simple task when you use the tools available in Visual Studio.NET. These examples demonstrate how to work with a single database table. Let's see how XML works with data from more than one table.

CREATING RELATIONSHIPS IN XML SCHEMAS

The Dataset schema in the last section represents structured data in XML format. You can also represent related database tables as an XML schema and associate this schema with an XML data file. In this case, the related records appear as hierarchical data in the file. The following example demonstrates how to create a Dataset schema named *XMLPayroll* that includes two related elements.

One of the strengths of the relational database model is being able to relate data between tables. Figure 11.30 shows a Microsoft Access database named *Payroll.mdb*.

> **Tip**
> The XML data does not include information about the data types for the elements. The XML file includes a reference to the Employees.xsd schema file, which contains information about the elements.

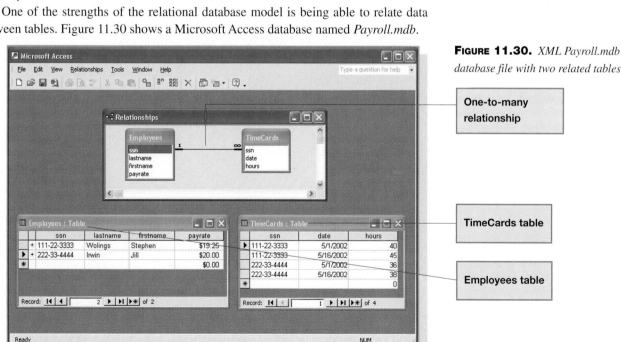

FIGURE 11.30. *XML Payroll.mdb database file with two related tables*

The database contains two tables. The *Employees* table stores the Social Security number, last name, first name, and pay rate of each employee. The *TimeCards* table stores time-card records for each pay period the employee worked. The database includes a one-to-many relationship between the *Employees* and *TimeCards* tables. This relationship means that for any employee in the database, there can be zero or more than one related time card records. The *Employees* table contains two associated *TimeCards* records for each of the two employees in the database.

Your data files for this chapter include a solution named *XMLPayroll*. The solution includes a Dataset schema and an XML data file. Figure 11.31 shows the two elements stored in the schema.

FIGURE 11.31. *XML schema with two related elements*

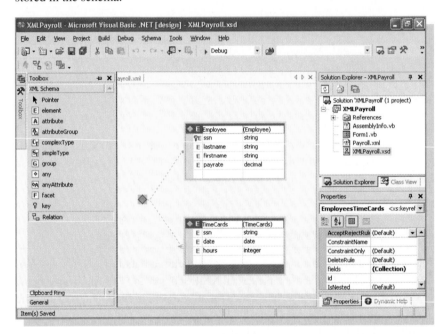

The Toolbox displays additional tags added to this schema: a ***Key tag*** for setting the primary key field in the *Employee* element, and a ***Relation tag*** for establishing a relationship between the *Employee* and *TimeCards* elements. The Relation tag establishes the hierarchical structure in the XML file that represents the relationship between these two tables. Figure 11.32 shows how to configure the Relation tag to enable this structure.

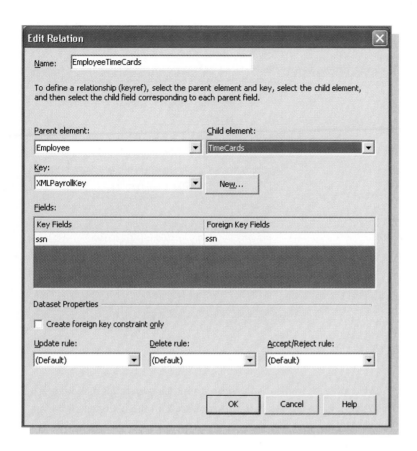

FIGURE 11.32. *Configuring a Relation tag*

If you click the **XML** tab in the Designer, you can see the XML tags that link the two elements. For this example, the XML tags in the Dataset schema that link the two elements are as follows:

```
<xs:key name="XMLPayrollKey" msdata:PrimaryKey="true">
    xs:selector xpath=".//mstns:Employee" />
    <xs:field xpath="mstns:ssn" />
 </xs:key>
 <xs:keyref name="EmployeeTimeCards" refer="XMLPayrollKey">
    <xs:selector xpath=".//mstns:TimeCards" />
    <xs:field xpath="mstns:ssn" />
 </xs:keyref>
```

After you establish a relationship, you can enter data into an XML file by using the XML Designer in the same way you enter data into a single table. If you display the XML file in the Designer and click the **Data** tab, the XML elements display in Data view. Figure 11.33 shows the Data view for the *Employee* XML elements. You will notice that each employee in the grid has an Expand button for expanding the data and entering associated time-card records.

FIGURE 11.33. *Data view displaying the related TimeCard data elements for each Employee element*

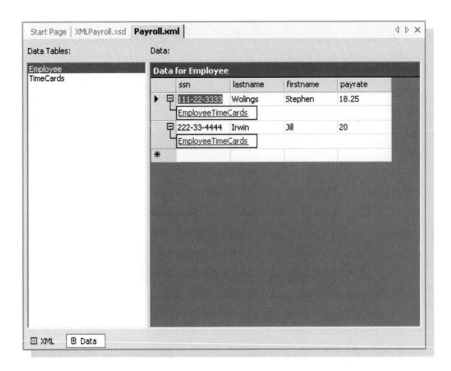

Also note that the Data view contains two related elements (*Employee* and *TimeCards*). Clicking the *TimeCards* element in the list opens the Data view shown in Figure 11.34.

FIGURE 11.34. *Displaying the TimeCards data in Data view*

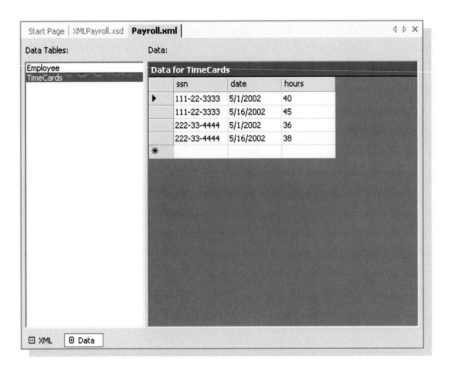

When you use the XML Designer to enter records into an XML data file, Visual Studio enforces the structure of the data represented by the associated Dataset schema. The well-formed XML data for the records shown in Figures 11.33 and 11.34 follows:

```
<?xml version="1.0" encoding="utf-8" ?>
<XMLPayroll xmlns="http://tempuri.org/XMLPayroll.xsd">
    <Employee>
        <ssn>111-22-3333</ssn>
        <lastname>Wolings</lastname>
        <firstname>Stephen</firstname>
        <payrate>18.25</payrate>
    </Employee>
    <TimeCards>
        <ssn>111-22-3333</ssn>
        <date>2002-05-01T00:00:00.0000000-06:00</date>
        <hours>40</hours>
    </TimeCards>
    <TimeCards>
        <ssn>111-22-3333</ssn>
        <date>2002-05-16T00:00:00.0000000-06:00</date>
        <hours>45</hours>
    </TimeCards>
    <Employee>
        <ssn>222-33-4444</ssn>
        <lastname>Irwin</lastname>
        <firstname>Jill</firstname>
        <payrate>20</payrate>
    </Employee>
    <TimeCards>
        <ssn>222-33-4444</ssn>
        <date>2002-05-01T00:00:00.0000000-06:00</date>
        <hours>36</hours>
    </TimeCards>
    <TimeCards>
        <ssn>222-33-4444</ssn>
        <date>2002-05-16T00:00:00.0000000-06:00</date>
        <hours>38</hours>
    </TimeCards>
</XMLPayroll>
```

As you can see, you can use XML as the data source for your Visual Basic.NET applications that work with structured information. You can use existing XML data files, or create new XML data files with the XML Designer. Now let's see how to use XML as the data format for the Employee Address Book application.

☞ HANDS-ON PROGRAMMING EXAMPLE

Creating an Address Book Application for Managing XML Records

In Chapter 6 you created an Employee Address Book application for manipulating database records in a bound Microsoft Access database. In this example you will create an application with a similar user interface but a different data source. The application manipulates employee information in a disconnected dataset, but the dataset is bound to an XML file. Figure 11.35 shows the interface for the *XML Employee Address Book* application.

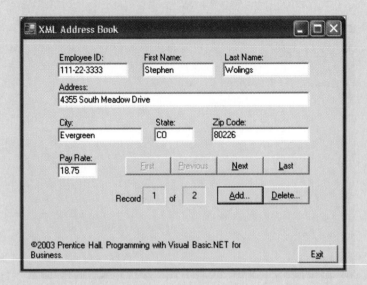

The Employee Address Book application is a form bound to an external XML data source. XML Address Book is for managing employee records and supports the following functionality:

1. Reads data from and writes data to the external XML file.
2. Contains navigation buttons for moving through the dataset.
3. Includes buttons for adding and deleting records.
4. Includes record counters that display the current record number and the total number of records.

Although the requirements for this application are relatively simple, you will need to add a Dataset schema to the application, add elements to the schema, create an XML file, and associate the XML file with the Dataset schema.

Plan the Application

The first step in planning an application is determining the inputs and outputs. This version of the Employee Address Book application has the same requirement as the address book you created in Chapter 6: entering, editing, and displaying database records. The inputs and outputs are as follows:

Inputs	Outputs
Fields and records	Fields and records
(entered on the keyboard)	(read from an XML file)

The Address Book application consists of one form with text box, label, and button controls.

Draw a visual representation of the application on a blank piece of paper. Figure 11.36 shows a drawing of the user interface, with the name and approximate position of each control on the form.

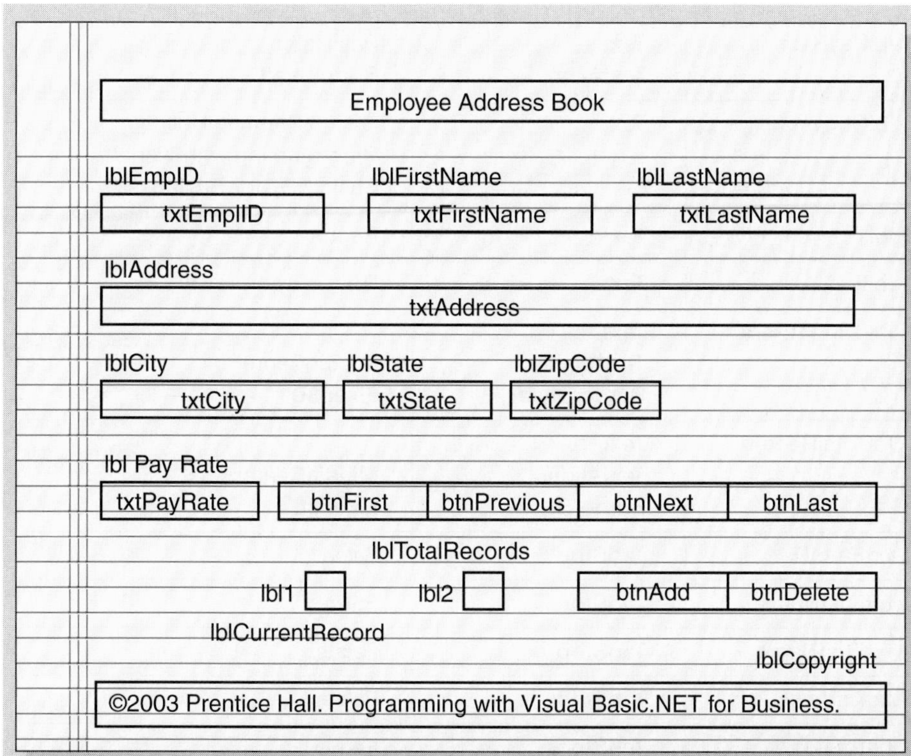

FIGURE 11.36. *Interface for the Employee Address Book application*

Table 11.3 lists the controls and properties for the user interface.

Table 11.3: *Objects and properties for the XML Employee Address Book application*

Object	Property	Setting
Form1	Text StartPosition Size	XML Address Book CenterScreen 455, 345
lblEmpID	Text TextAlign	Employee ID: BottomLeft
lblLastName	Text TextAlign	Last Name: BottomLeft
lblFirstName	Text TextAlign	First Name: BottomLeft
lblAddress	Text TextAlign	Address: BottomLeft
lblCity	Text TextAlign	City: BottomLeft
lblState	Text TextAlign	State: BottomLeft
lblZipCode	Text TextAlign	Zip Code: BottomLeft

lblPayRate	Text TextAlign	Pay Rate: BottomLeft
lblCopyright	Text	©2003 Prentice Hall. Programming with Visual Basic.NET for Business.
lbl1	Text	Record
lbl2	Text	Of
lblCurrentRecord	Text TextAlign BorderStyle	 MiddleCenter Fixed3D
lblTotalRecord	Text TextAlign BorderStyle	 MiddleCenter Fixed3D
txtEmpID	TabStop	False
txtLastName	TabStop	False
txtFirstName	TabStop	False
txtAddress	TabStop	False
txtCity	TabStop	False
txtState	TabStop	False
txtZipCode	TabStop	False
txtPayRate	TabStop	False
btnFirst	Text TabStop; Tab Index	First True, 0
btnPrevious	Text TabStop; Tab Index	Previous True, 1
btnNext	Text TabStop; Tab Index	Next True, 2
btnLast	Text TabStop; Tab Index	Last True, 3
btnAdd	Text TabStop; Tab Index	Add. . . True, 4
btnDelete	Text TabStop	Delete. . . True, 5
btnExit	Text TabStop	E&xit True, 6

The form's primary features are the text boxes for displaying field data and the buttons for navigating the dataset and adding and deleting records. Table 11.4 lists the pseudocode describing the application's functionality.

Table 11.4: *Pseudocode for the XML Address Book application*

Event Procedure	Action
btnFirst	Displays the first record in the dataset.
btnPrevious	Displays the previous record in the dataset.
btnNext	Displays the next record in the dataset.
btnLast	Displays the last record in the dataset.
btnAdd	1. Adds the data entered into input boxes. 2. Updates the XML data source.
btnDelete	1. Verifies the deletion and continues or cancels. 2. If the user clicks "Yes", deletes the current record from the dataset and updates the XML data source.
btnExit	1. Verifies the user's intent to exit. 2. Terminates the application.

Now that you have created the planning documents for the application, you are ready to begin designing the user interface in the IDE.

Design the User Interface

In addition to adding controls to the application's form and setting control properties, you will need to add a Dataset schema to the project, add elements to the schema, create an XML file, and assign the Dataset schema to the XML file. You will also need to bind the text box controls to the dataset.

If you have not launched Visual Studio.NET, do so now. Use the Start Page to set the profile to Visual Studio Developer. Complete each task that follows to complete this application.

To create a new Windows Application project:

1. Click **File**, **New Project**. The **New Project** dialog box appears.
2. Select Windows Application as the project template and type `XMLAddressBook` as the name for the project.

You are now ready to create the user interface by adding controls to the form.

To design the user interface:

1. Add each object listed in Table 11.3 to the form.
2. Click **File**, **Save All** to save your changes.
3. Set the object properties as specified. When you finish, your form should look like Figure 11.37.

FIGURE 11.37. *Controls added to the form*

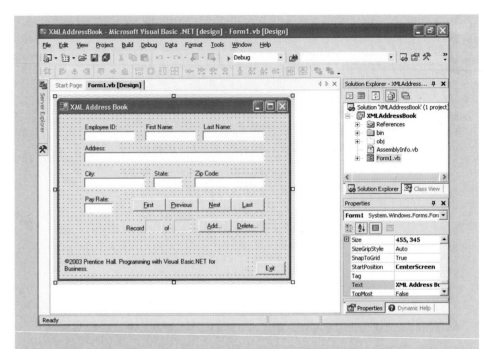

You are now ready to create the Dataset schema for the application.

To add a DataSet schema to the application:

1. Click **Project**, **Add New Item**.
2. Select the **DataSet** template in the **Templates** pane.
3. Type `XMLEmployees` as the name for the dataset.
4. Click **Open**. Visual Studio adds a Dataset schema to the project and displays the XML Designer.

To add an element to the DataSet schema:

1. Click the **Data** tab in the Toolbox and choose the **Element** object.
2. Drag an Element object to the XML Designer, as shown in Figure 11.38.

FIGURE 11.38. *Adding an element to the DataSet schema*

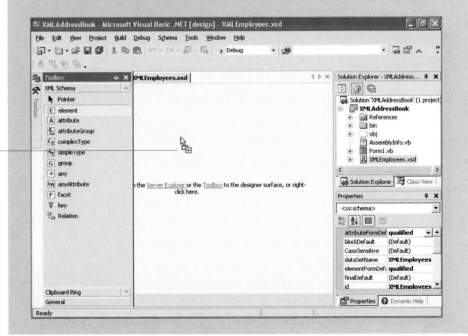

3. Name the element `Employee`.

4. Add the elements listed in Figure 11.39 to the DataSet schema.

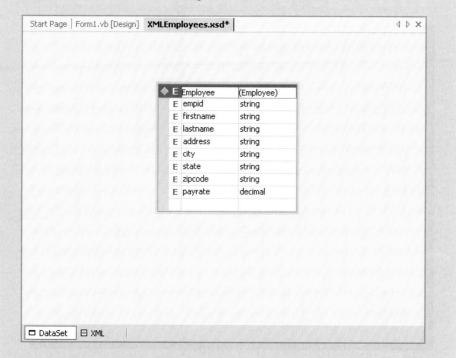

FIGURE 11.39. *Adding elements to the schema*

5. Save your changes. You are now ready to create the XML file that will store the employee records.

To add an XML file to the XML Designer and associate the file with the DataSet schema:

To store the employee records, you need to create an XML file and associate the file with the *XMLEmployees* dataset. By storing the file in the *bin* directory for this project, you write code for the file path so the application reads the records into the dataset whenever the application runs.

1. Click **File**, **New**, **File**.

2. Select the **XML File** in the **Templates** pane, and click **Open** to add a blank XML file to the XML Designer.

3. Click **File**, **Save XMLFile1**.

4. Navigate to the *bin* directory for the current project.

5. Type `Employees.xml` as the name for the file and click **Save**.

6. In the **targetSchema** row of the **Properties** pane for the XML file, click the drop-down list.

7. Select **http://tempuri.org/XMLEmployees.xsd** as the schema to associate with this file.

8. Save your changes. You are now ready to add data to the XML source.

To add data to the XML source:

1. Click the **Data** tab in the XML Designer for the *Employees.xml* file.
2. Add the following two records to the XML file:

    111-22-3333

    Stephen

    Wolings

    4355 South Meadow Drive

    Evergreen

    CO

    80226

    18.75

    222-33-4444

    Jill

    Irwin

    21329 Brook Forest Lane

    Conifer

    CO

    80291

    20.00

3. Save your changes.
4. Switch to XML view. The well-formed data should look like Figure 11.40.

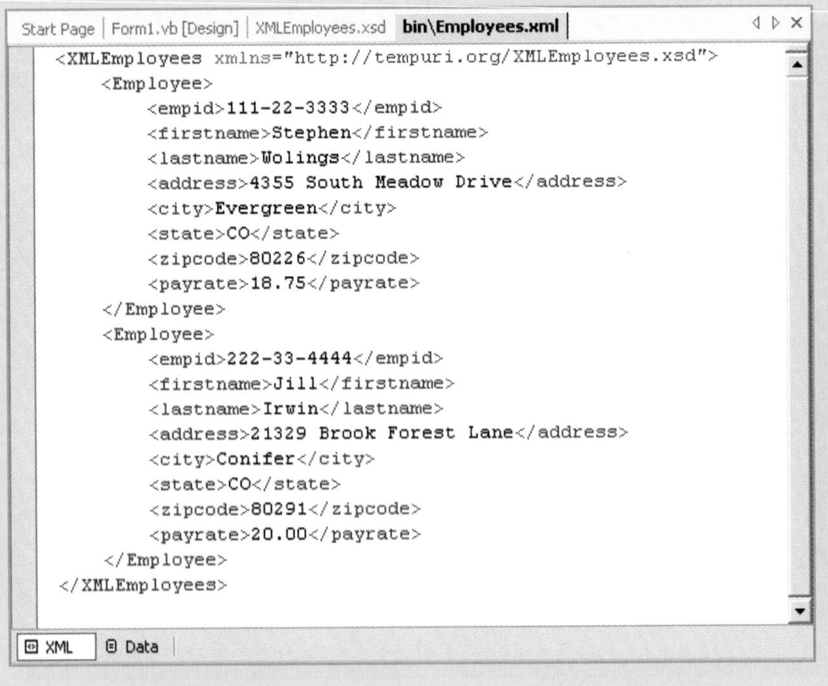

FIGURE 11.40. *XML data for the Employee Address Book*

```
Start Page  Form1.vb [Design]  XMLEmployees.xsd  bin\Employees.xml          ◁ ▷ ✕

   <XMLEmployees xmlns="http://tempuri.org/XMLEmployees.xsd">
       <Employee>
           <empid>111-22-3333</empid>
           <firstname>Stephen</firstname>
           <lastname>Wolings</lastname>
           <address>4355 South Meadow Drive</address>
           <city>Evergreen</city>
           <state>CO</state>
           <zipcode>80226</zipcode>
           <payrate>18.75</payrate>
       </Employee>
       <Employee>
           <empid>222-33-4444</empid>
           <firstname>Jill</firstname>
           <lastname>Irwin</lastname>
           <address>21329 Brook Forest Lane</address>
           <city>Conifer</city>
           <state>CO</state>
           <zipcode>80291</zipcode>
           <payrate>20.00</payrate>
       </Employee>
   </XMLEmployees>

 ⊞ XML   ⊟ Data
```

5. Right-click the tab for the *Employees.xml* file and choose Close.
6. Use the same method to close the *XMLEmployees.xsd* schema file.

Now that you have completed the interface and data components for the XML Employee Address Book, you are ready to write the code.

Write the Code

Your first tasks are to add comments to the Code Editor, define variables for holding the record counters, and initialize the form. You can then write the code that provides each button its functionality.

To add comments to the application and declare variables:

1. Press ⌷F7⌷ to display the Code Editor. If the region displaying the Windows Form Designer generated code region is expanded, collapse it.
2. Place the insertion point at the top of the Code Editor and type the following comments to document the application:

```
'©2003 Prentice Hall
'By [Enter your name here…]
'Created/Revised: [Enter the date here…]
'XML Address Book Windows Application
```

3. Place the insertion point immediately below the **Inherits System.Windows.Forms.Form** statement, and type the following statements:

```
Dim intCurrentRecord As Integer
Dim intTotalRecords As Integer
Dim dsEmployees As New System.Data.DataSet("XMLEmployees")
```

The first two statements declare the variables to store the counters for the current and total records. The last statement declares an instance of the *XMLEmployees* dataset.

4. Save your changes.

The application will contain three functions: one for reading XML data, one for writing XML data, and one for initializing the interface by updating the record counters and displaying the appropriate buttons, depending on the current record. In addition, the Form_Load event will use a **Try. . . Catch** statement to determine if the XML file exists. If the file exists, the procedure will bind the elements in the file to the controls on the form and call the function to initialize the interface.

To write functions and code the Form_Load event:

1. Place the insertion point below the Windows Form Designer generated code region.
2. Type #Region "Functions" and press ⌷←Enter⌷ to create a region for two functions.
3. Add the following function procedure to read XML data from the *Employees.xml* file:

```
Friend Sub ReadXML()
    Dim strDirectory As String
    strDirectory = Environment.CurrentDirectory
    Dim strFile As String
    strFile = strDirectory & "\Employees.xml"
```

```
    Dim fsReadXML As New System.IO.FileStream _
    (strFile, System.IO.FileMode.Open)
    dsEmployees.ReadXml(fsReadXML)
    fsReadXML.Close()
End Sub
```

This function determines the path for the XML file and assigns a filename. The function then declares an instance of a **FileStream** object to read the XML data from the file into the dataset.

4. Press ⏎Enter twice to separate this function from the function for writing XML data.

5. Add the following function to write XML data to the *Employees.xml* file:

```
Friend Sub WriteXML()
    Dim strDirectory As String
    strDirectory = Environment.CurrentDirectory
    Dim strFile As String

    strFile = strDirectory & "\Employees.xml"
    Dim fsWriteXML As New System.IO.FileStream _
    (strFile, System.IO.FileMode.Truncate)
    dsEmployees.WriteXml(fsWriteXML)
    fsWriteXML.Close()
End Sub
```

This function determines the path for the XML file and assigns a filename. The function then declares an instance of a FileStream object to write the XML data from the dataset to the XML file.

6. Press ⏎Enter twice to separate this function from the function for writing XML data.

7. Add the following function to initialize the interface:

```
Friend Sub InitializeInterface()
'Determine the number of records in the Dataset
    intTotalRecords = BindingContext(dsEmployees,
        "Employee").Count
    lblTotalRecords.Text = intTotalRecords

'Set the current record variable (first record has an index of
  0, so add 1)
    intCurrentRecord = BindingContext(dsEmployees,
        "Employee").Position + 1
    lblCurrentRecord.Text = intCurrentRecord

    'Configure buttons
    If intTotalRecords = 1 Then
        btnFirst.Visible = True
        btnPrevious.Visible = True
        btnNext.Visible = True
        btnLast.Visible = True
    Else
        Select Case intCurrentRecord
            Case Is = 1
```

```
                btnPrevious.Visible = False
                btnFirst.Visible = False
                btnNext.Visible = True
                btnLast.Visible = True

            Case Is = intTotalRecords
                btnPrevious.Visible = True
                btnFirst.Visible = True
                btnNext.Visible = False
                btnLast.Visible = False
            Case Is > 1 And intCurrentRecord < intTotalRecords
                btnPrevious.Visible = True
                btnFirst.Visible = True
                btnNext.Visible = True
                btnLast.Visible = True
            End Select
        End If
End Sub
```

This function first determines the total number of records and the current record and then updates the labels for the record counters. The function then determines which navigation buttons to display on the form, depending on the total number of records and the current record. If the total number of records is equal to 1, all navigation buttons display. Otherwise, a Select Case statement determines the position of the current record in the dataset and sets the visible property of each navigation button accordingly.

8. Move the insertion point below the region containing the two functions you just created.
9. Type #Region "Form Load" and press ⏎Enter to create a region to contain the code for the Form_Load event.
10. Create a Form_Load event inside the region you just created. Type the following statements for the event:

```
Try
    Call ReadXML()
    'Bind XML data to text box controls
    Me.txtEmpID.DataBindings.Add("Text", dsEmployees,
      "Employee.empid")
    Me.txtFirstName.DataBindings.Add("Text", dsEmployees,
      "Employee.firstname")
    Me.txtLastName.DataBindings.Add("Text", dsEmployees,
      "Employee.lastname")
    Me.txtAddress.DataBindings.Add("Text", dsEmployees,
      "Employee.address")
    Me.txtCity.DataBindings.Add("Text", dsEmployees,
      "Employee.city")
    Me.txtState.DataBindings.Add("Text", dsEmployees,
      "Employee.state")
    Me.txtZipCode.DataBindings.Add("Text", dsEmployees,
      "Employee.zipcode")
    Me.txtPayRate.DataBindings.Add("Text", dsEmployees,
      "'Employee.payrate")
```

```
            'Set the current record variable (first record has an index
               of 0, so add 1)
            intCurrentRecord = BindingContext(dsEmployees,
               "Employee").Position + 1
            'Determine the number of records in the Dataset
            intTotalRecords = BindingContext(dsEmployees, "Employee").Count
            Call InitializeInterface()
   Catch
            MsgBox("Cannot find the XML data source.",
               MsgBoxStyle.Critical, "File Error")
   End Try
```

The procedure uses the **Try. . . Catch** statement to call the **ReadXML** function and fill the dataset. If the file is not present or is corrupted, the procedure displays an error message and the application terminates. Otherwise, the procedure fills the dataset, binds the controls to the data elements, and calls the InitializeInterface function to configure the record counters and navigation buttons.

11. Save your changes.

The procedures for navigating among records will be familiar to you because these are similar to the procedures you used in Chapters 6 and 10 for record navigation. In addition to changing the position in the dataset, each procedure disables the appropriate navigation buttons and changes the value of the current record counter.

To write procedures for navigating among records:

1. Place the insertion point below the region containing the procedures for the Form Load event.

2. Type `#Region "Record Navigation"` and press ⏎Enter to create a region for the procedures for navigating among records.

3. Create a procedure for the btnFirst_Click event. Add the following statements to the procedure:

```
Me.BindingContext(dsEmployees, "Employee").Position = 0
Call InitializeInterface()
```

4. Create a procedure for the btnPrevious_Click event. Add the following statements to the procedure:

```
Me.BindingContext(dsEmployees, "Employee").Position -= 1
'Reset the CurrentRecord variable
intCurrentRecord = BindingContext(dsEmployees,
   "Employee").Position + 1
Call InitializeInterface()
```

5. Create a procedure for the btnNext_Click event. Add the following statements to the procedure:

```
Me.BindingContext(dsEmployees, "Employee").Position += 1
'Reset the CurrentRecord variable
intCurrentRecord = BindingContext(dsEmployees,
   "Employee").Position + 1
Call InitializeInterface()
```

6. Create a procedure for the btnLast_Click event. Add the following statements to the procedure:

```
Me.BindingContext(dsEmployees, "Employee").Position =
   BindingContext(dsEmployees, "Employee").Count - 1


'Reset the CurrentRecord variable
intCurrentRecord = BindingContext(dsEmployees,
   "Employee").Position + 1
Call InitializeInterface()
```

7. Save your changes.

You are now ready to write procedures for adding and deleting records from the dataset and the XML file.

To write procedures for adding and deleting records:

1. Place the insertion point below the region containing the procedures for navigating records.
2. Type `#Region "Record Management"` and press ⏎Enter to create a region for the procedures for adding and deleting records.
3. Create a procedure for the btnAdd_Click event. Add the following statements to the procedure:

```
Dim AddRow As DataRow
AddRow = dsEmployees.Tables("Employee").NewRow


'Populate the new dataset row with data from the form
AddRow("empid") = InputBox("Please enter an Employee ID...")
AddRow("firstname") = InputBox("Please the First Name...")
AddRow("lastname") = InputBox("Please enter the Last Name...")
AddRow("address") = InputBox("Please enter the Address ...")
AddRow("city") = InputBox("Please enter the a City ...")
AddRow("state") = InputBox("Please enter the State...")
AddRow("zipcode") = InputBox("Please enter the Zip Code...")
AddRow("payrate") = InputBox("Please enter the Pay Rate...")


Try
    'Add the new row to the dataset and notify user
    dsEmployees.Tables("Employees").Rows.Add(AddRow)

    WriteXML()

    MsgBox("You have successfully added a record.",
       MsgBoxStyle.Information, "Record Added")


    'Determine the number of records in the Dataset
    intTotalRecords = BindingContext(dsEmployees,
       "Employee").Count
```

```
        'Navigate to the last record
        Me.BindingContext(dsEmployees, "Employee").Position =
            intTotalRecords

        Call InitializeInterface()
Catch
        MsgBox("File Error: Cannot save this record.",
            MsgBoxStyle.Critical, "Save Operation Failed")
        Exit Try
End Try
```

This procedure adds a row to the dataset. Because the text box controls are
bound to the dataset, the procedure uses an input box to obtain user input for
each element in the dataset. The Try. . . Catch routine updates the XML file
with the new record. After the record is added, a message verifies the new
record, the application displays the last record in the dataset, and the counter
variables and navigation are updated.

4. Create a procedure for the btnDelete_Click event. Add the following state-
    ments to the procedure:

```
intCurrentRecord = BindingContext(dsEmployees,
    "Employee").Position

If MsgBox("Delete Record? Click 'Yes' to delete, 'No' to
    cancel.", MsgBoxStyle.YesNo, "Delete Record Operation") =
    MsgBoxResult.No Then

    MsgBox("Delete operation cancelled and record not deleted.",
        MsgBoxStyle.Information, "Record Not Deleted")
Else
    'Remove the current record from the dataset
    Try
        BindingContext(dsEmployees,
            "Employee").RemoveAt(intCurrentRecord)

        'Call the WriteXML Function to rewrite the XML File
        WriteXML()

        'Get the current record number (using the position
          property)
        intCurrentRecord = BindingContext(dsEmployees,
            "Employee").Position + 1
        Call InitializeInterface()
        MsgBox("The record has successfully been deleted.",
            MsgBoxStyle.Information, "Delete Record")
    Catch
        MsgBox("There was an error deleting the record. Please
            try again.", MsgBoxStyle.Critical, "Error Deleting
            Record")
    End Try
End If
```

This procedure begins by verifying the user's intent to delete a record. A Try. . . Catch routine attempts to remove the record from the dataset and then update the XML file. A message is displayed when the application successfully deletes the record.

5. Save your changes.

You have almost finished writing the code. You have one remaining task: writing a procedure to exit the application.

To write a procedure for exiting the application:

1. Place the insertion point below the region for Record Management.
2. Create a procedure for the btnExit_Click event. Add the following statements to the procedure:

```
Dim response As Integer
        response = MsgBox("Do you want to exit this
            application?", vbYesNo, "XML Address Book
            Application")
        If response = vbYes Then
              End
        End If
```

3. Save your changes.

Run the Application

You are now ready to run the XML Employee Address Book application and test its functionality.

To run the application:

1. Click the Start button or press the F5 key to run the application.
2. If the application locates the XML file, it displays the first record. You will receive an error message if the application cannot find the file or if the file is corrupted.
3. Test the navigation buttons, taking note of which buttons are disabled as you navigate through the dataset.
4. Navigate to the last record and try deleting it. You should receive a verification message.
5. Click the **Add** button. Enter each element as the application prompts you to do so. You should receive a verification message.
6. Continue testing your application to check its functionality. When you finish, click the **Exit** button.

Summary

● XML is a significant data format for today's business applications. The XML data format includes both data and the structure of the data. Because many applications read XML files, it has become a common way of transferring information between computers by using the Internet.

● Extensible Markup Language (XML) is a subset of the Standardized General Markup Language (SGML). XML is a generalized tag-based language that differs from other markup languages such as RTF and HTML that define how data appears.

● XML is self-describing, which means an XML document contains data and information about the structure of the data. Thus applications that support XML can share structured information that can be sent over common channels such as the Internet.

● You can easily create well-formed XML documents by using the Visual Studio.NET XML Designer. One advantage of using the XML Designer to create and edit XML files is that you can use built-in tools for validating the structure and content of the files. To use the XML Designer, you add a new XML file to a project. Although you can use either HTML view or Data view to add elements to the file, Data view is easier to use. In HTML view, you can use the XML menu to validate the structure of the XML data.

● You can use the ReadXML method to read XML data from an external XML file into a Visual Studio.NET dataset.

● You can use the WriteXML method to write XML data from a Visual Studio.NET dataset to an external file.

● XML schemas are text files with an .xsd file extension. A schema defines the structure of an XML file, including the root element, the data elements, and optional attributes. Because Visual Studio.NET supports the built-in XML data types, you can also specify data types in your schema definition files.

● You can use the XML Designer to create schemas, schema elements, and XML files. To create a schema, you add a new item to the project by using the XML schema template.

● To add elements to a schema, use the XML Designer to name the root element for the schema and to define each of the schema's elements. You can also assign a built-in data type by using the XML Designer.

● By associating a Dataset schema with an XML file, you can validate that the XML data is well-formed and conforms to the specifications contained in the schema. To validate XML data, switch to XML view and then click XML, Validate XML Data.

● You can use the tools available in Visual Studio.NET to add keys to XML schemas and establish relationships between schemas.

Key Terms

attribute

Data view

element

end-tag

Extensible Markup Language (XML)

generalized markup language

Hypertext Markup Language (HTML)

Key tag

Relation tag

Rich Text Format (RTF)

self-describing

specific markup language

Standard Generalized Markup Language (SGML)

start-tag

type

well-formed document

XML Designer

XML schema

XML Schema Definition Language (XSD)

XML view

Study Questions

Multiple-Choice Questions

1. Extensible Markup Language is a subset of:
   a. HTML
   b. RTF
   c. VBA
   d. SGML
   e. ASCII text

2. Which characteristic differentiates XML from other markup languages?
   a. XML includes tags that specify how to format data.
   b. XML is a specific markup language.
   c. XML is self-describing.
   d. XML is text-based.
   e. XML includes markup tags.

3. Consider the following XML statement:

   <lastname>Smith</LastName>

   Is this a well-formed statement?
   a. Yes, because it includes tags.
   b. No, because the end-tag includes a backslash character.
   c. Yes, because it contains both a start- and an end-tag.
   d. No, because the end-tag is in a different case.
   e. Yes, because both tags refer to the last-name element.

4. Which object links data in one XML element to the associated data in another XML element?
   a. Schema
   b. Attribute
   c. Key
   d. Built-in data type
   e. Complex element

5. Which of the following statements violates the recommended naming conventions for an XML element?
   a.
   b. <2Lastname></2Lastname>
   c.
   d.
   e.

6. A file has an extension of .XSD. What kind of file is it?
   a. RTF file
   b. SGML file
   c. HTML file
   d. XML data file
   e. XML schema file

7. You are using Visual Studio to create an XML document. How can you add this document to your project?
   a. Add a DataSet object to the application's form.
   b. Use the Add menu to add a new item to the project.
   c. Add XML tags to information appearing in Data view of the XML Designer.
   d. Use an OLEDB or SQLDB connection object to import XML into the project.
   e. Add XML tags to information appearing in XML view of the XML Designer.

8. Which of the following is a characteristic of an XML data source?
   a. It is external to a Visual Basic.NET application.
   b. XML data cannot be read or modified in a text editor.
   c. XML can be read into a dataset.
   d. A and B
   e. A and C

9. The tag </address> is what kind of tag?
   a. HTML heading tag.
   b. XML start-tag.
   c. SGML document tag.
   d. XML end-tag.
   e. RTF tag.

10. When you create a schema from an existing XML file, what is the default data type for all elements?
    a. Integer
    b. Decimal
    c. String
    d. Double
    e. Boolean

True/False Questions

1. XML contains information about how to format the text the document contains.

2. XML is a self-describing markup language.

3. A well-formed XML document corresponds to the definition provided in an associated schema.

4. You can bind objects on a Visual Basic form to elements in an XML file.

5. You can associate a schema with an XML file by using the Data view in the XML Designer.

Short Answer Questions

1. Describe how XML differs from RTF and HTML.

2. What is a self-describing document?

3. What is a well-formed XML document?

4. What is an XML schema? How are schemas associated with XML files?

5. Why might you use the ReadXML and WriteXML methods in your application?

Guided Exercises

Creating an Application with a DataGrid to Display XML Inventory Data

The Visual Basic DataGrid control is useful for displaying data stored in an external XML data source. In this chapter, you learned how to create an application that reads and writes XML data. In this exercise you will create an application for displaying and changing inventory records. The application displays inventory records from the *Inventory.xml* file on your data files. Figure 11.41 shows the completed Windows application.

FIGURE 11.41. *Interface for the Inventory application*

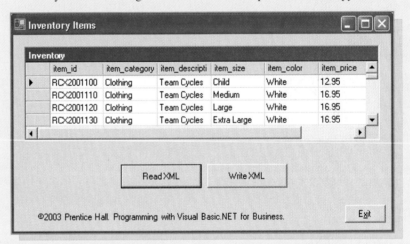

To create an Inventory Windows application:

1. Launch Visual Studio.NET if it is not already running.
2. Click **File**, **New Project**. Create a new Windows application and name it `XMLInventory`.
3. Using Figure 11.41 as a guide, add the following controls to the form and set the control properties as specified.

Name	Property	Setting
DataGrid1	TabStop	False
btnReadXML	Text TabStop, TabIndex	&ReadXML Yes, 0
btnWriteXML	txtDescription TabStop, TabIndex	&WriteXML Yes, 1
btnExit	Text	E&xit
lblCopyright	txtValue	©2003 Prentice Hall. Programming with Visual Basic.NET for Business.

4. Add the following code to the project:

Comments:

```
'©2003 Prentice Hall
'By Philip A. Koneman
'Created/Revised: 05/10/02
'XML Inventory Windows Form Application
```

Variable Declarations:

```
'Declare a dataset
    Dim dsInventory As New DataSet("Inventory")
```

Procedure for Reading XML Data:

```
Private Sub btnReadXML_Click(ByVal sender As System.Object,
  ByVal e As System.EventArgs) Handles btnReadXML.Click

        Dim strDirectory As String
        strDirectory = Environment.CurrentDirectory
        Dim strFile As String
        strFile = strDirectory & "\Inventory.xml"

        Dim fsReadXML As New System.IO.FileStream _
        (strFile, System.IO.FileMode.Open)
        dsInventory.ReadXml(fsReadXML)
        fsReadXML.Close()

        With DataGrid1
            .DataSource = dsInventory
            .DataMember = "Inventory"
            .CaptionText = .DataMember
        End With
    End Sub
```

Procedure for Writing XML Data:

```
Private Sub btnWriteXML_Click(ByVal sender As System.Object,
  ByVal e As System.EventArgs) Handles btnWriteXML.Click

    Dim strDirectory As String
    strDirectory = Environment.CurrentDirectory
    Dim strFile As String
    strFile = strDirectory & "\Inventory.xml"

    Dim fsWriteXML As New System.IO.FileStream _
    (strFile, System.IO.FileMode.Truncate)
    dsInventory.WriteXml(fsWriteXML)
    fsWriteXML.Close()

    MsgBox("The file has been updated.",
        MsgBoxStyle.Information, "Write XML")
End Sub
```

Procedure for Exiting the Application:

```
Private Sub btnExit_Click(ByVal sender As System.Object, ByVal e
    As System.EventArgs) Handles btnExit.Click
    Dim response As Integer
    response = MsgBox("Do you want to exit this application?",
        vbYesNo, "XML Inventory Application")
    If response = vbYes Then
        End
    End If
End Sub
```

5. Copy the *Inventory.xml* file from the folder containing the data files for this chapter to the *bin* folder for this project.
6. Save your changes.
7. Run and test the application.
8. Switch to design time and make any necessary changes to the application.
9. Save your changes, and close the solution.

Creating a Form to Display One Inventory Item at a Time

The application you created in the previous exercise is a convenient way to display XML data on a form, but many databases have a user interface that displays one record on the form at a time. In this exercise you will create a Windows application that is similar to the XML Address Book in this chapter, except the application in this exercise displays inventory data. Figure 11.42 shows the completed Windows application.

FIGURE 11.42. *Interface for the Inventory application for displaying a single inventory item*

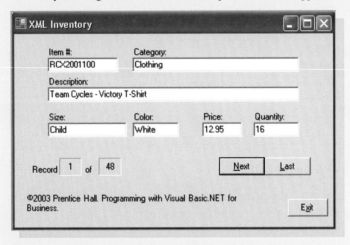

To create an Inventory Windows application:

1. Launch Visual Studio.NET if it is not already running.
2. Click **File**, **New**, **Project**. Create a new Windows application and name it `XMLInventoryForm`.
3. Using Figure 11.42 as a guide, add the following controls to the form and set the control properties as specified.

Object	Property	Setting
Form1	Text	XML Inventory
	StartPosition	CenterScreen
lblItemID	Text	Item #:
lblCategory	Text	Category:
lblDescription	Text	Description:

lblSize	Text	Size:
lblColor	Text	Color:
lblPrice	Text	Price:
lblQuantity	Text	Quantity:
lblCopyright	Text	©2003 Prentice Hall. Programming with Visual Basic.NET for Business.
lbl1	Text	Record
lbl2	Text	of
lblCurrentRecord	Text TextAlign BorderStyle	 MiddleCenter Fixed3D
lblTotalRecord	Text TextAlign BorderStyle	 MiddleCenter Fixed3D
txtItemID	TabStop	False
txtCategory	TabStop	False
txtDescription	TabStop	False
txtSize	TabStop	False
txtColor	TabStop	False
txtPrice	TabStop	False
txtQuantity	TabStop	False
btnFirst	Text TabStop; Tab Index	First True, 0
btnPrevious	Text TabStop; Tab Index	Previous True, 1
btnNext	Text TabStop; Tab Index	Next True, 2
btnLast	Text TabStop; Tab Index	Last True, 3

4. Open the *Inventory.xml* file from your data files.
5. Click **File**, **Save Inventory.xml As**. Save a copy of the file in the *bin* directory for this project.
6. With the file in XML view, click the **XML** menu item and choose **Create Schema**. Associate the schema with the XML file.
7. Use the Hands-On Programming Example for this project as a guide for writing the code. Create the following code elements:

Variable Declarations:

```
Dim CurrentRecord As Integer
Dim TotalRecords As Integer
Public dsInventory As New DataSet("Inventory")
```

Functions:

ReadXML( )

WriteXML( )

Form Load:

Make sure you create a DataBinding
for each text to its associated element
in the XML file, as follows:

item_id

item_category

item_description

item_size

item_color

item_price

item_quantity

Record Navigation:

btnFirst

btnPrevious

btnNext

btnLast

Exit Procedure:

Create an event procedure for exiting
the application.

8. Save your changes.
9. Run and test the application.
10. Switch to Design view and make any necessary changes to the application.
11. Save your changes, and close the solution.

Case Studies

Creating an XML Student Grade Book

In this chapter you learned how to bind a DataGrid control to an XML data source. In this case
study you will create a Windows application for storing student grades. The XML data file bound
to the data grid will display the following information for each student:

Student ID

Last Name

First Name

Score for Assignment #1

Score for Assignment #2

Midterm Exam Score

Score for Assignment #3

Score for Assignment #4

Final Exam Score

Each assignment and exam is worth 100 points, for a total of 700 points for the semester. Create
a Windows application named XMLGradeBook. Store the scores, using the built-in Decimal
data type. Save the XML file as Scores.xml. Add data for five students to the XML file, and
set the Form_Load event to fill the data grid with data from the XML data source. Save and test
the application.

Creating a Modified Version of the Student Grade Book Application

The Student Grade Book application is useful for entering student scores, but it does not display
the scores for one student at a time. Create a version of the Student Gradebook application named
XMLStudentGrades. The application consists of one form with text boxes for displaying
the student name and score information. Include a label on the form that displays the overall percent score and another label that displays a letter grade, using the following scale:

90% or above: A

80% to 89%: B

70% to 79%: C

60% - 69%: D

Less than 60%: F

Add navigation buttons to move through the student records. Save and test the application.

Graphics, Printing, and Reporting with Crystal Reports

Displaying graphics and printing information are features included in many of today's applications. Graphics provide rich content that enhances a program's interface, and e-commerce Websites frequently include pictures of the products that are for sale. Visual Studio.NET provides support for multimedia and graphics. Because images play a role in both Windows and Web applications, you will sometimes include images in your applications.

At other times you will need to print and distribute information from your applications. You can preview and print text by using built-in controls, or for more sophisticated reporting, you can use Crystal Reports. In this chapter, you will learn how to create and display graphics and preview, print, and report information.

Performance Objectives

At the conclusion of this chapter, you will be able to:

■ Display vector and raster graphics in Visual Basic.NET applications.

■ Use the Image Editor to create bitmap graphics.

■ Display bitmap images in Windows applications and Web Forms applications.

■ Use the PrintPreviewDialog and PrintDialog controls to preview and print text in Visual Basic.NET applications.

■ Create a report by using one of the Crystal Reports Experts.

■ Display reports by using the Windows Forms Viewer.

Displaying Graphics in Applications

Undoubtedly you have heard the saying, "A picture is worth a thousand words." The word *graphic* is just another term for picture. The applications you use in business support graphic capabilities, and the Web uses graphics extensively. You can add a variety of graphical elements to Visual Basic.NET Windows and Web applications. Common graphics you might use include lines, shapes, text rendered for display, or bitmapped graphics. Alternatively, you might want to add graphic images to buttons or other interface elements to enhance the appearance of an application. A common use for graphics is adding images to buttons. If you completed the Hands-On Programming Example in Chapter 10, you added graphical images to the buttons for navigating among records in a Web Forms project. The Windows environment supports two kinds of graphics, vector graphics and raster graphics. Let's examine these two graphic types in more detail.

USING VECTOR GRAPHICS IN APPLICATIONS

Vector graphics are simple images that draw shapes on the screen. Vector graphics represent images as coordinates, shapes, and colors. Many drawing programs, including Visio and the drawing tools available in software suites such as Microsoft Office, support vector graphics for creating simple shapes such as lines, rectangles, circles, curves, and figures. Other examples of vector graphics are graphs and charts that represent numeric relationships visually. Figure 12.1 shows a simple vector graphic in a Microsoft Excel workbook.

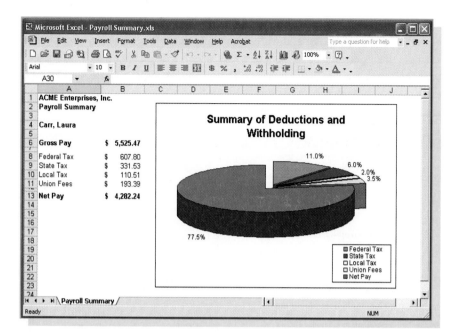

FIGURE 12.1. *Excel workbook displaying a vector graphic*

A line vector is defined by two endpoints. The first point defines the start of the line, and the second point identifies where the line ends. A rectangle vector is specified by the location of its upper left corner and a pair of numbers giving its width and height. A circle (ellipse) vector uses the coordinates of its upper left bounds and the size of the circle.

In Visual Basic.NET you can use the **OnPaint method** to raise a **Paint event**. The OnPaint method has one required argument: the data for the event, represented by the character **e**. A Paint event paints the graphic specified by e on the screen. The data files for this chapter include a solution named *VectorGraphic* that contains the following code:

```
Protected Overrides Sub OnPaint(ByVal e As PaintEventArgs)

    'Declare graphics object and pen object
    Dim myGraphic As Graphics
    myGraphic = e.Graphics
    Dim myPen As New Pen(Color.Red, 3)

    'Draw a rectangle
    myGraphic.DrawRectangle(myPen, 20, 10, 100, 50)

    'Draw a line
    myGraphic.DrawLine(myPen, 10, 100, 175, 100)

    'Draw a circle
    myGraphic.DrawEllipse(myPen, 10, 130, 100, 100)
End Sub
```

Visual Studio.NET uses an advanced Windows graphics design interface (GDI) called GDI+. You use GDI+ to create graphics, draw text, and manipulate graphical images as objects. GDI+ is the only way to render graphics programmatically in Windows Forms applications. The VectorGraphic application uses the **Advanced Graphics Interface (GDI+)** to create a graphics object and a pen object. To draw vector graphics, you must first declare a **Graphics object** to contain the graphic and a **Pen object** specifying the color and width of the line that will represent the graphics. In this example, the code creates an instance of a form for displaying the vector objects, and then declares a graphic and a pen. The **DrawLine**, **DrawRectangle**, and **DrawEllipse** methods use the graphic and pen objects to draw a line, rectangle, and ellipse on the form. Figure 12.2 shows the screen output when this application runs.

FIGURE 12.2. *Application displaying three vector graphics*

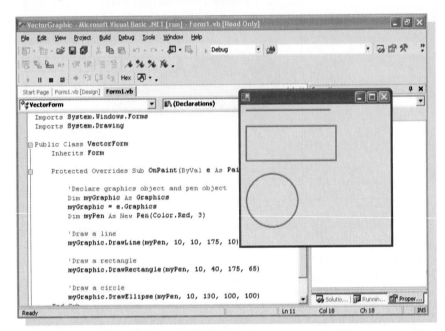

Why would you add vector graphic capabilities to an application? Programs that chart data, such as the example in Figure 12.1, use vector graphics to represent numeric relationships visually. Applications that draw flowcharts or model processes also use vector graphics for representing business rules, business processes, and procedures.

Although vector graphics are useful in applications, images appearing on toolbars or buttons or as program icons are difficult to display with the techniques for creating vector graphics from a collection of coordinates. Digital photographs are even more difficult to create as vector graphics. For these kinds of images, you need to use raster graphics.

USING RASTER GRAPHICS IN APPLICATIONS

A **raster graphic** is an image made up of thousands of small squares called **pixels**. Each pixel can be a color, and the combination of colors makes the image. An image made up of pixels is a **bitmap**, which is a two-dimensional representation of a collection of pixels. Figure 12.3 displays a bitmapped image of 32 by 32 pixels. The combination of red, white, and grey pixels creates an icon of a stop sign.

FIGURE 12.3. *A grid of pixels defining a raster graphic*

Icons created from pixels are the simplest kinds of raster graphics. Icons are familiar to you because most applications for Windows include buttons with icons indicating what the buttons do. In fact, the Visual Studio.NET IDE includes numerous buttons with icons indicating the task each button performs. To create raster graphics, you need an application for defining the pixels that make up the image. Many applications include an editor for creating simple raster graphics. Visual Studio.NET includes the Image Editor for creating raster graphics. Let's take a look at how to use the Image Editor to create icons you can associate with buttons.

USING THE VISUAL STUDIO.NET IMAGE EDITOR

The Visual Basic.NET *Image Editor* has an extensive set of tools for creating and editing images and for creating toolbar bitmaps. You can use the Image Editor to create bitmap images at design time and use them later in your applications.

The easiest way to open the Image Editor is to create a new bitmap or icon file. Figure 12.4 shows the **New File** dialog box that appears when you click **File, New, File**.

FIGURE 12.4. *Creating a new icon file with the Image Editor*

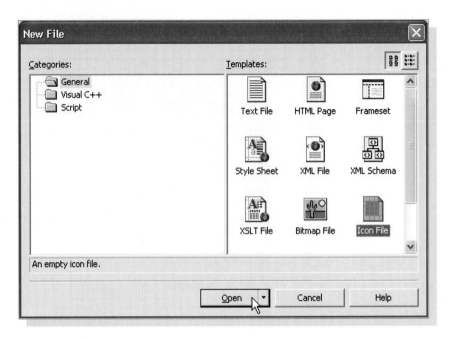

The Image Editor toolbar does not display by default when you are using the Visual Studio Developer profile. To display the Image Editor toolbar, click **View**, **Toolbars**, **Image Editor**, as shown in Figure 12.5.

FIGURE 12.5. *Displaying the Image Editor toolbar*

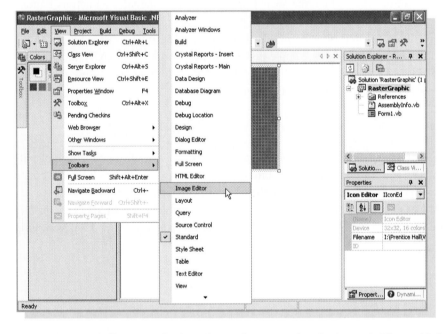

The Image Editor now displays the workspace and tools shown in Figure 12.6.

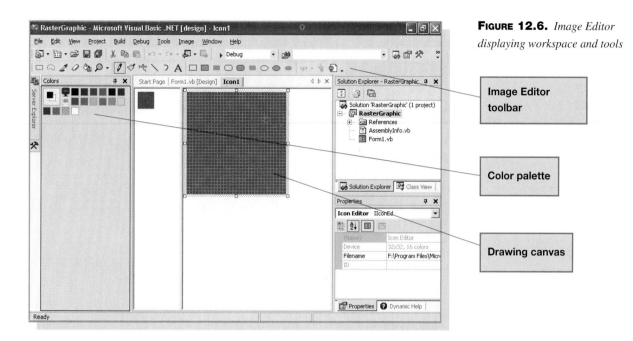

FIGURE 12.6. *Image Editor displaying workspace and tools*

The Image Editor window displays the current image in two panes separated by a splitter bar. The left pane shows the icon or image at its actual size; the right pane shows an enlarged view in which you can distinguish individual pixels. The right pane is updated automatically as you create the icon.

The Image Editor toolbar contains a variety of tools for adding lines, rectangles, curves, ellipses, and circles to the canvas. Table 12.1 summarizes the more common tools you will use when creating icons and bitmap images.

Table 12.1: Image Editor tools

Tool	Icon	Purpose
Rectangle Selection tool		Select an area of the image.
Color Selection tool		Select a color in the color palette.
Erase tool		Erase a series of pixels.
Fill tool		Fill an area of contiguous pixels with the current color.
Magnification tool		Change the zoom factor of the right pane.
Pencil tool		Draw a freeform line.
Brush tool		Draw a freeform line with a brush pattern.
Airbrush tool		Draw a freeform line with an airbrush pattern.
Line tool		Draw a line.
Curve tool		Draw a curve.
Text tool		Create a bitmap representation of text.
Rectangle tool		Draw a rectangle.
Ellipse tool		Draw an ellipse.

The best way to learn to draw icons and images in the Image Editor is to experiment with the tools. The Image Editor supports multiple levels of Undo, so you can easily repair any mistakes you make. You can use the Line and Fill tools to create the icon shown in Figure 12.7.

FIGURE 12.7. *Icon created in the Image Editor*

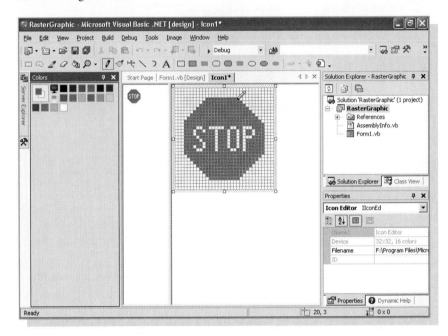

To save an image file created with the Image Editor, click **File**, **Save Icon1 As**. Recall from Chapter 11 that you can use the *bbin* folder for the project to store associated files. Figure 12.8 shows how to name the icon file *Stop.ico* and save it to the *bbin* folder.

FIGURE 12.8. *Entering the filename to save an icon*

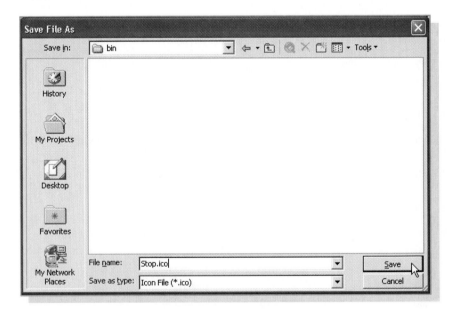

When you save an image or an icon, you have a choice of file types. Table 12.2 summarizes the kinds of bitmap files supported by Visual Studio.NET.

Table 12.2: Visual Studio.NET bitmap image types

File Type	File Extension	Purpose
Icon file	*.ico	Image file for creating a custom icon.
Bitmap file	*.bmp	BMP is a standard format used by Windows to store device-independent and application-independent images.
DIB file	*.dib	Device Independent Bitmap: Designed to ensure that bitmapped graphics created with one application can be loaded and displayed in another application.
GIF file	*.gif	Graphics Interchange Format: Compressed format for storing images that appear on Web pages. Works well with shapes.
JPEG file	*.jpg, *.jpe, *.jpeg	Joint Photographic Experts Group: Compressed file format popular for images displayed on the Web. Works best for digital photographs.

Once you save an icon file, you can use it in your projects. The form in *RasterGraphic* application that is included with your data files has a button with the **Name** property set to *btnStop*. Figure 12.9 displays the button on the form after the **Image** property has been set to the *Stop.ico* file.

If you are creating images to use in Web Forms projects, make sure you save the image files as GIF or JPEG images. These are the file formats the Web supports.

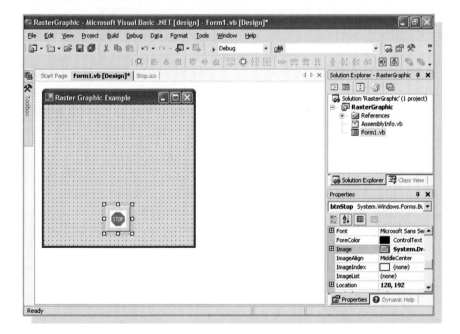

FIGURE 12.9. *Button with the image property set to display an icon*

Tools like the Image Editor are useful for creating simple raster graphics for icons. More sophisticated images, such as digital photographs, are made up of individual pixels that display different colors. For example, Figure 12.10 shows a portion of a digital photograph you will add to an application later in this chapter. With the image enlarged to 900 percent of normal size, the pixels that make up the image of a watch are clearly seen.

FIGURE 12.10. *Digital image enlarged to 900 percent to display individual pixels*

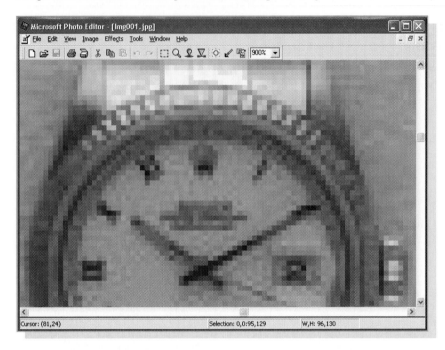

Obviously, it would be impractical to use an Image Editor to create a raster graphic with the detail shown in Figure 12.10. You can use other computer tools, such as image scanners and photo-editing programs to create bitmapped (raster) graphics. After you create the image files, you can display the images in your Visual Basic.NET programs.

DISPLAYING BITMAP IMAGES IN WINDOWS APPLICATIONS

Multimedia applications—applications that contain text and other media such as image—are popular for communicating information. At a basic level, *multimedia* can be defined as any application that represents information in two or more formats, such as text and images. You are familiar with multimedia because most Websites include both text and images. From online product catalogs to computer-based encyclopedias, combining text, graphics, and other rich media types is an essential skill for today's Windows or Web programmer.

Visual Basic.NET includes the ***PictureBox control*** for displaying bitmap images and icon files. The ***Image property*** determines the image that a PictureBox control displays at run time. You can set this property at design time by using the Image row in the Property window. You can also set the Image property code to respond to a specific user event, such as a command to change the image the control displays.

Let's look at an example of a simple multimedia application that combines text and images. In 1999, the United States Mint rolled out a program for commemorating all 50 states by releasing a special version of the quarter for each state. The 50 States program issues five coins a year, in the order in which the state's constitution was ratified. In 1999, for example, the Mint issued State Quarters for Delaware, Pennsylvania, New Jersey, Georgia, and Connecticut.

Assume you want to develop a Windows application that will display information about each coin and an image of the reverse of each coin. Figure 12.11 shows an interface for this application.

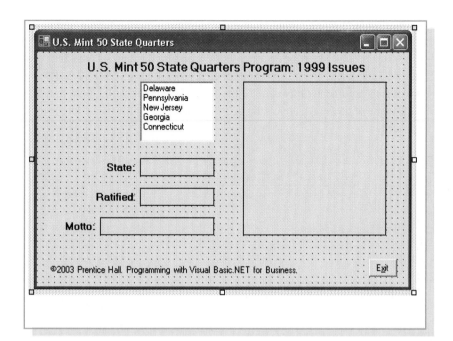

FIGURE 12.11. *Interface for the 50 State Quarters application*

As you can see, the application consists of a single form with a list box for changing the information and image of the specific state quarter displayed on the form. Table 12.3 displays the information for each state that will display on the form.

Table 12.3: Information for the 50 States Quarters issued in 1999

State	Date Ratified	Motto	Image File
Delaware	1787	The First State	DE.jpg
Pennsylvania	1787	The Keystone State	PA.jpg
New Jersey	1787	The Garden State	NJ.jpg
Georgia	1788	The Peach State	GA.jpg
Connecticut	1788	The Constitution State	CT.jpg

Selecting Delaware in the list will display the information shown in Figure 12.12.

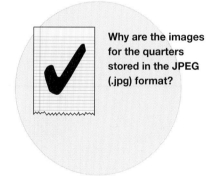

Why are the images for the quarters stored in the JPEG (.jpg) format?

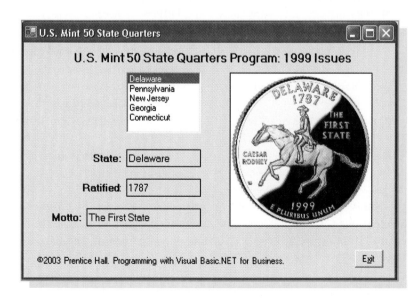

FIGURE 12.12. *50 State Quarters application displaying information about Delaware*

The data files for this chapter include a folder named *State Quarters* that contains this application. The application has a sub procedure named *DisplayState* that sets the **Image** property and **SizeMode** property of the picture box and sets the **Text** property of each label, displaying the information for each state listed in Table 12.3. The procedure receives four arguments: the name of the state, the date of ratification, the state motto, and the name of the image appearing on the reverse side of the coin. Here is the code for the procedure:

```
Friend Sub DisplayState(ByVal stName, ByVal stDate, ByVal
    stMotto, ByVal stImage)
    'Get directory and set image path and filename
    strDirectory = Environment.CurrentDirectory
    strFileName = strDirectory & "\" & stImage
    picReverse.Image = Image.FromFile(strFileName)
    picReverse.SizeMode = PictureBoxSizeMode.StretchImage
    'Set label data
    lblStateName.Text = stName
    lblDateRatified.Text = stDate
    lblStateMotto.Text = stMotto
End Sub
```

In Chapter 11 you learned how to use the **Environment.CurrentDirectory** method to return the path for the *bbin* directory for a project. All the images for the *States Quarters* application are stored in the *bin* folder so the procedure can use this information, in conjunction with the name of the image, to change the **Image** property of the **PictureBox** control.

The images you include in a Visual Basic.NET application may be of different sizes. The **SizeMode** property has settings that determine how an image displays. Table 12.4 summarizes the property settings for a picture box supported in Visual Studio.NET:

Table 12.4: Supported settings for the SizeMode property of a PictureBox control

Setting	Purpose
PictureBoxSizeMode.Normal	This value places the image in the upper left corner of the picture box and clips any part of the image too big for the control.
PictureBoxSizeMode.StretchImage	This value causes the image to stretch or be resized to fit the picture box.
PictureBoxSizeMode.AutoSize	This value causes the control to resize to the size of the image.
PictureBoxSizeMode.CenterImage	This value causes the image to appear centered in the client area.

The *DisplayState* procedure uses the PictureBoxSizeMode .StretchImage value. How will this setting affect the images displayed in the application?

Notice that the *DisplayState* procedure sets the **SizeMode** property to **StretchImage**. This is necessary, because each image is larger than the bounds of the control. If this property is set to **Normal**, only a portion of the image displays, as in Figure 12.13.

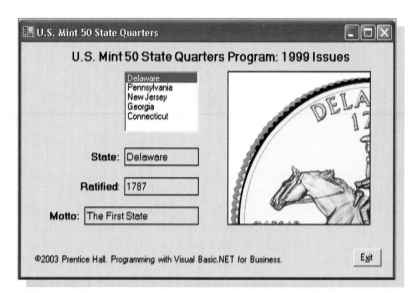

FIGURE 12.13. *Image displayed in a PictureBox control with the SizeMode property set to Normal*

The list box on the form for each state passes the appropriate arguments to the procedure, and the procedure uses these arguments to change the text and image that displays. The **SelectedIndexChanged** event for a list box occurs whenever the **SelectedIndex** property changes, which is the case when an item in the list is clicked. The code for the **SelectedIndexChanged** event is as follows:

```
Private Sub lstStates_SelectedIndexChanged(ByVal sender As
   System.Object, ByVal e As System.EventArgs) Handles
   lstStates.SelectedIndexChanged
    Select Case lstStates.SelectedIndex
        Case 0
            DisplayState("Delaware", "1787", "The First State",
            "DE.jpg")
        Case 1
            DisplayState("Pennsylvania", "1787", "The Keystone
                State",
            "PA.jpg")
        Case 2
            DisplayState("New Jersey", "1787", "The Garden
                State",
            "NJ.jpg")
        Case 3
            DisplayState("Georgia", "1788", "The Peach State",
            "GA.jpg")
        Case 4
            DisplayState("Connecticut", "1788", "The
                Constitution
            State", "CT.jpg")
    End Select
End Sub
```

As you can see, the procedure uses a Select Case decision structure to pass the appropriate arguments to the *DisplayState* procedure. Notice that all the information listed in Table 12.3 is included in the arguments.

Tip

Using a database or XML file to store the information for each button is more efficient than including this information in the arguments for each procedure. You will learn how to store text and image information in a database in the Hands-On Programming example later in this chapter.

Adding bitmap images to a Windows application is easy. As you might anticipate, certain Web Forms projects also require images. Visual Basic.NET includes a Web Server Image control for adding bitmap images to Web forms.

DISPLAYING BITMAP IMAGES IN WEB FORMS APPLICATIONS

Most likely the Websites you often visit provide interactivity so you are able to display information by using the controls that are a part of the Web interface. Images and other graphic media are an essential part of the Web. As you learned in Chapter 10, creating Web Forms applications in the Visual Studio.NET IDE is very similar to the way you create Windows applications. Therefore, replicating the 50 State Quarters Windows application as a Web Forms application should be fairly straightforward.

The .NET framework library includes the Web Server *Image control* for displaying images on Web forms. The *ImageURL property* of a Web Forms Image control specifies the image to display on the page. Figure 12.14 displays a Web Forms version of the application for displaying the 50 States Quarters issued by the United States Mint in 1999.

FIGURE 12.14. *Interface for the Web Forms 50 State Quarters application*

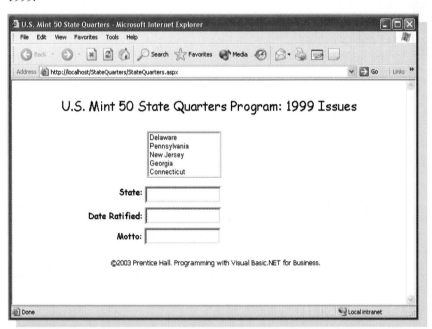

Tip

To view this solution do the following:

1. Copy the *StateQuarters* folder from your data files to the *\\InetPub\wwwroot* folder on your computer.

2. From the Windows Taskbar, Click **Start**, select **Run**, type *inetmgr.exe* into the Open box and click OK.

3. When IIS opens select Default Web Site in the left pane, look for the application folder in the right pane.

4. Right-click the *StateQuarters* folder and select Properties.

5. Click **Create**, and then click **OK**.

You will now be able to run this solution.

The interface for this version of the application is similar to the Windows form version. The main difference is that the Web Forms version uses an **Image** control, and the Windows application uses a **PictureBox** control. Otherwise, the names for the controls and the code routines are similar. The code for the *DisplayState* sub procedure is as follows:

```
Friend Sub DisplayState(ByVal stName, ByVal stDate, ByVal
  stMotto, ByVal stImage)
    imgReverse.ImageUrl = stImage
    imgReverse.Visible = True
    lblStateName.Text = stName
    lblDateRatified.Text = stDate
    lblStateMotto.Text = stMotto
End Sub
```

This procedure is actually simpler than the same procedure in the Windows application, because the procedure does not need to determine the path for the image files. Since the images for the Web Forms procedure are located in the same folder as the other files for the application, a relative reference to the images is all that is required to display the images. The procedure uses the *stName* argument to assign the image name to the **ImageURL** property. The procedure that handles the **SelectedIndexChanged** event for the Web Server Image control is as follows:

```
Private Sub lstStates_SelectedIndexChanged(ByVal sender As
   Object, ByVal e As System.EventArgs) Handles
   lstStates.SelectedIndexChanged
     Select Case lstStates.SelectedIndex
         Case 0
             DisplayState("Delaware", "1787", "The First State",
             "DE.jpg")
         Case 1
             DisplayState("Pennsylvania", "1787", "The Keystone
                 State",
             "PA.jpg")
         Case 2
             DisplayState("New Jersey", "1787", "The Garden
                 State",
             "NJ.jpg")
         Case 3
             DisplayState("Georgia", "1788", "The Peach State",
             "GA.jpg")
         Case 4
             DisplayState("Connecticut", "1788", "The
                 Constitution
             State", "CT.jpg")
     End Select
End Sub
```

The **Visible** property of the Image control is set to **False** at design time. The *DisplayImage* procedure, which is called by this procedure, changes the **Visible** property to **True** once the **ImageURL** property is set. Figure 12.15 displays the image and information for the New Jersey State Quarter.

FIGURE 12.15. *Web Forms 50 State Quarters application displaying information about New Jersey*

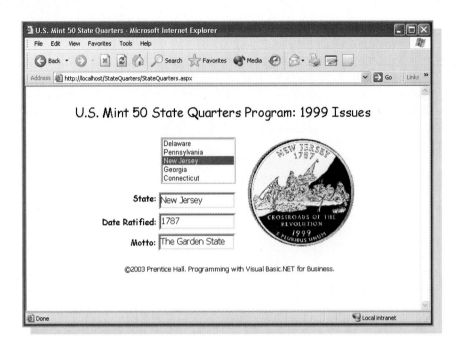

As you can see, displaying images in Windows and Web Forms applications is relatively simple. By using the appropriate control, you can easily build multimedia applications that combine text and graphics to provide useful information to the user.

Displaying vector and raster images in applications is one way to enhance the usefulness of your programs. At times you will need to generate program output that can be previewed and then sent to a printer. Let's learn how to preview and print documents in Visual Basic.NET.

Previewing and Printing Text by Using the PrintPreviewDialog and PrintDialog Controls

In Chapter 1 you learned about the Input, Processing, Output, and Storage (IPOS) cycle that defines what computer programs do. In the preceding chapters you have developed programs that accept input from the keyboard or by reading information from a file. You have also learned to store data for later use by writing information to a sequential or random text file or by updating records in a database. Up to this point, however, output has been limited to information displayed on the computer screen or information written to a text file. These kinds of output can be described as ***soft-copy output***, because the form of the output is represented electronically (on the screen and in the computer's memory) or magnetically (on a computer disk). Soft-copy output cannot be used independent of a computer and is viewed on the computer screen. Sometimes you need to distribute information in printed form. Printing produces ***hard-copy output***— information someone can use without looking at a computer screen. You can read and understand a printed document independent of a computer.

In Chapter 5 you learned how to use common dialog controls (OpenFileDialog, SaveFileDialog, and FontDialog) for file input and output (file IO). Visual Basic.NET also provides predefined dialog box controls for previewing and printing documents. The ***PrintDialog control*** displays a dialog box for selecting a printer and printing a document. The ***PrintPreviewDialog control*** displays a dialog box for previewing a document and then printing it. Both of these controls work in conjunction with the ***PrintDocument object*** to preview and print documents. Figure 12.16 shows the interface of an application for opening text files and previewing and printing the text appearing in the text box control. This application is contained in the *Printing* solution included in your data files.

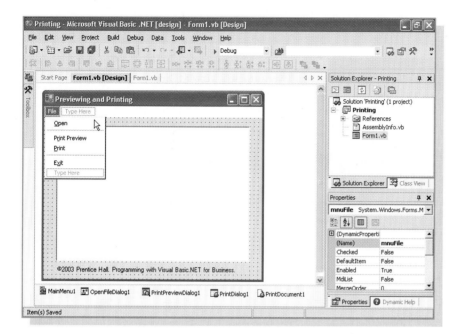

FIGURE 12.16. *Application for previewing and printing text*

Notice the components and objects in the component tray in Figure 12.16. The *MainMenu1* control displays the File Open, Preview, Print, and Exit menu items. The *OpenFileDialog1* control displays the dialog box for opening a text file for printing. The *PrintPreviewDialog1* and *PrintDialog1* controls display common dialog boxes for previewing and printing the document. The *PrintDocument1* object specifies exactly what will be previewed or printed.

Because the application supports both file IO and printing, the general declarations section of the code includes the following two statements:

```
Imports System.IO
Imports System.Drawing.Printing
```

You used the **System.IO** namespace in Chapter 5; it is required for file input and output. The **System.Drawing.Printing** namespace is required for rendering and printing a PrintDocument object.

Now let's see how the application works. The **Open** menu item on the **File** menu displays a common dialog box for opening the file to print. Here's the code for opening a text file:

```
Private Sub mnuFileOpen_Click(ByVal sender As System.Object,
  ByVal e As System.EventArgs) Handles mnuFileOpen.Click
    OpenFileDialog1().Filter = "txt files (*.txt)|*.txt"
    OpenFileDialog1().InitialDirectory =
      Environment.CurrentDirectory

    If OpenFileDialog1().ShowDialog() = DialogResult().OK Then
        Dim myStream As Stream
        myStream = OpenFileDialog1().OpenFile()
        Dim strReader As New StreamReader(myStream)
        txtFile().Text = strReader.ReadToEnd()
```

```
            txtFile().SelectionLength = 0
            strReader.Close()
        End If
    End Sub
```

This procedure is almost identical to the code you used in Chapter 5 to open a text file, except in this case the **Environment.CurrentDirectory** property sets the default directory where the text files are located. Clicking **File**, **Open** displays the dialog box shown in Figure 12.117. In this case, we are selecting the *Addresses.txt* file for previewing and printing.

FIGURE 12.17. *File Open dialog box displaying two text files*

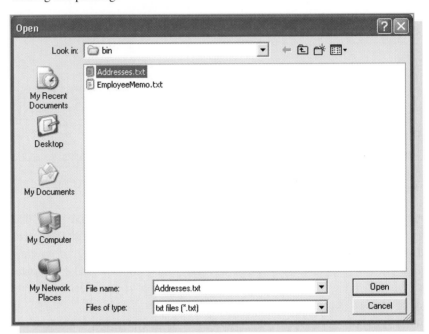

After you specify a file, the text file is read into the text box on the form. Figure 12.18 shows how the employee addresses appear in the text box.

FIGURE 12.18. *The contents of the Addresses.txt file*

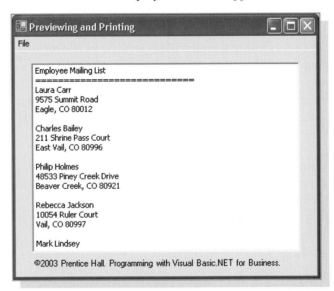

Now let's see how to preview the document before printing. Clicking **File**, **Print Preview** displays the **Print Preview** dialog box shown in Figure 12.19.

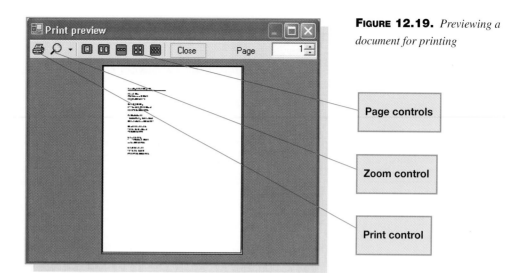

FIGURE 12.19. *Previewing a document for printing*

Page controls

Zoom control

Print control

The **Print Preview** dialog box includes standard controls for previewing and printing the document. In addition to changing the magnification of the preview by using the Zoom control, you can change the preview layout for multi-page documents to display from a single page up to six pages, and you can print the document by using the **Print** control. Here's the code that displays the **Print Preview** dialog box:

```
Private Sub MenuItemPreview_Click(ByVal sender As System.Object,
  ByVal e As System.EventArgs) Handles mnuFilePreview.Click
    PrintPreviewDialog1.ShowDialog()
End Sub
```

The procedure displays the **Print Preview** dialog box by using the **ShowDialog** method. As you can see, there is no code within the procedure for actually previewing the document. Previewing and printing are handled by the *PrintDocument1* object. Here's the code for the *PrintDocument1* object that specifies what to preview and to print:

```
Private Sub PrintDocument1_PrintPage(ByVal sender As Object,
  ByVal e As System.Drawing.Printing.PrintPageEventArgs) Handles
  PrintDocument1.PrintPage
    'Set the document to print
    Dim strTextToPrint As String
    strTextToPrint = txtFile.Text
    e.Graphics.DrawString(strTextToPrint, New Font("Arial", 10,
      FontStyle.Regular), Brushes.Black, 150, 125)
End Sub
```

The procedure declares a string variable named *strTextToPrint*. The contents of the text box are assigned to this variable. The data for the preview and print events is represented by *e*, and the ***Graphics.Drawstring method*** renders the contents of the *strTextToPrint* variable for previewing and printing, using the font and brush specified in the procedure. The font specifies the font face for the printed text. The Brushes class specifies the color of the printed output.

The code for the *PrintDocument1* object also supports the *PrintDialog1* control. Clicking **File**, **Print** displays the **Print** dialog box shown in Figure 12.20.

The Brushes class differs from the Brush tool that is included in the Image Editor.

FIGURE 12.20. *The Print dialog box*

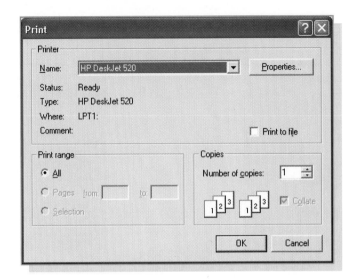

From this common dialog box you can select the printer and the page range to print. The code for the *mnuFilePrint* item is as follows:

```
Private Sub mnuFilePrint_Click(ByVal sender As Object, ByVal e
   As System.EventArgs) Handles mnuFilePrint.Click
     PrintDialog1.Document = PrintDocument1
     If PrintDialog1.ShowDialog() = DialogResult.OK Then
         PrintDocument1.Print()
     End If
End Sub
```

This procedure begins by setting the document to print as the *PrintDocument1* object. The procedure uses an If statement to determine whether the **OK** button in the dialog box has been clicked. If so, the ***Print method*** performs the printing.

The preceding procedures demonstrate the basics of printing simple text documents. Now let's learn how to use Crystal Reports for more sophisticated printing.

Tip

Because the printing originates from a common dialog control, the control handles any errors, such as if the printer is not turned on or is out of paper.

Reporting and Printing Information by Using Crystal Reports

Although you can use the **PrintDialog** control and *PrintDocument* object to print the text in a file or a text box control, there are times when you need more sophisticated printing and reporting capabilities, such as for printing specific records in a database. *Crystal Reports* is the reporting tool for Visual Studio.NET. This tool enables you to create interactive, presentation-quality reports. Because Crystal Reports is integrated with Visual Studio.NET, you can use its features and capabilities for creating and printing reports.

CREATING A REPORT BY USING THE REPORT EXPERT

You create the reports for your applications by using the ***Crystal Report Designer***. This design interface provides the tools you need for creating sophisticated reports. The Crystal Report Designer launches automatically when you add a Crystal Reports object to a project or when you double-click a Crystal Reports object that already exists. You can add predefined functionality to a report by using one of the ***Crystal Reports***

Experts, which will walk you through the process of creating the report. A ***Report Expert*** is a preconfigured report you can use to design a new report.

Your data files for this chapter include a solution named *CrystalReports*, with the form shown in Figure 12.21. The data connection object is bound to a query in the database. The fields displayed in the data grid include a calculated field that lists the total value for each inventory item in the database.

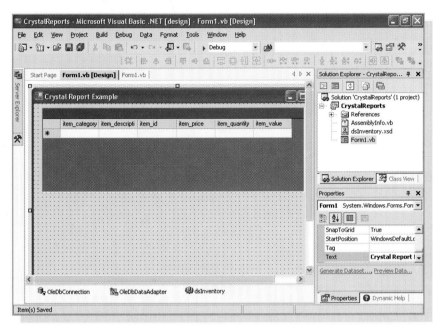

FIGURE 12.21. *Application with a data grid for displaying inventory data*

To open the Crystal Report Designer, add a new Crystal Report object to the project by clicking **File**, **Add New Item**. Choose a **Crystal Report** object in the **New Item** dialog box, name the report `Inventory.rpt`, and click **Open**, as shown in Figure 12.22.

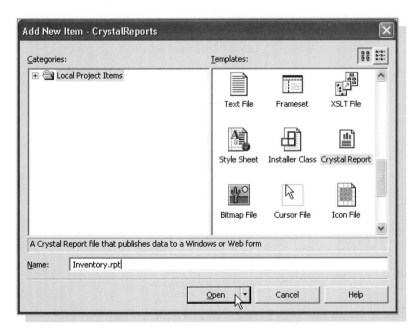

If you intend to open the CrystalReports project in Visual Basic.NET, make sure you copy the *Products.mdb* database from the Start folder to a formatted disk in Drive A, or the Data Connection object will not be able to locate the database.

FIGURE 12.22. *Adding a Crystal Report to a project*

The ***Crystal Report Gallery*** appears. This is a tool for designing a report. You have three options for creating a report: using the Report Expert, creating a blank report, or creating a new report from an existing report. If you use the Report Expert, you can choose the type of report. Figure 12.23 shows how to create a Standard report by using the Report Expert.

FIGURE 12.23. *Creating a report by using the Report Expert*

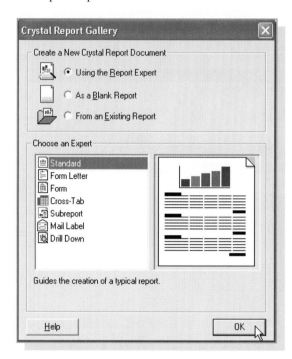

The Report Expert presents a series of dialog boxes in which you can specify the design of the report. The first step is to assign the data source for the report. Figure 12.24 demonstrates how to insert the *inventory_value* query into the report. You must expand the list for the database located on Drive A, and then open the query, also called a *view*.

FIGURE 12.24. *Choosing the data for a report*

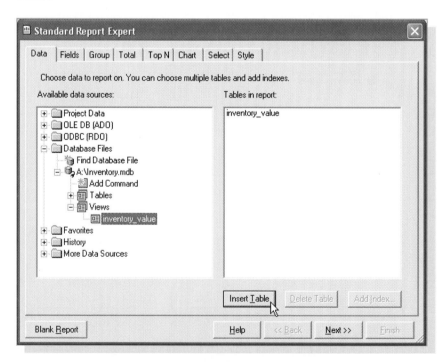

After identifying the data source, you must specify the field data for the report. In addition to adding fields from the **Available Fields:** list to the **Fields to Display:** list, you can specify the column heading for each field. By default, Crystal Reports uses the name of the field in the data source as the column heading. Figure 12.25 displays the five fields for the report. The Column headings are Category, Item #, Price, Quantity, and Value.

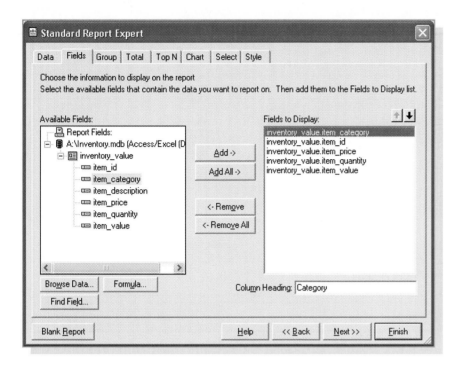

FIGURE 12.25. *Adding five fields to the report*

When you click the **Next** button, the **Group** tab appears. Grouping specifies the data groupings in the report. Figure 12.26 shows the group specification for a report grouped by item category.

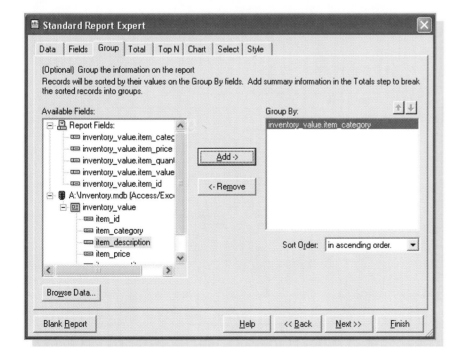

FIGURE 12.26. *Grouping data in the report*

You can also add summary information (totals) to the report. Figure 12.27 shows the default setting for adding grand totals to the fields in the report. By default the summary type is **Sum**, and the check box for adding Grand Totals is checked.

FIGURE 12.27. *Accepting the default to add grand totals to the report*

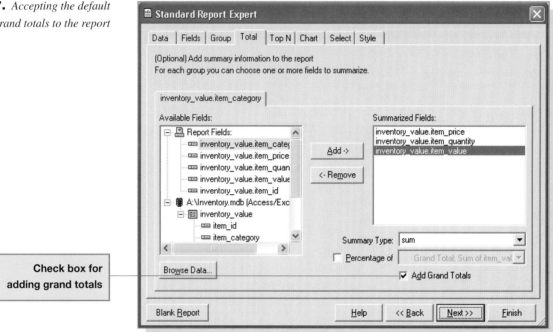

Check box for adding grand totals

The last step in creating the report is to select a formatting style and add a title to the report. Use Standard as the formatting style, type `Inventory Value` as the report title, and click **Finish**, as shown in Figure 12.28.

FIGURE 12.28. *Specifying the style and title for the report*

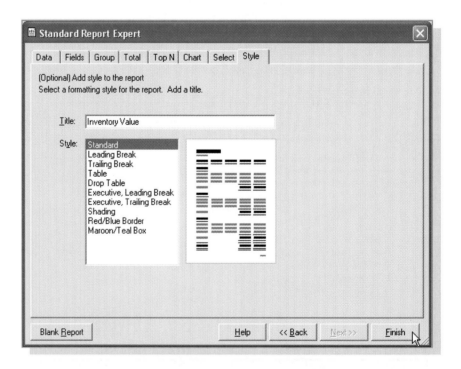

Visual Basic.NET adds the report design shown in Figure 12.29 to the project.

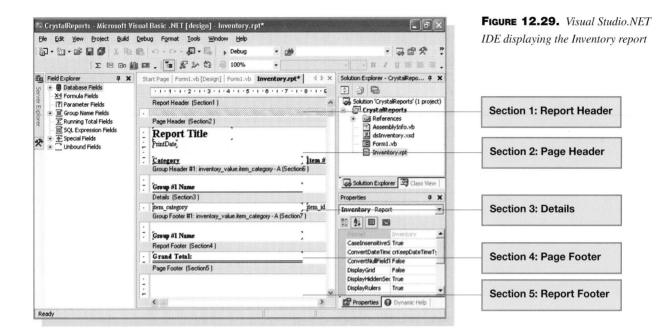

FIGURE 12.29. *Visual Studio.NET IDE displaying the Inventory report*

By default, a report consists of five *Sections*, each holding objects that reference the data to appear in the report. The report sections included in a Standard report and shown in Figure 12.29 are as follows:

Report Header (Section 1): Contains information that appears at the beginning of the report, such as the report title and date on a report with multiple sections.

Page Header (Section 2): Contains information that appears at the top of each page of the report, such as the headings above columns of data. On a simple report, this section may also contain the report title and date.

Details (Section 3): Contains the information from the data source that is of interest in the report.

Report Footer (Section 4): Contains information that appears at the end of the page, such as grand totals.

Page Footer (Section 5): Contains information that appears at the bottom of each page, such as the page number.

The Details section contains the primary information that is of interest. This is where you define the report objects that are linked to the records in the database. These objects act as placeholders, and the number of records in the data source determines the length of the report. If you add any grouping or summary fields, the report will include additional sections. As with any object created with a wizard or designer, you might need to modify the design of the reports you create.

Once you have created a report, the *Report Engine* processes the formatting, grouping, and charting criteria specified in your report.

After you create a report, you must determine how to deploy or display it. Let's look at the simplest way to do so.

DISPLAYING A REPORT

The most common method for making a report available is to host it on a Windows form with the *Windows Forms Viewer*, which is available as a *CrystalReportViewer control* in the Visual Studio toolbox. Figure 12.30 shows the control to add to a Windows application to display a Crystal Report.

Tip

In this example, all sections of the report except the Report Header contain data. To see the report sections not currently visible in the IDE, use the horizontal scroll bar in the report to display these sections.

Tip

If you have created reports in a database application such as Microsoft Access, the areas of the report design will be familiar to you. If you are new to reporting, you might want to experiment with creating reports by using the Report Expert.

FIGURE 12.30. *Using the toolbox to add a CrystalReportViewer control to a Windows form*

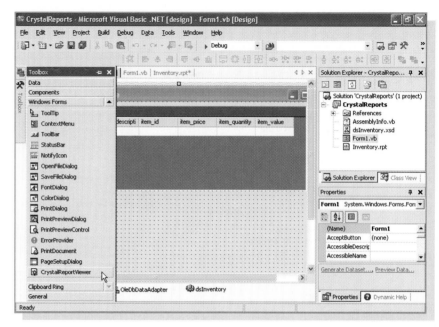

When you add a **CrystalReportViewer** control to an **ASP.NET** Web application, Visual Studio.NET adds a *Web Forms Viewer* to the solution.

After adding the CrystalReportViewer control to the form, you can resize it to maximize the area for displaying the report. Before the control will display a report, you must bind a report object to the viewer. You can do this by assigning a report to the ***ReportSource property*** of the Windows Forms Viewer. Setting this property of the Crystal Reports Viewer control determines the data displayed in the report. After you bind the report to a viewer, the Windows Forms Viewer displays the report with data from the database at run time.

The Crystal Report Viewer control contains a toolbar for scrolling through the report a page at a time, changing the zoom factor for the report, modifying how the report displays, and printing the report. Figure 12.31 shows the Inventory Value report with the Group Tree hidden and the zoom set to 50%.

FIGURE 12.31. *Viewing the Inventory report*

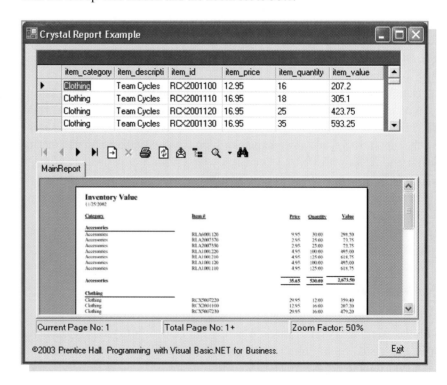

As you can see, Crystal Reports makes it easy to add sophisticated reporting capabilities to your applications. Whether the data source for a Visual Basic.NET Windows application or Web Forms project is a database or an XML file, the .NET framework works in conjunction with Crystal Reports to provide the reporting capabilities you need to address the business requirements of the application you create.

To hide and display the Group Tree, click the Group Tree button in the report, which is to the left of the Zoom Control button.

☞ HANDS-ON PROGRAMMING EXAMPLE

Creating an Address Book Application that Incorporates Graphics and Reporting Capabilities

In previous chapters you worked with Windows applications and Web Forms projects that connect to an external data source. You learned how to create the data connection and data adapter, create a disconnected dataset, and navigate among records. In this chapter you saw how to add images to Windows applications and create and display Crystal Reports for reporting the data your application displays. In this exercise you will learn to create a Windows application that displays employee payroll information in a manner similar to the application you created in Chapter 7, except that in this case the form will display each employee's picture in addition to specific data for each employee. The application also includes a Crystal Report that summarizes the payroll for all employees, grouped by employee name. A separate form contains a Crystal Report Viewer for previewing the report.

The application supports the following functionality:

1. Payroll data for each employee is read-only.
2. Only employees earning an annual salary are included in the database.
3. The application calculates employee pay according to 24 pay periods annually.
4. The application calculates withholding for each employee as follows:

   a. Federal tax: 15% of gross pay for the period
   b. FICA/Medicare: 8% of gross pay for the period
   c. State tax: 5% of gross pay for the period

5. The Year-To-Date Payroll Report is bound to a query in the ABPayroll.mdb database.

Plan the Application

The Address Book Payroll application consists of two forms. One form displays each employee's Social Security number, last name, first name, and annual salary and the employee's picture. The form also calculates the gross pay, taxes, and net pay for each pay period. Figure 12.32 displays this form.

FIGURE 12.32. *Interface for the Address Book Payroll Employee form*

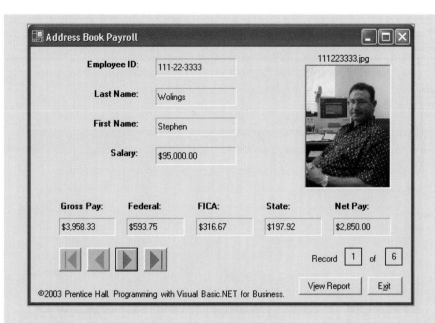

A second form appears if the user clicks the **View Report** button on the first form. The Payroll Report form includes a Windows Forms Viewer that displays the payroll report. Figure 12.33 shows this form displaying the report.

FIGURE 12.33. *Interface for the Address Book Payroll Report form*

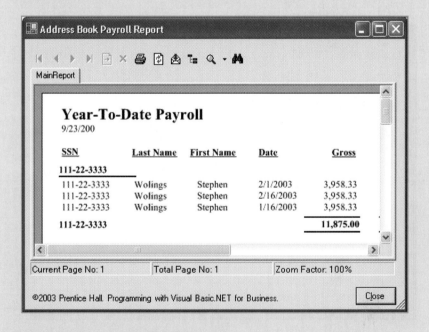

Draw a visual representation of each form on a blank piece of paper. Figures 12.34 and 12.35 represent the user interface for each form and the approximate position of each control.

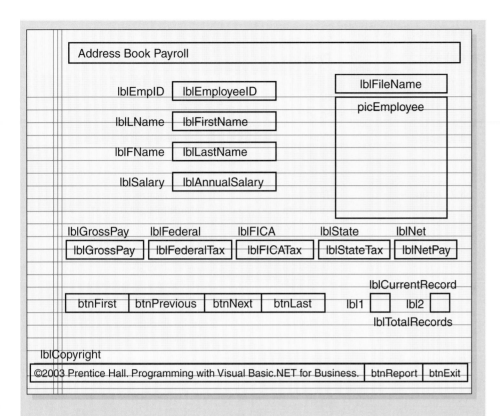

FIGURE 12.34. *Drawing of the Payroll form*

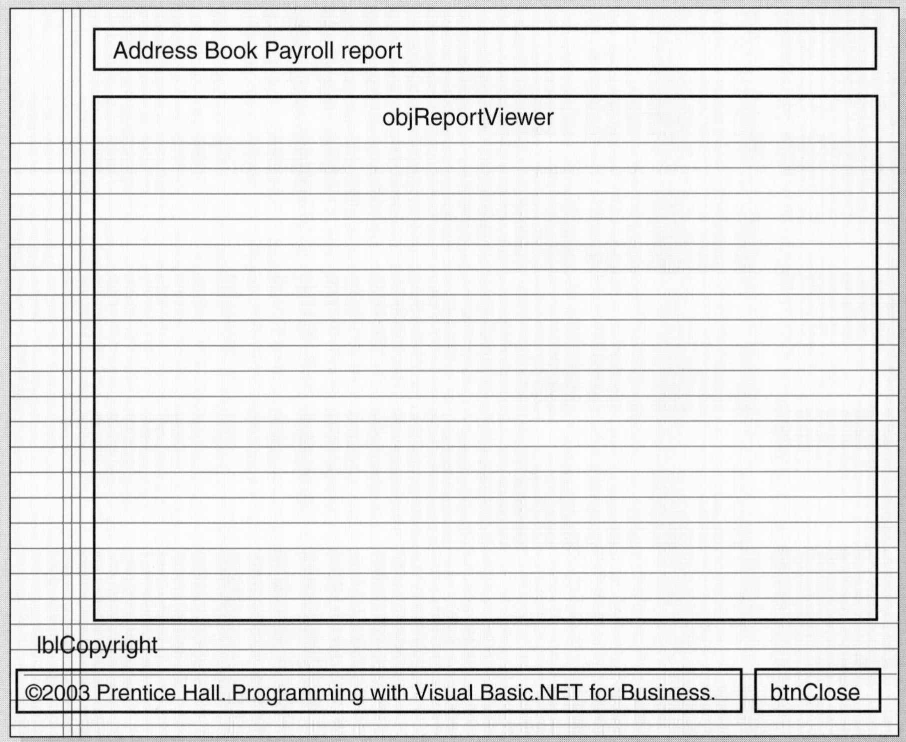

FIGURE 12.35. *Drawing of the Report form*

The Address Book Payroll application displays employee payroll data and a form for previewing the Payroll report. Table 12.5 lists the controls and properties for the user interface.

Table 12.5: *Objects and properties for the Address Book Payroll application*

Object	Property	Setting
frmPayroll.vb	Text Size StartPosition	Address Book Payroll 540,380 CenterScreen
lblEmpID	Text TextAlign Font Style	Employee ID: MiddleRight Bold
lblLName	Text TextAlign Font Style	Last Name: MiddleRight Bold
lblFName	Text TextAlign Font Style	First Name: MiddleRight Bold
lblSalary	Text TextAlign Font Style	Salary: MiddleRight Bold
lblEmployeeID	Text BorderStyle TextAlign	 Fixed3D MiddleLeft
lblLastName	Text BorderStyle TextAlign	 Fixed3D MiddleLeft
lblFirstName	Text BorderStyle TextAlign	 Fixed3D MiddleLeft
lblAnnualSalary	Text BorderStyle TextAlign	 Fixed3D MiddleLeft
lblGross	Text TextAlign Font Style	Gross Pay: MiddleLeft Bold
lblFederal	Text TextAlign Font Style	Federal: MiddleLeft Bold
lblFICA	Text TextAlign Font Style	FICA: MiddleLeft Bold
lblState	Text TextAlign Font Style	State: MiddleLeft Bold
lblNet	Text TextAlign Font Style	Net Pay: MiddleLeft Bold

lblGrossPay	Text	
	TextAlign	MiddleLeft
	BorderStyle	Fixed3D
lblFederalTax	Text	
	TextAlign	MiddleLeft
	BorderStyle	Fixed3D
lblFICATax	Text	
	TextAlign	MiddleLeft
	BorderStyle	Fixed3D
lblStateTax	Text	
	TextAlign	MiddleLeft
	BorderStyle	Fixed3D
lblNetPay	Text	
	TextAlign	MiddleLeft
	BorderStyle	Fixed3D
picEmployee	BorderStyle	Fixed3D
lblFileName	Text	
	TextAlign	MiddleCenter
btnFirst	TabStop/TabIndex	Yes, 0
	Image	First.ico
btnPrevious	TabStop/TabIndex	Yes, 1
	Image	Previous.ico
btnNext	TabStop/TabIndex	Yes, 2
	Image	Next.ico
btnLast	TabStop/TabIndex	Yes, 3
	Image	Last.ico
btnReport	Text	View &Report
	TabStop/TabIndex	Yes, 4
btnExit	Text	E&xit
	TabStop/TabIndex	Yes, 5
lblCurrentRecord	Text	
	TextAlign	MiddleCenter
	BorderStyle	FixedSingle
lbl1	Text	Record
lbl2	Text	of
lblTotalRecords	Text	
	TextAlign	MiddleCenter
	BorderStyle	FixedSingle
lblCopyright	Text	©2003 Prentice Hall. Programming with Visual Basic.NET for Business.
frmReport.vb	Text	Address Book Payroll Report
	Size	540, 400
	StartPosition	CenterScreen

objReportViewer		
lblCopyright		©2003 Prentice Hall. Programming with Visual Basic.NET for Business.
btnClose	Text TabStop/TabIndex	C&lose Yes, 0

The application's primary features are the labels for displaying field data and the buttons for navigating the dataset and viewing the Payroll report. Table 12.6 lists the pseudocode describing the application's functionality.

Table 12.6: *Pseudocode for the Address Book Payroll application*

Event Procedure	Action
btnFirst	Displays the first record in the dataset.
btnPrevious	Displays the previous record in the dataset.
btnNext	Displays the next record in the dataset.
btnLast	Displays the last record in the dataset.
btnReport	Displays the frmReport form.
btnClose	Closes the frmReport form.
btnExit	1. Verifies the user's intent to exit. 2. Terminates the application.

Now that you have created the planning documents for the application, you are ready to design the user interface in the IDE.

Design the User Interface

Launch Visual Studio.NET, if it is not currently running. Use the Profile link on the Start Page to set the profile to Visual Studio Developer.

To create a new Windows Application project:

1. Copy the *ABPayroll.mdb* database file from your data files to a floppy disk.
2. Click **File**, **New Project**. The **New Project** dialog box appears.
3. Select **Windows Application** as the project template, and type `ABPayroll` as the name for the project.
4. Copy the following image files from the folder containing the data files for this chapter to the bin folder for this project: *111223333.jpg, 222334444.jpg, 333445555.jpg, 444556666.jpg, 555667777.jpg, 666778888.jpg*. These are the employee photographs that display for each employee.

You are now ready to create the user interface by adding the controls listed in Table 12.5.

To design the user interface:

1. Right-click Form1 in the Solution Explorer. Rename the form as `frmPayroll.vb`.
2. Add each object listed in Table 12.5 to the form.

3. Set the object properties as specified. Because you have not created the icons for the navigation buttons, you will not be able to set the image properties to the icons listed the table.

4. Click **Save All** to save your changes. Your form should look like Figure 12.36.

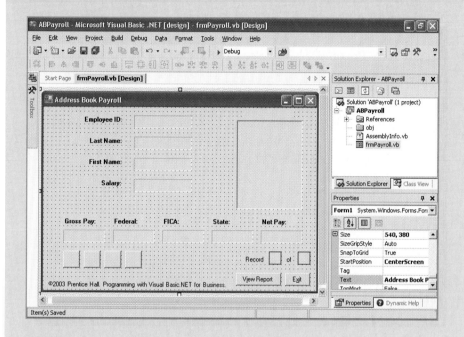

FIGURE 12.36. *Controls added to the frmPayroll form*

5. Click **File**, **Add New Item**. Add a form named `frmReport.vb` to the project.

6. Add the controls and set the properties as specified in Table 12.5.

7. Click **Save All** to save your changes. Your form should look like Figure 12.37.

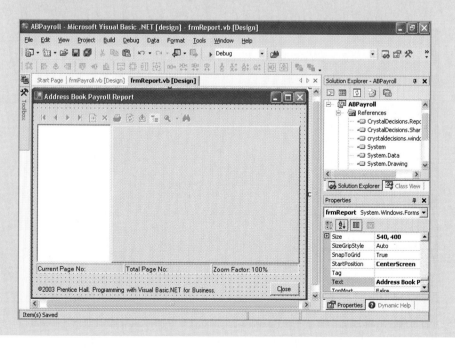

FIGURE 12.37. *Controls added to the frmReport form*

You are now ready to create a data connection, add the appropriate data adapter, and generate the required dataset for the *frmPayroll* form.

To create an OleDB Connection, OleDB adapter, and dataset for the project:

1. Move the pointer over the Server Explorer to open it.
2. Right-click inside the Server Explorer and choose **Add Connection**. The **Data Link Properties** dialog box appears.
3. Click the **Provider** tab, and select **Microsoft JET 4.0 OLE DB Provider** from the list.
4. Click the **Connection** tab, and navigate to the *ABPayroll.mdb* database included with the data files for this chapter.
5. Click the **Test Connection** button to verify that the database connection is working properly. Click **OK** in the **Microsoft Data Link** dialog box displaying the message that the test is successful, and then click **OK** in the Data Link dialog box.
6. Expand the tree for the connection you just created until you can see the tables contained in the connection.
7. Drag the *Employees* table from the Server Explorer window to the *frmPayroll* form.
8. Rename the *OleDbDataConnection1* object as `dcPayroll`.
9. Rename the *OleDbDataAdapter1* object as `daPayroll`.
10. Click the *daPayroll* adapter once to select it.
11. Click **Data**, **Generate Dataset**.
12. Change the **Name** property of the DataSet object from *Dataset1* to `dsPayroll` and click **OK**.
13. Save your changes. The form should look like Figure 12.38.

FIGURE 12.38. *Data adapter, data connector, and dataset added to the form*

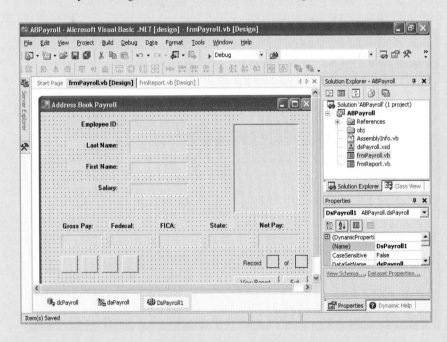

Tip

Notice that Visual Basic.NET adds the number "1" to the name of the dataset, so it appears as *DsPayroll1* in the Component Tray.

You are now ready to add the appropriate data adapter and dataset for the frmReport form.

To add an OleDbDataAdapter and dataset to the frmReport form:

1. Click the *frmReport.vb* tab in the IDE to change to the *frmReport* form.
2. Open the toolbox and click the **Data** tab.
3. Drag an OleDbDataAdapter from the Data tab to the form. The Data Adapter Configuration Wizard appears.
4. Click the **Next** button. Accept the setting for the current data connector, and click **Next** again.
5. Accept the default for SQL query types by clicking **Next**.
6. Type `SELECT payroll.* FROM payroll` as the SQL statement for the adapter, as shown in Figure 12.39. Then click **Next**.

FIGURE 12.39. *Entering an SQL statement*

7. Figure 12.40 shows the message that appears. Since you will not need to update rows in the database to display the report, you do not need to be concerned about these warnings. Click **Finish**.

FIGURE 12.40. *The results of configuring the data adapter*

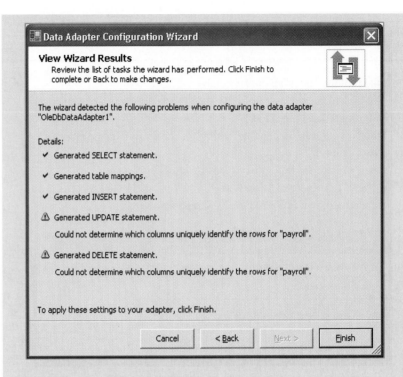

FIGURE 12.40. *The results of configuring the data adapter*

8.   Rename the *OleDbDataConnection1* object as `dcPayroll`.
9.   Rename the *OleDbDataAdapter1* object as `daReport`.
10. Save your changes.

To create icons for the navigation buttons:

Because you know how to create icons by using the Image Designer, create four icons for each of the navigation buttons.

1.   Click **File**, **New**, **File**.
2.   Add an Icon file to the project.
3.   Using the Image Editor, create an icon for the *btnFirst* control.
4.   Save the icon as `First.ico` in the *bin* folder for this project. Figure 12.41 shows the icon for the *btnFirst* control.

FIGURE 12.41. *Creating the First.ico icon*

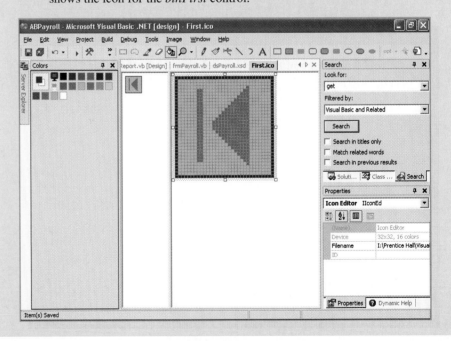

5. Create three additional icons and name them `Previous.ico`, `Next.ico`, and `Last.ico`, respectively.

6. Assign the appropriate icon to each navigation button control.

7. Save your changes.

To create the Crystal Report:

The second form in the application displays a report bound to a query (called a view) in the database. Before setting the Crystal Report Viewer control to the report, you must create it.

1. Click **File**, **Add New Item**.

2. Add a Crystal Report named `PayrollReport.rpt` to the project, as shown in Figure 12.42.

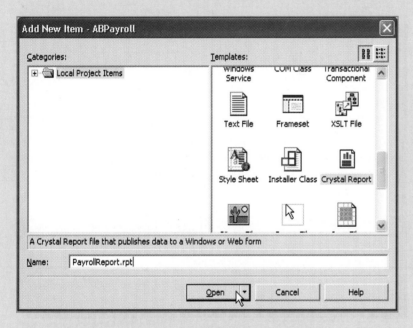

FIGURE 12.42. *Adding the PayrollReport.rpt Crystal Report to the solution*

3. The Crystal Report Gallery appears. Select the default options to use the Report Expert to create a Standard report. Click **OK**.

4. When the **Data** tab appears, expand the Database Files folder and navigate to the *ABPayroll.mdb* database on your data disk.

5. Open the database and expand the **Views** page. Highlight the *Payroll* view and click **Insert Table**. The *Payroll* view is added to the **Tables in Report:** pane, as shown in Figure 12.43. Click **Next**.

FIGURE 12.43. *Adding the Payroll view to the Tables in Report: pane*

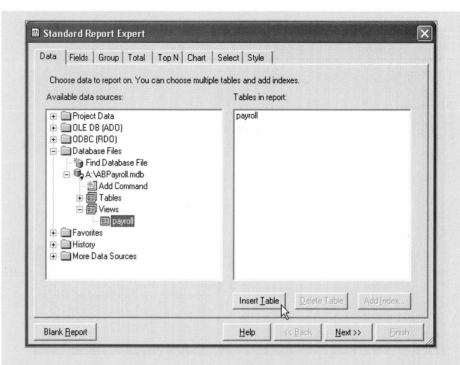

6. Add the fields shown in Figure 12.44 to the report. Change the column names of the first four fields to SSN, Last Name, First Name, and Date, respectively.

FIGURE 12.44. *Specifying fields for the report*

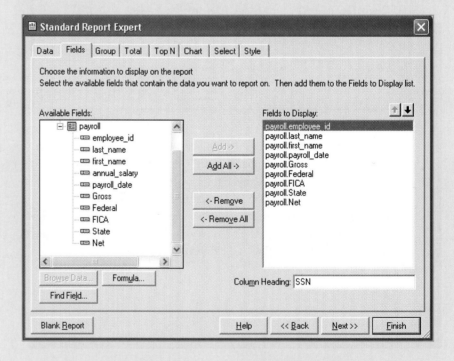

7. Click **Next**. Group the report by *employee_id* in ascending order.

8. Click **Next**. Accept the default settings for the summarized fields.

9. Click the **Style** tab. Type Year-To-Date Payroll as the title for the report, as shown in Figure 12.45. Accept the default of Standard as the report style. Then click **Finish**.

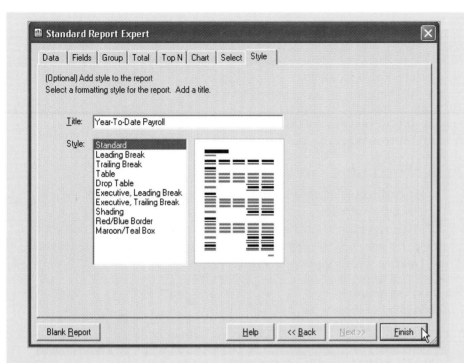

FIGURE 12.45. *Entering a title for the report*

10. Save your changes. Right-click the *PayrollReport.rpt* tab and choose **Close**.
11. Click the **frmReport.vb** tab.
12. Click the *objReportViewer* control, and click the **ReportSource** row.
13. Click the drop-down list, and select **Browse**.
14. Navigate to the *PayrollReport.rpt* file, select it, and click **Open**. This sets the report as the source for the control.
15. Click **File**, **Save All** to save your changes.

Now that you have completed the interface and data components for the Address Book Payroll application, you are ready to write the code.

Write the Code

Your first task is to add comments to the Code Editor and declare variables for the record counters. You will then write procedures for displaying an image, calculating the payroll, and initializing the record counters on the form. The Form_Load event will set up the data bindings. You can then write the code that initializes the form, loads the form, and provides each button its functionality.

To add comments to the application and declare variables:

1. Right-click the *frmPayroll.vb* form in the Solution Explorer and choose **View Code**.
2. Place the insertion point at the top of the Code Editor, and then type the following comments:

```
'©2003 Prentice Hall
'By [Enter your name here...]
'Created/Revised: [Enter the date here...]
'Address Book Payroll Application
```

You might need to reposition specific elements on your report after viewing it.

3. Place the insertion point below the Windows Form Designer generated code region.
4. Type #Region "Declarations" and press ↵Enter to create a region for the variable declarations.
5. Add the following statements to the region:

```
Friend intCurrentRecord As Integer
Friend intTotalRecords As Integer
```

To declare procedures:

1. Place the insertion point below the region containing the procedures for declaring variables.
2. Type #Region "Procedures" and press ↵Enter to create a region for the procedures for displaying the employee images and calculating payroll data.
3. Add the following procedures to the region:

```
Sub DisplayImage()
    Dim strDirectory As String
    Dim strFileName As String
    strDirectory = Environment.CurrentDirectory & "\"
    strFileName = lblFileName.Text
    strFileName = strDirectory & strFileName
    picEmployee.Image = Image.FromFile(strFileName)
    picEmployee.SizeMode = PictureBoxSizeMode.StretchImage
End Sub
```

This procedure determines the path for the image files, using the Environment's current directory. The name of each image file is contained in the database and bound to the *lblFileName* label, from which the filename is retrieved.

```
Sub CalculatePayroll()
    Dim sngGross As Single
    Dim sngFederal As Single
    Dim sngFICA As Single
    Dim sngState As Single
    Dim sngNet As Single

    sngGross = (CSng(lblAnnualSalary.Text) / 24)
    lblGrossPay.Text = Format(sngGross, "C")

    sngFederal = (sngGross * 0.15)
    lblFederalTax.Text = Format(sngFederal, "C")

    sngFICA = (sngGross * 0.08)
    lblFICATax.Text = Format(sngFICA, "C")

    sngState = (sngGross * 0.05)
    lblStateTax.Text = Format(sngState, "C")

    sngNet = sngGross - sngFederal - sngFICA - sngState
```

```
        lblNetPay.Text = Format(sngNet, "C")


        'Format the Salary label as Currency
        lblAnnualSalary.Text = Format(lblAnnualSalary.Text,
            "Currency")
End Sub
```

This procedure declares a series of variables for calculating the payroll data from the annual salary amount. Because there are 24 pay periods per year, the gross pay for each pay period is equal to the annual salary divided by 24. The tax rates are determined according to the business rules for the application.

```
Sub InitializeInterface()
    'Reset the CurrentRecord variable
    intCurrentRecord = BindingContext(DsPayroll1,
        "employees").Position + 1

    If intCurrentRecord = 1 Then
        btnFirst.Enabled = False
        btnPrevious.Enabled = False
        btnNext.Enabled = True
        btnLast.Enabled = True

    ElseIf intCurrentRecord < intTotalRecords Then

        btnPrevious.Enabled = True
        btnFirst.Enabled = True
        btnNext.Enabled = True
        btnLast.Enabled = True
    Else
        btnPrevious.Enabled = True
        btnFirst.Enabled = True
        btnNext.Enabled = False
        btnLast.Enabled = False
    End If
    lblCurrentRecord.Text = intCurrentRecord
End Sub
```

This procedure resets the current record variable as the records change and sets the Enabled property of the navigation buttons, depending on the position of the record within the dataset.

4. Save your changes.

To code the Form_Load event:

1. Place the insertion point below the region containing the procedures.
2. Type #Region "Form Load" and press ↵Enter to create a region for the procedures for adding and deleting records.
3. Create a procedure for the Form_Load event. Add the following statements within the procedure:

```
Private Sub Form1_Load(ByVal sender As Object, ByVal e As
    System.EventArgs) Handles MyBase.Load
```

```
Try
    'Populate the DataSet
    daPayroll.Fill(DsPayroll1)

    'Determine the number of records in the Dataset
    intTotalRecords = BindingContext(DsPayroll1,
        "employees").Count
    lblTotalRecords.Text = intTotalRecords
    'Set the current record variable (first record has an
        index of 0, so add 1)
    intCurrentRecord = BindingContext(DsPayroll1,
        "employees").Position + 1
    lblCurrentRecord.Text = intCurrentRecord
    'Disable the buttons
    btnFirst.Enabled = False
    btnPrevious.Enabled = False
    'Bind controls to the dataset
    lblEmployeeID.DataBindings.Add(New Binding("Text",
        DsPayroll1, "employees.employee_id"))
    lblLastName.DataBindings.Add(New Binding("Text",
        DsPayroll1, "employees.last_name"))
    lblFirstName.DataBindings.Add(New Binding("Text",
        DsPayroll1, "employees.first_name"))
    lblAnnualSalary.DataBindings.Add(New Binding("Text",
        DsPayroll1, "employees.annual_salary"))
    lblFileName.DataBindings.Add(New Binding("Text",
        DsPayroll1, "employees.photo_file"))
    'Call the procedure to display the employee picture
    DisplayImage()
    CalculatePayroll()
Catch
    MsgBox("Database not found. Please try again.",
        MsgBoxStyle.Critical, "File Error")
    'Terminate the application
    End
End Try
End Sub
```

In addition to populating the dataset, this routine binds the controls to the dataset at run time and initializes the buttons when the first record is displayed. This procedure also calls the DisplayImage and CalculatePayroll procedures so that the information for the first record appears on the form.

4.   Save your changes.

To write procedures for record navigation:

1.   Place the insertion point below the region containing the procedure for loading the form.

2.   Type #Region "Navigation" and press ←Enter to create a region for the procedures for adding and deleting records.

3.   Add the following procedures:

How do you bind
controls to a dataset
at design time?

```
Private Sub btnFirst_Click(ByVal sender As Object, ByVal e As
   System.EventArgs) Handles btnFirst.Click
      Me.BindingContext(DsPayroll1, "employees").Position = 0
      Call DisplayImage()
      Call CalculatePayroll()
      Call InitializeInterface()
End Sub

Private Sub btnPrevious_Click(ByVal sender As Object, ByVal e As
   System.EventArgs) Handles btnPrevious.Click
      Me.BindingContext(DsPayroll1, "employees").Position -= 1
      Call DisplayImage()
      Call CalculatePayroll()
      Call InitializeInterface()
End Sub

Private Sub btnNext_Click(ByVal sender As Object, ByVal e As
   System.EventArgs) Handles btnNext.Click
      Me.BindingContext(DsPayroll1, "employees").Position += 1
      Call DisplayImage()
      Call CalculatePayroll()
      Call InitializeInterface()
End Sub

Private Sub btnLast_Click(ByVal sender As Object, ByVal e As
   System.EventArgs) Handles btnLast.Click
      Me.BindingContext(DsPayroll1, "employees").Position =
         BindingContext(DsPayroll1, "Employees").Count - 1

      Call DisplayImage()
      Call CalculatePayroll()
      Call InitializeInterface()
End Sub
```

These procedures should be familiar, because you have used them in other applications in this book. Each navigation event calls the two procedures declared earlier so that the correct image displays and the payroll data is calculated when a different record displays.

4. Save your changes.

To write code for exiting the application, displaying the report, and closing the report:

1. Place the insertion point below the region for navigating records.
2. Type #Region "Misc" and press ↵Enter to create a region for the procedures for exiting the application and viewing the report.
3. Add the following procedures:

```
Private Sub btnExit_Click(ByVal sender As Object, ByVal e As
   System.EventArgs) Handles btnExit.Click
Dim intResponse As Integer
```

```
intResponse = MsgBox("Do you really want to exit this
  application?", 276, "Exit?")
If intResponse = 6 Then
End
End If
End Sub
```

```
    Private Sub btnReport_Click(ByVal sender As System.Object,
        ByVal e As System.EventArgs) Handles btnReport.Click
          Dim ShowForm As frmReport = New frmReport()
          ShowForm.ShowDialog()
    End Sub
```

The Report form is opened as a Modal form (using the .ShowDialog() method), so that the form must be closed prior to evoking any other events.

4. Display the *frmReport.vb* form in the designer.

5. Create an Event procedure for the *btnClose* click event. Add the following code:

```
Private Sub btnClose_Click(ByVal sender As System.Object, ByVal
  e As System.EventArgs) Handles btnClose.Click
        Close()
    End Sub
```

6. Save your changes.

Run the Application

You are now ready to run the Address Book Payroll application and test its functionality.

To run the application:

1. Click the Start button or press the [F5] key to run the application.

2. If the application locates the *ABPayroll.mdb* database, it displays the first record. You will receive an error message if the application cannot find the file or if the file is corrupted.

3. Test the navigation buttons, taking note of which buttons are disabled as you navigate through the dataset.

4. Click the **View Report** button. Modify the view for the report, noting any changes you want to make to the report. Click **Close** when you finish viewing the report.

5. Continue testing your application to check its functionality. When you are finished, click the **Exit** button.

6. If you need to modify the layout of the report, right-click the *PayrollReport.rpt* file in the Solution Explorer and choose **Open**.

7. Reposition and resize the controls in the report sections as necessary.

8. Save any changes you make to the project.

9. Close the solution.

Summary

- Vector graphics create a line or shape on the screen by defining the coordinates of the shape and the width of the line that creates the line or shape. Raster graphics create images by setting the color for small dots, called pixels, which make up the image. To display vector graphics in an application, you include a Paint event on the procedure that draws the graphic. To display raster (bitmap) graphics, add a PictureBox control (Windows application) or an Image control (Web Forms application) to a form, and set the Image (PictureBox control) or ImageURL (Image control) to the graphic.

- Visual Studio.NET includes the Image Editor, which is a powerful tool for creating and editing icons and images for your applications. To create an image, use the individual tools to draw the individual pixels in the workspace. After you save the images to a file, you can display them in your applications.

- To display bitmap images and graphics, use the PictureBox control in Windows applications and the Image control in Web Forms applications.

- You can print text from Visual Basic applications by using the PrintPreviewDialog and PrintDialog controls. These two controls display common dialog boxes for previewing and printing documents. These controls require a PrintDocument object, which uses the DrawString method to print a text string. To print text, include a procedure that uses a PrintDialog control to display a dialog box, and then use the Print method of the PrintDocument object to print the text string.

- Crystal Reports is a powerful tool available in Visual Studio.NET for creating sophisticated reports to display, summarize, and print data. Use the Report Expert to create a Crystal Report, and add a Crystal Report Viewer control to the application to display a Crystal Report in Visual Basic.NET.

- The Windows Forms Viewer is a control that displays a report in a Visual Studio.NET application. The Crystal Reports Form Viewer control in the toolbox adds a Windows Forms Viewer to the form. This viewer displays a Crystal Report and provides a toolbar and a Group Tree for changing the preview for the report.

Key Terms

Advanced Graphics Interface (GDI+)

bitmap

Crystal Report Designer

Crystal Report Gallery

Crystal Reports

Crystal Reports Experts

Crystal Report Viewer

CrystalReportViewer control

Details

e

Graphics object

Graphics.Drawstring method

hard-copy output

Image control

Image Editor

Image property

ImageURL property

multimedia

OnPaint method

Page Footer

Page Header

Paint event

Pen object

PictureBox control

pixels

Print method

PrintDialog control

PrintDocument object

PrintPreviewDialog control

raster graphics

Report Engine

Report Expert

Report Footer

Report Header

ReportSource property

Sections

SizeMode property

soft-copy output

StretchImage

vector graphics

view

Web Forms Viewer

Windows Forms Viewer

Study Questions

Multiple-Choice Questions

1. Which of the following is an example of a vector graphic?
   a. A high-resolution photograph displayed in a Windows application.
   b. An ellipse displayed in a PictureBox control on a Windows form.
   c. An icon file created with the Visual Studio.NET Image Editor.
   d. A rectangle created with the Rectangle tool in the Image Editor and stored as a Device Independent Bitmap.
   e. A rectangle defined by the coordinates 20, 10, 100, and 50.

2. Which of the following tools included in the Image Editor sets the color of multiple pixels?
   a. Erase tool
   b. Line tool
   c. Color Selection tool
   d. Fill tool
   e. Ellipse tool

3. Which of the following file types supports images displayed in Web Forms projects?
   a. BMP
   b. JPG
   c. ICO
   d. DIB
   e. TIF

4. Which of the following property settings resizes a bitmap image to fit a PictureBox control?
   a. PictureBoxSizeMode.Normal
   b. PictureBoxSizeMode.Expanded
   c. PictureBoxSizeMode.StretchImage
   d. PictureBoxSizeMode.AutoSize
   e. PictureBoxSizeMode.CenterImage

5. Which of the following controls displays an image in a Web Forms project?
   a. Picture
   b. Image
   c. PictureBox
   d. Panel
   e. ImageList

6. Which report section of a Crystal Report contains placeholders for records in the data source?
   a. Report Header
   b. Page Header
   c. Details
   d. Page Footer
   e. Report Footer

7. Which object is required for printing text with the PrintDocument control?
   a. PrintPreviewDialog
   b. Report Expert
   c. Crystal Reports Viewer
   d. PrintDialog
   e. Report Engine

8. Which section of a report usually includes summarized totals for all the sections of a report?
   a. Report Header
   b. Page Header
   c. Details
   d. Page Footer
   e. Report Footer

9. How many sections are contained in a Crystal Report by default?
   a. One
   b. Two
   c. Three
   d. Four
   e. Five

10. Which property of a Crystal Reports Viewer control determines the data that is displayed in a report?
    a. RecordSource
    b. DataSource
    c. DetailSource
    d. ImageURL
    e. ReportSource

True/False Questions

1. A bitmapped graphic is an example of a vector graphic.

2. The PrintDialog control must use a PrintDocument object that specifies what to print.

3. To view a Crystal Report in a Visual Basic.NET application, you must add a Report Viewer object to a form.

4. The Crystal Reports Viewer control is required for viewing a report in an application.

5. The Page Header section of a report usually lists field data from a data source.

Short Answer Questions

1. Explain the differences between vector graphics and raster graphics. When would you use one type of graphic over the other in your applications?

2. Explain the procedure for displaying bitmap images in both Windows applications and Web Forms applications.

3. What are the steps for previewing or printing text with the PrintPreviewDialog control?

4. What is the procedure for adding a Crystal Report to a Visual Basic.NET application?

5. After you have created a Crystal Report, how do you make it available in an application?

Guided Exercises

Creating a Windows Application to Display Inventory Items

Retail businesses often use multimedia applications to provide customers with information about their products. For example, realtors create interactive listings of homes for sale, where the potential buyer can take a virtual tour of a house before setting an appointment to see it.

In this exercise you will create an interactive Windows application that displays inventory of pre-owned watches for sale. Figure 12.46 displays the interface for the application.

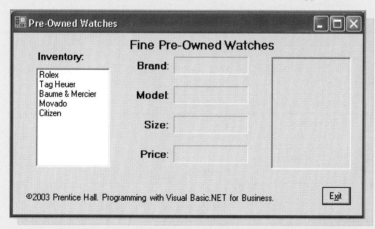

FIGURE 12.46. *Interface for the Pre-owned Watches application*

The application includes five inventory items. The watches available for sale are listed in Table 12.7.

Table 12.7: Inventory items for the Pre-Owned Watches application

Brand	Model	Date	Size	Price	Image
Rolex	DateJust	1993	36mm	$2950.00	Img001.jpg
Tag Heuer	2000 Classic	1999	37mm	$575.00	Img002.jpg
Baume & Mercier	Ladies Linea	2000	27mm	$550.00	Img003.jpg
Movado	Olympian	2002	34mm	$495.00	Img004.jpg
Citizen	Eco-Drive	2001	36mm	$165.00	Img005.jpg

To create the application and design the user interface:

1. Create a new Windows Application and name it `Watches`.
2. Copy the following files from the data files for this chapter to the *bbin* folder for this solution: *Img001.jpg, Img002.jpg, Img003.jpg, Img004.jpg,* and *Img005.jpg.*
3. Using Table 12.8 and Figure 12.46 as guides, create the user interface for the Watches application.

Table 12.8: Objects and properties for the Pre-owned Watches application

Object	Property	Setting
Form1	Text	Pre-Owned Watches
	Size	495, 280
	StartPosition	CenterScreen
lstInventory	BorderStyle	Fixed3D
lblTitle	Text	Fine Pre-Owned Watches
	Font Size	12 pt
	Font Style	Bold
	TextAlign	MiddleCenter
lblInventory	Text	Inventory:
	Text Style	Bold
	TextAlign	MiddleLeft
lblBrand	Text	Brand:
	Font Style	Bold
	TextAlign	MiddleRight
lblModel	Text	Model:
	Font Style	Bold
	TextAlign	MiddleRight
lblSize	Text	Size:
	Font Style	Bold
	TextAlign	MiddleRight
lblPrice	Text	Price:
	Font Style	Bold
	TextAlign	MiddleRight
picItem	BorderStyle	Fixed3D
lblWatchBrand	Text	
	BorderStyle	Fixed3D
lblWatchModel	Text	
	BorderStyle	Fixed3D
lblWatchSize	Text	
	BorderStyle	Fixed3D
lblWatchPrice	Text	
	BorderStyle	Fixed3D
lblCopyright	Text	©2003 Prentice Hall. Programming with Visual Basic.NET for Business.
btnExit	Text	E&xit

4. Add the following items to the collection for the *lstInventory* control:

Rolex

Tag Heuer

Baume & Mercier

Movado

Citizen

5. Save your changes.

To write the code:

1. Press F7 to open the Code Editor. Add the following statements at the top of the Code pane:

```
'©2003 Prentice Hall
'By [Enter your name here…]
'Created/Revised: [Enter the date here…]
'Windows Application Pre-Owned Watches Exercise
```

2. Create the following procedure below the Windows Form Designer generated code region:

```
Friend Sub DisplayItem(ByVal wBrand, ByVal wModel, ByVal wDate,
  ByVal wSize, ByVal wPrice, ByVal wImage)
      Dim strDirectory As String
      Dim strFileName As String
      'Get directory and set image path and filename
      strDirectory = Environment.CurrentDirectory
      strFileName = strDirectory & "\" & wImage
      picItem.Image = Image.FromFile(strFileName)
      picItem.SizeMode = PictureBoxSizeMode.StretchImage
      'Set label data
      lblWatchBrand.Text = wBrand
      lblWatchModel.Text = wModel
      lblWatchSize.Text = wSize
      lblWatchPrice.Text = wPrice
  End Sub
```

3. Double-click the *lstInventory* control, and add the following statements to handle the **SelectedIndexChanged** event procedure:

```
Private Sub lstInventory_SelectedIndexChanged(ByVal sender
  As System.Object, ByVal e As System.EventArgs) Handles
  lstInventory.SelectedIndexChanged
    Dim i As Integer
    i = lstInventory.SelectedIndex
    Select Case i
        Case 0
            DisplayItem("Rolex", "DateJust", "1993",
              "36mm", "$2350.00", "Img001.jpg")
        Case 1
            DisplayItem("Tag Heuer", "2000 Classic",
              "1999", "    37mm", "$575.00", "Img002.jpg")
        Case 2
            DisplayItem("Baume/Mercier", "Ladies Linea",
              "2000", "27mm", "$550.00", "Img003.jpg")
```

```
                    Case 3
                         DisplayItem("Movado", "Olympian", "2002",
                             "34mm", "$495.00", "Img004.jpg")
                    Case 4
                         DisplayItem("Citizen", "Eco-Drive", "2001",
                             "36mm", "$165.00", "Img005.jpg")
            End Select
    End Sub
```

4. Add the following code to the *btnExit* click event:

```
Private Sub btnExit_Click(ByVal sender As System.Object,
    ByVal e As System.EventArgs) Handles btnExit.Click
        Dim response As Integer
        response = MsgBox("Do you want to exit this
            application?", vbYesNo, "Pre-Owned Watches
            Application")
        If response = vbYes Then
            End
        End If
End Sub
```

5. Save your changes.

Run the application and test its functionality. Figure 12.47 displays one inventory item from the application.

FIGURE 12.47. *The Pre-owned Watches application displaying an inventory item*

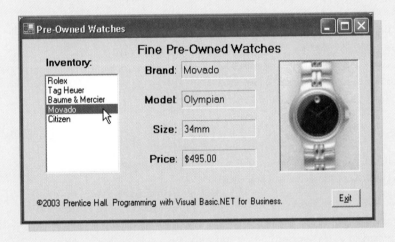

Creating a Report from a Database

As you learned in this chapter, Crystal Reports is a powerful tool for displaying and printing data from a Visual Basic.NET application. In the Hands-On Example for this chapter, you created a report for a database connected to the application. In this exercise you will create a Crystal Report without creating a data connection, data adapter, or dataset.

Many businesses require their employees to obtain certification in one or more technical products. In this exercise you will create a Crystal Report that reports the certification exam scores for the company's employees. An Access database named *Scores.mdb* contains a query that displays employee, exam, and score information in a single view. Figure 12.48 shows how your report should look after you create it.

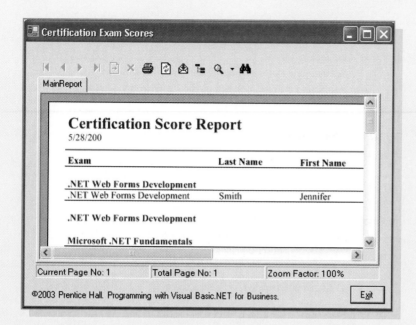

FIGURE 12.48. *Certification Score Report*

To create the application and design the user interface:

1. Copy the *Scores.mdb* database file from the data files for this chapter to a floppy disk.
2. Create a new Visual Basic project and name it `ExamScores`.
3. Using Table 12.9 and Figure 12.48 as guides, create the user interface for the Exam Scores application.

Table 12.9: Objects and properties for the Exam Scores application

Object	Property	Setting
Form1	Text	Certification Exam Scores
	Size	520, 390
	StartPosition	CenterScreen
objScores	ReportSource	(The report must exist before setting this property.)
btnExit	Text	E&xit
lblCopyright	Text	©2003 Prentice Hall. Programming with Visual Basic.NET for Business.

4. Save your changes.

To create the report:

1. Click **File**, **Add New Item** and add a Crystal Report named *ScoreReport.rpt* to the project.
2. Use the Report Expert to create a Standard report.
3. Set the data source for the report to the *Scores.mdb* database.
4. The database contains a query named *score_report*. Add this view as the table for the report.
5. Add the last six fields in the view to the report. Rename the report columns to `Last Name`, `First Name`, `Exam`, `Passing Score`, `Obtained Score`, and `Pass?`.
6. Group the report by the *exam_name* field.

7. Remove any summarized fields from the report.
8. Click the **Style** tab. Type `Certification Score Report` as the title for the report.
9. Set the Style as **Red/Blue Border** and click **Finish**.
10. Reposition the report objects in the Page Header and Details sections of the report.
11. Save your changes to the report.

To write the code:

1. Press ⒇F7⒈ to open the Code Editor. Add the following statements at the top of the Code pane:

```
'©2003 Prentice Hall
'By [Enter your name here…]
'Created/Revised: [Enter the date here…]
'Windows Application Certification Exam Scores Exercise
```

2. Create the following procedure to handle the *btnExit_click* event:

```
Private Sub btnExit_Click(ByVal sender As System.Object,
    ByVal e As System.EventArgs) Handles btnExit.Click
      Dim response As Integer
      response = MsgBox("Do you want to exit this
          application?", vbYesNo, "Certification Score Report
          Application")
      If response = vbYes Then
            End
      End If
End Sub
```

3. Set the **ReportSource** property of the *crvScores* Crystal Report Viewer object to the *ScoreReport.rpt* object.
4. Save your changes.
5. Run the application, and view the report.
6. Close the solution when you finish viewing the report.

Case Studies

Creating a Web Forms Project to Display Pre-owned Watches Inventory

In the first Exercise you created a Windows application for displaying information about pre-owned watches for sale. In this case study, you will create a Web Forms project displaying the same information and images. Create a new ASP.NET Web application and name it `PreOwnedWatches`. Copy the image files into the *bin* folder for this project. Add the appropriate Web Server controls to the form. Using the Web version of the 50 State Quarters application shown earlier in this chapter, add the code necessary to navigate among inventory items.

Previewing and Printing Text from the Enhanced Text Editor

In Chapter 5 you learned how to create a text editor that reads and writes both simple ASCII text and RTF documents. Create a copy of your solution from Chapter 5, and add common dialog controls for previewing and printing the text from the application. Add menu items for previewing and printing the text contained on the form. Using the code shown in this chapter as a guide, write the code to preview and print the text.

Packaging and Deploying Visual Basic.NET Applications

When you create Visual Basic.NET Windows and Web Forms projects, you are able to run them because the development version of Visual Studio.NET includes the .NET Framework. The goal of programming is to distribute programs to end users, who will install your programs on their computers. After you create a Windows or Web Forms application, you need to make it available to users who do not have Visual Studio.NET installed on their computers. The computer on which your programs will run is called the *client*. Any .NET application—either a Windows application or an ASP.NET Web forms application—requires the .NET Framework to be installed on the client computer. Figure A.1 shows how the .NET Framework supports Windows and ASP.NET applications.

FIGURE A.1. *Client requirements for running a .NET Windows or ASP.NET application*

Client Requirements for .NET Applications

Windows Application	ASP.NET Application
	Web Browser
.NET Framework	
Operating System	

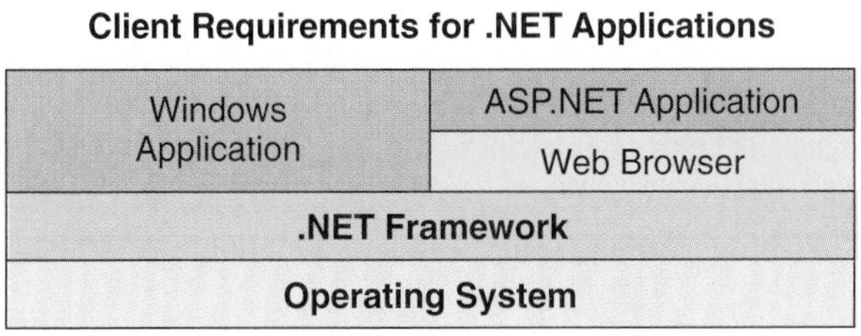

The .NET Framework is available as a download from Microsoft. The *.NET Framework redistributable* is a file that includes everything the client must have to run .NET Framework applications, including the Common Language Runtime, the .NET Framework class library, and ASP.NET.

Once a client has the .NET Framework installed, it can run the Windows or ASP.NET applications you create. To run a program, you must have an executable file installed on the client. An *executable file* is a program file with an .exe file extension that is used to load a program into memory. For example, if you use Visual Basic.NET to create a solution named *Cash Bonus*, the executable file for your program might be named *Cash Bonus.exe*. For a client to run the *Cash Bonus.exe* program, you need to provide a way for installing it on the client. Most programs use a file named *Setup.exe* or *Install.exe* to install the executable file and its associated components.

To distribute an executable file for installation on a client you must first follow a process known as packaging and deploying the application. *Packaging and deploying* a Visual Basic.NET solution means creating a *Setup.exe* program that contains the executable file and any other required program components, such as data files.

In this Appendix you will learn how to create an installation package consisting of a *Setup.exe* file and all the associated components for installing your Windows and Web applications on a client, or target, computer. The three steps to follow in packaging and deploying your application on a target computer are as follows:

1. Install .NET Framework on the client.
2. Create a Setup and Deployment project for the Windows or Web forms (ASP.NET) solution.
3. Use the Windows Installer to install the program on the client.

Installing .NET Framework Components

You can download the .NET Framework Redistributable from the Microsoft Website, or you can run the *dotnetredist.exe* file included with your data files.

To install the .NET Framework on a client, copy *dotnetredist.exe* to the client and double-click the file in My Computer or Windows Explorer to run it. After accepting the License Agreement, accept a location for the redistributable file. The *dotnetfx.exe* file will be installed in the location you specify. Run the *dotnetfx.exe* file to complete the installation.

The Windows Installer and Setup Projects

The **Microsoft Windows Installer** is an installation and configuration service that ships as part of the Microsoft Windows 2000, Windows XP, and Windows Millennium Edition (Windows Me) operating systems. The Windows Installer is also available as a Service Pack for Windows 95, Windows 98, and Microsoft Windows NT version 4.0.

The Visual Studio.NET deployment tools build on the foundation of Windows Installer, giving you the capability to create installation files for your Visual Studio.NET applications. After you create a deployment project for your Windows or ASP.NET application, you can use the Windows Installer to install the application on the client computer.

Now let's learn how to create setup and deployment projects.

Creating Setup and Deployment Projects

You create a setup and deployment project by selecting a template that defines the kind of deployment project you will create. You can create a setup project by using the appropriate template. You also have the option of using the Setup Wizard to walk through the process of creating a deployment project. The template you choose depends on the complexity of your application and whether it is a distributed application that will be installed on multiple computers. The templates for setup projects support one of four possible deployment projects. The four types of deployment projects are

- Merge Module project
- Setup project
- Web Setup project
- Cab project

Table A.1 lists the purpose of each deployment option.

Table A.1: Visual Studio.NET Deployment Options

Deployment Project Type	Purpose
Merge Module project	Packages components that might be shared by multiple applications.
Setup project	Builds an installer for a Windows-based application. This option uses the Windows Installer.
Web Setup project	Builds an installer for a Web application. This option uses the Windows Installer.
Cab project	Creates a cabinet file for downloading to a legacy Web browser.

Now let's learn how to create a setup and deployment project for a Windows application.

CREATING A SETUP AND DEPLOYMENT PROJECT BY USING THE WINDOWS INSTALLER FOR A WINDOWS APPLICATION

This example demonstrates how to create a setup and deployment project that uses the Windows Installer to install on a client the Cash Bonus solution you created in Chapter 7. To complete this example, you need to copy the *Cash Bonus* folder from your data files for Chapter 7 to a disk or network location where you can store your setup and deployment projects.

To create a setup and deployment project for the Cash Bonus application:

1. Launch Visual Studio.NET and open the *Cash Bonus* project.

2. Click **Build** and choose **Build Cash Bonus** to build the solution. Accept the default filename and location for the solution file and click **Save**.

3. Click **File**, **Add Project**, and choose **New Project**.

4. In the **Add New Project** dialog box, select **Setup and Deployment Projects** in the **Project Type** pane, and then choose **Setup Project** in the **Templates** pane. In the **Name** box, type Cash Bonus Setup and click **OK**, as shown in Figure A.2.

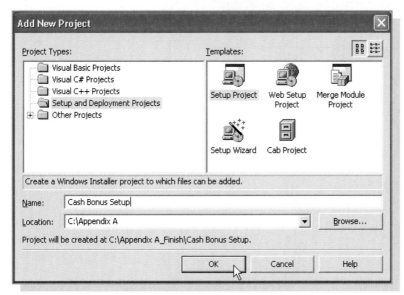

FIGURE A.2. *Adding a Setup project to the solution*

Tip
The **ProductName** property determines the name that displays for the application in folder names and in the Add/Remove Programs dialog box.

5.   Visual Studio.NET adds the project to the Solution Explorer, and the File System Editor opens.

6.   Select the *Cash Bonus Setup* project in Solution Explorer. In the Properties window, select the **ProductName** property and change the name from *Cash Bonus Setup* to Cash Bonus.

You are now ready to add the program to the installer.

To add the Windows application to the Windows Installer:

1.   The *Cash Bonus Setup* project is still selected in the Solution Explorer. Click the **Application Folder** node in the File System Editor.

2.   Click **Action** and choose **Add**, **Project Output**, as shown in Figure A.3.

FIGURE A.3. *Adding a project output group to the setup project*

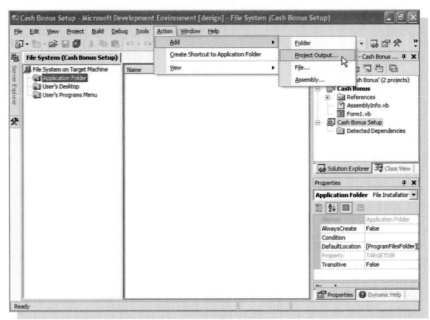

3.   The **Add Project Output Group** dialog box shown in Figure A.4 appears. Accept the defaults and click **OK**.

FIGURE A.4. *Adding the Cash Bonus project as the primary output*

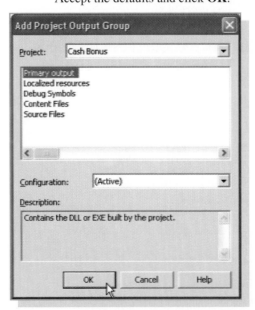

4. Click the **User's Programs Menus** node in the File System Editor.

5. Click **Action** and choose **Add**, **Project Output**. The **Add Project Output Group** dialog box appears.

6. Accept the defaults and click **OK**. This adds *Cash Bonus* to the **Start** Menu of the computer on which the application is installed.

7. Click **Build** and choose **Build Cash Bonus Setup**, as shown in Figure A.5. This builds the Setup components.

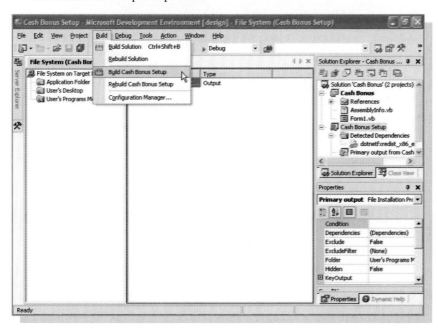

FIGURE A.5. *Building the Cash Bonus solution*

8. Save and close the solution.

You are now ready to install the application you have created. The files required for installation are included in the *Debug* folder for the *Cash Bonus Setup* project, as shown in Figure A.6.

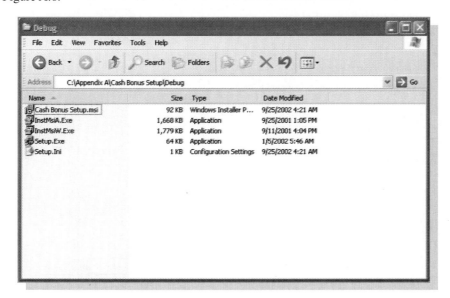

FIGURE A.6. *Installation files for the Cash Bonus application*

You can now install the Cash Bonus application on a client with the .NET Framework installed.

To deploy the application to a client with the .NET Framework installed:

1. Copy the files contained in the Debug folder to a network location or removable media, such as a CDR disc, to perform the setup.

2. Click the *Setup.exe* program icon to launch the Windows Installer. Figure A.7 shows the opening screen of the Setup Wizard.

FIGURE A.7. *Opening screen for the Cash Bonus Setup Wizard*

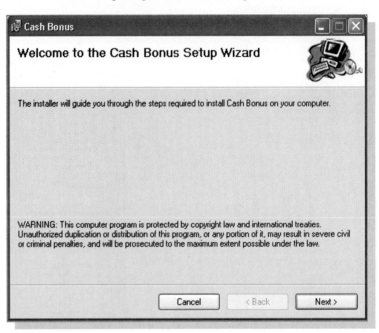

3. Click **Next** and select an installation location. Figure A.8 shows the location we have chosen. You click the **Browse** button to choose a location on your computer.

FIGURE A.8. *Selecting an installation location for the Cash Bonus application*

4. Click **Next**. The **Cash Bonus Setup Wizard** indicates that you are ready to install, as shown in Figure A.9. Click **Next**.

5. The installation progress is displayed in the screen, as shown in Figure A.10.

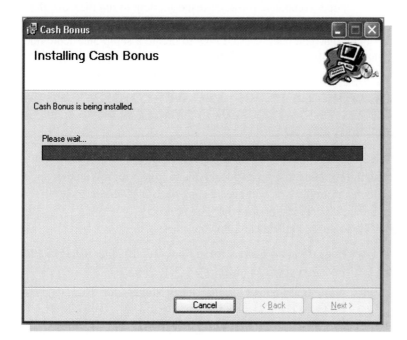

FIGURE A.10. *Installation progress*

When the installation is complete, the **Cash Bonus Setup Wizard** displays the message shown in Figure A.11. Click **Close**.

You can use the Add or Remove Programs option in the Windows Control Panel to uninstall the Cash Bonus application.

6.   After you install the application, a shortcut appears on the Start Menu of the target computer. You can use the shortcut to run the *Cash Bonus* application.

Now that you have learned how to create a setup and deployment project for a Windows application, let's learn how to install a Web application.

CREATING A SETUP AND DEPLOYMENT PROJECT BY USING THE WINDOWS INSTALLER FOR A WEB FORMS APPLICATION

The procedure for creating a setup and deployment project for a Web Forms project is similar to creating a setup and deployment project for a Windows application. To complete this example, you will need a copy the *StateQuarters* ASP.NET Web Application on the local host location for your Web projects.

To do this, complete the following steps:

1.   Copy the *StateQuarters* folder from your data files to the *\\InetPub\wwwroot* folder on your computer.

2.   From the Windows Taskbar, Click **Start**, select **Run**, type *inetmgr.exe* in the Open box and click **OK**.

3.   When IIS opens select **Default Web Site** in the left pane, and look for the application folder in the right pane.

4.   Right-click the *StateQuarters* folder and select **Properties**.

5.   Click **Create**, and then click **OK**.

To create a setup and deployment project for the State Quarters Web Forms project:

1.   Launch Visual Studio.NET and open the *StateQuarters* solution located on the local host.

2.   Click **Build** and choose **Build StateQuarters** to build the solution.

3.   Click **File**, **Add Project**, and choose **New Project**.

In the **Add New Project** dialog box, select **Setup and Deployment Projects** in the **Project Type** pane, and then choose **Web Setup Project** in the **Templates** pane. In the **Name** box, type `50StateQuarters` and click **OK**, as shown in Figure A.12.

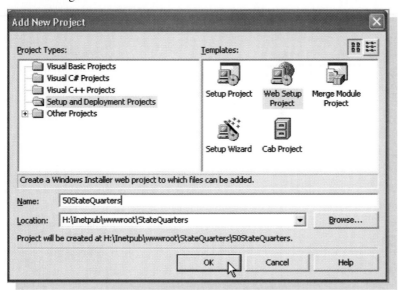

FIGURE A.12. *Adding a Setup project to the solution*

To add the output of the State Quarters Web Forms application project to the deployment project:

1.   In the File System Editor, select the **Web Application Folder**. On the **Action** menu, point to **Add** and then choose **Project Output**.

2.   Use the `Ctrl` key to select the **Primary output** and **Content Files** groups from the list. Then click **OK**, as shown in Figure A.13.

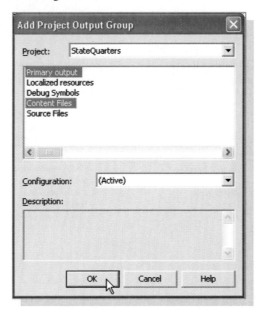

FIGURE A.13. *Adding a project output group to the setup project*

To set properties for the Windows Installer:

1. Click the **Web Application Folder** again to select it. In the **Properties** window, set the **DefaultDocument** property to `StateQuarters.aspx`, as shown in Figure A.14.

FIGURE A.14. *Setting the DefaultDocument property*

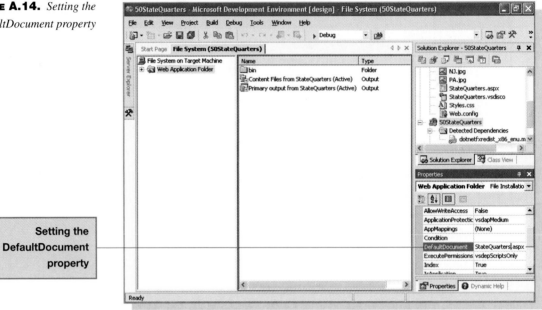

Setting the DefaultDocument property

2. On the **Build** menu, choose **Build 50StateQuarters**.

3. Save and close the solution.

4. Exit Visual Studio.NET.

To deploy the Web application:

To deploy a Web application to a Web server, copy the Windows Installer files to the Web server computer. Figure A.15 shows the installation files created in this example.

FIGURE A.15. *Installation files for the State Quarters Web application*

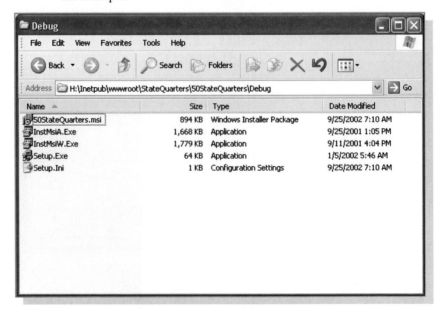

After you run Setup, the Web Forms application will be available in the *50StateQuarters* folder on the local host, using the following URL:

http://localhost/50StateQuarters/StateQuarters.aspx

To view the application, launch Internet Explorer and enter this URL. The project appears as shown in Figure A.16.

Tip

To deploy to a Web server, you must have administrative access privileges for that computer.

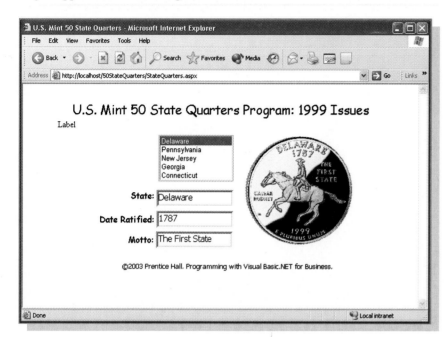

FIGURE A.16. *Internet Explorer displaying the installed application*

Summary

With packaging and deployment, a client must have the .NET Framework installed to run a program you create in Visual Basic.NET. You create a setup and deployment project that uses the Windows installer to install your program on the client.

Key Terms

client
executable file
Microsoft Windows Installer
.NET Framework redistributable
packaging and deploying

Numeric Data Types and Type Conversions

In Chapter 2 you learned to declare variables with different data types. You will recall that the data type you select for a variable depends on the kind of information your application must store for performing calculations or making comparisons. You also learned to use the *Option Explicit statement*, which requires that variables are explicitly declared before they are assigned values. As you know, the data type for a variable is important because when an expression contains variables of differing data types, Visual Basic.NET must convert one data type to another before performing a calculation or making a comparison.

In the Examples, Exercises, and Case Studies used throughout this book, we have used the **Val** function to convert user input obtained from text boxes or input boxes into numeric values that can be used in calculations. The **Val** function is a *conversion function*, which is a function that converts string data to a numeric value. The **Val** function explicitly converts the digits (numbers) contained in a string to a number that can be used in a calculation or in a comparison. Visual Basic.NET includes other conversion functions as well, which we will discuss shortly.

New to Visual Basic.NET is the Option Strict statement. The *Option Strict statement* does not allow data conversions from one data type to another where the conversion might result in data loss. Option Strict has two settings, **On** or **Off**. The default in Visual Basic is **Off**, and the statement is not required. To set **Option Strict** to **On**, add the following statement to the General Declarations section of the code for a project:

```
Option Strict On
```

Using the Option Strict Statement

Option Strict restricts implicit data type conversions to only widening conversions. This explicitly disallows any data type conversion in which data loss would occur and any conversion between numeric types and strings. Visual Basic .NET generally allows implicit conversions of any data type to any other data type. The **Val** function is an example of *permissive semantics*, meaning that it allows data conversions that might not be optimally efficient and can potentially result in data loss. Data loss can occur when the value of one data type is converted to a data type with less precision (fewer digits to the right of the decimal point) or a smaller capacity (integral or nonintegral). Such conversions are called narrowing conversions.

Strict semantics do not allow narrowing conversions. The **Option Strict** statement allows widening conversions and ensures that narrowing conversions are not permitted. Let's learn more about widening and narrowing conversions.

Widening and Narrowing Conversions

An important characteristic of a type conversion is whether the result of the conversion is within the range of the data type the value is being converted to.

WIDENING CONVERSIONS

A *widening conversion* changes a value to a data type that can accommodate any value of the original data. Table B.1 shows the widening conversions available in Visual Basic.NET for numeric values.

Table B.1: Widening Conversions for Numeric Data Types

Data Type	Widens to Data Types
Byte	Byte, Short, Integer, Long, Decimal, Single, Double
Short	Short, Integer, Long, Decimal, Single, Double
Integer	Integer, Long, Decimal, Single, Double
Long	Long, Decimal, Single, Double
Decimal	Decimal, Single, Double
Single	Single, Double
Double	Double

Conversions from Integer to Single, from Long to Single or Double, or from Decimal to Single or Double might result in loss of precision but never in loss of magnitude. Therefore, these conversions are allowed.

Widening conversions always succeed and can always be performed implicitly. You will learn about implicit and explicit conversions after the discussion of narrowing conversions.

NARROWING CONVERSIONS

A *narrowing conversion* changes a value to a data type that might not be able to hold some of the possible values. For example, a Double data type stores a decimal value with 14 digits of precision, while an Integer data type stores whole numbers. Converting a Double type to an Integer type is a narrowing conversion, because precision may be lost.

The standard narrowing conversions include the following:

- Any conversion that is the reverse of the direction of a widening conversion shown in Table B.1.

- Conversions in either direction between Boolean and any numeric type.

- Conversions in either direction between String and any numeric type, Boolean, or Date.

If a narrowing conversion fails at run time, an error occurs if the destination data type cannot receive the value being converted. You use a narrowing conversion when you know the value to convert can be converted to a specific data type without error. If Option Strict is On, Visual Basic.NET does not allow narrowing conversions.

Option Strict and Implicit and Explicit Conversions

If you use the Option Strict statement in your applications to disallow narrowing conversions, you need to be aware of the difference between implicit and explicit conversions. An *implicit conversion* does not require any special syntax in the source code. For example, consider the following code statements, where **Option Strict** is set to **On**:

```
Dim intValue As Integer
Dim dblValue As Double

intValue = 432
dblValue = intValue
```

Visual Basic .NET implicitly converts the value of *intValue* to single-precision floating point before assigning it to *dblValue*.

Now consider the following code statements, which attempt to assign text entered into a text box to an Integer value and then convert the Integer value to a Single value:

```
Dim intValue As Integer
Dim sngValue As Single
intValue = Val(txtValue.Text)
sngValue = intValue
```

This code generates the message shown in Figure B.1.

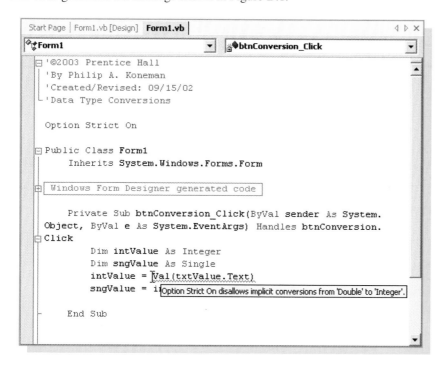

FIGURE B.1. *Message indicating that an implicit function is disallowed*

As you can see in Figure B.1, the first conversion fails. The code window highlights the error by marking the statement that contains the error. Moving your pointer over the error statement displays the error message. Because **Option Strict** is **On**, the

Val function cannot be used to convert the value in the text box to a numeric value. In this case, an explicit statement is required.

An *explicit conversion* requires a *type conversion keyword* to perform the conversion. Visual Basic.NET provides these keywords to explicitly convert an expression in parentheses to a specific data type. A type conversion keyword acts like a function but compiles without making a call, so execution is slightly faster than with a function call. Here's how to fix the error shown in Figure B.1 by using an explicit conversion:

```
Dim intValue As Integer
Dim sngValue As Single
intValue = CInt(txtValue.Text)
sngValue = intValue
```

As Figure B.2 shows, the **CInt** type conversion keyword explicitly converts the string value in the text box to an Integer data type.

FIGURE B.2. *Message using the* **CInt** *type conversion keyword to explicitly convert a String value to an Integer value*

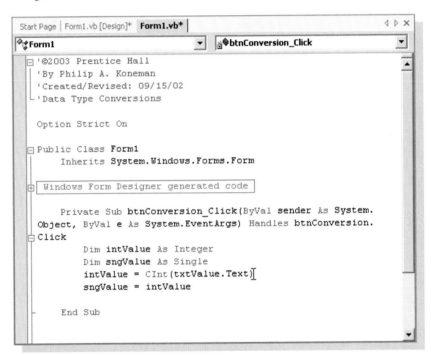

Table B.2 lists the Type Conversion keywords available in Visual Basic.NET for explicitly converting numeric values.

Table B.2: Type Conversion Keywords

Type Conversion Keyword	Converts an Expression to Data Type	Data Types Allowed in the Conversion
Cbool	Boolean	Any numeric type, String, Object
Cbyte	Byte	Any numeric type, Boolean, String, Object
CDate	Date	String, Object
CDbl	Double	Any numeric type (including Byte), Boolean, String, Object
CDec	Decimal	Any numeric type (including Byte), Boolean, String, Object
CInt	Integer	Any numeric type (including Byte), Boolean, String, Object
CLng	Long	Any numeric type (including Byte), Boolean, String, Object
CShort	Short	Any numeric type (including Byte), Boolean, String, Object
CSng	Single	Any numeric type (including Byte), Boolean, String, Object
CStr	String	Any numeric type (including Byte), Boolean, Char, Char() array, Date, Object

The **Option Strict** statement limits implicit data type conversions to only widening conversions. This explicitly disallows any data type conversions in which data loss would occur and any conversion between numeric types and strings. You need to use the appropriate type conversion keyword to explicitly perform conversions with Option Strict turned on.

Key Terms

conversion function

explicit conversion

implicit conversion

narrowing conversion

Option Explicit statement

Option Strict statement

permissive semantics

strict semantics

type conversion keyword

Val function

widening conversion

Glossary

 # End Region statement—Statement that defines the end of a code region. The # Region and End Region statements specify a block of code you can expand or collapse when using the outlining feature of the Visual Studio Code Editor.

 # Region statement—Statement that defines the beginning of a code region.

.NET Framework Redistributable—The .NET Framework components available as a download from the Microsoft Corporation. The .NET Framework must be installed on a client computer to run a Visual Studio.NET application.

abstraction—Hiding the internal details of an object from the user.

access key—An underlined character in the text of a menu, menu item, or the label of a control such as a button that runs a procedure when the Alt key is pressed in combination with the predefined access key.

accessibility (procedure)—The accessibility of a sub procedure determines the range of procedures that can make a call to the sub procedure.

accessibility (variable)—Characteristic of a variable that defines what procedures have access to the value stored in the variable.

ADO provider—Data provider that connects ADO.NET applications to non-SQL databases.

Advanced DataBinding property—Property of a text box, combo box, or list box control that defines the specific item in a list the control is bound to.

Advanced Graphics Interface (GDI+)—Windows graphics design interface (GDI) for creating graphics, drawing text, and manipulating graphical images as objects in Visual Studio.NET.

ampersand symbol—The ampersand character (&) has two purposes in Visual Basic.NET: concatenating (joining) variable values and text strings and setting the accelerator key for a menu or context menu. See *concatenation*.

append mode—File write mode for writing text to the end of a file.

applications—Programs that run on a computer. A computer program (application) is a set of instructions that tells the computer hardware how to obtain input, what action to perform, and the output to produce.

argument—Value that is passed to or from a procedure.

arguments—A function can accept one or more arguments, which are values passed to it.

array—Variable that stores multiple values.

array variable—Another term for an array, because an array is a variable with a declared size.

ArrayList—Collection you can use to create an array of items.

ASCII (American Standard Code for Information Interchange)—Standard designation of characters and symbols shared among computer systems. ASCII values 32 to 127 represent the numbers, the special characters, and the uppercase and lowercase characters contained in many text strings.

ASP.NET—New .NET Framework Web development technology that includes both the objects and controls you create at design time and the code that executes at run time from a Web server.

attribute—Characteristic of an XML element that is like a property and provides further definition about an element in the same way that properties describe the characteristics of objects and classes.

AutoFormat—Predefined set of formats that apply to the database fields displayed in the DataGrid control.

Auto Hide—Feature of a Visual Studio.NET tool window that determines whether the window will display and hide automatically.

base class—Class from which a new class inherits its functionality.

bitmap—Two-dimensional collection of pixels that creates an image.

Boolean data type—Data type for storing dichotomous values (true or false).

Boolean value—Value assigned to a Boolean variable. Many procedures return a Boolean value.

bounds—Description of the size of an array.

bug—Error in a program that causes program execution to stop or yields inaccurate data. See *debugging*.

button—Visual Basic.NET control contained on a form that runs an event procedure.

ByRef keyword—Specifies that an argument is passed by reference, meaning that the value can be changed by the function that receives it.

Byte data type—Data type for storing a single ASCII character (ASCII code 0-255).

ByVal keyword—Specifies that an argument is passed by value, meaning that the value cannot be changed by the function that receives it.

call—When a calling procedure references a called procedure, the calling procedure is said to make a call.

calling code—Statement or expression within a code sequence that makes a call to a called procedure.

calling procedure—Procedure that contains a calling statement.

calling statement—Code statement that contains calling code.

case—In a Select Case statement, the case is the individual condition being tested.

case block—Defines the set of cases being tested in a Select Case statement.

CausesValidation property—Property of a Visual Basic.NET control that determines whether the control causes validation to be performed when the control is clicked.

Char data type—Data type for storing Unicode characters from 0 to 65535.

check box control—Control for storing a value that may be on or off (true or false).

checked property—Property of radio button and check box controls specifying whether the control is checked at run time.

class—Set of characteristics differentiating one category of objects from another.

Class Name list—Drop-down list at the top left of the Code Editor for selecting a control and creating an event procedure.

Class statement—Used to define a class. You define a class by using the Class statement, providing a name for the class, entering the code statements that define the class, and completing the class declaration with the End Class statement.

Clear method—Clears the contents of a list box or combo box control.

client—Computer on which a program runs.

client (Web)—Computer requesting a Web page from the server. To open a Web page, the client must have a Web browser installed.

client-server computing model—Computing model where a Web document is posted on a Web server, and a client computer with Internet access and a Web browser can open the document.

client-side scripting—Technology for interactivity in Web pages where the code that defines the interactivity is either embedded in the HTML or contained in a separate program downloaded with the page and run by the browser.

Close method—Method used by a StreamReader or StreamWriter to close the file opened for reading or writing.

code—Program statements or commands written as instructions that describe exactly what the program will do. In Visual Basic.NET, you can enter the code for an event by using the Code Editor.

Code Editor—Visual Studio.NET IDE window that displays all the code statements for an application. The Code Editor is the document window you use to enter the program statements that give your program its functionality. The area where you enter and edit code is called the Code pane.

code-behind scripting—When the programming code in a Web application is separated from the user interface, it is called code-behind scripting. "Code-behind" means that the HTML and controls that define the Web Form interface are contained in a separate file from the code statements that provide the functionality.

collection—Ordered set of items in a list box or combo box that can be referred to as a unit and manipulated at run time. Each item in the collection has a unique index.

ComboBox control—Visual Basic.NET control with a list of items from which one or more items can be selected at run time. A combo box has characteristics of both a list box and a text box. The lower portion of the control contains a list of items, and the upper portion contains a text box for adding an item not in the list.

Command object—Managed provider object used to create commands telling the database what actions to perform.

command prompt—Location in a text-based interface where you enter a command by typing a statement at the prompt and pressing the ↵Enter key.

comments—The code for your application typically begins with remarks, also called comments, which are internal documentation that explains what the code accomplishes. Comments begin with the asterisk character (*) and are color-coded green in the Code Editor.

common dialog box—Predefined dialog box for performing useful functions such as opening and saving files, changing fonts, or printing.

common dialog control—Displays a common dialog box in a Windows application.

CompareValidator—Control that compares an entry with a constant value, or the property value of another control.

compile errors—Any error in a program's code that prevents the application from running.

component tray—Area of the IDE that appears below a form. The component tray contains controls that do not appear at run time but need to be available at design time for setting their properties.

compound condition—Expression made up of multiple logical operators used to test a condition.

computer program—Set of instructions that tells the computer hardware how to obtain input, what action to perform, and the output to produce. See *applications*.

concatenation—To join multiple text strings so the information displayed in the text property of the text box appears on multiple lines, you use the ampersand symbol (&) between the strings to connect the individual text strings into a single string. The process of joining multiple elements such as text is concatenation. The ampersand character concatenates, or joins, the text strings.

condition—Expression that uses a relational operator to perform a test.

Connection object—ADO.NET object that connects an application to a database so the application can read and write database records.

Const keyword—Used to declare a constant. When declaring a constant, you provide a name, data type, and value; for example, Const conTaxRate As Decimal = 0.745.

constant—Declared value specified at design time that remains the same (or constant) and cannot change while the application is running.

ContextMenu control—Visual Basic.NET control for creating context menus.

continuation character—Character consisting of an underscore (_) that you can use to continue a line of code in the Code Editor. By placing an underscore at the end of a line of code, you can press ⏎Enter and continue the code statement on the next line.

controls—Objects such as buttons, text boxes, list boxes, labels, or other interface elements that make up the user interface on a form, which is a container for controls.

conversion function—Converts string data to a numeric value.

counter variable—Variable, usually of the Integer data type, that increases or decreases in value during each repetition of the loop.

Crystal Report Designer—Crystal Reports design interface that provides the tools you need to create sophisticated reports.

Crystal Report Gallery—Crystal Reports tool that displays predefined reports you can use to create a new report.

CrystalReportViewer—Control that allows a Crystal Report to be viewed in an application. The control appearing in a Crystal Report that contains a toolbar for scrolling through the report a page at a time, changing the zoom factor for the report, modifying how the report displays, and printing the report.

Crystal Reports—Reporting tool in Visual Studio.NET for creating interactive, presentation-quality reports.

Crystal Reports Experts—Component of Crystal Reports that allows you to add predefined functionality to a report by presenting a series of dialog boxes for creating and formatting the report.

Crystal Report Viewer—Term used to describe a control for hosting a report in an application. There are two report viewers—see *Web Forms Viewer* and *Windows forms Viewer*.

Currency keyword—Keyword used in conjunction with the Format function to format a number displayed in a text box or label as currency.

CustomValidator control—Control for checking an entry against validation logic that you define. This type of validation supports a check against values derived at run time.

data adapter—Managed provider object used to create a disconnected dataset.

data file—Stores information used by a program.

data type—Specification of the kind of data a variable or constant will hold. Examples include String, Integer, and Single.

data validation—Checking data entered into a program by a user.

Data view—View in the XML Designer that displays XML elements in a data grid.

DataAdapter object—ADO.NET object that manages all communications between the program and the database after a data connection is established.

database—Collection of related information organized on a computer.

database management system (DBMS)—Application for creating and using databases consisting of tables, queries, forms, reports, and other database objects.

DataGrid control—Windows Forms control that displays data from a dataset as a series of rows and columns.

DataMember property—Property of a DataGrid control that specifies which table or query contains the records to display.

DataReader object—Managed provider object that connects to a database and delivers read-only data that cannot be edited.

dataset—Disconnected copy of a database.

DataSource property—Property of a DataGrid control that specifies which dataset the control is bound to.

Date data type—Data type for storing calendar dates in an eight-character format.

debug mode—When you run an application, Visual Studio switches to debug mode. In debug mode, Visual Studio flags errors that occur when the application is running.

Debug.WriteLine statement—Statement you can add to your code to test the results of a procedure. This statement displays output in the Output window that appears on the screen when you run an application from the Visual Studio.NET IDE.

debugging—A program error is a bug, so debugging is the process of identifying, correcting, and eliminating errors in your application.

Decimal data type—Data type for storing decimal values with up to 28 places to the right of the decimal point.

decision statement—Visual Basic.NET statement for handling decision structures. You can use a decision statement to test whether a condition is true or false, to test a series of conditions, to make a selection when a condition is true, or to run a series of statements if an exception occurs in testing a condition.

decision structure—Programming structure that makes a comparison between program statements.

declaration statement—Nonexecutable code statement that creates (declares) a variable or constant. The Dim statement declares a local variable; the Const statement declares a constant. For variables, the accessibility is declared by using the appropriate keyword in the declaration: Dim, Public, Protected, Friend, Protected Friend, or Private.

decrement—In a For...Next loop, a decrement is a decrease in the counter variable by the step value.

derived class—Inherits all the properties, methods, and events of a base class.

design time—State of the Visual Studio.NET development environment while a project is being developed, in contrast to run time (when the application is running) and break mode (when the application is being debugged with the Visual Studio debugger).

Design view—View in the Web Forms IDE that displays the Web page as a form. You can add controls to the form by using the Toolbox, and you can manipulate the controls directly on the form.

Details—A section of a Crystal Report that contains information from the data source that is of interest in the report.

development environment—Computer application with a comprehensive set of tools and features that allow you to create, debug, and deploy applications.

development tool—Set of programs for developing applications. See *development environment*.

dialog box—Window that appears on the screen and presents one or more options.

Dim keyword—Begins a Dim statement for declaring a variable.

dimension—The dimensionality of an array refers to the number of columns in the array.

Do...Loop statement—Creates a loop that executes a block of statements while a condition is true or until a condition is satisfied.

dockable—You can dock and undock a tool window by selecting or clearing Dockable on the Window menu. When a tool window is dockable, it floats on top of the other windows or snaps to a side of the application window.

document window—Window that is dynamically created when you open or create files or other items in the IDE.

documentation—Documentation includes anything that helps someone understand the program. See *internal documentation* and *external documentation*.

Double data type—Data type for storing double-precision floating-point numbers with 14 digits of accuracy.

dynamic array—Array that can be resized at run time.

e—Required argument for the OnPaint method that represents the data for the event. A Paint event paints on the screen the vector graphic specified by *e*.

element (array)—Value stored in an array.

element (XML)—Unique unit of data stored in an XML file.

encapsulation—Literally meaning to enclose something. In object-oriented programming, this means the characteristics and behaviors of an object are wrapped up in a self-contained unit.

End Class statement—Indicates the end of a class statement. You define a class by using the Class statement, providing a name for the class, entering the code statements that define the class, and completing the class declaration with the End Class statement.

End Function statement—Terminates the definition of a function procedure.

End Get statement—Terminates a Get property procedure.

End Region statement—Defines the end of a code region. The # Region and End Region statements specify a block of code you can expand or collapse when using the outlining feature of the Visual Studio Code Editor.

End Set statement—Statement that is required to end a Function procedure definition. When the program execution encounters an End Function statement, control is returned to the calling code.

End Structure keyword—Statement that is required to end a structure definition.

End sub statement—Statement required to terminate the definition of a procedure or block.

endless loop—Loop that never reaches the end value. Also called an infinite loop.

end-tag—XML tag indicating the end of an element. The end of an element is identified within an end-tag, which uses the less-than symbol (<), the name of the element, and a forward-slash and greater-than symbols together (/>).

enumeration—Symbolic name for a set of values.

event—Action that triggers a program instruction.

Event procedure—Procedure that belongs to a specific object or event. An example is the procedure that handles the click event for a button control.

event-driven language—Visual Basic.NET is an event-driven language, meaning you write program code that responds to specific events. The program logic in an event-driven language is not limited to any specific sequence of events you must anticipate while developing the program.

exception—Any error condition or unexpected behavior that occurs in a procedure during run time.

executable file—Program file with an .exe file extension that is used to load a program into memory.

Exit Loop statement—Statement that will exit a loop before a condition is met.

explicit conversion—Data conversion required by strict semantics where a type conversion keyword is required to perform the conversion.

explicit variable declaration—Requirement in Visual Basic.NET that every variable must be declared before you use it. The Option Explicit statement forces explicit variable declaration. To allow implicit variable declaration, set Option Explicit to Off.

exposed—In object-oriented programming, the action of making the characteristics and methods of an object available to other objects.

Extensible Markup Language (XML)—Tag-based language for storing data in a way that also describes the structure of the data.

external documentation—Refers to any documents that explain the application. For commercial programs, external documentation usually includes the user's manual and online help system.

field—Item of information contained in a database or random access data file that defines a characteristic of a data record. Examples of fields are the first and last names in an address book application.

fields (OOP)—In object-oriented programming, public variables exposed by a class.

RequiredFieldValidator—Control that verifies that a required control used for data entry contains a value.

field variables—Variables that define the data contained within the structure.

file input/output—Processes for reading data from files and writing data to files. See *file I/O*.

file I/O—Process of reading data from and writing data to external files.

FileClose function—Function that concludes file input or output to a file opened using the FileOpen function.

FileOpen function—Implicit function for opening a sequential file to input, output, or append data.

files—In the context of a Visual Basic.NET project, a project is composed of files that provide the solution with its functionality.

Fill command—Visual Basic.NET command that fills a dataset with records from the data source.

financial functions—Intrinsic functions in Visual Basic.NET for performing financial calculations. The Pmt, PPmt, and IPmt functions are examples of financial functions.

floating-point numbers—Numbers that are expressed as a power of 10 and therefore have an exponent, which is represented by an E. You can use these to store numbers that are either extremely small (a number with a negative exponent) or extremely large (a number with a positive exponent).

flowchart—Drawing that uses standardized symbols to model the steps required to handle decision statements.

flowcharting—Modeling technique for planning the flow of a program's code to handle decision statements.

FlowLayout mode—View supported by the Web Forms IDE where you create a Web page by building the page from top to bottom.

flowlines—Lines that connect the symbols and model the flow of a decision in a flowchart.

FontDialog control—Common dialog control that displays a dialog box with a list of the fonts currently installed on the system.

For Each...Next statement—Looping structure that executes the statements in the loop for each element in a collection.

For...Next statement—Looping structure that repeats a statement or procedure a specific number of times.

foreign key—Field in a relational database that links information in a child table with the parent table.

form-level variable—Variable that is available to any procedure on a form. Also called a module-level variable because it has module scope.

Form load method—Method for a form that specifies any actions you wish to accomplish when a form is loaded into memory at run time.

Format function—Returns a string that is formatted according to the instructions specified by the function. The statement Format (txtTaxes.Text,"Currency") formats the string contained in the text box as currency.

Friend access—Variables declared with the Friend keyword have friend access, and are accessible from within the program that contains their declaration.

function—Procedure that returns a value.

function procedure—Procedure that performs a series of actions or tasks and returns a value.

Function statement—A statement that declares the name, arguments, and code that define a Function procedure.

FV function—An intrinsic function that calculates the future value of an annuity based on periodic, fixed payments and a fixed interest rate.

Generalized Markup Language—Class of languages that define the structure and meaning of the text in a document, without specifying how the text should be used. XML is derived from a Generalized Markup Language.

Get property procedure—Used to retrieve a value from a property.

Get statement—The statement that begins a Get Property procedure for obtaining the value stored in a property.

glyph—Small green marker indicating that a control on a Web form is a Web Server control.

graphics object—Used to declare and display a vector graphic.

Graphical user interface (GUI)—A program interface that includes visual elements for interacting with the program.

Graphics.Drawstring method—Draws a text string at the specified location by using the specified Brush and Font objects.

GridLayout mode—View supported by the Web Forms IDE where you create a Web page by adding controls to the grid in the same way you do when creating a Windows form.

group box control—Contains a set of radio button or check box controls that are treated as a unit.

hard-copy output—Computer output, such as a printed document, that can be used and interpreted independent of the computer.

HTML—See *Hypertext Markup Language*.

HTML controls—Controls that use tags to send data input to the server. The functionality of an HTML control is not visible to the server.

HTML Server controls—Visual Basic.NET controls that are similar to HTML controls except that the functionality of an HTML Server control is visible to the server.

HTML view—View in the Web Forms IDE that displays the HTML markup that defines the user interface.

Hypertext Markup Language (HTML)—HTML is a markup language for developing Web pages. HTML consists of the textual information to display, references to graphic elements, and instructions for how to display the page.

If...ElseIf...Else statement—Decision structure used as an alternative to nested If statements for testing multiple conditions. To create this structure, add one or more Else If statements to If...Then...Else to test additional conditions if the first condition is False.

If...Then statement—Simplest kind of decision structure that performs a logical test. If the test evaluates to True, the program code specifies what action to take.

If...Then...Else statement—Decision structure that tests for a condition and specifies one option if the test evaluates to True and another if it evaluates to False.

Image control—Web Server control for displaying images on Web forms.

Image Editor—Visual Studio.NET component with an extensive set of tools for creating and editing images and for creating toolbar bitmaps.

Image property—Property of a PictureBox control that specifies the image displayed at run time.

ImageURL property—Property of a Web Forms Image control that specifies the image to display on the page.

implicit conversion—Type conversion that is allowed when Option Strict is set to Off and therefore does not require a type conversion keyword.

implicit function—Predefined function procedure that is a part of Visual Basic.NET. Examples include the Val, Format, and Pmt functions.

implicit variable declaration—When Option Explicit is set to Off, you can declare a variable implicitly by including a statement in the code that makes a reference to the variable.

increment—In a For...Next loop, an increase in the counter variable by the step value.

index—Expression that specifies the position of a member of the collection, or an integer that identifies each element in an array.

inheritance—In object-oriented programming, the ability to create new classes based on an existing class.

Inherits keyword—Keyword that designates the base class from which a derived class will inherit its functionality.

Input box function—Intrinsic function that displays a dialog box on the screen with a text box for obtaining user input.

input mode—File access mode for reading data from a file.

InputString function—Implicit function that reads a character string from a text file.

instance—An object is a specific occurrence of a class called an *instance* of the class.

instantiation—Act of creating a specific object from a class.

Integer data type—Data type for storing whole numbers ranging from –2,147,483,648 to 2,147,483,647.

integral data types—Data types that store whole numbers only. Examples include Integer, Short, and Long.

integrated development environment (IDE)—Development environment where all features are made available within a common interface.

interface—What users see on the screen and what they interact with when using a program. Also called the user interface.

interface design—Discipline of designing the components of a computer program that the user interacts with when using the program.

internal documentation—Usually consists of comments added to the program statements to help programmers understand the purpose of the program code.

IPmt function—Intrinsic function that calculates the portion of a loan payment that applies to the loan interest.

IsNumeric function—Intrinsic function that determines whether a text string entered into a text box or input box can be evaluated as a number.

IsPostBack keyword—Keyword that returns a value indicating whether the page is being loaded and accessed for the first time or in response to a client request being sent back to the server.

Item property—Property of a combo box or list box that defines the items in the list.

Items.Add method—Method you can use with combo box and list box controls to add items to the collection at run time.

iteration—Single execution of a loop.

key tag—Tag in the Toolbox for setting the primary key field for an element.

keyword—The function of any keyword is known to Visual Basic.NET. When Visual Basic.NET executes the keyword, it performs the known function. Variables and objects cannot take on the name of a keyword.

label—Control that displays text as a caption that cannot be edited by the user. It is common to use labels for titles on forms.

Lbound keyword—Keyword for determining the lower bounds of an array.

LCase function—Intrinsic function that converts all values from lowercase to uppercase.

Len function—Intrinsic function that determines the record length for the structure variable.

Length of File (LOF) function—Intrinsic function that obtains the number of characters contained in a file that has been opened by using the FileOpen function.

length property—Property of an array that returns the size of the array as an integer value.

ListBox control—Visual Basic.NET control that contains a list of items from which one or more items can be selected. A list box is similar to a combo box but does not include a text box for entering a new value.

local variable—Accessible only to the procedure in which it is declared. Local variables are declared by using the Dim statement.

logic errors—Errors in formulas or calculations that do not prevent an application from running but produce inaccurate information.

logical operators—Used to compare two statements or conditions. The most common logical operators are And, Or, and Not.

logical test—Test that compares two statements to determine if the comparison is true or false.

Long data type—Data type for storing whole numbers ranging from -9,223,372,036,854,775,808 to 9,223,372,036,854,775,807.

loop—Procedure or set of statements that is repeated. See *repetition structure*.

looping—Process of repeating a set of instructions until a condition is met in a repetition structure.

MainMenu control—Control for adding menus to Visual Basic.NET Windows applications.

managed providers—Set of ADO.NET objects that establish and manage a connection between a Visual Basic.NET program and a database.

markup language—Language of text and tags that defines the standards for what each tag must include. HTML and XML are examples of markup languages.

Me keyword—Refers to the specific instance of a class where the code is currently executing.

menu—Graphical element in a program that contains associated commands.

Menu Designer—Visual Studio.NET tool for creating and editing menus.

menu items—Items appearing on a menu and used to perform commands or functions.

message box—Box that appears on the screen and displays a message. Contains a caption in the title bar and one or more command buttons.

method—Behavior (action) supported by an object that determines which actions an event can trigger. A specific action an object can perform when the application is running.

Method Name list—Drop-down list at the top right of the Code Editor for determining which method of a control will evoke an event procedure.

Microsoft Windows Installer—Installation and configuration service that ships as part of the Microsoft Windows 2000, Windows XP, and Windows Millennium Edition (Windows Me) operating systems.

Modified-Hungarian Notation—Standard naming convention for naming controls in Visual Studio.NET, using a three-character designation for each control. Became widely used inside Microsoft and is accepted in the programming community.

module—Visual Basic.NET project component for organizing functions and other program elements, such as variables, that are used anywhere (globally) in a solution.

module-level variable—Available to any procedure contained in a form and has module scope. Also called a form-level variab*le*.

module scope—Applies to modules, classes, and structures. You can declare elements at this level by placing the declaration statement outside any procedure or block within the module, class, or structure.

MsgBox function—Intrinsic function you include in a program statement to display a message box on the screen. Requires a prompt that defines the message appearing in the dialog box.

multidimensional array—Array with more than one column. See *dimension*.

multimedia—Computer application that represents information by using two or more formats, such as text and images. Examples are Websites that include both text and images and computer-based encyclopedias that combine text, graphics, and other rich media types.

Name property—One of the first properties you normally set for the objects in a project. You refer to an object by its name when you reference it in code.

narrowing conversion—Data conversion that changes a value to a data type that might not be able to hold some of the possible values.

nested If statements—Decision structure with If statements that contain additional If statements.

non-integral data types—Data types that store numbers with both integer and fractional parts, which are commonly used in calculations. Decimal, Single, and Double are all non-integral data types.

object—Anything that is a part of your Visual Basic.NET application. An object is a combination of code and data you can treat as a single unit. Can be part of your application, such as a menu, button, text box, or other control on a form.

Object data type—Data type for storing any value. This is the default if no data type is assigned.

object variable—Variable that refers to a Visual Basic.NET object to simplify the code that refers to the object. For example, an object variable can refer to the elements in a collection.

object-oriented programming (OOP)—Programming approach that emphasizes working with objects and building programs by defining categories of objects that share common characteristics.

OleDbConnection object—One of two ADO.NET connection objects that connects an application to a data source. You can use the OleDbConnection object to connect to a non-SQL database.

OleDbDataAdapter object—ADO.NET data adapter that works in conjunction with the OLE DB managed provider.

one-to-many relationship—Database relationship that links one record in a parent table to zero or many records in a child table.

OnPaint method—Visual Basic.NET method that raises a Paint event.

OpenFileDialog—Control that displays a dialog box on the screen for browsing and opening files.

operator—Character or combination of characters that accomplishes a specific computation. Visual Basic.NET supports six different kinds of operators: arithmetic, assignment, comparison, concatenation, logical, and miscellaneous.

operator precedence—Predetermined order that determines which part of an expression is evaluated first when several operations occur in an expression.

Option Explicit statement—Statement that appears at the end of the General Declarations section of your code to enable and disable explicit (and therefore implicit) variable declaration. Option Explicit requires variables to be explicitly declared before they are assigned values.

Option Strict statement—Code statement that enforces strict semantics and thereby requires a type conversion keyword for all type conversions.

output mode—File access mode that overwrites the existing file.

Overridable keyword—Used by a derived class to override a method in the base class.

override—If you cannot use the inherited member of a base class, you can modify it in the derived class. The action of modifying the inherited member is called *overriding*.

Overrides keyword—Keyword in a derived class indicating that a method inherited from the base class will be overridden.

Packaging and deploying—Process of creating a Setup.exe file that installs the required components in a .NET solution on a client.

Page Header—A section of a Crystal Report that contains information appearing at the top of each page of the report, such as the headings appearing above columns of data.

Page Footer—A section of a Crystal Report that contains information appearing at the bottom of each page, such as the page number.

Page_Load event—An event contained in an ASP.NET Web Application that determines what happens the first time the page is loaded.

Paint event—Raised by the OnPaint method to paint a vector graphic on the screen.

parameter—Named part of a function that receives an argument passed to it.

parent-child relationship—See *one-to-many relationship*.

Pascal-case—Naming convention for variables in which the first character of each word is capitalized when the descriptive name includes more than one word.

pass, passing—Sending an argument to a procedure.

Pen object—Object that works in conjunction with a graphic object that specifies the color and width of the line that will represent a vector graphic.

permissive semantics—Code statement that allows implicit conversion of any data type to any other data type, where the conversion might not be optimally efficient and can potentially result in data loss. The Val function is an example of permissive semantics.

PictureBox control—Box for displaying an image on a Windows form.

pixels—Small dots that make up a bitmap image. Each pixel is a small square that contains a specific color. The collection of pixels creates the image.

Pmt function—Intrinsic function that calculates the monthly payment for a loan.

polymorphism—Literally meaning "many forms," this central concept in OOP means that a derived class can implement the properties and methods of the base class differently than another derived class of the same base class.

populate—Adding information to a list box, combo box, or database table.

Position property—Property of the data binding mechanism that determines which record in a dataset is bound to a control.

postback event—Event supported by Visual Basic.NET Web Forms that retains changes made by the user when data on a page is changed and a new page is loaded.

PostTest—Test for a condition in a looping structure where the test occurs after entering the loop.

PmtFunction—An intrinsic function that calculates the monthly payment for a loan.

PPmtfunction—Intrinsic function that calculates the portion of a loan payment that applies to the principal.

Preserve keyword—Used to retain the current data in the array as the array is resized.

PreTest—Test for a condition in a looping structure where the test occurs before entering the loop.

primary key—Database field that uniquely identifies each record in a database.

Print function—Intrinsic function that writes each character in a text string to a sequential file.

Print method—Method for the PrintDocument object that starts the printing of a document.

PrintDialog component—Common dialog control that displays a dialog box for selecting a printer and printing a document.

PrintDocument object—Visual Basic.NET component that sets the properties that describe what to print and how to print a document within Windows applications. Can be used in conjunction with the PrintDialog component to control the printing of a document.

PrintPreviewDialog control—Common dialog control that displays a dialog box for previewing and printing a document.

Private—Accessibility for a variable where the value is accessible only within the procedure where it is declared.

Private keyword—Declares a variable with procedure scope.

Procedure—Series of code statements that perform specific actions. There are two kinds of procedures in Visual Basic.NET: sub procedures and function procedures.

procedure scope—Scope of a variable declared with the Dim statement (local). A local variable is available only to the procedure in which it is declared.

profile—Collection of settings that defines the appearance of the Visual Studio.NET IDE.

program files—Files a computer uses to run and support a program.

programming language—Program code written according to a defined syntax.

programming structure—Sequence in which the program statements are executed at run time. Programmers use programming structures to organize code. Program statements are organized in one of three ways: by using a sequence structure, a decision structure, or a repetition structure.

projects—Solutions you create in Visual Basic.NET contain one or more projects. You can create a project by using any Visual Studio.NET Language. A project contains the files that provide the solution with its functionality. The IDE organizes solutions, projects, and files and holds all your work in a hierarchy that is visible in the Solution Explorer.

property—Characteristic of an object.

Property Builder—Visual tool in the Visual Basic.NET IDE for setting the display options for a data grid.

Property keyword—Used to declare a local variable for storing data in a property.

property procedure—Procedure used to get or set the properties of an object.

Public keyword—Keyword used to declare a public variable. Variables declared as Public have public access, and there are no restrictions on the accessibility of public variables.

pseudocode—English-like statements that express in simple terms what a program's procedures will do.

pushpin—Small icon in a Visual Studio.NET tool window that determines whether the window will display and hide automatically.

radio button control—Control for selecting one option from a list of possible options. Radio buttons are typically grouped by using a Group Box control.

random file access—Accesses any record in the file directly, because each field and record has a fixed length.

RangeValidator—Web Forms validation control that limits data entry to a specified range.

rank—Number of dimensions in an array.

raster graphic—Image made up of thousands of small squares called pixels. Each pixel can be a color, and the combination of colors makes the image.

ReadOnly property—An optional statement in a property procedure indicating that the value in a property can be retrieved but not modified.

ReadToEnd method—Reads all characters from the current position to the end of a TextReader and returns them as one string.

record—Collection of fields that distinguish one item in a database or data file.

ReDim statement—Used to resize an array. ReDim is short for Redimension. When you redimension an array, you change its size.

region—Area of the Code Editor that contains code you can display or hide by expanding and collapsing the region. See *# Region*.

RegularExpressionValidator—Web forms validation control that checks that the entry matches a pattern defined by a regular expression, such as those in social security numbers and e-mail addresses.

relation tag—Tag in the Toolbox for establishing a relationship between two related table elements.

relational database management system (RDBMS)—Database management system that stores database records in separate tables that can be related to one another.

relational operator—Character used in making comparisons, including less than (<), greater than (>), and equals (=).

remark—Comment the programmer adds to the code, often to document what the program is doing. See *comment*.

repetition structure—Programming structure that repeats the execution of a series of program statements.

Report Engine—Crystal Reports component that processes the formatting, grouping, and charting criteria specified in a report.

Report Expert—Specific predefined report available in the Crystal Report Expert Report Gallery.

Report Footer—A section of a Crystal Report that contains information appearing at the end of the report, such as grand totals.

Report Header—A section of a Crystal Report that contains information appearing at the beginning of the report, such as the report title and date on a report with multiple sections.

ReportSource property—Property of a Windows Forms Viewer that determines which Crystal Report to display in the viewer.

RequiredFieldValidator control—A validation control that makes input in a control mandatory.

Return statement—Statement in a called procedure that returns a result to the calling procedure.

rich controls—Visual Basic.NET Web Forms controls that include properties you can set to customize the look and feel of the control.

Rich Text Format (RTF)—File format that uses codes, or tags (also called tokens), added to plain text to change the way the text appears.

RichTextBox control—Control that stores and displays Rich Text Format (RTF) data.

run time—State of the Visual Studio.NET development environment when a program is running.

run-time errors—Any error that causes an application to halt when it is running.

Runat attribute—Code statement required to use Web Server controls.

SaveFile method—Saves the contents of the RichTextBox to a file.

scalar variable—Variable consisting of a single element.

Sections—The areas of a Crystal report that hold objects that reference the data to appear in the report.

Select...Case statement—Programming statement that compares an expression or a value to a case block to determine which case applies.

SelectionMode property—Property of a list box that specifies the items in the list that can be selected. The settings for this property are None, One, MultiSimple, and

MultiExtended. Setting the MultiSimple and MultiExtended properties to True allows multiple items in the list to be selected.

self-describing—Characteristic of XML documents where the document contains both data and information about the data's structure.

self-service application—The user can view and update data directly rather than relying on a customer service representative.

separator line—A line that appears between groups of items on a menu or context menu.

sequence structure—Program statements that are executed in the order in which the statements appear.

sequential file access—File access method where text is read from a file or written to a file as a continuous stream of data.

Server Explorer—Visual Studio.Net tool for viewing all the resources on your system, including databases. You can use the Server Explorer to create an ADO.NET data connection.

Set property procedure—Procedure for storing a value in a property. Begins with the Set statement, includes the assignment statement, and concludes with End Set.

Set statement—Starts a Set property procedure used to set the value of a property.

SetSelected method—Method for a list box that selects a specified item in the list.

Short data type—Data type for storing whole numbers ranging from -32,768 to 32,767.

ShowDialog Method—Method that runs a common dialog box.

Single data type—Data type for storing single-precision floating-point numbers with six digits of accuracy.

single-dimension array—Array consisting of one column.

size—Specification that determines how many rows are contained in an array.

SizeMode property—Property of a PictureBox control that specifies how an image is sized within the control. Settings include Normal, StretchImage, AutoSize, and CenterImage.

soft-copy output—Program output that is represented electronically (on the screen and in the computer's memory) or magnetically (stored on a computer disk).

solution—Starting point for creating applications in Visual Studio.NET. Think of a solution as the container or receptacle (like a box or package) that manages all the individual pieces that make up your application. You create a solution in Visual Studio.NET. The solutions you create contain one or more projects.

sort method—Method for sorting the elements in a one-dimensional array.

specific markup language—Markup language that accomplishes a specific purpose. For example, HTML has the purpose of formatting documents for the Web, and RTF formats text.

SQL Server Provider—SQL connection object for connecting a Visual Basic.NET application to a SQL database.

SQLConnection object—Visual Basic.NET connection object for connecting to a SQL database.

SqlDataAdapter object—ADO.NET data adapter that works in conjunction with the SQL Server managed provider.

Standard Generalized Markup Language (SGML)—XML derives from another markup language called the Standard Generalized Markup Language, on which XML is based. See *Generalized Markup Language*.

Start Value—The initial value of a counter variable in a looping structure.

start-tag—XML tag indicating the beginning of an element. The beginning of an element is identified within a start-tag, designated with the less-than symbol (<), the name of the element, and a greater-than symbol (>).

static array—Declared array with a size that will not change during program execution.

Step keyword—Specifies an increment value for a loop counter.

Step Value—The amount by which the counter in a looping structure is incremented each cycle of the loop.

StreamReader object—Object used by controls such as an OpenFileDialog control to read a stream of characters from a sequential access file.

StreamWriter object—Object used by controls such as a SaveFileDialog control to write a stream of characters to a sequential access file.

StretchImage—Property of a PictureBox control that stretches the bitmap image to the size of the control.

strict semantics—Code statements that do not allow narrowing conversions. Setting Option Strict to On enforces strict semantics in Visual Basic.NET applications.

String Collection Editor—Editor available in Visual Basic.NET for adding a collection of items to a list box or combo box.

String data type—Data type for storing alphanumeric data: letters, digits, and other characters. "Adam Smith" is an example of a text string.

Structure keyword—Keyword used to begin the definition of a structure.

structure variable—Variable declared as the data type of a defined structure.

structured data—Data elements in a random access file that have the same length and a consistent format.

structured exception handling—Coding approach that uses code structures that detect and respond to exceptions raised by errors.

Sub keyword—Keyword used to define the beginning of a sub procedure.

sub procedure—Procedure that performs an action without returning a value.

subscript—Index that identifies each element in an array.

subscripted variables—Arrays are also called subscripted variables because the array includes an index that determines the number of elements reserved in memory.

syntax—Rules that specify how code statements are written in a specific programming language.

System.IO namespace—The .NET Framework namespace that includes classes for reading and writing data to different I/O devices such as drives and printers.

tables—Database fields and records are stored in rows and columns called tables.

tags—Characters appearing in a RTF or HTML file that indicate how text is displayed. Tags are also called *tokens*.

testing—Running the application to locate any errors.

text box—Control on a form that contains text the user can enter and change.

text literals—Text string consisting of text values enclosed in quotation marks.

Text property—Property of a text box or label control that defines the text displayed in the control.

text string—Series of one or more characters enclosed in quote symbols. Often used in assignment statements, such as txtLastName.Text = "Smith".

Toolbox—Object in the Visual Studio.NET IDE that holds a series of vertically oriented tabs containing the tools you need for creating controls.

Tool window—Window available from the View menu for displaying the tools available in the IDE.

Try...Catch...Finally statement—Visual Basic.NET statement that uses a decision structure to handle an exception.

two-dimensional array—Array with more than one column. Each column is a dimension.

type—Defines the valid content for an XML element.

type conversion keyword—Visual Basic .NET keyword that explicitly converts an expression in parentheses to a specific data type.

Ubound keyword—Determines the upper bounds of an array.

UCase function—Intrinsic function that converts all values from uppercase to lowercase.

Until keyword—Keyword you can use in a Do...Loop to repeat the iterations of the loop until the specified condition evaluates to True.

Update command—Used by a data adapter to write additions, deletions, and changes back to the data source.

User Defined Data Type—Custom data type for storing structured information.

user-defined data type (UDT)—Special kind of variable that contains one or more variables for defining the structure for each record in a random access file.

user-defined function—Created by a programmer to perform an action and return a result.

User-defined sub procedure—Visual Basic.NET procedure that is not associated with a specific object but can be called by more than one object.

user interface—Everything a user sees on the screen for interacting with a program.

Val function—Intrinsic function that converts a text string to a numeric value.

Val keyword—Keyword for using the Val function to convert a text value to a number that can be used in a calculation.

Validating event—Event raised by a control when the CausesValidation property is set to True and the validation condition is not met.

Validation control—Category of Web Server controls for performing data validation.

variable scope—The scope of a variable determines which procedures have access to the value stored in the variable. See *accessibility*.

variables—Memory location for storing a value that can change and be retrieved while the application is running. A variable is referred to by a name and stores a specific data type.

vbTab—Internal constant that adds a tab character to a text string.

vector graphics—Simple images that draw shapes on the screen by using coordinates, shapes, and colors.

view—Group of settings that define how the interface elements appear on the screen.

Web application—Visual Basic.NET application that includes Web Forms pages with a Web interface that runs from a Web server and displays the user interface by using a Web browser.

Web browser—Software program that interprets the contents of a Web page and displays the page on the screen. Microsoft Internet Explorer is an example of a Web browser.

Web document—Simple HTML document that contains the information to display as well as the instructions for how to display it. Also called a Web page.

Web Forms pages—Pages in an ASP.NET project that have a Web interface, run from a Web server, and display the user interface by using a Web browser.

Web Forms Viewer—An ASP.NET Web Forms control running inside Microsoft Internet Information Server (IIS) that hosts and updates Crystal Report pages.

Web server—Stores Web documents that are available to anyone with Internet access and a Web browser.

Web Server controls—Visual Basic.NET controls available on the Web Forms tab of the Toolbox. Include not only form-type controls such as buttons and text boxes but also special-purpose controls such as a calendar or data grid.

well-formed document—XML file in which both the data and the structure are consistent.

While keyword—Keyword you can use in a Do...Loop to repeat the iterations of the loop while the specified condition is True.

widening conversion—Data conversion in which the new data type can accommodate any value of the original data.

Windows application—Program designed to run on a desktop computer in the Microsoft Windows environment. Includes the graphical interface supported by the Windows operating system.

Windows Form Designer—Visual workspace for creating the interface for your application.

Windows Forms Viewer—Control for hosting a Crystal Report in a Windows Application.

Write method—Method that writes the contents of a text box on a form to a file opened for writing.

WriteOnly property—An optional statement in a property procedure indicating that a property can be the target of assignment but its value cannot be retrieved.

XML (Extensible Markup Language)—Text-based language for storing data in a way that contains both the data and information describing the structure of the data.

XML Designer—Visual Studio.NET tool for working with XML files in the IDE.

XML schema—Document that defines and validates the content and structure of XML data.

XML schema definition language (XSD)—For defining XML schemas.

XML view—Displays XML elements in the XML Designer.

zero-based—Designation of an array where the first element has an index of zero.

INDEX

Symbols

Index

1263-125

Assignment - 143

550

prenhall.com / Koneman.
student resources